The ability to shut out all aspects of my life and concentrate on the task at hand

4/14/85

Some people are parasitic or I guess?

If you're in so much control of your life as you seem to think from your obsession with your actions then guide your future — follow a path

THE
ENDURING
QUESTIONS

FOURTH EDITION

THE ENDURING QUESTIONS

MAIN PROBLEMS OF PHILOSOPHY

Melvin Rader
UNIVERSITY OF WASHINGTON

HOLT, RINEHART AND WINSTON
NEW YORK   CHICAGO   SAN FRANCISCO   DALLAS
MONTREAL   TORONTO   LONDON   SYDNEY

Library of Congress Cataloging in Publication Data
Rader, Melvin Miller, 1903-
    The enduring questions.
    Bibliography p. 609
    Includes index.
    1. Philosophy. I. Title.
BD31.R32 1980   100   80-10970
ISBN: 0-03-055406-3

    456789 038 987654

Preface

The Enduring Questions has grown out of the conviction, based on many years of teaching, that the most compelling problems of philosophy are best approached through the great philosophers, ancient and modern. Twenty-five centuries of philosophical thought have left a wonderfully rich heritage that students should share. This book invites them to join in an exciting intellectual adventure.

As in most introductory texts in philosophy, the emphasis is upon knowledge (epistemology) and reality (metaphysics). The two are so intertwined that I have combined them in Part One. Ethics in Part Two and social philosophy in Part Three comprise the other divisions. Chapter 1 introduces the student to philosophy through the fascinating character of Socrates. This portrait of a philosopher in his search for wisdom helps to give the book a personal and humanistic orientation. The biographical notes that precede the readings reenforce this personal approach and spark interest. Major figures such as Plato, Descartes, Berkeley, Hume, Kant, and Mill are represented by ample selections. Snippets are avoided, and each reading is integral and unmutilated by removal from its original context. The bibliography helps the student who embarks on a term paper, or who wishes to explore a problem or study an author more extensively.

I have borne in mind two objectives: to keep the philosophical content at a high level of quality and to make the book interesting and understandable to the beginning student. In the unavoidable instances in which a reading is especially difficult but too important to omit, the student is helped over the rough spots with editorial commentary. The instructor can take as his starting point the student's acquaintance with the readings as illuminated by the Comments, going on from there to spontaneous discussion, rather than being bogged down by interminable questions about the meaning of passages. The Comments, which are more extensive than in most books of readings, are thus intended to help both student and instructor.

By emphasizing clashing points of view, such as theism and agnosticism, monism and pluralism, rationalism and empiricism, free will and determinism, duty and utility, liberalism and communism, the book acquires a sharply interrogative character. The fourth edition strongly accentuates this feature. Walter T. Stace's essay, restored from the second edition, is a provocative challenge to the arguments of Anselm, Saint Thomas, and other theists in the book. Bertrand Russell's insistence on the problematic character of materialism contrasts with the speculative but confident materialism of Lucretius. Alan M. Turing's mechanism, with its attempt to close the gulf that divides the mind of man from the machine, is an arresting alternative to the dualism of Descartes and the idealism of Berkeley and Hegel. Gilbert Ryle's behaviorism and Karl Popper's "three worlds" doctrine, each in its own way, attack Descartes' dualistic answer to the body–mind problem. Gerald Dworkin's exceptionally lucid exposition of the free will *versus* determinism controversy, to which Lucretius, Spinoza, Hume, and Kant give alternative answers, clarifies the issues and the arguments pro and con. Martin Buber's interpretation of interpersonal relations, while representing a different kind of existentialism than Kierkegaard's intense individualism, is at the opposite pole from Turing's mechanism and Skinner's behavioristic technology. John Dewey's reconstruction of philosophy is a bold repudiation of older modes of thought, such as the rationalism of Plato, Spinoza, and Descartes. A. C. Ewing's defence of unselfishness contrasts with Bentham's theory of egoistic motivation and illuminates the perennial egoism–altruism question. These readings, which distinguish the fourth edition from its predecessors, will excite controversy. The problems with which they deal are important and "teach well."

I have deleted more than I have added. The reduction in size is a significant improvement, because the third edition was too large and contained marginal readings. Much as I have hesitated to omit Locke, Pascal, Nietzsche, Bergson, Lovejoy, Whitehead, Santayana, Montague, Blake, Wittgenstein, and Kolakowski, and to reduce the excerpts from Aristotle, Peirce, and James, these deleted selections were less essential for an introduction to philosophy than the ones that I have added. I have somewhat abbreviated but I have not eliminated my editorial comments, because too many teachers and students have assured me that great reduction or elimination would be a mistake. Although the fourth edition is briefer than the second and third editions, there is abundant material for an introductory course.

I am very grateful to all who advised me in preparing this edition: Albert Lataner of Nassau Community College, Donald R. Gregory of Northern Virginia Community College, Joseph P. Boyle of Hillsborough Community College and the University of South Florida, Oliver A. Johnson of the University of California at Riverside, and Paul Dietrichson of the University of Washington.

February 1980   M. R.

Contents

Introduction

THE NATURE
OF PHILOSOPHY

THE GENERAL INTERPRETATION
OF EXPERIENCE

If philosophers can be called "specialists," they are specialists in the general. Socrates (in Plato's *Republic*) defines the philosopher as "the spectator of all time and all existence"; and William James declares that philosophy deals "with the principles of explanation that underlie all things without exception, the elements common to gods and men and animals and stones, the first *whence* and the last *whither* of the whole cosmic procession, the conditions of all knowing, and the most general rules of human conduct."[1]

C. D. Broad similarly characterizes philosophy. He distinguishes between critical and *speculative* philosophy, both of which deal with what is general. The task of critical philosophy is to analyze and define our most fundamental and general concepts, such as "goodness," "truth," "reality," and "causation." The object of speculative philosophy is "to take over the results of the various sciences, to add to them the results of the religious and ethical experiences of mankind, and then to reflect upon the whole" in an attempt "to reach some general conclusions as to the nature of the Universe, and as to our position and prospects in it."[2]

These characterizations seem to fit the problems that philosophers most often discuss: What is a good life? What is the relation between mind and body? Do we have free will? Is there a God? Is the world fundamentally material or spiri-

[1] *Some Problems of Philosophy* (New York: Longmans, Green, 1911), p. 5.
[2] *Scientific Thought* (New York: Harcourt, Brace & World, 1923).
herein, pp. 146–153. See p. 152.

tual? Can we know the ultimate nature of reality? These are basic questions involved in a general interpretation of the world. Accordingly, Herbert Spencer defines philosophy as "knowledge of the highest degree of generality."[3]

There are certain difficulties in this view. First, science also is sometimes *very* general. Newton's theory of gravitation, for example, characterizes the nearest and the most remote, the least and the greatest of objects—the pin in one's bedroom as well as the most distant galaxy. Similarly, modern atomic physics is applicable to every material entity in the universe; and the theory of evolution, summarizing the whole history of life from the first germs in the primordial sea to the highest stages of human life, is also exceedingly wide in scope. Secondly, the synthesis of all the sciences, or the interpretation of the whole of reality, is a pretty big order. A person would need to be a kind of god, or at least a universal genius, to succeed at so prodigious an undertaking. But philosophy is not the peculiar business of the gods or of rare geniuses; it is everyman's business.

THE PURSUIT OF MEANING

Such considerations have led many philosophers to define their field in a more restricted way. One of the most widely accepted definitions is that philosophy is the analysis, or systematic study, of meanings. This definition would in effect limit the field to what C. D. Broad calls critical philosophy.

Those who adopt this interpretation sometimes cite Socrates as an example of a philosopher. In employing his favorite conversational method of giving and receiving questions and answers, he is usually trying to analyse the meaning of some basic concept, such as "knowledge," "justice," "courage," "friendship," or "beauty."

One of the most influential philosophers of modern times, Moritz Schlick (1882–1936), has said:

> . . . Socrates' philosophy consists of what we may call "The Pursuit of Meaning." He tried to clarify thought by analyzing the meaning of our expressions and the real sense of our propositions. Here then we find a definite contrast between this philosophic method, which has for its object the discovery of meaning, and the method of the sciences, which have for their object the discovery of truth. . . . Science should be defined as the "pursuit of truth" and philosophy as the "pursuit of meaning." Socrates has set the example of the true philosophic method for all times.[4]

I do not believe that this is an adequate characterization of the method of Socrates or the nature of philosophy. Socrates was engaged not only in the pursuit of meaning but also in the pursuit of truth, and the former was largely instrumental

---

[3] *First Principles* (New York: Burt, 1880), p. 111.

[4] "The Future of Philosophy," in D. J. Bronstein, Y. H. Krikorian, and P. P. Wiener, *Basic Problems of Philosophy* (Englewood Cliffs, N.J.: Prentice Hall, 1947), p. 739.

to the latter. His definitions were intended not as arbitrary or merely verbal: they were what philosophers call "real" definitions—that is, they sought to characterize actually existent things. When Socrates asserted that justice or friendship or beauty was this or that, he implied that justice or friendship or beauty really existed and actually bore the character marked off and fixed in the definition. Consequently, he kept referring to the facts of experience so as to make his definitions truthful. Also, he was interested in fitting together the various insights thus gained into a critical interpretation of man's nature, his destiny, and his values.

To define philosophy as the pursuit of meaning is at once too broad and too narrow. It is too broad because scientists as well as philosophers seek to clarify meanings. As C. J. Ducasse has said:

> To mention but a few, such concepts as salt, acid, gas, liquid, solid, water, air, iron, etc. are concepts the exact meaning of which is investigated and discovered not by metaphysicians, logicians, or mathematicians, but by chemists and physicists; and the same is true of such even more basic physical concepts as light, electricity, matter, mass, etc. Moreover, although physicists do give us precise accounts of the meaning of these and numerous other concepts, they do so in their capacity as natural scientists, *i.e.*, on the basis, ultimately, of observations and experiments. . . .[5]

In another sense, Schlick's definition of philosophy is too narrow. If Plato, Aristotle, Aquinas, Descartes, Spinoza, and Kant, for example, are to be considered philosophers—and no one has a better claim—it would appear that their field includes what Broad calls "speculative philosophy." Schlick seeks to dismiss the problems of speculative philosophy as either nonsensical or nonphilosophical. "Some of them will disappear by being shown to be mistakes and misunderstandings of our language," he declares, "and the others will be found to be ordinary scientific questions in disguise."[6] But it is unlikely that all the problems of speculative philosophy will either vanish when they are stated clearly or will turn out to be nonphilosophical problems, more appropriately treated by science. Moreover, the sharp distinction between the pursuit of meaning and the pursuit of truth is artificial, for the clarification of meaning and the discovery of truth go hand in hand. Broad rightly includes under "critical philosophy" not only the clarification of concepts but the resolute criticism of our fundamental beliefs.

THE CULTIVATION OF WISDOM

Philosophy, we conclude, involves both the analysis of meanings and the search for generic truths. To complete our definition, we need to distinguish the kinds

[5] *Philosophy as a Science* (New York: Oskar Piest, 1941), pp. 77–78.
[6] *Philosophy as a Science*, p. 745.

of meanings and generic truths that are essentially philosophical from the kinds that are scientific.

It will help us to consider the original meaning of "philosophy." Etymologically, philosophy means "the love of wisdom" (from the Greek *"philein,"* to love, and *"sophia,"* wisdom). The word has ordinarily been used to designate an activity rather than an emotion—the activity of pursuing wisdom rather than the emotion motivating that pursuit. The essential question that we need to consider is what, exactly, is the wisdom that the philosopher seeks.

"Wisdom" has been used in two senses. First, it is contrasted with ignorance. The wise person is one who knows and therefore is not ignorant. This meaning, however, does not help us to distinguish philosophy from science, since the scientist also, of course, is trying to replace ignorance by knowledge. In the second sense, wisdom is contrasted with foolishness. The wise person is one who has good judgment and therefore is not foolish. The fool may have a great deal of knowledge about ordinary matter of fact, but lacks the balance and maturity and ripe insight that make it possible not only to live but to live well.

If philosophy is the pursuit of wisdom as contrasted with foolishness, it *is* marked off from ordinary science. The subject matter of science is facts, and science attempts to discover verifiable laws—regularities—among these facts. These laws give a *description* of the facts. It is obvious that the physicist does not talk about wicked atoms or beneficent motions, and even the sociologist, in the purely scientific role, tries to *describe* rather than to *evaluate* the behavior of social groups. If philosophy, on the other hand, seeks wisdom as the opposite of foolishness, it must be a kind of critical activity concerned with appraisals. Matthew Arnold has defined poetry as "the criticism of life," but this definition fits philosophy better than poetry. It is similar to the definition of Ducasse, who maintains that "philosophy is the general theory of criticism,"[7] and the definition of Dewey, who declares that "philosophy is inherently criticism, having its distinctive position among various modes of criticism in its generality: a criticism of criticisms, as it were."[8]

It is characteristic of criticism that it is yea-saying or nay-saying—a favoring or a disfavoring. The ways of saying "yea" or "nay" are quite various, and they correspond to different pairs of adjectives. In logic, for example, we speak of *valid* or *fallacious;* in epistemology, of *true* or *false;* in metaphysics, of *real* or *unreal;* in theology, of *holy* or *unholy;* in esthetics, of *beautiful* or *ugly;* in ethics, of *right* or *wrong.* In using these adjectives, we are making judgments. The function of philosophy is to provide the intellectual bases of sound judgments about the great issues of life.

Even when philosophy wears the garb of science, it is distinctive. For example, Lucretius was not primarily concerned with the hypotheses of atoms and evolution as scientific descriptions of the nature of things: he was concerned with the

---

[7] *The Philosophy of Art* (New York: Dial, 1929), p. 3.

[8] *Experience and Nature* (Chicago: Open Court, 1925), p. 398.

right way to think and live in the sort of universe that he regarded as real. Metaphysics should not be interpreted—as it often is—as potential or generalized natural science; rather, it should be regarded as the attempt to achieve a true understanding of humanity and its place in the cosmos so that we can distinguish the deep and permanent from the superficial and temporary, the important from the unimportant. Thus to distinguish is to *judge,* and metaphysics, like other branches of philosophy, provides a basis for judgment.

Philosophy resembles science not so much in its aim as in its method. Both employ reason and evidence as means to the discovery of truth and the clarification of meaning. Both are forms of inquiry—science being an inquiry into the laws of nature; philosophy, into the norms of criticism. The faith of the philosopher, like that of the scientist, is that inquiry is worth while. In the *Apology,* Socrates expresses the fundamental conviction of all true philosophers: "The unexamined life," he declares, "is not worth living." Likewise, in the *Meno,* his faith rings out sharp and clear:

> Some things I have said of which I am not altogether confident. But that we shall be better and braver and less helpless if we think that we ought to inquire, than we should have been if we indulged in the idle fancy that there was no knowing and no use in seeking to know what we do not know;—that is a theme upon which I am ready to fight, in word and deed, to the utmost of my power.[9]

We can fully appreciate the brave words of Socrates only if we too engage in the quest for wisdom. The proof of the pudding is in the eating—we can best judge the value of philosophy after we have philosophized. We must all taste of the pudding; no one can do it for us. Of course, it is immensely helpful to study the great thinkers, such as Plato, Aristotle, Hume, and Kant, or nearer to us, William James, Santayana, and Russell. As Descartes declares in the opening chapter of his *Discourse on Method,* "The reading of good books is, as it were, to engage in talk with their authors, the finest minds of past ages, artfully contrived talk in which they give us none but the best and most select of their thoughts."[10] But like all the very good things of life, wisdom is something that cannot be given and that each must attain personally.

In thumbing through some old lecture notes, I have found a definition of philosophy that sums up much that I have said: "Philosophy is an effort to give unity to human arts and sciences by a critical examination of the grounds of our meanings, values, and beliefs."

[9] *The Dialogues of Plato,* trans. by Benjamin Jowett (London: Oxford, 1924), II, p. 47.
[10] *Discourse on Method,* in *Descartes' Philosophical Writings* (London: Macmillan, 1952), p. 119.

Part One

KNOWLEDGE
AND
REALITY

One of the main divisions of philosophy is epistemology, or the theory of knowledge. Epistemology asks such fundamental questions as these: How much do we know? How much *can* we know? *How* do we know? How can we distinquish between appearance and reality? What is the nature of truth, and how can we separate it from falsehood? We shall be dealing with such questions in Part One.

It is difficult, if not impossible, to separate epistemology, the theory of knowledge, from metaphysics, the theory of reality. In this part, we shall examine the philosophies of Descartes, Berkeley, Hume, and Kant, all of whom have contributed greatly to both metaphysics and epistemology. Hence Part One is entitled "Knowledge and Reality."

We shall consider the question "What is the fundamental nature of man and the surrounding universe?" This question directs attention to "the metaphysics of the microcosm"—of the "I" or self as a small part of the whole scheme of things—and "to the metaphysics of the macrocosm"—of the great, all-enveloping system of reality. We shall not attempt to separate these two inquiries, and, indeed, any sharp separation would be artificial. Each of the theories that we shall consider will throw light upon the nature of the human person and the nature of his total environment.

We shall scrutinize the career of Socrates, who personifies, as well as anyone, the commitment to philosophy as a way of life. Plato's stirring portrayal of his teacher, Socrates, will be followed by selections from ancient and modern philosophers. These readings are an exciting introduction to the great problems of epistemology and metaphysics.

1

The Quest for Wisdom

PLATO (428/7–348/7 B.C.)
and
SOCRATES (c.470–399 B.C.)

As a member of one of the most distinguished families in Athens, Plato was in touch with political and social developments from his early childhood. He grew to manhood during the long, turbulent period of the Peloponnesian War, and his mind must have been deeply disturbed by war and revolution. Athens was finally defeated by Sparta when Plato was twenty-three, and he watched the ensuing oligarchical dictatorship, of which his uncle Charmides and his cousin Critias were leaders, with great hope. It soon turned to horror and anger, however, when his old friend Socrates was eventually tried and executed by the restored democratic faction. The shock of this event, occurring when he was just twenty-eight, was the decisive influence upon his entire career. He concluded that good government depends upon the rare union of power and wisdom, and resolved to emulate and so far as possible complete the work of Socrates. Retiring from Athens to Megara, he began to write his famous dialogues which lovingly portray his old master.

He is said to have spent the next ten years traveling in Greece, Italy, Egypt, and Asia Minor. For a time he lived at the court of Dionysius I, the tyrant of Syracuse, whose son-in-law, Dion, became Plato's friend and ardent admirer. At the age of forty he returned to Athens to found the Academy, a school for philosophers, mathematicians, and statesmen. This school was the main center of his interest for the remainder of his long life. In addition to teaching, he continued to write dialogues, which became more technical as he grew older. This quiet, academic life was interrupted in 367 B.C., when he was close on sixty. Dion, his old friend, persuaded him to return to Syracuse as tutor to Dionysius II, a young man of thirty, who had succeeded to the throne. The venture turned out badly. Dionysius and Dion eventually quarreled and Plato went back to Athens. Not easily dismayed, he returned to Syracuse six years later in the hope of remedying the situation—and once again met with broken promises and barely escaped with his life. Then he settled down in the Academy to spend the last years of his life teaching and writing. He died at the age of eighty or eighty-one and, according to Cicero, was hard at work at the very end. Generally considered the greatest of the Greek philosophers, he has exercised an immense influence on the thought and literature of the world ever since his death.

More than anyone else, Plato's friend and teacher, Socrates, represents the very type and ideal of the philosopher. In the *Apology,* Plato portrays his magnificent defense in the trial that culminated in his death sentence. By his independence, his critical spirit, and his unceasing quest for wisdom, Socrates had offended both the democratic and oligarchical parties in strife-torn Athens.

Political motives, combined with their intense dislike of Socrates' unconventional teachings, prompted Anytus, a prominent democratic politician, and two lesser associates, Meletus and Lycon, to bring charges against Socrates in 339 B.C. The indictment, as recorded by the later historian Diogenes Laertius, read:

> Socrates is guilty of not worshipping the gods whom the State worships, but introducing new and unfamiliar religious practices; and, further, of corrupting the young. The prosecutor demands the death penalty.

The charges in the case were motivated by widespread hostility against Socrates for his critical spirit and his unremitting search for a new rationale and norm for life. In the eyes of conservatives, he *had* blasphemed and corrupted youth. Indeed, he had questioned the very foundation of the social order, and the guardians of the *status quo,* hurt to the quick, retaliated by seeking to impose the ultimate penalty—death.

Tried before five hundred jurors selected by lot, Socrates spoke with such uncompromising independence that he angered the jury and provoked the death penalty. Some of his friends made a last-minute attempt to effect his escape, but he would brook no such disgraceful tactics. After a serene philosophical conversation with a group of intimates in his prison cell, he drank the fatal hemlock. Now let us see how Plato portrayed Socrates in his defense.

The Apology

SCENE.—The Court of Justice.

Socrates. I cannot tell what impression my accusers have made upon you, Athenians: for my own part, I know that they nearly made me forget who I was, so plausible were they; and yet they have scarcely uttered one single word of truth. But of all their many falsehoods, the one which astonished me most, was when they said that I was a clever speaker, and that you must be careful not to let me mislead you. I thought that it was most impudent of them not to be ashamed to talk in that way; for as soon as I open my mouth the lie will be exposed, and I shall prove that I am not a clever speaker in any way at all: unless, indeed, by a clever speaker they mean a man who speaks the truth. If that is their meaning, I agree with them that I am a much greater orator than they. My accusers, then I repeat, have said little or nothing that is true; but from me you shall hear the whole truth. Certainly you will not hear an elaborate speech, Athenians, drest up, like theirs, with

The following dialogue of Plato is from the translation of F. J. Church, first published by Macmillan and Company, London, 1880.

words and phrases. I will say to you what I have to say, without preparation, and in the words which come first, for I believe that my cause is just; so let none of you expect anything else. Indeed, my friends, lt would hardly be seemly for me, at my age, to come before you like a young man with his specious falsehoods. But there is one thing, Athenians, which I do most earnestly beg and entreat of you. Do not be surprised and do not interrupt, if in my defence I speak in the same way that I am accustomed to speak in the market-place, at the tables of the money-changers, where many of you have heard me, and elsewhere. The truth is this. I am more than seventy years old, and this is the first time that I have ever come before a Court of Law; so your manner of speech here is quite strange to me. If I had been really a stranger, you would have forgiven me for speaking in the language and the fashion of my native country: and so now I ask you to grant me what I think I have a right to claim. Never mind the style of my speech—it may be better or it may be worse—give your whole attention to the question, Is what I say just, or is it not? That is what makes a good judge, as speaking the truth makes a good advocate.

I have to defend myself, Athenians, first against the old false charges of my old accusers, and then against the later ones of my present accusers. For many men have been accusing me to you, and for very many years, who have not uttered a word of truth: and I fear them more than I fear Anytus and his companions, formidable as they are. But, my friends, those others are still more formidable; for they got hold of most of you when you were children, and they have been more persistent in accusing me with lies, and in trying to persuade you that there is one Socrates, a wise man, who speculates about the heavens, and who examines into all things that are beneath the earth, and who can "make the worse appear the better reason." These men, Athenians, who spread abroad this report, are the accusers whom I fear; for their hearers think that persons who pursue such inquiries never believe in the gods. And then they are many, and their attacks have been going on for a long time: and they spoke to you when you were at the age most readily to believe them: for you were all young, and many of you were children: and there was no one to answer them when they attacked me. And the most unreasonable thing of all is that commonly I do not even know their names: I cannot tell you who they are, except in the case of the comic poets. But all the rest who have been trying to prejudice you against me, from motives of spite and jealousy, and sometimes, it may be, from conviction, are the enemies whom it is hardest to meet. For I cannot call any one of them forward in Court, to cross-examine him: I have, as it were, simply to fight with shadows in my defence, and to put questions which there is no one to answer. I ask you, therefore, to believe that, as I say, I have been at-tacked by two classes of accusers—first by Meletus and his friends, and then by those older ones of whom I have spoken. And, with your leave, I will defend myself first against my old enemies; for you heard their accusations first, and they were much more persistent than my present accusers are.

Well, I must make my defence, Athenians, and try in the short time allowed me to remove the prejudice which you have had against me for a long time. I hope that I may manage to do this, if it be good for you and for me, and that my defence may be successful; but I am quite aware of the nature of my task, and I know that it is a difficult one. Be the issue, however, as God wills, I must obey the law, and make my defence.

Let us begin again, then, and see what is the charge which has given rise to the prejudice against me, which was what Meletus relied on when he drew his indictment. What is the calumny which my enemies have been spreading about me? I must assume that they are formally accusing me, and read their indictment. It would run somewhat in this fashion: "Socrates is an evil-doer, who meddles with inquiries into things beneath the earth, and in heaven, and who 'makes the worse appear the better reason,' and who teaches others these same things." That is what they say; and in the Comedy of Aristophanes [*The Clouds*] you yourselves saw a man called Socrates swinging round in a basket, and saying that he walked the air, and talking a great deal of nonsense about matters of which I understand nothing, either more or less. I do not mean to disparage that kind of knowledge, if there is any man who possesses it. I trust Meletus may never be able to prosecute me for that. But, the truth is, Athenians, I have nothing to do with these matters, and almost all of you are yourselves my witnesses of this. I beg all of you who have ever heard me converse, and they are many, to inform your neighbors and tell them if any of you have ever heard me conversing about such matters, either more or less. That will show you that the other common stories about me are as false as this one.

But, the fact is, that not one of these stories is true; and if you have heard that I undertake to educate men, and exact money from them for so doing, that is not true either; though I think that it would be a fine thing to be able to educate men, as Gorgias of Leontini, and Prodicus of Ceos, and Hippias of Elis do. For each of them, my friends, can go into any city, and persuade the young men to leave the society of their fellow-citizens, with any of whom they might associate for nothing, and to be only too glad to be allowed to pay money for the privilege of associating with themselves. And I believe that there is another wise man from Paros residing in Athens at this moment. I happened to meet Callias, the son of Hipponicus, a man who has spent more money on the Sophists than every one else put together. So I said to him—he has two sons—Callias, if your two sons had been foals or calves, we could have hired a trainer for them who would have made them perfect in the excellence which belongs to their nature. He would have been either a groom or a farmer. But whom do you intend to take to train them, seeing that they are men? Who understands the excellence which belongs to men and to citizens? I suppose that you must have thought of this, because of your sons. Is there such a person, said I, or not? Certainly there is, he replied. Who is he, said I, and where does he come from, and what is his fee? His name is Evenus, Socrates, he replied: he comes from Paros, and his fee is five minæ. Then I thought that Evenus was a fortunate person if he really understood this art and could teach so cleverly. If I had possessed knowledge of that kind, I should have given myself airs and prided myself on it. But, Athenians, the truth is that I do not possess it.

Perhaps some of you may reply: But, Socrates, what is this pursuit of yours? Whence come these calumnies against you? You must have been engaged in some pursuit out of the common. All these stories and reports of you would never have gone about, if you had not been in some way different from other men. So tell us what your pursuits are, that we may not give our verdict in the dark. I think that that is a fair question, and I will try to explain to you what it is that has raised these calumnies against me, and given me this name. Listen, then: some of you perhaps will think that I am jesting; but I assure you that I will tell you the whole truth. I have gained this name, Athenians, simply by reason of a certain wisdom. But by what kind of wisdom? It is by just that wisdom which is, I believe, possible to men. In that, it may be, I am really wise. But the men of whom I was speaking just now must be wise in a wisdom which is greater than human wisdom, or in some way which I cannot describe, for certainly I know nothing of it myself, and if any man says that I do, he lies and wants to slander me. Do not interrupt me, Athenians, even if you think that I am speaking arrogantly. What I am going to say is not my own: I will tell you who says it, and he is worthy of your credit. I will bring the god of Delphi to be the witness of the fact of my wisdom and of its nature. You remember Chærephon. From youth upwards he was my comrade; and he went into exile with the people,[1] and with the people he returned. And you remember, too, Chærephon's character; how vehement he was in carrying through whatever he took in hand. Once he went to Delphi and ventured to put this question to the oracle—I entreat you again, my friends, not to cry out—he asked if there was any man who was wiser than I: and the priestess answered that there was no man. Chærephon himself is dead, but his brother here will confirm what I say.

Now see why I tell you this. I am going to explain to you the origin of my unpopularity. When I heard of the oracle I began to reflect: What can God mean by this dark saying? I know very well that I am not wise, even in the smallest degree. Then what can he mean by saying that I am the wisest of men? It cannot be that he is speaking falsely, for he is a god and cannot lie. And for a long time I was at a loss to understand his meaning: then, very reluctantly, I turned to seek for it in

[1] Chærephon was forced into exile during the anti-democratic dictatorship of the Thirty in 404 B.C.

this manner. I went to a man who was reputed to be wise, thinking that there, if anywhere, I should prove the answer wrong, and meaning to point out to the oracle its mistake, and to say, "You said that I was the wisest of men, but this man is wiser than I am." So I examined the man—I need not tell you his name, he was a politician—but this was the result, Athenians. When I conversed with him I came to see that, though a great many persons, and most of all he himself, thought that he was wise, yet he was not wise. And then I tried to prove to him that he was not wise, though he fancied that he was: and by so doing I made him, and many of the bystanders, my enemies. So when I went away, I thought to myself, "I am wiser than this man: neither of us probably knows anything that is really good, but he thinks that he has knowledge, when he has not, while I, having no knowledge, do not think that I have. I seem, at any rate, to be a little wiser than he is on this point: I do not think that I know what I do not know." Next I went to another man who was reputed to be still wiser than the last, with exactly the same result. And there again I made him, and many other men, my enemies.

Then I went on to one man after another, seeing that I was making enemies every day, which caused me much unhappiness and anxiety: still I thought that I must set God's command above everything. So I had to go to every man who seemed to possess any knowledge, and search for the meaning of the oracle: and, Athenians, I must tell you the truth; verily, by the dog of Egypt, this was the result of the search which I made at God's bidding. I found that the men, whose reputation for wisdom stood highest, were nearly the most lacking in it; while others, who were looked down on as common people, were much better fitted to learn. Now, I must describe to you the wanderings which I undertook, like a series of Heraclean labors, to make full proof of the oracle. After the politicians, I went to the poets, tragic, dithyrambic, and others, thinking that there I should find myself manifestly more ignorant than they. So I took up the poems on which I thought that they had spent most pains, and asked them what they meant, hoping at the same time to learn something from them. I am ashamed to tell you the truth, my friends, but I must say it. Almost any one of the bystanders could have talked about the works of these poets better than the poets themselves. So I soon found that it is not by wisdom that the poets create their works, but by a certain natural power and by inspiration, like soothsayers and prophets, who say many fine things, but who understand nothing of what they say. The poets seemed to me to be in a similar case. And at the same time I perceived that, because of their poetry, they thought that they were the wisest of men in other matters too, which they were not. So I went away again, thinking that I had the same advantage over the poets that I had over the politicians.

Finally, I went to the artisans, for I knew very well that I possessed no knowledge at all, worth speaking of, and I was sure that I should find that they knew many fine things. And in that I was not mistaken. They knew what I did not know, and so far they were wiser than I. But, Athenians, it seemed to me that the skilled artisans made the same mistake as the poets. Each of them believed himself to be extremely wise in matters of the greatest importance, because he was skillful in his own art: and this mistake of theirs threw their real wisdom into the shade. So I asked myself, on behalf of the oracle, whether I would choose to remain as I was, without either wisdom or their ignorance, or to possess both, as they did. And I made answer to myself and to the oracle that it was better for me to remain as I was.

By reason of this examination, Athenians, I have made many enemies of a very fierce and bitter kind, who have spread abroad a great number of calumnies about me, and people say that I am "a wise man." For the bystanders always think that I am wise myself in any matter wherein I convict another man of ignorance. But, my friends, I believe that only God is really wise: and that by this oracle he meant that men's wisdom is worth little or nothing. I do not think that he meant that Socrates was wise. He only made use of my name, and took me as an example, as though he would say to men, "He among you is the wisest, who, like Socrates, knows that in very truth his wisdom is worth nothing at all." And therefore I still go about testing and examining every man whom I think wise, whether he be a citizen or a stranger, as God has commanded me; and whenever I find that he is not wise, I point out to him on the part of God that he is not wise. And I am so busy in this pursuit that I have never had leisure to take any part worth mentioning in public matters, or to look after my private affairs. I am in very great poverty by reason of my service to God.

And besides this, the young men who follow me about, who are the sons of wealthy persons and have a great deal of spare time, take a natural pleasure in hearing men cross-examined: and they often imitate me among themselves: then they try their hands at cross-examining other people. And, I imagine, they find a great abundance of men who think that they know a great deal, when in fact they know little or nothing. And then the persons who are cross-examined, get angry with me instead of with themselves, and say that Socrates is an abominable fellow who corrupts young men. And when they are asked, "Why, what does he do? what does he teach?" they do not know what to say; but, not to seem at a loss, they repeat the stock charges against all philosophers, and allege that he investigates things in the air and under the earth, and that he teaches people to disbelieve in the gods, and "to make the worse appear the better reason." For, I fancy, they would not like to confess the truth, which is that they are shown up as ignorant pretenders to knowledge that they do not possess. And so they have been filling your ears with their bitter calumnies for a long time, for they are zealous and numerous and bitter against me; and they are well disciplined and plausible in speech. On these grounds Meletus and Anytus and Lycon have attacked me. Meletus is indignant with me on the part of the poets, and Any-

tus on the part of the artisans and politicians, and Lycon on the part of the orators. And so, as I said at the beginning, I shall be surprised if I am able, in the short time allowed me for my defence, to remove from your minds this prejudice which has grown so strong. What I have told you, Athenians, is the truth: I neither conceal, nor do I suppress anything, small or great. And yet I know that it is just this plainness of speech which makes me enemies. But that is only a proof that my words are true, and that the prejudice against me, and the causes of it, are what I have said. And whether you look for them now or hereafter, you will find that they are so.

What I have said must suffice as my defence against the charges of my first accusers. I will try next to defend myself against that "good patriot" Meletus, as he calls himself, and my later accusers. Let us assume that they are a new set of accusers, and read their indictment, as we did in the case of the others. It runs thus. He says that Socrates is an evil-doer who corrupts the youth, and who does not believe in the gods whom the city believes in, but in other new divinities. Such is the charge. Let us examine each point in it separately. Meletus says that I do wrong by corrupting the youth: but I say, Athenians, that he is doing wrong; for he is playing off a solemn jest by bringing men lightly to trial, and pretending to have a great zeal and interest in matters to which he has never given a moment's thought. And now I will try to prove to you that it is so.

Come here, Meletus. Is it not a fact that you think it very important that the younger men should be as excellent as possible?

Meletus. It is.

Socr. Come then: tell the judges, who is it who improves them? You take so much interest in the matter that of course you know that. You are accusing me, and bringing me to trial, because, as you say, you have discovered that I am the corrupter of the youth. Come now, reveal to the judges who improves them. You see, Meletus, you have nothing to say; you are silent. But don't you think that this is a scandalous thing? Is not your silence a conclusive proof of what I say, that you have never given a moment's thought to the matter? Come, tell us, my good sir, who makes the young men better citizens?

Mel. The laws.

Socr. My excellent sir, that is not my question. What man improves the young, who starts with a knowledge of the laws?

Mel. The judges here, Socrates.

Socr. What do you mean, Meletus? Can they educate the young and improve them?

Mel. Certainly.

Socr. All of them? or only some of them?

Mel. All of them.

Socr. By Hêrê that is good news! There is a great abundance of benefactors. And do the listeners here improve them, or not?

Mel. They do.

Socr. And do the senators?

Mel. Yes.

Socr. Well then, Meletus; do the members of the Assembly corrupt the younger men? or do they again all improve them?

Mel. They too improve them.

Socr. Then all the Athenians, apparently, make the young into fine fellows except me, and I alone corrupt them. Is that your meaning?

Mel. Most certainly; that is my meaning.

Socr. You have discovered me to be a most unfortunate man. Now tell me: do you think that the same holds good in the case of horses? Does one man do them harm and every one else improve them? On the contrary, is it not one man only, or a very few—namely, those who are skilled in horses—who can improve them; while the majority of men harm them, if they use them, and have to do with them? Is it not so, Meletus, both with horses and with every other animal? Of course it is, whether you and Anytus say yes or no. And young men would certainly be very fortunate persons if only one man corrupted them, and every one else did them good. The truth is, Meletus, you prove conclusively that you have never thought about the youth in your life. It is quite clear, on your own showing, that you take no interest at all in the matters about which you are prosecuting me.

Now, be so good as to tell us, Meletus, is it better to live among good citizens or bad ones? Answer, my friend: I am not asking you at all a difficult question. Do not bad citizens do harm to their neighbors and good citizens good.

Mel. Yes.

Socr. Is there any man who would rather be injured than benefited by his companions? Answer, my good sir:

you are obliged by the law to answer. Does any one like to be injured?

Mel. Certainly not.

Socr. Well then; are you prosecuting me for corrupting the young, and making them worse men, intentionally or unintentionally?

Mel. For doing it intentionally.

Socr. What, Meletus? Do you mean to say that you, who are so much younger than I, are yet so much wiser than I, that you know that bad citizens always do evil, and that good citizens always do good, to those with whom they come in contact, while I am so extraordinarily stupid as not to know that if I make any of my companions a rogue, he will probably injure me in some way, and as to commit this great crime, as you allege, intentionally? You will not make me believe that, nor any one else either, I should think. Either I do not corrupt the young at all; or if I do, I do so unintentionally: so that you are a liar in either case. And if I corrupt them unintentionally, the law does not call upon you to prosecute me for a fault like that, which is an involuntary one: you should take me aside and admonish and instruct me: for of course I shall cease from doing wrong involuntarily, as soon as I know that I have been doing wrong. But you declined to instruct me: you would have nothing to do with me: instead of that, you bring me up before the Court, where the law sends persons, not for instruction, but for punishment.

The truth is, Athenians, as I said, it is quite clear that Meletus has never paid the slightest attention to these matters. However, now tell us, Meletus, how do you say that I corrupt the younger men? Clearly, according to your indictment, by teaching them not to believe in the gods of the city, but in other new divinities instead. You mean that I corrupt young men by that teaching, do you not?

Mel. Yes: most certainly; I mean that.

Socr. Then in the name of these gods of whom we are speaking, explain yourself a little more clearly to me and to the judges here. I cannot understand what you mean. Do you mean that I teach young men to believe in some gods, but not in the gods of the city? Do you accuse me of teaching them to believe in strange gods? If that is your meaning, I myself believe in some gods, and my crime is not that of absolute atheism. Or do you mean that I do not believe in the gods at all myself, and that I teach other people not to believe in them either?

Mel. I mean that you do not believe in the gods in any way whatever.

Socr. Wonderful, Meletus! Why do you say that? Do you mean that I believe neither the sun nor the moon to be gods, like other men?

Mel. I swear he does not, judges: he says that the sun is a stone, and the moon earth.

Socr. My dear Meletus, do you think that you are prosecuting Anaxagoras? You must have a very poor opinion of the judges, and think them very unlettered men, if you imagine that they do not know that the works of Anaxagoras of Clazomenæ are full of these doctrines. And so young men learn these things from me, when they can often buy places in the theater[2] for a

---

[2] Socrates here alludes to the references to

drachma at most, and laugh Socrates to scorn, were he to pretend that these doctrines, which are very peculiar doctrines, too, were his. But please tell me, do you really think that I do not believe in the gods at all?

Mel. Most certainly I do. You are a complete atheist.

Socr. No one believes that, Meletus, and I think that you know it to be a lie yourself. It seems to me, Athenians, that Meletus is a very insolent and wanton man, and that he is prosecuting me simply in the insolence and wantonness of youth. He is like a man trying an experiment on me, by asking me a riddle that has no answer. "Will this wise Socrates," he says to himself, "see that I am jesting and contradicting myself? or shall I outwit him and every one else who hears me?" Meletus seems to me to contradict himself in his indictment: it is as if he were to say, "Socrates is a wicked man who does not believe in the gods, but who believes in the gods." But that is mere trifling.

Now, my friends, let us see why I think that this is his meaning. Do you answer me, Meletus: and do you, Athenians, remember the request which I made to you at starting, and do not interrupt me if I talk in my usual way.

Is there any man, Meletus, who believes in the existence of things pertaining to men and ·not in the existence of men? Make him answer the question, my friends, without these absurd interruptions. Is there any man who

Anaxagoras by Aristophanes, Euripedes, and other Greek dramatists. Anaxagoras' doctrine that the sun is a stone is mentioned in the *Orestes* of Euripedes.

believes in the existence of horsemanship and not in the existence of horses? or in flute-playing and not in flute-players? There is not, my excellent sir. If you will not answer, I will tell both you and the judges that. But you must answer my next question. Is there any man who believes in the existence of divine things and not in the existence of divinities?

Mel. There is not.

Socr. I am very glad that the judges have managed to extract an answer from you. Well then, you say that I believe in divine beings, whether they be old or new ones, and that I teach others to believe in them; at any rate, according to your statement, I believe in divine beings. That you have sworn in your deposition. But if I believe in divine beings, I suppose it follows necessarily that I believe in divinities. Is it not so? It is. I assume that you grant that, as you do not answer. But do we not believe that divinities are either gods themselves or the children of the gods? Do you admit that?

Mel. I do.

Socr. Then you admit that I believe in divinities: now, if these divinities are gods, then, as I say, you are jesting and asking a riddle, and asserting that I do not believe in the gods, and at the same time that I do, since I believe in divinities. But if these divinities are the illegitimate children of the gods, either by the nymphs or by other mothers, as they are said to be, then, I ask, what man could believe in the existence of the children of the gods, and not in the existence of the gods? That would be as strange as believing in the existence of the offspring of horses and asses, and not in the existence of horses and asses. You must have indicted me in this manner, Meletus, either to test my skill, or because you could not find any crime that you could accuse me of with truth. But you will never contrive to persuade any man, even of the smallest understanding, that a belief in divine things and things of the gods does not necessarily involve a belief in divinities, and in the gods, and in heroes.

But in truth, Athenians, I do not think that I need say very much to prove that I have not committed the crime for which Meletus is prosecuting me. What I have said is enough to prove that. But, I repeat, it is certainly true, as I have already told you, that I have incurred much unpopularity and made many enemies. And that is what will cause my condemnation, if I am condemned; not Meletus, nor Anytus either, but the prejudice and suspicion of the multitude. They have been the destruction of many good men before me, and I think that they will be so again. There is no fear that I shall be their last victim.

Perhaps some one will say: "Are you not ashamed, Socrates, of following pursuits which are very likely now to cause your death?" I should answer him with justice, and say: My friend, if you think that a man of any worth at all ought to reckon the chances of life and death when he acts, or that he ought to think of anything but whether he is acting rightly or wrongly, and as a good or a bad man would act, you are grievously mistaken. According to you, the demigods who died at Troy would be men of no great worth, and among them the son of Thetis, who thought nothing of

danger when the alternative was disgrace. For when his mother, a goddess, addressed him, as he was burning to slay Hector, I suppose in this fashion, "My son, if thou avengest the death of thy comrade Patroclus, and slayest Hector, thou wilt die thyself, for 'fate awaits thee straightway after Hector's death,'" he heard what she said, but he scorned danger and death; he feared much more to live a coward, and not to avenge his friend. "Let me punish the evil-doer and straightway die," he said, "that I may not remain here by the beaked ships, a scorn of men, encumbering the earth." Do you suppose that he thought of danger or of death? For this, Athenians, I believe to be the truth. Wherever a man's post is, whether he has chosen it of his own will, or whether he has been placed at it by his commander, there it is his duty to remain and face the danger, without thinking of death, or of any other thing, except dishonor.

When the generals whom you chose to command me, Athenians, placed me at my post at Potidæa, and at Amphipolis, and at Delium, I remained where they placed me, and ran the risk of death, like other men: and it would be very strange conduct on my part if I were to desert my post now from fear of death or of any other thing, when God has commanded me, as I am persuaded that he has done, to spend my life in searching for wisdom, and in examining myself and others. That would indeed be a very strange thing: and then certainly I might with justice be brought to trial for not believing in the gods: for I should be disobeying the oracle, and fearing death, and thinking myself wise, when I was not wise. For to fear death, my friends, is only to think ourselves wise, without being wise: for it is to think that we know what we do not know. For anything that men can tell, death may be the greatest good that can happen to them: but they fear it as if they knew quite well that it was the greatest of evils. And what is this but that shameful ignorance of thinking that we know what we do not know? In this matter too, my friends, perhaps I am different from the mass of mankind: and if I were to claim to be at all wiser than others, it would be because I do not think that I have any clear knowledge about the other world, when, in fact, I have none. But I do know very well that it is evil and base to do wrong, and to disobey my superior, whether he be man or god. And I will never do what I know to be evil, and shrink in fear from what, for all that I can tell, may be a good. And so, even if you acquit me now, and do not listen to Anytus' argument that, if I am to be acquitted, I ought never to have been brought to trial at all; and that, as it is, you are bound to put me to death, because, as he said, if I escape, all your children will forthwith be utterly corrupted by practising what Socrates teaches; if you were therefore to say to me, "Socrates, this time we will not listen to Anytus: we will let you go; but on this condition, that you cease from carrying on this search of yours, and from philosophy; if you are found following those pursuits again, you shall die": I say, if you offered to let me go on these terms, I should reply: —Athenians, I hold you in the highest regard and love; but I will obey God rather than you: and as long as I have breath and strength I will not cease from philosophy, and from exhorting you, and declaring the truth to every one of you whom I meet, saying, as I am wont: "My excellent friend, you are a citizen of Athens, a city which is very great and very famous for wisdom and power of mind; are you not ashamed of caring so much for the making of money, and for reputation, and for honor? Will you not think or care about wisdom and truth, and the perfection of your soul?" And if he disputes my words, and says that he does care about these things, I shall not forthwith release him and go away: I shall question him and cross-examine him and test him: and if I think that he has not virtue, though he says that he has, I shall reproach him for setting the lower value on the most important things, and a higher value on those that are of less account. This I shall do to every one whom I meet, young or old, citizen or stranger: but more especially to the citizens, for they are more nearly akin to me. For, know well, God has commanded me to do so. And I think that no better piece of fortune has ever befallen you in Athens than my service to God. For I spend my whole life in going about and persuading you all to give your first and chiefest care to the perfection of your souls, and not till you have done that to think of your bodies, or your wealth; and telling you that virtue does not come from wealth, but that wealth, and every other good thing which men have, whether in public, or in private, comes from virtue. If then I corrupt the youth by this teaching, the mischief is great: but if any man says that I teach anything else, he speaks falsely. And therefore, Athenians, I say, either listen to Anytus, or do not listen to him: either acquit me, or do not acquit me: but be sure that I shall not alter my way of life; no, not if I have to die for it many times.

Do not interrupt me, Athenians. Remember the request which I made to you, and listen to my words. I think that it will profit you to hear them. I am going to say something more to you, at which you may be inclined to cry out: but do not do that. Be sure that if you put me to death, who am what I have told you that I am, you will do yourselves more harm than me. Meletus and Anytus can do me no harm: that is impossible: for I am sure that God will not allow a good man to be injured by a bad one. They may indeed kill me, or drive me into exile, or deprive me of my civil rights; and perhaps Meletus and others think those things great evils. But I do not think so: I think that it is a much greater evil to do what he is doing now, and to try to put a man to death unjustly. And now, Athenians, I am not arguing in my own defence at all, as you might expect me to do: I am trying to persuade you not to sin against God, by condemning me, and rejecting his gift to you. For if you put me to death, you will not easily find another man to fill my place. God has sent me to attack the city, as if it were a great and noble horse, to use a quaint simile, which was rather sluggish from its size, and which needed to be aroused by a gadfly: and I think that I am the gadfly that God has sent to the city to attack it; for I never cease from settling upon you, as it were, at every point, and rousing, and exhorting, and reproaching each man of you all day long. You will not easily find any one else, my friends, to fill my place: and if you take my advice, you will spare my life. You are vexed, as drowsy persons are, when they are awakened, and of course, if you listened to Anytus, you could easily kill me with a single blow, and then sleep on undisturbed for the rest of your lives, unless God were to care for you enough to send another man to arouse you. And you may easily see that it is God who has given me to your city: a mere human impulse would never have led me to neglect all my own interests, or to endure seeing my private affairs neglected now for so many years, while it made me busy myself unceasingly in your interests, and go to each man of you by himself, like a father, or an elder brother, trying to persuade him to care for virtue. There would have been a reason for it, if I had gained any advantage by this conduct, or if I had been paid for my exhortations; but you see yourselves that my accusers, though they accuse me of everything else without blushing, have not had the effrontery to say that I ever either exacted or demanded payment. They could bring no evidence of that. And I think that I have sufficient evidence of the truth of what I say in my poverty.

Perhaps it may seem strange to you that, though I am so busy in going about in private with my counsel, yet I do not venture to come forward in the assembly, and take part in the public councils. You have often heard me speak of my reason for this, and in many places: it is that I have a certain divine sign from God, which is the divinity that Meletus has caricatured in his indictment. I have had it from childhood: it is a kind of voice, which whenever I hear it, always turns me back from something which I was going to do, but never urges me to act. It is this which forbids me to take part in politics. And I think that it does well to forbid me. For, Athenians, it is quite certain that if I had attempted to take part in politics, I should have perished at once and long ago, without doing any good either to you or to myself. And do not be vexed with me for telling the truth. There is no man who will preserve his life for long, either in Athens or elsewhere, if he firmly opposes the wishes of the people, and tries to prevent the commission of much injustice and illegality in the State. He who would really fight for injustice, must do so as a private man, not in public, if he means to preserve his life, even for a short time.

I will prove to you that this is so by very strong evidence, not by mere words, but by what you value highly, actions. Listen then to what has happened to me, that you may know that there is no man who could make me consent to do wrong from the fear of death; but that I would perish at once rather than give way. What I am going to tell you may be a commonplace in the Courts of Law; nevertheless it is true. The only office that I ever held in the State, Athenians, was that of Senator. When you wished to try the ten generals, who did not rescue their men after the battle of Arginusæ, in a body, which was illegal, as you all came to think afterwards, the tribe Antiochis, to which I belong, held

the presidency. On that occasion I alone of all the presidents opposed your illegal action, and gave my vote against you. The speakers were ready to suspend me and arrest me; and you were clamoring against me, and crying out to me to submit. But I thought that I ought to face the danger out in the cause of law and justice, rather than join with you in your unjust proposal, from fear of imprisonment or death. That was before the destruction of the democracy. When the oligarchy came, the Thirty sent for me, with four others, to the Council-Chamber, and ordered us to bring over Leon the Salaminian from Salamis, that they might put him to death. They were in the habit of frequently giving similar orders to many others, wishing to implicate as many men as possible in their crimes. But then I again proved, not by mere words, but by my actions, that, if I may use a vulgar expression, I do not care a straw for death; but that I do care very much indeed about not doing anything against the laws of God or man. That government with all its power did not terrify me into doing anything wrong; but when we left the Council-Chamber, the other four went over to Salamis, and brought Leon across to Athens; and I went away home: and if the rule of the Thirty had not been destroyed soon afterwards, I should very likely have been put to death for what I did then. Many of you will be my witnesses in this matter.

Now do you think that I should have remained alive all these years, if I had taken part in public affairs, and had always maintained the cause of justice like an honest man, and had held it a paramount duty, as it is, to do so? Certainly not, Athenians, nor any other man either. But throughout my whole life, both in private, and in public, whenever I have had to take part in public affairs, you will find that I have never yielded a single point in a question of right and wrong to any man; no, not to those whom my enemies falsely assert to have been my pupils.[3] But I was never any man's teacher. I have never withheld myself from any one, young or old, who was anxious to hear me converse while I was about my mission; neither do I converse for payment, and refuse to converse without payment: I am ready to ask questions of rich and poor alike, and if any man wishes to answer me, and then listen to what I have to say, he may. And I cannot justly be charged with causing these men to turn out good or bad citizens: for I never either taught, or professed to teach any of them any knowledge whatever. And if any man asserts that he ever learnt or heard any thing from me in private, which every one else did not hear as well as he, be sure that he does not speak the truth.

Why is it, then, that people delight in spending so much time in my company? You have heard why, Athenians. I told you the whole truth when I said that they delight in hearing me examine persons who think that they are wise when they are not wise. It is certainly very amusing to listen to that. And, I say, God has commanded me to examine men in oracles, and in dreams, and in every way in which the divine will was ever declared to man. This is the truth, Athenians, and if it were not the truth,

it would be easily refuted. For if it were really the case that I have already corrupted some of the young men, and am now corrupting others, surely some of them, finding as they grew older that I had given them evil counsel in their youth, would have come forward today to accuse me and take their revenge. Or if they were unwilling to do so themselves, surely their kinsmen, their fathers, or brothers, or other relatives, would, if I had done them any harm, have remembered it, and taken their revenge. Certainly I see many of them in Court. Here is Crito, of my own deme and of my own age, the father of Critobulus; here is Lysanias of Sphettus, the father of Æschinus: here is also Antiphon of Cephisus, the father of Epigenes. Then here are others, whose brothers have spent their time in my company; Nicostratus, the son of Theozotides, and brother of Theodotus—and Theodotus is dead, so he at least cannot entreat his brother to be silent: here is Paralus, the son of Demodocus, and the brother of Theages: here is Adeimantus, the son of Ariston, whose brother is Plato here: and Æantodorus, whose brother is Aristodorus. And I can name many others to you, some of whom Meletus ought to have called as witnesses in the course of his own speech: but if he forgot to call them then, let him call them now—I will stand aside while he does so—and tell us if he has any such evidence. No, on the contrary, my friends, you will find all these men ready to support me, the corrupter, the injurer of their kindred, as Meletus and Anytus call me. Those of them who have been already corrupted might perhaps have some reason for supporting

---

[3] For example, Critias and Alcibiades.

me: but what reason can their relatives, who are grown up, and who are uncorrupted, have, except the reason of truth and justice, that they know very well that Meletus is a liar, and that I am speaking the truth?

Well, my friends, this, together it may be with other things of the same nature, is pretty much what I have to say in my defence. There may be some one among you who will be vexed when he remembers how, even in a less important trial than this, he prayed and entreated the judges to acquit him with many tears, and brought forward his children and many of his friends and relatives in Court, in order to appeal to your feelings; and then finds that I shall do none of these things, though I am in what he would think the supreme danger. Perhaps he will harden himself against me when he notices this: it may make him angry, and he may give his vote in anger. If it is so with any of you—I do not suppose that it is, but in case it should be so—I think that I should answer him reasonably if I said: "My friend, I have kinsmen too, for, in the words of Homer, 'I am not born of stocks and stones,' but of woman"; and so, Athenians, I have kinsmen, and I have three sons, one of them a lad, and the other two still children. Yet I will not bring any of them forward before you, and implore you to acquit me. And why will I do none of these things? It is not from arrogance, Athenians, nor because I hold you cheap: whether or no I can face death bravely is another question: but for my own credit, and for your credit, and for the credit of our city, I do not think it well, at my age, and with my name, to do anything of that kind.

Rightly or wrongly, men have made up their minds that in some way Socrates is different from the mass of mankind. And it will be a shameful thing if those of you who are thought to excel in wisdom, or in bravery, or in any other virtue, are going to act in this fashion. I have often seen men with a reputation behaving in a strange way at their trial, as if they thought it a terrible fate to be killed, and as though they expected to live for ever, if you did not put them to death. Such men seem to me to bring discredit on the city: for any stranger would suppose that the best and most eminent Athenians, who are selected by their fellow-citizens to hold office, and for other honors, are no better than women. Those of you, Athenians, who have any reputation at all, ought not to do these things: and you ought not to allow us to do them: you should show that you will be much more merciless to men who make the city ridiculous by these pitiful pieces of acting, than to men who remain quiet.

But apart from the question of credit, my friends, I do not think that it is right to entreat the judge to acquit us, or to escape condemnation in that way. It is our duty to convince his mind by reason. He does not sit to give away justice to his friends, but to pronounce judgment: and he has sworn not to favor any man whom he would like to favor, but to decide questions according to law. And therefore we ought not to teach you to forswear yourselves; and you ought not to allow yourselves to be taught, for then neither you nor we would be acting righteously. Therefore, Athenians, do not require me to do these things, for I believe them to be neither good nor just nor holy; and, more especially do not ask me to do them today, when Meletus is prosecuting me for impiety. For were I to be successful, and to prevail on you by my prayers to break your oaths, I should be clearly teaching you to believe that there are no gods; and I should be simply accusing myself by my defence of not believing in them. But, Athenians, that is very far from the truth. I do believe in the gods as no one of my accusers believes in them: and to you and to God I commit my cause to be decided as is best for you and for me.

[*He is found guilty by 281 votes to 220.*]

I am not vexed at the verdict which you have given, Athenians, for many reasons. I expected that you would find me guilty; and I am not so much surprised at that, as at the numbers of the votes. I, certainly, never thought that the majority against me would have been so narrow. But now it seems that if only thirty votes had changed sides, I should have escaped. So I think that I have escaped Meletus, as it is: and not only have I escaped him; for it is perfectly clear that if Anytus and Lycon had not come forward to accuse me too, he would not have obtained the fifth part of the votes, and would have had to pay a fine of a thousand drachmæ.

So he proposes death as the penalty. Be it so. And what counter-penalty shall I propose to you, Athenians? What I deserve, of course, must I not? What then do I deserve to pay or to suffer for having determined not to spend my life in ease? I neglected the things which most men value, such as wealth, and family interests, and military commands, and popular oratory, and all the political appointments, and clubs, and factions, that there are in Athens; for I thought that I was really too conscientious a man to preserve my life if I engage in these matters. So I did not go where I should have done no good either to you or to myself. I went instead to each one of you by himself, to do him, as I say, the greatest of services, and strove to persuade him not to think of his affairs, until he had thought of himself, and tried to make himself as perfect and wise as possible; nor to think of the affairs of Athens, until he had thought of Athens herself; and in all cases to bestow his thoughts on things in the same manner. Then what do I deserve for such a life? Something good, Athenians, if I am really to propose what I deserve; and something good which it would be suitable to me to receive. Then what is a suitable reward to be given to a poor benefactor, who requires leisure to exhort you? There is no reward, Athenians, so suitable for him as a public maintenance in the Prytaneum. It is a much more suitable reward for him than for any of you who has won a victory at the Olympic games with his horse or his chariots. Such a man only makes you seem happy, but I make you really happy: and he is not in want, and I am. So if I am to propose the penalty which I really deserve, I propose this, a public maintenance in the Prytaneum.

Perhaps you think me stubborn and arrogant in what I am saying now, as in what I said about the entreaties and tears. It is not so, Athenians; it is rather that I am convinced that I never wronged any man intentionally, though

I cannot persuade you of that, for we have conversed together only a little time. If there were a law at Athens, as there is elsewhere, not to finish a trial of life and death in a single day, I think that I could have convinced you of it: but now it is not easy in so short a time to clear myself of the gross calumnies of my enemies. But when I am convinced that I have never wronged any man, I shall certainly not wrong myself, or admit that I deserve to suffer any evil, or propose any evil for myself as a penalty. Why should I? Lest I should suffer the penalty which Meletus proposes, when I say that I do not know whether it is a good or an evil? Shall I choose instead of it something which I know to be an evil, and propose that as a penalty? Shall I propose imprisonment? And why should I pass the rest of my days in prison, the slave of successive officials? Or shall I propose a fine, with imprisonment until it is paid? I have told you why I will not do that. I should have to remain in prison for I have no money to pay a fine with. Shall I then propose exile? Perhaps you would agree to that. Life would indeed be very dear to me, if I were unreasonable enough to expect that strangers would cheerfully tolerate my discussions and reasonings, when you who are my fellow-citizens cannot endure them, and have found them so burdensome and odious to you, that you are seeking now to be released from them. No, indeed, Athenians, that is not likely. A fine life I should lead for an old man, if I were to withdraw from Athens, and pass the rest of my days in wandering from city to city, and continually being expelled. For I know very well that the young men will listen to me, wherever I go, as they do here; and if I drive them away, they will persuade their elders to expel me: and if I do not drive them away, their fathers and kinsmen will expel me for their sakes.

Perhaps some one will say, "Why cannot you withdraw from Athens, Socrates, and hold your peace?" It is the most difficult thing in the world to make you understand why I cannot do that. If I say that I cannot hold my peace, because that would be to disobey God, you will think that I am not in earnest and will not believe me. And if I tell you that no better thing can happen to a man than to converse every day about virtue and the other matters about which you have heard me conversing and examining myself and others, and that an unexamined life is not worth living, then you will believe me still less. But that is the truth, my friends, though it is not easy to convince you of it. And, what is more, I am not accustomed to think that I deserve any punishment. If I had been rich, I would have proposed as large a fine as I could pay: that would have done me no harm. But I am not rich enough to pay a fine, unless you are willing to fix it at a sum within my means. Perhaps I could pay you a mina: so I propose that. Plato here, Athenians, and Crito, and Critobulus, and Apollodorus bid me propose thirty minæ, and they will be sureties for me. So I propose thirty minæ. They will be sufficient sureties to you for the money.

[He is condemned to death.]

You have not gained very much time, Athenians, and, as the price of it, you will have an evil name from all who wish to revile the city, and they will cast in your teeth that you put Socrates, a wise man, to death. For they will certainly call me wise, whether I am wise or not, when they want to reproach you. If you would have waited for a little while, your wishes would have been fulfilled in the course of nature; for you see that I am an old man, far advanced in years, and near to death. I am speaking not to all of you, only to those who have voted for my death. And now I am speaking to them still. Perhaps, my friends, you think that I have been defeated because I was wanting in the arguments by which I could have persuaded you to acquit me, if, that is, I had thought it right to do or to say anything to escape punishment. It is not so. I have been defeated because I was wanting, not in arguments, but in overboldness and effrontery: because I would not plead before you as you would have liked to hear me plead, or appeal to you with weeping and wailing, or say and do many other things, which I maintain are unworthy of me, but which you have been accustomed to from other men. But when I was defending myself, I thought that I ought not to do anything unmanly because of the danger which I ran, and I have not changed my mind now. I would very much rather defend myself as I did, and die, than as you would have had me do, and live. Both in a law suit, and in war, there are some things which neither I nor any other man may do in order to escape from death. In battle a man often sees that he may at least escape from death by throwing down his arms and falling on his knees before the pursuer to beg for his life. And there are many other ways

of avoiding death in every danger, if a man will not scruple to say and to do anything. But, my friends, I think that it is a much harder thing to escape from wickedness than from death; for wickedness is swifter than death. And now I, who am old and slow, have been overtaken by the slower pursuer: and my accusers, who are clever and swift, have been overtaken by the swifter pursuer, which is wickedness. And now I shall go hence, sentenced by you to death; and they will go hence, sentenced by truth to receive the penalty of wickedness and evil. And I abide by this award as well as they. Perhaps it was right for these things to be so: and I think that they are fairly measured.

And now I wish to prophesy to you, Athenians who have condemned me. For I am going to die, and that is the time when men have most prophetic power. And I prophesy to you who have sentenced me to death, that a far severer punishment than you have inflicted on me, will surely overtake you as soon as I am dead. You have done this thing, thinking that you will be relieved from having to give an account of your lives. But I say that the result will be very different from that. There will be more men who will call you to account, whom I have held back, and whom you did not see. And they will be harder masters to you than I have been, for they will be younger, and you will be more angry with them. For if you think that you will restrain men from reproaching you for your evil lives by putting them to death, you are very much mistaken. That way of escape is hardly possible, and it is not a good one. It is much better, and much easier, not to silence reproaches, but to make yourselves as perfect as you can. This is my parting prophecy to you who have condemned me.

With you who have acquitted me I should like to converse touching this thing that has come to pass, while the authorities are busy, and before I go to the place where I have to die. So, I pray you, remain with me until I go hence: there is no reason why we should not converse with each other while it is possible. I wish to explain to you, as my friends, the meaning of what has befallen me. A wonderful thing has happened to me, judges—for you I am right in calling judges. The prophetic sign, which I am wont to receive from the divine voice, has been constantly with me all through my life till now, opposing me in quite small matters if I were not going to act rightly. And now you yourselves see what has happened to me; a thing which might be thought, and which is sometimes actually reckoned, the supreme evil. But the sign of God did not withstand me when I was leaving my house in the morning, nor when I was coming up hither to the Court, nor at any point in my speech, when I was going to say anything: though at other times it has often stopped me in the very act of speaking. But now, in this matter, it has never once withstood me, either in my words or my actions. I will tell you what I believe to be the reason of that. This thing that has come upon me must be a good: and those of us who think that death is an evil must needs be mistaken. I have a clear proof that that is so; for my accustomed sign would certainly have opposed me, if I had not been going to fare well.

And if we reflect in another way we shall see that we may well hope that death is a good. For the state of death is one of two things: either the dead man wholly ceases to be, and loses all sensation; or, according to the common belief, it is a change and a migration of the soul unto another place. And if death is the absence of all sensation, and like the sleep of one whose slumbers are unbroken by any dreams, it will be a wonderful gain. For if a man had to select that night in which he slept so soundly that he did not even see any dreams, and had to compare with it all the other nights and days of his life, and then had to say how many days and nights in his life he had spent better and more pleasantly than this night, I think that a private person, nay, even the great King [of Persia] himself, would find them easy to count, compared with the others. If that is the nature of death, I for one count it a gain. For then it appears that eternity is nothing more than a single night. But if death is a journey to another place, and the common belief be true, that there are all who have died, what good could be greater than this, my judges? Would a journey not be worth taking, at the end of which, in the other world, we should be released from the self-styled judges who are here, and should find the true judges, who are said to sit in judgment below, such as Minos, and Rhadamanthus, and Æacus, and Triptolemus, and the other demi-gods who were just in their lives? Or what would you not give to converse with Orpheus and Musæus and Hesiod and Homer?

I am willing to die many times, if this be true. And for my own part I should have a wonderful interest in meeting there Palamedes, and Ajax the son of Telamon, and the other men of old who have died through an unjust judgment, and in comparing my experiences with theirs. That I think would be no small pleasure. And, above all, I could spend my time in examining those who are there, as I examine men here, and in finding out which of them is wise, and which of them thinks himself wise, when he is not wise. What would we not give, my judges, to be able to examine the leader of the great expedition against Troy, or Odysseus, or Sisyphus, or countless other men and women whom we could name? It would be an infinite happiness to converse with them, and to live with them, and to examine them. Assuredly there they do not put men to death for doing that. For besides the other ways in which they are happier than we are, they are immortal, at least if the common belief be true.

And you too, judges, must face death with a good courage, and believe this as a truth, that no evil can happen to a good man, either in life, or after death. His fortunes are not neglected by the gods; and what has come to me today has not come by chance. I am persuaded that it was better for me to die now, and to be released from trouble: and that was the reason why the sign never turned me back. And so I am hardly angry with my accusers, or with those who have condemned me to die. Yet it was not with this mind that they accused me and condemned me, but meaning to do me an injury. So far I may find fault with them.

Yet I have one request to make of them. When my sons grow up, visit them with punishment, my friends, and vex them in the same way that I have vexed you, if they seem to you to care for riches, or for any other thing, before virtue: and if they think that they are something, when they are nothing at all, reproach them, as I have reproached you, for not caring for what they should, and for thinking that they are great men when in fact they are worthless. And if you will do this, I myself and my sons will have received our deserts at your hands.

But now the time has come, and we must go hence; I to die, and you to live. Whether life or death is better is known to God, and to God only.

COMMENT

The importance of Socrates as an exemplar of philosophy lies not so much in his teachings as in his method. He was trying to explore the human mind and to reach the truth by dint of question and answer, dialogue, and debate. This give-and-take method of investigation by discussion is called "dialectic" or "the Socratic method"—and it is still the essential method of the philosopher. It may be carried on between two or more persons or within the mind of a single inquirer, as you put questions to yourself and wrestle with the answers. Usually its objective is to establish a definition, to fix in mind the essential reality of some basic value or property. Each proposed definition is tested by a process of critical examination. Is it internally consistent? Does it fit the facts? Does it agree with what we already know? In formulating and testing the definition, the philosopher continually refers to the particular data of experience; but he examines the particulars as instances of a type, and he defines the type—the "idea," "form," or "universal"—by establishing its significance in the particulars.

Basic to the method is the attitude of inquiry. Although Socrates spoke of an "inner voice" of conscience which forbade disgraceful acts, he insisted that "the unexamined life is not worth living." He realized that conscience reflects the norms of custom, but he subjected these norms to reflection and unfettered discussion. He distinguished between various attitudes:

Dogmatic belief—"It is so."
Dogmatic disbelief—"It is not so."
Agnostic nonbelief—"We can never know."
Tentativity—"It may or may not be so."
Inquirism—"We may not know, but let us try to find out."

Dogmatic belief and disbelief and agnostic nonbelief cut off inquiry, but tentativity and inquirism stimulate free and hopeful wonder. Socrates attacked the attitudes that block the way to truth and praised the attitudes that open the path. He differed from the Sophists, who tended to be dogmatic agnostics, and from the traditionalists, who tended to be dogmatic believers. Although he was a man of intense convictions, and was prepared to die for their sake, he subjected his own ideas to the same unsparing criticism that he directed toward others.

I shall not attempt to analyse the ideas implicit in his defence that (1) freedom of inquiry is a service to the state, (2) that the dialectical method is the best way to separate truth from falsehood, (3) that wisdom is virtue, (4) that virtue can be taught, (5) that wrong-doing is involuntary, (6) that spiritual goods are superior to material goods, and (7) that an honorable death is better than a dishonorable life. The examination of these ideas is best left to the reader.

2

God and Man

SAINT ANSELM (1033?–1109)

Although Italian by birth, Saint Anselm ended his career as Archbishop of Canterbury. He is famous not only for his philosophical works but also for his interpretation of Christian theology. As Abbot of a monastery in Normandy and as Archbishop in England, he was a zealous defender of the Church against the expansion of secular power.

Proslogium

. . . I do not seek to understand that I may believe, but I believe in order to understand. For this also I believe,— that unless I believed, I should not understand.

And so, Lord, do thou, who dost give understanding to faith, give me, so far as thou knowest it to be profitable, to understand that thou art as we believe; and that thou art that which we believe. And, indeed, we believe that thou art a being than which nothing greater can be conceived. Or is there no such nature, since the fool hath said in his heart, there is no God? (Psalms xiv. 1). But, at any rate, this very fool, when he hears of this being

Translated by Sidney Norton Deane, Open Court Publishing Co., 1903. Reprinted by permission.

of which I speak—a being than which nothing greater can be conceived—understands what he hears, and what he understands is in his understanding; although he does not understand it to exist.

For, it is one thing for an object to be in the understanding, and another to understand that the object exists. When a painter first conceives of what he will afterwards perform, he has it in his understanding, but he does not yet understand it to be, because he has not yet performed it. But after he has made the painting, he both has it in his understanding, and he understands that it exists, because he has made it.

Hence, even the fool is convinced that something exists in the understanding, at least, than which nothing greater can be conceived. For, when he hears of this, he understands it. And whatever is understood, exists in the understanding. And assuredly that, than which nothing greater can be conceived, cannot exist in the understanding alone. For, suppose it exists in the understanding alone: then it can be conceived to exist in reality; which is greater.

Therefore, if that, than which nothing greater can be conceived, exists in the understanding alone, the very being, than which nothing greater can be conceived, is one, than which a greater can be conceived. But obviously this is impossible. Hence, there is no doubt that there exists a being, than which nothing greater can be conceived, and it exists both in the understanding and in reality.

And it assuredly exists so truly, that it cannot be conceived not to exist. For, it is possible to conceive of a being which cannot be conceived not to exist; and this is greater than one which can be conceived not to exist. Hence, if that, than which nothing greater can be conceived, can be conceived not to exist, it is not that, than which nothing greater can be conceived. But this is an irreconcilable contradiction. There is, then, so truly a being than which nothing greater can be conceived to exist, that it cannot even be conceived not to exist; and this being thou art, O Lord, our God.

So truly, therefore, dost thou exist, O Lord, my God, that thou canst not be conceived not to exist; and rightly. For, if a mind could conceive of a being better than thee, the creature would rise above the Creator; and this is most absurd. And, indeed, whatever else there is, except thee alone, can be conceived not to exist. To thee alone, therefore, it belongs to exist more truly than all other beings, and hence in a higher degree than all others. For, whatever else exists does not exist so truly, and hence in a less degree it belongs to it to exist. Why, then, has the fool said in his heart, there is no God, since it is so evident, to a rational mind, that thou dost exist in the highest degree of all? Why, except that he is dull and a fool?

SAINT THOMAS AQUINAS (1225?–1274)

Thomas, the son of Count Landolfo, of Aquino, was born at the ancestral castle near Naples. At the age of five, he was sent to the Benedictine monastery of Monte Cassino to be educated. When ten years old, he entered the University of Naples, where he remained for six years. He then joined the Dominican Order, very much against the will of his parents and so much to the disgust of his brothers that they kidnaped and imprisoned him in the family stronghold for two years. At last he escaped and continued his education at Paris and Cologne. In 1256, he became a Master of Theology, and thereafter taught at the University of Paris and elsewhere. During his career, he succeeded in constructing the greatest of all systems of Catholic philosophy. He died at the age of forty-nine. Three years after his death he was censured by the Bishop of Paris for his alleged heterodoxy, but in 1323 he was canonized by Pope John XXII.

Summa Theologica

and

Summa Contra Gentiles

1. [The Argument From Change]

[*In his first argument, St. Thomas argues from the fact of change to an Unmoved Mover; in his second argument, from the fact of causation to an Uncaused Cause; in his third argument, from the fact of non-necessary being to a Necessary Being. In each case the reasoning is an inference from something dependent (change, causation, or contingent being) to something independent and self-sufficient—namely, God. Motion, movement, change, as employed in the first argument, are synonymous. Note that the argument is not restricted to change of place (motion as we ordinarily use the term), but refers to all change whatsoever.*]

From St. Thomas Aquinas, *Philosophical Texts,* trans. by Thomas Gilby, Oxford University Press, London, New York, Toronto, 1951. Reprinted by permission.

The first and most open way is presented by change or motion. It is evident to our senses and certain that in the world some things are in motion.

Whatever is in motion is set in motion by another. For nothing is in

35

motion unless it be potential to that to which it is in motion; whereas a thing sets in motion inasmuch as it is actual, because to set in motion is naught else than to bring a thing from potentiality to actuality, and from potentiality a subject cannot be brought except by a being that is actual; actually hot makes potentially hot become actually hot, as when fire changes and alters wood. Now for the same thing to be simultaneously and identically actual and potential is not possible, though it is possible under different respects; what is actually hot cannot simultaneously be potentially hot, though it may be potentially cold. It is impossible, therefore, for a thing both to exert and to suffer motion in the same respect and according to the same motion.

If that which sets in motion is itself in motion then it also must be set in motion by another, and that in its turn by another again. But here we cannot proceed to infinity, otherwise there would be no first mover, and consequently no other mover, seeing that subsequent movers do not initiate motion unless they be moved by a former mover, as stick by hand.

Therefore we are bound to arrive at the first mover set in motion by no other, and this everyone understands to be God.

Summa Theologica, Ia. ii. 3

Having indicated that the attempt to prove God's existence is not hopeless from the outset, we proceed now to fix on the arguments of philosophers and theologians alike, beginning with Aristotle who sets off from the concept of change. His argument takes two directions, of which the first is as follows.

Everything in a process of change is set in motion by another. Our senses tell us that things are in motion, the sun for instance. Therefore they are set in motion by another. Now this setter-in-motion is either itself in motion or it is not. If not, then we have our conclusion, namely the necessity of inferring a motionless mover which we term God. But if it is itself in motion then it must be set in motion by another. Either we have an infinite series or we arrive at a changeless mover. But we cannot go back infinitely. Therefore we must infer a first changeless mover.

There are two propositions to be proved; first, that everything in motion is set in motion by another; second, that an infinite series of things setting and set in motion is impossible.

Summa Contra Gentiles, I, 13

2. [The Argument from Efficient Causality]

The second approach starts from the nature of efficient causality. Among phenomena we discover an order of efficient causes. But we never come across, nor ever shall, anything that is an efficient cause of itself; such a thing would be prior to itself, which is impossible. It is also impossible to go on to infinity with efficient causes, for in an ordered series the first is the cause of the intermediate and the intermediate is the cause of the last. Whether or not the intermediate causes be one or many is irrelevant. Take away the cause and the effect also goes. Therefore if there were not a first among efficient causes—which would be the case in an infinite series—there would be no intermediate causes nor an ultimate effect. This plainly is not the case. A first cause, generally termed God, must therefore be inferred.

Summa Theologica, Ia. ii. 3

An infinite series of efficient causes in essential subordination is impossible. Causes essentially required for the production of a determinate effect cannot consequently be infinitely multiplied, as if a block could be shifted by a crowbar, which in turn is levered by a hand, and so on to infinity.

But an infinite series of causes in accidental subordination is not reputed impossible, so long as all the causes thus multiplied are grouped as one cause and their multiplication is incidental to the causality at work. For instance a blacksmith may work with many hammers because one after another breaks in his hand, but that one particular hammer is used after another particular one is incidental. Similarly that in begetting a child a man was himself begotten by another man; for he is father as man, not as son. In a genealogy of efficient causes all men have the same status of particular generator. Hence, for such a line to stretch back to infinity is not unthinkable.

Summa Theologica, Ia. xlvi. 2, ad 7

3. [The Argument from Contingent Being]

We observe in our environment how things are born and die away; they may or may not exist; to be or not to be—

they are open to either alternative. All things cannot be so contingent, for what is able not to be may be reckoned as once a non-being, and were everything like that once there would have been nothing at all. Now were this true, nothing would ever have begun, for what is does not begin to be except because of something which is, and so there would be nothing even now. This is clearly hollow. Therefore all things cannot be might-not-have-beens; among them must be being whose existence is necessary.

Summa Theologica, Ia. ii. 3

Everything that is a possible-to-be has a cause, since its essence as such is equally uncommitted to the alternatives of existing and not existing. If it be credited with existence, then this must be from some cause. Causality, however, is not an infinite process. Therefore a necessary being is the conclusion. The principle of its necessity is either from outside or not. If not, then the being is inwardly necessary. If necessity comes from without, we must still propose a first being necessary of itself, since we cannot have an endless series of derivatively necessary beings.

Summa Contra Gentiles, I, 15

4. [The Argument from Degrees of Excellence]

The fourth argument is taken from the degrees of reality we discover in things. Some are truer and better and nobler than others, so also with other perfections. But more or less are attributed to different things in proportion as they variously approach something which is the maximum.

Hence, there is something truest, and best, and noblest, and in consequence the superlative being, for the greatest truths are the greatest beings. Now the maximum in any order is the cause of all the other realities of that order. Therefore there is a real cause of being and goodness and all perfections whatsoever in everything; and this we term God.

Summa Theologica, Ia. ii. 3

The argument can be gathered from words let fall by Aristotle in the *Metaphysics*. He says that the truest things are also the most real; and again, that there is a superlative truth. One piece of architecture is more sham than another, one more genuine; throughout a comparison is implied with what is true without qualification and most of all. We can go farther and conclude that there is something most real, and this we call God.

Summa Contra Gentiles, I, 13

5. [The Argument from Purpose or Design]

Contrary and discordant elements . . . cannot always, or nearly always, work harmoniously together unless they be directed by something providing each and all with their tendencies to a definite end. Now in the universe we see things of diverse natures conspiring together in one scheme, not rarely or haphazardly, but approximately always or for the most part. There must be

something, therefore, whose providence directs the universe.

Summa Contra Gentiles, I, 13

We observe that things without consciousness, such as physical bodies, operate with a purpose, as appears from their co-operating invariably, or almost so, in the same way in order to obtain the best result. Clearly then they reach this end by intention and not by chance. Things lacking knowledge move towards an end only when directed by someone who knows and understands, as an arrow by an archer. There is consequently an intelligent being who directs all natural things to their ends; and this being we call God.

Summa Theologica, Ia. ii. 3

When diverse things are co-ordinated the scheme depends on their directed unification, as the order of battle of a whole army hangs on the plan of the commander-in-chief. The arrangement of diverse things cannot be dictated by their own private and divergent natures; of themselves they are diverse and exhibit no tendency to make a pattern. It follows that the order of many among themselves is either a matter of chance or it must be resolved into one first planner who has a purpose in mind. What comes about always, or in the great majority of cases, is not the result of accident. Therefore the whole of this world has but one planner or governor.

Summa Contra Gentiles, I, 42

DAVID HUME (1711–1776)

Born in Edinburgh, Hume was the youngest son of a gentleman landowner. His father died when he was an infant, and he was reared by his mother, who, somewhat critical of his bookish tendencies, is said to have remarked that "oor Davie's a fine good-natured crater but uncommon wake-minded." Hume's studies at the University of Edinburgh instilled in him a love of literature and philosophy which kept him from settling down to a legal or business career. He decided to devote his life to scholarly pursuits, and at the age of twenty-three crossed the Channel to live in France, studying at La Flèche, where Descartes had gone to school.

There he completed, before he reached the age of twenty-five, his greatest philosophical work, the *Treatise of Human Nature.* In his brief autobiography he remarked that the book "fell dead-born from the press." Although this remark is an exaggeration, it suggests Hume's great disappointment that his ideas did not find a wider public. His *An Enquiry Concerning Human Understanding* (1748) and *An Enquiry Concerning the Principles of Morals* (1751), which restated principal parts of the *Treatise,* were somewhat more popular, but his literary reputation was based mainly upon his *Political Discourses* (1752) and his *History of England,* published in 1755 and following years. He also wrote *Dialogues Concerning Natural Religion,* which he regarded as a bit too shocking to publish during his own lifetime.

Although the income from his books gradually increased and he remained a frugal bachelor, he had to find other means of livelihood. Early in his career, he applied first to the University of Edinburgh and then to the University of Glasgow for a teaching position, but both universities rejected him because of the heterodoxy of his views. For a short time he was tutor to a lunatic, the Marquis of Annandale, and then secretary to a general, St. Clair. Thereafter he secured a six-year post as Keeper of Advocates' Library in Edinburgh, and from 1763 to 1765 served as secretary to the British Embassy in Paris. His French acquaintances included the most famous intellectuals of the period—D'Alembert, Diderot, Holbach, and Rousseau. After his sojourn in France, he spent two years in London (1767–1769) as Under Secretary of State for Scotland. In Great Britain as in France, he was a friend of distinguished wits, such as Burke, Gibbon, and Adam Smith. Having received a moderate pension, he finally retired to Edinburgh, where he lived quietly with his sister until his death in 1776.

In a self-obituary, he describes himself as follows:

> I was a man of mild disposition, of command of temper, of an open, social and cheerful humor, capable of attachment but little susceptible of enmity, and of great moderation in all my passions. Even my love of literary fame, my ruling passion, never soured my temper, notwithstanding my frequent disappointments.

This characterization appears to be entirely accurate. Hume was a canny Scot, with a kindly, humorous, equable disposition.

Dialogues Concerning Natural Religion

1. [The Argument for a First Cause]

The argument, replied Demea, which I would insist on is the common one. Whatever exists must have a cause or reason of its existence, it being absolutely impossible for anything to produce itself or be the cause of its own existence. In mounting up, therefore, from effects to causes, we must either go on in tracing an infinite succession, without any ultimate cause at all, or must at last have recourse to some ultimate cause that is *necessarily* existent. Now that the first supposition is absurd may be thus proved. In the infinite chain or succession of causes and effects, each single effect is determined to exist by the power and efficacy of that cause which immediately preceded; but the whole eternal chain or succession, taken together, is not determined or caused by anything, and yet it is evident that it requires a cause or reason, as much as any particular object which begins to exist in time. The question is still reasonable why this particular succession of causes existed from eternity, and not any other succession or no succession at all. If there be no necessarily existent being, any supposition which can be formed is equally possible; nor is there any more absurdity in *nothing's* having existed from eternity than there is in that succession of causes which constitutes the universe. What was it, then, which determined *something* to exist rather than *nothing,* and bestowed being on a particular possibility, exclusive of the rest? *External causes,* there are supposed to be none. *Chance* is a word without a meaning. Was it *nothing?* But that can never produce anything. We must, therefore, have recourse to a necessarily existent Being who carries the *reason* of his existence in himself, and who cannot be supposed not to

Published in London, 1779. Critical edition by Norman Kemp Smith, Oxford University Press, 1935.

exist, without an express contradiction. There is, consequently, such a Being—that is, there is a Deity.

I shall not leave it to Philo, said Cleànthes, though I know that the starting objections is his chief delight, to point out the weakness of this metaphysical reasoning. It seems to me so obviously ill-grounded, and at the same time of so little consequence to the cause of true piety and religion, that I shall myself venture to show the fallacy of it.

I shall begin with observing that there is an evident absurdity in pretending to demonstrate a matter of fact, or to prove it by any arguments *a priori*. Nothing is demonstrable unless the contrary implies a contradiction. Nothing that is distinctly conceivable implies a contradiction. Whatever we conceive as existent, we can also conceive as non-existent. There is no being, therefore, whose non-existence implies a contradiction. Consequently there is no being whose existence is demonstrable. I propose this argument as entirely decisive, and am willing to rest the whole controversy upon it.

It is pretended that the Deity is a necessarily existent being; and this necessity of his existence is attempted to be explained by asserting that, if we knew his whole essence or nature, we should perceive it to be as impossible for him not to exist, as for twice two not to be four. But it is evident that this can never happen, while our faculties remain the same as at present. It will still be possible for us, at any time, to conceive the non-existence of what we formerly conceived to exist; nor can the mind ever lie under a necessity of sup-posing any object to remain always in being; in the same manner as we lie under a necessity of always conceiving twice two to be four. The words, therefore, *necessary existence* have no meaning or, which is the same thing, none that is consistent.

But further, why may not the material universe be the necessarily existent Being, according to this pretended explication of necessity? We dare not affirm that we know all the qualities of matter; and, for aught we can determine, it may contain some qualities which, were they known, would make its non-existence appear as great a contradiction as that twice two is five. I find only one argument employed to prove that the material world is not the necessarily existent Being; and this argument is derived from the contingency both of the matter and the form of the world. "Any particle of matter," it is said, "may be *conceived* to be annihilated, and any form may be *conceived* to be altered. Such an annihilation or alteration, therefore, is not impossible."[1] But it seems a great partiality not to perceive that the same argument extends equally to the Deity, so far as we have any conception of him, and that the mind can at least imagine him to be non-existent or his attributes to be altered. It must be some unknown, inconceivable qualities which can make his non-existence appear impossible or his attributes unalterable; and no reason can be assigned why these qualities may not belong to matter. As they are altogether unknown

[1] Dr. Clarke.

and inconceivable, they can never be proved incompatible with it.

Add to this that in tracing an eternal succession of objects it seems absurd to inquire for a general cause or first author. How can anything that exists from eternity have a cause, since that relation implies a priority in time and a beginning of existence?

In such a chain, too, or succession of objects, each part is caused by that which preceded it, and causes that which succeeds it. Where then is the difficulty? But the *whole*, you say, wants a cause. I answer that the uniting of these parts into a whole, like the uniting of several distinct countries into one kingdom, or several distinct members into one body, is performed merely by an arbitrary act of the mind, and has no influence on the nature of things. Did I show you the particular causes of each individual in a collection of twenty particles of matter, I should think it very unreasonable should you afterwards ask me what was the cause of the whole twenty. This is sufficiently explained in explaining the cause of the parts.

Though the reasonings which you have urged, Cleanthes, may well excuse me, said Philo, from starting any further difficulties, yet I cannot forbear insisting still upon another topic. It is observed by arithmeticians that the products of 9 compose always either 9 or some lesser product of 9 if you add together all the characters of which any of the former products is composed. Thus, of 18, 27, 36, which are products of 9, you make 9 by adding 1 to 8, 2 to 7, 3 to 6. Thus 369 is a product also of 9; and if you add 3, 6, and 9, you make

18, a lesser product of 9. To a superficial observer so wonderful a regularity may be admired as the effect either of chance or design; but a skilful algebraist immediately concludes it to be the work of necessity, and demonstrates that it must for ever result from the nature of these numbers. Is it not probable, I ask, that the whole economy of the universe is conducted by a like necessity, though no human algebra can furnish a key which solves the difficulty? And instead of admiring the order of natural beings, may it not happen that, could we penetrate into the intimate nature of bodies, we should clearly see why it was absolutely impossible they could ever admit of any other disposition? So dangerous is it to introduce this idea of necessity into the present question! and so naturally does it afford an inference directly opposite to the religious hypothesis!

2. [The Argument from Design]

Not to lose any time in circumlocutions, said Cleanthes, . . . I shall briefly explain how I conceive this matter. Look round the world, contemplate the whole and every part of it: you will find it to be nothing but one great machine, subdivided into an infinite number of lesser machines, which again admit of subdivisions to a degree beyond what human senses and faculties can trace and explain. All these various machines, and even their most minute parts, are adjusted to each other with an accuracy which ravishes into admiration all men who have ever contemplated them. The curious adapting of means to ends, throughout all nature, resembles exactly, though it much exceeds, the productions of human contrivance—of human design, thought, wisdom, and intelligence. Since therefore the effects resemble each other, we are led to infer, by all the rules of analogy, that the causes also resemble, and that the Author of nature is somewhat similar to the mind of man, though possessed of much larger faculties, proportioned to the grandeur of the work which he has executed. By this argument *a posteriori,* and by this argument alone, do we prove at once the existence of a Deity and his similarity to human mind and intelligence.

I shall be so free, Cleanthes, said Demea, as to tell you that from the beginning I could not approve of your conclusion concerning the similarity of the Deity to men, still less can I approve of the mediums by which you endeavor to establish it. What! No demonstration of the Being of God! No abstract arguments! No proofs *a priori!* Are these which have hitherto been so much insisted on by philosophers all fallacy, all sophism? Can we reach no farther in this subject than experience and probability? I will not say that this is betraying the cause of a Deity; but surely, by this affected candor, you give advantages to atheists which they never could obtain by the mere dint of argument and reasoning.

What I chiefly scruple in this subject, said Philo, is not so much that all religious arguments are by Cleanthes reduced to experience, as that they appear not to be even the most certain and irrefragable of that inferior kind. That a stone will fall, that fire will burn, that the earth has solidity, we have observed a thousand and a thousand times; and when any new instance of this nature is presented, we draw without hesitation the accustomed inference. The exact similarity of the cases gives us a perfect assurance of a similar event, and a stronger evidence is never desired nor sought after. But wherever you depart, in the least, from the similarity of the cases, you diminish proportionably the evidence, and may at last bring it to a very weak *analogy,* which is confessedly liable to error and uncertainty. After having experienced the circulation of the blood in human creatures, we make no doubt that it takes place in Titius and Maevius; but from its circulation in frogs and fishes it is only a presumption, though a strong one, from analogy that it takes place in men and other animals. The analogical reasoning is much weaker when we infer the circulation of the sap in vegetables from our experience that the blood circulates in animals; and those who hastily followed that imperfect analogy are found, by more accurate experiments, to have been mistaken.

If we see a house, Cleanthes, we conclude, with the greatest certainty, that it had an architect or builder because this is precisely that species of effect which we have experienced to proceed from that species of cause. But surely you will not affirm that the universe bears such a resemblance to a house that we can with the same certainty infer a similar cause, or that the analogy is here entire and perfect. The dissimilitude is so striking that the utmost you can here pretend to is a guess, a conjecture, a presumption concerning a similar cause; and how that pretension will be received in the world, I leave you to consider. . . .

That all inferences, Cleanthes, concerning fact are founded on experience, and that all experimental reasonings are founded on the supposition that similar causes prove similar effects, and similar effects similar causes, I shall not at present much dispute with you. But observe, I entreat you, with what extreme caution all just reasoners proceed in the transferring of experiments to similar cases. Unless the cases be exactly similar, they repose no perfect confidence in applying their past observation to any particular phenomenon. Every alteration of circumstances occasions a doubt concerning the event; and it requires new experiments to prove certainly that the new circumstances are of no moment or importance. A change in bulk, situation, arrangement, age, disposition of the air, or surrounding bodies—any of these particulars may be attended with the most unexpected consequences. And unless the objects be quite familiar to us, it is the highest temerity to expect with assurance, after any of these changes, an event similar to that which before fell under our observation. The slow and deliberate steps of philosophers here, if anywhere, are distinguished from the precipitate march of the vulgar, who, hurried on by the smallest similitude, are incapable of all discernment or consideration.

But can you think, Cleanthes, that your usual phlegm and philosophy have been preserved in so wide a step as you have taken when you compared to the universe houses, ships, furniture, machines, and, from their similarity in some circumstances, inferred a similarity in their causes? Thought, design, intelligence, such as we discover in men and other animals, is no more than one of the springs and principles of the universe, as well as heat or cold, attraction or repulsion, and a hundred others which fall under daily observation. It is an active cause by which some particular parts of nature, we find, produce alterations on other parts. But can a conclusion, with any propriety, be transferred from parts to the whole? Does not the great disproportion bar all comparison and inference? From observing the growth of a hair, can we learn anything concerning the generation of a man? Would the manner of a leaf's blowing, even though perfectly known, afford us any instruction concerning the vegetation of a tree?

But allowing that we were to take the *operations* of one part of nature upon another for the foundation of our judgment concerning the *origin* of the whole (which never can be admitted), yet why select so minute, so weak, so bounded a principle as the reason and design of animals is found to be upon this planet? What peculiar privilege has this little agitation of the brain which we call *thought,* that we must thus make it the model of the whole universe? Our partiality in our own favor does indeed present it on all occasions, but sound philosophy ought carefully to guard against so natural an illusion.

So far from admitting, continued Philo, that the operations of a part can afford us any just conclusion concerning the origin of the whole, I will not allow any one part to form a rule for another part if the latter be very remote from the former. Is there any reasonable ground to conclude that the inhabitants of other planets possess thought, intelligence, reason, or anything similar to these faculties in men? When nature has so extremely diversified her manner of operation in this small globe, can we imagine that she incessantly copies herself throughout so immense a universe? And if thought, as we may well suppose, be confined merely to this narrow corner and has even there so limited a sphere of action, with what propriety can we assign it for the original cause of all things? The narrow views of a peasant who makes his domestic economy the rule for the government of kingdoms is in comparison a pardonable sophism.

But were we ever so much assured that a thought and reason resembling the human were to be found throughout the whole universe, and were its activity elsewhere vastly greater and more commanding than it appears in this globe, yet I cannot see why the operations of a world constituted, arranged, adjusted, can with any propriety be extended to a world which is in its embryo state, and is advancing towards that constitution and arrangement. By observation we know somewhat of the economy, action, and nourishment of a finished animal, but we must transfer with great caution that observation to the growth of a fœtus in the womb, and still more to the formation of an animalcule in the loins of its male parent. Nature, we find, even from our limited experience, possesses an infinite number of springs and principles which incessantly discover themselves on every change of her

position and situation. And what new and unknown principles would actuate her in so new and unknown a situation as that of the formation of a universe, we cannot, without the utmost temerity, pretend to determine.

A very small part of this great system, during a very short time, is very imperfectly discovered to us; and do we thence pronounce decisively concerning the origin of the whole?

Admirable conclusion! Stone, wood, brick, iron, brass, have not, at this time, in this minute globe of earth, an order or arrangement without human art and contrivance; therefore, the universe could not originally attain its order and arrangement without something similar to human art. But is a part of nature a rule for another part very wide of the former? Is it a rule for the whole? Is a very small part a rule for the universe? Is nature in one situation a certain rule for nature in another situation vastly different from the former?

And can you blame me, Cleanthes, if I here imitate the prudent reserve of Simonides, who, according to the noted story, being asked by Hiero, *What God was?* desired a day to think of it, and then two days more; and after that manner continually prolonged the term, without ever bringing in his definition or description? Could you even blame me if I had answered, at first, *that I did not know,* and was sensible that this subject lay vastly beyond the reach of my faculties? You might cry out sceptic and rallier, as much as you pleased; but, having found in so many other subjects much more familiar the imperfections and even contradictions of human reason, I never should expect any success from its feeble conjectures in a subject so sublime and so remote from the sphere of our observation. When two *species* of objects have always been observed to be conjoined together, I can *infer,* by custom, the existence of one wherever I *see* the existence of the other; and this I call an argument from experience. But how this argument can have place where the objects, as in the present case, are single, individual, without parallel or specific resemblance, may be difficult to explain. And will any man tell me with a serious countenance that an orderly universe must arise from some thought and art like the human because we have experience of it? To ascertain this reasoning it were requisite that we had experience of the origin of worlds; and it is not sufficient, surely, that we have seen ships and cities arise from human art and contrivance. . . .

. . . I shall endeavor to show you, a little more distinctly, the inconveniences of that anthropomorphism which you have embraced, and shall prove that there is no ground to suppose a plan of the world to be formed in the Divine mind, consisting of distinct ideas, differently arranged, in the same manner as an architect forms in his head the plan of a house which he intends to execute.

It is not easy, I own, to see what is gained by this supposition, whether we judge of the matter by *reason* or by *experience.* We are still obliged to mount higher in order to find the cause of this cause which you had assigned as satisfactory and conclusive.

If *reason* (I mean abstract reason derived from inquiries *a priori*) be not alike mute with regard to all questions concerning cause and effect, this sentence at least it will venture to pronounce: that a mental world or universe of ideas requires a cause as much as does a material world or universe of objects, and, if similar in its arrangement, must require a similar cause. For what is there in this subject which should occasion a different conclusion or inference? In an abstract view, they are entirely alike; and no difficulty attends the one supposition which is not common to both of them.

Again, when we will needs force *experience* to pronounce some sentence, even on these subjects which lie beyond her sphere, neither can she perceive any material difference in this particular between these two kinds of worlds, but finds them to be governed by similar principles, and to depend upon an equal variety of causes in their operations. We have specimens in miniature of both of them. Our own mind resembles the one; a vegetable or animal body the other. Let experience, therefore, judge from these samples. Nothing seems more delicate, with regard to its causes, than thought; and as these causes never operate in two persons after the same manner, so we never find two persons who think exactly alike. Nor indeed does the same person think exactly alike at any two different periods of time. A difference of age, of the disposition of his body, of weather, of food, of company, of books, of passions—any of these particulars, or others more minute, are sufficient to alter the curious machinery of thought and communicate to it very different movements and operations. As far as we can judge, vegetables and animal bodies are not more delicate in their motions, nor depend upon a greater variety or more curious adjustment of springs and principles.

How, therefore, shall we satisfy ourselves concerning the cause of that Being whom you suppose the Author of nature, or, according to your system of anthropomorphism, the ideal world into which you trace the material? Have we not the same reason to trace that ideal world into another ideal world or new intelligent principle? But if we stop and go no farther, why go so far? why not stop at the material world? How can we satisfy ourselves without going on *in infinitum?* And, after all, what satisfaction is there in that infinite progression? Let us remember the story of the Indian philosopher and his elephant. It was never more applicable than to the present subject. If the material world rests upon a similar ideal world, this ideal world must rest upon some other, and so on without end. It were better, therefore, never to look beyond the present material world. By supposing it to contain the principle of its order within itself, we really assert it to be God; and the sooner we arrive at that Divine Being, so much the better. When you go one step beyond the mundane system, you only excite an inquisitive humor which it is impossible ever to satisfy.

To say that the different ideas which compose the reason of the Supreme Being fall into order of themselves and by their own nature is really to talk without any precise meaning. If it has a meaning, I would fain know why it is not as good sense to say that the parts of the material world fall into order of themselves and by their own nature. Can the one opinion be intelligible, while the other is not so?

We have, indeed, experience of ideas which fall into order of themselves and without any *known* cause. But, I am sure, we have a much larger experience of matter which does the same, as in all instances of generation and vegetation where the accurate analysis of the cause exceeds all human comprehension. We have also experience of particular systems of thought and of matter which have no order; of the first in madness, of the second in corruption. Why, then, should we think that order is more essential to one than the other? And if it requires a cause in both, what do we gain by your system, in tracing the universe of objects into a similar universe of ideas? The first step which we make leads us on for ever. It were, therefore, wise in us to limit all our inquiries to the present world, without looking farther. No satisfaction can ever be attained by these speculations which so far exceed the narrow bounds of human understanding. . . .

But to show you still more inconveniences, continued Philo, in your anthropomorphism, please to take a new survey of your principles. *Like effects prove like causes.* This is the experimental argument; and this, you say too, is the sole theological argument. . . .

Now, Cleanthes, said Philo, with an air of alacrity and triumph, mark the consequences. *First,* by this method of reasoning you renounce all claim to infinity in any of the attributes of the Deity. For, as the cause ought only to be proportioned to the effect, and the effect, so far as it falls under our cognizance, is not infinite, what pretensions have we, upon your suppositions, to ascribe that attribute to the Divine Being? You will still insist that, by removing him so much from all similarity to human creatures, we give in to the most arbitrary hypothesis, and at the same time weaken all proofs of his existence.

Secondly, you have no reason, on your theory, for ascribing perfection to the Deity, even in his finite capacity, or for supposing him free from every error, mistake, or incoherence, in his undertakings. There are many inexplicable difficulties in the works of nature which, if we allow a perfect author to be proved *a priori,* are easily solved, and become only seeming difficulties from the narrow capacity of man, who cannot trace infinite relations. But according to your method of reasoning, these difficulties become all real, and, perhaps, will be insisted on as new instances of likeness to human art and contrivance. At least, you must acknowledge that it is impossible for us to tell, from our limited views, whether this system contains any great faults or deserves any considerable praise if compared to other possible and even real systems. Could a peasant, if the *Æneid* were read to him, pronounce that poem to be absolutely faultless, or even assign to it its proper rank among the productions of human wit, he who had never seen any other production?

But were this world ever so perfect a production, it must still remain uncertain whether all the excellences of the work can justly be ascribed to the workman. If we survey a ship, what an exalted idea must we form of the in-

genuity of the carpenter who framed so complicated, useful, and beautiful a machine? And what surprise must we feel when we find him a stupid mechanic who imitated others, and copied an art which, through a long succession of ages, after multiplied trials, mistakes, corrections, deliberations, and controversies, had been gradually improving? Many worlds might have been botched and bungled, throughout an eternity, ere this system was struck out; much labor lost, many fruitless trials made, and a slow but continued improvement carried on during infinite ages in the art of world-making. In such subjects, who can determine where the truth, nay, who can conjecture where the probability lies, amidst a great number of hypotheses which may be proposed, and a still greater which may be imagined?

And what shadow of an argument, continued Philo, can you produce from your hypothesis to prove the unity of the Deity? A great number of men join in building a house or ship, in rearing a city, in framing a commonwealth; why may not several deities combine in contriving and framing a world? This is only so much greater similarity to human affairs. By sharing the work among several, we may so much further limit the attributes of each, and get rid of that extensive power and knowledge which must be supposed in one deity, and which, according to you, can only serve to weaken the proof of his existence. And if such foolish, such vicious creatures as man can yet often unite in framing and executing one plan, how much more those deities or demons, whom we may suppose several degrees more perfect! . . . .

It must be a slight fabric, indeed, said Demea, which can be erected on so tottering a foundation. While we are uncertain whether there is one deity or many, whether the deity or deities, to whom we owe our existence, be perfect or imperfect, subordinate or supreme, dead or alive, what trust or confidence can we repose in them? What devotion or worship address to them? What veneration or obedience pay them? To all the purposes of life the theory of religion becomes altogether useless; and even with regard to speculative consequences its uncertainty, according to you, must render it totally precarious and unsatisfactory.

To render it still more unsatisfactory, said Philo, there occurs to me another hypothesis which must acquire an air of probability from the method of reasoning so much insisted on by Cleanthes. That like effects arise from like causes—this principle he supposes the foundation of all religion. But there is another principle of the same kind, no less certain and derived from the same source of experience, that, where several known circumstances are observed to be similar, the unknown will also be found similar. Thus, if we see the limbs of a human body, we conclude that it is also attended with a human head, though hid from us. Thus, if we see, through a chink in a wall, a small part of the sun, we conclude that were the wall removed we should see the whole body. In short, this method of reasoning is so obvious and familiar that no scruple can ever be made with regard to its solidity.

Now, if we survey the universe, so far as it falls under our knowledge, it bears a great resemblance to an animal or organized body, and seems actuated with a like principle of life and motion. A continual circulation of matter in it produces no disorder; a continual waste in every part is incessantly repaired; the closest sympathy is perceived throughout the entire system; and each part or member, in performing its proper offices, operates both to its own preservation and to that of the whole. The world, therefore, I infer, is an animal; and the Deity is the *soul* of the world, actuating it, and actuated by it.

You have too much learning, Cleanthes, to be at all surprised at this opinion which, you know, was maintained by almost all the theists of antiquity, and chiefly prevails in their discourses and reasonings. For though, sometimes, the ancient philosophers reason from final causes, as if they thought the world the workmanship of God, yet it appears rather their favorite notion to consider it as his body whose organization renders it subservient to him. And it must be confessed that, as the universe resembles more a human body than it does the works of human art and contrivance, if our limited analogy could ever, with any propriety, be extended to the whole of nature, the inference seems juster in favor of the ancient than the modern theory.

There are many other advantages, too, in the former theory which recommended it to the ancient theologians. Nothing more repugnant to all their notions, because nothing more repugnant to common experience, than mind without body, a mere spiritual substance which fell not under their senses nor comprehension, and of which they had not observed one single instance throughout all nature. Mind and body they knew because they felt both; an order, arrangement, organization, or internal machinery, in both they likewise knew, after the same manner; and it could not but seem reasonable to transfer this experience to the universe, and to suppose the divine mind and body to be also coeval and to have, both of them, order and arrangement naturally inherent in them and inseparable from them.

Here, therefore, is a new species of anthropomorphism, Cleanthes, on which you may deliberate, and a theory which seems not liable to any considerable difficulties. You are too much superior, surely, to systematical prejudices to find any more difficulty in supposing an animal body to be, originally, of itself or from unknown causes, possessed of order and organization, than in supposing a similar order to belong to mind. But the vulgar prejudice that body and mind ought always to accompany each other ought not, one should think, to be entirely neglected; since it is founded on vulgar experience, the only guide which you profess to follow in all these theological inquiries. And if you assert that our limited experience is an unequal standard by which to judge of the unlimited extent of nature, you entirely abandon your own hypothesis, and must thenceforward adopt our mysticism, as you call it, and admit of the absolute incomprehensibility of the Divine Nature.

This theory, I own, replied Cleanthes, has never before occurred to me, though a pretty natural one; and I cannot readily, upon so short an examination and reflection, deliver any opinion with regard to it. You are very scrupulous, indeed, said Philo; were I to examine any system of yours, I should not have acted with half that caution and reserve, in stating objections and difficulties to it. However, if anything occur to you, you will oblige us by proposing it.

Why then, replied Cleanthes, it seems to me that, though the world does, in many circumstances, resemble an animal body, yet is the analogy also defective in many circumstances the most material: no organs of sense; no seat of thought or reason; no one precise origin of motion and action. In short, it seems to bear a stronger resemblance to a vegetable than to an animal, and your inference would be so far inconclusive in favor of the soul of the world. . . .

But here, continued Philo, in examining the ancient system of the soul of the world there strikes me, all on a sudden, a new idea which, if just, must go near to subvert all your reasoning, and destroy even your first inferences on which you repose such confidence. If the universe bears a greater likeness to animal bodies and to vegetables than to the works of human art, it is more probable that its cause resembles the cause of the former than that of the latter, and its origin ought rather to be ascribed to generation or vegetation than to reason or design. Your conclusion, even according to your own principles, is therefore lame and defective.

Pray open up this argument a little further, said Demea, for I do not rightly apprehend it in that concise manner in which you have expressed it.

Our friend Cleanthes, replied Philo, as you have heard, asserts that, since no question of fact can be proved otherwise than by experience, the existence of a Deity admits not of proof from any other medium. The world, says he, resembles the works of human contrivance; therefore its cause must also resemble that of the other. Here we may remark that the operation of one very small part of nature, to wit, man, upon another very small part, to wit, that inanimate matter lying within his reach, is the rule by which Cleanthes judges of the origin of the whole; and he measures objects, so widely disproportioned, by the same individual standard. But to waive all objections drawn from this topic, I affirm that there are other parts of the universe (besides the machines of human invention) which bear still a greater resemblance to the fabric of the world, and which, therefore, afford a better conjecture concerning the universal origin of this system. These parts are animals and vegetables. The world plainly resembles more an animal or a vegetable than it does a watch or a knitting-loom. Its cause, therefore, it is more probable, resembles the cause of the former. The cause of the former is generation or vegetation. The cause, therefore, of the world we may infer to be something similar or analogous to generation or vegetation.

. . . In this little corner of the world alone, there are four principles, *reason, instinct, generation, vegetation,* which are similar to each other, and are the causes of similar effects. What a number of other principles may we naturally suppose in the immense extent and variety of the universe could we travel from planet to planet, and from system to system, in order to examine each part of this mighty fabric? Any one of these four principles above mentioned (and a hundred others which lie open to our conjecture) may afford us a theory by which to judge of the origin of the world; and it is a palpable and egregious partiality to confine our view entirely to that principle by which our own minds operate. Were this principle more intelligible on that account, such a partiality might be somewhat excusable; but reason, in its internal fabric and structure, is really as little known to us as instinct or vegetation; and perhaps, even that vague, undeterminate word *nature* to which the vulgar refer everything is not at the bottom more inexplicable. The effects of these principles are all known to us from experience; but the principles themselves and their manner of operation are totally unknown; nor is it less intelligible or less conformable to experience to say that the world arose by vegetation, from a seed shed by another world, than to say that it arose from a divine reason or contrivance, according to the sense in which Cleanthes understands it.

But methinks, said Demea, if the world had a vegetative quality and could sow the seeds of new worlds into the infinite chaos, this power would be still an additional argument for design in its author. For whence could arise so wonderful a faculty but from design? Or how can order spring from anything which perceives not that order which it bestows?

You need only look around you, replied Philo, to satisfy yourself with regard to this question. A tree bestows order and organization on that tree which springs from it, without knowing the order; an animal in the same manner on its offspring; a bird on its nest; and instances of this kind are even more frequent in the world than those of order which arise from reason and contrivance. To say that all this order in animals and vegetables proceeds ultimately from design is begging the question; nor can that great point be ascertained otherwise than by proving, *a priori,* both that order is, from its nature, inseparably attached to thought and that it can never of itself or from original unknown principles belong to matter. . . .

I must confess, Philo, replied Cleanthes, that, of all men living, the task which you have undertaken, of raising doubts and objections, suits you best and seems, in a manner, natural and unavoidable to you. So great is your fertility of invention that I am not ashamed to acknowledge myself unable, on a sudden, to solve regularly such out-of-the-way difficulties as you incessantly start upon me, though I clearly see, in general, their fallacy and error. And I question not, but you are yourself, at present, in the same case, and have not the solution so ready as the objection, while you must be sensible that common sense and reason are entirely against you, and that such whimsies as you have delivered may puzzle but never can convince us.

What you ascribe to the fertility of my invention, replied Philo, is entirely owing to the nature of the subject. In subjects adapted to the narrow compass of human reason there is commonly but one determination which carries probability or conviction with it; and to a man of sound judgment all other suppositions but that one appear

entirely absurd and chimerical. But in such questions as the present, a hundred contradictory views may preserve a kind of imperfect analogy, and invention has here full scope to exert itself. Without any great effort of thought, I believe that I could, in an instant, propose other systems of cosmogony which would have some faint appearance of truth, though it is a thousand, a million to one if either yours or any one of mine be the true system.

For instance, what if I should revive the old Epicurean hypothesis? This is commonly, and I believe justly, esteemed the most absurd system that has yet been proposed; yet I know not whether, with a few alterations, it might not be brought to bear a faint appearance of probability. Instead of supposing matter infinite, as Epicurus did, let us suppose it finite. A finite number of particles is only susceptible of finite transpositions; and it must happen, in an eternal duration, that every possible order or position must be tried an infinite number of times. This world, therefore, with all its events, even the most minute, has before been produced and destroyed, and will again be produced and destroyed, without any bounds and limitations. No one who has a conception of the powers of infinite, in comparison of finite, will ever scruple this determination.

But this supposes, said Demea, that matter can acquire motion without any voluntary agent or first mover.

And where is the difficulty, replied Philo, of that supposition? Every event, before experience, is equally difficult and incomprehensible; and every event, after experience, is equally easy and intelligible. Motion, in many instances, from gravity, from elasticity, from electricity, begins in matter, without any known voluntary agent; and to suppose always, in these cases, an unknown voluntary agent is mere hypothesis and hypothesis attended with no advantages. The beginning of motion in matter itself is as conceivable *a priori* as its communication from mind and intelligence.

Besides, why may not motion have been propagated by impulse through all eternity, and the same stock of it, or nearly the same, be still upheld in the universe? As much as is lost by the composition of motion, as much is gained by its resolution. And whatever the causes are, the fact is certain that matter is and always has been in continual agitation, as far as human experience or tradition reaches. There is not probably, at present, in the whole universe, one particle of matter at absolute rest.

And this very consideration, too, continued Philo, which we have stumbled on in the course of the argument suggests a new hypothesis of cosmogony that is not absolutely absurd and improbable. Is there a system, an order, an economy of things, by which matter can preserve that perpetual agitation which seems essential to it, and yet maintain a constancy in the forms which it produces? There certainly is such an economy, for this is actually the case with the present world. The continual motion of matter, therefore, in less than infinite transpositions, must produce this economy or order, and, by its very nature, that order, when once established, supports itself for many ages if not to eternity. But wherever matter is so poised, arranged, and adjusted, as to continue in perpetual motion, and yet preserve a constancy in the forms, its situation must, of necessity, have all the same appearance of art and contrivance which we observe at present. All the parts of each form must have a relation to each other and to the whole; and the whole itself must have a relation to the other parts of the universe, to the element in which the form subsists, to the materials with which it repairs its waste and decay, and to every other form which is hostile or friendly. A defect in any of these particulars destroys the form, and the matter of which it is composed is again set loose, and is thrown into irregular motions and fermentations till it unite itself to some other regular form. If no such form be prepared to receive it, and if there be a great quantity of this corrupted matter in the universe, the universe itself is entirely disordered, whether it be the feeble embryo of a world in its first beginnings that is thus destroyed or the rotten carcass of one languishing in old age and infirmity. In either case, a chaos ensues till finite though innumerable revolutions produce, at last, some forms whose parts and organs are so adjusted as to support the forms amidst a continued succession of matter.

Suppose (for we shall endeavor to vary the expression) that matter were thrown into any position by a blind, unguided force; it is evident that this first position must, in all probability, be the most confused and most disorderly imaginable, without any resemblance to those works of human contrivance which, along with a symmetry of parts, discover an adjustment of means to ends and a tendency to self-preservation. If the actuating force cease after this operation, matter must remain for ever in disorder and continue an immense chaos, without any proportion or activity. But suppose that the actuating force, whatever it be, still continues in matter, this first position will immediately give place to a second which will likewise, in all probability, be as disorderly as the first, and so on through many successions of changes and revolutions. No particular order or position ever continues a moment unaltered. The original force, still remaining in activity, gives a perpetual restlessness to matter. Every possible situation is produced, and instantly destroyed. If a glimpse or dawn of order appears for a moment, it is instantly hurried away and confounded by that never-ceasing force which actuates every part of matter.

Thus the universe goes on for many ages in a continued succession of chaos and disorder. But is it not possible that it may settle at last, so as not to lose its motion and active force (for that we have supposed inherent in it), yet so as to preserve an uniformity of appearance, amidst the continual motion and fluctuation of its parts? This we find to be the case with the universe at present. Every individual is perpetually changing, and every part of every individual; and yet the whole remains, in appearance, the same. May we not hope for such a position or rather be assured of it from the eternal revolutions of unguided matter; and may not this account for all the appearing wisdom and contrivance which is in the universe? Let us contemplate the subject a little, and we shall find that this adjustment, if attained by matter, of a seeming stability in the forms, with a real and perpetual revolution or motion of parts,

affords a plausible, if not a true, solution of the difficulty.

It is in vain, therefore, to insist upon the uses of the parts in animals or vegetables, and their curious adjustment to each other. I would fain know how an animal could subsist unless its parts were so adjusted? Do we not find that it immediately perishes whenever this adjustment ceases, and that its matter, corrupting, tries some new form? It happens indeed that the parts of the world are so well adjusted that some regular form immediately lays claim to this corrupted matter; and if it were not so, could the world subsist? Must it not dissolve, as well as the animal, and pass through new positions and situations till in great but finite succession it fall, at last, into the present or some such order?

It is well, replied Cleanthes, you told us that this hypothesis was suggested on a sudden, in the course of the argument. Had you had leisure to examine it, you would soon have perceived the insuperable objections to which it is exposed. No form, you say, can subsist unless it possess those powers and organs requisite for its subsistence; some new order or economy must be tried, and so on, without intermission, till at last some order which can support and maintain itself is fallen upon. But according to this hypothesis, whence arise the many conveniences and advantages which men and all animals possess? Two eyes, two ears are not absolutely necessary for the subsistence of the species. Human race might have been propagated and preserved without horses, dogs, cows, sheep, and those innumerable fruits and products which serve to our satisfaction and enjoyment.

If no camels had been created for the use of man in the sandy deserts of Africa and Arabia, would the world have been dissolved? If no loadstone had been framed to give that wonderful and useful direction to the needle, would human society and the human kind have been immediately extinguished? Though the maxims of nature be in general very frugal, yet instances of this kind are far from being rare; and any one of them is a sufficient proof of design—and of a benevolent design—which gave rise to the order and arrangement of the universe.

At least, you may safely infer, said Philo, that the foregoing hypothesis is so far incomplete and imperfect, which I shall not scruple to allow. But can we ever reasonably expect greater success in any attempts of this nature? Or can we ever hope to erect a system of cosmogony that will be liable to no exceptions, and will contain no circumstance repugnant to our limited and imperfect experience of the analogy of nature? Your theory itself cannot surely pretend to any such advantage, even though you have run into *anthropomorphism,* the better to preserve a conformity to common experience. Let us once more put it to trial. In all instances which we have ever seen, ideas are copied from real objects, and are ectypal, not archetypal, to express myself in learned terms. You reverse this order and give thought the precedence. In all instances which we have ever seen, thought has no influence upon matter except where that matter is so conjoined with it as to have an equal reciprocal influence upon it. No animal can move immediately anything but the members of its own body; and, indeed, the equality of action and reaction seems to be an universal law of nature; but your theory implies a contradiction to this experience. These instances, with many more which it were easy to collect (particularly the supposition of a mind or system of thought that is eternal or, in other words, an animal ingenerable and immortal)—these instances, I say, may teach all of us sobriety in condemning each other, and let us see that as no system of this kind ought ever to be received from a slight analogy, so neither ought any to be rejected on account of a small incongruity. For that is an inconvenience from which we can justly pronounce no one to be exempted.

All religious systems, it is confessed, are subject to great and insuperable difficulties. Each disputant triumphs in his turn, while he carries on an offensive war, and exposes the absurdities, barbarities, and pernicious tenets of his antagonist. But all of them, on the whole, prepare a complete triumph for the *sceptic,* who tells them that no system ought ever to be embraced with regard to such subjects: for this plain reason than no absurdity ought ever to be assented to with regard to any subject. A total suspense of judgment is here our only reasonable resource. And if every attack, as is commonly observed, and no defense among theologians is successful, how complete must be *his* victory who remains always, with all mankind, on the offensive, and has himself no fixed station or abiding city which he is ever, on any occasion, obliged to defend?

WALTER T. STACE (1886–1965)

Stace was born in London and educated at Edinburgh and Trinity College, Dublin. From 1910 to 1932 he served in the British Civil Service in Ceylon, where he became a District Judge and eventually Mayor of Colombo. While in Ceylon he studied Hinduism and Buddhism and wrote extensively on philosophical subjects. In 1932 he came to the United States to teach at Princeton, and remained at the University until his academic retirement in 1955. His publications include books on Greek philosophy, Hegel, aesthetics, metaphysics and theory of knowledge, morals and politics, and religion. In his later life he became intensely interested in mysticism, which he sought to reconcile with empiricism. The following essay represents his more sceptical period.

Man Against Darkness

1

The Catholic bishops of America recently issued a statement in which they said that the chaotic and bewildered state of the modern world is due to man's loss of faith, his abandonment of God and religion. For my part I believe in no religion at all. Yet I entirely agree with the bishops. It is no doubt an oversimplification to speak of *the* cause of so complex a state of affairs as the tortured condition of the world today. Its causes are doubtless multitudinous. Yet allowing for some element of oversimplification, I say that the bishops' assertion is substantially true.

M. Jean-Paul Sartre, the French existentialist philosopher, labels himself an atheist. Yet his views seem to me plainly to support the statement of the bishops. So long as there was believed to be a God in the sky, he says, men could regard him as the source of their moral ideals. The universe, created and governed by a fatherly God, was a

friendly habitation for man. We could be sure that, however great the evil in the world, good in the end would triumph and the forces of evil would be routed. With the disappearance of God from the sky all this has changed. Since the world is not ruled by a spiritual being, but rather by blind forces, there cannot be any ideals, moral or otherwise, in the universe outside us. Our ideals, therefore, must proceed only from our own minds; they are our own inventions. Thus the world which surrounds us is nothing but an immense spiritual emptiness. It is a dead universe. We do no live in a universe which is on the side of our values. It is completely indifferent to them.

Years ago Mr. Bertrand Russell, in his essay *A Free Man's Worship,* said much the same thing.

> Such in outline, but even more purposeless, more void of meaning, is the world which Science presents for our belief. Amid such a world, if anywhere, our ideals henceforward must find a home. . . . Blind to good and evil, reckless of destruction, omnipotent matter rolls on its relentless

From *The Atlantic Monthly*, September 1948. Reprinted by permission of the editors and Mrs. Walter T. Stace.

way; for man, condemned today to lose his dearest, tomorrow himself to pass through the gate of darkness, it remains only to cherish, ere yet the blow falls, the lofty thoughts that ennoble his little day; . . . to worship at the shrine his own hands have built; . . . to sustain alone, a weary but unyielding Atlas, the world that his own ideals have fashioned despite the trampling march of unconscious power.

It is true that Mr. Russell's personal attitude to the disappearance of religion is quite different from either that of M. Sartre or the bishops or myself. The bishops think it a calamity. So do I. M. Sartre finds it "very distressing." And he berates as shallow the attitude of those who think that without God the world can go on just the same as before, as if nothing had happened. This creates for mankind, he thinks, a terrible crisis. And in this I agree with him. Mr. Russell, on the other hand, seems to believe that religion has done more harm than good in the world, and that its disappearance will be a blessing. But his picture of the world, and of the modern mind, is the same as that of M. Sartre. He stresses the *purposelessness* of the universe, the facts that man's ideals are his own creations, that the universe outside him in no way supports them, that man is alone and friendless in the world.

Mr. Russell notes that it is science which has produced this situation. There is no doubt that this is correct. But the way in which it has come about is not generally understood. There is a popular belief that some particular scientific discoveries or theories, such as the Darwinian theory of evolution, or the views of geologists about the age of the earth, or a series of such discoveries, have done the damage. It would be foolish to deny that these discoveries have had a great effect in undermining religious dogmas. But this account does not at all go to the root of the matter. Religion can probably outlive any scientific discoveries which could be made. It can accommodate itself to them. The root cause of the decay of faith has not been any particular discovery of science, but rather the general spirit of science and certain basic assumptions upon which modern science, from the seventeenth century onwards, has proceeded.

2

It was Galileo and Newton—notwithstanding that Newton himself was a deeply religious man—who destroyed the old comfortable picture of a friendly universe governed by spiritual values. And this was effected, not by Newton's discovery of the law of gravitation nor by any of Galileo's brilliant investigations, but by the general picture of the world which these men and others of their time made the basis of the science, not only of their own day, but of all succeeding generations down to the present. That is why the century immediately following Newton, the eighteenth century, was notoriously an age of religious skepticism. Skepticism did not have to wait for the discoveries of Darwin and the geologists in the nineteenth century. It flooded the world immediately after the age of the rise of science.

Neither the Copernican hypothesis nor any of Newton's or Galileo's particular discoveries were the real causes. Religious faith might well have accommodated itself to the new astronomy. The real turning point between the medieval age of faith and the modern age of unfaith came when the scientists of the seventeenth century turned their backs upon what used to be called "final causes." The final cause of a thing or event meant the purpose which it was supposed to serve in the universe, its cosmic purpose. What lay back of this was the presupposition that there is a cosmic order or plan and that everything which exists could in the last analysis be explained in terms of its place in this cosmic plan, that is, in terms of its purpose.

Plato and Aristotle believed this, and so did the whole medieval Christian world. For instance, if it were true that the sun and the moon were created and exist for the purpose of giving light to man, then this fact would explain why the sun and the moon exist. We might not be able to discover the purpose of everything, but everything must have a purpose. Belief in final causes thus amounted to a belief that the world is governed by purposes, presumably the purposes of some overruling mind. This belief was not the invention of Christianity. It was basic to the whole of Western civilization, whether in the ancient pagan world or in Christendom, from the time of Socrates to the rise of science in the seventeenth century.

The founders of modern science—for instance, Galileo, Kepler, and Newton—were mostly pious men who did not doubt God's purposes. Nevertheless they took the revolutionary step of consciously and deliberately expelling the idea of purpose as controlling nature from their new science of nature. They did this on the ground that inquiry into purposes is useless for what science aims at: namely, the prediction and control of events. To predict an eclipse, what you have to know is not its purpose but its causes. Hence science from the seventeenth century onwards became exclusively an inquiry into causes. The conception of purpose in the world was ignored and frowned on. This, though silent and almost unnoticed, was the greatest revolution in human history, far outweighing in importance any of the political revolutions whose thunder has reverberated through the world.

For it came about in this way that for the past three hundred years there has been growing up in men's minds, dominated as they are by science, a new imaginative picture of the world. The world, according to this new picture, is purposeless, senseless, meaningless. Nature is nothing but matter in motion. The motions of matter are governed, not by any purpose, but by blind forces and laws. Nature on this view, says Whitehead—to whose writings I am indebted in this part of my paper—is "merely the hurrying of material, endlessly, meaninglessly." You can draw a sharp line across the history of Europe dividing it into two epochs of very unequal length. The line passes through the lifetime of Galileo. European man before Galileo—whether ancient pagan or more recent Christian—thought of the world as controlled by plan and purpose. After Galileo European man thinks of it as utterly purposeless. This is the great revolution of which I spoke.

It is this which has killed religion. Religion could survive the discoveries that the sun, not the earth, is the center; that men are descended from simian ancestors; that the earth is hundreds of millions of years old. These discoveries may render out of date some of the details of older theological dogmas, may force their restatement in new intellectual frameworks. But they do not touch the essence of the religious vision itself, which is the faith that there is plan and purpose in the world, that the world is a moral order, that in the end all things are for the best. This faith may express itself through many different intellectual dogmas, those of Christianity, of Hinduism, of Islam. All and any of these intellectual dogmas may be destroyed without destroying the essential religious spirit. But that spirit cannot survive destruction of belief in a plan and purpose of the world, for that is the very heart of it. Religion can get on with any sort of astronomy, geology, biology, physics. But it cannot get on with a purposeless and meaningless universe.

If the scheme of things is purposeless and meaningless, then the life of man is purposeless and meaningless too. Everything is futile, all effort is in the end worthless. A man may, of course, still pursue disconnected ends, money, fame, art, science, and may gain pleasure from them. But his life is hollow at the center. Hence the dissatisfied, disillusioned, restless, spirit of modern man.

The picture of a meaningless world, and a meaningless human life, is, I think, the basic theme of much modern art and literature. Certainly it is the basic theme of modern philosophy. According to the most characteristic philosophies of the modern period from Hume in the eighteenth century to the so-called positivists of today, the world is just what it is, and that is the end of all inquiry. There is no reason for its being what it is. Everything might just as well have been quite different, and there would have been no reason for that either. When you have stated what things are, what things the world contains, there is nothing more which could be said, even by an omniscient being. To ask any question about *why* things are thus, or what purpose their being so serves, is to ask a senseless question, because they serve no purpose at all. For instance, there is for modern philosophy no such thing as the ancient problem of evil. For this once famous question presupposes that pain and misery, though they seem so inexplicable and irrational to us, must ultimately subserve some rational purpose, must have their places in the cosmic plan. But this is nonsense. There is no such overruling rationality in the universe. Belief in the ultimate irrationality of everything is the quintessence of what is called the modern mind.

It is true that, parallel with these philosophies which are typical of the modern mind, preaching the meaninglessness of the world, there has run a line of idealistic philosophies whose contention is that the world is after all spiritual in nature and that moral ideals and values are inherent in its structure. But most of these idealisms were simply philosophical expressions of romanticism, which was itself no more than an unsuccessful counterattack of the religious against the scientific view of things. They perished, along with romanticism in literature and art, about the beginning of the present century, though of course they still have a few adherents.

At the bottom these idealistic systems of thought were rationalizations of man's wishful thinking. They were born of the refusal of men to admit the cosmic darkness. They were comforting illusions within the warm glow of which the more tender-minded intellectuals sought to shelter themselves from the icy winds of the universe. They lasted a little while. But they are shattered now, and we return once more to the vision of a purposeless world.

3

Along with the ruin of the religious vision there went the ruin of moral principles and indeed of all values. If there is a cosmic purpose, if there is in the nature of things a drive towards goodness, then our moral systems will derive their validity from this. But if our moral rules do not proceed from something outside us in the nature of the universe—whether we say it is God or simply the universe itself—then they must be our own inventions. Thus it came to be believed that moral rules must be merely an expression of our own likes and dislikes. But likes and dislikes are notoriously variable. What pleases one man, people, or culture displeases another. Therefore morals are wholly relative.

This obvious conclusion from the idea of a purposeless world made its appearance in Europe immediately after the rise of science, for instance in the philosophy of Hobbes. Hobbes saw at once that if there is no purpose in the world there are no values either. "Good and evil," he writes, "are names that signify our appetites and aversions; which in different tempers, customs, and doctrines of men are different. . . . Every man calleth that which pleaseth him, good; and that which displeaseth him, evil."

This doctrine of the relativity of morals, though it has recently received an impetus from the studies of anthropologists, was thus really implicit in the whole scientific mentality. It is disastrous for morals because it destroys their entire traditional foundation. That is why philosophers who see the danger signals, from the time at least of Kant, have been trying to give to morals a new foundation, that is, a secular or nonreligious foundation. This attempt may very well be intellectually successful. Such a foundation, independent of the religious view of the world, might well be found. But the question is whether it can ever be a *practical* success, that is, whether apart from its logical validity and its influence with intellectuals, it can ever replace among the masses of men the lost religious foundation. On that question hangs perhaps the future of civilization. But meanwhile disaster is overtaking us.

The widespread belief in "ethical relativity" among philosophers, psychologists, ethnologists, and sociologists is the theoretical counterpart of the repudiation of principle which we see all around us, especially in international affairs, the field in which morals have always had the weakest foothold.

No one any longer effectively believes in moral principles except as the private prejudices either of individual men or of nations or cultures. This is the inevitable consequence of the doctrine of ethical relativity, which in turn is the inevitable consequence of believing in a purposeless world.

Another characteristic of our spiritual state is loss of belief in the freedom of the will. This also is a fruit of the scientific spirit, though not of any particular scientific discovery. Science has been built up on the basis of determinism, which is the belief that every event is completely determined by a chain of causes and is therefore theoretically predictable beforehand. It is true that recent physics seems to challenge this. But so far as its practical consequences are concerned, the damage has long ago been done. A man's actions, it was argued, are as much events in the natural world as is an eclipse of the sun. It follows that men's actions are as theoretically predictable as an eclipse. But if it is certain now that John Smith will murder Joseph Jones at 2.15 P.M. on January 1, 1963, what possible meaning can it have to say that when that time comes John Smith will be *free* to choose whether he will commit the murder or not? And if he is not free, how can he be held responsible?

It is true that the whole of this argument can be shown by a competent philosopher to be a tissue of fallacies— or at least I claim that it can. But the point is that the analysis required to show this is much too subtle to be understood by the average entirely unphilosophical man. Because of this, the argument against free will is generally swallowed whole by the unphilosophical. Hence the thought that man is not free, that he is the helpless plaything of forces over which he has no control, has deeply penetrated the modern mind. We hear of economic determinism, cultural determinism, historical determinism. We are not responsible for what we do because our glands control us, or because we are the products of environment or heredity. Not moral self-control, but the doctor, the psychiatrist, the educationist, must save us from doing evil. Pills and injections in the future are to do what Christ and the prophets have failed to do. Of course I do not mean to deny that doctors and educationists can and must help. And I do not mean in any way to belittle their efforts. But I do wish to draw attention to the weakening of moral controls, the greater or less repudiation of personal responsibility which, in the popular thinking of the day, result from these tendencies of thought.

4

What, then, is to be done? Where are we to look for salvation from the evils of our time? All the remedies I have seen suggested so far are, in my opinion, useless. Let us look at some of them.

Philosophers and intellectuals generally can, I believe, genuinely do something to help. But it is extremely little. What philosophers can do is to show that neither the relativity of morals nor the denial of free will really follows from the grounds which have been supposed to support them. They can also try to discover a genuine secular basis for morals to replace the religious basis which has disappeared. Some of us are trying to do these things. But in the first place philosophers unfortunately are not agreed about these matters, and their disputes are utterly confusing to the nonphilosophers. And in the second place their influence is practically negligible because their analyses necessarily take place on a level on which the masses are totally unable to follow them.

The bishops, of course, propose as remedy a return to belief in God and in the doctrines of the Christian religion. Others think that a new religion is what is needed. Those who make these proposals fail to realize that the crisis in man's spiritual condition is something unique in history for which there is no sort of analogy in the past. They are thinking perhaps of the collapse of the ancient Greek and Roman religions. The vacuum then created was easily filled by Christianity, and it might have been filled by Mithraism if Christianity had not appeared. By analogy they think that Christianity might now be replaced by a new religion, or even that Christianity itself, if revivified, might bring back health to men's lives.

But I believe that there is no analogy at all between our present state and that of the European peoples at the time of the fall of paganism. Men had at that time lost their belief only in particular dogmas, particular embodiments of the religious view of the world. It had no doubt become incredible that Zeus and the other gods were living on the top of Mount Olympus. You could go to the top and find no trace of them. But the imaginative

picture of a world governed by purpose, a world driving towards the good —which is the inner spirit of religion —had at that time received no serious shock. It had merely to re-embody itself in new dogmas, those of Christianity or some other religion. Religion itself was not dead in the world, only a particular form of it.

But now the situation is quite different. It is not merely that particular dogmas, like that of the virgin birth, are unacceptable to the modern mind. That is true, but it constitutes a very superficial diagnosis of the present situation of religion. Modern skepticism is of a wholly different order from that of the intellectuals of the ancient world. It has attacked and destroyed not merely the outward forms of the religious spirit, its particularized dogmas, but the very essence of that spirit itself, belief in a meaningful and purposeful world. For the founding of a new religion a new Jesus Christ or Buddha would have to appear, in itself a most unlikely event and one for which in any case we cannot afford to sit and wait. But even if a new prophet and a new religion did appear, we may predict that they would fail in the modern world. No one for long would believe in them, for modern men have lost the vision, basic to all religion, of an ordered plan and purpose of the world. They have before their minds the picture of a purposeless universe, and such a world-picture must be fatal to any religion at all, not merely to Christianity.

We must not be misled by occasional appearances of a revival of the religious spirit. Men, we are told, in their disgust and disillusionment at the emptiness of their lives, are turning once more to religion, or are searching for a new message. It may be so. We must expect such wistful yearnings of the spirit. We must expect men to wish back again the light that is gone, and to try to bring it back. But however they may wish and try, the light will not shine again,—not at least in the civilization to which we belong.

Another remedy commonly proposed is that we should turn to science itself, or the scientific spirit, for our salvation. Mr. Russell and Professor Dewey both make this proposal, though in somewhat different ways. Professor Dewey seems to believe that discoveries in sociology, the application of scientific method to social and political problems, will rescue us. This seems to me to be utterly naïve. It is not likely that science, which is basically the cause of our spiritual troubles, is likely also to produce the cure for them. Also it lies in the nature of science that, though it can teach us the best means for achieving our ends, it can never tell us what ends to pursue. It cannot give us any ideals. And our trouble is about ideals and ends, not about the means for reaching them.

5

No civilization can live without ideals, or to put it in another way, without a firm faith in moral ideas. Our ideals and moral ideas have in the past been rooted in religion. But the religious basis of our ideals has been undermined, and the superstructure of ideals is plainly tottering. None of the commonly suggested remedies on examination seems likely to succeed. It would therefore look as if the early death of our civilization were inevitable.

Of course we know that it is perfectly possible for individual men, very highly educated men, philosophers, scientists, intellectuals in general, to live moral lives without any religious convictions. But the question is whether a whole civilization, a whole family of peoples, composed almost entirely of relatively uneducated men and women, can do this.

It follows, of course, that if we could make the vast majority of men as highly educated as the very few are now, we might save the situation. And we are already moving slowly in that direction through the techniques of mass education. But the critical question seems to concern the time-lag. Perhaps in a few hundred years most of the population will, at the present rate, be sufficiently highly educated and civilized to combine high ideals with an absence of religion. But long before we reach any such stage, the collapse of our civilization may have come about. How are we to live through the intervening period?

I am sure that the first thing we have to do is to face the truth, however bleak it may be, and then next we have to learn to live with it. Let me say a word about each of these two points. What I am urging as regards the first is complete honesty. Those who wish to resurrect Christian dogmas are not, of course, consciously dishonest. But they have that kind of unconscious dishonesty which consists in lulling oneself with opiates and dreams. Those who talk of a new religion are merely hoping for a new opiate. Both alike refuse to face the truth that there is, in the universe outside man, no spirituality, no regard for values, no friend in the sky, no help or comfort for man of any sort. To be perfectly honest in the admission of this fact, not to seek shelter in new or old illusions, not to indulge in wishful dreams about this matter, this is the first thing we shall have to do.

I do not urge this course out of any special regard for the sanctity of truth in the abstract. It is not self-evident to me that truth is the supreme value to which all else must be sacrificed. Might not the discoverer of a truth which would be fatal to mankind be justified in suppressing it, even in teaching men a falsehood? Is truth more valuable than goodness and beauty and happiness? To think so is to invent yet another absolute, another religious delusion in which Truth with a capital T is substituted for God. The reason why we must now boldly and honestly face the truth that the universe is nonspiritual and indifferent to goodness, beauty, happiness, or truth is not that it would be wicked to suppress it, but simply that it is too late to do so, so that in the end we cannot do anything else but face it. Yet we stand on the brink, dreading the icy plunge. We need courage. We need honesty.

Now about the other point, the necessity of learning to live with the truth. This means learning to live virtuously and happily, or at least contentedly, without illusions. And this is going to be extremely difficult because what we have now begun dimly to perceive is that human life in the past, or at least human happiness, has almost wholly depended upon illusions. It has been said that man lives by truth, and that the truth will make us free. Nearly the opposite seems to me to be the case. Mankind has managed to live only by means of lies, and the truth may very well destroy us. If one were a Bergsonian one might believe that nature deliberately puts illusions into our souls in order to induce us to go on living.

The illusions by which men have lived seem to be of two kinds. First, there is what one may perhaps call the Great Illusion—I mean the religious illusion that the universe is moral and good, that it follows a wise and noble plan, that it is gradually generating some supreme value, that goodness is bound to triumph in it. Secondly, there is a whole host of minor illusions on which human happiness nourishes itself. How much of human happiness notoriously comes from the illusions of the lover about his beloved? Then again we work and strive because of the illusions connected with fame, glory, power, or money. Banners of all kinds, flags, emblems, insignia, ceremonials, and rituals are invariably symbols of some illusion or other. The British Empire, the connection between mother country and dominions, is partly kept going by illusions surrounding the notion of kingship. Or think of the vast amount of human happiness which is derived from the illusion of supposing that if some nonsense syllable, such as "sir" or "count" or "lord" is pronounced in conjunction with our names, we belong to a superior order of people.

There is plenty of evidence that human happiness is almost wholly based upon illusions of one kind or another. But the scientific spirit, or the spirit of truth, is the enemy of illusions and therefore the enemy of human happiness. That is why it is going to be so difficult to live with the truth.

There is no reason why we should have to give up the host of minor illusions which render life supportable. There is no reason why the lover should be scientific about the loved one. Even the illusions of fame and glory may persist. But without the Great Illusion, the illusion of a good, kindly, and purposeful universe, we shall *have* to learn to live. And to ask this is really no more than to ask that we become genuinely civilized beings and not merely sham civilized beings.

I can best explain the difference by a reminiscence. I remember a fellow student in my college days, an ardent Christian, who told me that if he did not believe in a future life, in heaven and hell, he would rape, murder, steal, and be a drunkard. That is what I call being a sham civilized being. On the other hand, not only could a Huxley, a John Stuart Mill, a David Hume, live great and fine lives without any religion, but a great many others of us,

quite obscure persons, can at least live decent lives without it.

To be genuinely civilized means to be able to walk straightly and to live honorably without the props and crutches of one or another of the childish dreams which have so far supported men. That such a life is likely to be ecstatically happy I will not claim. But that it can be lived in quiet content, accepting resignedly what cannot be helped, not expecting the impossible, and thankful for small mercies, this I would maintain. That it will be difficult for men in general to learn this lesson I do not deny. But that it will be impossible I would not admit since so many have learned it already.

Man has not yet grown up. He is not adult. Like a child he cries for the moon and lives in a world of fantasies. And the race as a whole has perhaps reached the great crisis of its life. Can it grow up as a race in the same sense as individual men grow up? Can man put away childish things and adolescent dreams? Can he grasp the real world as it actually is, stark and bleak, without its romantic or religious halo, and still retain his ideals, striving for great ends and noble achievements? If he can, all may yet be well. If he cannot, he will probably sink back into the savagery and brutality from which he came, taking a humble place once more among the lower animals.

WILLIAM JAMES (1842–1910)

Born in New York City in 1842, William James grew up in a family remarkable for its high spirits, intelligence, and congeniality. His father, Henry James, Senior, a man of intense religious and philosophical disposition, used his considerable inherited fortune to surround his five children with an atmosphere of culture. The family traveled a great deal, and William, like his sister and three brothers, was educated in various schools in the United States, England, France, Germany, and Switzerland. Thus he acquired the cosmopolitanism and *savoir faire* which distinguished him throughout his life. Uncertain of the choice of a career, he dabbled in painting, then studied chemistry, physiology, and medicine at Harvard. Still unable to reach a decision, he accompanied Louis Agassiz, the great naturalist, on a field trip up the Amazon, and spent the next two years studying in Europe, mainly Germany. During this period and the subsequent three years spent in America, he suffered from a profound mental depression, at times even considering suicide.

Although he completed the work for his Doctor's degree at the Harvard Medical School in 1869, it was not until 1872, when he was appointed to the post of Instructor in Physiology at Harvard, that he found regular employment. This appointment, which he called "a perfect God-send to me," contributed to a happier outlook. The last traces of his morbid mental state had apparently disappeared by 1878, when he married Alice Gibbens.

By this time, aged 36, he was an established teacher of physiology and psychology at Harvard. In 1880, he became Assistant Professor of Philosophy and before long Professor. During his tenure, the Department of Philosophy attained a high point of distinction, including among its faculty Josiah Royce, Hugo Münsterberg, and George Santayana. James' own importance as an original thinker was established with the publication, in 1890 of his master work, *Principles of Psychology*, the product of eleven years of labor. Although he finally won great acclaim as a philosopher, he never succeeded in writing a philosophical work as substantial and comprehensive as this great treatise in psychology.

Among his favorite recreations was mountain climbing. In June 1899, while climbing alone in the Adirondacks, he lost his way and overstrained his heart in a desperate thirteen-hour scramble. The result was an irreparable lesion, which forced him to curtail his intellectual activities. Finally, in 1910, his heart trouble became very serious, and he died in his New Hampshire home in August of that year.

Witty, kindly, urbane, but restless and neurasthenic, James was a remarkably complex and attractive character—"a being," to quote his sister, "who would bring life and charm to a treadmill." This charm he communicated in his writing, which often lends a rollicking sprightliness to the most abstruse subjects. Despite his artistic flair, he had the scientist's keen sense of fact and the moralist's high seriousness. But his seriousness was never stuffy—he was always opposed to the snobs, the dogmatists, the dry-as-dusts, and the goody-goodies that would fence in the human spirit.

The Will to Believe

In the recently published Life by Leslie Stephen of his brother, Fitz-James, there is an account of a school to which the latter went when he was a boy. The teacher, a certain Mr. Guest, used to converse with his pupils in this wise: "Gurney, what is the difference between justification and sanctification?—Stephen, prove the omnipotence of God!" etc. In the midst of our Harvard freethinking and indifference we are prone to imagine that here at your good old orthodox College conversation continues to be somewhat upon this order; and to show you that we at Harvard have not lost all interest in these vital subjects, I have brought with me tonight something like a sermon on justification by faith to read to you—I mean an essay in justification *of* faith, a defense of our right to adopt a believing attitude in religious matters, in spite of the fact that our merely logical intellect may not have been coerced. "The Will to Believe," accordingly, is the title of my paper.

I have long defended to my own students the lawfulness of voluntarily adopted faith; but as soon as they have got well imbued with the logical spirit, they have as a rule refused to admit my contention to be lawful philosophically, even though in point of fact they were personally all the time chock-full of some faith or other themselves. I am all the while, however, so profoundly convinced that my own position is correct, that your invitation has seemed to me a good occasion to make my statements more clear. Perhaps your minds will be more open than those with which I have hitherto had to deal. I will be as little technical as I can, though I must begin by setting up some technical distinctions that will help us in the end.

I

Let us give the name of *hypothesis* to anything that may be proposed to our belief; and just as the electricians speak of live and dead wires, let us

An Address to the Philosophical Clubs of Yale and Brown Universities. Published in the *New World*, June 1896.

speak of any hypothesis as either *live* or *dead*. A live hypothesis is one which appeals as a real possibility to him to whom it is proposed. If I ask you to believe in the Mahdi, the notion makes no electric connection with your nature —it refuses to scintillate with any credibility at all. As an hypothesis it is completely dead. To an Arab, however (even if he be not one of the Mahdi's followers), the hypothesis is among the mind's possibilities: it is alive. This shows that deadness and liveness in an hypothesis are not intrinsic properties, but relations to the individual thinker. They are measured by his willingness to act. The maximum of liveness in an hypothesis means willingness to act irrevocably. Practically, that means belief; but there is some believing tendency wherever there is willingness to act at all.

Next, let us call the decision between two hypotheses an *option*. Options may be of several kinds. They may be —first, *living* or *dead;* secondly, *forced* or *avoidable;* thirdly, *momentous* or *trivial;* and for our purposes we may call an option a genuine option when it is of the forced, living, and momentous kind.

1. A living option is one in which both hypotheses are live ones. If I say to you: "Be a theosophist or be a Mohammedan," it is probably a dead option, because for you neither hypothesis is likely to be alive. But if I say: "Be an agnostic or be a Christian," it is otherwise: trained as you are, each hypothesis makes some appeal, however small, to your belief.

2. Next, if I say to you: "Choose between going out with your umbrella or without it," I do not offer you a genuine option, for it is not forced. You can easily avoid it by not going out at all. Similarly, if I say, "Either love me or hate me," "Either call my theory true or call it false," your option is avoidable. You may remain indifferent to me, neither loving nor hating, and you may decline to offer any judgment as to my theory. But if I say, "Either accept this truth or go without it," I put on you a forced option, for there is no standing place outside of the alternative. Every dilemma based on a complete logical disjunction, with no possibility of not choosing, is an option of this forced kind.

3. Finally, if I were Dr. Nansen and proposed to you to join my North Pole expedition, your option would be momentous; for this would probably be your only similar opportunity, and your choice now would either exclude you from the North Pole sort of immortality altogether or put at least the chance of it into your hands. He who refuses to embrace a unique opportunity loses the prize as surely as if he tried and failed. *Per contra,* the option is trivial when the opportunity is not unique, when the stake is insignificant, or when the decision is reversible if it later prove unwise. Such trivial options abound in the scientific life. A chemist finds an hypothesis live enough to spend a year in its verification: he believes in it to that extent. But if his experiments prove inconclusive either way, he is quit for his loss of time, no vital harm being done.

It will facilitate our discussion if we keep all these distinctions well in mind.

II

The next matter to consider is the actual psychology of human opinion. When we look at certain facts, it seems as if our passional and volitional nature lay at the root of all our convictions. When we look at others, it seems as if they could do nothing when the intellect had once said its say. Let us take the latter facts up first.

Does it not seem preposterous on the very face of it to talk of our opinions being modifiable at will? Can our will either help or hinder our intellect in its perceptions of truth? Can we, by just willing it, believe that Abraham Lincoln's existence is a myth, and that the portraits of him in *McClure's Magazine* are all of some one else? Can we, by an effort of our will, or by any strength of wish that it were true, believe ourselves well and about when we are roaring with rheumatism in bed, or feel certain that the sum of the two one-dollar bills in our pocket must be a hundred dollars? We can *say* any of these things, but we are absolutely impotent to believe them; and of just such things is the whole fabric of the truths that we do believe in made up —matters of fact, immediate or remote, as Hume said, and relations between ideas, which are either there or not there for us if we see them so, and which if not there cannot be put there by any action of our own.

In Pascal's *Thoughts* there is a celebrated passage known in literature as Pascal's wager. In it he tries to force us into Christianity by reasoning as if our concern with truth resembled our concern with the stakes in a game of chance. Translated freely his words are these: You must either believe or not believe that God is—which will you do? Your human reason cannot say. A game is going on between you and the nature of things which at the day of judgment will bring out either heads or tails. Weigh what your gains and your losses would be if you should stake all you have on heads, or God's existence: if you win in such case, you gain eternal beatitude; if you lose, you lose nothing at all. If there were an infinity of chances, and only one for God in this wager, still you ought to stake your all on God; for though you surely risk a finite loss by this procedure, any finite loss is reasonable, even a certain one is reasonable, if there is but the possibility of infinite gain. Go, then, and take holy water, and have masses said; belief will come and stupefy your scruples—*Cela vous fera croire et vous abêtira* [This will make you believe and stupefy you]. Why should you not? At bottom, what have you to lose?

You probably feel that when religious faith expresses itself thus, in the language of the gaming-table, it is put to its last trumps. Surely Pascal's own personal belief in masses and holy water had far other springs; and this celebrated page of his is but an argument for others, a last desperate snatch at a weapon against the hardness of the unbelieving heart. We feel that a faith in masses and holy water adopted wilfully after such a mechanical calculation would lack the inner soul of faith's reality; and if we were ourselves in the place of the Deity, we should probably take particular pleasure in cutting off believers of this pattern from their infinite reward. It is evident that unless there be some pre-existing tendency to believe in masses and holy water, the option offered to the will by Pascal is not a living option. Certainly no Turk ever took to masses and holy water on its account; and even to us Protestants these means of salvation seem such foregone impossibilities that Pascal's logic, invoked for them specifically, leaves us unmoved. As well might the Mahdi write to us, saying, "I am the Expected One whom God has created in his effulgence. You shall be infinitely happy if you confess me; otherwise you shall be cut off from the light of the sun. Weigh, then, your infinite gain if I am genuine against your finite sacrifice if I am not!" His logic would be that of Pascal; but he would vainly use it on us, for the hypothesis he offers us is dead. No tendency to act on it exists in us to any degree.

The talk of believing by our volition seems, then, from one point of view, simply silly. From another point of view it is worse than silly, it is vile. When one turns to the magnificent edifice of the physical sciences, and sees how it was reared; what thousands of disinterested moral lives of men lie buried in its mere foundations; what patience and postponement, what choking down of preference, what submission to the icy laws of outer fact are wrought into its very stones and mortar; how absolutely impersonal it stands in its vast augustness—then how besotted and contemptible seems every little sentimentalist who comes blowing his voluntary smoke-wreaths, and pretending to decide things from out

of his private dream! Can we wonder if those bred in the rugged and manly school of science should feel like spewing such subjectivism out of their mouths? The whole system of loyalties which grow up in the schools of science go dead against its toleration; so that it is only natural that those who have caught the scientific fever should pass over to the opposite extreme, and write sometimes as if the incorruptibly truthful intellect ought positively to prefer bitterness and unacceptableness to the heart in its cup.

> It fortifies my soul to know
> That though I perish, Truth is so—

sings Clough, while Huxley exclaims: "My only consolation lies in the reflection that, however bad our posterity may become, so far as they hold by the plain rule of not pretending to believe what they have no reason to believe, because it may be to their advantage so to pretend [the word 'pretend' is surely here redundant], they will not have reached the lowest depth of immorality." And that delicious *enfant terrible* Clifford writes: "Belief is desecrated when given to unproved and unquestioned statements for the solace and private pleasure of the believer.... Whoso would deserve well of his fellows in this matter will guard the purity of his belief with a very fanaticism of jealous care, lest at any time it should rest on an unworthy object, and catch a stain which can never be wiped away. . . . If [a] belief has been accepted on insufficient evidence [even though the belief be true, as Clifford on the same page explains] the pleasure is a stolen one. . . . It is sinful because it is stolen in defiance of our duty to mankind. That duty is to guard ourselves from such beliefs as from a pestilence which may shortly master our own body and then spread to the rest of the town. . . . It is wrong always, everywhere, and for every one, to believe anything upon insufficient evidence."

III

All this strikes one as healthy, even when expressed, as by Clifford, with somewhat too much of robustious pathos in the voice. Free will and simple wishing do seem, in the matter of our credences, to be only fifth wheels to the coach. Yet if any one should thereupon assume that intellectual insight is what remains after wish and will and sentimental preference have taken wing, or that pure reason is what then settles our opinions, he would fly quite as directly in the teeth of the facts.

It is only our already dead hypotheses that our willing nature is unable to bring to life again. But what has made them dead for us is for the most part a previous action of our willing nature of an antagonistic kind. When I say "willing nature," I do not mean only such deliberate volitions as may have set up habits of . belief that we cannot now escape from—I mean all such factors of belief as fear and hope, prejudice and passion, imitation and partisanship, the circumpressure of our caste and set. As a matter of fact we find ourselves believing, we hardly know how or why. Mr. Balfour gives the name of "authority" to all those influences, born of the intellectual climate, that make hypotheses possible or impossible for us, alive or dead. Here in this room, we all of us believe in molecules and the conservation of energy, in democracy and necessary progress, in Protestant Christianity and the duty of fighting for "the doctrine of the immortal Monroe," all for no reasons worthy of the name. We see into these matters with no more inner clearness, and probably with much less, than any disbeliever in them might possess. His unconventionality would probably have some grounds to show for its conclusions; but for us, not insight, but the *prestige* of the opinions, is what makes the spark shoot from them and light up our sleeping magazines of faith. Our reason is quite satisfied, in nine hundred and ninety-nine cases out of every thousand of us, if it can find a few arguments that will do to recite in case our credulity is criticized by some one else. Our faith is faith in some one else's faith, and in the greatest matters this is most the case. Our belief in truth itself, for instance, that there is a truth, and that our minds and it are made for each other—what is it but a passionate affirmation of desire, in which our social system backs us up? We want to have a truth; we want to believe that our experiments and studies and discussions must put us in a continually better and better position towards it; and on this line we agree to fight out our thinking lives. But if a Pyrrhonistic sceptic asks us *how we know* all this, can our logic find a reply? No! certainly it cannot. It is just one volition against another—we willing to go in for life upon a trust or assumption which he, for his part, does not care to make.

As a rule we disbelieve all facts and theories for which we have no use. Clifford's cosmic emotions find no use for Christian feelings. Huxley belabors the bishops because there is no use for sacerdotalism in his scheme of life. Newman, on the contrary, goes over to Romanism, and finds all sorts of reasons good for staying there, because a priestly system is for him an organic need and delight. Why do so few "scientists" even look at the evidence for telepathy, so called? Because they think, as a leading biologist, now dead, once said to me, that even if such a thing were true, scientists ought to band together to keep it suppressed and concealed. It would undo the uniformity of Nature and all sorts of other things without which scientists cannot carry on their pursuits. But if this very man had been shown something which as a scientist he might *do* with telepathy, he might not only have examined the evidence, but even have found it good enough. This very law which the logicians would impose upon us—if I may give the name of logicians to those who would rule out our willing nature here—is based on nothing but their own natural wish to exclude all elements for which they, in their professional quality of logicians, can find no use.

Evidently, then, our non-intellectual nature does influence our convictions. There are passional tendencies and volitions which run before and others which come after belief, and it is only the latter that are too late for the fair; and they are not too late when the previous passional work has been already in their own direction. Pascal's argument, instead of being powerless, then seems a regular clincher, and is the last stroke needed to make our faith in masses and holy water complete. The state of things is evidently far from simple; and pure insight and logic, whatever they might do ideally, are not the only things that really do produce our creeds.

IV

Our next duty, having recognized this mixed-up state of affairs, is to ask whether it be simply reprehensible and pathological, or whether, on the contrary, we must treat it as a moral element in making up our minds. The thesis I defend is, briefly stated, this: *Our passional nature not only lawfully may, but must, decide an option between propositions, whenever it is a genuine option that cannot by its nature be decided on intellectual grounds; for to say, under such circumstances, "Do not decide, but leave the question open," is itself a passional decision— just like deciding yes or no—and is attended with the same risk of losing the truth.* The thesis thus abstractly expressed will, I trust, soon become quite clear. . . .

VII

One more point, small but important, and our preliminaries are done. There are two ways of looking at our duty in the matter of opinion—ways entirely different, and yet ways about whose difference the theory of knowledge seems hitherto to have shown very little concern. *We must know the truth; and we must avoid error*—these are our first and great commandments as would-be knowers; but they are not two ways of stating an identical commandment, they are two separable laws. Although it may indeed happen that when we believe the truth *A,* we escape as an incidental consequence from believing the falsehood *B,* it hardly ever happens that by merely disbelieving *B* we necessarily believe *A.* We may in escaping *B* fall into believing other falsehoods, *C* or *D,* just as bad as *B;* or we may escape *B* by not believing anything at all, not even *A.*

Believe truth! Shun error!—these, we see, are two materially different laws; and by choosing between them we may end by coloring differently our whole intellectual life. We may regard the chase for truth as paramount, and the avoidance of error as secondary; or we may, on the other hand, treat the avoidance of error as more imperative, and let truth take its chance. Clifford, in the instructive passage which I have quoted, exhorts us to the latter course. Believe nothing, he tells us, keep your mind in suspense for ever, rather than by closing it on insufficient evidence incur the awful risk of believing lies. You, on the other hand, may think that the risk of being in error is a very small matter when compared with the blessings of real knowledge, and be ready to be duped many times in your investigation rather than postpone indefinitely the chance of guessing true. I myself find it impossible to go with Clifford. We must remember that these feelings of our duty about either truth or error

are in any case only expressions of our passional life. Biologically considered, our minds are as ready to grind out falsehood as veracity, and he who says, "Better go without belief forever than believe a lie!" merely shows his own preponderant private horror of becoming a dupe. He may be critical of many of his desires and fears, but this fear he slavishly obeys. He cannot imagine any one questioning its binding force. For my own part, I have also a horror of being duped; but I can believe that worse things than being duped may happen to a man in this world: so Clifford's exhortation has to my ears a thoroughly fantastic sound. It is like a general informing his soldiers that it is better to keep out of battle forever than to risk a single wound. Not so are victories either over enemies or over nature gained. Our errors are surely not such awfully solemn things. In a world where we are so certain to incur them in spite of all our caution, a certain lightness of heart seems healthier than this excessive nervousness on their behalf. At any rate, it seems the fittest thing for the empiricist philosopher.

VIII

And now, after all this introduction, let us go straight at our question. I have said, and now repeat it, that not only as a matter of fact do we find our passional nature influencing us in our opinions, but that there are some options between opinions in which this influence must be regarded both as an inevitable and as a lawful determinant of our choice.

I fear here that some of you my hearers will begin to scent danger, and lend an inhospitable ear. Two first steps of passion you have indeed had to admit as necessary—we must think so as to avoid dupery, and we must think so as to gain truth; but the surest path to those ideal consummations, you will probably consider, is from now onwards to take no further passional step.

Well, of course, I agree as far as the facts will allow. Wherever the option between losing truth and gaining it is not momentous, we can throw the chance of *gaining truth* away, and at any rate save ourselves from any chance of *believing falsehood,* by not making up our minds at all till objective evidence has come. In scientific questions, this is almost always the case; and even in human affairs in general, the need of acting is seldom so urgent that a false belief to act on is better than no belief at all. Law courts, indeed, have to decide on the best evidence attainable for the moment, because a judge's duty is to make law as well as to ascertain it, and (as a learned judge once said to me) few cases are worth spending much time over: the great thing is to have them decided on *any* acceptable principle, and got out of the way. But in our dealings with objective nature we obviously are recorders, not makers, of the truth; and decisions for the mere sake of deciding promptly and getting on to the next business would be wholly out of place. Throughout the breadth of physical nature facts are what they are quite independently of us, and seldom is there any such hurry about them that the risks of being duped by believing a premature theory need be faced. The questions here are always trivial options, the hypotheses are hardly living (at any rate not living for us spectators), the choice between believing truth or falsehood is seldom forced. The attitude of sceptical balance is therefore the absolutely wise one if we would escape mistakes. What difference, indeed, does it make to most of us whether we have or have not a theory of the Röentgen rays, whether we believe or not in mind-stuff, or have a conviction about the causality of conscious states? It makes no difference. Such options are not forced on us. On every account it is better not to make them, but still keep weighing reasons *pro et contra* with an indifferent hand.

I speak, of course, here of the purely judging mind. For purposes of discovery such indifference is to be less highly recommended, and science would be far less advanced than she is if the passionate desires of individuals to get their own faiths confirmed had been kept out of the game. See for example the sagacity which Spencer and Weismann now display. On the other hand, if you want an absolute duffer in an investigation, you must, after all, take the man who has no interest whatever in its results: he is the warranted incapable, the positive fool. The most useful investigator, because the most sensitive observer, is always he whose eager interest in one side of the question is balanced by an equally keen nervousness lest he become deceived. Science has organized this nervousness into a regular *technique,* her so-called method of verification; and she has fallen so deeply in love with the method that one may even say she has ceased to care for truth by itself at all. It is only truth as technically verified that interests her. The truth of truths might come in merely affirmative form, and she would decline to touch it. Such truth as that, she might repeat with Clifford, would be stolen in defiance of her duty to mankind. Human passions, however, are stronger than technical rules. *"Le cœur a ses raisons,"* as Pascal says, *"que la raison ne connaît pas"* [The heart has its reasons which the reason does not know]; and however indifferent to all but the bare rules of the game the umpire, the abstract intellect, may be, the concrete players who furnish him the materials to judge of are usually, each one of them, in love with some pet "live hypothesis" of his own. Let us agree, however, that wherever there is no forced option, the dispassionately judicial intellect with no pet hypothesis, saving us, as it does, from dupery at any rate, ought to be our ideal.

The question next arises: Are there not somewhere forced options in our speculative questions, and can we (as men who may be interested at least as much in positively gaining truth as in merely escaping dupery) always wait with impunity till the coercive evidence shall have arrived? It seems *a priori* improbable that the truth should be so nicely adjusted to our needs and powers as that. In the great boarding-house of nature, the cakes and the butter and the syrup seldom come out so even and leave the plates so clean. Indeed, we should view them with scientific suspicion if they did.

IX

Moral questions immediately present themselves as questions whose solution cannot wait for sensible proof. A moral question is a question not of what sensibly exists, but of what is good, or would be good if it did exist. Science can tell us what exists; but to compare the *worths,* both of what exists and of what does not exist, we must consult not science, but what Pascal calls our heart. Science herself consults her heart when she lays it down that the infinite ascertainment of fact and correction of false belief are the supreme goods for man. Challenge the statement, and science can only repeat it oracularly, or else prove it by showing that such ascertainment and correction bring man all sorts of other goods which man's heart in turn declares. The question of having moral beliefs at all or not having them is decided by our will. Are our moral preferences true or false, or are they only odd biological phenomena, making things good or bad for *us,* but in themselves indifferent? How can your pure intellect decide? If your heart does not *want* a world of moral reality, your head will assuredly never make you believe in one. Mephistophelian scepticism, indeed, will satisfy the head's play-instincts much better than any rigorous idealism can. Some men (even at the student age) are so naturally cool-hearted that the moralistic hypothesis never has for them any pungent life, and in their supercilious presence the hot young moralist always feels strangely ill at ease. The appearance of knowingness is on their side, of *naïveté* and gullibility on his.

Yet, in the inarticulate heart of him, he clings to it that he is not a dupe, and that there is a realm in which (as Emerson says) all their wit and intellectual superiority is no better than the cunning of a fox. Moral scepticism can no more be refuted or proved by logic than intellectual scepticism can. When we stick to it that there *is* truth (be it of either kind), we do so with our whole nature, and resolve to stand or fall by the results. The sceptic with his whole nature adopts the doubting attitude; but which of us is the wiser, Omniscience only knows.

Turn now from these wide questions of good to a certain class of questions of fact, questions concerning personal relations, states of mind between one man and another. *Do you like me or not?*—for example. Whether you do or not depends, in countless instances, on whether I meet you half-way, am willing to assume that you must like me, and show you trust and expectation. The previous faith on my part in your liking's existence is in such cases what makes your liking come. But if I stand aloof, and refuse to budge an inch until I have objective evidence, until you shall have done something apt, as the absolutists say, *ad extorquendum assensum meum* [to compel my assent], ten to one your liking never comes. How many women's hearts are vanquished by the mere sanguine insistence of some man that they *must* love him! he will not consent to the hypothesis that they cannot. The desire for a certain kind of truth here brings about that special truth's existence; and so it is in innumerable cases of other sorts. Who gains promotions, boons, appoint-ments, but the man in whose life they are seen to play the part of live hypotheses, who discounts them, sacrifices other things for their sake before they have come, and takes risks for them in advance? His faith acts on the powers above him as a claim, and creates its own verification.

A social organism of any sort whatever, large or small, is what it is because each member proceeds to his own duty with a trust that the other members will simultaneously do theirs. Wherever a desired result is achieved by the cooperation of many independent persons, its existence as a fact is a pure consequence of the precursive faith in one another of those immediately concerned. A government, an army, a commercial system, a ship, a college, an athletic team, all exist on this condition, without which not only is nothing achieved, but nothing is even attempted. A whole train of passengers (individually brave enough) will be looted by a few highwaymen, simply because the latter can count on one another, while each passenger fears that if he makes a movement of resistance, he will be shot before any one else backs him up. If we believed that the whole car-full would rise at once with us, we should each severally rise, and train-robbing would never even be attempted. There are, then, cases where a fact cannot come at all unless a preliminary faith exists in its coming. *And where faith in a fact can help create the fact,* that would be an insane logic which should say that faith running ahead of scientific evidence is the "lowest kind of immorality" into which a thinking being can fall. Yet such is the logic by which our scientific absolutists pretend to regulate our lives!

X

In truths dependent on our personal action, then, faith based on desire is certainly a lawful and possibly an indispensable thing.

But now, it will be said, these are all childish human cases, and have nothing to do with great cosmical matters, like the question of religious faith. Let us then pass on to that. Religions differ so much in their accidents that in discussing the religious question we must make it very generic and broad. What then do we now mean by the religious hypothesis? Science says things are; morality says some things are better than other things; and religion says essentially two things.

First, she says that the best things are the more eternal things, the overlapping things, the things in the universe that throw the last stone, so to speak, and say the final word. "Perfection is eternal"—this phrase of Charles Secrétan seems a good way of putting this first affirmation of religion, an affirmation which obviously cannot yet be verified scientifically at all.

The second affirmation of religion is that we are better off even now if we believe her first affirmation to be true.

Now, let us consider what the logical elements of this situation are *in case the religious hypothesis in both its branches be really true.* (Of course, we must admit that possibility at the outset. If we are to discuss the question at all, it must involve a living option. If for any of you religion be a hypothesis that cannot, by any living possibility, be true, then you need go no farther. I speak to the "saving remnant" alone.) So proceeding, we see, first, that religion offers itself as a *momentous* option. We are supposed to gain, even now, by our belief, and to lose by our non-belief, a certain vital good. Secondly, religion is a *forced* option, so far as that good goes. We cannot escape the issue by remaining sceptical and waiting for more light, because, although we do avoid error in that way *if religion be untrue,* we lose the good, *if it be true,* just as certainly as if we positively chose to disbelieve. It is as if a man should hesitate indefinitely to ask a certain woman to marry him because he was not perfectly sure that she would prove an angel after he brought her home. Would he not cut himself off from that particular angel-possibility as decisively as if he went and married some one else? Scepticism, then, is not avoidance of option; it is option of a certain particular kind of risk. *Better risk loss of truth than chance of error*—that is your faith-vetoer's exact position. He is actively playing his stake as much as the believer is; he is backing the field against the religious hypothesis, just as the believer is backing the religious hypothesis against the field. To preach scepticism to us as a duty until "sufficient evidence" for religion be found, is tantamount therefore to telling us, when in presence of the religious hypothesis, that to yield to our fear of its being error is wiser and better than to yield to our hope that it may be true. It is not intellect against all passions, then; it is only intellect with one passion laying down its law. And by what, forsooth, is the supreme wisdom of this passion warranted? Dupery for dupery, what proof is there that dupery through hope is so much worse than dupery through fear? I, for one, can see no proof; and I simply refuse obedience to the scientist's command to imitate his kind of option, in a case where my own stake is important enough to give me the right to choose my own form of risk. If religion be true and the evidence for it be still insufficient, I do not wish, by putting your extinguisher upon my nature (which feels to me as if it had after all some business in this matter), to forfeit my sole chance in life of getting upon the winning side—that chance depending, of course, on my willingness to run the risk of acting as if my passional need of taking the world religiously might be prophetic and right.

All this is on the supposition that it really may be prophetic and right, and that, even to us who are discussing the matter, religion is a live hypothesis which may be true. Now, to most of us religion comes in a still further way that makes a veto on our active faith even more illogical. The more perfect and more eternal aspect of the universe is represented in our religions as having personal form. The universe is no longer a mere *It* to us, but a *Thou,* if we are religious; and any relation that may be possible from person to person might be possible here. For instance, although in one sense we are passive portions of the universe, in another we show a curious autonomy, as if we were small active centers on our own account. We feel, too, as if the appeal

of religion to us were made to our own active good-will, as if evidence might be forever withheld from us unless we met the hypothesis half-way. To take a trivial illustration: just as a man who in a company of gentlemen made no advances, asked a warrant for every concession, and believed no one's word without proof, would cut himself off by such churlishness from all the social rewards that a more trusting spirit would earn—so here, one who should shut himself up in snarling logicality and try to make the gods extort his recognition willy-nilly, or not get it at all, might cut himself off forever from his only opportunity of making the gods' acquaintance. This feeling, forced on us we know not whence, that by obstinately believing that there are gods (although not to do so would be so easy both for our logic and our life) we are doing the universe the deepest service we can, seems part of the living essence of the religious hypothesis. If the hypothesis *were* true in all its parts, including this one, then pure intellectualism, with its veto on our making willing advances, would be an absurdity; and some participation of our sympathetic nature would be logically required. I, therefore, for one, cannot see my way to accepting the agnostic rules for truth-seeking, or wilfully agree to keep my willing nature out of the game. I cannot do so for this plain reason, that *a rule of thinking which would absolutely prevent me from acknowledging certain kinds of truth if those kinds of truth were really there, would be an irrational rule.* That for me is the long and short of the formal logic of the situation, no matter what the kinds of truth might materially be.

I confess I do not see how this logic can be escaped. But sad experience makes me fear that some of you may still shrink from radically saying with me, *in abstracto,* that we have the right to believe at our own risk any hypothesis that is live enough to tempt our will. I suspect, however, that if this is so, it is because you have got away from the abstract logical point of view altogether, and are thinking (perhaps without realizing it) of some particular religious hypothesis which for you is dead. The freedom to "believe what we will" you apply to the case of some patent superstition; and the faith you think of is the faith defined by the schoolboy when he said, "Faith is when you believe something that you know ain't true." I can only repeat that this is misapprehension. *In concreto,* the freedom to believe can only cover living options which the intellect of the individual cannot by itself resolve; and living options never seem absurdities to him who has them to consider. When I look at the religious question as it really puts itself to concrete men, and when I think of all the possibilities which both practically and theoretically it involves, then this command that we shall put a stopper on our heart, instincts, and courage, and *wait*—acting of course meanwhile more or less as if religion were *not* true[1]—till

doomsday, or till such time as our intellect and senses working together may have raked in evidence enough—this command, I say, seems to me the queerest idol ever manufactured in the philosophic cave. Were we scholastic absolutists, there might be more excuse. If we had an infallible intellect with its objective certitudes, we might feel ourselves disloyal to such a perfect organ of knowledge in not trusting to it exclusively, in not waiting for its releasing word. But if we are empiricists, if we believe that no bell in us tolls to let us know for certain when truth is in our grasp, then it seems a piece of idle fantasticality to preach so solemnly our duty of waiting for the bell. Indeed we *may* wait if we will—I hope you do not think that I am denying that—but if we do so, we do so at our peril as much as if we believed. In either case we *act,* taking our life in our hands. No one of us ought to issue vetoes to the other, nor should we bandy words of abuse. We ought, on the contrary, delicately and profoundly to respect one another's mental freedom: then only shall we bring about the intellectual republic; then only shall we have that spirit of inner tolerance without which all our outer tolerance is soulless, and which is empiricism's glory;

---

[1] Since belief is measured by action, he who forbids us to believe religion to be true, necessarily also forbids us to act as we should if we did believe it to be true. The whole defense of religious faith hinges upon action. If the action required or inspired by the religious hypothesis is in no way different from that dictated by the naturalistic hypothesis, then religious faith is a pure superfluity, better pruned away, and controversy about its legitimacy is a piece of idle trifling, unworthy of serious minds. I myself believe, of course, that the religious hypothesis gives to the world an expression which specifically determines our reactions, and makes them in a large part unlike what they might be on a purely naturalistic scheme of belief.

then only shall we live and let live, in speculative as well as in practical things.

I began by a reference to Fitz-James Stephen; let me end by a quotation from him. "What do you think of yourself? What do you think of the world? . . . These are questions with which all must deal as it seems good to them. They are riddles of the Sphinx, and in some way or other we must deal with them. . . . In all important transactions of life we have to take a leap in the dark. . . . If we decide to leave the riddles unanswered, that is a choice; if we waver in our answer, that, too, is a choice: but whatever choice we make, we make it at our peril. If a man chooses to turn his back altogether on God and the future, no one can prevent him; no one can show beyond reasonable doubt that he is mis-taken. If a man thinks otherwise and acts as he thinks, I do not see that any one can prove that *he* is mistaken. Each must act as he thinks best; and if he is wrong, so much the worse for him. We stand on a mountain pass in the midst of whirling snow and blinding mist, through which we get glimpses now and then of paths which may be deceptive. If we stand still we shall be frozen to death. If we take the wrong road we shall be dashed to pieces. We do not certainly know whether there is any right one. What must we do? 'Be strong and of a good courage.' Act for the best, hope for the best, and take what comes. . . . If death ends all, we cannot meet death better."[2]

[2] *Liberty, Equality, Fraternity,* p. 353, 2d edition. London, 1874.

COMMENT

The Meaning of Theism

For the theist, the key to reality lies in God and his design. A theist can be a teleologist, a dualist, or an idealist; but he cannot be a complete materialist or an absolute sceptic.

God has been defined as "a being who is personal, supreme, and good." This definition is in accord with what most people mean when they use the word "God." They think of Him as personal—that is, as conscious mind or spirit. Of course, God's mind is conceived as much larger or greater than any human mind, but still somewhat like mind or spirit as we know it. God is also thought of as supreme—if not omnipotent, at least immensely great and powerful—so powerful, indeed, that He can profoundly affect the whole world. Finally, a personal and supreme being would not be called God if He were not also good—perhaps not perfect, but at least good in a measure that far surpasses our poor human capacities.

If it be granted that the concept of God should be so defined, the question arises whether the belief in God is mature and defensible—whether it is consistent with the life of reason, which Socrates declared is alone worth living. Is faith in God, as Freud maintained, a mere illusory compensation for fear, repression, and catastrophe? Or is it an inalienable possession of man's spiritual life, as rational as it is emotionally satisfying? Can this faith withstand the criticism of philosophy? What *reasons* are there for believing in the existence of God, and how valid are these reasons?

The main arguments *pro* and *con* are contained in this chapter. The ontological proof ("ontological" means "pertaining to the nature of being") as stated by St. Anselm is an *a priori* argument. From his definition of God as "that being than which no greater can be conceived," he reasons that we cannot, without contradiction, assert that God does not exist. St. Thomas rejected this form of proof, his five arguments all being *a posteriori*. They start with some fact given in experience—change, causality, nonnecessary being, degrees of excellence, or design—and they proceed to reason from this fact to the conclusion that God exists. The arguments of both St. Anselm and St. Thomas are intended to prove the existence of a perfect and omnipotent God. The argument of Cleanthes in Hume's *Dialogues* resembles the fifth proof of St. Thomas but concludes that God must be limited in power.

Hume's *Dialogues Concerning Natural Religion* are conversations (sometimes long speeches) between three characters: Demea, a partisan of "the argument for a first cause," Cleanthes, a defender of "the argument from design," and Philo, who is sceptical of both arguments. Demea's argument resembles the first three proofs of St. Thomas, but Demea also falls back upon St. Anselm's contention that the nonexistence of God would be a logical contradiction. Cleanthes' argument is like the fifth proof of St. Thomas.

I shall not restate the arguments because the reader, perhaps with help from his instructor, should be able to understand them, but I will say something about the criticisms that have been brought to bear against these arguments.

Criticism of the Ontological Argument

The ontological argument has had a chequered history. It was immediately criticized by an aged monk, Gaunilo, and was rejected by the greatest medieval philosopher, St. Thomas Aquinas. Then it was revived by Descartes, restated by Spinoza and Leibniz, and sharply criticized by Locke, Hume, and Kant. Relatively few philosophers in more recent times have accepted it.

The import of the argument is clarified by Gaunilo's objection and Anselm's reply. As interpreted by Gaunilo, the argument can be restated as follows: God is thought of as perfect; existence is necessary to perfection; therefore, God exists. This argument, said Gaunilo, is fallacious because by the same kind of reasoning I could "prove" the existence of a perfect island, to wit: If the island did not exist it would lack one of the elements of perfection, namely, real existence, and hence it would not be a perfect island. But the conclusion that a perfect island must exist is obviously absurd, and hence this type of argument is fallacious.

Anselm promptly replied to this attempted *reductio ad absurdum* by pointing out that a "perfect island" is perfect only in a weak and limited sense. By its very nature, an island is finite, and hence can be "perfect" only in a relative or inaccurate manner of speaking—it cannot be *infinitely* perfect. God, and not the hypothetical island, is that being than which no greater can be conceived—a being perfect in the sense of being incomparably greatest. Such absolute and infinite perfection applies to God and to God alone, and only such perfection requires existence.

Another objection was advanced by St. Thomas Aquinas. Going to the root of the argument, he questioned whether we really have in mind the concept of an utterly infinite or perfect being. He pointed out that we finite human beings have only an inadequate and indirect knowledge of God. Because of the infirmity of our understanding, we cannot discern God as He is in Himself, but only by the effects that He produces. If we could know God's essence absolutely, we would surely see that His essence involves His existence. But since we know God only relatively, His existence is not self-evident to us. We cannot leap from our imperfect idea of God to the conclusion that an absolutely perfect being exists.

Perhaps the most profound criticism of the ontological argument was advanced by Kant, whose objection turns on the meaning of the word "exists." Suppose I say that God exists. Am I making the same sort of statement as when I say that God is omnipotent? Kant would say no. The first statement asserts nothing about the *characteristics* of God; it merely tells me that God, whatever He is, exists, just as a rabbit, a cabbage, a stone, or a planet exists. This statement can be denied in only one way—namely, by denying that God exists. The second statement, that God is omnipotent, does tell me something about the *character* of God, and this statement, unlike the first, can be denied in *two* ways—either by denying that there is a God, or by denying that God is omnipotent.

Since the question of a thing's existence is thus *additional* to the question of its characteristics, we can grasp its characteristics without knowing whether it exists. Take the following illustration. As I sit at my desk I wonder whether there is a dollar bill in my pocket. Before I reach into my pocket to find out, I have in mind what the dollar bill would be like. The characteristics of the dollar bill which I have in mind are the same whether or not there really is a dollar bill in my pocket. Hence, I can grasp the characteristics of a dollar bill without knowing that it exists. Can we likewise grasp God's characteristics without knowing whether He exists? Yes, declares Kant. It is logically possible to think of an infinite and perfect Being without knowing that there *is* such a Being. But suppose we *mean* by God a necessarily existent God. It would still not follow that there really is such a Being. It would merely follow that *if* there is a God, then He is a necessarily existent Being—because that is what we mean. At best, Anselm's argument shows only that the thought of God implies the *thought* of God's existence. The thought of perfection implies the thought of existence, and real perfection implies real existence. But the *thought* of perfection does imply *real* existence. This is the tenor of Kant's criticism.

I shall leave to the reader the evaluation of the original argument and these criticisms. Regardless of the criticisms, Anselm's distinction between "essence" and "existence" has had a very stimulating influence on later philosophical thought. Existentialism, which we shall examine in Chapter 10, is based in large measure on this distinction. The ontological proof, moreover, still fascinates both students and philosophers. Two very able American philosophers, Norman Malcolm and Charles Hartshorne, have reformulated and defended the argument. If the reader wishes to pursue the matter, he will find references to their discussions in my suggestions for further reading at the end of this chapter.

Criticism of the Cosmological Proof

The term "cosmological proof" has been used in a blanket way to cover arguments like the first three of St. Thomas. These arguments are alike in maintaining that the insufficiency of nature requires the self-sufficiency of God to explain it. *Change* ("motion" in the sense of actualization of potentialities) cannot explain itself but requires an Unchanged Changer ("Unmoved Mover"—a fully actualized being) for its explanation. *Causation* (in the sense of bringing something into existence) cannot explain itself but requires an Uncaused Cause. *Contingent being* cannot explain itself but requires a Necessary Being for its explanation. Because these proofs are parallel they can be grouped together. It is the third that we shall take as the most instructive and consider in some detail.

Fundamental to the third argument is the contention that we cannot explain one dependent event merely by another or yet another dependent event, even if we push back the regress indefinitely. St. Thomas is prepared to admit, apart from Revelation, that contingent events may be causally linked to one another in a never-ending regress. What he denies is that we can have a *sufficient* explanation in terms of such an infinite regress of *dependent* causes.

So long as we have merely series of causes of causes, however infinitely extended, we are explaining one dependent event by another dependent event by still another dependent event, and so on and on. This is unsatisfactory for two reasons. First, each event is dependent upon its antecedents, and hence no event is more than *conditionally* necessary. If everything is dependent upon something else, the whole process hangs upon nothing. An explanation that thus never gives us an *ultimate* necessity is incomplete, and hence is not a full and satisfactory explanation. Secondly, even if there is an infinite regress of causes, we can always ask why this chain occurs rather than some other chain. Or even if we consider the sum total of nature, we can ask why we have *this* totality rather than some quite different totality. The only *sufficient* explanation is that natural events, and even the whole of nature, must ultimately depend upon a necessary Being. Such a Being cannot have had an external cause, because it is an infinite and eternal Being—namely, God—whose essence is to exist. The argument arrives at the same conclusion as the ontological proof but via a different route.

This argument can be criticized in a number of ways. First, we can ask what is meant by saying that God is a necessary Being. The word "necessity" applies to *propositions* whose denial would be contradictory. "Two plus two equals four" is a necessary proposition, since it would be contradictory to deny it. But does "necessity" apply to *things* as well as to propositions? The character Cleanthes, in Hume's dialogue, answers: "Nothing is demonstrable unless the contrary implies a contradiction. Nothing that is distinctly conceivable implies a contradiction. Whatever we conceive as existent, we can also conceive as nonexistent. There is no being, therefore, whose nonexistence implies a contradiction." If necessity thus applies to logically necessitated propositions and not to things, nothing, not even God, is a necessary Being.

If, in some mysterious way, a Being can be necessary, why might not the natural universe be this necessarily existent Being? If you reply that every natural event is seen to be non-necessary (in the sense that its absence involves no contradiction), it does not follow that the whole of nature is non-necessary. A whole need not have the character of its parts. It does not follow from the fact that every note in a musical composition is short that the whole composition is short. Similarly, it does not follow from the fact that every natural thing or event is non-necessary that the whole of nature is non-necessary. If we are to insist upon a necessity that we do not understand, this necessity would seem as applicable to nature as to supernature.

But should we demand such an ultimate necessity? Why not simply suppose that the causal series of linked events stretches back infinitely and that there is no other explanation? If each part is determined by its antecedents, is not the whole sufficiently determined? It would seem to be absurd to demand an external cause for an infinite regress without beginning, since the causal relation implies priority in time and hence a beginning of existence. Our whole experience of causal connections, moreover, lies *within* nature, and we have no sufficient basis for projecting this relation *outside* of nature. Can we assume that what is true of particular things in the world—namely, that *they* are caused—is true of the universe in its totality? Must the universe have a cause outside its own nature? Or must it have any cause at all? To a consistent empiricist, such as Hume, the extension of the concept of causation beyond the field of all actual or possible experience offers special difficulties. On the other hand, if we understand the "necessity" of a necessary Being as logical rather than causal, we are faced by the difficulty already mentioned—that the necessity here involved is mysterious and seems applicable to the whole of nature no less than to supernature.

Despite these objections of Hume, most Catholic and some non-Catholic philosophers believe that the argument retains its cogency. It seems to them that the evident self-insufficiency of natural events requires an ultimate self-sufficient foundation. Nature as a composite whole, moreover, seems *not* self-sufficient, because any composite *could* be composed in a different way. Why should there be this total natural constellation rather than some other? Does not the existence of such dependent and conditioned being require existence of independent and unconditioned Being? Only an infinite, eternal, completely actualized, and noncomposite Being—a pure spirit—could be thus independent and unconditioned, the guarantor of its own existence and all else besides. We may have to fall back upon other arguments to establish some of the attributes of God, but the cosmological argument at least proves that nature is dependent upon supernature, and this conclusion carries us a long way—or so the believer in the cosmological argument would continue to maintain.

Criticism of the Teleological Argument

The teleological argument, or argument from design, is very ancient but still popular. It was first expressly formulated by Plato, in the *Laws*, and has been restated by innumerable philosophers, among them St. Augustine, St. Thomas (in his Fifth Proof), Locke, and Rousseau. It was especially popular in the seventeenth and eighteenth centuries, when the astronomy and physics of Newton were interpreted as the disclosure of a wonderful natural order requiring God as its source.

The criticisms of Hume, as set forth by the character Philo in the *Dialogues Concerning Natural Religion*, constitute a powerful attack upon the design argument. Are these criticisms conclusive? Evidently Hume did not think so. The criticisms are not presented as his but are put in the mouth of Philo, one of the three characters in the *Dialogues*. Hume abstains from indicating his own sympathies except at the very end of the book, where he suggests that "the opinions" of Cleanthes, the proponent of the design argument, are nearer to the truth than those of Philo. In a letter to a friend, George Elliot (dated March 10, 1751), Hume refers to Cleanthes as the "hero" of the dialogues, and asks for any suggestions which will strengthen that side of the dispute. Even Philo, in a final passage not quoted here, is made to remark that the apparent design in nature proves that its cause bears an analogy, though somewhat remote, to the human mind. Probably Hume felt that Philo's criticisms were weighty but by no means decisive.

One thing to note about most of these criticisms is that they do not tend to prove the *absence* of a designing agency or agencies. They indicate limitations rather than fatal defects in the design argument. They show that the finite order and goodness of nature are an insufficient basis for inferring an infinite, perfect, unitary, external, and conscious designer. Kant later pointed out an additional limitation—that the design argument can prove only a kind of architect, but it cannot prove a creator who makes the world out of nothing. Just as a watch-maker uses materials already in existence to make a watch, so the designer of a natural order may use pre-existing materials to compose his design. But these considerations are consistent with some kind of teleological explanation of the goodness and higher levels of order to be found in nature. It is true that Philo's final point, that the natural order may be the result of mere natural selection, is opposed to a teleological hypothesis, but the further course of the dialogue suggests that neither Cleanthes nor Philo regarded natural selection as sufficient, in itself, to explain the whole order of nature. It is also noteworthy that John Stuart Mill and William James could not bring themselves to the view that the Darwinian hypothesis of natural selection was alone sufficient to explain the higher levels of evolution. They preferred to believe in a finite God, struggling against evil but not wholly able to eliminate it. Moreover, this finite God need not be thought of as an external, transcendent Deity but can be construed as the total society of natural forces that are pushing on toward the good. Admittedly, this concept alters the usual meaning of "God," but some modern philosophers nevertheless prefer it.

I shall not discuss St. Thomas' Fourth Proof except to remark that it appears to me inconclusive. That there are degrees of excellence I do not doubt, but I see no reason to suppose that there must be Perfection at the top of the scale or that lower degrees of excellence must depend for their existence upon the highest degree.

An Alternative to Theism

Suppose that all the proofs of the existence of God fail, and that neither argument nor faith suffices as a basis for belief in Him? What then? The essay of Stace is an honest and forthright answer. It speaks for itself more eloquently than any commentary.

Stace felt, on later reflection, that mystical experience may open up another dimension of truth. But he never abandoned the view, here so finely stated, that it is possible to live without fantasies, and that to maintain noble human ideals, disentangled from superstitition, is the mature answer to the problem of life. There is an undercurrent of sadness in what he writes, but also of hope and courage.

One generalization we might question. He characterizes the universe revealed by science as "stark and bleak." "There is, in the universe outside man," he says, "no spirituality, no values. . . ." Is this not a hazardous generalization? It implies that there is no extra-terrestrial life on a level as high as man. Modern science scarcely supports this conclusion. The cosmos is so vast and so mysterious that we can only conjecture. The chemical building blocks of life are dispersed very widely throughout the known universe, and life may have emerged at many stations beyond our solar system. As an eminent scientist has written:

> It has been estimated that about 100 billion galaxies float within view of our larger telescopes and that the population of stars in an average galaxy such as our own is roughly 100 billion. . . . Planets are a normal product of stellar condensation and should be associated with . . . more than half of all the stars in the visible universe.[1]

Among the billions of planets there may be some where life has evolved to a level at least as high as man. No human being can know what exists in the infinitude of time and space, but there is little occasion for characterizing the universe beyond earth as utterly devoid of life and intelligence.

Aside from this questionable generalization, the contrast that Stace draws between humanism and theism presents one of the great issues in the religious life of mankind. This issue William James regards as of paramount importance.

James' Defense of the Right To Believe in Theism

James' purpose is to defend not any and all kinds of faith but only belief entertained under the conditions that he specifies. He points out that we are often confronted by the problem of choosing between two mutually incompatible hypotheses. Such a choice he calls an "option," and he classifies options into three pairs of opposites: (1) *living* or *dead,* (2) *forced* or *avoidable,* and (3) *momentous* or *trivial.* A *living* option offers a choice sufficiently exciting to tempt our will; a *dead* option presents a choice that leaves us cold. A *forced* option cannot be escaped; an *avoidable* option can be indefinitely postponed or evaded. Finally, a *momentous* option makes an important difference; a *trivial* option has no significant consequences.

James cites many illustrations to clarify these distinctions, but we shall confine ourselves to a single example. Suppose you were critically ill and had to decide whether to risk a very dangerous operation. You would be confronted by two hypotheses: (1) that your chances of recovery would be better if you were to have the operation, and (2) that your chances would be better if you were to avoid the operation. Obviously, this option would be living, since you could not be in-

[1] Preston Cloud, *Cosmos, Earth, and Man* (New Haven: Yale University Press, 1978), pp. 279–280.

different to it; forced, since you could not delay or evade a decision (nondecision being equivalent to negative decision); and momentous, since it would be a life-and-death matter. James calls an option *genuine* when it is living, forced, and momentous.

He then distinguishes between three attitudes towards an hypothesis: belief, nonbelief, and disbelief. In terms of consequences, nonbelief and disbelief are sometimes identical. In the illustration cited above, the *failure* to decide (nonbelief) is practically equivalent to disbelief in the advisability of the operation. In either case, there would be no operation.

Having thus defined his terms, James states three conditions which must be present in order for faith to be justified:

1. when we are confronted by a *genuine* option—living, forced, and momentous;

2. when we do not have enough reason or evidence to prove that one hypothesis (*e.g.,* that God exists) is more probable than the alternative hypothesis (that God does not exist); and

3. when the result of believing is to make life substantially better.

There is a final twist to the argument. James points out that belief in a proposition sometimes helps to make that proposition came true. He cites the example of a man's faith that his sweetheart really loves him. This faith helps to create a relation of confidence and intimacy that ensures, or helps to ensure, the very love which is the object of belief. In such case, faith is doubly justified.

James' argument is ingenious, and many people regard it as valid. It should not be used to justify credulity, however, and it should be hedged with qualifications. First, if we believe on the basis of faith, we should be clear-headed about what we are doing. We should recognize that it *is* faith and not reason. We should distinguish between *valuable* and *probable,* between *allurement* and *evidence,* between *wishful thinking* and *rational demonstration.* The mere fact that we desire a certain state to be the case is no evidence that it *is* the case. I may desire immortality, but my desire will not make me immortal. Believing in God may make me happier, but this has no bearing on the truth of my belief. "If wishes were horses, beggars would ride." James himself insists that the will to believe comes into play only when the option is live, forced, and momentous and reason is unable to provide an answer.

Second, James speaks as if there were no intermediate shades of opinion between complete belief and complete disbelief. Actually there are many shades of belief and doubt. We rightly distinguish between probability and certainty, and we recognize that there are innumerable degrees of probability, depending upon the strength of the evidence. In a rational mind, the degree of credence is generally proportional to the degree of probability.

Third, James is perhaps too much inclined to interpret nonbelief as practically equivalent to disbelief. In some situations, there is indeed no practical difference between them, but very often there is a difference. Moreover, the nonbelief of an agnostic is quite different from the nonbelief of an inquirist such as Socrates. Complete belief, complete disbelief, and agnostic nonbelief tend to cut off inquiry, whereas inquiristic nonbelief tends to stimulate inquiry. Here is a practical difference of great importance—a difference which James seems to overlook.

Fourth, James' point that faith sometimes creates its own verification has limited validity. When the outcome of one's endeavors depends upon one's morale, faith in the venture may help to ensure success. A football team's faith that it will win may help to make it win; a man's faith that he will get well may help him to recover from a psychological or psychosomatic illness. No one will argue, however, that a man's faith in God will ensure, or even help to ensure, God's existence. The truth or falsity of most beliefs depends upon objective factors, independent of how one feels or thinks. Of course, *if* God exists and *if* he is a Being that enters into personal relations with individuals, the faith that one can commune with God may be very helpful in establishing the communion.

These considerations do not disprove the need for faith. Certain kinds of facts, such as the beauty and power of love, can be known only if we open ourselves to their influence; and if our attitude is negative to begin with, this is impossible. The data of life are often ambiguous, and we may interpret them in very different ways. In some instances, the only way to realize the higher possibilities may be to respond with hope and trust. It is up to the reader to consider how far such faith is justified, and to what extent it should be hedged about by qualifications and exceptions.

3

One or Many

BARUCH SPINOZA (1632–1677)

Born into the Jewish community of Amsterdam, Spinoza was educated in the Rabbinical tradition but studied such non-Jewish philosphers as Bruno and Descartes. By the time he was twenty-three he rebelled against orthodox Judaism, even refusing a bribe to conceal his views. In consequence, he was cursed in the name of God and his Holy Angels by the Jewish authorities and excommunicated from the Synagogue. Changing his Jewish name, Baruch, to its Latin equivalent, Benedictus, he dwelt for many years in a nearby village earning a modest living by polishing optical lenses. Later he moved to The Hague. As an excommunicated Jew, he had few ties with either his Dutch or his Jewish neighbors, but he was loved and respected by the few who knew him.

He devoted much of his time to studying philosophy and corresponding with the great scientists, mathematicians, and philosophers of the period. In 1663 he published an expository account of Descartes' philosophy and in 1670 published his *Tractatus Theologico-Politicus*. The latter, a work of biblical criticism and political theory, although prohibited by both Catholics and Protestants, achieved fame in learned and emancipated circles. As result, Spinoza was offered a professorship at the University of Heidelberg if he would promise not to disturb the established religion. He refused the offer because the proviso would restrict his freedom of speech and the academic duties would cut into his studies.

The grinding of lenses may have brought on or aggravated the tuberculosis of which he died at the age of forty-three. At the time of his death, he left behind a few personal belongings and some unpublished manuscripts, including the *Ethics*. It was one of the richest estates ever left by any man.

Ethics

I have now explained the nature of God and its properties. I have shown that He necessarily exists; that He is one God; that from the necessity alone of His own nature He is and acts; that He is, and in what way He is, the free cause of all things; that all things are in Him, and so depend upon Him that without Him they can neither be nor can be conceived; and, finally, that all things have been predetermined by Him, not indeed from freedom of will or from absolute good pleasure, but from His absolute nature or infinite power.

Moreover, wherever an opportunity was afforded, I have endeavoured to remove prejudices which might hinder the perception of the truth of what I have demonstrated; but because not a few still remain which have been and are now sufficient to prove a very great hindrance to the comprehension of the connection of things in the manner in which I have explained it, I have thought it worth while to call them up to be examined by reason. But all these prejudices which I here undertake to point out depend upon this solely: that it is commonly supposed that all things in nature, like men, work to some end;

From Benedict Spinoza, *Ethics*, Appendix to Part I. Translated from the Latin by William Hale White. London: Trübner and Company, 1883.

and indeed it is thought to be certain that God himself directs all things to some sure end, for it is said that God has made all things for man, and man that he may worship God. This, therefore, I will first investigate by inquiring, firstly, why so many rest in this prejudice, and why all are so naturally inclined to embrace it? I shall then show its falsity, and, finally, the manner in which there have arisen from it prejudices concerning *good* and *evil, merit* and *sin, praise* and *blame, order* and *disorder, beauty* and *deformity,* and so forth. This, however, is not the place to deduce these things from the nature of the human mind. It will be sufficient if I here take as an axiom that which no one ought to dispute, namely that man is born ignorant of the causes of things, and that he has a desire, of which he is conscious, to seek that which is profitable to him. From this it follows, firstly, that he thinks himself free because he is conscious of his wishes and appetites, whilst at the same time he is ignorant of the causes by which he is led to wish and desire, not dreaming what they are; and, secondly, it follows that man does everything for an end, namely, for that which is profitable to him, which is what he seeks. Hence it happens that he attempts to discover merely the final causes of that which has happened; and when he has heard them he is satisfied, because there is no longer any cause for further uncertainty. But if he cannot hear from another what these final causes are, nothing remains but to turn to himself and reflect upon the ends which usually determine him to the like actions, and thus by his own mind he necessarily judges that of another. Moreover, since he discovers, both within and without himself, a multitude of means which contribute not a little to the attainment of what is profitable to himself—for example, the eyes, which are useful for seeing, the teeth for mastication, plants and animals for nourishment, the sun for giving light, the sea for feeding fish, &c. —it comes to pass that all natural objects are considered as means for obtaining what is profitable. These too being evidently discovered and not created by man, hence he has a cause for believing that some other person exists, who has prepared them for man's use. For having considered them as means it was impossible to believe that they had created themselves, and so he was obliged to infer from the means which he was in the habit of providing for himself that some ruler or rulers of nature exist, endowed with human liberty, who have taken care of all things for him, and have made all things for his use. Since he never heard anything about the mind of these rulers, he was compelled to judge of it from his own, and hence he affirmed that the gods direct everything for his advantage, in order that he may be bound to them and hold them in the highest honour. This is the reason why each man has devised for himself, out of his own brain, a different mode of

worshipping God, so that God might love him above others, and direct all nature to the service of his blind cupidity and insatiable avarice.

Thus has this prejudice been turned into a superstition and has driven deep roots into the mind—a prejudice which was the reason why every one has so eagerly tried to discover and explain the final causes of things. The attempt, however, to show that nature does nothing in vain (that is to say, nothing which is not profitable to man), seems to end in showing that nature, the gods, and man are alike mad.

Do but see, I pray, to what all this has led. Amidst so much in nature that is beneficial, not a few things must have been observed which are injurious, such as storms, earthquakes, diseases, and it was affirmed that these things happened either because the gods were angry because of wrongs which had been inflicted on them by man, or because of sins committed in the method of worshipping them; and although experience daily contradicted this, and showed by an infinity of examples that both the beneficial and the injurious were indiscriminately bestowed on the pious and the impious, the inveterate prejudices on this point have not therefore been abandoned. For it was much easier for a man to place these things aside with others of the use of which he was ignorant, and thus retain his present and inborn state of ignorance, than to destroy the whole superstructure and think out a new one. Hence it was looked upon as indisputable that the judgments of the gods far surpass our comprehension; and this opinion alone would have been sufficient to keep the human race in darkness to all eternity, if mathematics, which does not deal with ends, but with the essences and properties of forms, had not placed before us another rule of truth. In addition to mathematics, other causes also might be assigned, which it is superfluous here to enumerate, tending to make men reflect upon these universal prejudices, and leading them to a true knowledge of things.

I have thus sufficiently explained what I promised in the first place to explain. There will now be no need of many words to show that nature has set no end before herself, and that all final causes are nothing but human fictions. For I believe that this is sufficiently evident both from the foundations and causes of this prejudice, and from Prop. 16 and Corol. Prop. 32, as well as from all those propositions in which I have shown that all things are begotten by a certain eternal necessity of nature and in absolute perfection. Thus much, nevertheless, I will add, that this doctrine concerning an end altogether overturns nature. For that which is in truth the cause it considers as the effect, and *vice versa*. Again, that which is first in nature it puts last; and, finally, that which is supreme and most perfect it makes the most imperfect. For (passing by the first two assertions as self-evident) it is plain from Props. 21, 22, and 23, that that effect is the most perfect which is immediately produced by God, and in proportion as intermediate causes are necessary for the production of a thing is it imperfect. But if things which are immediately produced by God were made in order that He might obtain the end He had in view, then the last things for the sake of which the first exist, must be the most perfect of all. Again, this doctrine does away with God's perfection. For if God works to obtain an end, He necessarily seeks something of which he stands in need. And although theologians and metaphysicians distinguish between the end of want and the end of assimilation (*finem indegentiæ et finem assimilationis*), they confess that God has done all things for His own sake, and not for the sake of the things to be created, because before the creation they can assign nothing excepting God for the sake of which God could do anything; and therefore they are necessarily compelled to admit that God stood in need of and desired those things for which He determined to prepare means. This is self-evident. Nor is it here to be overlooked that the adherents of this doctrine, who have found a pleasure in displaying their ingenuity in assigning the ends of things, have introduced a new species of argument, not the *reductio ad impossible,* but the *reductio ad ignorantiam,* to prove their position, which shows that it had no other method of defence left. For, by way of example, if a stone has fallen from some roof on somebody's head and killed him, they will demonstrate in this manner that the stone has fallen in order to kill the man. For if it did not fall for that purpose by the will of God, how could so many circumstances concur through chance (and a number often simultaneously do concur)? You will answer, perhaps, that the event happened because the wind blew and the man was passing that way. But, they will urge, why did the wind blow at that time, and why did the man pass that way precisely at the same moment? If you again reply that the wind rose then because the sea on the preceding day began to be stormy, the weather hitherto having been calm, and that the man had been invited by a friend, they will urge again—because there is no end of questioning—But why was the sea agitated? why was the man invited at that time? And so they will not cease from asking the causes of causes, until at last you fly to the will of God, the refuge for ignorance.

So, also, when they behold the structure of the human body, they are amazed; and because they are ignorant of the causes of such art, they conclude that the body was made not by mechanical but by a supernatural or divine art, and has been formed in such a way so that the one part may not injure the other. Hence it happens that the man who endeavours to find out the true causes of miracles, and who desires as a wise man to understand nature, and not to gape at it like a fool, is generally considered and proclaimed to be a heretic and impious by those whom the vulgar worship as the interpreters both of nature and the gods. For these know that if ignorance be removed, amazed stupidity, the sole ground on which they rely in arguing or in defending their authority, is taken away also. But these things I leave and pass on to that which I determined to do in the third place.

After man has persuaded himself that all things which exist are made for him, he must in everything adjudge that to be of the greatest importance which is most useful to him, and he must esteem that to be of surpassing worth by which he is most beneficially affected. In this way he is compelled to form those notions by which he explains nature; such, for instance, as *good, evil, order, confusion, heat, cold, beauty,* and *deformity,* &c.; and because he supposes himself to be free, notions like those of *praise* and *blame, sin* and *merit,* have arisen. These latter I shall hereafter explain when I have treated of human nature; the former I will here briefly unfold.

It is to be observed that man has given the name *good* to every thing which leads to health and the worship of God; on the contrary, everything which does not lead thereto he calls *evil.* But because those who do not understand nature affirm nothing about things themselves, but only imagine them, and take the imagination to be understanding, they therefore, ignorant of things and their nature, firmly believe an *order* to be in things; for when things are so placed that, if they are represented to us through the senses, we can easily imagine them, and consequently easily remember them, we call them well arranged; but if they are not placed so that we can imagine and remember them, we call them badly arranged or *confused.* Moreover, since those things are more especially pleasing to us which we can easily imagine, men therefore prefer order to confusion, as if order were something in nature apart from our own imagination; and they say that God has created everything in order, and in this manner they ignorantly attribute imagination to God, unless they mean perhaps that God, out of consideration for the human imagination, has disposed things in the manner in which they can most easily be imagined. No hesitation either seems to be caused by the fact that an infinite number of things are discovered which far surpass our imagination, and very many which confound it through its weakness. But enough of this. The other notions which I have mentioned are nothing but modes in which the imagination is affected in different ways, and nevertheless they are regarded by the ignorant as being specially attributes of things, because, as we have remarked, men consider all things as made for themselves, and call the nature of a thing good, evil, sound, putrid, or corrupt, just as they are affected by it. For example if the motion by which the nerves are affected by means of objects represented to the eye conduces to well-being, the objects by which it is caused are called *beautiful;* while those exciting a contrary motion are called *deformed.* Those things, too, which stimulate the senses through the nostrils are called sweet-smelling or stinking; those which act through the taste are called sweet or bitter, full-flavoured or insipid; those which act through the touch, hard or soft, heavy or light; those, lastly, which act through the ears are said to make a noise, sound, or harmony, the last having caused men to lose their senses to such a degree that they have believed that God even is delighted with it. Indeed, philosophers may be found who have persuaded themselves that the celestial motions beget a harmony. All these things sufficiently show that every

one judges things by the constitution of his brain, or rather accepts the affections of his imagination in the place of things. It is not, therefore, to be wondered at, as we may observe in passing, that all those controversies which we see have arisen amongst men, so that at last scepticism has been the result. For although human bodies agree in many things, they differ in more, and therefore that which to one person is good will appear to another evil, that which to one is well arranged to another is confused, that which pleases one will displease another, and so on in other cases which I pass by both because we cannot notice them at length here, and because they are within the experience of every one. For every one has heard the expressions: So many heads, so many ways of thinking; Every one is satisfied with his own way of thinking; Differences of brains are not less common than differences of taste;—all which maxims show that men decide upon matters according to the constitution of their brains, and imagine rather than understand things. If men understood things, they would, as mathematics prove, at least be all alike convinced if they were not all alike attracted. We see, therefore, that all those methods by which the common people are in the habit of explaining nature are only different sorts of imaginations, and do not reveal the nature of anything in itself, but only the constitution of the imagination; and because they have names as if they were entities existing apart from the imagination, I call them entities not of the reason but of the imagination. All argument, therefore, urged against us based upon such notions can be easily refuted. Many people, for instance, are accustomed to argue thus:—If all things have followed from the necessity of the most perfect nature of God, how is it that so many imperfections have arisen in nature—corruption, for instance, of things till they stink; deformity, exciting disgust; confusion, evil, crime, &c.? But, as I have just observed, all this is easily answered. For the perfection of things is to be judged by their nature and power alone; nor are they more or less perfect because they delight or offend the human senses, or because they are beneficial or prejudicial to human nature. But to those who ask why God has not created all men in such a manner that they might be controlled by the dictates of reason alone, I give but this answer: Because to Him material was not wanting for the creation of everything, from the highest down to the very lowest grade of perfection; or, to speak more properly, because the laws of His nature were so ample that they suffered for the production of everything which can be conceived by an infinite intellect, as I have demonstrated in Prop. 16.

These are the prejudices which I undertook to notice here. If any others of a similar character remain, they can easily be rectified with a little thought by any one.

Correspondence

Letter XXXII

To the Very Noble and Learned Mr. HENRY OLDENBURG.

Most noble Sir,

I thank you and the very Noble Mr. Boyle very much for kindly encouraging me to go on with my Philosophy. I do indeed proceed with it, as far as my slender powers allow, not doubting meanwhile of your help and goodwill.

When you ask me what I think about the question which turns on *the Knowl-*

From *The Correspondence of Spinoza,* translated and edited by Abraham Wolf, 1928, new impression, 1966. By permission of George Allen & Unwin, London, and Russell & Russell, New York.

edge how each part of Nature accords with the whole of it, and in what way it is connected with the other parts, I think you mean to ask for the reasons on the strength of which we believe that each part of Nature accords with the whole of it, and is connected with the other parts. For I said in my preceding letter that I do not know how the parts are really interconnected, and how each part accords with the whole; for to know this it would be necessary to know the whole of Nature and all its Parts.

I shall therefore try to show the reason which compels me to make this assertion; but I should like first to warn you that I do not attribute to Nature beauty or ugliness, order or confusion. For things cannot, except with respect to our imagination, be called beautiful, or ugly, ordered or confused.

By connection of the parts, then, I mean nothing else than that the laws, or nature, of one part adapt themselves to the laws, or nature, of another part in such a way as to produce the least possible opposition. With regard to whole and parts, I consider things as parts of some whole, in so far as their natures are mutually adapted so that they are in accord among themselves, as far as possible; but in so far as things differ among themselves, each produces an idea in our mind, which is distinct from the others, and is therefore considered to be a whole, not a part. For instance, since the motions of the particles of lymph, chyle, etc., are so mutually adapted in respect of magnitude and figure that they clearly agree among themselves, and all together constitute one fluid, to that extent only, chyle, lymph, etc., are considered to be parts of the blood: but in so far as we conceive the lymph particles as differing in respect of figure and motion from the particles of chyle, to that extent we consider them to be a whole, not a part.

Let us now, if you please, imagine that a small worm lives in the blood, whose sight is keen enough to distinguish the particles of blood, lymph, etc., and his reason to observe how each part on collision with another either rebounds, or communicates a part of its own motion, etc. That worm would live in this blood as we live in this part of the universe, and he would consider each particle of blood to be a whole, and not a part. And he could not know

how all the parts are controlled by the universal nature of blood, and are forced, as the universal nature of blood demands, to adapt themselves to one another, so as to harmonize with one another in a certain way. For if we imagine that there are no causes outside the blood to communicate new motions to the blood, and that outside the blood there is no space, and no other bodies, to which the particles of blood could transfer their motion, it is certain that the blood would remain always in its state, and its particles would suffer no changes other than those which can be conceived from the given relation of the motion of the blood to the lymph and chyle, etc., and so blood would have to be considered always to be a whole and not a part. But, since there are very many other causes which in a certain way control the laws of the nature of blood, and are in turn controlled by the blood, hence it comes about that other motions and other changes take place in the blood, which result not only from the mere relation of the motion of its parts to one another, but from the relation of the motion of the blood and also the external causes to one another: in this way the blood has the character of a part and not of a whole. I have only spoken of whole and part.

Now, all the bodies of nature can and should be conceived in the same way as we have here conceived the blood: for all bodies are surrounded by others, and are mutually determined to exist and to act in a definte and determined manner, while there is preserved in all together, that is, in the whole universe, the same proportion of motion and rest. Hence it follows that every body, in so far as it exists modified in a certain way, must be considered to be a part of the whole universe, to be in accord with the whole of it, and to be connected with the other parts. And since the nature of the universe is not limited, like the nature of the blood, but absolutely infinite, its parts are controlled by the nature of this infinite power in infinite ways, and are compelled to suffer infinite changes. But I conceive that with regard to substance each part has a closer union with its whole. For as I endeavoured to show in my first letter, which I wrote to you when I was still living at Rhynsburg, since it is of the nature of substance to be infinite, it follows that each part belongs to the nature of corporeal substance, and can neither exist nor be conceived without it.

You see, then, in what way and why I think that the human Body is a part of Nature. As regards the human Mind I think it too is a part of Nature: since I state that there exists in Nature an infinite power of thought, which in so far as it is infinite, contains in itself subjectively the whole of Nature, and its thoughts proceed in the same way as Nature, which, to be sure, is its ideatum.

Then I declare that the human mind is this same power, not in so far as it is infinite, and perceives the whole of Nature, but in so far as it is finite and perceives only the human Body, and in this way I declare that the human Mind is a part of a certain infinite intellect. . . .

In all affection yours

B. de SPINOZA

[Voorburg, 20 November 1665]

Letter LVI

To the Very Honourable and Prudent
Mr. HUGO BOXEL.

Most honourable Sir,

I hasten to answer your letter, which I received yesterday, because if I go on delaying longer I shall be compelled to postpone my reply longer than I should wish. Your health would cause me anxiety if I had not heard that you are better, and I hope you are now entirely recovered.

How difficult it is for two persons who follow different principles to meet one another and agree on a subject which depends on many others, would be clear from this question alone, even if no argument demonstarted it. Tell me, I pray, whether you have seen or read any Philosophers who hold the opinion that the world was made by chance, that is, in the sense in which you understand it, namely, that God, when creating the world had set Himself a definite aim, and yet transgressed His own decree. I do not know that such a thing even occurred to any man's thought. Similarly, I am in the dark about the arguments by which you endeavour to persuade me to believe that *Fortuitious* and *Necessary* are not contraries. As soon as I realize that the three angles of a triangle are necessarily equal to two right angles, I also deny that this is the result of chance. Similarly as soon as I realize that heat is the necessary effect of fire, I also deny that it occurs by chance. It seems no less absurd and opposed to reason to suppose that *Necessary* and *Free* are contraries. For no one can deny that God knows

Himself and everything else freely, and yet all are agreed in admitting that God knows Himself necessarily. Thus you seem to me to make no distinction between coercion or force, and Necessity. That man desires to live, to love, etc., is not a compulsory activity, but it is none the less necessary, and much more so is God's will to be, and to know, and to act. If, apart from these remarks, you turn over in your mind the fact that indifference is nothing but ignorance or doubt, and that a will ever constant and determined in all things is a virtue, and a necessary property of the intellect, then you will see that my words are thoroughly in accord with the truth. If we assert that God had it in His power not to will a thing, and did not have it in His power not to understand it, then we attribute to God two different kinds of freedom, one being that of necessity, the other that of indifference, and consequently we shall conceive the will of God as differing from His essence and His intellect, and in that case we shall fall into one absurdity after another. . . .

Further, when you say that if I deny to God the acts of seeing, of hearing, of attending and of willing, etc., and their occurrence in Him in an eminent degree, then you do not know what kind of God I have, I suspect therefrom that you believe that there is no perfection greater than that which is unfolded in the said attributes. I do not wonder at this, since I believe that a triangle, if only it had the power of speech, would say in like manner that God is eminently triangular, and a circle would say that the Divine Nature is eminently circular, and in this way each thing would ascribe its own attributes to God,

and make itself like unto God, while all else would appear to it deformed.

The small compass of a letter, and limitation of time, do not permit me to explain in detail my opinion about the Divine Nature, or the other Questions which you put forward, to say nothing of the fact that to raise difficulties is not the same as to advance reasons. It is true that in the world we often act on conjecture; but it is false that our reflections are based on conjecture. In ordinary life we must follow what is most probable, but in philosophical speculations, the truth. Man would perish of thirst and hunger if he would not eat or drink until he had obtained a perfect proof that food and drink would do him good. But in contemplation this has no place. On the contrary, we must be cautious not to admit as true something which is merely probable. For when we admit one falsity, countless others follow.

Further, from the fact that divine and human sciences are full of disputes and controversies it cannot be inferred that all the things which are treated therein are uncertain: for there have been very many people who were so possessed by the love of contradiction that they laughed even at Geometrical proofs. Sextus Empiricus and other Sceptics whom you cite say that it is not true that the whole is greater than its part, and they have the same view of the other axioms.

But, putting aside and admitting the fact that in default of proofs we must be satisfied with probabilities, I say that a probable Proof ought to be such that, although we can doubt it, yet we cannot contradict it; because that which can be contradicted is not likely to be true, but likely to be false. If, for instance, I say that Peter is alive, because I saw him in good health yesterday, this is indeed likely to be true so long as no one can contradict me; but if someone else says that yesterday he saw Peter suffering from loss of consciousness, and that he believes that Peter died from it, he makes my words seem false. That your conjecture about spectres and ghosts seems false and not even probable, I have so clearly shown that I find nothing worthy of consideration in your answer.

To your question whether I have as clear an idea of God as I have of a triangle, I answer in the affirmative. But if you ask me whether I have as clear a mental image of God as I have of a triangle, I shall answer No. For we cannot imagine God, but we can, indeed, conceive Him. Here also it should be noted that I do not say that I know God entirely, but only that I understand some of His attributes, though not all, nor even the greater part of them, and it is certain that our ignorance of the majority of them does not hinder our having a knowledge of some of them. When I learnt Euclid's elements I first understood that the three angles of a triangle are equal to two right angles, and I clearly perceived this property of a triangle although I was ignorant of many others.

As regards spectres, or ghosts, I have never yet heard of an intelligible property of theirs, but only of Phantasies which no-one can grasp. When you say that spectres, or ghosts, here in this lower region (I follow your form of expression, although I do not know that the matter here in this lower region is less valuable than that above) consist of the finest, thinnest, and most subtle substance, you seem to be speaking of spiders' webs, of air, or of vapours. To say that they are invisible means for me as much as if you said what they are not, but not what they are; unless perhaps you want to indicate that, according as they please, they make themselves now visible, now invisible, and that in these as in other impossibilities, the imagination will find no difficulty.

The authority of Plato, Aristotle, and Socrates has not much weight with me. I should have been surprised had you mentioned Epicurus, Democritus, Lucretius or any one of the Atomists, or defenders of the atoms. It is not surprising that those who invented occult Qualities, intentional Species, substantial Forms, and a thousand other trifles, should have devised spectres and ghosts, and put their faith in old women, in order to weaken the authority of Democritus, of whose good repute they were so envious that they burnt all his books, which he had published amidst so much praise. If you have a mind to put faith in them, what reasons have you for denying the miracles of the Holy Virgin, and of all the Saints, which have been described by so many very famous Philosophers, Theologians, and Historians that I can produce an hundred of them to scarcely one of the others?

Lastly, most honoured Sir, I have gone further than I intended. I do not wish to annoy you further with things which (I know) you will not admit, since you follow other principles which differ widely from my own, etc.

[The Hague, October 1674]

Letter LVIII

To the Very Learned and Expert
Mr. G. H. SCHULLER.

Most Expert Sir,

. . . I say that that thing is free which exists and acts solely from the necessity of its own nature; but that that thing is under compulsion which is determined by something else to exist, and to act in a definite and determined manner. For example, God, although He exists necessarily, nevertheless exists freely, since He exists solely from the necessity of His own nature. So also God freely understands Himself and absolutely all things, since it follows solely from the necessity of His own nature that He should understand everything. You see, therefore, that I do not place Freedom in free decision, but in free necessity.

Let us, however, descend to created things, which are all determined by external causes to exist, and to act in a definite and determined manner. In order that this may be clearly understood, let us think of a very simple thing. For instance, a stone receives from an external cause, which impels it, a certain quantity of motion, with which it will afterwards necessarily continue to move when the impact of the external cause has ceased. This continuance of the stone in its motion is compelled, not because it is necessary, but because it must be defined by the impact of an external cause. What is here said of the stone must be understood of each individual thing, however composite and however adapted to various ends it may be thought to be: that is, that each thing

is necessarily determined by an external cause to exist and to act in a definite and determinate manner.

Next, conceive, if you please, that the stone while it continues in motion thinks, and knows that it is striving as much as possible to continue in motion. Surely this stone, inasmuch as it is conscious only of its own effort, and is far from indifferent, will believe that it is completely free, and that it continues in motion for no other reason than because it wants to. And such is the human freedom which all men boast that they possess, and which consists solely in this, that men are conscious of their desire, and ignorant of the causes by which they are determined. So the infant believes that it freely wants milk; the boy when he is angry that he freely wants revenge; the timid that he wants to escape. Then too the drunkard believes that, by the free decision of his mind, he says those things which afterwards when sober he would prefer to have left unsaid. So the delirious, the garrulous and many others of the same sort, believe that they are acting in accordance with the free decision of their mind, and not that they are carried away by impulse. Since this preconception is innate in all men, they are not so easily freed from it. For, although experience teaches sufficiently and more than sufficiently that the last thing that men can do is to moderate their appetites, and that often, when they are tormented by conflicting feelings, they see the better and follow the worse, yet they believe themselves to be free, because they desire some things slightly, and their appetites for these can easily be repressed by the memory of some other thing, which we frequently call to mind.

With these remarks, unless I am mistaken, I have sufficiently explained what my view is about free and compelled necessity, and about imaginary human freedom: and from this it will be easy to answer the objections of your friend. For, when he says with Descartes, that he is free who is compelled by no external cause, if by a man who is compelled he means one who acts against his will, I admit that in certain matters we are in no way compelled, and that in this respect we have a free will. But if by compelled he means one who, although he does not act against his will, yet acts necessarily (as I explained above), then I deny that we are free in anything.

Your friend, on the contrary, asserts that *we can exercise our reason with complete freedom, that is, absolutely.* He persists in this opinion with sufficient, not to say too much, confidence. *For who,* he says, *without contradicting his own consciousness, would deny that in my thoughts I can think that I want to write, and that I do not want to do so.* I should very much like to know of what consciousness he speaks, other than that which I explained above in my example of the stone. Indeed, in order not to contradict my consciousness, that is, my reason and experience, and in order not to foster preconceived ideas and ignorance, I deny that I can, by any absolute power of thought, think that I want, and that I do not want to write. But I appeal to his own consciousness, for he has doubtless experienced the fact that in dreams he has not the power of thinking that he

wants, and does not want to write; and that when he dreams that he wants to write he has not the power of not dreaming that he wants to write. I believe he has had no less experience of the fact that the mind is not always equally capable of thinking about the same subject; but that according as the body is more fit for the excitation of the image of this or that object, so the mind is more capable of contemplating this or that object.

When he adds, further, that the causes of his applying himself to writing have stimulated him to write, but have not compelled him, he means nothing else (if you will examine the matter fully) than that his mind was at that time so constituted that the causes which on other occasions, that is, when they were in conflict with some powerful feeling, could not influence him, could now influence him easily, that is, that causes which on other occasions could not compel him, have now compelled him, not to write against his will, but necessarily to desire to write.

Again, as to his statement that *if we were compelled by external causes then no one would be able to acquire the habit of virtue,* I do not know who has told him that we cannot be of a firm and constant disposition as a result of fatalistic necessity, but only from the free decision of the Mind.

As to his last addition, that *if this were granted all wickedness would be excusable*; what then? For wicked men are no less to be feared, and no less pernicious, when they are necessarily wicked. But on these things, look up, if you please, Part II, Chapter VIII, of my *Appendix to Descartes' Principles,*

Books I and II, geometrically demon-strated.

Lastly, I should like your friend, who makes these objections to my theory, to tell me how he conceives human virtue, which he says arises from the free decision of the mind, together with the preordination of God. For if, with Descartes, he admits that he does not know how to reconcile them, then he is endeavouring to hurl against me the weapon by which he has already been pierced. But in vain. For if you will attentively examine my view, you will see that it is entirely consistent, etc.

[The Hague, October 1674]

WILLIAM JAMES

(For biographical note see page 66.)

The One and the Many

. . . Philosophy has often been defined as the quest or the vision of the world's unity. Few persons ever challenge this definition, which is true as far as it goes, for philosophy has indeed manifested above all things its interest in unity. But how about the *variety* in things? Is that such an irrelevant matter? If instead of using the term philosophy, we talk in general of our intellect and its needs, we quickly see that unity is only one of them. Acquaintance with the details of fact is always reckoned, along with their reduction to system, as an indispensable mark of mental greatness. Your 'scholarly' mind, of encyclopedic, philo-

logical type, your man essentially of *learning*, has never lacked for praise along with your philosopher. What our intellect really aims at is neither variety nor unity taken singly, but *totality*. In this, acquaintance with reality's diversities is as important as understanding their connexion. Curiosity goes *pari passu* with the systematizing passion.

In spite of this obvious fact the unity of things has always been considered more *illustrious*, as it were, than their variety. When a young man first conceives the notion that the whole world forms one great fact, with all its parts moving abreast, as it were, and interlocked, he feels as if he were enjoying a great insight, and looks superciliously on all who still fall short of this sublime conception. Taken thus abstractly as it first comes to one, the monistic insight

From *Pragmatism: A New Name for Some Old Ways of Thinking*. New York: Longmans, Green & Co., Inc., 1907.

is so vague as hardly to seem worth defending intellectually. Yet probably every one in this audience in some way cherishes it. A certain abstract monism, a certain emotional response to the character of oneness, as if it were a feature of the world not co-ordinate with its manyness, but vastly more excellent and eminent, is so prevalent in educated circles that we might almost call it a part of philosophic common sense. Of *course* the world is One, we say. How else could it be a world at all? Empiricists as a rule, are as stout monists of this abstract kind as rationalists are.

The difference is that the empiricists are less dazzled. Unity doesn't blind them to everything else, doesn't quench their curiosity for special facts, whereas there is a kind of rationalist who is sure to interpret abstract unity mystically and to forget everything else, to treat it as a principle; to admire and worship it; and thereupon to come to a full stop intellectually.

'The world is One!'—the formula may become a sort of number-worship. 'Three' and 'seven' have, it is true, been reckoned sacred numbers; but, abstractly taken, why is 'one' more excellent than 'forty-three,' or than 'two million and ten'? In this first vague conviction of the world's unity, there is so little to take hold of that we hardly know what we mean by it.

The only way to get forward with our notion is to treat it pragmatically. Granting the oneness to exist, what facts will be different in consequence? What will the unity be known as? The world is One—yes, but *how* one. What

is the practical value of the oneness for *us*.

Asking such questions, we pass from the vague to the definite, from the abstract to the concrete. Many distinct ways in which a oneness predicated of the universe might make a difference, come to view. I will note successively the more obvious of these ways.

1. First, the world is at least *one subject of discourse*. If its manyness were so irremediable as to permit *no* union whatever of its parts, not even our minds could 'mean' the whole of it at once: they would be like eyes trying to look in opposite directions. But in point of fact we mean to cover the whole of it by our abstract term 'world' or 'universe,' which expressly intends that no part shall be left out. Such unity of discourse carries obviously no farther monistic specifications. A 'chaos,' once so named, has as much unity of discourse as a cosmos. It is an odd fact that many monists consider a great victory scored for their side when pluralists say 'the universe is many.' " 'The Universe'!" they chuckle—"his speech betrayeth him. He stands confessed of monism out of his own mouth." Well, let things be one in so far forth! You can then fling such a word as universe at the whole collection of them, but what matters it? It still remains to be ascertained whether they are one in any further or more valuable sense.

2. Are they, for example, *continuous*? Can you pass from one to another, keeping always in your one universe without any danger of falling out? In other words, do the parts of our universe *hang together,* instead of being like detached grains of sand?

Even grains of sand hang together through the space in which they are embedded, and if you can in any way move through such space, you can pass continuously from number one of them to number two. Space and time are thus vehicles of continuity by which the world's parts hang together. The practical difference to us, resultant from these forms of union, is immense. Our whole motor life is based upon them.

3. There are innumerable other paths of practical continuity among things. Lines of *influence* can be traced by which they hang together. Following any such line you pass from one thing to another till you may have covered a good part of the universe's extent. Gravity and heat-conduction are such all-uniting influences, so far as the physical world goes. Electric, luminous and chemical influences follow similar lines of influence. But opaque and inert bodies interrupt the continuity here, so that you have to step round them, or change your mode of progress if you wish to get farther on that day. Practically, you have then lost your universe's unity, *so far as it was constituted by those first lines of influence.*

There are innumerable kinds of connexion that special things have with other special things; and the *ensemble* of any one of these connexions forms one sort of *system* by which things are conjoined. Thus men are conjoined in a vast network of *acquaintanceship.* Brown knows Jones, Jones knows Robinson, etc.; and *by choosing your farther intermediaries rightly* you may carry a message from Jones to the Empress of China, or the Chief of the African Pigmies, or to any one else in the inhabited world. But you are stopped short, as by a non-conductor, when you choose one man wrong in this experiment. What may be called love-systems are grafted on the acquaintance-system. A loves (or hates) B; B loves (or hates) C, etc. But these systems are smaller than the great acquaintance-system that they presuppose.

Human efforts are daily unifying the world more and more in definite systematic ways. We found colonial, postal, consular, commercial systems, all the parts of which obey definite influences that propagate themselves within the system but not to facts outside of it. The result is innumerable little hangings-together of the world's parts within the larger hangings-together, little worlds, not only of discourse but of operation, within the wider universe. Each system exemplifies one type or grade of union, its parts being strung on that peculiar kind of relation, and the same part may figure in many different systems, as a man may hold various offices and belong to several clubs. From this 'systematic' point of view, therefore, the pragmatic value of the world's unity is that all these definite networks actually and practically exist. Some are more enveloping and extensive, some less so; they are superposed upon each other; and between them all they let no individual elementary part of the universe escape. Enormous as is the amount of disconnexion among things (for these systematic influences and conjunctions follow rigidly exclusive paths), everything that exists is influenced in *some* way by something else, if you can only pick the way out rightly. Loosely speaking, and in general, it may be said that all things cohere and adhere to each other *somehow*, and that the universe exists practically in reticulated or concatenated forms which make of it a continuous or 'integrated' affair. Any kind of influence whatever helps to make the world one, so far as you can follow it from next to next. You may then say that 'the world *is* One,'—meaning in these respects, namely, and just so far as they obtain. But just as definitely is it *not* One, so far as they do not obtain; and there is no species of connexion which will not fail, if, instead of choosing conductors for it you choose non-conductors. You are then arrested at your very first step and have to write the world down as a pure *many* from that particular point of view. If our intellect had been as much interested in disjunctive as it is in conjunctive relations, philosophy would have equally successfully celebrated the world's *disunion*.

The great point is to notice that the oneness and the manyness are absolutely co-ordinate here. Neither is primordial or more essential or excellent than the other. Just as with space, whose separating of things seems exactly on a par with its uniting of them, but sometimes one function and sometimes the other is what comes home to us most, so, in our general dealings with the world of influences, we now need conductors and now need non-conductors, and wisdom lies in knowing which is which at the appropriate moment.

4. All these systems of influence or non-influence may be listed under the general problem of the world's *causal unity*. If the minor causal influences among things should converge towards one common causal origin of them in the past, one great first cause for all that is, one might then speak of the absolute causal unity of the world. God's *fiat* on creation's day has figured in traditional philosophy as such an absolute cause and origin. Transcendental Idealism, translating 'creation' into 'thinking' (or 'willing to think') calls the divine act 'eternal' rather than 'first'; but the union of the many here is absolute, just the same—the many would not *be*, save for the One. Against this notion of the unity of origin of all things there has always stood the pluralistic notion of an eternal self-existing many in the shape of atoms or even of spiritual units of some sort. The alternative has doubtless a pragmatic meaning, but perhaps, as far as these lectures go, we had better leave the question of unity of origin unsettled.

5. The most important sort of union that obtains among things, pragmatically speaking, is their *generic unity*. Things exist in kinds, there are many specimens in each kind, and what the 'kind' implies for one specimen, it implies also for every other specimen of that kind. We can easily conceive that every fact in the world might be singular, that is, unlike any other fact and sole of its kind. In such a world of singulars our logic would be useless, for logic works by predicating of the single instance what is true of all its kind. With no two things alike in the world, we should be unable to reason from our past experiences to our future ones. The existence of so much generic unity in things is thus perhaps the most

momentous pragmatic specification of what it may mean to say 'the world is One.' *Absolute* generic unity would obtain if there were one *summum genus* under which all things without exception could be eventually subsumed. 'Beings,' 'thinkables,' 'experiences,' would be candidates for this position. Whether the alternatives expressed by such words have any pragmatic significance or not, is another question which I prefer to leave unsettled just now.

6. Another specification of what the phrase 'the world is one' may mean is *unity of purpose*. An enormous number of things in the world subserve a common purpose. All the man-made systems, administrative, industrial, military, or what not, exist each for its controlling purpose. Every living being pursues its own peculiar purposes. They co-operate, according to the degree of their development, in collective or tribal purposes, larger ends thus enveloping lesser ones, until an absolutely single, final and climacteric purpose subserved by all things without exception might conceivably be reached. It is needless to say that the appearances conflict with such a view. Any resultant, as I said in my third lecture, *may* have been purposed in advance, but none of the results we actually know in this world have in point of fact been purposed in advance in all their details. Men and nations start with a vague notion of being rich, or great, or good. Each step they make brings unforeseen chances into sight, and shuts out older vistas, and the specifications of the general purpose have to be daily changed. What is reached in the end may be better or worse than what was proposed, but it is always more complex and different.

Our different purposes also are at war with each other. Where one can't crush the other out, they compromise; and the result is again different from what any one distinctly proposed beforehand. Vaguely and generally, much of what was purposed may be gained; but everything makes strongly for the view that our world is incompletely unified teleologically and is still trying to get its unification better organized.

Whoever claims *absolute* teleological unity, saying that there is one purpose that every detail of the universe subserves, dogmatizes at his own risk. Theologians who dogmatize thus find it more and more impossible, as our acquaintance with the warring interests of the world's parts grows more concrete, to imagine what the one climacteric purpose may possibly be like. We see indeed that certain evils minister to ulterior goods, that the bitter makes the cocktail better, and that a bit of danger or hardship puts us agreeably to our trumps. We can vaguely generalize this into the doctrine that all the evil in the universe is but instrumental to its greater perfection. But the scale of the evil actually in sight defies all human tolerance; and transcendental idealism, in the pages of a Bradley or a Royce, brings us no farther than the book of Job did—God's ways are not our ways, so let us put our hands upon our mouth. A God who can relish such superfluities of horror is no God for human beings to appeal to. His animal spirits are too high. In other words the 'Absolute' with his one purpose, is not the man-like God of common people.

7. *Aesthetic union* among things also obtains, and is very analogous to teleological union. Things tell a story. Their parts hang together so as to work out a climax. They play into each other's hands expressively. Retrospectively, we can see that altho no definite purpose presided over a chain of events, yet the events fell into a dramatic form, with a start, a middle, and a finish. In point of fact all stories end; and here again the point of view of a many is the more natural one to take. The world is full of partial stories that run parallel to one another, beginning and ending at odd times. They mutually interlace and interfere at points, but we can not unify them completely in our minds. In following your life-history, I must temporarily turn my attention from my own. Even a biographer of twins would have to press them alternately upon his reader's attention.

It follows that whoever says that the whole world tells one story utters another of those monistic dogmas that a man believes at his risk. It is easy to see the world's history pluralistically, as a rope of which each fibre tells a separate tale; but to conceive of each cross-section of the rope as an absolutely single fact, and to sum the whole longitudinal series into one being living an undivided life, is harder. We have indeed the analogy of embryology to help us. The microscopist makes a hundred flat cross-sections of a given embryo, and mentally unites them into one solid whole. But the great world's ingredients, so far as they are beings, seem, like the rope's fibres, to be discontinuous, cross-wise, and to cohere only in the longitudinal direction. Followed in

that direction they are many. Even the embryologist, when he follows the *development* of his object, has to treat the history of each single organ in turn. *Absolute* aesthetic union is thus another barely abstract ideal. The world appears as something more epic than dramatic.

So far, then, we see how the world is unified by its many systems, kinds, purposes, and dramas. That there is more union in all these ways than openly appears is certainly true. That there *may* be one sovereign purpose, system, kind, and story, is a legitimate hypothesis. All I say here is that it is rash to affirm this dogmatically without better evidence than we possess at present.

8. The *great* monistic *denkmittel* for a hundred years past has been the notion of *the one Knower*. The many exist only as objects for his thought—exist in his dream, as it were; and *as he knows* them, they have one purpose, form one system, tell one tale for him. This notion of an *all enveloping noetic unity* in things is the sublimest achievement of intellectualist philosophy. Those who believe in the Absolute, as the all-knower is termed, usually say that they do so for coercive reasons, which clear thinkers can not evade. The Absolute has far-reaching practical consequences, to some of which I drew attention in my second lecture. Many kinds of difference important to us would surely follow from its being true. I can not here enter into all the logical proofs of such a Being's existence, farther than to say that none of them seem to me sound. I must therefore treat the notion of an All-Knower simply as an hypothesis, exactly on a par logically with the pluralist notion that there is no

point of view, no focus of information extant, from which the entire content of the universe is visible at once. "God's conscience," says Professor Royce,[1] "forms in its wholeness one luminously transparent conscious moment"—this is the type of noetic unity on which rationalism insists. Empiricism on the other hand is satisfied with the type of noetic unity that is humanly familiar. Everything gets known by *some* knower along with something else; but the knowers may in the end be irreducibly many, and the greatest knower of them all may yet not know the whole of everything, or even know what he does know at one single stroke:—he may be liable to forget. Whichever type obtained, the world would still be a universe noetically. Its parts would be cojoined by knowledge, but in the one case the knowledge would be absolutely unified, in the other it would be strung along and overlapped.

The notion of one instantaneous or eternal Knower—either adjective here means the same thing—is, as I said, the great intellectualist achievement of our time. It has practically driven out that conception of 'Substance' which earlier philosophers set such store by, and by which so much unifying work used to be done—universal substance which alone has being in and from itself, and of which all the particulars of experience are but forms to which it gives support. Substance has succumbed to the pragmatic criticisms of the English school. It appears now only as another name for the fact that phenomena as

they come are actually grouped and given in coherent forms, the very forms in which we finite knowers experience or think them together. These forms of conjunction are as much parts of the tissue of experience as are the terms which they connect; and it is a great pragmatic achievement for recent idealism to have made the world hang together in these directly representable ways instead of drawing its unity from the "inherence" of its parts—whatever that may mean—in an unimaginable principle behind the scenes.

'The world is One,' therefore, just so far as we experience it to be concatenated, One by as many definite conjunctions as appear. But then also *not* One by just as many definite *dis*junctions as we find. The oneness and the manyness of it thus obtain in respects which can be separately named. It is neither a universe pure and simple nor a multiverse pure and simple. And its various manners of being One suggest, for their accurate ascertainment, so many distinct programs of scientific work. Thus the pragmatic question 'What is the oneness known as? What practical difference will it make?' saves us from all feverish excitement over it as a principle of sublimity and carries us forward into the stream of experience with a cool head. The stream may indeed reveal far more connexion and union than we now suspect, but we are not entitled on pragmatic principles to claim absolute oneness in any respect in advance.

It is so difficult to see definitely what absolute oneness can mean, that probably the majority of you are satisfied with the sober attitude which we have

[1] *The Conception of God,* New York, 1897, p. 292.

reached. Nevertheless there are possibly some radically monistic souls among you who are not content to leave the one and the many on a par. Union of various grades, union of diverse types, union that stops at non-conductors, union that merely goes from next to next, and means in many cases outer nextness only, and not a more internal bond, union of concatenation, in short; all that sort of thing seems to you a halfway stage of thought. The oneness of things, superior to their manyness, you think must also be more deeply true, must be the more real aspect of the world. The pragmatic view, you are sure, gives us a universe imperfectly rational. The real universe must form an unconditional unit of being, something consolidated, with its parts co-implicated through and through. Only then could we consider our estate completely rational.

There is no doubt whatever that this ultramonistic way of thinking means a great deal to many minds. "One Life, One Truth, one Love, one Principle, One Good, One God"—I quote from a Christian Science leaflet which the day's mail brings into my hands—beyond doubt such a confession of faith has pragmatically an emotional value, and beyond doubt the word 'one' contributes to the value quite as much as the other words. But if we try to realize *intellectually* what we can possibly *mean* by such a glut of oneness we are thrown right back upon our pragmatistic determinations again. It means either the mere name One, the universe of discourse; or it means the sum total of all the ascertainable particular conjunctions and concatenations; or, fin-

ally, it means some one vehicle of conjunction treated as all-inclusive, like one origin, one purpose, or one knower. In point of fact it always means one *knower* to those who take it intellectually to-day. The one knower involves, they think, the other forms of conjunction. His world must have all its parts co-implicated in the one logical-aesthetical-teleological unit-picture which is his eternal dream.

The character of the absolute knower's picture is however so impossible for us to represent clearly, that we may fairly suppose that the authority which absolute monism undoubtedly possesses, and probably always will possess over some persons, draws its strength far less from intellectual than from mystical grounds. To interpret absolute monism worthily, be a mystic. Mystical states of mind in every degree are shown by history, usually tho not always, to make for the monistic view. This is no proper occasion to enter upon the general subject of mysticism, but I will quote one mystical pronouncement to show just what I mean. The paragon of all monistic systems is the Vedânta philosophy of Hindostan, and the paragon of Vedântist missionaries was the late Swami Vivekananda who visited our land some years ago. The method of Vedântism is the mystical method. You do not reason, but after going through a certain discipline *you see*, and having seen, you can report the truth. Vivekananda thus reports the truth in one of his lectures here:

"Where is there any more misery for him who sees this Oneness in the universe, this Oneness of life, Oneness of everything? . . . This separation between man and man, man and woman, man and child, nation from nation, earth from moon, moon from sun, this separation between atom and atom is the cause really of all the misery, and the Vedânta says this separation does not exist, it is not real. It is merely apparent, on the surface. In the heart of things there is unity still. If you go inside you find that unity between man and man, women and children, races and races, high and low, rich and poor, the gods and men: all are One, and animals too, if you go deep enough, and he who has attained to that has no more delusion. . . . Where is there any more delusion for him? What can delude him? He knows the reality of everything, the secret of everything. Where is there any more misery for him? What does he desire? He has traced the reality of everything unto the Lord, that centre, that Unity of everything, and that is Eternal Bliss, Eternal Knowledge, Eternal Existence. Neither death nor disease nor sorrow nor misery nor discontent is There . . . In the Centre, the reality, there is no one to be mourned for, no one to be sorry for. He has penetrated everything, the Pure One, the Formless, the Bodiless, the Stainless, He the Knower, He the great Poet, the Self-Existent, He who is giving to every one what he deserves."

Observe how radical the character of the monism here is. Separation is not simply overcome by the One, it is denied to exist. There is no many. We are not parts of the One; It has no parts; and since in a sense we undeniably *are*, it must be that each of us *is* the One, indivisibly and totally. *An Absolute One, and I that One,*—surely we have

here a religion which, emotionally considered, has a high pragmatic value; it imparts a perfect sumptuosity of security. As our Swami says in another place:

"When man has seen himself as One with the infinite Being of the universe, when all separateness has ceased, when all men, all women, all angels, all gods, all animals, all plants, the whole universe has been melted into that oneness, then all fear disappears. Whom to fear? Can I hurt myself? Can I kill myself? Can I injure myself? Do you fear yourself? Then will all sorrow disappear. What can cause me sorrow? I am the One Existence of the universe. Then all jealousies will disappear; of whom to be jealous? Of myself? Then all bad feelings disappear. Against whom shall I have this bad feeling? Against myself? There is none in the universe but me . . . kill out this differentiation, kill out this superstition that there are many. 'He who, in this world of many, sees that One; he who, in this mass of insentiency, sees that One Sentient Being; he who in this world of shadow, catches that Reality, unto him belongs eternal peace, unto none else, unto none else.'"

We all have some ear for this monistic music: it elevates and reassures. We all have at least the germ of mysticism in us. And when our idealists recite their arguments for the Absolute, saying that the slightest union admitted anywhere carries logically absolute Oneness with it, and that the slightest separation admitted anywhere logically carries disunion remediless and complete, I cannot help suspecting that the palpable weak places in the intellectual reasonings they use are protected from their own criticism by a mystical feeling that, logic or no logic, absolute Oneness must somehow at any cost be true. Oneness overcomes *moral* separateness at any rate. In the passion of love we have the mystic germ of what might mean a total union of all sentient life. This mystical germ wakes up in us on hearing the monistic utterances, acknowledges their authority, and assigns to intellectual considerations a secondary place. . . .

Leave . . . out of consideration for the moment the authority which mystical insights may be conjectured eventually to possess; treat the problem of the One and the Many in a purely intellectual way; and we see clearly enough where pragmatism stands. With her criterion of the practical differences that theories make, we see that she must equally abjure absolute monism and absolute pluralism. The world is One just so far as its parts hang together by any definite connexion. It is many just so far as any definite connexion fails to obtain. And finally it is growing more and more unified by those systems of connexion at least which human energy keeps framing as time goes on.

It is possible to imagine alternative universes to the one we know, in which the most various grades and types of union should be embodied. Thus the lowest grade of universe would be a world of mere *withness*, of which the parts were only strung together by the conjunction 'and.' Such a universe is even now the collection of our several inner lives. The spaces and times of your imagination, the objects and events of your day-dreams are not only more or less incoherent *inter se*, but are wholly out of definite relation with the similar contents of any one else's mind. Our various reveries now as we sit here compenetrate each other idly without influencing or interfering. They coexist, but in no order and in no receptacle, being the nearest approach to an absolute 'many' that we can conceive. We can not even imagine any reason why they *should* be known all together, and we can imagine even less, if they were known together, how they could be known as one systematic whole.

But add our sensations and bodily actions, and the union mounts to a much higher grade. Our *audita et visa* and our acts fall into those receptacles of time and space in which each event finds its date and place. They form 'things' and are of 'kinds' too, and can be classed. Yet we can imagine a world of things and of kinds in which the causal interactions with which we are so familiar should not exist. Everything there might be inert towards everything else, and refuse to propagate its influence. Or gross mechanical influences might pass, but no chemical action. Such worlds would be far less unified than ours. Again there might be complete physio-chemical interaction, but no minds; or minds, but altogether private ones, with no social life; or social life limited to acquaintance, but no love; or love, but no customs or institutions that should systematize it. No one of these grades of universe would be absolutely irrational or disintegrated, inferior tho it might appear when looked at from the higher grades. For instance, if our minds should ever become 'telepathically' connected, so that we knew immediately, or could under certain conditions know immediately, each what the other was thinking, the world we now live in would appear to the thinkers in that world to have been of an inferior grade.

With the whole of past eternity open for our conjectures to range in, it may be lawful to wonder whether the various kinds of union now realized in the universe that we inhabit may not possibly have been successively evolved after the fashion in which we now see human systems evolving in consequence of human needs. If such an hypothesis were legitimate, total oneness would appear at the end of things rather than at their origin. In other words the notion of the 'Absolute' would have to be replaced by that of the 'Ultimate.' The two notions would have the same content—the maximally unified content of fact, namely—but their time-relations would be positively reversed.[2]

After discussing the unity of the universe in this pragmatic way, you ought to see why I said in my second lecture, borrowing the word from my friend G. Papini, that pragmatism tends to *unstiffen* all our theories. The world's oneness has generally been affirmed abstractly only, and as if any one who questioned it must be an idiot. The temper of monists has been so vehement, as almost at times to be convulsive; and this way of holding a doctrine does not easily go with reasonable discussion and the drawing of distinctions. The theory of the Absolute, in particular, has had to be an article of faith, affirmed dogmatically and exclusively.

The One and All, first in the order of being and of knowing, logically necessary itself, and uniting all lesser things in the bonds of mutual necessity, how could it allow of any mitigation of its inner rigidity? The slightest suspicion of pluralism, the minutest wiggle of independence of any one of its parts from the control of the totality would ruin it. Absolute unity brooks no degrees,— as well might you claim absolute purity for a glass of water because it contains but a single little cholera-germ. The independence, however infinitesimal, of a part, however small, would be to the Absolute as fatal as a cholera-germ.

Pluralism on the other hand has no need of this dogmatic rigoristic temper. Provided you grant *some* separation among things, some tremor of independence, some free play of parts on one another, some real novelty or chance, however minute, she is amply satisfied, and will allow you any amount, however great, of real union. How much of union there may be is a question that she thinks can only be decided empirically. The amount may be enormous, colossal; but absolute monism is shattered if, along with all the union, there has to be granted the slightest modicum, the most incipient nascency, or the most residual trace, of a separation that is not 'overcome.'

Pragmatism, pending the final empirical ascertainment of just what the balance of union and disunion among things may be, must obviously range herself upon the pluralistic side. Some day, she admits, even total union, with one knower, one origin, and a universe consolidated in every conceivable way, may turn out to be the most acceptable

---

[2] Compare on the Ultimate, Mr. Schiller's essay "Activity and Substance," in his book entitled *Humanism*, p. 204.

of all hypotheses. Meanwhile the opposite hypothesis, of a world imperfectly unified still, and perhaps always to remain so, must be sincerely entertained. This latter hypothesis is pluralism's doctrine. Since absolute monism forbids its being even considered seriously, branding it as irrational from the start, it is clear that pragmatism must turn its back on absolute monism, and follow pluralism's more empirical path. This leaves us with the common-sense world, in which we find things partly joined and partly disjoined. . . .

COMMENT

Spinoza's Monism

"Monism" is the name commonly given to theories that stress the oneness of reality. "Dualism" is the doctrine that there are at least two distinct kinds of things—mind and matter. "Pluralism" is the doctrine that there is not one (Monism), not two (Dualism), but a larger number of ultimate kinds or things.

How many things are there in the world? Quantitative monism is the doctrine that there is only one thing. Spinoza is a quantitative monist. How many *kinds* are there in the world? Qualitative monism answers "Only one kind." Spinoza distinguishes between mind and matter as qualitatively different aspects ("attributes") of the one cosmic being. Hence he is not a qualitative monist in the sense of maintaining that all reality is mental (Idealism) or that all reality is material (Materialism). But in another sense he is a monist. He believes that mind and matter pervade the entire universe and are attributes of the same ultimate substance. In the human being, as well as in the universe at large, mind is not reducible to matter nor matter to mind, but both are aspects of a single reality. This view is sometimes called "the double-aspect theory." Finally Spinoza believes that the one cosmic being is infinite in an infinite number of others ways, each of which is as ultimate and unique as mind and matter. In addition to the one substance and its infinite attributes, there are so-called individual things—a rock, a horse, a man, a planet—which Spinoza calls "modes." To call them modes is to emphasize their adjectival nature—they are merely modifications of the single substance.

Spinoza seizes upon the Cartesian notion (derived from Aristotle) that substance is an enduring thing independent of other things, but he rejects utterly the notion of a finite substance or a plurality of substances. "By substance," he says, "I understand that which is in itself and is conceived through itself; in other words, that the conception of which does not need the conception of another thing from which it must be formed."[1] Substance is thus, by definition absolutely independent and self-sustaining. Spinoza then proceeds to prove that there can be only one

[1] *Ethics,* First Part, Def. III.

substance, and that this substance is infinite and all-inclusive. Finally he "proves" that this single substance, which he calls God or Nature, must exist. The argument, which we shall not trace, is modeled after geometry, being based upon definitions and axioms from which various propositions are deduced.

In the Appendix reproduced above, Spinoza sums up his argument briefly and combats misconceptions of Nature or God. These all arise from the idea that the God-Universe works toward some goal or "final cause." Human beings interpret themselves as goal-seeking and God as like themselves. They think that God has created every natural object and guided every event for an end or purpose. According to Spinoza, this whole approach is false, because God, who is absolutely infinite and self-complete, is made to appear in need of, and dependent upon, an end not yet attained. Those who accept this anthropomorphic belief make the will of God a "refuge of ignorance" by referring every event of which they do not know the cause to God.

Pitted against these "superstitions" is Spinoza's own interpretation of the nature of things. God's causality, far from being teleological, must be conceived on the analogy of logical ground and consequent. ". . . From the supreme power of God, or from God's infinite nature, infinite things in infinite ways, that is to say, all things, have necessarily flowed, or continually follow by the same necessity, in the same way as it follows from the nature of a triangle, from eternity to eternity, that its three angles are equal to two right angles."[2] This kind of causality precludes all chance anywhere and anytime. "Necessary" alone expresses what is, and "impossible" what is not. Hence there is no divine purpose and no indeterminism. People, in distinction from God, think they act freely and purposively, but ultimately their action is determined by forces over which they have no exclusive control, since the only completely adequate ground, and the only real and ultimate agent, is God, from whom everything follows by logical necessity.

According to Spinoza, happiness depends upon the quality of the object of one's love, and love toward the greatest of objects, God or Nature, feeds the mind with a profound joy. This joy, accompanied with a clear understanding of its cause, is called by Spinoza "intellectual love." They who have comprehensive knowledge of themselves and the natural world love God: their intellectual love, in effect, is that very love of God whereby God loves God's self. The finite human being is then virtually at one with the eternal nature of things. Our life is a communion with that sublime and marvellous order of nature in which God is manifest. Whoever loves God in this "intellectual" way is free; he is caught up into the impersonal infinitude of being, and knows the deepest happiness of which a human being is capable. Because his account of the nature of things culminates in this ecstatic vision, Spinoza regarded metaphysics as a prelude to ethics and gave to his great metaphysical treatise the name of "Ethics."

Even highly trained philosophers find the *Ethics* a very difficult book to under-

[2] *Ethics,* Prop. XVII, Scholium.

stand. But in the Appendix and the Correspondence that we have quoted the doctrine is easier to grasp.

No one today would altogether accept Spinoza's rationalism and extreme monism. To set up cosmic monism and determinism as necessary truths, and to demonstrate them in the style of Euclid's geometry, with definitions, axioms, and theorems, is no longer plausible. Nevertheless, his vision of an integrated, deterministic, and nonpurposive universe retains a kind of impersonal grandeur, and his conception of freedom as the understanding of necessity has a deep and enduring appeal.

James' Concatenism

When we turn from the austere monism of Spinoza to the genial pragmatism of James, we seem to have entered another world. Spinoza would have been profoundly shocked by James' question, "What is the practical value of oneness for *us*?" and the suggestion that this value may serve as a criterion for the truth or falsity of monism. James comes close to characterizing the God-Universe of Spinoza when he refers to "the One and All, first in the order of being and of knowing, logically necessary itself, and uniting all lesser things in the bonds of mutual necessity." His dislike for this concept of absolute unity and his feeling that it does not truly serve the needs of humanity are implicit in his statement: "The slightest suspicion of pluralism, the minutest wiggle of any one of its parts from the control of the totality would ruin it."

It is characteristic of his concrete, empirical approach to metaphysical problems that he is not content with the idea of unity in its abstract generality. He distinguishes between various forms of oneness: one in discourse, one cause, one kind, one purpose, one story, one knower, one in mystical trance. Each of these he examines in terms of its meaningfulness for human thought and action. Although he concedes that oneness in each of these modes is alluring, he finds that manyness is a stubborn fact of experience and an ineradicable human need.

Note that James is presenting an alternative to both extreme monism and extreme pluralism. He is indicating that things may be related in some ways without being related in others; that these relations may be of various degrees of intensity; that the world is a mixture of conductors and nonconductors; and that in a long concatenation, the connections become nonexistent when interrupted by nonconductors, or increasingly tenuous as the links are farther and farther apart. His metaphor of a chain conveys the notion that things may be connected next to next without being connected in any significant way across great distances of time and space or across great disparities in kind. Your present thought may have no real connection, or the very slightest, with a particular grain of sand in the Sahara desert. The coughing of someone near you in a theater is annoying, but the coughing of someone in an ancient Greek theater, very far removed in time and space, has no discernible effect upon you. Every movement of your eyelash may influence every star in the universe, but the influence is so slight as to be negligible. Such homely considerations as these lead James to adopt an intermediate theory, which may be called "concatenism" in distinction from either monism or pluralism pure and simple.

So vivid is James' literary style, and so keen and clear is his analysis, that no further comment is needed to aid understanding or awaken interest. He makes such old problems as the One and the Many come alive. The oversimplification that may exist in his pragmatism is outweighed by his ability to rescue philosophical questions from the fog of abstraction and to make them relevant to our practical and personal concerns.

Conclusion

This chapter has been devoted to very difficult subject-matter, and the reader should not be surprised if it is found hard to understand. In the effort to do so, you may wish to consider the following questions: How does Spinoza's "geometrical method" differ from James' "pragmatic method"? How does Spinoza answer the question of the nature and relation of mind and matter? How does this answer respond to the "mind-body problem"? In what sense is the philosophy of Spinoza (1) monistic, (2) dualistic, and (3) pluralistic? What is his doctrine of freedom and determinism? How are his determinism and monism related to his ethics? Turning to James we may ask: How does he distinguish the various forms of oneness? Why is he dissatisfied with each of these forms? How does his theory of relations differ from Spinoza's? To what extent does his "concatenism" mediate between extreme monism and extreme pluralism? If students answer these questions they will be in a better position to consider the great over-arching question—the problem of the One and the Many. This problem will bob up in various forms in the chapters that follow.

4

Materialism

TITUS LUCRETIUS CARUS (95?–52? B.C.)

We know nothing certain about the life of Lucretius. St. Jerome, a hostile critic, declared that he had fits of madness, composed his poem during intervals of sanity, and killed himself in his forty-fourth year. This report, as George Santayana has remarked, must be taken with a large grain of salt. From his book we discover that he revered Epicurus, detested religious superstition, and delighted in the bounty of nature.

On the Nature
of the Universe

1. [*Prayer to the creative force of Nature (personified as Venus)*

Translated by Robert Latham. Penguin Books, 1951. Reprinted by permission of Penguin Books, Ltd., Harmondsworth, Middlesex.

to inspire the poet, to bless his patron Memmius, and to bring peace to the world.]

Mother of Aeneas and his race, delight of men and gods, life-giving

119

Venus, it is your doing that under the wheeling constellations of the sky all nature teems with life, both the sea that buoys up our ships and the earth that yields our food. Through you all living creatures are conceived and come forth to look upon the sunlight. Before you the winds flee, and at your coming the clouds forsake the sky. For you the inventive earth flings up sweet flowers. For you the ocean levels laugh, the sky is calmed and glows with diffused radiance. When first the day puts on the aspect of spring, when in all its force the fertilizing breath of Zephyr is unleashed, then, great goddess, the birds of air give the first intimation of your entry; for yours is the power that has pierced them to the heart. Next the cattle run wild, frisk through the lush pastures and swim the swift-flowing streams. Spell-bound by your charm, they follow your lead with fierce desire. So throughout seas and uplands, rushing torrents, verdurous meadows and the leafy shelters of the birds, into the breasts of one and all you instil alluring love, so that with passionate longing they reproduce their several breeds.

Since you alone are the guiding power of the universe and without you nothing emerges into the shining sunlit world to grow in joy and loveliness, yours is the partnership I seek in striving to compose these lines *On the Nature of the Universe* for my noble Memmius. For him, great goddess, you have willed outstanding excellence in every field and everlasting fame. For his sake, therefore, endow my verse with everlasting charm.

Meanwhile, grant that this brutal business of war by sea and land may everywhere be lulled to rest. For you alone have power to bestow on mortals the blessing of quiet peace. In your bosom Mars himself, supreme commander in this brutal business, flings himself down at times, laid low by the irremediable wound of love. Gazing upward, his neck a prostrate column, he fixes hungry eyes on you, great goddess, and gluts them with love. As he lies outstretched, his breath hangs upon your lips. Stoop, then, goddess most glorious, and enfold him at rest in your hallowed bosom and whisper with those lips sweet words of prayer, beseeching for the people of Rome untroubled peace. In this evil hour of my country's history, I cannot pursue my task with a mind at ease, as an illustrious scion of the house of Memmius cannot at such a crisis withhold his service from the common weal.

2. [*Exhortation to Memmius to listen to an exhortation of "true reason."*]

For what is to follow, my Memmius, lay aside your cares and lend undistracted ears and an attentive mind to true reason. Do not scornfully reject, before you have understood them, the gifts I have marshalled for you with zealous devotion. I will set out to discourse to you on the ultimate realities of heaven and the gods. I will reveal those *atoms* from which nature creates all things and increases and feeds them and into which, when they perish, nature again resolves them. To these in my discourse I commonly give such names as the 'raw material', or 'generative bodies' or 'seeds' of things. Or I may call them 'primary particles', because they come first and everything else is composed of them.

3. [*Praise of Epicurus for delivering mankind from superstition.*]

When human life lay groveling in all men's sight, crushed to the earth under the dead weight of superstition whose grim features loured menacingly upon mortals from the four quarters of the sky, a man of Greece was first to raise mortal eyes in defiance, first to stand erect and brave the challenge. Fables of the gods did not crush him, nor the lightning flash and the growling menace of the sky. Rather, they quickened his manhood, so that he, first of all men, longed to smash the constraining locks of nature's doors. The vital vigour of his mind prevailed. He ventured far out beyond the flaming ramparts of the world and voyaged in mind throughout infinity. Returning victorious, he proclaimed to us what can be and what cannot: how a limit is fixed to the power of everything and an immovable frontier post. Therefore superstition in its turn lies crushed beneath his feet, and we by his triumph are lifted level with the skies.

4. [*Superstition, its cause and cure.*]

One thing that worries me is the fear that you may fancy yourself embarking on an impious course, setting your feet on the path of sin. Far from it. More often it is this very superstition that is the mother of sinful and impious deeds.

Remember how at Aulis the altar of the Virgin Goddess was foully stained with the blood of Iphigeneia by the leaders of the Greeks, the patterns of chivalry. The headband was bound about her virgin tresses and hung down evenly over both her cheeks. Suddenly she caught sight of her father standing sadly in front of the altar, the attendants beside him hiding the knife and her people bursting into tears when they saw her. Struck dumb with terror, she sank on her knees to the ground. Poor girl, at such a moment it did not help her that she had been first to give the name of father to a king. Raised by the hands of men, she was led trembling to the altar. Not for her the sacrament of marriage and the loud chant of Hymen. It was her fate in the very hour of marriage to fall a sinless victim to a sinful rite, slaughtered to her greater grief by a father's hand, so that a fleet might sail under happy auspices. Such are the heights of wickedness to which men are driven by superstition.

You yourself, if you surrender your judgement at any time to the blood-curdling declamations of the prophets, will want to desert our ranks. Only think what phantoms they can conjure up to overturn the tenor of your life and wreck your happiness with fear. And not without cause. For, if men saw that a term was set to their troubles, they would find strength in some way to withstand the hocus-pocus and intimidations of the prophets. As it is, they have no power of resistance, because they are haunted by the fear of eternal punishment after death. They know nothing of the nature of the spirit. Is it born, or is it implanted in us at birth? Does it perish with us, dissolved by death, or does it visit the murky depths and dreary sloughs of Hades? Or is it transplanted by divine power into other creatures, as described in the poems of our own Ennius, who first gathered on the delectable slopes of Helicon an evergreen garland destined to win renown among the nations of Italy? Ennius indeed in his immortal verses proclaims that there is also a Hell, which is peopled not by our actual spirits or bodies but only by shadowy images, ghastly pale. It is from this realm that he pictures the ghost of Homer, of unfading memory, as appearing to him, shedding salt tears and revealing the nature of the universe.

I must therefore give an account of celestial phenomena, explaining the movements of sun and moon and also the forces that determine events on earth. Next, and no less important, we must look with keen insight into the make-up of spirit and mind: we must consider those alarming phantasms that strike upon our minds when they are awake but disordered by sickness, or when they are buried in slumber, so that we seem to see and hear before us men whose dead bones lie in the embraces of earth.

I am well aware that it is not easy to elucidate in Latin verse the obscure discoveries of the Greeks. The poverty of our language and the novelty of the theme compel me often to coin new words for the purpose. But your merit and the joy I hope to derive from our delightful friendship encourage me to face any task however hard. This it is that leads me to stay awake through the quiet of the night, studying how by choice of words and the poet's art I can display before your mind a clear light by which you can gaze into the heart of hidden things.

5. [*Nothing is ever created out of nothing.*]

This dread and darkness of the mind cannot be dispelled by the sunbeams, the shining shafts of day, but only by an understanding of the outward form and inner workings of nature. In tackling this theme, our starting-point will be this principle: *Nothing can ever be created by divine power out of nothing.* The reason why all mortals are so gripped by fear is that they see all sorts of things happening on the earth and in the sky with no discernible cause, and these they attribute to the will of a god. Accordingly, when we have seen that nothing can be created out of nothing, we shall then have a clearer picture of the path ahead, the problem of how things are created and occasioned without the aid of the gods.

First then, if things were made out of nothing, any species could spring from any source and nothing would require seed. Men could arise from the sea and scaly fish from the earth, and birds could be hatched out of the sky. Cattle and other domestic animals and every kind of wild beast, multiplying indiscriminately, would occupy cultivated and waste lands alike. The same fruits would not grow constantly on the same trees, but they would keep changing: any tree might bear any fruit. If each species were not composed of its own generative bodies, why should each be born always of the same kind of mother? Actually, since each is formed out of specific seeds, it is born and emerges into the sunlit world only from a place where there exists the right material, the right kind of atoms. This is why everything cannot be born of everything, but a specific power of generation inheres in specific objects.

Again, why do we see roses appear in spring, grain in summer's heat, grapes under the spell of autumn? Surely, because it is only after specific seeds have drifted together at their own proper time that every created thing stands revealed, when the season is favourable and the life-giving earth can safely deliver delicate growths into the sunlit world. If they were made out of nothing, they would spring up suddenly after varying lapses of time and at abnormal seasons, since there would of course be no primary bodies which could be prevented by the harshness of the season from entering into generative unions. Similarly, in order that things might grow, there would be no need of any lapse of time for the accumulation of seed. Tiny tots would turn suddenly into grown men, and trees would shoot up spontaneously out of the earth. But it is obvious that none of these things happens, since everything grows gradually, as is natural, from a specific seed and retains its specific character. It is a fair inference that each is increased and nourished by its own raw material.

Here is a further point. Without seasonable showers the earth cannot send up gladdening growths. Lacking food, animals cannot reproduce their kind or sustain life. This points to the conclusion that many elements are common to many things, as letters are to words, rather than to the theory that anything can come into existence without atoms.

Or again, why has not nature been able to produce men on such a scale that they could ford the ocean on foot or demolish high mountains with their hands or prolong their lives over many generations? Surely, because each thing requires for its birth a particular material which determines what can be produced. It must therefore be admitted that nothing can be made out of nothing, because everything must be generated from a seed before it can emerge into the unresisting air.

Lastly, we see that tilled plots are superior to untilled, and their fruits are improved by cultivation. This is because the earth contains certain atoms which we rouse to productivity by turning the fruitful clods with the ploughshare and stirring up the soil. But for these, you would see great improvements arising spontaneously without any aid from our labours.

6. [*Nothing is ever annihilated.*]

The second great principle is this: *nature resolves everything into its component atoms and never reduces anything to nothing.* If anything were perishable in all its parts, anything might perish all of a sudden and vanish from sight. There would be no need of any force to separate its parts and loosen their links. In actual fact, since everything is composed of indestructible seeds, nature obviously does not allow anything to perish till it has encountered a force that shatters it with a blow or creeps into chinks and unknits it.

If the things that are banished from the scene by age are annihilated through the exhaustion of their material, from what source does Venus bring back the several races of animals into the light of life? And, when they are brought back, where does the inventive earth find for each the special food required for its sustenance and growth? From what fount is the sea replenished by its native springs and the streams that flow into it from afar? Whence does the ether draw nutriment for the stars? For everything consisting of a mortal body must have been exhausted by the long day of time, the illimitable past. If throughout this bygone eternity there have persisted bodies from which the universe has been perpetually renewed, they must certainly be possessed of immortality. Therefore things cannot be reduced to nothing.

Again, all objects would regularly be destroyed by the same force and the same cause, were it not that they are sustained by imperishable matter more or less tightly fastened together. Why, a mere touch would be enough to bring about destruction supposing there were no imperishable bodies whose union could be dissolved only by the appropriate force. Actually, because the fastenings of the atoms are of various kinds while their matter is imperishable, compound objects remain intact until one of them encounters a force that proves strong enough to break up its particular constitution. Therefore nothing returns to nothing, but everything is resolved into its constituent bodies.

Lastly, showers perish when father ether has flung them down into the lap of mother earth. But the crops spring up fresh and gay; the branches on the trees burst into leaf; the trees themselves grow and are weighed down with fruit. Hence in turn man and brute draw nourishment. Hence we see flourishing cities blest with children and every leafy thicket loud with new broods of songsters. Hence in lush pastures cattle wearied by their bulk fling down their bodies, and the white milky juice oozes from their swollen udders. Hence a new generation frolic friskily on wobbly legs through the fresh grass, their young minds tipsy with undiluted milk. Visible objects therefore do not perish utterly, since nature repairs one thing from another and allows nothing to be born without the aid of another's death.

7. [*Matter exists in the form of invisible particles (atoms).*]

Well, Memmius, I have taught you that things cannot be created out of nothing nor, once born be summoned back to nothing. Perhaps, however, you are becoming mistrustful of my words, because these atoms of mine are not visible to the eye. Consider, therefore, this further evidence of *bodies whose existence you must acknowledge though they cannot be seen*. First, wind, when its force is roused, whips up waves, founders tall ships and scatters cloud-rack. Sometimes scouring plains with hurricane force it strews them with huge trees and batters mountain peaks with blasts that hew down forests. Such is wind in its fury, when it whoops aloud with a mad menace in its shouting. Without question, therefore, there must be invisible particles of wind which sweep sea and land and the clouds in the sky, swooping upon them and whirling them along in a headlong hurricane. In the way they flow and the havoc they spread they are no different from a torrential flood of water when it rushes down in a sudden spate from the mountain heights, swollen by heavy rains, and heaps together wreckage from the forest and entire trees. Soft though it is by nature, the sudden shock of oncoming water is more than even stout bridges can withstand, so furious is the force with which the turbid, storm-flushed torrent surges against their piers. With a mighty roar it lays them low, rolling huge rocks under its waves and brushing aside every obstacle from its course. Such, therefore, must be the movement of blasts of wind also. When they have come surging along some course like a rushing river, they push obstacles before them and buffet them with repeated blows; and sometimes, eddying round and round, they snatch them up and carry them along in a swiftly circling vortex. Here then is proof upon proof that winds have invisible bodies, since in their actions and behaviour they are found to rival great rivers, whose bodies are plain to see.

Then again, we smell the various scents of things though we never see them approaching our nostrils. Similarly, heat and cold cannot be detected by our eyes, and we do not see sounds. Yet all these must be composed of bodies, since they are able to impinge upon our senses. For nothing can touch or be touched except body.

Again, clothes hung out on a surf-beaten shore grow moist. Spread in the sun they grow dry. But we do not see how the moisture has soaked into them, nor again how it has been dispelled by the heat. It follows that the moisture is split up into minute parts which the eye cannot possibly see.

Again, in the course of many annual revolutions of the sun a ring is worn thin next to the finger with continual rubbing. Dripping water hollows a stone. A curved ploughshare, iron though it is, dwindles imperceptibly in the furrow. We see the cobble-stones of the highway worn by the feet of many wayfarers. The bronze statues by the city gates show their right hands worn thin by the touch of travellers who have greeted them in passing. We see that all these are being diminished, since they are worn away. But to perceive what particles drop off at any particular time is a power grudged to us by our ungenerous sense of sight.

To sum up, whatever is added to things gradually by nature and the passage of days, causing a cumulative increase, eludes the most attentive scrutiny of our eyes. Conversely, you cannot see what objects lose by the wastage of age—sheer sea-cliffs, for instance, exposed to prolonged erosion by the mordant brine—or at what time the loss occurs. It follows that nature works through the agency of invisible bodies.

8. [*Besides matter, the universe contains empty space (vacuity).*]

On the other hand, things are not hemmed in by the pressure of solid bodies in a tight mass. This is because *there is vacuity in things*. A grasp of this fact will be helpful to you in many respects and will save you from much bewildered doubting and questioning about the universe and from mistrust of my teaching. Well then, by vacuity I mean intangible and empty space. If it did not exist, things could not move at all. For the distinctive action of matter, which is counteraction and obstruction, would be in force always and everywhere. Nothing could proceed, because nothing would give it a starting-point by receding. As it is, we see with our own eyes at sea and on land and high up in the sky that all sorts of things in all sorts of ways are on the move. If there were no empty space, these things would be denied the power of restless movement—or rather, they could not possibly have come into existence, embedded as they would have been in motionless matter.

Besides, there are clear indications that things that pass for solid are in fact porous. Even in rocks a trickle of water seeps through into caves, and copious drops ooze from every surface. Food percolates to every part of an animal's body. Trees grow and bring forth their fruit in season, because their food is distributed throughout their length from the tips of the roots through the trunk and along every branch. Noises pass through walls and fly into closed buildings. Freezing cold penetrates to the bones. If there were no vacancies through which the various bodies could make their way, none of these phenomena would be possible.

Again, why do we find some things outweigh others of equal volume? If there is as much matter in a ball of wool as in one of lead, it is natural that it should weigh as heavily, since it is the function of matter to press everything downwards, while it is the function of space on the other hand to remain weightless. Accordingly, when one thing is not less bulky than another but obviously lighter, it plainly declares that there is more vacuum in it, while the heavier object proclaims that there is more matter in it and much less empty space. We have therefore reached the goal of our diligent inquiry: there is in things an admixture of what we call vacuity.

In case you should be misled on this question by the idle imagining of certain theorists, I must anticipate their argument. They maintain that water yields and opens a penetrable path to scaly bodies of fish that push against it, because they leave spaces behind them into which the yielding water can flow together. In the same way, they suppose, other things can move by mutually changing places, although every place remains filled. This theory has been adopted utterly without warrant. For how can the fish advance till the water has given way? And how can the water retire when the fish cannot move? There are thus only two alternatives: either all bodies are devoid of movement, or you must admit that things contain an admixture of vacuity whereby each is enabled to make the first move.

Lastly, if two bodies suddenly spring apart from contact on a broad surface, all the intervening space must be void until it is occupied by air. However quickly the air rushes in all round, the entire space cannot be filled instantaneously. The air must occupy one spot after another until it has taken possession of the whole space. If anyone supposes that this consequence of such springing apart is made possible by the condensation of air, he is mistaken. For condensation implies that something that was full becomes empty, or *vice versâ*. And I contend that air could not condense so as to produce this effect; or at any rate, if there were no vacuum, it could not thus shrink into itself and draw its parts together.

However many pleas you may advance to prolong the argument, you must end by admitting that there is vacuity in things. There are many other proofs I could add to the pile in order to strengthen conviction; but for an acute intelligence these small clues should suffice to enable you to discover the rest for yourself. As hounds that range the hills often smell out the lairs of wild beasts screened in thickets, when once they have got on to the right trail, so in such questions one thing will lead on to another, till you can succeed by yourself in tracking down the truth to its lurking-places and dragging it forth. If you grow weary and relax from the chase, there is one thing, Memmius, that I can safely promise you: my honeyed tongue will pour from the treasury of my breast such generous draughts, drawn from inexhaustible springs, that I am afraid slow-plodding age may creep through my limbs and unbolt the bars of my life before the full flood of my arguments on any single point has flowed in verse through your ears.

9. [*The universe consists of matter (with its properties and accidents) and of vacuity and nothing else.*]

To pick up the thread of my discourse, all nature as it is in itself consists of two things—bodies and the vacant space in which the bodies are situated and through which they move in different directions. The existence of bodies is vouched for by the agreement of the senses. If a belief resting directly on this foundation is not valid, there will be no standard to which we can refer any doubt on obscure questions for rational confirmation. If there were no place and space, which we call vacuity, these bodies could not be situated anywhere or move in any direction whatever. This I have just demonstrated. It remains to show that *nothing exists that is distinct both from body and from vacuity* and could be ranked with the others as a third substance. For whatever *is* must also be something. If it offers resistance to touch, however light and slight, it will increase the mass of body by such amount, great or small, as it may amount to, and will rank with it. If, on the other hand, it is intangible, so that it offers no resistance whatever to anything passing through it, then it will be that empty space which we call vacuity. Besides, whatever it may be in itself, either it will act in some way, or react to other things acting upon it, or else it will be such that things can be and happen in it. But without body nothing can act or react; and nothing can afford a place except emptiness and vacancy. Therefore, besides matter and vacuity, we cannot include in the number of things any third substance that can either affect our senses at any time or be grasped by the reasoning of our minds.

You will find that anything that can be named is either a property or an accident of these two. A *property* is something that cannot be detached or separated from a thing without destroying it, as weight is a property of rocks, heat of fire, fluidity of water, tangibility of all bodies, intangibility of vacuum. On the other hand, servitude and liberty, poverty and riches, war and peace, and all other things whose advent or departure leaves the essence of a thing intact, all these it is our practice to call by their appropriate name, *accidents*.

Similarly, time by itself does not exist; but from things themselves there results a sense of what has already taken place, what is now going on and what is to ensue. It must not be claimed that anyone can sense time by itself apart from the movement of things or their restful immobility.

Again, when men say it *is* a fact that Helen was ravished or the Trojans were conquered, do not let anyone drive you to the admission that any such event *is* independently of any object, on the ground that the generations of men of whom these events were accidents have been swept away by the irrevocable lapse of time. For we could put it that whatever has taken place is an accident of a particular tract of earth or of the space it occupied. If there had been no matter and no space or place in which things could happen, no spark of love kindled by the beauty of Tyndareus' daughter would ever have stolen into the breast of Phrygian Paris to light that dazzling blaze of pitiless war; no Wooden Horse, unmarked by the sons of Troy, would have set the towers of Ilium aflame through the midnight issue of Greeks from its womb. So you may see that events cannot be said to *be* by themselves like matter or in the same sense as space. Rather, you should describe them as accidents of matter, or of the place in which things happen.

10. [*The atoms are indestructible.*]

Material objects are of two kinds, atoms and compounds of atoms. The atoms themselves cannot be swamped by any force, for they are preserved indefinitely by their absolute solidity. Admittedly, it is hard to believe that anything can exist that is absolutely solid. The lightning stroke from the sky penetrates closed buildings, as do shouts and other noises. Iron glows molten in the fire, and hot rocks are cracked by untempered scorching. Hard gold is softened and melted by heat; and bronze, ice-like, is liquefied by flame. Both heat and piercing cold seep through silver, since we feel both alike when a cooling shower of water is poured into a goblet that we hold ceremonially in our hands. All these facts point to the conclusion that nothing is really solid. But sound reasoning and nature itself drive us to the opposite conclusion. Pay attention, therefore, while I demonstrate in a few lines that there exist certain bodies that are absolutely solid and indestructible, namely those atoms which according to our teaching are the seeds or prime units of things from which the whole universe is built up.

In the first place, we have found that nature is twofold, consisting of two totally different things, matter and the space in which things happen. Hence each of these must exist by itself without admixture of the other. For, where there is empty space (what we call vacuity), there matter is not; where matter exists, there cannot be a vacuum. Therefore the prime units of matter are solid and free from vacuity.

Again, since composite things contain some vacuum, the surrounding matter must be solid. For you cannot reasonably maintain that anything can hide vacuity and hold it within its body unless you allow that the container itself is solid. And what contains the vacuum in things can only be an accumulation of matter. Hence matter, which possesses absolute solidity, can be everlasting when other things are decomposed.

Again, if there were no empty space, everything would be one solid mass; if there were no material objects with the property of filling the space they occupy, all existing space would be utterly void. It is clear, then, that there is an alternation of matter and vacuity, mutually distinct, since the whole is neither completely full nor completely empty. There are therefore solid bodies, causing the distinction between empty space and full. And these, as I have just shown, can be neither decomposed by blows from without nor invaded and unknit from within nor destroyed by any other form of assault. For it seems that a thing without vacuum can be neither knocked to bits nor snapped nor chopped in two by cutting; nor can

it let in moisture or seeping cold or piercing fire, the universal agents of destruction. The more vacuum a thing contains within it, the more readily it yields to these assailants. Hence, if the units of matter are solid and without vacuity, as I have shown, they must be everlasting.

Yet again, if the matter in things had not been everlasting, everything by now would have gone back to nothing, and the things we see would be the product of rebirth out of nothing. But, since I have already shown that nothing can be created out of nothing nor any existing thing be summoned back to nothing, the atoms must be made of imperishable stuff into which everything can be resolved in the end, so that there may be a stock of matter for building the world anew. The atoms, therefore, are absolutely solid and unalloyed. In no other way could they have survived throughout infinite time to keep the world in being.

Furthermore, if nature had set no limit to the breaking of things, the particles of matter in the course of ages would have been ground so small that nothing could be generated from them so as to attain in the fullness of time to the summit of its growth. For we see that anything can be more speedily disintegrated than put together again. Hence, what the long day of time, the bygone eternity, has already shaken and loosened to fragments could never in the residue of time be reconstructed. As it is, there is evidently a limit set to breaking, since we see that everything is renewed and each according to its kind has a fixed period in which to grow to its prime.

Here is a further argument. Granted that the particles of matter are absolutely solid, we can still explain the composition and behaviour of soft things—air, water, earth, fire—by their intermixture with empty space. On the other hand, supposing the atoms to be soft, we cannot account for the origin of hard flint and iron. For there would be no foundation for nature to build on. Therefore there must be bodies strong in their unalloyed solidity by whose closer clustering things can be knit together and display unyielding toughness.

If we suppose that there is no limit set to the breaking of matter, we must still admit that material objects consist of particles which throughout eternity have resisted the forces of destruction. To say that these are breakable does not square with the fact that they have survived throughout eternity under a perpetual bombardment of innumerable blows.

Again, there is laid down for each thing a specific limit to its growth and its tenure of life, and the laws of nature ordain what each can do and what it cannot. No species is ever changed, but each remains so much itself that every kind of bird displays on its body its own specific markings. This is a further proof that their bodies are composed of changeless matter. For, if the atoms could yield in any way to change, there would be no certainty as to what could arise and what could not, at what point the power of everything was limited by an immovable frontier-post; nor could successive generations so regularly repeat the nature, behaviour, habits and movements of their parents.

To proceed with our argument, there is an ultimate point in visible objects which represents the smallest thing that can be seen. So also there must be an ultimate point in objects that lie below the limit of perception by our senses. This point is without parts and is the smallest thing that can exist. It never has been and never will be able to exist by itself, but only as one primary part of something else. It is with a mass of such parts, solidly jammed together in order, that matter is filled up. Since they cannot exist by themselves, they must needs stick together in a mass from which they cannot by any means be pried loose. The atoms therefore are absolutely solid and unalloyed, consisting of a mass of least parts tightly packed together. They are not compounds formed by the coalescence of their parts, but bodies of absolute and everlasting solidity. To these nature allows no loss or diminution, but guards them as seeds for things. If there are no such least parts, even the smallest bodies will consist of an infinite number of parts, since they can always be halved and their halves halved again without limit. On this showing, what difference will there be between the whole universe and the very least of things? None at all. For, however endlessly infinite the universe may be, yet the smallest things will equally consist of an infinite number of parts. Since true reason cries out against this and denies that the mind can believe it, you must needs give in and admit that there are least parts which themselves are partless. Granted that these parts exist, you must needs admit that the atoms they compose are also solid and everlasting. But, if all things were compelled by all-creating nature to be broken up into these least parts, nature would lack the power to rebuild anything out of them. For partless objects cannot have the essential properties of generative matter—those varieties of attachment, weight, impetus, impact and movement on which everything depends. . . .

11. [*Occasionally they swerve slightly from the vertical.*]

. . . There is another fact that I want you to grasp. *When the atoms are travelling straight down through empty space by their own weight, at quite indeterminate times and places they swerve ever so little from their course,* just so much that you can call it a change of direction. If it were not for this swerve, everything would fall downwards like rain-drops through the abyss of space. No collision would take place and no impact of atom on atom would be created. Thus nature would never have created anything.

If anyone supposes that heavier atoms on a straight course through empty space could outstrip lighter ones and fall on them from above, thus causing impacts that might give. rise to generative motions, he is going far astray from the path of truth. The reason why objects falling through water or thin air vary in speed according to their weight is simply that the matter composing water or air cannot obstruct all objects equally, but is forced to give way more speedily to heavier ones. But empty space can offer no resistance to any object in any quarter at any time, so as not to yield free passage as its own nature demands. Therefore, through undisturbed vacuum all bodies must travel at equal speed though impelled by unequal weights. The heavier will never be able to fall on the lighter from above or generate of themselves impacts leading to that variety of motions out of which nature can produce things. We are thus forced back to the conclusion that the atoms swerve a little— but only a very little, or we shall be caught imagining slantwise movements, and the facts will prove us wrong. For we see plainly and palpably that weights, when they come tumbling down, have no power of their own to move aslant, so far as meets the eye. But who can possibly perceive that they do not diverge in the very least from a vertical course?

Again, if all movement is always interconnected, the new arising from the old in a determinate order—if the atoms never swerve so as to originate some new movement that will snap the bonds of fate, the everlasting sequence of cause and effect—what is the source of the free will possessed by living things throughout the earth? What, I repeat, is the source of that will-power snatched from the fates, whereby we follow the path along which we are severally led by pleasure, swerving from our course at no set time or place but at the bidding of our own hearts? There is no doubt that on these occasions the will of the individual originates the movements that trickle through his limbs. Observe, when the starting barriers are flung back, how the race-horses in the eagerness of their strength cannot break away as suddenly as their hearts desire. For the whole supply of matter must first be mobilized throughout every member of the body: only then, when it is mustered in a continuous array, can it respond to the prompting of the heart. So you may see that the beginning of movement is generated by the heart; starting from the voluntary action of the mind, it is then transmitted throughout the body and the limbs. Quite different is our experience when we are shoved along by a blow inflicted with compulsive force by someone else. In that case it is obvious that all the matter of our body is set going and pushed along involuntarily, till a check is imposed through the limbs by the will. Do you see the difference? Although many men are driven by an external force and often constrained involuntarily to advance or to rush headlong, yet there is within the human breast something that can fight against this force and resist it. At its command the supply of matter is forced to take a new course through our limbs and joints or is checked in its course and brought once more to a halt. So also in the atoms you must recognize the same possibility: besides weight and impact there must be a third cause of movement, the source of this inborn power of ours, since we see that nothing can come out of nothing. For the weight of an atom prevents its movements from being completely determined by the impact of other atoms. But the fact that the mind itself has no internal necessity to determine its every act and compel it to suffer in helpless passivity—this is due to the slight swerve of the atoms at no determinate time or place.

12. [*The atoms themselves are devoid of colour.*]

Give ear now to arguments that I have searched out with an effort that was also a delight. Do not imagine that white objects derive the snowy aspect they present to your eyes from white atoms, or that black objects are composed of a black element. And in general do not believe that anything owes the colour it displays to the fact that its atoms are tinted correspondingly. *The primary particles of matter have no colour whatsoever,* neither the same colour as the objects they compose nor a different one. If you think the mind cannot lay hold of such bodies, you are quite wrong. Men who are blind from birth and have never looked on the sunlight have knowledge by touch of bodies that have never from the beginning been associated with any colour. It follows that on our minds also an image can impinge of bodies not marked by any tint. Indeed the things that we ourselves touch in pitch darkness are not felt by us as possessing any colour.

Having proved that colourless bodies are not unthinkable, I will proceed to demonstrate that the atoms must be such bodies.

First, then, any colour may change completely to any other. But the atoms cannot possibly change colour. For something must remain changeless, or everything would be absolutely annihilated. For, if ever anything is so transformed as to overstep its own limits, this means the immediate death of what was before. So do not stain the atoms with colour, or you will find everything slipping back into nothing.

Let us suppose, then, that the atoms are naturally colourless and that it is through the variety of their shapes that they produce the whole range of colours, a great deal depending on their combinations and positions and their reciprocal motions. You will now find it easy to explain without more ado why things that were dark-coloured a moment since can suddenly become as white as marble—as the sea, for instance, when its surface is ruffled by a fresh breeze, is turned into white wavecrests of marble lustre. You could say that something we often see as dark is promptly transformed through the churning up of its matter and a reshuffling of atoms, with some additions and subtractions, so that it is seen as bleached and white. If, on the other hand, the waters of the sea were composed of blue atoms, they could not possibly be whitened; for, however you may stir up blue matter, it can never change its colour to the pallor of marble.

It might be supposed that the uniform lustre of the sea is made up of particles of different colours, as for instance a single object of a square shape is often made up of other objects of various shapes. But in the square we discern the different shapes. So in the surface of the sea or in any other uniform lustre we ought, on this hypothesis, to discern a variety of widely different colours. Besides, differences in the shapes of the parts are no hindrance to the whole being square in outline. But differences in colour completely prevent it from displaying an unvariegated lustre.

The seductive argument that sometimes tempts us to attribute colours to the atoms is demolished by the fact that white objects are not created from white material nor black from black, but both from various colours. Obviously, white could much more readily spring from no colour at all than from black, or from any other colour that interferes and conflicts with it.

Again, since there can be no colours without light and the atoms do not emerge into the light, it can be inferred that they are not clothed in any colour. For what colour can there be in blank darkness? Indeed, colour is itself changed by a change of light, according as the beams strike it vertically or aslant. Observe the appearance in sunlight of the plumage that rings the neck of a dove and crowns its nape: sometimes it is tinted with the brilliant red of a ruby; at others it is seen from a certain point of view to mingle emerald greens with the blue of the sky. In the same way a peacock's tail, profusely illumined, changes colour as it is turned this way or that. These colours, then, are created by a particular incidence of light. Hence, no light, no colour.

When the pupil of the eye is said to perceive the colour white, it experiences in fact a particular kind of impact. When it perceives black, or some other colour, the impact is different. But, when you touch things, it makes no odds what colour they may be, but only what is their shape. The inference is that the atoms have no need of colour, but cause various sensations of touch according to their various shapes.

Since there is no natural connexion

dung when the earth is soaked and rotted by intemperate showers. Besides, we see every sort of substance transformed in the same way. Rivers, foliage and lush pastures are transformed into cattle; the substance of cattle is transformed into our bodies; and often enough our bodies go to build up the strength of predatory beasts or the bodies of the lords of the air. So nature transforms all foods into living bodies and generates from them all the senses of animate creatures, just as it makes dry wood blossom out in flame and transfigures it wholly into fire. So now do you see that it makes a great difference in what order the various atoms are arranged and with what others they are combined so as to impart and take over motions?

What is it, then, that jogs the mind itself and moves and compels it to express certain sentiments, so that you do not believe that the sentient is generated by the insentient? Obviously it is the fact that a mixture of water and wood and earth cannot of itself bring about vital sensibility. There is one relevant point you should bear in mind: I am not maintaining that sensations are generated automatically from all the elements out of which sentient things are created. Everything depends on the size and shape of the sense-producing atoms and on their appropriate motions, arrangements and positions. None of these is found in wood or clods. And yet these substances, when they are fairly well rotted by showers, give birth to little worms, because the particles of matter are jolted out of their old arrangements by a new factor and combined in such a way that animate objects must result.

Again, those who would have it that sensation can be produced only be sensitive bodies, which originate in their turn from others similarly sentient—these theorists are making the foundations of our senses perishable, because they are making them soft. For sensitivity is always associated with flesh, sinews, veins—all things that we see to be soft and composed of perishable stuff.

Let us suppose, for argument's sake, that particles of these substances could endure everlastingly. The sensation with which they are credited must be either that of a part or else similar to that of an animate being as a whole. But it is impossible for parts by themselves to experience sensation: all the sensations felt in our limbs are felt by us as a whole; a hand or any other member severed from the whole body is quite powerless to retain sensation on its own. There remains the alternative that such particles have senses like those of an animate being as a whole. They must then feel precisely what we feel, so as to share in all our vital sensations. How then can they pass for elements and escape the path of death, since they are animate beings, and animate and mortal are one and the same thing? Even supposing they could escape death, yet they will make nothing by their combination and conjunction but a mob or horde of living things, just as men and cattle and wild beasts obviously could not combine so as to give birth to a single thing. If we suppose that they shed their own sentience from their bodies and acquire another one, what is between particular colours and particular shapes, atoms (if they were not colourless) might equally well be of any colour irrespective of their form. Why then are not their compounds tinted with every shade of colour irrespective of their kind? We should expect on this hypothesis that ravens in flight would often emit a snowy sheen from snowy wings; and that some swans would be black, being composed of black atoms, or would display some other uniform or variegated colour.

Again, the more anything is divided into tiny parts, the more you can see its colour gradually dimming and fading out. When red cloth, for instance, is pulled to pieces thread by thread, its crimson or scarlet colour, than which there is none brighter, is all dissipated. From this you may gather that, before its particles are reduced right down to atoms, they would shed all their colour.

Finally, since you acknowledge that not all objects emit noise or smell, you accept that as a reason for not attributing sounds and scents to everything. On the same principle, since we cannot perceive everything by eye, we may infer that some things are colourless, just as some things are scentless and soundless, and that these can be apprehended by the percipient mind as readily as things that are lacking in some other quality.

13. [*The atoms are also devoid of heat, sound, taste, and smell.*]

Do not imagine that colour is the only quality that is denied to the atoms. *They are also wholly devoid of warmth and cold and scorching heat; they are barren of sound and starved of savour,*
and emit no inherent odour from their bodies. When you are setting out to prepare a pleasant perfume of marjoram or myrrh or flower of spikenard, breathing nectar into our nostrils, your first task is to select so far as possible an oil that is naturally odourless and sends out no exhalation to our nostrils. This will be least liable to corrupt the scents blended and concocted with its substance by contamination with its own taint. For the same reason the atoms must not impart to things at their birth a scent or sound that is their own property, since they can send nothing out of themselves; nor must they contribute any flavour or cold or heat, whether scorching or mild, or anything else of the kind.

These qualities, again, are perishable things, made pliable by the softness of their substance, breakable by its crumbliness and penetrable by its looseness of texture. They must be kept far apart from the atoms, if we wish to provide the universe with imperishable foundations on which it may rest secure; or else you will find everything slipping back into nothing.

14. [*And of sentience.*]

At this stage you must admit that *whatever is seen to be sentient is nevertheless composed of atoms that are insentient.* The phenomena open to our observation do not contradict this conclusion or conflict with it. Rather, they lead us by the hand and compel us to believe that the animate is born, as I maintain, of the insentient.

As a particular instance, we can point to living worms, emerging from foul the point of giving them the one that is taken away? Besides, as we saw before, from the fact that we perceive eggs turning into live fledgelings and worms swarming out when the earth has been rotted by intemperate showers, we may infer that sense can be generated from the insentient.

Suppose someone asserts that sense can indeed emerge from the insentient, but only by some transformation or some creative process comparable to birth. He will be adequately answered by a clear demonstration that birth and transformation occur only as the result of union or combination. Admittedly sensation cannot arise in any body until an animate creature has been born. This of course is because the requisite matter is dispersed through air and streams and earth and the products of earth: it has not come together in the appropriate manner, so as to set in mutual operation those vitalizing motions that kindle the all-watchful senses which keep watch over every animate creature.

When any animate creature is suddenly assailed by a more powerful blow than its nature can withstand, all the senses of body and mind are promptly thrown into confusion. For the juxtapositions of the atoms are unknit, and the vitalizing motions are inwardly obstructed, until the matter, jarred and jolted throughout every limb, loosens the vital knots of the spirit from the body and expels the spirit in scattered particles through every pore. What other effect can we attribute to the infliction of a blow than this of shaking and shattering everything to bits? Besides, it often happens, when the blow is less

violently inflicted, that such vitalizing motions as survive emerge victorious; they assuage the immense upheavals resulting from the shock, recall every particle to its own proper courses, break up the lethal motion when it is all but master of the body and rekindle the well-nigh extinguished senses. How else could living creatures on the very threshold of death rally their consciousness and return to life rather than make good their departure by a route on which they have already travelled most of the way?

Again, pain occurs when particles of matter have been unsettled by some force within the living flesh of the limbs and stagger in their inmost stations. When they slip back into place, that is blissful pleasure. It follows that the atoms cannot be afflicted by any pain or experience any pleasure in themselves, since they are not composed of any primal particles, by some reversal of whose movements they might suffer anguish or reap some fruition of vitalizing bliss. They cannot therefore be endowed with any power of sensation.

Again, if we are to account for the power of sensation possessed by animate creatures in general by attributing sentience to their atoms, what of those atoms that specifically compose the human race? Presumably they are not merely sentient, but also shake their sides with uproarious guffaws and besprinkle their cheeks with dewy teardrops and even discourse profoundly and at length about the composition of the universe and proceed to ask of what elements they are themselves composed. If they are to be likened to entire mortals, they must certainly consist of other elemental particles, and these again of others. There is no point at which you may call a halt, but I will follow you there with your argument that whatever speaks or laughs or thinks is composed of particles that do the same. Let us acknowledge that this is stark madness and lunacy: one can laugh without being composed of laughing particles, can think and proffer learned arguments though sprung from seeds neither thoughtful nor eloquent. Why then cannot the things that we see gifted with sensation be compounded of seeds that are wholly senseless?

Lastly, we are all sprung from heavenly seed. All alike have the same father, from whom all-nourishing mother earth receives the showering drops of moisture. Thus fertilized, she gives birth to smiling crops and lusty trees, to mankind and all the breeds of beasts. She it is that yields the food on which they all feed their bodies, lead their joyous lives and renew their race. So she has well earned the name of mother. In like manner this matter returns: what came from earth goes back into the earth; what was sent down from the ethereal vault is readmitted to the precincts of heaven. Death does not put an end to things by annihilating the component particles but by breaking up their conjunction. Then it links them in new combinations, making everything change in shape and colour and give up in an instant its acquired gift of sensation. So you may realize what a difference it makes in what combinations and positions the same elements occur, and what motions they mutually pass on and take over. You

will thus avoid the mistake of conceiving as permanent properties of the atoms the qualities that are seen floating on the surface of things, coming into being from time to time and as suddenly perishing. Obviously it makes a great difference in these verses of mine in what context and order the letters are arranged. If not all, at least the greater part is alike. But differences in their position distinguish word from word. Just so with actual objects: when there is a change in the combination, motion, order, position or shapes of the component matter, there must be a corresponding change in the object composed. . . .

15. [*Mind and spirit were born and will die.*]

A tree cannot exist high in air, or clouds in the depths of the sea, as fish cannot live in the fields, or blood flow in wood or sap in stones. There is a determined and allotted place for the growth and presence of everything. So mind cannot arise alone without body or apart from sinews and blood. If it could do this, then surely it could much more readily function in head or shoulders or the tips of the heels and be born in any other part, so long as it was held in the same container, that is to say in the same man. Since, however, even in the human body we see a determined and allotted place set aside for the growth and presence of spirit and mind, we have even stronger grounds for denying that they could survive or come to birth outside the body altogether. You must admit, therefore, that when the body has perished there is an end also of the spirit diffused through it. It is surely crazy to couple a mortal object with an eternal and suppose that they can work in harmony and mutually interact. What can be imagined more incongruous, what more repugnant and discordant, than that a mortal object and one that is immortal and everlasting should unite to form a compound and jointly weather the storms that rage about them?

Again, there can be only three kinds of everlasting objects. The first, owing to the absolute solidity of their substance, can repel blows and let nothing penetrate them so as to unknit their close texture from within. Such are the atoms of matter, whose nature I have already demonstrated. The second kind can last for ever because it is immune from blows. Such is empty space, which remains untouched and unaffected by any impact. Last is that which has no available place surrounding it into which its matter can disperse and disintegrate. It is for this reason that the sum total of the universe is everlasting, having no space outside it into which the matter can escape and no matter that can enter and disintegrate it by the force of impact.

Equally vain is the suggestion that the spirit is immortal because it is shielded by life-preserving powers; or because it is unassailed by forces hostile to its survival; or because such forces, if they threaten, are somehow arrested before we are conscious of the threat. Apart from the spirit's participation in the ailments of the body, it has maladies enough of its own. The prospect of the future torments it with fear and wearies it with worry, and past misdeeds leave the sting of remorse. Lastly, it may fall a prey to the mind's own specific afflictions, madness and amnesia, and plunge into the black waters of oblivion.

From all this it follows that *death is nothing to us* and no concern of ours, since our tenure of the mind is mortal. In days of old, we felt no disquiet when the hosts of Carthage poured in to battle on every side—when the whole earth, dizzied by the convulsive shock of war, reeled sickeningly under the high ethereal vault, and between realm and realm the empire of mankind by land and sea trembled in the balance. So, when we shall be no more—when the union of body and spirit that engenders us has been disrupted—to us, who shall then be nothing, nothing by any hazard will happen any more at all. Nothing will have power to stir our senses, not though earth be fused with sea and sea with sky. . . .

16. [*Happiness lies in cheerful acceptance of the universal lot.*]

Here is something that you might well say to yourself from time to time: 'Even good king Ancus looked his last on the daylight—a better man than you, my presumptuous friend, by a long reckoning. Death has come to many another monarch and potentate, who lorded it over mighty nations. Even that King of Kings who once built a highway across the deep—who gave his legions a path to tread among the waves and taught them to march on foot over the briny gulfs and with his charger trampled scornfully upon the ocean's roar—even he was robbed of the light and poured out the spirit from a dying frame. Scipio, that thunderbolt of war, the terror of Carthage, gave his bones to the earth as if he had been the meanest of serfs. Add to this company the discoverers of truth and beauty. Add the attendants of the Muses, among them Homer who in solitary glory bore the sceptre but has sunk into the same slumber as the rest. Democritus, when ripe age warned him that the mindful motions of his intellect were running down, made his unbowed head a willing sacrifice to death. And the Master himself, when his daylit race was run, Epicurus himself died, whose genius outshone the race of men and dimmed them all, as the stars are dimmed by the rising of the fiery sun. And will *you* kick and protest against your sentence? You, whose life is next-door to death while you are still alive and looking on the light. You, who waste the major part of your time in sleep and, when you are awake, are snoring still and dreaming. You, who bear a mind hagridden by baseless fear and cannot find the commonest cause of your distress, hounded as you are, poor creature, by a pack of troubles and drifting in a drunken stupor upon a wavering tide of fantasy.'

Men feel plainly enough within their minds, a heavy burden, whose weight depresses them. If only they perceived with equal clearness the causes of this depression, the origin of this lump of evil within their breasts, they would not lead such a life as we now see all too commonly—no one knowing what he really wants and everyone for ever trying to get away from where he is, as though mere locomotion could throw off the load. Often the owner of some

stately mansion, bored stiff by staying at home, takes his departure, only to return as speedily when he feels himself no better off out of doors. Off he goes to his country seat, driving his carriage and pair hot-foot, as though in haste to save a house on fire. No sooner has he crossed its doorstep than he starts yawning or retires moodily to sleep and courts oblivion, or else rushes back to revisit the city. In so doing the individual is really running away from himself. Since he remains reluctantly wedded to the self whom he cannot of course escape, he grows to hate him, because he is a sick man ignorant of the cause of his malady. If he did but see this, he would cast other thoughts aside and devote himself first to studying the nature of the universe. It is not the fortune of an hour that is in question, but of all time—the lot in store for mortals throughout the eternity that awaits them after death.

What is this deplorable lust of life that holds us trembling in bondage to such uncertainties and dangers? A fixed term is set to the life of mortals, and there is no way of dodging death. In any case the setting of our lives remains the same throughout, and by going on living we do not mint any new coin of pleasure. So long as the object of our craving is unattained, it seems more precious than anything besides. Once it is ours, we crave for something else. So an unquenchable thirst for life keeps us always on the gasp. There is no telling what fortune the future may bring—what chance may throw in our way, or what upshot lies in waiting. By prolonging life, we cannot subtract or whittle away one jot from the duration of our death. The time after our taking off remains constant. However many generations you may add to your store by living, there waits for you none the less the same eternal death. The time of not-being will be no less for him who made an end of life with yesterday's daylight than for him who perished many a moon and many a year before.

BERTRAND RUSSELL (1872–1970)

The second son of Viscount Amberly and grandson of Lord John Russell, a famous liberal Prime Minister, Bertrand Russell was born on May 18, 1872, in the lovely valley of the Wye (described in Wordsworth's *Tintern Abbey*). His mother died when he was two years old and his father when he was three, so the boy was brought up in the home of his grandfather. Until he went to Cambridge University, at the age of eighteen, he lived a solitary life, supervised by German and Swiss governesses and English tutors and seeing little of other children. But Cambridge opened to him "a new world of infinite delight." Here he found mathematics and philosophy extremely exciting and formed warm friendships with a number of brilliant young men, including the philosophers McTaggart, Moore, and Whitehead.

The next two decades were the most intellectually productive in his long career. During this period he wrote a series of important books, including *A Critical Exposition of the Philosophy of Leibniz* (1900), *The Principles of Mathematics* (1903), *Principia Mathematica* (with Whitehead, 1910–1913), and *Our Knowledge of the External World* (1914). These books, especially *Principia Mathematica* which was the result of twelve years of intense labor, firmly established Russell's reputation as one of the great figures in modern thought.

Always interested in politics, Russell was profoundly disturbed by the outbreak of World War I and was quite unsatisfied with the melodramatic pronouncements of the belligerent governments. His bold defense of conscientious objectors and his anti-war publications brought him fines and imprisonment, as well as loss of his position as Fellow at Trinity College, Cambridge. He emerged from the war a changed man, aware of great social perils and pathological evils in human nature that he had never suspected. Ever after, he devoted a large part of his time and energy to writing about human political, educational, and moral affairs.

In 1921, after seventeen years of married life, his first marriage was dissolved, and he then wed Dora Winifred Black, who bore him a daughter and son, and from whom he was later divorced. Upon the death of his elder brother in 1931, he succeeded to the family earldom; and in 1934 he remarried, thus making Helen Patricia Spence, a young and beautiful woman, the Countess Russell. In 1950 he received the Nobel prize for literature. Despite his advanced age, he continued to live a busy and adventurous life, writing prolifically and espousing the cause of peace.

The Existence and Nature of Matter

1. The Existence of Matter

In this chapter we have to ask ourselves whether, in any sense at all, there is such a thing as matter. Is there a table which has a certain intrinsic nature, and continues to exist when I am not looking, or is the table merely a product of my imagination, a dream-table in a very prolonged dream? This question is of the greatest importance. For if we cannot be sure of the independent existence of objects, we cannot be sure of the independent existence of other people's bodies, and therefore still less of other people's minds, since we have no grounds for believing in their minds except such as are derived from observing their bodies. Thus if we cannot be sure of the independent existence of objects, we shall be left alone in a desert—it may be that the whole outer world is nothing but a dream, and that we alone exist. This is an uncomfortable possibility; but although it cannot be strictly *proved* to be false, there is not the slightest reason to suppose that it is true. In this chapter we have to see why this is the case.

Before we embark upon doubtful matters, let us try to find some more or less fixed point from which to start.

From Bertrand Russell, *The Problems of Philosophy*. London, New York, and Toronto: Oxford University Press, 1912. Reprinted by permission.

Although we are doubting the physical existence of the table, we are not doubting the existence of the sense-data which made us think there was a table; we are not doubting that, while we look, a certain colour and shape appear to us, and while we press, a certain sensation of hardness is experienced by us. All this, which is psychological, we are not calling in question. In fact, whatever else may be doubtful, some at least of our immediate experiences seem absolutely certain.

Descartes (1596–1650), the founder of modern philosophy, invented a method which may still be used with profit—the method of systematic doubt. He determined that he would believe nothing which he did not see quite clearly and distinctly to be true. Whatever he could bring himself to doubt, he would doubt, until he saw reason for not doubting it. By applying this method he gradually became convinced that the only existence of which he could be *quite* certain was his own. He imagined a deceitful demon, who presented unreal things to his senses in a perpetual phantasmagoria; it might be very improbable that such a demon existed, but still it was possible, and therefore doubt concerning things perceived by the senses was possible.

But doubt concerning his own existence was not possible, for if he did not exist, no demon could deceive him. If he doubted, he must exist; if he had any experiences whatever, he must exist. Thus his own existence was an absolute certainty to him. 'I think, therefore I am,' he said (*Cogito, ergo sum*); and on the basis of this certainty he set to work to build up again the world of knowledge which his doubt had laid in ruins. By inventing the method of doubt, and by showing that subjective things are the most certain, Descartes performed a great service to philosophy, and one which makes him still useful to all students of the subject.

But some care is needed in using Descartes' argument. '*I* think, therefore *I* am' says rather more than is strictly certain. It might seem as though we were quite sure of being the same person to-day as we were yesterday, and this is no doubt true in some sense. But the real Self is as hard to arrive at as the real table, and does not seem to have that absolute, convincing certainty that belongs to particular experiences. When I look at my table and see a certain brown colour, what is quite certain at once is not '*I* am seeing a brown colour', but rather, 'a brown colour is being seen'. This of course involves something (or somebody) which (or who) sees the brown colour; but it does not of itself involve that more or less permanent person whom we call 'I'. So far as immediate certainty goes, it might be that the something which sees the brown colour is quite momentary, and not the same as the something which has some different experience the next moment.

Thus it is our particular thoughts and feelings that have primitive certainty. And this applies to dreams and hal-lucinations as well as to normal perceptions: when we dream or see a ghost, we certainly do have the sensations we think we have, but for various reasons it is held that no physical object corresponds to these sensations. Thus the certainty of our knowledge of our own experiences does not have to be limited in any way to allow for exceptional cases. Here, therefore, we have, for what it is worth, a solid basis from which to begin our pursuit of knowledge.

The problem we have to consider is this: Granted that we are certain of our own sense-data, have we any reason for regarding them as signs of the existence of something else, which we can call the physical object? When we have enu-merated all the sense-data which we should naturally regard as connected with the table, have we said all there is to say about the table, or is there still something else—something not a sense-datum, something which persists when we go out of the room? Common sense unhesitatingly answers that there is. What can be bought and sold and pushed about and have a cloth laid on it, and so on, cannot be a *mere* collec-tion of sense-data. If the cloth com-pletely hides the table, we shall derive no sense-data from the table, and there-fore, if the table were merely sense-data, it would have ceased to exist, and the cloth would be suspended in empty air, resting, by a miracle, in the place where the table formerly was. This seems plainly absurd; but whoever wishes to become a philosopher must learn not to be frightened by absurdities.

One great reason why it is felt that we must secure a physical object in addition to the sense-data, is that we want the *same* object for different people. When ten people are sitting round a dinner-table, it seems preposterous to maintain that they are not seeing the same tablecloth, the same knives and forks and spoons and glasses. But the sense-data are private to each separate person; what is immediately present to the sight of one is not immediately present to the sight of another: they all see things from slightly different points of view, and therefore see them slightly differently. Thus, if there are to be public neutral objects, which can be in some sense known to many different people, there must be something over and above the private and particular sense-data which appear to various people. What reason, then, have we for believing that there are such public neutral objects?

The first answer that naturally occurs to one is that, although different people may see the table slightly differently, still they all see more or less similar things when they look at the table, and the variations in what they see follow the laws of perspective and reflection of light, so that it is easy to arrive at a permanent object underlying all the different people's sense-data. I bought my table from the former occupant of my room; I could not buy *his* sense-data, which died when he went away, but I could and did buy the confident expectation of more or less similar sense-data. Thus it is the fact that different people have similar sense-data, and that one person in a given place at different times has similar sense-data, which makes us suppose that over and above the sense-data there is a permanent public object which underlies or causes the sense-data of various people at various times.

Now in so far as the above considerations depend upon supposing that there are other people besides ourselves, they beg the very question at issue. Other people are represented to me by certain sense-data, such as the sight of them or the sound of their voices, and if I had no reason to believe that there were physical objects independent of my sense-data, I should have no reason to believe that other people exist except as part of my dream. Thus, when we are trying to show that there must be objects independent of our own sense-data, we cannot appeal to the testimony of other people, since this testimony itself consists of sense-data, and does not reveal other people's experiences unless our own sense-data are signs of things existing independently of us. We must therefore, if possible, find, in our own purely private experiences, characteristics which show, or tend to show, that there are in the world things other than ourselves and our private experiences.

In one sense it must be admitted that we can never *prove* the existence of things other than ourselves and our experiences. No logical absurdity results from the hypothesis that the world consists of myself and my thoughts and feelings and sensations, and that everything else is mere fancy. In dreams a very complicated world may seem to be present, and yet on waking we find it was a delusion; that is to say, we find that the sense-data in the dream do not appear to have corresponded with such physical objects as we should naturally infer from our sense-data. (It is true that, when the physical world is assumed, it is possible to find physical causes for the sense-data in dreams: a door banging, for instance, may cause us to dream of a naval engagement. But although, in this case, there is a physical *cause* for the sense-data, there is not a physical object *corresponding* to the sense-data in the way in which an actual naval battle would correspond.) There is no logical impossibility in the supposition that the whole of life is a dream, in which we ourselves create all the objects that come before us. But although this is not logically impossible, there is no reason whatever to suppose that it is true; and it is, in fact, a less simple hypothesis, viewed as a means of accounting for the facts of our own life, than the common-sense hypothesis that there really are objects independent of us, whose action on us causes our sensations.

The way in which simplicity comes in from supposing that there really are physical objects is easily seen. If the cat appears at one moment in one part of the room, and at another in another part, it is natural to suppose that it has moved from the one to the other, passing over a series of intermediate positions. But if it is merely a set of sense-data, it cannot have ever been in any place where I did not see it; thus we shall have to suppose that it did not exist at all while I was not looking, but suddenly sprang into being in a new place. If the cat exists whether I see it or not, we can understand from our own experience how it gets hungry between one meal and the next; but if it does not exist when I am not seeing it, it seems odd that appetite should grow during non-existence as fast as

during existence. And if the cat consists only of sense-data, it cannot be *hungry,* since no hunger but my own can be a sense-datum to me. Thus the behaviour of the sense-data which represent the cat to me, though it seems quite natural when regarded as an expression of hunger, becomes utterly inexplicable when regarded as mere movements and changes of patches of colour, which are as incapable of hunger as a triangle is of playing football.

But the difficulty in the case of the cat is nothing compared to the difficulty in the case of human beings. When human beings speak—that is, when we hear certain noises which we associate with ideas, and simultaneously see certain motions of lips and expressions of face—it is very difficult to suppose that what we hear is not the expression of a thought, as we know it would be if we emitted the same sounds. Of course similar things happen in dreams, where we are mistaken as to the existence of other people. But dreams are more or less suggested by what we call waking life, and are capable of being more or less accounted for on scientific principles if we assume that there really is a physical world. Thus every principle of simplicity urges us to adopt the natural view, that there really are objects other than ourselves and our sense-data which have an existence not dependent upon our perceiving them.

Of course it is not by argument that we originally come by our belief in an independent external world. We find this belief ready in ourselves as soon as we begin to reflect: it is what may be called an *instinctive* belief. We should never have been led to question this belief but for the fact that, at any rate in the case of sight, it seems as if the sense-datum itself were instinctively believed to be the independent object, whereas argument shows that the object cannot be identical with the sense-datum. This discovery, however—which is not at all paradoxical in the case of taste and smell and sound, and only slightly so in the case of touch—leaves undiminished our instinctive belief that there *are* objects *corresponding* to our sense-data. Since this belief does not lead to any difficulties, but on the contrary tends to simplify and systematize our account of our experiences, there seems no good reason for rejecting it. We may therefore admit—though with a slight doubt derived from dreams— that the external world does really exist, and is not wholly dependent for its existence upon our continuing to perceive it.

The argument which has led us to this conclusion is doubtless less strong than we could wish, but it is typical of many philosophical arguments, and it is therefore worth while to consider briefly its general character and validity. All knowledge, we find, must be built up upon our instinctive beliefs, and if these are rejected, nothing is left. But among our instinctive beliefs some are much stronger than others, while many have, by habit and association, become entangled with other beliefs, not really instinctive, but falsely supposed to be part of what is believed instinctively.

Philosophy should show us the hierarchy of our instinctive beliefs, beginning with those we hold most strongly, and presenting each as much isolated and as free from irrelevant additions as possible. It should take care to show that, in the form in which they are finally set forth, our instinctive beliefs do not clash, but form a harmonious system. There can never be any reason for rejecting one instinctive belief except that it clashes with others; thus, if they are found to harmonize, the whole system becomes worthy of acceptance.

It is of course *possible* that all or any of our beliefs may be mistaken, and therefore all ought to be held with at least some slight element of doubt. But we cannot have *reason* to reject a belief except on the ground of some other belief. Hence, by organizing our instinctive beliefs and their consequences, by considering which among them is most possible, if necessary, to modify or abandon, we can arrive, on the basis of accepting as our sole data what we instinctively believe, at an orderly systematic organization of our knowledge, in which, though the *possibility* of error remains, its likelihood is diminished by the interrelation of the parts and by the critical scrutiny which has preceded acquiescence.

This function, at least, philosophy can perform. Most philosophers, rightly or wrongly, believe that philosophy can do much more than this—that it can give us knowledge, not otherwise attainable, concerning the universe as a whole, and concerning the nature of ultimate reality. Whether this be the case or not, the more modest function we have spoken of can certainly be performed by philosophy, and certainly suffices, for those who have once begun to doubt the adequacy of common sense, to justify the arduous and difficult labours that philosophical problems involve.

2. The Nature of Matter

In the preceding chapter we agreed, though without being able to find demonstrative reasons, that it is rational to believe that our sense-data—for example, those which we regard as associated with my table—are really signs of the existence of something independent of us and our perceptions. That is to say, over and above the sensations of colour, hardness, noise, and so on, which make up the appearance of the table to me, I assume that there is something else, *of* which these things are appearances. The colour ceases to exist if I shut my eyes, the sensation of hardness ceases to exist if I remove my arm from contact with the table, the sound ceases to exist if I cease to rap the table with my knuckles. But I do not believe that when all these things cease the table ceases. On the contrary, I believe that it is because the table exists continuously that all these sense-data will reappear when I open my eyes, replace my arm, and begin again to rap with my knuckles. The question we have to consider in this chapter is: What is the nature of this real table, which persists independently of my perception of it?

To this question physical science gives an answer, somewhat incomplete it is true, and in part still very hypothetical, but yet deserving of respect so far as it goes. Physical science, more or less unconsciously, has drifted into the view that all natural phenomena ought to be reduced to motions. Light and heat and sound are all due to wave-motions, which travel from the body emitting them to the person who sees light or feels heat or hears sound. That which has the wave-motion is either aether or 'gross matter', but in either case is what the philosopher would call matter. The only properties which science assigns to it are position in space, and the power of motion according to the laws of motion. Science does not deny that it *may* have other properties; but if so, such other properties are not useful to the man of science, and in no way assist him in explaining the phenomena.

It is sometimes said that 'light *is* a form of wave-motion', but this is misleading, for the light which we immediately see, which we know directly by means of our senses, is *not* a form of wave-motion, but something quite different—something which we all know if we are not blind, though we cannot describe it so as to convey our knowledge to a man who is blind. A wave-motion, on the contrary, could quite well be described to a blind man, since he can acquire a knowledge of space by the sense of touch; and he can experience a wave-motion by a sea voyage almost as well as we can. But this, which a blind man can understand, is not what we mean by *light*: we mean by *light* just that which a blind man can never understand, and which we can never describe to him.

Now this something, which all of us who are not blind know, is not, according to science, really to be found in the outer world: it is something caused by the action of certain waves upon the eyes and nerves and brain of the person who sees the light. When it is said that light *is* waves, what is really meant is that waves are the physical cause of our sensations of light. But light itself, the thing which seeing people experience and blind people do not, is not supposed by science to form any part of the world that is independent of us and our senses. And very similar remarks would apply to other kinds of sensations.

It is not only colours and sounds and so on that are absent from the scientific world of matter, but also *space* as we get it through sight or touch. It is essential to science that its matter should be in *a* space, but the space in which it is cannot be exactly the space we see or feel. To begin with, space as we see it is not the same as space as we get it by the sense of touch; it is only by experience in infancy that we learn how to touch things we see, or how to get a sight of things which we feel touching us. But the space of science is neutral as between touch and sight; thus it cannot be either the space of touch or the space of sight.

Again, different people see the same object as of different shapes, according to their point of view. A circular coin, for example, though we should always *judge* it to be circular, will *look* oval unless we are straight in front of it. When we judge that it *is* circular, we are judging that it has a real shape which is not its apparent shape, but belongs to it intrinsically apart from its appearance. But this real shape, which is what concerns science, must be in a real space, not the same as anybody's *apparent* space. The real space is public, the apparent space is private to the percipient. In different people's *private* spaces the same object seems to have different shapes; thus the real space, in which it has its real shape, must be different from the private spaces. The space of science, therefore, though *connected* with the spaces we see and feel, is not identical with them, and the manner of its connexion requires investigation.

We agreed provisionally that physical objects cannot be quite like our sense-data, but may be regarded as *causing* our sensations. These physical objects are in the space of science, which we may call 'physical' space. It is important to notice that, if our sensations are to be caused by physical objects, there must be a physical space containing these objects and our sense-organs and nerves and brain. We get a sensation of touch from an object when we are in contact with it; that is to say, when some part of our body occupies a place in physical space quite close to the space occupied by the object. We see an object (roughly speaking) when no opaque body is between the object and our eyes in physical space. Similarly, we only hear or smell or taste an object when we are sufficiently near to it, or when it touches the tongue, or has some suitable position in physical space relatively to our body. We cannot begin to state what different sensations we shall derive from a given object under different circumstances unless we regard the object and our body as both in one physical space, for it is mainly the relative positions of the object and our body that determine what sensations we shall derive from the object.

Now our sense-data are situated in

our private spaces, either the space of sight or the space of touch or such vaguer spaces as other senses may give us. If, as science and common sense assume, there is one public all-embracing physical space in which physical objects are, the relative positions of physical objects in physical space must more or less correspond to the relative positions of sense-data in our private spaces. There is no difficulty in supposing this to be the case. If we see on a road one house nearer to us than another, our other senses will bear out the view that it is nearer; for example, it will be reached sooner if we walk along the road. Other people will agree that the house which looks nearer to us is nearer; the ordnance map will take the same view; and thus everything points to a spatial relation between the houses corresponding to the relation between the sense-data which we see when we look at the houses. Thus we may assume that there is a physical space in which physical objects have spatial relations corresponding to those which the corresponding sense-data have in our private spaces. It is this physical space which is dealt with in geometry and assumed in physics and astronomy.

Assuming that there is physical space, and that it does thus correspond to private spaces, what can we know about it? We can know *only* what is required in order to secure the correspondence. That is to say, we can know nothing of what it is like in itself, but we can know the sort of arrangement of physical objects which results from their spatial relations. We can know, for example, that the earth and moon and sun are in one straight line during an eclipse, though we cannot know what a physical straight line is in itself, as we know the look of a straight line in our visual space. Thus we come to know much more about the *relations* of distances in physical space than about the distances themselves; we may know that one distance is greater than another, or that it is along the same straight line as the other, but we cannot have that immediate acquaintance with physical distances that we have with distances in our private spaces, or with colours or sounds or other sense-data. We can know all those things about physical space which a man born blind might know through other people about the space of sight; but the kind of things which a man born blind could never know about the space of sight we also cannot know about physical space. We can know the properties of the relations required to preserve the correspondence with sense-data, but we cannot know the nature of the terms between which the relations hold.

With regard to time, our *feeling* of duration or of the lapse of time is notoriously an unsafe guide as to the time that has elapsed by the clock. Times when we are bored or suffering pain pass slowly, times when we are agreeably occupied pass quickly, and times when we are sleeping pass almost as if they did not exist. Thus, in so far as time is constituted by duration, there is the same necessity for distinguishing a public and a private time as there was in the case of space. But in so far as time consists in an *order* of before and after, there is no need to make such a distinction; the time-order which events seem to have is, so far as we can see, the same as the time-order which they do have. At any rate no reason can be given for supposing that the two orders are not the same. The same is usually true of space: if a regiment of men are marching along a road, the *shape* of the regiment will look different from different points of view, but the men will appear arranged in the same *order* from all points of view. Hence we regard the *order* as true also in physical space, whereas the shape is only supposed to correspond to the physical space so far as is required for the preservation of the order.

In saying that the time-order which events *seem to have* is the same as the time-order which they *really have*, it is necessary to guard against a possible misunderstanding. It must not be supposed that the various states of different physical objects have the same time-order as the sense-data which constitute the perceptions of those objects. Considered as physical objects, the thunder and lightning are simultaneous; that is to say, the lightning is simultaneous with the disturbance of the air in the place where the disturbance begins, namely, where the lightning is. But the sense-datum which we call hearing the thunder does not take place until the disturbance of the air has travelled as far as to where we are. Similarly, it takes about eight minutes for the sun's light to reach us; thus, when we see the sun we are seeing the sun of eight minutes ago. So far as our sense-data afford evidence as to the physical sun they afford evidence as to the physical sun of eight minutes ago; if the physical sun had ceased to exist within the last eight minutes, that would make no

difference to the sense-data which we call 'seeing the sun'. This affords a fresh illustration of the necessity of distinguishing between sense-data and physical objects.

What we have found as regards space is much the same as what we find in relation to the correspondence of the sense-data with their physical counterparts. If one object looks blue and another red, we may reasonably presume that there is some corresponding difference between the physical objects; if two objects both look blue, we may presume a corresponding similarity. But we cannot hope to be acquainted directly with the quality in the physical object which makes it look blue or red. Science tells us that this quality is a certain sort of wave-motion, and this sounds familiar, because we think of wave-motions in the space we see. But the wave-motions must really be in physical space, with which we have no direct acquaintance; thus the real wave-motions have not that familiarity which we might have supposed them to have. And what holds for colours is closely similar to what holds for other sense-data. Thus we find that, although the *relations* of physical objects have all sorts of knowable properties, derived from their correspondence with the relations of sense-data, the physical objects themselves remain unknown in their intrinsic nature, so far at least as can be discovered by means of the senses. The question remains whether there is any other method of discovering the intrinsic nature of physical objects.

The most natural, though not ultimately the most defensible, hypothesis to adopt in the first instance, at any rate as regards visual sense-data, would be that, though physical objects cannot, for the reasons we have been considering, be *exactly* like sense-data, yet they may be more or less like. According to this view, physical objects will, for example, really have colours, and we might, by good luck, see an object as of the colour it really is. The colour which an object seems to have at any given moment will in general be very similar, though not quite the same, from many different points of view; we might thus suppose the 'real' colour to be a sort of medium colour, intermediate between the various shades which appear from the different points of view.

Such a theory is perhaps not capable of being definitely refuted, but it can be shown to be groundless. To begin with, it is plain that the colour we see depends only upon the nature of the light-waves that strike the eye, and is therefore modified by the medium intervening between us and the object, as well as by the manner in which light is reflected from the object in the direction of the eye. The intervening air alters colours unless it is perfectly clear, and any strong reflection will alter them completely. Thus the colour we see is a result of the ray as it reaches the eye, and not simply a property of the object

from which the ray comes. Hence, also, provided certain waves reach the eye, we shall see a certain colour, whether the object from which the waves start has any colour or not. Thus it is quite gratuitous to suppose that physical objects have colours, and therefore there is no justification for making such a supposition. Exactly similar arguments will apply to other sense-data.

It remains to ask whether there are any general philosophical arguments enabling us to say that, if matter is real, it *must* be of such and such a nature. As explained above, very many philosophers, perhaps most, have held that whatever is real must be in some sense mental, or at any rate that whatever we can know anything about must be in some sense mental. Such philosophers are called 'idealists'. Idealists tell us that what appears as matter is really something mental; namely, either (as Leibniz held) more or less rudimentary minds, or (as Berkeley contended) ideas in the minds which, as we should commonly say, 'perceive' the matter. Thus idealists deny the existence of matter as something intrinsically different from mind, though they do not deny that our sense-data are signs of something which exists independently of our private sensations. . . . `

ALAN M. TURING (1912–1954)

Turing was educated and taught mathematics at Cambridge University. While still in his early twenties, he contributed substantially to pure and applied mathematics. He was a pioneer in the theory and construction of computing machinery, being interested not only in the construction of actual machines but in the computational powers and limitations of computers in the predictable future. In his famous article, "Computing Machinery and Intelligence," partly reproduced below, he argued that it would eventually be possible to build machines that would exhibit highly sophisticated intelligence. Only prejudice against a mechanistic theory of mind, he contended, would prevent us from attributing thought and intelligence to these machines. This contention, echoed in so much science fiction (see, for example, Isaac Asimov, *I, Robot*), has been an influential contribution to a materialistic theory of the human mind.

Computing Machinery and Intelligence

The Imitation Game

I propose to consider the question "Can machines think?" This should begin with definitions of the meaning of the terms "machine" and "think." The definitions might be framed so as to reflect so far as possible the normal use of the words, but this attitude is dangerous. If the meaning of the words "machine" and "think" are to be found by examining how they are commonly used it is difficult to escape the conclusion that the meaning and the answer to the question, "Can machines think?" is to be sought in a statistical survey such as a Gallup poll. But this is absurd. Instead of attempting such a definition I shall replace the question by another, which is closely related to it and is expressed in relatively unambiguous words.

The new form of the problem can be described in terms of a game which we call the "imitation game." It is played with three people, a man (A), a woman (B), and an interrogator (C) who may be of either sex. The interrogator stays in a room apart from the other two.

From Alan M. Turing, "Computing Machinery and Intelligence," *Mind*, Vol. 59 (1950). Reprinted by permission of the Editor of *Mind*. (The most difficult passages have been omitted. An advanced student, familiar with this type of subject-matter, may prefer to read the entire article in *Mind*.)

The object of the game for the interrogator is to determine which of the other two is the man and which is the woman. He knows them by labels X and Y, and at the end of the game he says either "X is A and Y is B" or "X is B and Y is A." The interrogator is allowed to put questions to A and B thus:

C: Will X please tell me the length of his or her hair? Now suppose X is actually A, then A must answer. It is A's object in the game to try to cause C to make the wrong identification. His answer might therefore be

"My hair is shingled, and the longest strands are about nine inches long."

In order that tones of voice may not help the interrogator the answers should be written, or better still, typewritten. The ideal arrangement is to have a teleprinter communicating between the two rooms. Alternatively the question and answers can be repeated by an intermediary. The object of the game for the third player (B) is to help the interrogator. The best strategy for her is probably to give truthful answers. She can add such things as "I am the woman, don't listen to him!" to her answers, but it will avail nothing as the man can make similar remarks.

We now ask the question, "What will happen when a machine takes the part of A in this game?" Will the interrogator decide wrongly as often when the game is played like this as he does when the game is played between a man and a woman? These questions replace our original, "Can machines think?"

Critique of the New Problem

As well as asking, "What is the answer to this new form of the question," one may ask, "Is this new question a worthy one to investigate?" This latter question we investigate without further ado, thereby cutting short an infinite regress.

The new problem has the advantage of drawing a fairly sharp line between the physical and the intellectual capacities of a man. No engineer or chemist claims to be able to produce a material which is indistinguishable from the human skin. It is possible that at some time this might be done, but even supposing this invention available we should feel there was little point in trying to make a "thinking machine" more human by dressing it up in such artificial flesh. The form in which we have set the problem reflects this fact in the condition which prevents the interrogator from seeing or touching the other competitors, or hearing their voices. Some other advantages of the proposed criterion may be shown up by specimen questions and answers. Thus:

Q: Please write me a sonnet on the subject of the Forth Bridge.
A: Count me out on this one. I never could write poetry.
Q: Add 34957 to 70764.
A: (Pause about 30 seconds and then give as answer) 105721.

Q: Do you play chess?
A: Yes.
Q: I have K at my K1, and no other pieces. You have only K at K6 and R at R1. It is your move. What do you play?
A: (After a pause of 15 seconds) R-R8 mate.

The question and answer method seems to be suitable for introducing almost any one of the fields of human endeavor that we wish to include. We do not wish to penalize the machine for its inability to shine in beauty competitions, nor to penalize a man for losing in a race against an airplane. The conditions of our game make these disabilities irrelevant. The "witnesses" can brag, if they consider it advisable, as much as they please about their charms, strength or heroism, but the interrogator cannot demand practical demonstrations. . . .

The present interest in "thinking machines" has been aroused by a particular kind of machine, usually called an "electronic computer" or "digital computer." Following this suggestion we only permit digital computers to take part in our game.

This restriction appears at first sight to be a very drastic one. I shall attempt to show that it is not so in reality. To do this necessitates a short account of the nature and properties of these computers. . . .

Digital Computers

The idea behind digital computers may be explained by saying that these machines are intended to carry out any operations which could be done by a human computer. The human computer is supposed to be following fixed rules; he has no authority to deviate from them in any detail. We may suppose that these rules are supplied in a book which is altered whenever he is put on to a new job. He has also an unlimited supply of paper on which he does his calculations. He may also do his multiplications and additions on a "desk machine," but this is not important.

If we use the above explanation as a definition we shall be in danger of circularity of argument. We avoid this by giving an outline of the means by which the desired effect is achieved. A digital computer can usually be regarded as consisting of three parts:

(1) Store.
(2) Executive unit.
(3) Control.

The store is a store of information, and corresponds to the human computer's paper, whether this is the paper on which he does his calculations or that on which his book of rules is printed. Insofar as the human computer does calculations in his head a part of the store will correspond to his memory.

The executive unit is the part which carries out the various individual operations involved in a calculation. What these individual operations are will vary from machine to machine. Usually fairly lengthy operations can be done such as "Multiply 3540675445 by 7076345687" but in some machines only very simple ones such as "Write down o" are possible.

We have mentioned that the "book of rules" supplied to the computer is replaced in the machine by a part of the store. It is then called the "table of instructions." It is the duty of the control to see that these instructions are obeyed correctly and in the right order. The control is so constructed that this necessarily happens.

The information in the store is usually broken up into packets of moderately small size. In one machine, for instance, a packet might consist of ten decimal digits. Numbers are assigned to the parts of the store in which the various packets of information are stored, in some systematic manner. A typical instruction might say—

Add the number stored in position 6809 to that in 4302 and put the result back into the latter storage position.

Needless to say it would not occur in the machine expressed in English. It would more likely be coded in a form such as 6809430217. Here 17 says which of various possible operations is to be performed on the two numbers. In this case the operation is that described above, viz. "Add the number. . . ." It will be noticed that the instruction takes up 10 digits and so forms one packet of information, very conveniently. The control will normally take the instructions to be obeyed in the order of the positions in which they are stored, but occasionally an instruction such as

Now obey the instruction stored in position 5606, and continue from there

may be encountered, or again

If position 4505 contains 0 obey next the instruction stored in 6707, otherwise continue straight on.

Instructions of these latter types are very important because they make it possible for a sequence of operations to be repeated over and over again until some condition is fulfilled, but in doing so to obey, not fresh instructions on each repetition, but the same ones over and over again. To take a domestic analogy. Suppose Mother wants Tommy to call at the cobbler's every morning on his way to school to see if her shoes are done: she can ask him afresh every morning. Alternatively she can stick up a notice once and for all in the hall which he will see when he leaves for school and which tells him to call for the shoes, and also to destroy the notice when he comes back if he has the shoes with him.

The reader must accept it as a fact that digital computers can be constructed, and indeed have been constructed, according to the principles we have described, and that they can in fact mimic the actions of a human computer very closely. . . .

I believe that at the end of the century the use of words and general educated opinion will have altered so much that one will be able to speak of machines thinking without expecting to be contradicted. I believe further that no useful purpose is served by concealing these beliefs. The popular view that scientists proceed inexorably from well-established fact, never being influenced by any unproved conjecture, is quite mistaken. Provided it is made clear which are proved facts and which are conjectures, no harm can result. Conjectures are of great importance since they suggest useful lines of research.

I now proceed to consider opinions opposed to my own.

The Theological Objection

Thinking is a function of man's immortal soul. God has given an immortal soul to every man and woman, but not to any other animal or to machines. Hence no animal or machine can think.

I am unable to accept any part of this, but will attempt to reply in theological terms. I should find the argument more convincing if animals were classed with men, for there is a greater difference, to my mind, between the typical animate and the inanimate than there is between man and the other animals. The arbitrary character of the orthodox view becomes clearer if we consider how it might appear to a member of some other religious community. How do Christians regard the Moslem view that women have no souls? But let us leave this point aside and return to the main argument. It appears to me that the argument quoted above implies a serious restriction of the omnipotence of the Almighty. It is admitted that there are certain things that He cannot do such as making one equal to two, but should we not believe that He has freedom to confer a soul on an elephant if He sees fit? We might expect that He would only exercise this power in conjunction with a mutation which provided the elephant with an appropriately improved brain to minister to the needs of this soul. An argument of exactly similar form may be made for the case of machines. It may seem different because it is more difficult to "swallow." But this really only means that we think it would be less likely that He would consider the circumstances suitable for conferring a soul. The circumstances in question are discussed in the rest of this paper. In attempting to construct such machines we should not be irreverently usurping His power of creating souls, any more than we are in the procreation of children: rather we are, in either case, instruments of His will providing mansions for the souls that He creates.

However, this is mere speculation. I am not very impressed with theological arguments whatever they may be used to support. Such arguments have often been found unsatisfactory in the past. In the time of Galileo it was argued that the texts, "And the sun stood still . . . and hasted not to go down about a whole day" (Joshua x. 13) and "He laid the foundations of the earth, that it should not move at any time" (Psalm cv. 5) were an adequate refutation of the Copernican theory. With our present knowledge such an argument appears futile. When that knowledge was not available it made a quite different impression.

The "Heads in the Sand" Objection

"The consequences of machines thinking would be too dreadful. Let us hope and believe that they cannot do so."

This argument is seldom expressed quite so openly as in the form above. But it affects most of us who think about it at all. We like to believe that Man is in some subtle way superior to the rest of creation. It is best if he can be shown to be *necessarily* superior, for then there is no danger of him losing his commanding position. The popularity of the theological argument is clearly connected with this feeling. It is likely to be quite strong in intellectual people, since they value the power of thinking more highly than others, and are more inclined to base their belief in the superiority of Man on this power.

I do not think that this argument is sufficiently substantial to require refutation. Consolation would be more appropriate: perhaps this should be sought in the transmigration of souls. . . .

The Argument from Consciousness

This argument is very well expressed in Professor Jefferson's Lister Oration for 1949, from which I quote. "Not until a machine can write a sonnet or compose a concerto because of thoughts and emotions felt, and not by the chance fall of symbols, could we agree that machine equals brain—that is, not only write it but know that it had written it. No mechanism could feel (and not merely artificially signal, an easy contrivance) pleasure at its successes, grief when its valves fuse, be warmed by flattery, be made miserable by its mistakes, be charmed by sex, be angry or depressed when it cannot get what it wants."[1]

[1] G. Jefferson, "The Mind of Mechanical Man," *British Medical Journal*, Vol. 1 (1949). M.R.

This argument appears to be a denial of the validity of our test. According to the most extreme form of this view the only way by which one could be sure that a machine thinks is to *be* the machine and to feel oneself thinking. One could then describe these feelings to the world, but of course no one would be justified in taking any notice. Likewise according to this view the only way to know that a *man* thinks is to be that particular man. It is in fact the solipsist point of view. It may be the most logical view to hold but it makes communication of ideas difficult. A is liable to believe "A thinks but B does not" while B believes "B thinks but A does not." Instead of arguing continually over this point it is usual to have the polite convention that everyone thinks.

I am sure that Professor Jefferson does not wish to adopt the extreme and solipsist point of view. Probably he would be quite willing to accept the imitation game as a test. The game (with the player B omitted) is frequently used in practice under the name of *viva voce* to discover whether someone really understands something or has "learned it parrot fashion." Let us listen in to a part of such a *viva voce:*

Interrogator: In the first line of your sonnet which reads "Shall I compare thee to a summer's day," would not "a spring day" do as well or better?
Witness: It wouldn't scan.
Interrogator: How about "a winter's day." That would scan all right.
Witness: Yes, but nobody wants to be compared to a winter's day.

Interrogator: Would you say Mr. Pickwick reminded you of Christmas?
Witness: In a way.
Interrogator: Yet Christmas is a winter's day, and I do not think Mr. Pickwick would mind the comparison.
Witness: I don't think you're serious. By a winter's day one means a typical winter's day, rather than a special one like Christmas.

And so on. What would Professor Jefferson say if the sonnet-writing machine was able to answer like this in the *viva voce?* I do not know whether he would regard the machine as "merely artificially signaling" these answers, but if the answers were as satisfactory and sustained as in the above passage I do not think he would describe it as "an easy contrivance." This phrase is, I think, intended to cover such devices as the inclusion in machine of a record of someone reading a sonnet, with appropriate switching to turn it on from time to time.

In short then, I think that most of those who support the argument from consciousness could be persuaded to abandon it rather than be forced into the solipsist position. They will then probably be willing to accept our test.

I do not wish to give the impression that I think there is no mystery about consciousness. There is, for instance, something of a paradox connected with any attempt to localize it. But I do not think these mysteries necessarily need to be solved before we can answer the question with which we are concerned in this paper.

Arguments from Various Disabilities

These arguments take the form, "I grant you that you can make machines do all the things you have mentioned but you will never be able to make one to do X." Numerous features X are suggested in this connection. I offer a selection:

> Be kind, resourceful, beautiful, friendly (p. 19), have initiative, have a sense of humor, tell right from wrong, make mistakes (p. 19), fall in love, enjoy strawberries and cream (p. 19), make someone fall in love with it, learn from experience (pp. 25f.), use words properly, be the subject of his own thought (p. 20), have as much diversity of behavior as a man, do something really new (p. 20). (Some of these disabilities are given special consideration as indicated by the page numbers.)

No support is usually offered for these statements. I believe they are mostly founded on the principle of scientific induction. A man has seen thousands of machines in his lifetime. From what he sees of them he draws a number of general conclusions. They are ugly, each is designed for a very limited purpose, when required for a minutely different purpose they are useless, the variety of behavior of any one of them is very small, etc., etc. Naturally he concludes that these are necessary properties of machines in general. Many of these limitations are associated with the very small storage capacity of most machines. (I am assuming that the idea of storage capacity is extended in some way to cover machines other than discrete state machines. The exact definition does not matter as no mathematical accuracy is claimed in the present discussion.) A few years ago, when very little had been heard of digital computers, it was possible to elicit much incredulity concerning them, if one mentioned their properties without describing their construction. That was presumably due to a similar application of the principle of scientific induction. These applications of the principle are of course largely unconscious. When a burned child fears the fire and shows that he fears it by avoiding it, I should say that he was applying scientific induction. (I could of course also describe his behavior in many other ways.) The works and customs of mankind do not seem to be very suitable material to which to apply scientific induction. A very large part of space-time must be investigated if reliable results are to be obtained. Otherwise we may (as most English children do) decide that everybody speaks English, and that it is silly to learn French.

There are, however, special remarks to be made about many of the disabilities that have been mentioned. The inability to enjoy strawberries and cream may have struck the reader as frivolous. Possibly a machine might be made to enjoy this delicious dish, but any attempt to make one do so would be idiotic. . . .

The claim that "machines cannot make mistakes" seems a curious one. One is tempted to retort, "Are they any the worse for that?" But let us adopt a more sympathetic attitude, and try to see what is really meant. I think this criticism can be explained in terms of the imitation game. It is claimed that the interrogator could distinguish the machine from the man simply by setting them a number of problems in arithmetic. The machine would be unmasked because of its deadly accuracy. The reply to this is simple. The machine (programed for playing the game) would not attempt to give the *right* answers to the arithmetic problems. It would deliberately introduce mistakes in a manner calculated to confuse the interrogator. A mechanical fault would probably show itself through an unsuitable decision as to what sort of a mistake to make in the arithmetic. Even this interpretation of the criticism is not sufficiently sympathetic. But we cannot afford the space to go into it much further. It seems to me that this criticism depends on a confusion between two kinds of mistakes. We may call them "errors of functioning" and "errors of conclusion." Errors of functioning are due to some mechanical or electrical fault which causes the machine to behave otherwise than it was designed to do. In philosophical discussions one likes to ignore the possibility of such errors; one is therefore discussing "abstract machines." These abstract machines are mathematical fictions rather than physical objects. By definition they are incapable of errors of functioning. In this sense we can truly say that "machines can never make mistakes." Errors of conclusion can only arise when some meaning is attached to the output signals from the machine. The machine might, for instance, type out mathematical equations, or sentences in English. When a false proposition is typed we say that the machine has committed an error of conclusion. There is clearly no reason at all for saying that a machine cannot make this kind of mistake. It might do nothing but type out repeatedly "0 = 1." To take a less perverse example, it might have some method for drawing conclusions by scientific induction. We must expect such a method to lead occasionally to erroneous results.

The claim that a machine cannot be the subject of its own thought can of course only be answered if it can be shown that the machine has *some* thought with *some* subject matter. Nevertheless, "the subject matter of a machine's operations" does seem to mean something, at least to the people who deal with it. If, for instance, the machine was trying to find a solution of equation $x^2 - 40x - 11 = 0$ one would be tempted to describe this equation as part of the machine's subject matter at that moment. In this sort of sense a machine undoubtedly can be its own subject matter. It may be used to help in making up its own programs, or to predict the effect of alterations in its own structure. By observing the results of its own behavior it can modify its own programs so as to achieve some purpose more effectively. These are possibilities of the near future, rather than Utopian dreams.

The criticism that a machine cannot have much diversity of behavior is just a way of saying that it cannot have much storage capacity. Until fairly recently a storage capacity of even a thousand digits was very rare.

The criticisms that we are considering here are often disguised forms of the argument from consciousness. Usually if one maintains that a machine *can* do one of these things, and describes the kind of method that the machine could use, one will not make much of an impression. It is thought that the method (whatever it may be, for it must be mechanical) is really rather base. Compare the parenthesis in Jefferson's statement quoted above.

Lady Lovelace's Objection.[2] . . .

A variant of Lady Lovelace's objection states that a machine can "never do anything really new." This may be parried for a moment with the saw, "There is nothing new under the sun." Who can be certain that "original work" that he has done was not simply the growth of the seed planted in him by teaching, or the effect of following well-known general principles. A better variant of the objection says that a machine can never "take us by surprise." This statement is a more direct challenge and can be met directly. Machines take me by surprise with great frequency. This is largely because I do not do sufficient calculation to decide what to expect them to do, or rather because, although I do a calculation, I do it in a hurried, slipshod fashion, taking risks. Perhaps I say to myself, "I suppose the voltage here ought to be the same as there: anyway let's assume it is." Naturally I am often wrong, and the result

is a surprise for me, for by the time the experiment is done these assumptions have been forgotten. These admissions lay me open to lectures on the subject of my vicious ways, but do not throw any doubt on my credibility when I testify to the surprises I experience.

I do not expect this reply to silence my critic. He will probably say that such surprises are due to some creative mental act on my part, and reflect no credit on the machine. This leads us back to the argument from consciousness, and far from the idea of surprise. It is a line of argument we must consider closed, but it is perhaps worth remarking that the appreciation of something as surprising requires as much of a "creative mental act" whether the surprising event originates from a man, a book, a machine or anything else.

The view that machines cannot give rise to surprises is due, I believe, to a fallacy to which philosophers and mathematicians are particularly subject. This is the assumption that as soon as a fact is presented to a mind all consequences of that fact spring into the mind simultaneously with it. It is a very useful assumption under many circumstances, but one too easily forgets that it is false. A natural consequence of doing so is that one then assumes that there is no virtue in the mere working out of consequences from data and general principles. . .

The reader will have anticipated that I have no very convincing arguments of a positive nature to support my views. If I had I should not have taken such pains to point out the fallacies in contrary views. Such evidence as I have I shall now give.

[2] Characterizing a project to construct a computer, the Countess of Lovelace declared that a machine cannot originate anything—it can only perform what human beings "order it to perform." (*Scientific Memoirs*, 1842)—M.R.

Let us return for a moment to Lady Lovelace's objection, which stated that the machine can only do what we tell it to do. One could say that a man can "inject" an idea into the machine, and that it will respond to a certain extent and then drop into quiescence, like a piano string struck by a hammer. Another simile would be an atomic pile of less than critical size: an injected idea is to correspond to a neutron entering the pile from without. Each such neutron will cause a certain disturbance which eventually dies away. If, however, the size of the pile is sufficiently increased, the disturbance caused by such an incoming neutron will very likely go on and on increasing until the whole pile is destroyed. Is there a corresponding phenomenon for minds, and is there one for machines? There does seem to be one for the human mind. The majority of them seem to be "subcritical," i.e., to correspond in this analogy to piles of subcritical size. An idea presented to such a mind will on an average give rise to less than one idea in reply. A smallish proportion are supercritical. An idea presented to such a mind may give rise to a whole "theory" consisting of secondary, tertiary and more remote ideas. Animals' minds seem to be very definitely subcritical. Adhering to this analogy we ask, "Can a machine be made to be supercritical?"

The "skin of an onion" analogy is also helpful. In considering the functions of the mind or the brain we find certain operations which we can explain in purely mechanical terms. This we say does not correspond to the real mind: it is a sort of skin which we must strip off if we are to find the real mind. But then in what remains we find a further skin to be stripped off, and so on. Proceeding in this way do we ever come to the "real" mind, or do we eventually come to the skin which has nothing in it? In the latter case the whole mind is mechanical. (It would not be a discrete state machine however. We have discussed this.)

These last two paragraphs do not claim to be convincing arguments. They should rather be described as "recitations tending to produce belief." . . .

As I have explained, the problem is mainly one of programing. Advances in engineering will have to be made too, but it seems unlikely that these will not be adequate for the requirements. Estimates of the storage capacity of the brain vary from 10^{10} to 10^{15} binary digits. I incline to the lower values and believe that only a very small fraction is used for the higher types of thinking. Most of it is probably used for the retention of visual impressions. I should be surprised if more than 10^9 was required for satisfactory playing of the imitation game, at any rate against a blind man. (Note: The capacity of the *Encyclopaedia Britannica*, eleventh edition, is 2×10^9.) A storage capacity of 10^7 would be a very practicable possibility even by present techniques. It is probably not necessary to increase the speed of operations of the machines at all. Parts of modern machines which can be regarded as analogues of nerve cells work about a thousand times faster than the latter. This should provide a "margin of safety" which could cover losses of speed arising in many ways. Our problem then is to find out how to program these machines to play the game. At my present rate of working I produce about a thousand digits of program a day, so that about sixty workers, working steadily through the fifty years might accomplish the job, if nothing went into the wastepaper basket. Some more expeditious method seems desirable. . . .

We may hope that machines will eventually compete with men in all purely intellectual fields. But which are the best ones to start with? Even this is a difficult decision. Many people think that a very abstract activity, like the playing of chess, would be best. It can also be maintained that it is best to provide the machine with the best sense organs that money can buy, and then teach it to understand and speak English. This process could follow the normal teaching of a child. Things would be pointed out and named, etc. Again I do not know what the right answer is, but I think both approaches should be tried.

We can only see a short distance ahead, but we can see plenty there that needs to be done.

COMMENT

Ancient and Modern Materialism

Although Lucretius wrote his poem over two thousand years ago, his vision of a materialistic universe remains as fresh and vivid as ever it was. This may seem strange to a reader familiar with the history of ideas. Have not science and the naturalistic philosophy based upon it undergone an immense revolution since the time of Lucretius? Even the more modern materialism of Hobbes and La Mettrie appears quaint and archaic in the light of recent science and philosophy. We can no longer conceive of matter in the form of tiny indivisible particles, like the motes of dust that we see dancing about in a shaft of sunlight. The atomic theory has been transplanted from metaphysical speculation to experimental research, and the resulting discoveries have radically transformed it.

Few people would now question the existence of atoms, but the atoms are no longer conceived as inert, eternal, and indivisible particles moving·in a featureless void. Instead of being inert, they are made up of electrical charges which behave like waves. Instead of being eternal, they emit radiations and are subject to splittings and fusions. Instead of being indivisible, they can be analyzed into electrons, protons, neutrons, mesons, positrons, and so on. Instead of moving in a void, they are enmeshed in "electromagnetic fields" within "curved" space-time. These modern concepts of radiation, fission, quanta, waves, fields, and relativity are a far cry from Lucretius.

Yet the naturalistic temper of his philosophy as distinguished from the archaic details of his science remains as up-to-date as ever. Nothing in modern physics contradicts his vision of all things arising from and returning to a material base. The view of the world that some philosophers prefer to call naturalism rather than materialism remains as plausible as ever. This is the view that the universe as revealed in the physical sciences is primary and fundamental in the nature of things.

Can Materialism Explain Perceptual Appearances?

Extreme materialism tries to explain every process in terms of matter and motion quantitatively described. "Primary qualities," which are abstract and measurable, are conceived to be more ultimate or objective, whereas "secondary qualities," which are concrete and unmeasurable, are regarded as more derivative or subjective. This distinction was first clearly stated by Democritus:

> There are two kinds of knowledge: real knowledge and obscure knowledge. To obscure knowledge belong all things of sight, sound, odor, taste, and touch; real knowledge is distinct from this . . . Sweet and bitter, heat and cold, and color, are only opinions; there is nothing true but atoms and the void.[1]

For Democritus, the only objective properties of things are size, shape, weight, and motion. All other qualities, such as sound, color, odor, taste, and touch, are sensations in us caused by the motions and arrangements of the atoms.

This theory was revived by Galileo and was reformulated by Hobbes, Locke, Newton, and other influential modern thinkers. It has figured very prominently in modern theories of perception. Warmth, for example, is explained as the reaction of our sense organs and nervous systems to molecular motions; sound, as our reaction to air waves; color, as our reaction to electromagnetic vibrations. Thus the "secondary qualities"—colors, sounds, odors, and so on—exist, as such, only for our minds. In the absence of our mental reactions, the universe is a pretty dull and abstract affair—a collection of soundless, colorless, and odorless particles, in various arrangements, drifting through space and time.

Lucretius, departing from the views of Democritus, had a different theory. He agreed that the atoms individually are without any of the secondary qualities, but maintained that these qualities spring into existence when the atoms are combined in certain ways. "The first-bodies," he tells us, are not only "bereft . . . of color, they are also sundered altogether from warmth and cold, and fiery heat, and are carried along barren of sound and devoid of taste, nor do they give off any scent of their own from their body." But these qualities *are* properties of compounds, formed by combinations of atoms. The compounds, being new and different entities, have color, sound, odor, taste, and heat, none of which can belong to the

[1] Translated by Philip Wheelwright, *The Way of Philosophy* (New York: Odyssey Press, 1954), p. 162.

atoms as individual particles. When we perceive these secondary qualities we are grasping real objective properties, for the complex body perceived by our senses is as real as the atoms.

Whatever interpretation is adopted, whether that of Democritus, Lucretius, or a modern materialist, is subject to all the difficulties discussed by Bertrand Russell in this chapter. The qualities of perception belong to appearances ("sense-data") which depend at least in part on the reactions of the sentient organism. To profess to know what is behind the sensory appearances is to leap into conjecture. Russell indicates just how conjectural this leap is.

Even if we accept the conclusions drawn from modern physical science, the electrons, protons, neutrons, mesons, positrons, and other abstract entities, with their fields of force and curved space-time environment, are very unlike human perceptions. To what extent are the appearances verifiable? To what extent are the *inferences* from these appearances also verifiable? To what extent are the appearances merely reactions in us? To what extent are they like "things" in the real external world? These are questions that should not be answered without reviewing the difficulties pointed out by Russell.

Can Materialism Explain Life?

Can a materialist account for the difference between animate and inanimate things?

An extreme materialist will not admit any such fundamental cleavage. Plant and animal activity, he will maintain, is reducible simply to physical and chemical forces exactly like those found in inorganic bodies. Living things are composed exclusively of substances that may also be found in nonliving things, and there are no teleological or vitalistic forces that explain life. In opposition to this point of view, "vitalists" such as Henri Bergson maintain that life is distinct and fundamentally different from nonlife.

Vitalism is not as plausible as it was earlier in this century. We are now aware of intermediate forms such as viruses that cannot be easily classified as either organic or inorganic. There are chemical substances which grow and multiply—they behave in some ways as if they were alive and in other ways as if they were not. Even machines, as Turing points out, display marks of behavior which were hitherto regarded as characteristic of living things only. It has become increasingly difficult to differentiate between the behavior of living and lifeless things.

More plausible than a sharp and everlasting dualism of the inorganic and the organic is the doctrine of emergence. This is the theory that life and mind evolve out of the nonliving and the nonmental. Lucretius can be called a believer in emergence. He pointed out that men can speak and laugh and think whereas it would be absurd to attribute these capacities to atoms. A human organism, made up of innumerable atoms, has vital characteristics which the atoms taken singly do not possess. Just as the meaning of a sentence results from the combinations of meaningless letters, so life and mind result from the meetings and configurations of lifeless and mindless atoms. Applied to evolution, this theory means the recognition of diverse levels of complexity and organization, each with its emergent qualities, and the interpretation of these levels as successive stages in an evolutionary process. We associate this type of theory with such modern philosophers as Samuel Alexander (1859–1938), but it was maintained by Lucretius two thousand years ago.

Its implications are, in the wide sense of the word, "materialistic." Mind, it declares, arises out of matter and is a function of complex material bodies. "Out of dust man arises and to dust will he return." Vital processes, including thought, cannot survive the dissolution of the body any more than a football game can continue after the disbanding of the opposing teams.

The type of materialism called "epiphenomenalism" admits that there are mental processes but regards them as mere ineffectual byproducts of physical processes. The only causal relations are between physical events and other physical events, or between physical antecedents and mental consequents. Our thoughts and feelings are caused by molecular changes in the brain or other physical processes and have no causal efficacy of their own. The mind has as little to do with the movement of the body as the shadow cast by a locomotive has to do with the racing of the locomotive.

Lucretius is not consistent enough to be called an epiphenomenalist, but for the most part he clings to a materialistic interpretation of the *causes* of mental events. He maintains, for example, that all knowledge is derived from sensations caused by the impact on the mind-atoms of surface-films emanating from external physical objects. But he departs from epiphenomenalism with its extreme mechanistic implications in his theory of "swerving" atoms and concomitant free will.

Consideration of these alternative theories—vitalism, emergence, and epiphenomenalism—will provide ample ground for discussion.

Can Materialism Explain Mind?

Can a materialist account for mental characteristics?

The most extreme kind of materialism, exemplified by some radical mechanists and behaviorists, is the virtual denial that we have minds at all. Since we are all aware that there are mental processes, such as reasoning, willing, feeling, perceiving, remembering, and imagining, we need not argue the point.

More sensible than the denial that human beings experience mental processes is the contention that machines can, in a sense, "think." Since World War II there has been an amazing development of "electronic brains" or "thinking machines." They can perform lightning computations of the most complex kind—they can play chess, prove theorems, translate from one language to another, and guide rockets through interplanetary space. These astounding performances have reinforced the contention that the human mind is just a very complicated mechanism. In his article "Computing Machines and Intelligence," A. M. Turing argues that technicians will eventually be able to create machines with artificial intelligence so sophisticated that it cannot, under certain conditions (for example, "the imitation game"), be distinguished from human intelligence. Turing contends that we should then concede that machines can think.

An opponent would object that we cannot determine whether a machine can think by the mere observation of outputs, however cleverly they might simulate human behavior. It is not simply *what* the machine does but *how* it does it that must be considered. If by thought one means *conscious* deliberations and initiatives the machine does not think.

Every conscious human being is aware of his or her own mental life—the sensations, feelings of pleasure and pain, hopes and dreams and fancies, loves and hates, plans and purposes. No machine has such an "inner life" or any self-conscious awareness. As Wladyslaw Sluckin, who is both a psychologist and an engineer, has written:

> Machines do not form their purposes in the manner of human beings, the purposes of machines are decided for them by their inventors or operators. It would be absurd to praise or blame a machine for results of its operations other than in a metaphorical way. Machines have no ethical sentiments and no effective attitudes. In no situation are machines expected to pass moral judgment. The question as to whether machines could possibly exhibit purpose in this sense of the word is nonsensical because it does not appear in any way feasible to describe robot behavior in terms which ascribe to it morality.[2]

Do these considerations refute extreme materialism? If so, is there a good defence of materialism of a less sweeping and reductive kind? The near-behaviorism of Gilbert Ryle in Chapter 6 or the full-fledged behaviorism of B. F. Skinner in Chapter 18 may supply the answer. Whether there are sound approximations to materialism the reader may wish to consider now or later.

---

[2] *Minds and Machines* (Baltimore: Penguin Boooks Inc., revised edition, 1960), p. 213.

5

Idealism

GEORGE BERKELEY (1685–1753)

Berkeley was born in Kilkenny County, Ireland. His parents, having a comfortable income, gave him a good education at Kilkenny School and Trinity College, Dublin. While scarcely more than a boy, he began to fill notebooks with original philosophical reflections. His first major publication, *An Essay Toward a New Theory of Vision,* appeared when he was twenty-four, and *Principles of Human Knowledge,* which set forth his whole idealistic philosophy, was published only a year later. Finding that his ideas were ridiculed, if not neglected, he reformulated his argument in *Three Dialogues Between Hylas and Philonous,* which appeared in 1713. Thus, by the time he was twenty-eight, he had published his three major works, remarkable both for the felicity of their style and for the daring and profundity of their thought.

During this period of his greatest literary activity, Berkeley was a fellow and tutor at Trinity College, but he spent the next years after publishing his *Dialogues* in London, France, and Italy. In London, he became the friend of Pope, Steele, Addison, and Swift. Subsequently he traveled in Europe as secretary and chaplain to an earl and tutor to a bishop's son. While in Sicily, he lost the manuscript of the second part of *The Principles of Human Knowledge* and never had the heart to rewrite it.

Returning to Ireland, he was appointed Lecturer in Greek and Theology at Trinity College and eventually an ecclesiastical Dean (1724). Shortly thereafter, to his immense surprise, he inherited three thousand pounds from Hester Van Homrigh (Swift's former friend "Vanessa"), a lady whom he had met once and then only casually.

At about the same time, he conceived the project of founding a college in the Bermudas for training missionaries to the Indians and clergymen for the American colonists. By his eloquence and personal charm, he was able to obtain a considerable sum to finance his project from private donors and the promise of twenty thousand pounds from the House of Commons. With a new wife, he set sail for America in 1728. But Walpole, the Prime Minister, refused to fulfill the promise of Parliament, and Berkeley remained for three years at Newport, Rhode Island, his hopes gradually diminishing. Finally, in 1731, despairing of further aid and saddened by the death of an infant daughter, he sailed with his wife and tiny son back to England.

His later life was spent as Bishop of Cloyne and head of a growing family. He divided his time between ecclesiastical duties, philosophical studies, agitation for social reform, and family affairs. His main publication in these years was *Siris* (1744), a rather odd work in which he extolled the medicinal virtues of tar-water and expounded an idealistic interpretation of the Universe. In the final year of his life, Berkeley and his family moved to Oxford, where, "suddenly and without the least previous notice or pain," he died in 1753.

Mind and Its Objects

The First Dialogue

Philonous. Good morning, *Hylas:* I did not expect to find you abroad so early.

Hyl. It is indeed something unusual;

London, 1713. Second unchanged edition, 1725. Third edition, 1734. The present text is that of A. Campbell Fraser, *The Works of George Berkeley*. Oxford: Clarendon Press, 1871. (With omissions.)

but my thoughts were so taken up with a subject I was discoursing of last night, that finding I could not sleep, I resolved to rise and take a turn in the garden.

Phil. It happened well, to let you see what innocent and agreeable pleasures you lose every morning. Can there be a pleasanter time of the day, or a more delightful season of the year? That purple sky, those wild but sweet notes of birds, the fragrant bloom upon the trees and flowers, the gentle influence of the rising sun, these and a thousand nameless beauties of nature inspire the soul with secret transports; its faculties too being at this time fresh and lively, are fit for these meditations, which the solitude of a garden and tranquillity of the morning naturally dispose us to. But I am afraid I interrupt your thoughts: for you seemed very intent on something.

Hyl. It is true, I was, and shall be obliged to you if you will permit me to go on in the same vein; not that I would by any means deprive myself of your company, for my thoughts always flow more easily in conversation with a friend, than when I am alone: but my request is, that you would suffer me to impart my reflections to you.

Phil. With all my heart, it is what I should have requested myself if you had not prevented me.

Hyl. I was considering the odd fate of those men who have in all ages, through an affectation of being distinguished from the vulgar, or some unaccountable turn of thought, pretended either to believe nothing at all, or to believe the most extravagant things in the world. This however might be borne, if their paradoxes and scepticism did not draw after them some consequences of general disadvantage to mankind. But the mischief lieth here; that when men of less leisure see them who are supposed to have spent their whole time in the pursuits of knowledge professing an entire ignorance of all things, or advancing such notions as are repugnant to plain and commonly

received principles, they will be tempted to entertain suspicions concerning the most important truths, which they had hitherto held sacred and unquestionable.

Phil. I entirely agree with you, as to the ill tendency of the affected doubts of some philosophers, and fantastical conceits of others. . . .

Hyl. I am glad to find there was nothing in the accounts I heard of you.

Phil. Pray, what were those?

Hyl. You were represented in last night's conversation, as one who maintained the most extravagant opinion that ever entered into the mind of man, to wit, that there is no such thing as *material substance* in the world.

Phil. That there is no such thing as what Philosophers call *material substance,* I am seriously persuaded: but, if I were made to see anything absurd or sceptical in this, I should then have the same reason to renounce this that I imagine I have now to reject the contrary opinion.

Hyl. What! can anything be more fantastical, more repugnant to common sense, or a more manifest piece of Scepticism, than to believe there is no such thing as *matter?*

Phil. Softly, good *Hylas.* What if it should prove, that you, who hold there is, are, by virtue of that opinion, a greater sceptic, and maintain more paradoxes and repugnances to common sense, than I who believe no such thing?

Hyl. You may as soon persuade me, the part is greater than the whole, as that, in order to avoid absurdity and Scepticism, I should ever be obliged to give up my opinion in this point.

Phil. Well then, are you content to admit that opinion for true, which, upon examination, shall appear most agreeable to common sense, and remote from Scepticism?

Hyl. With all my heart. Since you are for raising disputes about the plainest things in nature, I am content for once to hear what you have to say. . . .

Phil. Shall we therefore examine which of us it is that denies the reality of sensible things, or professes the greatest ignorance of them; since, if I take you rightly, he is to be esteemed the greatest *sceptic?*

Hyl. That is what I desire.

Phil. What mean you by Sensible Things?

Hyl. Those things which are perceived by the senses. Can you imagine that I mean anything else?

Phil. Pardon me, *Hylas,* if I am desirous clearly to apprehend your notions, since this may much shorten our inquiry. Suffer me then to ask you this further question. Are those things only perceived by the senses which are perceived immediately? Or, may those things properly be said to be *sensible* which are perceived mediately, or not without the intervention of others?

Hyl. I do not sufficiently understand you.

Phil. In reading a book, what I immediately perceive are the letters, but mediately, or by means of these, are suggested to my mind the notions of God, virtue, truth, &c. Now, that the letters are truly sensible things, or perceived by sense, there is no doubt: but I would know whether you take the things suggested by them to be so too.

Hyl. No, certainly; it were absurd to think *God* or *virtue* sensible things, though they may be signified and suggested to the mind by sensible marks, with which they have an arbitrary connection.

Phil. It seems then, that by *sensible things* you mean those only which can be perceived *immediately* by sense?

Hyl. Right.

Phil. Doth it not follow from this, that though I see one part of the sky red, and another blue, and that my reason doth thence evidently conclude there must be some cause of that diversity of colors, yet that cause cannot be said to be a sensible thing, or perceived by the sense of seeing?

Hyl. It doth.

Phil. In like manner, though I hear variety of sounds, yet I cannot be said to hear the causes of those sounds?

Hyl. You cannot.

Phil. And when by my touch I perceive a thing to be hot and heavy, I cannot say, with any truth or propriety, that I feel the cause of its heat or weight?

Hyl. To prevent any more questions of this kind, I tell you once for all, that by *sensible things* I mean those only which are perceived by sense, and that in truth the senses perceive nothing which they do not perceive immediately: for they make no inferences. The deducing therefore of causes or occasions from effects and appearances, which alone are perceived by sense, entirely relates to reason.

Phil. This point then is agreed between us—that *sensible things are those only which are immediately perceived by sense*. You will further inform me, whether we immediately perceive by sight anything beside light, and colors, and figures; or by hearing, anything but sounds; by the palate, anything beside tastes; by the smell, beside odors; or by the touch, more than tangible qualities.

Hyl. We do not.

Phil. It seems, therefore, that if you take away all sensible qualities, there remains nothing sensible?

Hyl. I grant it.

Phil. Sensible things therefore are nothing else but so many sensible qualities, or combinations of sensible qualities?

Hyl. Nothing else.

Phil. Heat is then a sensible thing?

Hyl. Certainly.

Phil. Doth the reality of sensible things consist in being perceived? or, is it something distinct from their being perceived, and that bears no relation to the mind?

Hyl. To *exist* is one thing, and to be *perceived* is another.

Phil. I speak with regard to sensible things only: and of these I ask, whether by their real existence you mean a subsistence exterior to the mind, and distinct from their being perceived?

Hyl. I mean a real absolute being, distinct from, and without any relation to their being perceived.

Phil. Heat therefore, if it be allowed a real being, must exist without the mind?

Hyl. It must.

Phil. Tell me, *Hylas,* is this real existence equally compatible to all degrees of heat, which we perceive; or is there

any reason why we should attribute it to some, and deny it to others? and if there be, pray let me know that reason.

Hyl. Whatever degree of heat we perceive by sense, we may be sure the same exists in the object that occasions it.

Phil. What! the greatest as well as the least?

Hyl. I tell you, the reason is plainly the same in respect of both: they are both perceived by sense; nay, the greater degree of heat is more sensibly perceived; and consequently, if there is any difference, we are more certain of its real existence than we can be of the reality of a lesser degree.

Phil. But is not the most vehement and intense degree of heat a very great pain?

Hyl. No one can deny it.

Phil. And is any unperceiving thing capable of pain or pleasure?

Hyl. No certainly.

Phil. Is your material substance a senseless being, or a being endowed with sense and perception?

Hyl. It is senseless without doubt.

Phil. It cannot therefore be the subject of pain?

Hyl. By no means.

Phil. Nor consequently of the greatest heat perceived by sense, since you acknowledge this to be no small pain?

Hyl. I grant it.

Phil. What shall we say then of your external object; is it a material Substance, or no?

Hyl. It is a material substance with the sensible qualities inhering in it.

Phil. How then can a great heat exist in it, since you own it cannot in a material substance? I desire you would clear this point.

Hyl. Hold, *Philonous,* I fear I was out in yielding intense heat to be a pain. It should seem rather, that pain is something distinct from heat, and the consequence or effect of it.

Phil. Upon putting your hand near the fire, do you perceive one simple uniform sensation, or two distinct sensations?

Hyl. But one simple sensation.

Phil. Is not the heat immediately perceived?

Hyl. It is.

Phil. And the pain?

Hyl. True.

Phil. Seeing therefore they are both immediately perceived at the same time, and the fire affects you only with one simple, or uncompounded idea, it follows that this same simple idea is both the intense heat immediately perceived, and the pain; and, consequently, that the intense heat immediately perceived, is nothing distinct from a particular sort of pain.

Hyl. It seems so.

Phil. Again, try in your thoughts, *Hylas,* if you can conceive a vehement sensation to be without pain or pleasure.

Hyl. I cannot.

Phil. Or can you frame to yourself an idea of sensible pain or pleasure, in general, abstracted from every particular idea of heat, cold, tastes, smells? &c.

Hyl. I do not find that I can.

Phil. Doth it not therefore follow, **that sensible pain is nothing distinct** from those sensations or ideas—in an intense degree?

Hyl. It is undeniable; and, to speak the truth, I begin to suspect a very great heat cannot exist but in a mind perceiving it.

Phil. What! are you then in that *sceptical* state of suspense, between affirming and denying?

Hyl. I think I may be positive in the point. A very violent and painful heat cannot exist without the mind.

Phil. It hath not therefore, according to you, any real being?

Hyl. I own it.

Phil. Is it therefore certain, that there is no body in nature really hot?

Hyl. I have ñot denied there is any real heat in bodies. I only say, there is no such thing as an intense real heat.

Phil. But, did you not say before that all degrees of heat were equally real; or, if there was any difference, that the greater were more undoubtedly real than the lesser?

Hyl. True: but it was because I did not then consider the ground there is for distinguishing between them, which I now plainly see. And it is this:—because intense heat is nothing else but a particular kind of painful sensation; and pain cannot exist but in a perceiving being; it follows that no intense heat can really exist in an unperceiving corporeal substance. But this is no reason why we should deny heat in an inferior degree to exist in such a substance.

Phil. But how shall we be able to discern those degrees of heat which exist only in the mind from those which exist without it?

Hyl. That is no difficult matter. You know the least pain cannot exist unperceived; whatever, therefore, degree of heat is a pain exists only in the mind. But, as for all other degrees of heat, nothing obliges us to think the same of them.

Phil. I think you granted before that no unperceiv.ng being was capable of pleasure, any more than of pain.

Hyl. I did.

Phil. And is not warmth, or a more gentle degree of heat than what causes uneasiness, a pleasure?

Hyl. What then?

Phil. Consequently, it cannot exist without the mind in an unperceiving substance, or body.

Hyl. So it seems.

Phil. Since, therefore, as well those degrees of heat that are not painful, as those that are, can exist only in a thinking substance; may we not conclude that external bodies are absolutely incapable of any degree of heat whatsoever?

Hyl. On second thoughts, I do not think it so evident that warmth is a pleasure, as that a great degree of heat is a pain.

Phil. I do not pretend that warmth is as great a pleasure as heat is a pain. But, if you grant it to be even a small pleasure, it serves to make good my conclusion.

Hyl. I could rather call it an *indolence*. It seems to be nothing more than a privation of both pain and pleasure. And that such a quality or state as this may agree to an unthinking substance, I hope you will not deny.

Phil. If you are resolved to maintain that warmth, or a gentle degree of heat, is no pleasure, I know not how to convince you otherwise, than by appealing to your own sense. But what think you of cold?

Hyl. The same that I do of heat. An intense degree of cold is a pain; for to feel a very great cold, is to perceive a great uneasiness: it cannot therefore exist without the mind; but a lesser degree of cold may, as well as a lesser degree of heat.

Phil. Those bodies, therefore, upon whose application to our own, we perceive a moderate degree of heat, must be concluded to have a moderate degree of heat or warmth in them; and those, upon whose application we feel a like degree of cold, must be thought to have cold in them.

Hyl. They must.

Phil. Can any doctrine be true that necessarily leads a man into an absurdity?

Hyl. Without doubt it cannot.

Phil. Is it not an absurdity to think that the same thing should be at the same time both cold and warm?

Hyl. It is.

Phil. Suppose now one of your hands hot, and the other cold, and that they are both at once put into the same vessel of water, in an intermediate state; will not the water seem cold to one hand, and warm to the other?

Hyl. It will.

Phil. Ought we not therefore, by our principles, to conclude it is really both cold and warm at the same time, that is, according to your own concession, to believe an absurdity?

Hyl. I confess it seems so.

Phil. Consequently, the principles themselves are false, since you have granted that no true principle leads to an absurdity.

Hyl. But, after all, can anything be more absurd than to say, *there is no heat in the fire?*

Phil. To make the point still clearer; tell me whether, in two cases exactly alike, we ought not to make the same judgment?

Hyl. We ought.

Phil. When a pin pricks your finger, doth it not rend and divide the fibers of your flesh?

Hyl. It doth.

Phil. And when a coal burns your finger, doth it any more?

Hyl. It doth not.

Phil. Since, therefore, you neither judge the sensation itself occasioned by the pin, nor anything like it to be in the pin; you should not, conformably to what you have now granted, judge the sensation occasioned by the fire, or anything like it, to be in the fire.

Hyl. Well, since it must be so, I am content to yield this point, and acknowledge that heat and cold are only sensations existing in our minds. But there still remain qualities enough to secure the reality of external things.

Phil. But what will you say, *Hylas,* if it shall appear that the case is the same with regard to all other sensible qualities, and that they can no more be supposed to exist without the mind, than heat and cold?

Hyl. Then indeed you will have done something to the purpose; but that is what I despair of seeing proved.

Phil. Let us examine them in order. What think you of *tastes*—do they exist without the mind, or no?

Hyl. Can any man in his senses doubt whether sugar is sweet, or wormwood bitter?

Phil. Inform me, *Hylas.* Is a sweet taste a particular kind of pleasure or pleasant sensation, or is it not?

Hyl. It is.

Phil. And is not bitterness some kind of uneasiness or pain?

Hyl. I grant it.

Phil. If therefore sugar and wormwood are unthinking corporeal substances existing without the mind, how can sweetness and bitterness, that is, pleasure and pain, agree to them?

Hyl. Hold, *Philonous,* I now see what it was deluded me all this time. You asked whether heat and cold, sweetness and bitterness, were not particular sorts of pleasure and pain; to which I answered simply, that they were. Whereas I should have thus distinguished:— those qualities, as perceived by us, are pleasures or pains; but not as existing in the external objects. We must not therefore conclude absolutely, that there is no heat in the fire, or sweetness in the sugar, but only that heat or sweetness, as perceived by us, are not in the fire or sugar. What say you to this?

Phil. I say it is nothing to the purpose. Our discourse proceeded altogether concerning sensible things, which you define to be, *the things we immediately perceive by our senses.* Whatever other qualities, therefore, you speak of, as distinct from these, I know nothing of them, neither do they at all belong to the point in dispute. You may, indeed, pretend to have discovered certain qualities which you do not perceive, and assert those insensible qualities exist in fire and sugar. But what use can be made of this to your present purpose, I am at a loss to conceive. Tell me then once more, do you acknowledge that heat and cold, sweetness and bitterness (meaning those qualities which are perceived by the senses), do not exist without the mind?

Hyl. I see it is to no purpose to hold out, so I give up the cause as to those mentioned qualities. Though I profess it sounds oddly, to say that sugar is not sweet.

Phil. But, for your further satisfaction, take this along with you: that which at other times seems sweet, shall, to a distempered palate, appear bitter. And, nothing can be plainer than that divers persons perceive different tastes in the same food; since that which one man delights in, another abhors. And how could this be, if the taste was something really inherent in the food?

Hyl. I acknowledge I know not how.

Phil. In the next place, *odors* are to be considered. And, with regard to these, I would fain know whether what has been said of tastes doth not exactly agree to them? Are they not so many pleasing or displeasing sensations?

Hyl. They are.

Phil. Can you then conceive it possible that they should exist in an unperceiving thing?

Hyl. I cannot.

Phil. Or, can you imagine that filth and ordure affect those brute animals that feed on them out of choice, with the same smells which we perceive in them?

Hyl. By no means.

Phil. May we not therefore conclude of smells, as of the other forementioned qualities, that they cannot exist in any but a perceiving substance or mind.

Hyl. I think so.

Phil. Then as to *sounds,* what must we think of them: are they accidents really inherent in external bodies, or not?

Hyl. That they inhere not in the sonorous bodies is plain from hence; because a bell struck in the exhausted receiver of an air-pump sends forth no sound. The air, therefore, must be thought the subject of sound.

Phil. What reason is there for that, *Hylas?*

Hyl. Because, when any motion is raised in the air, we perceive a sound greater or lesser, according to the air's motion; but without some motion in the air, we never hear any sound at all.

Phil. And granting that we never hear a sound but when some motion is produced in the air, yet I do not see how you can infer from thence, that the sound itself is in the air.

Hyl. It is this very motion in the external air that produces in the mind the sensation of *sound*. For, striking on the drum of the ear, it causeth a vibration, which by the auditory nerves being communicated to the brain, the soul is thereupon affected with the sensation called *sound*.

Phil. What! is sound then a sensation?

Hyl. I tell you, as perceived by us, it is a particular sensation in the mind.

Phil. And can any sensation exist without the mind?

Hyl. No, certainly.

Phil. How then can sound, being a

sensation, exist in the air, if by the *air* you mean a senseless substance existing without the mind?

Hyl. You must distinguish, *Philonous,* between sound as it is perceived by us, and as it is in itself; or (which is the same thing) between the sound we immediately perceive, and that which exists without us. The former, indeed, is a particular kind of sensation, but the latter is merely a vibrative or undulatory motion in the air.

Phil. I thought I had already obviated that distinction, by the answer I gave when you were applying it in a like case before. But, to say no more of that, are you sure then that sound is really nothing but motion?

Hyl. I am.

Phil. Whatever therefore agrees to real sound, may with truth be attributed to motion?

Hyl. It may.

Phil. It is then good sense to speak of *motion* as of a thing that is *loud, sweet, acute, or grave.*

Hyl. I see you are resolved not to understand me. Is it not evident those accidents or modes belong only to sensible sound, or *sound* in the common acceptation of the word, but not to *sound* in the real and philosophic sense; which, as I just now told you, is nothing but a certain motion of the air?

Phil. It seems then there are two sorts of sound—the one vulgar, or that which is heard, the other philosophical and real?

Hyl. Even so.

Phil. And the latter consists in motion?

Hyl. I told you so before.

Phil. Tell me, *Hylas,* to which of the senses, think you, the idea of motion belongs? to the hearing?

Hyl. No, certainly; but to the sight and touch.

Phil. It should follow then, that, according to you, real sounds may possibly be *seen* or *felt,* but never *heard.*

Hyl. Look you, *Philonous,* you may, if you please, make a jest of my opinion, but that will not alter the truth of things. I own, indeed, the inferences you draw me into, sound something oddly; but common language, you know, is framed by, and for the use of the vulgar: we must not therefore wonder, if expressions adapted to exact philosophic notions seem uncouth and out of the way.

Phil. Is it come to that? I assure you, I imagine myself to have gained no small point, since you make so light of departing from common phrases and opinions; it is being a main part of our inquiry, to examine whose notions are widest of the common road, and most repugnant to the general sense of the world. But, can you think it no more than a philosophical paradox, to say that *real sounds are never heard,* and that the idea of them is obtained by some other sense? And is there nothing in this contrary to nature and the truth of things?

Hyl. To deal ingenuously, I do not like it. And, after the concessions already made, I had as well grant that sounds too have no real being without the mind.

Phil. And I hope you will make no difficulty to acknowledge the same of *colors.*

Hyl. Pardon me: the case of colors is very different. Can anything be plainer than that we see them on the objects?

Phil. The objects you speak of are, I suppose, corporeal Substances existing without the mind?

Hyl. They are.

Phil. And have true and real colors inhering in them?

Hyl. Each visible object hath that color which we see in it.

Phil. How! is there anything visible but what we perceive by sight?

Hyl. There is not.

Phil. And, do we perceive anything by sense which we do not perceive immediately?

Hyl. How often must I be obliged to repeat the same thing? I tell you, we do not.

Phil. Have patience, good *Hylas;* and tell me once more, whether there is anything immediately perceived by the senses, except sensible qualities. I know you asserted there was not; but I would now be informed, whether you still persist in the same opinion.

Hyl. I do.

Phil. Pray, is your corporeal substance either a sensible quality, or made up of sensible qualities?

Hyl. What a question that is! who ever thought it was?

Phil. My reason for asking was, because in saying, *each visible object hath that color which we see in it,* you make visible objects to be corporeal substances; which implies either that corporeal substances are sensible qualities, or else that there is something beside sensible qualities perceived by sight: but, as this point was formerly agreed between us, and is still maintained by

you, it is a clear consequence, that your corporeal substance is nothing distinct from sensible qualities.

Hyl. You may draw as many absurd consequences as you please, and endeavor to perplex the plainest things; but you shall never persuade me out of my senses. I clearly understand my own meaning.

Phil. I wish you would make me understand it too. But, since you are unwilling to have your notion of corporeal substance examined, I shall urge that point no further. Only be pleased to let me know, whether the same colors which we see exist in external bodies, or some other?

Hyl. The very same.

Phil. What! are then the beautiful red and purple we see on yonder clouds really in them? Or do you imagine they have in themselves any other form than that of a dark mist or vapor?

Hyl. I must own, *Philonous,* those colors are not really in the clouds as they seem to be at this distance. They are only apparent colors.

Phil. Apparent call you them? how shall we distinguish these apparent colors from real?

Hyl. Very easily. Those are to be thought apparent which, appearing only at a distance, vanish upon a nearer approach.

Phil. And those, I suppose, are to be thought real which are discovered by the most near and exact survey.

Hyl. Right.

Phil. Is the nearest and exactest survey made by the help of a microscope, or by the naked eye?

Hyl. By a microscope, doubtless.

Phil. But a microscope often discovers colors in an object different from those perceived by the unassisted sight. And, in case we had microscopes magnifying to any assigned degree, it is certain that no object whatsoever, viewed through them, would appear in the same color which it exhibits to the naked eye.

Hyl. And what will you conclude from all this? You cannot argue that there are really and naturally no colors on objects: because by artificial managements they may be altered, or made to vanish.

Phil. I think it may evidently be concluded from your own concessions, that all the colors we see with our naked eyes are only apparent as those on the clouds, since they vanish upon a more close and accurate inspection which is afforded us by a microspace. Then, as to what you say by way of prevention: I ask you whether the real and natural state of an object is better discovered by a very sharp and piercing sight, or by one which is less sharp?

Hyl. By the former without doubt.

Phil. Is it not plain from *Dioptrics* that microscopes make the sight more penetrating, and represent objects as they would appear to the eye in case it were naturally endowed with a most exquisite sharpness?

Hyl. It is.

Phil. Consequently the microscopical representation is to be thought that which best sets forth the real nature of the thing, or what it is in itself. The colors, therefore, by it perceived are more genuine and real than those perceived otherwise.

Hyl. I confess there is something in what you say.

Phil. Besides, it is not only possible but manifest, that there actually are animals whose eyes are by nature framed to perceive those things which by reason of their minuteness escape our sight. What think you of those inconceivably small animals perceived by glasses? must we suppose they are all stark blind? Or, in case they see, can it be imagined their sight hath not the same use in preserving their bodies from injuries, which appears in that of all other animals? And if it hath, is it not evident they must see particles less than their own bodies, which will present them with a far different view in each object from that which strikes our senses? Even our own eyes do not always represent objects to us after the same manner. In the *jaundice* every one knows that all things seem yellow. Is it not therefore highly probable those animals in whose eyes we discern a very different texture from that of ours, and whose bodies abound with different humors, do not see the same colors in every object that we do? From all which, should it not seem to follow that all colors are equally apparent, and that none of those which we perceive are really inherent in any outward object?

Hyl. It should.

Phil. The point will be past all doubt, if you consider that, in case colors were real properties or affections inherent in external bodies, they could admit of no alteration without some change wrought in the very bodies themselves; but, is it not evident from what hath been said that, upon the use of microscopes, upon a change happening in the humors of the eye, or a variation of distance, without any manner of real alteration in the thing itself, the colors of any object are either changed, or totally disappear? Nay, all other circumstances remaining the same, change but the situation of some objects, and they shall present different colors to the eye. The same thing happens upon viewing an object in various degrees of light. And what is more known than that the same bodies appear differently colored by candlelight from what they do in the open day? Add to these the experiment of a prism which, separating the heterogeneous rays of light, alters the color of any object, and will cause the whitest to appear of a deep blue or red to the naked eye. And now tell me whether you are still of opinion that every body hath its true real color inhering in it; and, if you think it hath, I would fain know farther from you, what certain distance and position of the object, what peculiar texture and formation of the eye, what degree or kind of light is necessary for ascertaining that true color, and distinguishing it from apparent ones.

Hyl. I own myself entirely satisfied, that they are all equally apparent, and that there is no such thing as color really inhering in external bodies, but that it is altogether in the light. And what confirms me in this opinion is that in proportion to the light, colors are still more or less vivid; and if there be no light, then are there no colors perceived. Besides, allowing there are colors on external objects, yet, how is it possible for us to perceive them? For no external body affects the mind, unless it acts first on our organs of sense. But the only action of bodies is motion; and motion cannot be communicated otherwise than by impulse. A distant object therefore cannot act on the eye, nor consequently make itself or its properties perceivable to the soul. Whence it plainly follows that it is immediately some contiguous substance, which, operating on the eye, occasions a perception of colors: and such is light.

Phil. How! is light then a substance?

Hyl. I tell you, *Philonous,* external light is nothing but a thin fluid substance, whose minute particles being agitated with a brisk motion, and in various manners reflected from the different surfaces of outward objects to the eyes, communicate different motions to the optic nerves; which, being propagated to the brain, cause therein various impressions; and these are attended with the sensations of red, blue, yellow, &c.

Phil. It seems then the light doth no more than shake the optic nerves.

Hyl. Nothing else.

Phil. And, consequent to each particular motion of the nerves, the mind is affected with a sensation, which is some particular color.

Hyl. Right.

Phil. And these sensations have no existence without the mind.

Hyl. They have not.

Phil. How then do you affirm that colors are in the light; since by *light* you understand a corporeal substance external to the mind?

Hyl. Light and colors, as immediately perceived by us, I grant cannot exist without the mind. But, in themselves they are only the motions and configurations of certain insensible particles of matter.

Phil. Colors, then, in the vulgar

sense, or taken for the immediate objects of sight, cannot agree to any but a perceiving substance.

Hyl. That is what I say.

Phil. Well then, since you give up the point as to those sensible qualities which are alone thought colors by all mankind beside, you may hold what you please with regard to those invisible ones of the philosophers. It is not my business to dispute about them; only I would advise you to bethink yourself, whether, considering the inquiry we are upon, it be prudent for you to affirm—*the red and blue which we see are not real colors, but certain unknown motions and figures, which no man ever did or can see, are truly so.* Are not these shocking notions, and are not they subject to as many ridiculous inferences, as those you were obliged to renounce before in the case of sounds?

Hyl. I frankly own, *Philonous,* that it is in vain to stand out any longer. Colors, sounds, tastes, in a word all those termed *secondary qualities,* have certainly no existence without the mind. But, by this acknowledgment I must not be supposed to derogate anything from the reality of Matter or external objects; seeing it is no more than several philosophers maintain, who nevertheless are the farthest imaginable from denying Matter. For the clearer understanding of this, you must know sensible qualities are by philosophers divided into *primary* and *secondary.* The former are Extension, Figure, Solidity, Gravity, Motion, and Rest. And these they hold exist really in bodies. The latter are those above enumerated; or, briefly, all sensible qualities beside the Primary, which they assert are only so

many sensations or ideas existing nowhere but in the mind. But all this, I doubt not, you are apprised of. For my part, I have been a long time sensible there was such an opinion current among philosophers, but was never thoroughly convinced of its truth until now.

Phil. You are still then of opinion that *extension* and *figures* are inherent in external unthinking substances?

Hyl. I am.

Phil. But what if the same arguments which are brought against Secondary Qualities will hold good against these also?

Hyl. Why then I shall be obliged to think, they too exist only in the mind.

Phil. Is it your opinion the very figure and extension which you perceive by sense exist in the outward object or material substance?

Hyl. It is.

Phil. Have all other animals as good grounds to think the same of the figure and extension which they see and feel?

Hyl. Without doubt, if they have any thought at all.

Phil. Answer me, *Hylas.* Think you the senses were bestowed upon all animals for their preservation and wellbeing in life? or were they given to men alone for this end?

Hyl. I make no question but they have the same use in all other animals.

Phil. If so, it is not necessary they should be enabled by them to perceive their own limbs, and those bodies which are capable of harming them?

Hyl. Certainly.

Phil. A mite therefore must be supposed to see his own foot, and things equal or even less than it, as bodies of some considerable dimension; though at the same time they appear to you scarce discernible, or at best as so many visible points?

Hyl. I cannot deny it.

Phil. And to creatures less than the mite they will seem yet larger?

Hyl. They will.

Phil. Insomuch that what you can hardly discern will to another extremely minute animal appear as some huge mountain?

Hyl. All this I grant.

Phil. Can one and the same thing be at the same time in itself of different dimensions?

Hyl. That were absurd to imagine.

Phil. But, from what you have laid down it follows that both the extension by you perceived, and that perceived by the mite itself, as likewise all those perceived by lesser animals, are each of them the true extension of the mite's foot; that is to say, by your own principles you are led into an absurdity.

Hyl. There seems to be some difficulty in the point.

Phil. Again, have you not acknowledged that no real inherent property of any object can be changed without some change in the thing itself?

Hyl. I have.

Phil. But, as we approach to or recede from an object, the visible extension varies, being at one distance ten or a hundred times greater than at another. Doth it not therefore follow from hence likewise that it is not really inherent in the object?

Hyl. I own I am at a loss what to think.

Phil. Your judgment will soon be determined, if you will venture to think

as freely concerning this quality as you have done concerning the rest. Was it not admitted as a good argument, that neither heat nor cold was in the water, because it seemed warm to one hand and cold to the other?

Hyl. It was.

Phil. Is it not the very same reasoning to conclude there is no extension or figure in an object, because to one eye it shall seem little, smooth, and round, when at the same time it appears to the other, great, uneven, and angular?

Hyl. The very same. But does this latter fact ever happen?

Phil. You may at any time make the experiment, by looking with one eye bare, and with the other through a microscope.

Hyl. I know not how to maintain it, and yet I am loath to give up *extension,* I see so many odd consequences following upon such a concession.

Phil. Odd, say you? After the concessions already made, I hope you will stick at nothing for its oddness. But, on the other hand, should it not seem very odd, if the general reasoning which includes all other sensible qualities did not also include extension? If it be allowed that no idea nor anything like an idea can exist in an unperceiving substance, then surely it follows that no figure or mode of extension, which we can either perceive or imagine, or have any idea of, can be really inherent in Matter; not to mention the peculiar difficulty there must be in conceiving a material substance, prior to and distinct from extension, to be the *substratum* of extension. Be the sensible quality what it will—figure, or sound, or color; it seems alike impossible it should subsist in that which doth not perceive it.

Hyl. I give up the point for the present, reserving still a right to retract my opinion, in case I shall hereafter discover any false step in my progress to it.

Phil. That is a right you cannot be denied. Figures and extensions being dispatched, we proceed next to *motion. Can* a real motion in any external body be at the same time both very swift and very slow?

Hyl. It cannot.

Phil. Is not the motion of a body swift in a reciprocal proportion to the time it takes up in describing any given space? Thus a body that describes a mile in an hour moves three times faster than it would in case it described only a mile in three hours.

Hyl. I agree with you.

Phil. And is not time measured by the succession of ideas in our minds?

Hyl. It is.

Phil. And is it not possible ideas should succeed one another twice as fast in your mind as they do in mine, or in that of some spirit of another kind?

Hyl. I own it.

Phil. Consequently, the same body may to another seem to perform its motion over any space in half the time that it doth to you. And the same reasoning will hold as to any other proportion: that is to say, according to your principles (since the motions perceived are both really in the object) it is possible one and the same body shall be really moved the same way at once, both very swift and very slow. How is this consistent either with common sense, or with what you just now granted?

Hyl. I have nothing to say to it.

Phil. Then as for *solidity;* either you do not mean any sensible quality by that word, and so it is beside our inquiry: or if you do, it must be either hardness or resistance. But both the one and the other are plainly relative to our senses: it being evident that what seems hard to one animal may appear soft to another, who hath greater force and firmness of limbs. Nor is it less plain that the resistance I feel is not in the body.

Hyl. I own the very sensation of resistance, which is all you immediately perceive, is not in the *body,* but the cause of that sensation is.

Phil. But the causes of our sensations are not things immediately perceived, and therefore not sensible. This point I thought had been already determined.

Hyl. I own it was; but you will pardon me if I seem a little embarrassed: I know not how to quit my old notions.

Phil. To help you out, do but consider that if *extension* be once acknowledged to have no existence without the mind, the same must necessarily be granted of motion, solidity, and gravity —since they all evidently suppose extension. It is therefore superfluous to inquire particularly concerning each of them. In denying extension, you have denied them all to have any real existence. . . .

Hyl. It is just come into my head, *Philonous,* that I have somewhere heard of a distinction between absolute and sensible extension. Now, though it be acknowledged that *great* and *small,* consisting merely in the relation which other extended beings have to the parts of our own bodies, do not really inhere in the Substances themselves; yet nothing obliges us to hold the same with regard to *absolute extension,* which is something abstracted from *great* and *small,* from this or that particular magnitude or figure. So likewise as to motion; *swift* and *slow* are altogether relative to the succession of ideas in our own minds. But, it doth not follow, because those modifications of motion exist not without the mind, that therefore absolute motion abstracted from them doth not.

Phil. Pray what is it that distinguishes one motion, or one part of extension, from another? Is it not something sensible, as some degree of swiftness or slowness, some certain magnitude or figure peculiar to each?

Hyl. I think so.

Phil. These qualities, therefore, stripped of all sensible properties, are without all specific and numerical differences, as the schools call them.

Hyl. They are.

Phil. That is to say, they are extension in general, and motion in general.

Hyl. Let it be so.

Phil. But it is a universally received maxim that *Everything which exists is particular.* How then can motion in general, or extension in general, exist in any corporeal Substance?

Hyl. I will take time to solve your difficulty.

Phil. But I think the point may be speedily decided. Without doubt you can tell whether you are able to frame this or that idea. Now I am content to put our dispute on this issue. If you can frame in your thoughts a distinct abstract idea of motion or extension; divested of all those sensible modes, as swift and slow, great and small, round and square, and the like, which are acknowledged to exist only in the mind, I will then yield the point you contend for. But, if you cannot, it will be unreasonable on your side to insist any longer upon what you have no notion of.

Hyl. To confess ingenuously, I cannot.

Phil. Can you even separate the ideas of extension and motion from the ideas of all those qualities which they who make the distinction term *secondary?*

Hyl. What! is it not an easy matter to consider extension and motion by themselves, abstracted from all other sensible qualities? Pray how do the mathematicians treat of them?

Phil. I acknowledge, *Hylas,* it is not difficult to form general propositions and reasonings about those qualities, without mentioning any other; and, in this sense, to consider or treat of them abstractedly. But, how doth it follow that, because I can pronounce the word *motion* by itself, I can form the idea of it in my mind exclusive of body? Or, because theorems may be made of extension and figures, without any mention of *great* or *small,* or any other sensible mode or quality, that therefore it is possible such an abstract idea of extension, without any particular size or figure, or sensible quality, should be distinctly formed, and apprehended by the mind? Mathematicians treat of quantity, without regarding what other sensible qualities it is attended with, as being altogether indifferent to their demonstrations. But, when laying aside the words, they contemplate the bare ideas, I believe you will find, they are not the pure abstracted ideas of extension.

Hyl. But what say you to *pure intellect?* May not abstracted ideas be framed by that faculty?

Phil. Since I cannot frame abstract ideas at all, it is plain I cannot frame them by the help of *pure intellect;* whatsoever faculty you understand by those words. Besides, not to inquire into the nature of pure intellect and its spiritual objects, as *virtue, reason, God,* or the like, thus much seems manifest, that sensible things are only to be perceived by sense, or represented by the imagination. Figures, therefore, and extension, being originally perceived by sense, do not belong to pure intellect: but, for your further satisfaction, try if you can frame the idea of any figure, abstracted from all particularities of size, or even from other sensible qualities.

Hyl. Let me think a little. . . . I do not find that I can.

Phil. And can you think it possible that should really exist in nature which implies a repugnancy in its conception?

Hyl. By no means.

Phil. Since therefore it is impossible even for the mind to disunite the ideas of extension and motion from all other sensible qualities, doth it not follow, that where the one exist there necessarily the other exist likewise?

Hyl. It should seem so.

Phil. Consequently, the very same arguments which you admitted as conclusive against the Secondary Qualities are, without any further application of force, against the Primary too. Besides, if you will trust your senses, is it not plain all sensible qualities coexist, or to them appear as being in the same place? Do they ever represent a motion, or figure, as being divested of all other visible and tangible qualities?

Hyl. You need say no more on this head. I am free to own, if there be no secret error to oversight in our proceedings hitherto, that all sensible qualities are alike to be denied existence without the mind. But, my fear is that I have been too liberal in my former concessions, or overlooked some fallacy or other. In short, I did not take time to think.

Phil. For that matter, *Hylas,* you may take what time you please in reviewing the progress of our inquiry. You are at liberty to recover any slips you might have made, or offer whatever you have omitted which makes for your first opinion.

Hyl. One great oversight I take to be this—that I did not sufficiently distinguish the *object* from the *sensation.* Now, though this latter may not exist without the mind, yet it will not thence follow that the former cannot.

Phil. What object do you mean? The object of the senses?

Hyl. The same.

Phil. It is then immediately perceived?

Hyl. Right.

Phil. Make me to understand the difference between what is immediately perceived, and a sensation.

Hyl. The sensation I take to be an act of the mind perceiving; besides which, there is something perceived; and this I call the *object.* For example, there is red and yellow on that tulip. But then the act of perceiving those colors, is in me only, and not in the tulip.

Phil. What tulip do you speak of? Is it that which you see?

Hyl. The same.

Phil. And what do you see beside color, figure, and extension?

Hyl. Nothing.

Phil. What you would say then is that the red and yellow are coexistent with the extension; is it not?

Hyl. That is not all; I would say they have a real existence without the mind, in some unthinking substance.

Phil. That the colors are really in the tulip which I see is manifest. Neither can it be denied that this tulip may exist independent of your mind or mine; but, that any immediate object of the senses—that is, any idea, or combination of ideas—should exist in an unthinking substance, or exterior to all minds, is in itself an evident contradiction. Nor can I imagine how this follows from what you said just now, to wit, that the red and yellow were on the tulip *you saw,* since you do not pretend to *see* that unthinking substance. . . .

Hyl. Pray what think you of this? It is just come into my head that the ground of all our mistake lies in your treating of each quality by itself. Now, I grant that each quality cannot singly subsist without the mind. Color cannot without extension, neither can figure without some other sensible quality. But, as the several qualities united or blended together form entire sensible things, nothing hinders why such things

may not be supposed to exist without the mind.

Phil. Either, *Hylas,* you are jesting, or have a very bad memory. Though indeed we went through all the qualities by name one after another, yet my arguments, or rather your concessions, nowhere tended to prove that the Secondary Qualities did not subsist each alone by itself; but, that they were not *at all* without the mind. Indeed, in treating of figure and motion we concluded they could not exist without the mind, because it was impossible even in thought to separate them from all secondary qualities, so as to conceive them existing by themselves. But then this was not the only argument made use of upon that occasion. But (to pass by all that hath been hitherto said, and reckon it for nothing, if you will have it so) I am content to put the whole upon this issue. If you can conceive it possible for any mixture or combination of qualities, or any sensible object whatever, to exist without the mind, then I will grant it actually to be so.

Hyl. If it comes to that the point will soon be decided. What more easy than to conceive a ·tree or house existing by itself, independent of, and unperceived by, any mind whatsoever? I do at this present time conceive them existing after that manner.

Phil. How say you, *Hylas,* can you see a thing which is at the same time unseen?

Hyl. No, that were a contradiction.

Phil. Is it not as great a contradiction to talk of *conceiving* a thing which is *unconceived?*

Hyl. It is.

Phil. The tree or house therefore which you think of is conceived by you?

Hyl. How should it be otherwise?

Phil. And what is conceived is surely in the mind?

Hyl. Without question, that which is conceived is in the mind.

Phil. How then came you to say, you conceived a house or tree existing independent and out of all minds whatsoever?

Hyl. That was I own an oversight; but stay, let me consider what led me into it.—It is a pleasant mistake enough. As I was thinking of a tree in a solitary place where no one was present to see it, methought that was to conceive a tree as existing unperceived or unthought of—not considering that I myself conceived it all the while. But now I plainly see that all I can do is to frame ideas in my own mind. I may indeed conceive in my own thoughts the idea of a tree, or a house, or a mountain, but that is all. And his is far from proving that I can conceive them *existing out of the minds of all Spirits*.

Phil. You acknowledge then that you cannot possibly conceive how any one corporeal sensible thing should exist otherwise than in a mind? . . .

Hyl. To speak the truth, *Philonous,* I think there are two kinds of objects:—the one perceived immediately, which are likewise called *ideas;* the other are real things or external objects, perceived by the mediation of ideas, which are their images and representations. Now, I own ideas do not exist without the mind; but the latter sort of objects do. I am sorry I did not think of this dis-tinction sooner; it would probably have cut short your discourse.

Phil. Are those external objects perceived by sense, or by some other faculty?

Hyl. They are perceived by sense.

Phil. How! is there anything perceived by sense which is not immediately perceived?

Hyl. Yes, *Philonous,* in some sort there is. For example, when I look on a picture or statue of Julius Cæsar, I may be said after a manner to perceive him (though not immediately) by my senses.

Phil. It seems then you will have our ideas, which alone are immediately perceived, to be pictures of external things: and that these also are perceived by sense, inasmuch as they have a conformity or resemblance to our ideas?

Hyl. That is my meaning.

Phil. And, in the same way that Julius Cæsar, in himself invisible, is nevertheless perceived by sight; real things, in themselves imperceptible, are perceived by sense.

Hyl. In the very same.

Phil. Tell me, *Hylas,* when you behold the picture of Julius Cæsar, do you see with your eyes any more than some colors and figures, with a certain symmetry and composition of the whole?

Hyl. Nothing else.

Phil. And would not a man who had never known anything of Julius Cæsar see as much?

Hyl. He would.

Phil. Consequently he hath his sight, and the use of it, in as perfect a degree as you?

Hyl. I agree with you.

Phil. Whence comes it then that your thoughts are directed to the Roman emperor, and his are not? This cannot proceed from the sensations or ideas of sense by you then perceived; since you acknowledge you have no advantage over him in that respect. It should seem therefore to proceed from reason and memory: should it not?

Hyl. It should.

Phil. Consequently, it will not follow from that instance that anything is perceived by sense which is not immediately perceived. Though I grant we may, in one acceptation, be said to perceive sensible things mediately by sense—that is, when, from a frequently perceived connection, the immediate perception of ideas by one sense suggest to the mind others, perhaps belonging to another sense, which are wont to be connected with them. For instance, when I hear a coach drive along the streets, immediately I perceive only the sound; but, from the experience I have had that such a sound is connected with a coach, I am said to hear the coach. It is nevertheless evident that, in truth and strictness, nothing can be *heard* but *sound;* and the coach is not then properly perceived by sense, but suggested from experience. So likewise when we are said to see a red-hot bar of iron; the solidity and heat of the iron are not the objects of sight, but suggested to the imagination by the color and figure which are properly perceived by that sense. In short, those things alone are actually and strictly perceived by any sense, which would have been perceived in case that same sense had then been first conferred on us. As for other things, it is plain they are only suggested to the mind by experience, grounded on former perceptions. But, to return to your comparison of Cæsar's picture, it is plain, if you keep to that, you must hold the real things or archetypes of our ideas are not perceived by sense, but by some internal faculty of the soul, as reason or memory. I would therefore fain know what arguments you can draw from reason for the existence of what you call *real things* or *material objects.* Or, whether you remember to have seen them formerly as they are in themselves; or, if you have heard or read of any one that did.

Hyl. I see, *Philonous,* you are disposed to raillery; but that will never convince me.

Phil. My aim is only to learn from you the way to come at the knowledge of *material beings.* Whatever we perceive is perceived immediately or mediately: by sense; or by reason and reflection. But, as you have excluded sense, pray show me what reason you have to believe their existence; or what *medium* you can possibly make use of to prove it, either to mine or your own understanding.

Hyl. To deal ingenuously, *Philonous,* now I consider the point, I do not find I can give you any good reason for it. But, thus much seems pretty plain, that it is at least possible such things may really exist. And, as long as there is no absurdity in supposing them, I am resolved to believe as I did, till you bring good reasons to the contrary.

Phil. What! is it come to this, that you only believe the existence of material objects, and that your belief is founded barely on the possibility of its being true? Then you will have me bring reasons against it: though another would think it reasonable the proof should lie on him who holds the affirmative. And, after all, this very point which you are now resolved to maintain, without any reason, is in effect what you have more than once during this discourse seen good reason to give up. But, to pass over all this; if I understand you rightly, you say our ideas do not exist without the mind; but that they are copies, images, or representations, of certain originals that do?

Hyl. You take me right.

Phil. They are then like external things?

Hyl. They are.

Phil. Have those things a stable and permanent nature, independent of our senses; or are they in a perpetual change, upon our producing any motions in our bodies, suspending, exerting, or altering, our faculties or organs of sense?

Hyl. Real things, it is plain, have a fixed and real nature, which remains the same notwithstanding any change in our senses, or in the posture and motion of our bodies; which indeed may affect the ideas in our minds, but it were absurd to think they had the same effect on things existing without the mind.

Phil. How then is it possible that things perpetually fleeting and variable as our ideas should be copies or images of anything fixed and constant? Or, in other words, since all sensible qualities, as size, figure, colour, &c., that is, our ideas, are continually changing upon every alteration in the distance, medium, or instruments of sensation; how

can any determinate material objects be properly represented or painted forth by several distinct things, each of which is so different from and unlike the rest? Or, if you say it resembles some one only of our ideas, how shall we be able to distinguish the true copy from all the false ones?

Hyl. I profess, *Philonous,* I am at a loss. I know not what to say to this.

Phil. But neither is this all. Which are material objects in themselves—perceptible or imperceptible-

Hyl. Properly and immediately nothing can be perceived but ideas. All material things, therefore, are in themselves insensible, and to be perceived only by our ideas.

Phil. Ideas then are sensible, and their archetypes or originals insensible?

Hyl. Right.

Phil. But how can that which is sensible be like that which is insensible? Can a real thing, in itself *invisible,* be like a *colour;* or a real thing, which is not *audible,* be like a *sound?* In a word, can anything be like a sensation or idea, but another sensation or idea?

Hyl. I must own, I think not.

Phil. Is it possible there should be any doubt on the point? Do you not perfectly know your own ideas?

Hyl. I know them perfectly; since what I do not perceive or know can be no part of my idea.

Phil. Consider, therefore, and examine them, and then tell me if there be anything in them which can exist without the mind? or if you can conceive anything like them existing without the mind?

Hyl. Upon inquiry, I find it is impossible for me to conceive or understand how anything but an idea can be like an idea. And it is most evident that *no idea can exist without the mind.*

Phil. You are therefore, by our principles, forced to deny the reality of sensible things; since you made it to consist in an absolute existence exterior to the mind. That is to say, you are a downright sceptic. So I have gained my point, which was to show your principles led to Scepticism.

Hyl. For the present I am, if not entirely convinced, at least silenced. . . .

The Second Dialogue

Hylas. I beg your pardon, *Philonous,* for not meeting you sooner. All this morning my head was so filled with our late conversation that I had not leisure to think of the time of the day, or indeed of anything else.

Philonous. I am glad you were so intent upon it, in hopes if there were any mistakes in your concessions, or fallacies in my reasonings from them, you will now discover them to me. . . .

Hyl. I own there is a great deal in what you say. Nor can any one be more entirely satisfied of the truth of those odd consequences, so long as I have in view the reasonings that lead to them. But, when these are out of my thoughts, there seems, on the other hand, something so satisfactory, so natural and intelligible, in the modern way of explaining things that, I profess, I know not how to reject it.

Phil. I know not what way you mean.

Hyl. I mean the way of accounting for our sensations or ideas.

Phil. How is that?

Hyl. It is supposed the soul makes her residence in some part of the brain, from which the nerves take their rise, and are thence extended to all parts of the body; and that outward objects, by the different impressions they make on the organs of sense, communicate certain vibrative motions to the nerves; and these being filled with spirits propagate them to the brain or seat of the soul, which, according to the various impressions or traces thereby made in the brain, is variously affected with ideas.

Phil. And call you this an explication of the manner whereby we are effected with ideas?

Hyl. Why not, *Philonous;* have you anything to object against it?

Phil. I would first know whether I rightly understand your hypothesis. You make certain traces in the brain to be the causes or occasions of our ideas. Pray tell me whether by the *brain* you mean any sensible thing.

Hyl. What else think you I could mean?

Phil. Sensible things are all immediately perceivable; and those things which are immediately perceivable are ideas; and these exist only in the mind. Thus much you have, if I mistake not, long since agreed to.

Hyl. I do not deny it.

Phil. The brain therefore you speak of, being a sensible thing, exists only in the mind. Now, I would fain know whether you think it reasonable to suppose that one idea or thing existing in the mind occasions all other ideas. And, if you think so, pray how do you account for the origin of that primary idea or brain itself?

Hyl. I do not explain the origin of

our ideas by that brain which is perceivable to sense, this being itself only a combination of sensible ideas, but by another which I imagine.

Phil. But are not things imagined as truly *in the mind* as things perceived?

Hyl. I must confess they are.

Phil. It comes, therefore, to the same thing; and you have been all this while accounting for ideas by certain motions or impressions of the brain, that is, by some alterations in an idea, whether sensible or imaginable it matters not.

Hyl. I begin to suspect my hypothesis.

Phil. Besides spirits, all that we know or conceive are our own ideas. When, therefore, you say all ideas are occasioned by impressions in the brain, do you conceive this brain or no? If you do, then you talk of ideas imprinted in an idea causing that same idea, which is absurd. If you do not conceive it, you talk unintelligibly, instead of forming a reasonable hypothesis.

Hyl. I now clearly see it was a mere dream. There is nothing in it.

Phil. You need not be much concerned at it; for after all, this way of explaining things, as you called it, could never have satisfied any reasonable man. What connection is there between a motion in the nerves, and the sensations of sound or colour in the mind? Or how is it possible these should be the effect of that?

Hyl. But I could never think it had so little in it as now it seems to have.

Phil. Well then, are you at length satisfied that no sensible things have a real existence; and that you are in truth an arrant *sceptic?*

Hyl. It is too plain to be denied.

Phil. Look! are not the fields covered with a delightful verdure? Is there not something in the woods and groves, in the rivers and clear springs, that soothes, that delights, that transports the soul? At the prospect of the wide and deep ocean, or some huge mountain whose top is lost in the clouds, or of an old gloomy forest, are not our minds filled with a pleasing horror? Even in rocks and deserts is there not an agreeable wildness? How sincere a pleasure is it to behold the natural beauties of the earth! To preserve and renew our relish for them, is not the veil of night alternately drawn over her face, and doth she not change her dress with the seasons? How aptly are the elements disposed! What variety and use in the meanest productions of nature! What delicacy, what beauty, what contrivance, in animal and vegetable bodies! How exquisitely are all things suited, as well to their particular ends, as to constitute opposite parts of the whole! And, while they mutually aid and support, do they not also set off and illustrate each other? Raise now your thoughts from this ball of earth to all those glorious luminaries that adorn the high arch of heaven. The motion and situation of the planets, are they not admirable for use and order? Were those (miscalled *erratic*) globes ever known to stray, in their repeated journeys through the pathless void? Do they not measure areas round the sun ever proportioned to the times? So fixed, so immutable are the laws by which the unseen Author of nature actuates the universe. How vivid and radiant is the luster of the fixed stars! How magnificent and rich that negligent profusion with which they appear to be scattered throughout the whole azure vault! Yet, if you take the telescope, it brings into your sight a new host of stars that escape the naked eye. Here they seem contiguous and minute, but to a nearer view immense orbs of light at various distances, far sunk in the abyss of space. Now you must call imagination to your aid. The feeble narrow sense cannot descry innumerable worlds revolving round the central fires; and in those worlds the energy of an all-perfect Mind displayed in endless forms. But, neither sense nor imagination are big enough to comprehend the boundless extent, with all its glittering furniture. Though the laboring mind exert and strain each power to its utmost reach, there still stands out ungrasped a surplusage immeasurable. Yet all the vast bodies that compose this mighty frame, how distant and remote soever, are by some secret mechanism, some divine art and force, linked in a mutual dependence and intercourse with each other, even with this earth, which was almost slipped from my thoughts and lost in the crowd of worlds. Is not the whole system immense, beautiful, glorious beyond expression and beyond thought! What treatment, then, do those philosophers deserve, who would deprive these noble and delightful scenes of all reality? How should those Principles be entertained that lead us to think all the visible beauty of the creation a false imaginary glare? To be plain, can you expect this Scepticism of yours will not be thought extravagantly absurd by all men of sense?

Hyl. Other men may think as they please; but for your part you have nothing to reproach me with. My comfort is, you are as much a sceptic as I am.

Phil. There, *Hylas,* I must beg leave to differ from you.

Hyl. What have you all along agreed to the premises, and do you now deny the conclusion, and leave me to maintain those paradoxes by myself which you led me into? This surely is not fair.

Phil. I deny that I agreed with you in those notions that led to Scepticism. You indeed said the *reality* of sensible things consisted in an *absolute existence* out of the minds of spirits, or distinct from their being perceived. And, pursuant to this notion of reality, you are obliged to deny sensible things any real existence: that is, according to your own definition, you profess yourself a sceptic. But I neither said nor thought the reality of sensible things was to be defined after that manner. To me it is evident, for the reasons you allow of, that sensible things cannot exist otherwise than in a mind or spirit. Whence I conclude, not that they have no real existence, but that, seeing they depend not on my thought, and have an existence distinct from being perceived by me, *there must be some other mind wherein they exist.* As sure, therefore, as the sensible world really exists, so sure is there an infinite omnipresent Spirit, who contains and supports it.

Hyl. What! this is no more than I and all Christians hold, nay and all others too who believe there is a God, and that He knows and comprehends all things.

Phil. Aye, but here lies the difference.

Men commonly believe that all things are known or perceived by God, because they believe the being of a God; whereas I, on the other side, immediately and necessarily conclude the being of a God, because all sensible things must be perceived by him. . . . It is evident that the things I perceive are my own ideas, and that no idea can exist unless it be in a mind. Nor is it less plain that these ideas or things by me perceived, either themselves or their archetypes, exist independently of my mind; since I know myself not to be their author, it being out of my power to determine at pleasure what particular ideas I shall be affected with upon opening my eyes or ears. They must therefore exist in some other mind, whose will it is they should be exhibited to me. The things, I say, immediately perceived are ideas or sensations, call them which you will. But how can any idea or sensation exist in, or be produced by, anything but a mind or spirit? This indeed is inconceivable; and to assert that which is inconceivable is to talk nonsense: is it not?

Hyl. Without doubt.

Phil. But, on the other hand, it is very conceivable that they should exist in and be produced by a Spirit; since this is no more than I daily experience in myself, inasmuch as I perceive numberless ideas; and, by an act of my will, can form a great variety of them, and raise them up in my imagination: though, it must be confessed, these creatures of the fancy are not altogether so distinct, so strong, vivid, and permanent, as those perceived by my senses, which latter are called *real things.* From all which I conclude, *there is a Mind which affects me every moment with all the sensible impressions I perceive.* And, from the variety, order, and manner of these, I conclude the Author of them to be *wise, powerful, and good, and beyond comprehension.* . . .

[*The Third Dialogue is omitted.*]

COMMENT

The speakers in Berkeley's *Dialogues* are Hylas, a "materialist," and Philonous, who represents the point of view of the author. Physical objects, according to Philonous, have no existence independent of thought. The whole universe is made up of minds and the immaterial objects of minds, and nothing more. This doctrine, which is called "idealism" (idea-ism, with the "i" inserted for the sake of euphony), may strike beginning students as exceedingly odd; but it is quite possible that the Universe *is* very odd, and the arguments for idealism are strong. Since Berkeley's presentation of these arguments is lucid, I shall not summarize them.

Some of Berkeley's arguments are similar to the arguments of Russell in discussing the nature and existence of matter (see pages 141–150). Other arguments are unique to Berkeley. Altogether they constitute a powerful case for idealism. But certain critical questions are worth reviewing:

1. Is the Essence of an Object to be Perceived? Over and over again, Berkeley insisted that "things" are mere collections of "ideas" and that ideas cannot exist unless they are perceived. The plausibility of his contention depends upon his constant use of the word *idea*. We think of "idea" as something in the mind and therefore as incapable of existing apart from the mind. Hence, if we are told that an apple consists entirely of "ideas," it is natural for us to suppose that the apple can exist only in some mind. But "idea," as Berkeley used it, really means "immediate object of thought or experience" (including both imaginative and perceptual experience). If we understand idea in this sense, there is a possibility—not lightly to be dismissed—that an object known as a set of ideas may continue to exist when the thought of it ceases.

The point can be illustrated by an amusing passage from Lewis Carroll's *Through the Looking Glass*. Alice is warned by Tweedledum and Tweedledee not to awaken the Red King:

> "He's dreaming now," said Tweedledee: "and what do you think he's dreaming about?"
> Alice said, "Nobody can guess that."
> "Why about *you!*" Tweedledee exclaimed, clapping his hands triumphantly. "And if he left off dreaming about you, where do you suppose you'd be?"
> "Where I am now, of course," said Alice.
> "Not you!" Tweedledee retorted contemptuously. "You'd be nowhere. Why, you're only a sort of thing in his dream!"
> "If that there King was to wake," added Tweedledum, "you'd go out—bang! —just like a candle!"

The delicious absurdity of this passage depends upon the supposition of Tweedledum and Tweedledee that to *exist* is to be *borne in mind,* and that when Alice is not borne in mind by the Red King she cannot exist. But no real person is merely a thought or idea in anybody's mind.

This point would be admitted by Berkeley. His formula for summing up the nature of reality is *"esse est percipi aut percipere,"* [essence is to be perceived or to perceive] not just *"esse est percipi."* But if people can exist independently of someone's idea of them, why cannot a *thing* exist independently? To argue that an apple must be in our minds because we are thinking of it is like arguing that a person must be in our minds because we are thinking of him. If we distinguish clearly between the act of thinking and the object of thought, the act of perceiving and the object perceived, there is no absurdity in supposing that things may exist even when they are unperceived or unthought.

2. Is the "Egocentric Predicament" a Reason for Believing in Idealism? Berkeley pointed out that everyone's knowledge is incurably egocentric. Even when I think of the unobserved interior of the earth, I am *thinking* about it,

and, in that sense, it is an object before my mind. Every object we ever perceive or think about in any way stands *ipso facto* in relation to our minds. Does this "egocentric predicament"[1] provide a valid argument for idealism?

Ralph Barton Perry answers in the negative. The fact that we can not eliminate ourselves as the subject of our own experiences proves nothing at all about the nature of the external world. We may have good reason to suppose that there are unknown stars, unexperienced atoms, unsighted grains of sand in the Sahara Desert, and unobserved physical processes beneath the earth's crust. Our reasons for believing in them should be judged on the basis of logic and evidence and should not be rejected merely because no one can think about these matters without using one's mind.

3. DOES THE RELATIVITY OF PERCEPTION PROVE IDEALISM? The fact that sense data are relative to the perceiver can scarcely be denied; but does it prove idealism? So long as we can explain *why* things appear differently to different observers, we can still maintain that there are real objective qualities.

Let us consider one of Berkeley's own examples. He pointed out that if one hand has been chilled and the other warmed, and both hands are put simultaneously into the same pan of water, the water will seem warm to one hand and cool to the other. But this is just what we should expect if the water is *really tepid*. What the person who puts his hands in the water feels is not the temperature of the water but the temperature in his hands—and the preheated hand naturally has a different temperature than the prechilled hand. If the two hands remain in the water long enough, the temperature of the water will finally pervade them, and then the water will feel tepid to *both* hands. Similarly, if light and color are truly objective, an object will naturally appear to have a different color in a different light. Or if a microscope enables us to see features of an object that were before invisible, it is not surprising that we see colors and shapes that we did not see before. However variously things may *appear*, we can often distinguish between "appearances" and "realities." Whether we can do this in a sufficient number of cases to invalidate Berkeley's argument is a question worth debating.

4. DOES THE INSEPARABILITY OF PRIMARY AND SECONDARY QUALITIES COMMIT US TO IDEALISM? Suppose we grant Berkeley's contention that primary and secondary qualities are inseparable. We might therefore conclude that both are objective (*not* mind-dependent) rather than that both are subjective (mind-dependent). Some critics maintain that Berkeley's arguments fail to show that even secondary qualities are "in the mind." They believe that colors, sounds, odors, and textures (though perhaps not tastes) are no less objective than the primary qualities.

Another alternative would be the agnostic position that things-in-themselves are unknowable, and that consequently we can no more assert idealism than we can assert materialism. This is the position favored by Kant, Hume, and the positivists——all of whom admit the inseparability of primary and secondary qualities.

But it is also possible to reject Berkeley's thesis that primary and secondary qualities are inseparable. Actually, there is a very significant difference between the two sets of qualities. The secondary qualities are *sensory* properties, whereas the primary qualities are *formal* characteristics—the structures, relations, and quantities of things. This difference may justify the supposition that the primary qualities have a different epistemological status than the secondary qualities.

According to modern scientific theories of perception, the secondary qualities seem to depend upon physiological and mental factors and thus appear to be qualitative events in the perceiving organisms. Sounds seem to depend upon organic reactions to air-waves; colors upon organic reactions to electro-magnetic vibrations; and so on. Our *impressions* of primary qualities are similarly dependent upon our minds, but there is a significant difference: the laws of physics are framed in terms of abstract orders and quantitative relations—primary qualities—rather than in terms of concrete secondary qualities. We therefore have scientific warrant for believing that our impressions of primary but not of secondary qualities have objective counterparts—*if* science is dealing with a real objective world.

Relational properties cannot exist all by themselves; they must attach to the things related. On this point Berkeley is perfectly right. Yet it is conceivable that physical science reveals the relational structure of the real world without revealing its content. Atoms may exist and conform to Einstein's equations even though their ultimate qualitative nature remains a mystery.

5. Can We Test the Correspondence Between Ideas and Things? Once we distinguish between objects as we apprehend them and objects as they really are, how can we ever know that the former agree with the latter? Not only Berkeley, but Kant and Hegel as well, maintain that the correspondence test of truth is unworkable.

The impossibility of directly comparing ideas (or sense data) with things outside experience must be admitted. But we can *infer* things that we do not experience. No one, for example, *directly* observes another person's toothache, but one can be reasonably certain that the other person *is* suffering toothache. Such indirect knowledge involves the interpretation of signs, and we can often infer from signs what we cannot observe.

It is a striking fact that the signs of minds differ very markedly from the signs of external things. When we hear people talk, see them gesture, or read what they have written, we are interpreting signs of a very different sort than when we are

[1] See also Ralph Barton Perry, *Present Philosophical Tendencies* (Longmans, Green, 1929), pp. 129–132.

looking at a rock. The first set of signs are clearly indicative of thinking people and their thoughts, whereas the second set of signs, to all appearances, indicates something non-conscious and non-intelligent. It seems a bit fantastic and gratuitous to attribute a *mind* to the rock, or even to the system of nature of which the rock is a minute part. The sensible aspects of human behavior from which we infer a human mind have little resemblance to the sensible characteristics of nature from which Berkeley would have us infer God. Perhaps Kant and the positivists are right—perhaps we can never know the rock as a thing-in-itself—but such clues as we have for judging the nature of inorganic things are quite different from the clues whereby we infer the minds of our friends and acquaintances. Reality *appears* to be dualistic, made up of both mental and physical qualities, and it involves a sharp break with common sense to suppose that this appearance is quite illusory.

6. OTHER ISSUES. The contrast between Berkeley's pluralistic idealism and Hegel's absolute idealism suggests the great issue of monism *versus* pluralism—the question whether reality, in its basic structure, is one or many. This issue, in turn, gives rise to the question whether relations are "internal" or "external"—whether things are so interdependent that they are determined by the character of their relations, or whether they can enter or leave these relations without prejudice to their existence and basic characteristics. Berkeley recognized an internal relatedness between minds and their objects, since he believed that no mind can function without objects and no object can exist unperceived. Hegel extended the notion of internal relatedness to its uttermost limits, thinking of truth and reality in terms of an all-comprehensive and coherent system. Also, Berkeley's attack upon abstract ideas, his rejection of such abstract notions as "substance," "matter," and "primary qualities," involves the whole question of the meaning of universals and the validity of abstract thought. Hegel's theory of the "concrete universal" as the larger coherent pattern that embraces and gives meaning and interrelatedness to particular things, is an alternative to both abstract universalism and Berkeley's particularism. Finally, there is the question of the validity of Hegel's "dialectical" logic, with its implication that polarities and opposites are fundamental to the nature of things. This "dialectic" is reflected in his vision of history, which is conceived as the development of mind or spirit by means of a conflict of ideas or cultural forces. Hegel is not represented in this chapter, but the reader can turn to Chapter 15 for a represenative selection from Hegel's *Philosophy of History*.

Berkeley and Hegel have raised issues of profound and lasting importance. Perhaps their greatest service is to stimulate us to think rather than to give us final answers.

6

Dualism

RENÉ DESCARTES (1596–1650)

Descartes' father was Councillor of the Parliament of Brittany and owner of a fair amount of landed property. His mother, apparently consumptive, died during his infancy and left him with enfeebled health. Anxious to surround the delicate boy with every care, his father entrusted Descartes' education to the Jesuits. It was at the newly established Jesuit college at La Flèche that the young Descartes fell in love with geometry.

Leaving school at seventeen, Descartes spent the next four years in Paris studying law. Thereafter for several years, he lived as a traveler and a soldier, serving as a volunteer in three European armies, in the Netherlands, Bavaria, and Hungary. During this period, when he had a good deal of time to reflect, he came to doubt the value of everything he had learned with the single exception of mathematics.

On November 10, 1619, he had the remarkable experience to which he refers at the beginning of Part II of the *Discourse on Method*. He spent this cold November day in a stove-heated room, meditating about the mathematical and scientific ideas that had been tumbling through his mind for several days. Nervously exhausted, he finally fell asleep and had three strange dreams, which he interpreted as pointing to a life of philosophical reflection. As a result of these dreams, which he thought were inspired by God, and the intense intellectual activity that preceded them, he saw himself at the parting of the ways, and he resolved thenceforth to follow the path of philosophy and scientific research.

Although Descartes has not given us a detailed account of "the foundations of a wonderful science" which he discovered at this time, we know he had the conviction that the method of mathematics could be generalized to apply to all the sciences and that thereby certainty could be gained. Moreover, he conceived the method of applying algebraic symbolism to geometry and of using coordinates to describe geometrical figures; in other words, he founded analytical geometry. Finally, he was convinced that science and philosophy should form one whole, subject to a single method.

He vowed that no ties of marriage or society should deter him from a life of intellectual research devoted to the development of these insights. Although he continued to travel and to study "the great book of the world" for the next nine years (1619–1628), he still found time to work on various problems of mathematics and science. Growing tired of his wanderings at last, in 1628 he sold his inherited estates in France and settled in a quiet country house in Holland. With abundant leisure and a few servants to take care of his material needs, he formed the habit of staying in bed until about noon, reading, writing, or meditating. He soon acquired a wide reputation and was visited by, or corresponded with, many notable scientists and philosophers of the age. During this sojourn in Holland, he had what was apparently his only love affair. The daughter who was the product of this alliance died at the age of five, much to her father's sorrow.

In the autumn of 1649, Descartes accepted an invitation from Queen Christina of Sweden to spend a winter at her court. An imperious though learned monarch, Christina thought that she had the right to command his services at any hour she chose. Daily at five in the morning throughout the bitterly cold winter, Descartes was ushered into the presence of the Queen, where he discoursed to her about philosophy while he stood shivering on the marble floor. Unused to the biting climate and the rigors of such early rising, he caught pneumonia and died in March 1650, a few days before his fifty-fifth birthday.

Scepticism, Mind and Body

Meditation I

Of the things which may be brought within the sphere of the doubtful.

It is now some years since I detected how many were the false beliefs that I had from my earliest youth admitted as true, and how doubtful was everything I had since constructed on this basis; and from that time I was convinced that I must once for all seriously undertake to rid myself of all the opinions which I had formerly accepted, and commence to build anew from the foundation, if I wanted to establish any firm and permanent structure in the sciences. But as this enter-

The following excerpts from the *Meditations* are from *The Philosophical Works of Descartes*, translated from the Latin by Elizabeth S. Haldane and G. R. T. Ross, and published by Cambridge at the University Press, 1931. Where it seems desirable an alternative reading from the French is given in brackets. Reprinted by permission.

prise appeared to be a very great one, I waited until I had attained an age so mature that I could not hope that at any later date I should be better fitted to execute my design. This reason caused me to delay so long that I should feel that I was doing wrong were I to occupy in deliberation the time that yet remains to me for action. Today, then, since very opportunely for the plan I have in view I have delivered my mind from every care [and am happily agitated by no passions] and since I have procured for myself an assured leisure in a peaceable retirement, I shall at last seriously and freely address myself to the general upheaval of all my former opinions.

Now for this object it is not necessary that I should show that all of these are false—I shall perhaps never arrive at this end. But inasmuch as reason already persuades me that I ought no less carefully to withhold my assent from matters which are not entirely certain and indubitable than from those which appear to me manifestly to be false, if I am able to find in each one some reason to doubt, this will suffice to justify my rejecting the whole. And for that end it will not be requisite that I should examine each in particular, which would be an endless undertaking; for owing to the fact that the destruction of the foundations of necessity brings with it the downfall of the rest of the edifice, I shall only in the first place attack those principles upon which all my former opinions rested.

All that up to the present time I have accepted as most true and certain I have learned either from the senses or through the senses; but it is sometimes proved to me that these senses are deceptive, and it is wiser not to trust entirely to any thing by which we have once been deceived.

But it may be that although the senses sometimes deceive us concerning things which are hardly perceptible, or very far away, there are yet many others to be met with as to which we cannot reasonably have any doubt, although we recognize them by their means. For example, there is the fact that I am here, seated by the fire, attired in a dressing gown, having this paper in my hands and other similar matters. And how could I deny that these hands and this body are mine, were it not perhaps that I compare myself to certain persons, devoid of sense, whose cerebella are so troubled and clouded by the violent vapors of black bile, that they constantly assure us that they think they are kings when they are really quite poor, or that they are clothed in purple when they are really without covering, or who imag-

ine that they have an earthenware head or are nothing but pumpkins or are made of glass. But they are mad, and I should not be any the less insane were I to follow examples so extravagant.

At the same time I must remember that I am a man, and that consequently I am in the habit of sleeping, and in my dreams representing to myself the same things or sometimes even less probable things, than do those who are insane in their waking moments. How often has it happened to me that in the night I dreamt that I found myself in this particular place, that I was dressed and seated near the fire, whilst in reality I was lying undressed in bed! At this moment it does indeed seem to me that it is with eyes awake that I am looking at this paper; that this head which I move is not asleep, that it is deliberately and of set purpose that I extend my hand and perceive it; what happens in sleep does not appear so clear nor so distinct as does all this. But in thinking over this I remind myself that on many occasions I have in sleep been deceived by similar illusions, and in dwelling carefully on this reflection I see so manifestly that there are no certain indications by which we may clearly distinguish wakefulness from sleep that I am lost in astonishment. And my astonishment is such that it is almost incapable of persuading me that I now dream.

Now let us assume that we are asleep and that all these particulars, *e.g.* that we open our eyes, shake our head, extend our hands, and so on, are but false delusions; and let us reflect that possibly neither our hands nor our whole body are such as they appear to us to be. At the same time we must at least confess that the things which are represented to us in sleep are like painted representations which can only have been formed as the counterparts of something real and true, and that in this way those general things at least, *i.e.* eyes, a head, hands, and a whole body, are not imaginary things, but things really existent. For, as a matter of fact, painters, even when they study with the greatest skill to represent sirens and satyrs by forms the most strange and extraordinary, cannot give them natures which are entirely new, but merely make a certain medley of the members of different animals; or if their imagination is extravagant enough to invent something so novel that nothing similar has ever before been seen, and that then their work represents a thing purely fictitious and absolutely false, it is certain all the same that the colors of which this is composed are necessarily real. And for the same reason, although these general things, to wit, [a body], eyes, a head, and such like, may be imaginary, we are bound at the same time to confess that there are at least some other objects yet more simple and more universal, which are real and true; and of these just in the same way as with certain real colors, all these images of things which dwell in our thoughts, whether true and real or false and fantastic, are formed.

To such a class of things pertains corporeal nature in general, and its extension, the figure of extended things, their quantity or magnitude and number, as also the place in which they are, the time which measures their duration, and so on.

That is possibly why our reasoning is not unjust when we conclude from this that Physics, Astronomy, Medicine and all other sciences which have as their end the consideration of composite things, are very dubious and uncertain; but that Arithmetic, Geometry and other sciences of that kind which only treat of things that are very simple and very general, without taking great trouble to ascertain whether they are actually existent or not, contain some measure of certainty and an element of the indubitable. For whether I am awake or asleep, two and three together always form five, and the square can never have more than four sides, and it does not seem possible that truths so clear and apparent can be suspected of any falsity [or uncertainty].

Nevertheless I have long had fixed in my mind the belief that an all-powerful God existed by whom I have been created such as I am. But how do I know that He has not brought it to pass that there is no earth, no heaven, no extended body, no magnitude, no place, and that nevertheless [I possess the perceptions of all these things and that] they seem to me to exist just exactly as I now see them? And, besides, as I sometimes imagine that others deceive themselves in the things which they think they know best, how do I know that I am not deceived every time that I add two and three, or count the sides of a square, or judge of things yet simpler, if anything simpler can be imagined? But possibly God has not desired that I should be thus deceived, for He is said to be supremely good. If, however, it is contrary to His goodness to have made me such that I constantly deceive myself, it would also appear to be contrary to His goodness to permit me to be sometimes deceived, and nevertheless I cannot doubt that He does permit this.

There may indeed be those who would prefer to deny the existence of a God so powerful, rather than believe that all other things are uncertain. But let us not oppose them for the present, and grant that all that is said of a God is a fable; nevertheless in whatever way they suppose that I have arrived at the state of being that I have reached—whether they attribute it to fate or to accident, or make out that it is by a continual succession of antecedents, or by some other method—since to err and deceive oneself is a defect, it is clear that the greater will be the probability of my being so imperfect as to deceive myself ever, as is the Author to whom they assign my origin the less powerful. To these reasons I have certainly nothing to reply, but at the end I feel constrained to confess that there is nothing in all that I formerly believed to be true, of which I cannot in some measure doubt, and that not merely through want of thought or through levity, but for reasons which are very powerful and maturely considered; so that henceforth I ought not the less carefully to refrain from giving credence to these opinions than to that which is manifestly false, if I desire to arrive at any certainty [in the sciences].

But it is not sufficient to have made these remarks, we must also be careful to keep them in mind. For these ancient and commonly held opinions still revert frequently to my mind, long and familiar custom having given them the right to occupy my mind against my inclination and rendered them almost masters of my belief; nor will I ever lose the habit of deferring to them or of placing my confidence in them, so long as I consider them as they really are, *i.e.* opinions in some measure doubtful, as I have just shown, and at the same time highly probable, so that there is much more reason to believe than to deny them. That is why I consider that I shall not be acting amiss, if, taking of set purpose a contrary belief, I allow myself to be deceived, and for a certain time pretend that all these opinions are entirely false and imaginary, until at last, having thus balanced my former prejudices with my latter [so that they cannot divert my opinions more to one side than to the other], my judgment will no longer be dominated by bad usage or turned away from the right knowledge of the truth. For I am assured that there can be neither peril nor error in this course, and that I cannot at present yield too much to distrust, since I am not considering the question of action, but only of knowledge.

I shall then suppose, not that God who is supremely good and the fountain of truth, but some evil genius not less powerful than deceitful, has employed his whole energies in deceiving me; I shall consider that the heavens, the earth, colors, figures, sound, and all other external things are nought but the illusions and dreams of which this genius has availed himself in order to lay traps for my credulity; I shall consider myself as having no hands, no eyes, no flesh, no blood, nor any senses, yet falsely believing myself to possess all these things; I shall remain obstinately attached to this idea, and if by this means it is not in my power to arrive at the knowledge of any truth, I may at least do what is in my power [*i.e.* suspend my judgment], and with firm purpose avoid giving credence to any false thing, or being imposed upon by this arch deceiver, however powerful and deceptive he may be. But this task is a laborious one, and insensibly a certain lassitude leads me into the course of my ordinary life. And just as a captive who in sleep enjoys imaginary liberty, when he begins to suspect that his liberty is but a dream, fears to awaken, and conspires with these agreeable illusions that the deception may be prolonged, so insensibly of my own accord I fall back into my former opinions, and I dread awakening from this slumber, lest the laborious wakefulness which would follow the tranquillity of this repose should have to be spent not in daylight, but in the excessive darkness of the difficulties which have just been discussed.

Meditation II

Of the Nature of the Human Mind; and that it is more easily known than the Body.

The Meditation of yesterday filled my mind with so many doubts that it is no longer in my power to forget them. And yet I do not see in what manner I can resolve them; and, just as if I had all of a sudden fallen into very deep water, I am so disconcerted that I can neither make certain of setting my feet on the bottom, nor can I swim and so support myself on the surface. I shall nevertheless make an effort and follow anew the same path as that on which I yesterday entered, *i.e.* I shall proceed by setting aside all that in which the least doubt could be supposed to exist, just as if I had discovered that it was absolutely false; and I shall ever follow in this road until I have met with something which is certain, or at least, if I can do nothing else, until I have learned for certain that there is nothing in the world that is certain. Archimedes, in order that he might draw the terrestrial globe out of its place, and transport it elsewhere, demanded only that one point should be fixed and immovable; in the same way I shall have the right to conceive high hopes if I am happy enough to discover one thing only which is certain and indubitable.

I suppose, then, that all the things that I see are false; I persuade myself that nothing has ever existed of all that my fallacious memory represents to me. I consider that I possess no senses; I imagine that body, figure, extension, movement and place are but the fictions of my mind. What, then, can be esteemed as true? Perhaps nothing at all, unless that there is nothing in the world that is certain.

But how can I know there is not something different from those things that I have just considered, of which one cannot have the slightest doubt? Is there not some God, or some other being by whatever name we call it, who puts these reflections into my mind? That is not necessary, for is it not possible that I am capable of producing them myself? I myself, am I not at least something? But I have already denied that I had senses and body. Yet I hesitate, for what follows from that? Am I so dependent on body and senses that I cannot exist without these? But I was persuaded that there was nothing in all the world, that there was no heaven, no earth, that there were no minds, nor any bodies: was I not then likewise persuaded that I did not exist? Not at all; of a surety I myself did exist since I persuaded myself of something [or merely because I thought of something]. But there is some deceiver or other, very powerful and very cunning, who ever employs his ingenuity in deceiving me. Then without doubt I exist also if he deceives me, and let him deceive me as much as he will, he can never cause me to be nothing so long as I think that I am something. So that after having reflected well and carefully examined all things, we must come to the definite conclusion that this proposition: I am, I exist, is necessarily true each time that I pronounce it, or that I mentally conceive it.

But I do not yet know clearly enough what I am, I who am certain that I am; and hence I must be careful to see that I do not imprudently take some other object in place of myself, and thus that I do not go astray in respect of this knowledge that I hold to be the most certain and most evident of all that I have formerly learned. That is why I shall now consider anew what I believed myself to be before I embarked upon these last reflections; and of my former opinions I shall withdraw all that might even in a small degree be invalidated by the reasons which I have just brought forward, in order that there may be nothing at all left beyond what is absolutely certain and indubitable.

What then did I formerly believe myself to be? Undoubtedly I believed myself to be a man. But what is a man? Shall I say a reasonable animal? Certainly not; for then I should have to inquire what an animal is, and what is reasonable; and thus from a single question I should insensibly fall into an infinitude of others more difficult; and I should not wish to waste the little time and leisure remaining to me in trying to unravel subtleties like these. But I shall rather stop here to consider the thoughts which of themselves spring up in my mind, and which were not inspired by anything beyond my own nature alone when I applied myself to the consideration of my being. In the first place, then, I considered myself as having a face, hands, arms, and all that system of members composed of bones and flesh as seen in a corpse which I designated by the name of body. In addition to this I considered that I was nourished, that I walked, that I felt, and that I thought, and I referred all these actions to the soul: but I did not stop to consider what the soul was, or if I did stop, I imagined that it was something extremely rare and subtle like a wind, a flame, or an ether, which was spread throughout my grosser parts. As to body I had no manner of doubt about its nature, but thought I had a very clear knowledge of it; and if I had desired to explain it according to the notions that I had then formed of it, I should have described it thus: By the body I understand all that which can be defined by a certain figure: something which can be confined in a certain place, and which can fill a given space in such a way that every other body will be excluded from it; which can be perceived either by touch, or by sight, or by hearing, or by taste, or by smell: which can be moved in many ways not, in truth, by itself, but by something which is foreign to it, by which it is touched [and from which it receives impressions]: for to have the power of self-movement, as also of feeling or of thinking, I did not consider to appertain to the nature of body: on the contrary, I was rather astonished to find that faculties similar to them existed in some bodies.

But what am I, now that I suppose that there is a certain genius which is extremely powerful, and, if I may say so, malicious, who employs all his powers in deceiving me? Can I affirm that I possess the least of all those things which I have just said pertain to the nature of body? I pause to consider, I resolve all these things in my mind, and find none of which I can say that it pertains to me. It would be tedious to stop to enumerate them. Let us pass to the attributes of soul and see if there is any one which is in me? What of nutrition or walking [the first mentioned]? But if it is so that I have no body, it is also true that I can neither walk nor take nourishment. Another attribute is sensation. But one cannot feel without body, and besides I have thought I perceived many things during sleep that I recognized in my waking moments as not having been experienced at all. What of thinking? I find here that thought is an attribute that belongs to me; it alone cannot be separated from me. I am, I exist, that is certain. But how often? Just when I think; for it might possibly be the case if I ceased entirely to think, that I should likewise cease altogether to exist. I do not now admit anything which is not necessarily true: to speak accurately I am not more than a thing which thinks, that is to say a mind or a soul, or an understanding, or a reason, which are terms whose significance was formerly unknown to me. I am, however, a real thing and really exist; but what thing? I have answered: a thing which thinks.

And what more? I shall exercise my imagination [in order to see if I am not something more]. I am not a collection of members which we call the human body: I am not a subtle air distributed through these members, I am not a wind, a fire, a vapor, a breath, nor anything at all which I can imagine or conceive; because I have assumed that all these were nothing. Without changing that supposition I find that I only leave myself certain of the fact that I am somewhat. But perhaps it is true that these same things which I supposed were non-existent because they are unknown to me, are really not different from the self which I know. I am not sure about this, I shall not dispute about it now; I can only give judgment on things that are known to me. I know that I exist, and I inquire what I am, I whom I know to exist. But it is very certain that the knowledge of my existence taken in its precise significance does not depend on things whose existence is not yet known to me; consequently it does not depend on those which I can feign in imagination. And indeed the very term *feign* in imagination proves to me my error, for I really do this if I image myself a something, since to imagine is nothing else than to contemplate the figure or image of a corporeal thing. But I already know for certain that I am, and that it may be that all these images, and, speaking generally, all things that relate to the nature of body are nothing but dreams [and chimeras]. For this reason I see clearly that I have as little reason to say, "I shall stimulate my imagination in order to know more distinctly what I am," than if I were to say, "I am now awake," and I perceive somewhat that is real and true: but because I do not yet perceive it distinctly enough, I shall go to sleep of express purpose, so that my dreams may represent the perception with greatest truth and evidence." And, thus, I know for certain that nothing of all that I can understand by means of my imagination belongs to this knowledge which I have of myself, and that it is necessary to recall the mind from this mode of thought with the utmost diligence in order that it may be able to know its own nature with perfect distinctness.

But what then am I? A thing which thinks. What is a thing which thinks? It is a thing which doubts, understands, [conceives], affirms, denies, wills, refuses, which also imagines and feels.

Certainly it is no small matter if all these things pertain to my nature. But why should they not so pertain? Am I not that being who now doubts nearly everything, who nevertheless understands certain things, who affirms that one only is true, who denies all the others, who desires to know more, is averse from being deceived, who imagines many things, sometimes indeed despite his will, and who perceives many likewise, as by the intervention of the bodily organs? Is there nothing in all this which is as true as it is certain that I exist, even though I should always sleep and though he who has given me being employed all his ingenuity in deceiving me? Is there likewise any one of these attributes which can be distinguished from my thought, or which might be said to be separated from myself? For it is so evident of itself that it is I who doubts, who understands, and who desires, that there is no reason here to add anything to explain it. And I have certainly the power of imagining likewise; for although it may happen (as I formerly supposed) that none of the things which I imagine are true, nevertheless this power of imagining does not cease to be really in use, and it forms part of my thought. Finally, I am the same who feels, that is to say, who perceives certain things, as by the organs of sense, since in truth I see light, I hear noise, I feel heat. But it will be said that these phenomena are false and that I am dreaming. Let it be so; still it is at least quite certain that it seems to me that I see light, that I hear noise and that I feel heat. That cannot be false; properly speaking it is what is in me called feeling; and used in this precise sense that is no other thing than thinking.

From this time I begin to know what I am with a little more clearness and distinction than before; but nevertheless it still seems to me, and I cannot prevent myself from thinking, that corporeal things, whose images are framed by thought, which are tested by the senses, are much more distinctly known than that obscure part of me which does not come under the imagination. Although really it is very strange to say that I know and understand more distinctly these things whose existence seems to me dubious, which are unknown to me, and which do not belong to me, than others of the truth of which I am convinced, which are known to me and which pertain to my real nature, in a word, than myself. But I see clearly how the case stands: my mind loves to wander, and cannot yet suffer itself to be retained within the just limits of truth. Very good, let us once more give it the freest rein, so that, when afterwards we seize the proper occasion for pulling up, it may the more easily be regulated and controlled.

Let us begin by considering the commonest matters, those which we believe to be the most distinctly comprehended, to wit, the bodies which we touch and see; not indeed bodies in general, for these general ideas are usually a little more confused, but let us consider one body in particular. Let us take for example, this piece of wax: it has been taken quite freshly from the hive, and it has not yet lost the sweetness of the honey which it contains; it still retains somewhat of the odor of the flowers from which it has been culled; its color, its figure, its size are apparent; it is hard, cold, easily handled, and if you strike it with the finger, it will emit a sound. Finally all the things which are requisite to cause us distinctly to recognize a body, are met within it. But notice that while I speak and approach the fire what remained of the taste is exhaled, the smell evaporates, the color alters, the figure is destroyed, the size increases, it becomes liquid, it heats, scarcely can one handle it, and when one strikes it, no sound is emitted. Does the same wax remain after this change? We must confess that it remains; none would judge otherwise. What then did I know so distinctly in this piece of wax? It could certainly be nothing of all that the senses brought to my notice, since all these things which fall under taste, smell, sight, touch, and hearing, are found to be changed, and yet the same wax remains.

Perhaps it was what I now think, viz. that this wax was not that sweetness of honey, nor that agreeable scent of flowers, nor that particular whiteness, nor that figure, nor that sound, but simply a body which a little before appeared to me as perceptible under these forms, and which is now perceptible under others. But what, precisely, is that I imagine when I form such conceptions? Let us attentively consider this, and, abstracting from all that does not belong to the wax, let us see what remains. Certainly nothing remains excepting a certain extended thing which is flexible and movable. But what is the meaning of flexible and movable? Is it not that I imagine that this piece of wax being round is capable of becoming square and of passing from a square to a triangular figure? No, certainly it is not that, since I imagine it admits of an infinitude of similar changes, and I nevertheless do not know how to compass the infinitude by my imagination, and consequently this conception which I have of the wax is not brought about by the faculty of imagination. What now is this extension? Is it not also unknown? For it becomes greater when the wax is melted, greater when it is boiled, and greater still when the heat increases; and I should not conceive [clearly] according to truth what wax is, if I did not think that even this piece that we are considering is capable of receiving more variations in extension than I have ever imagined. We must then grant that I could not even understand through the imagination what this piece of wax is, and that it is my mind alone which perceives it. I say this piece of wax in particular, for as to wax in general it is yet clearer. But what is this piece of wax which cannot be understood excepting by the [understanding or] mind? It is certainly the same that I see, touch, imagine, and finally it is the same which I have always believed it to be from the beginning. But what must particularly be observed is that its perception is neither an act of vision, nor of touch, nor of imagination, and has never been such although it may have appeared formerly to be so, but only an intuition of the mind, which may be imperfect and confused as it was formerly, or clear and distinct as it is at present, according as my attention is more or less directed to the elements which are found in it, and of which it is composed.

Yet in the meantime I am greatly astonished when I consider [the great feebleness of mind] and its proneness to fall [insensibly] into error; for although without giving expression to my thoughts I consider all this in my own mind, words often impede me and I am almost deceived by the terms of ordinary language. For we say that we see the same wax, if it is present, and not that we simply judge that it is the same from its having the same color and figure. From this I should conclude that I knew the wax by means of vision and not simply by the intuition of the mind; unless by chance I remember that, when looking from a window and saying I see men who pass in the street, I really do not see them, but infer that what I see is men, just as I say that I see wax. And yet what do I see from the window but hats and coats which may cover automatic machines? Yet I judge these to be men. And similarly solely by the faculty of judgment which rests in my mind, I comprehend that which I believed I saw with my eyes.

A man who makes it his aim to raise his knowledge above the common should be ashamed to derive the occasion for doubting from the forms of speech invented by the vulgar; I prefer to pass on and consider whether I had a more evident and perfect conception of what the wax was when I first perceived it, and when I believed I knew it by means of the external senses or at least by the common sense as it is called, that is to say by the imaginative faculty, or whether my present conception is clearer now that I have most carefully examined what it is, and in what way it can be known. It would certainly be absurd to doubt as to this. For what was there in this first perception which was distinct? What was there which might not as well have been perceived by any of the animals? But when I distinguish the wax from its external forms, and when, just as if I had taken from it its vestments, I consider it quite naked, it is certain that although some error may still be found in my judgment, I can nevertheless not perceive it thus without a human mind.

But finally what shall I say of this mind, that is, of myself, for up to this point I do not admit in myself anything but mind? What then, I who seem to perceive this piece of wax distinctly, do I not know myself, not only with much more truth and certainty, but also with much more distinctness and clearness? For if I judge that the wax is or exists from the fact that I see it, it certainly follows much more clearly that I am or that I exist myself from the fact that I see it. For it may be that what I see is not really wax, it may also be that I do not possess eyes with which to see anything; but it cannot be that when I see, or (for I no longer take account of the distinction) when I think I see, that I myself who think am nought. So if I judge that the wax exists from the fact that I touch it, the same thing will follow, to wit, that I am; and if I judge that my imagination, or some other cause, whatever it is, persuades me that the wax exists, I shall still conclude the same. And what I have here remarked of wax may be applied to all other things which are external to me [and which are met with outside of me]. And further, if the [notion or] perception of wax has seemed to me

clearer and more distinct, not only after the sight or the touch, but also after many other causes have rendered it quite manifest to me, with how much more [evidence] and distinctness must it be said that I now know myself, since all the reasons which contribute to the knowledge of wax, or any other body whatever, are yet better proofs of the nature of my mind! And there are so many other things in the mind itself which may contribute to the elucidation of its nature, that those which depend on body such as these just mentioned, hardly merit being taken into account.

But finally here I am, having insensibly reverted to the point I desired, for, since it is now manifest to me that even bodies are not properly speaking known by the senses or by the faculty of imagination, but by the understanding only, and since they are not known from the fact that they are seen or touched, but only because they are understood, I see clearly that there is nothing which is easier for me to know than my mind. But because it is difficult to rid oneself so promptly of an opinion to which one was accustomed for so long, it will be well that I should halt a little at this point, so that by the length of my meditation I may more deeply imprint on my memory this new knowledge.

Meditation III

Of God: that He exists.

I shall now close my eyes, I shall stop my ears, I shall call away all my senses, I shall efface even from my thoughts all the images of corporeal things, or at least (for that is hardly possible). I shall esteem them as vain and false; and thus holding converse only with myself and considering my own nature, I shall try little by little to reach a better knowledge of and a more familiar acquaintanceship with myself. I am a thing that thinks, that is to say, that doubts, affirms, denies, that knows a few things, that is ignorant of many, [that loves, that hates], that wills, that desires, that also imagines and perceives; for as I remarked before, although the things which I perceive and imagine are perhaps nothing at all apart from me and in themselves, I am nevertheless assured that these modes of thought that I call perceptions and imaginations, inasmuch only as they are modes of thought, certainly reside [and are met with] in me.

And in the little that I have just said, I think I have summed up all that I really know, or at least all that hitherto I was aware that I knew. In order to try to extend my knowledge further, I shall now look around more carefully and see whether I cannot still discover in myself some other things which I have not hitherto perceived. I am certain that I am a thing which thinks; but do I not then likewise know what is requisite to render me certain of a truth? Certainly in this first knowledge there is nothing that assures me of its truth, excepting the clear and distinct perception of that which I state, which would not indeed suffice to assure me that what I say is true, if it could ever happen that a thing which I conceived so clearly and distinctly could be false; and accord-

ingly it seems to me that already I can establish as a general rule that all things which I perceive very clearly and very distinctly are true.

At the same time I have before received and admitted many things to be very certain and manifest, which yet I afterwards recognized as being dubious. What then were these things? They were the earth, sky, stars and all other objects which I apprehended by means of the senses. But what did I clearly [and distinctly] perceive in them? Nothing more than that the ideas or thoughts of these things were presented to my mind. And not even now do I deny that these ideas are met with in me. But there was yet another thing which I affirmed, and which, owing to the habit which I had formed of believing it, I thought I perceived very clearly, although in truth I did not perceive it at all, to wit, that there were objects outside of me from which these ideas proceeded, and to which they were entirely similar. And it was in this that I erred, or, if perchance my judgment was correct, this was not due to any knowledge arising from my perception.

But when I took anything very simple and easy in the sphere of arithmetic or geometry into consideration, *e.g.* that two and three together made five, and other things of the sort, were not these present to my mind so clearly as to enable me to affirm that they were true? Certainly if I judged that since such matters could be doubted, this would not have been so for any other reason than that it came into my mind that perhaps a God might have endowed me with such a nature that I may have been deceived even concerning things which seemed to me most manifest. But every time that this preconceived opinion of the sovereign power of a God presents itself to my thought, I am constrained to confess that it is easy to Him, if He wishes it, to cause me to err, even in matters in which I believe myself to have the best evidence. And, on the other hand, always when I direct my attention to things which I believe myself to perceive very clearly, I am so persuaded of their truth that I let myself break out into words such as these: Let who will deceive me, He can never cause me to be nothing while I think that I am, or some day cause it to be true to say that I have never been, it being true now to say that I am, or that two and three make more or less than five, or any such thing in which I see a manifest contradiction. And certainly, since I have no reason to believe that there is a God who is a deceiver, and as I have not yet satisfied myself that there is a God at all, the reason for doubt which depends on this opinion alone is very slight, and so to speak metaphysical. But in order to be able altogether to remove it, I must inquire whether there is a God as soon as the occasion presents itself; and if I find that there is a God, I must also inquire whether He may be a deceiver; for without a knowledge of these two truths I do not see that I can ever be certain of anything.

[*To answer this lingering doubt, Descartes "proves" that there is a God who, as perfect, would not deceive me. Since arguments for the existence of God have been considered in detail in Chapter 2, a brief summary of Descartes' arguments will here be sufficient.*

His first argument for the existence of God consists of four steps: (1) I have an idea of God. (2) Everything, including my idea, has a cause. (3) Since the greater cannot proceed from the less, nothing less than God is adequate to explain my idea of God. This step involves the notion that the idea of a Perfect Being is, in conception, perfect; that no imperfect being is capable of producing such an idea; and that hence it requires a perfect Cause to produce it. (4) Therefore God exists.

Descartes advances a second argument for God, once again starting with "I think, therefore I am." He argues (still using the first person pronoun) that God is the cause, not only of my idea of God, but of me. This is an argument by elimination: (1) I am not the cause of myself, for if I were, I would not be the highly imperfect and fallible being that I know myself to be. (2) No other finite being could be the sufficient cause of my existence, for if such a being existed, it in turn would have to be explained, as would any prior finite cause as well. I would thus have to trace the causal process back from stage to stage to the ultimate cause, an eternal and necessary being who requires no explanation beyond itself. Only such an infinite cause could be conceived as existing, not merely through my life, but through all the lives involved in the total succession of finite beings—and only such a cause would be adequate to maintain as well as to originate the entire succession.

(3) The ultimate cause could not be multiple, because I conceive of God as absolutely one, and the cause of this idea must be no less perfect than its effect, not falling short of the idea in its unity or in any other respect. (4) The only possibility that remains is that an infinite and monotheistic God is the cause. Therefore God exists.

In Meditation V which has been omitted in the present book, Descartes presents a third argument for God's existence—a restatement of the so-called Ontological Argument of Saint Anselm, an early medieval philosopher. Since this argument is dealt with in Chapter 14, we shall not consider it here.

The importance of God in Descartes' system is that God is used to guarantee not a system of dogma but science and philosophy. Science and philosophy are based upon reason and memory, and God is needed to guarantee their reliability. God, being perfect, would not deceive me—God would not, like a malignant demon, so mislead me as to invalidate my most vivid memory and careful reasoning. Descartes' constructive argument starts with "I think, therefore I am." But, almost surreptitiously, he admits three other "self-evident truths":

1. *Whatever is clearly and distinctly perceived is true.*

2. *Nothing can be without a cause.*

3. *The cause must be at least as great as the effect.*

From these premises he deduces two additional "truths":

4. *God exists.*

5. *God, being perfect, cannot deceive me.*

The rest of his argument follows rather quickly. He argues for the existence of other minds and material objects alike on the grounds of God's veracity. This means not that all my ideas are true but simply that the faculties God has given me are reliable when used correctly—without prejudice, hastiness, or naïveté. I can trust only "firm conceptions born in a sound and attentive mind from the light of reason alone" and rigorous deductions from these conceptions.

The remainder of Meditation III and Meditations IV and V are omitted.]

Meditation VI

Of the existence of Material Things, and of the real distinction between the Soul and Body of Man.

. . . First of all I shall recall to my memory those matters which I hitherto held to be true, as having perceived them through the senses, and the foundations on which my belief has rested; in the next place I shall examine the reasons which have since obliged me to place them in doubt; in the last place I shall consider which of them I must now believe.

First of all, then, I perceived that I had a head, hands, feet, and all other members of which this body—which I considered as a part, or possibly even as the whole, of myself—is composed. Further I was sensible that this body was placed amidst many others, from which it was capable of being affected in many different ways, beneficial and hurtful, and I remarked that a certain feeling of pleasure accompanied those that were beneficial, and pain those which were harmful. And in addition to this pleasure and pain, I also experienced hunger, thirst, and other similar appetites, as also certain corporeal inclinations towards joy, sadness, anger, and other similar passions. And outside myself, in addition to extension, figure, and motions of bodies, I remarked in them hardness, heat, and all other tactile qualities, and, further, light and color, and scents and sounds, the variety of which gave me the means of distinguishing the sky, the earth, the sea, and generally all the other bodies, one from the other. And certainly, considering the ideas of all these qualities which presented themselves to my mind, and which alone I perceived properly or immediately, it was not without reason that I believed myself to perceive objects quite different from my thought, to wit, bodies from which those ideas proceeded; for I found by experience that these ideas presented themselves to me without my consent being requisite, so that I could not perceive any object, however desirous I might be, unless it were present to the organs of sense; and it was not in my power not to perceive it, when it was present. And because the ideas which I perceived through the senses were much more lively, more clear, and even, in their own way, more distinct than any of those which I could of myself frame in meditation, or than those I found impressed on my memory, it appeared as though they could not have proceeded from my mind, so that they must necessarily have been produced in me by some other things.

And having no knowledge of those objects excepting the knowledge which the ideas themselves gave me, nothing was more likely to occur to my mind than that the objects were similar to the ideas which were caused. And because I likewise remembered that I had formerly made use of my senses rather than my reason, and recognized that the ideas which I formed of myself were not so distinct as those which I perceived through the senses, and that they were most frequently even composed of portions of these last, I persuaded myself easily that I had no idea in my mind which had not formerly come to me through the senses. Nor was it without some reason that I believed that this body (which by a certain special right I call my own) belonged to me more properly and more strictly than any other; for in fact I could never be separated from it as from other bodies; I experienced in it and on account of it all my appetites and affections, and finally I was touched by the feeling of pain and the titillation of pleasure in its parts, and not in the parts of other bodies which were separated from it. But when I inquired, why, from some, I know not what, painful sensation, there follows sadness of mind, and from the pleasurable sensation there arises joy, or why this mysterious emotion of the stomach which I call hunger causes me to desire to eat, and dryness of throat causes a desire to drink, and so on, I could give no reason excepting that nature taught me so; for there is certainly no affinity (that I at least can understand) between the craving of the stomach and the desire to eat, any more than between the perception of whatever causes pain and the thought of sadness which arises from this perception. And in the same way it appeared to me that I had learned from nature all the other judgments which I formed regarding the objects of my senses, since I remarked that these judgments were formed in me before I had the leisure to weigh and consider any reasons which might oblige me to make them.

But afterwards many experiences little by little destroyed all the faith which I had rested in my senses; for I from time to time observed that those towers which from afar appeared to me to be round, more closely observed seemed square, and that colossal statues raised on the summit of these towers, appeared as quite tiny statues when viewed from the bottom; and so in an infinitude of other cases I found error in judgments founded on the external senses. And not only in those founded on the external senses, but even in those founded on the internal as well; for is there anything more intimate or more internal than pain? And yet I have learned from some persons whose arms or legs have been cut off, that they sometimes seemed to feel pain in the part which had been amputated, which made me think that I could not be quite certain that it was a certain member which pained me, even although I felt pain in it. And to those grounds of doubt I have lately added two others, which are very general; the first is that I never have believed myself to feel anything in waking moments which I cannot also sometimes believe myself to feel when I sleep, and as I do not think that these things

which I seem to find in sleep, proceed from objects outside of me, I do not see any reason why I should have this belief regarding objects which I seem to perceive while awake. The other was that being still ignorant, or rather supposing myself to be ignorant, of the author of my being, I saw nothing to prevent me from having been so constituted by nature that I might be deceived even in matters which seemed to me to be most certain. And as to the grounds on which I was formerly persuaded of the truth of sensible objects, I had not much trouble in replying to them. For since nature seemed to cause me to lean towards many things from which reason repelled me, I did not believe that I should trust much to the teachings of nature. And although the ideas which I receive by the senses do not depend on my will, I did not think that one should for that reason conclude that they proceeded from things different from myself, since possibly some faculty might be discovered in me—though hitherto unknown to me—which produced them.

But now that I begin to know myself better, and to discover more clearly the author of my being, I do not in truth think that I should rashly admit all the matters which the senses seem to teach us, but, on the other hand, I do not think that I should doubt them all universally.

And first of all, because I know that all things which I apprehend clearly and distinctly can be created by God as I apprehend them, it suffices that I am able to apprehend one thing apart from another clearly and distinctly in order to be certain that the one is different from the other, since they may be made to exist in separation at least by the omnipotence of God; and it does not signify by what power this separation is made in order to compel me to judge them to be different: and, therefore, just because I know certainly that I exist, and that meanwhile I do not remark that any other thing necessarily pertains to my nature or essence, excepting that I am a thinking thing, I rightly conclude that my essence consists solely in the fact that I am a thinking thing [or a substance whose whole essence or nature is to think]. And although possibly (or rather certainly, as I shall say in a moment) I possess a body with which I am very intimately conjoined, yet because, on the one side, I have a clear and distinct idea of myself inasmuch as I am only a thinking and unextended thing, and as, on the other, I possess a distinct idea of body, inasmuch as it is only an extended and unthinking thing, it is certain that this I [that is to say, my soul by which I am what I am], is entirely and absolutely distinct from my body, and can exist without it. . . .

. . . There is a great difference between mind and body, inasmuch as body is by nature always divisible, and the mind is entirely indivisible. For, as a matter of fact, when I consider the mind, that is to say, myself inasmuch as I am only a thinking thing, I cannot distinguish in myself any parts, but apprehend myself to be clearly one and entire; and although the whole mind seems to be united to the whole body, yet if a foot, or an arm, or some other part, is separated from my body, I am aware that nothing has been taken away

from my mind. And the faculties of willing, feeling, conceiving, etc., cannot be properly speaking said to be its parts, for it is one and the same mind which employs itself in willing and in feeling and understanding. But it is quite otherwise with corporeal or extended objects, for there is not one of these imaginable by me which my mind cannot easily divide into parts, and which consequently I do not recognize as being divisible; this would be sufficient to teach me that the mind or soul of man is entirely different from the body, if I have not already learned it from other sources. . . .

From this it is quite clear that, notwithstanding the supreme goodness of God, the nature of man, inasmuch as it is composed of mind and body, cannot be otherwise than sometimes a source of deception. For if there is any cause which excites, not in the foot but in some parts of the nerves which are extended between the foot and the brain, or even the brain itself, the same movement which usually is produced when the foot is detrimentally affected, pain will be experienced as though it were in the foot, and the sense will thus naturally be deceived; for since the same movement in the brain is capable of causing but one sensation in the mind, and this sensation is much more frequently excited by a cause which hurts the foot than by another existing in some other quarter, it is reasonable that it should convey to the mind pain in the foot rather than in any other part of the body. And although the parchedness of the throat does not always proceed, as it usually does, from the fact that drinking is essential for the health of the body, but sometimes comes from quite a different cause, as is the case with dropsical patients, it is yet much better that it should mislead on this occasion than if, on the other hand, it were always to deceive us when the body is in good health; and so on in similar cases.

And certainly this consideration is of great service to me, not only in enabling me to recognize all the errors to which my nature is subject, but also in enabling me to avoid them or to correct them more easily. For knowing that all my senses more frequently indicate to me truth than falsehood respecting the things which concern that which is beneficial to the body, and being able almost always to avail myself of many of them in order to examine one particular thing, and, besides that, being able to make use of my memory in order to connect the present with the past, and of my understanding which already has discovered all the causes of my errors, I ought no longer to fear that falsity may be found in matters every day presented to me by my senses. And I ought to set aside all the doubts of these past days as hyperbolical and ridiculous, particularly that very common uncertainty respecting sleep, which I could not distinguish from the waking state; for at present I find a very notable difference between the two, inasmuch as our memory can never connect our dreams one with the other, or with the whole course of our lives, as it unites events which happen to us while we are awake. And, as a matter of fact, if someone, while I was awake, quite suddenly appeared to me and disappeared as fast as do the images which I see in sleep, so that I could not know from whence the form came nor whither it went, it would not be without reason that I should deem it a specter or a phantom formed by my brain [and similar to those which I form in sleep], rather than a real man. But when I perceive things as to which I know distinctly both the place from which they proceed, and that in which they are, and the time at which they appeared to me; and when, without any interruption, I can connect the perceptions which I have of them with the whole course of my life, I am perfectly assured that these perceptions occur while I am waking and not during sleep. And I ought in no wise to doubt the truth of such matters, if, after having called up all my senses, my memory, and my understanding, to examine them, nothing is brought to evidence by any one of them which is repugnant to what is set forth by the others. For because God is in no wise a deceiver, it follows that I am not deceived in this. But because the exigencies of action often oblige us to make up our minds before having leisure to examine matters carefully, we must confess that the life of man is very frequently subject to error in respect to individual objects, and we must in the end acknowledge the infirmity of our nature.

GILBERT RYLE (1900–1976)

As author, editor, and teacher, Ryle was a leader in the British school of analytical philosophy. He was associated with Oxford University since enrolling there as an undergraduate, later serving as tutor and lecturer. At the conclusion of military service in World War II, he was appointed Waynflete Professor of Metaphysical Philosophy at Oxford. In 1948 he succeeded G. E. Moore as editor of the distinguished philosophical journal, *Mind*. His books and articles cover a wide range of subject matter, but fall mainly in the fields of philosophical methodology, the philosophy of mind, and the history of philosophy. Master of the bold metaphor and terse epigram, he avoided learned jargon and wrote in a fresh and informal style.

The Ghost in the Machine

(1) The Official Doctrine

There is a doctrine about the nature and place of minds which is so prevalent among theorists and even among laymen that it deserves to be described as the official theory. Most philosophers, psychologists and religious teachers subscribe, with minor reservations, to its main articles and, although they admit certain theoretical difficulties in it, they tend to assume that these can be overcome without serious modifications being made to the architecture of the theory. It will be argued here that the central principles of the doctrine are unsound and conflict with the whole body of what we know about minds when we are not speculating about them.

The official doctrine, which hails chiefly from Descartes, is something

From *The Concept of Mind*, Chapter 1. Published by Hutchinson's University Library, London, and Barnes and Noble, Inc., New York, 1949. Reprinted by permission of Hutchinson Publishing Group Ltd. and Barnes and Noble, Inc. In the original volume, the title of this chapter is "Descartes' Myth."

like this. With the doubtful exceptions of idiots and infants in arms every human being has both a body and a mind. Some would prefer to say that every human being is both a body and a mind. His body and his mind are ordinarily harnessed together, but after the death of the body his mind may continue to exist and function.

Human bodies are in space and are subject to the mechanical laws which govern all other bodies in space. Bodily processes and states can be inspected by external observers. So a man's bodily life is as much a public affair as are the lives of animals and reptiles and even as the careers of trees, crystals and planets.

But minds are not in space, nor are their operations subject to mechanical laws. The workings of one mind are not witnessable by other observers; its career is private. Only I can take direct cognisance of the states and processes of my own mind. A person therefore lives through two collateral histories, one consisting of what happens in and to his body, the other consisting of what happens in and to his mind. The first is public, the second private. The events in the first history are events in the physical world, those in the second are events in the mental world.

It has been disputed whether a person does or can directly monitor all or only some of the episodes of his own private history; but, according to the official doctrine, of at least some of these episodes he has direct and unchallengeable cognisance. In consciousness, self-consciousness and introspection he is directly and authentically apprised of the present states and operations of his mind. He may have great or small uncertainties about concurrent and adjacent episodes in the physical world, but he can have none about at least part of what is momentarily occupying his mind.

It is customary to express this bifurcation of his two lives and of his two worlds by saying that the things and events which belong to the physical world, including his own body, are external, while the workings of his own mind are internal. This antithesis of outer and inner is of course meant to be construed as a metaphor, since minds, not being in space, could not be described as being spatially inside anything else, or as having things going on spatially inside themselves. But relapses from this good intention are common and theorists are found speculating how stimuli, the physical sources of which are yards or miles outside a person's skin, can generate mental responses inside his skull, or how decisions framed inside his cranium can set going movements of his extremities.

Even when "inner" and "outer" are construed as metaphors, the problem how a person's mind and body influence one another is notoriously charged with theoretical difficulties. What the mind wills, the legs, arms and the tongue execute; what affects the ear and the eye has something to do with what the mind perceives; grimaces and smiles betray the mind's moods and bodily castigations lead, it is hoped, to moral improvement. But the actual transactions between the episodes of the private history and those of the public history remain mysterious, since by definition they can belong to neither series. They could not be reported among the happenings described in a person's autobiography of his inner life, but nor could they be reported among those described in some one else's biography of that person's overt career. They can be inspected neither by introspection nor by laboratory experiment. They are theoretical shuttlecocks which are forever being bandied from the physiologist back to the psychologist and from the psychologist back to the physiologist.

Underlying this partly metaphorical representation of the bifurcation of a person's two lives there is a seemingly more profound and philosophical assumption. It is assumed that there are two different kinds of existence or status. What exists or happens may have the status of physical existence, or it may have the status of mental existence. Somewhat as the faces of coins are either heads or tails, or somewhat as living creatures are either male or female, so, it is supposed, some existing is physical existing, other existing is mental existing. It is a necessary feature of what has physical existence that it is in space and time; it is a necessary feature of what has mental existence that it is in time but not in space. What has physical existence is composed of matter, or else is a function of matter; what has mental existence consists of consciousness, or else is a function of consciousness.

There is thus a polar opposition between mind and matter, an opposition which is often brought out as follows. Material objects are situated in a common field, known as "space," and what happens to one body in one part of space is mechanically connected with what happens to other bodies in other parts of space. But mental happenings occur in insulated fields, known as "minds," and there is, apart maybe from telepathy, no direct causal connection between what happens in one mind and what happens in another. Only through the medium of the public physical world can the mind of one person make a difference to the mind of another. The mind is its own place and in his inner life each of us lives the life of a ghostly Robinson Crusoe. People can see, hear and jolt one another's bodies, but they are irremediably blind and deaf to the workings of one another's minds and inoperative upon them.

What sort of knowledge can be secured of the workings of a mind? On the one side, according to the official theory, a person has direct knowledge of the best imaginable kind of the workings of his own mind. Mental states and processes are (or are normally) conscious states and processes, and the consciousness which irradiates them can engender no illusions and leaves the door open for no doubts. A person's present thinkings, feelings and willings, his perceivings, rememberings and imaginings are intrinsically "phosphorescent"; their existence and their nature are inevitably betrayed to their owner. The inner life is a stream of consciousness of such a sort that it would be absurd to suggest that the mind whose life is that stream might be unaware of what is passing down it.

True, the evidence adduced recently by Freud seems to show that there exist channels tributary to this stream, which run hidden from their owner. People are actuated by impulses the existence of which they vigorously disavow; some of their thoughts differ from the thoughts which they acknowledge; and some of the actions which they think they will to perform they do not really will. They are thoroughly gulled by some of their own hypocrisies and they successfully ignore facts about their mental lives which on the official theory ought to be patent to them. Holders of the official theory tend, however, to maintain that anyhow in normal circumstances a person must be directly and authentically seized of the present state and workings of his own mind.

Besides being currently supplied with these alleged immediate data of consciousness, a person is also generally supposed to be able to exercise from time to time a special kind of perception, namely inner perception, or introspection. He can take a (non-optical) "look" at what is passing in his mind. Not only can he view and scrutinize a flower through his sense of sight and listen to and discriminate the notes of a bell through his sense of hearing; he can also reflectively or introspectively watch, without any bodily organ of sense, the current episodes of his inner life. This self-observation is also commonly supposed to be immune from illusion, confusion or doubt. A mind's reports of its own affairs have a certainty superior to the best that is possessed by its reports of matters in the physical world. Sense-perceptions can, but consciousness and introspection cannot, be mistaken or confused.

On the other side, one person has no direct access of any sort to the events of the inner life of another. He cannot do better than make problematic inferences from the observed behaviour of the other person's body to the states of mind which, by analogy from his own conduct, he supposes to be signalised by that behaviour. Direct access to the workings of a mind is the privilege of that mind itself; in default of such privileged access, the workings of one mind are inevitably occult to everyone else. For the supposed arguments from bodily movements similar to their own to mental workings similar to their own would lack any possibility of observational corroboration. Not unnaturally, therefore, an adherent of the official theory finds it difficult to resist this consequence of his premises, that he has no good reason to believe that there do exist minds other than his own. Even if he prefers to believe that to other human bodies there are harnessed minds not unlike his own, he cannot claim to be able to discover their individual characteristics, or the particular things that they undergo and do. Absolute solitude is on this showing the ineluctable destiny of the soul. Only our bodies can meet.

As a necessary corollary of this general scheme there is implicitly prescribed a special way of construing our ordinary concepts of mental powers and operations. The verbs, nouns and adjectives, with which in ordinary life we describe the wits, characters and higher-grade performances of the people with whom we have to do, are required to be construed as signifying special episodes in their secret histories, or else as signifying tendencies for such episodes to occur. When someone is described as knowing, believing or guessing something, as hoping, dreading, intending or shirking something, as designing this or being amused at that, these verbs are supposed to denote the occurrence of specific modifications in his (to us) occult stream of consciousness. Only his own privileged access to this stream in direct awareness and introspection could provide authentic testimony that these mental-conduct verbs were correctly or incorrectly applied. The on-looker, be he teacher, critic, biographer or friend, can never assure himself that his comments have any vestige of truth. Yet it was just because we do in fact all know how to make such comments, make them with general correctness and correct them when they turn out to be confused or mistaken, that philosophers found it necessary to construct their theories of the nature and place of minds. Finding mental-conduct concepts being regularly and effectively used, they properly sought to fix their logical geography. But the logical geography officially recommended would entail that there could be no regular or effective use of these mental-conduct concepts in our descriptions of, and prescriptions for, other people's minds.

(2) The Absurdity of the Official Doctrine

Such in outline is the official theory. I shall often speak of it, with deliberate abusiveness, as "the dogma of the Ghost in the Machine." I hope to prove that it is entirely false, and false not in detail but in principle. It is not merely an assemblage of particular mistakes. It is one big mistake and a mistake of a special kind. It is, namely, a category-mistake. It represents the facts of mental life as if they belonged to one logical type or category (or range of types or categories), when they actually belong to another. The dogma is therefore a philosopher's myth. In attempting to explode the myth I shall probably be taken to be denying well-known facts about the mental life of human beings, and my plea that I aim at doing nothing more than rectify the logic of mental-conduct concepts will probably be disallowed as mere subterfuge.

I must first indicate what is meant by the phrase "Category-mistake." This I do in a series of illustrations.

A foreigner visiting Oxford or Cambridge for the first time is shown a number of colleges, libraries, playing fields, museums, scientific departments and administrative offices. He then asks "But where is the University? I have seen where the members of the Colleges live, where the Registrar works, where the scientists experiment and the rest. But I have not yet seen the University in which reside and work the members of your University." It has then to be

explained to him that the University is not another collateral institution, some ulterior counterpart to the colleges, laboratories and offices which he has seen. The University is just the way in which all that he has already seen is organized. When they are seen and when their co-ordination is understood, the University has been seen. His mistake lay in his innocent assumption that it was correct to speak of Christ Church, the Bodleian Library, the Ashmolean Museum *and* the University, to speak, that is, as if "the University" stood for an extra member of the class of which these other units are members. He was mistakenly allocating the University to the same category as that to which the other institutions belong.

The same mistake would be made by a child witnessing the march-past of a division, who, having had pointed out to him such and such battalions, batteries, squadrons, etc., asked when the division was going to appear. He would be supposing that a division was a counterpart to the units already seen, partly similar to them and partly unlike them. He would be shown his mistake by being told that in watching the battalions, batteries and squadrons marching past he had been watching the division marching past. The march-past was not a parade of battalions, batteries, squadrons *and* a division; it was a parade of the battalions, batteries and squadrons *of* a division.

One more illustration. A foreigner watching his first game of cricket learns what are the functions of the bowlers, the batsmen, the fielders, the umpires and the scorers. He then says "But there is no one left on the field to contribute the famous element of team-spirit. I see who does the bowling, the batting and the wicket-keeping; but I do not see whose role it is to exercise *esprit de corps.*" Once more, it would have to be explained that he was looking for the wrong type of thing. Team-spirit is not another cricketing-operation supplementary to all of the other special tasks. It is, roughly, the keenness with which each of the special tasks is performed, and performing a task keenly is not performing two tasks. Certainly exhibiting team-spirit is not the same thing as bowling or catching, but nor is it a third thing such that we can say that the bowler first bowls *and* then exhibits team-spirit or that a fielder is at a given moment *either* catching *or* displaying *esprit de corps.*

These illustrations of category-mistakes have a common feature which must be noticed. The mistakes were made by people who did not know how to wield the concepts *University, division* and *team-spirit.* Their puzzles arose from inability to use certain items in the English vocabulary.

The theoretically interesting category-mistakes are those made by people who are perfectly competent to apply concepts, at least in the situations with which they are familiar, but are still liable in their abstract thinking to allocate those concepts to logical types to which they do not belong. An instance of a mistake of this sort would be the following story. A student of politics has learned the main differences between the British, the French and the American Constitutions, and has learned also the differences and connections between the Cabinet, Parliament, the various Ministries, the Judicature and the Church of England. But he still becomes embarrassed when asked questions about the connections between the Church of England, the Home Office and the British Constitution. For while the Church and the Home Office are institutions, the British Constitution is not another institution in the same sense of that noun. So inter-institutional relations which can be asserted or denied to hold between the Church and the Home Office cannot be asserted or denied to hold between either of them and the British Constitution. "The British Constitution" is not a term of the same logical type as "the Home Office" and "the Church of England." In a partially similar way, John Doe may be a relative, a friend, an enemy or a stranger to Richard Roe; but he cannot be any of these things to the Average Taxpayer. He knows how to talk sense in certain sorts of discussions about the Average Taxpayer, but he is baffled to say why he could not come across him in the street as he can come across Richard Roe.

It is pertinent to our main subject to notice that, so long as the student of politics continues to think of the British Constitution as a counterpart to the other institutions, he will tend to describe it as a mysteriously occult institution; and so long as John Doe continues to think of the Average Taxpayer as a fellow-citizen, he will tend to think of him as an elusive insubstantial man, a ghost who is everywhere yet nowhere.

My destructive purpose is to show that a family of radical category-mistakes is the source of the double-life theory. The representation of a person as a ghost mysteriously ensconced in a machine derives from this argument. Because, as is true, a person's thinking, feeling and purposive doing cannot be described solely in the idioms of physics, chemistry and physiology, therefore they must be described in counterpart idioms. As the human body is a complex organised unit, so the human mind must be another complex organised unit, though one made of a different sort of stuff and with a different sort of structure. Or, again, as the human body, like any other parcel of matter, is a field of causes and effects, so the mind must be another field of causes and effects, though not (Heaven be praised) mechanical causes and effects.

(3) The Origin of the Category-Mistake

One of the chief intellectual origins of what I have yet to prove to be the Cartesian category-mistake seems to be this. When Galileo showed that his methods of scientific discovery were competent to provide a mechanical theory which should cover every occupant of space, Descartes found in himself two conflicting motives. As a man of scientific genius he could not but endorse the claims of mechanics, yet as a religious and moral man he could not accept, as Hobbes accepted, the discouraging rider to those claims, namely that human nature differs only in degree of complexity from clockwork. The mental could not be just a variety of the mechanical.

He and subsequent philosophers naturally but erroneously availed themselves of the following escape-route. Since mental-conduct words are not to be construed as signifying the occurrence of mechanical processes, they must be construed as signifying the occurrence of non-mechanical processes; since mechanical laws explain movements in space as the effects of other movements in space, other laws must explain some of the non-spatial workings of minds as the effects of other non-spatial workings of minds. The difference between the human behaviours which we describe as intelligent and those which we describe as unintelligent must be a difference in their causation; so, while some movements of human tongues and limbs are the effects of mechanical causes, others must be the effects of non-mechanical causes, i.e., some issue from movements of particles of matter, others from workings of the mind.

The differences between the physical and the mental were thus represented as differences inside the common framework of the categories of "thing," "stuff," "attribute," "state," "process," "change," "cause" and "effect." Minds are things, but different sorts of things from bodies; mental processes are causes and effects, but different sorts of causes and effects from bodily movements. And so on. Somewhat as the foreigner expected the University to be an extra edifice, rather like a college but also considerably different, so the repudiators of mechanism represented minds as extra centers of causal processes, rather like machines but also considerably different from them. Their theory was a para-mechanical hypothesis.

That this assumption was at the heart of the doctrine is shown by the fact that there was from the beginning felt to be a major theoretical difficulty in explaining how minds can influence and be influenced by bodies. How can a mental process, such as willing, cause spatial movements like the movements of the tongue? How can a physical change in the optic nerve have among its effects a mind's perception of a flash of light? This notorious crux by itself shows the logical mould into which Descartes pressed his theory of the mind. It was the self-same mould into which he and Galileo set their mechanics. Still unwittingly adhering to the grammar of mechanics, he tried to avert disaster by describing minds in what was merely an obverse vocabulary. The workings of minds had to be described by the mere negatives of the specific descriptions given to bodies; they are not in space, they are not motions, they are not modifications of matter, they are not accessible to public observation. Minds are not bits of clockwork, they are just bits of not-clockwork.

As thus represented, minds are not merely ghosts harnessed to machines, they are themselves just spectral machines. Though the human body is an engine, it is not quite an ordinary engine, since some of its workings are governed by another engine inside it—this interior governor-engine being one of a very special sort. It is invisible, inaudible and it has no size or weight. It cannot be taken to bits and the laws it obeys are not those known to ordinary engineers. Nothing is known of how it governs the bodily engine.

A second major crux points the same moral. Since, according to the doctrine, minds belong to the same category as bodies and since bodies are rigidly governed by mechanical laws, it seemed to many theorists to follow that minds must be similarly governed by rigid non-mechanical laws. The physical world is a deterministic system, so the mental world must be a deterministic system. Bodies cannot help the modifications that they undergo, so minds cannot help pursuing the careers fixed for them. *Responsibility, choice, merit* and *demerit* are therefore inapplicable concepts—unless the compromise solution is adopted of saying that the laws governing mental processes, unlike those governing physical processes, have the congenial attribute of being only rather rigid. The problem of the Freedom of the Will was the problem how to reconcile the hypothesis that minds are to be described in terms drawn from the categories of mechanics with the knowledge that higher-grade human conduct is not of a piece with the behaviour of machines.

It is an historical curiosity that it was not noticed that the entire argument was broken-backed. Theorists correctly assumed that any sane man could already recognise the differences between, say, rational and non-rational utterances or between purposive and automatic behaviour. Else there would have been nothing requiring to be salved from mechanism. Yet the explanation given presupposed that one person could in principle never recognise the difference between the rational and the irrational utterances issuing from other human bodies, since he could never get access to the postulated immaterial causes of some of their utterances. Save for the doubtful exception of himself, he could never tell the difference beween a man and a Robot. It would have to be conceded, for example, that, for all that we can tell, the inner lives of persons who are classed as idiots or lunatics are as rational as those of anyone else. Perhaps only their overt behaviour is disappointing; that is to say, perhaps "idiots" are not really idiotic, or "lunatics" lunatic. Perhaps, too, some of those who are classed as sane are really idiots. According to the theory, external observers could never know how the overt behaviour of others is correlated with their mental powers and processes and so they could never know or even plausibly conjecture whether their applications of mental-conduct concepts to these other people were correct or incorrect. It would then be hazardous or impossible for a man to claim sanity or logical consistency even for himself, since he would be debarred from comparing his own performances with those of others. In short, our characterisations of persons and their performances as intelligent, prudent and virtuous or as stupid, hypocritical and cowardly could never have been made, so the problem of providing a special causal hypothesis to serve as the basis of such diagnoses would never have arisen. The question, "How do persons differ from machines?" arose just because everyone already knew how to apply mental-conduct concepts before the new causal hypothesis was introduced. This causal hypothesis could not therefore be the source of the criteria used in those applications. Nor, of course, has the causal hypothesis in any degree improved our handling of those criteria.

We still distinguish good from bad arithmetic, politic from impolitic conduct and fertile from infertile imaginations in the ways in which Descartes himself distinguished them before and after he speculated how the applicability of these criteria was compatible with the principle of mechanical causation.

He had mistaken the logic of his problem. Instead of asking by what criteria intelligent behaviour is actually distinguished from non-intelligent behaviour, he asked "Given that the principle of mechanical causation does not tell us the difference, what other causal principle will tell it us?" He realised that the problem was not one of mechanics and assumed that it must therefore be one of some counterpart to mechanics. Not unnaturally psychology is often cast for just this role.

When two terms belong to the same category, it is proper to construct conjunctive propositions embodying them. Thus a purchaser may say that he bought a left-hand glove and a right-hand glove, but not that he bought a left-hand glove, a right-hand glove and a pair of gloves. "She came home in a flood of tears and a sedan-chair" is a well-known joke based on the absurdity of conjoining terms of different types. It would have been equally ridiculous to construct the disjunction "She came home either in a flood of tears or else in a sedan-chair." Now the dogma of the Ghost in the Machine does just this. It maintains that there exist both bodies and minds; that there occur physical processes and mental processes; that there are mechanical causes of corporeal movements and mental causes of corporeal movements. I shall argue that these and other analogous conjunctions are absurd; but, it must be noticed, the argument will not show that either of the illegitimately conjoined propositions is absurd in itself. I am not, for example, denying that there occur mental processes. Doing long division is a mental process and so is making a joke. But I am saying that the phrase "there occur mental processes" does not mean the same sort of thing as "there occur physical processes," and, therefore, that it makes no sense to conjoin or disjoin the two.

If my argument is successful, there will follow some interesting consequences. First, the hallowed contrast between Mind and Matter will be dissipated, but dissipated not by either of the equally hallowed absorptions of Mind by Matter or of Matter by Mind, but in quite a different way. For the seeming contrast of the two will be shown to be as illegitimate as would be the contrast of "she came home in a flood of tears" and "she came home in a sedan-chair." The belief that there is a polar opposition between Mind and Matter is the belief that they are terms of the same logical type.

It will also follow that both Idealism and Materialism are answers to an improper question. The "reduction" of the material world to mental states and processes, as well as the "reduction" of mental states and processes to physical states and processes, presuppose the legitimacy of the disjunction "Either there exist minds or there exist bodies (but not both)." It would be like saying, "Either she bought a left-hand and a right-hand glove or she bought a pair of gloves (but not both)."

It is perfectly proper to say, in one logical tone of voice, that there exist minds and to say, in another logical tone of voice, that there exist bodies. But these expressions do not indicate two different species of existence, for "existence" is not a generic word like "coloured" or "sexed." They indicate two different senses of "exist," somewhat as "rising" has different senses in "the tide is rising," "hopes are rising," and "the average age of death is rising." A man would be thought to be making a poor joke who said that three things are now rising, namely the tide, hopes and the average age of death. It would be just as good or bad a joke to say that there exist prime numbers and Wednesdays and public opinions and navies; or that there exist both minds and bodies. . . .

KARL R. POPPER (1902–   )

Popper was born in Vienna and reared in a family devoted to books and music. His father, a lawyer, had received a doctor of law degree at the University of Vienna, and his mother was an accomplished musician. Karl studied mathematics, physics, and philosophy at the University from 1919 to 1928. In the depressed city of Vienna following World War I, he struggled to earn a living with a variety of occupations—as a cabinet-maker, a social worker with neglected children, and a teacher in secondary schools. Eventually he published a number of philosophical papers and a book on scientific method (*Logik der Forschung*, 1935, translated twenty five years later as *The Logic of Scientific Method*).

Escaping from Austria before it capitulated to Hitler, he taught in the University of New Zealand from 1937 to 1945. He was then appointed to the University of London, where he is now Professor Emeritus. He is the author of more than one hundred articles in academic journals, and his books include *The Open Society and Its Enemies* (1945), *The Poverty of Historicism* (1957), *Conjectures and Refutations* (1963), *Objective Knowledge* (1972), and in collaboration with Sir John Eccles, *The Self and Its Brain* (1977). In 1964 he was knighted in recognition of his achievements. Many have not only recognized his eminence as a social philosopher, but regard him as perhaps the greatest living philosopher of science.

The Three Worlds

Our main task as philosophers is, I think, to enrich our picture of the world by helping to produce imaginative and at the same time argumentative and critical theories, preferably of methodological interest. Western philosophy consists very largely of world pictures which are variations of the theme of body-mind dualism, and of problems of method connected with them. The main departures from this Western dualistic theme were attempts to replace it by some kind of monism. It seems to me that these attempts were unsuccessful, and that behind the veil of monistic protestations there still lurks the dualism of body and mind.

1. Pluralism and the Thesis of the Three Worlds

There were, however, not only monistic deviations, but also some *pluralistic* ones. This is almost obvious if we think of polytheism, and even of its monotheistic variants. Yet to the philosopher it may seem doubtful whether the various religious interpretations of the world offer any genuine alternative to the dualism of body and

From Karl R. Popper, *Objective Knowledge: An Evolutionary Approach,* Oxford University Press, 1972. © Karl R. Popper, 1972. Reprinted by permission of the publisher.

mind. The gods, whether many or few, are either minds endowed with immortal bodies, or else pure minds, in contrast to ourselves.

However, some philosophers have made a serious beginning towards a philosophical pluralism, by pointing out the existence of a *third world*. I am thinking of Plato, the Stoics, and some moderns such as Leibniz, Bolzano, and Frege (but not of Hegel who embodied strong monistic tendencies).

Plato's world of Forms or Ideas was, in many respects, a religious world, a world of higher realities. Yet it was neither a world of personal gods nor a world of consciousness, nor did it consist of the contents of some consciousness. It was an objective, autonomous third world which existed in addition to the physical world and the world of the mind.

I follow those interpreters of Plato who hold that Plato's Forms or Ideas are different not only from bodies and from minds, but also from 'Ideas in the mind', that is to say, from conscious or unconscious experiences: Plato's Forms or Ideas constitute a third world *sui generis*. Admittedly, they are virtual or possible *objects* of thought—*intelligibilia*. Yet for Plato, these *intelligibilia* are as objective as the *visibilia* which are physical bodies: virtual or possible objects of sight.[1]

Thus Platonism goes beyond the duality of body and mind. It introduces a tripartite world, or, as I prefer to say, a third world.

I will not argue here about Plato, however; rather I will argue about pluralism. And even if I and others should be mistaken in attributing this pluralism to Plato, even then could I appeal to a well-known *interpretation* of Plato's theory of Forms or Ideas as an example of a philosophy which genuinely transcends the dualistic schema.

I wish to make this pluralistic philosophy the starting-point of my discussion, even though I am neither a Platonist nor a Hegelian.[2]

In this pluralistic philosophy the world consists of at least three ontologically distinct sub-worlds; or, as I shall say, there are three worlds: the first is the physical world or the world of physical states; the second is the mental world or the world of mental states; and the third is the world of intelligibles, or of *ideas in the objective sense*; it is the world of possible objects of thought: the world of theories in themselves, and their logical relations; of arguments in themselves; and of problem situations in themselves.

One of the fundamental problems of this pluralistic philosophy concerns the relationship between these three 'worlds'. The three worlds are so re-

---

[1] For Plato's distinction between the visible (*horaton*) and the intelligible (*noeton*) see, for example, Plato's *Republic*, 509 E. (Cp. *Theaetetus*, 185 D ff.) The physiology of the eye has shown that the processes of visually perceiving *visibilia* closely resemble an elaborate interpretation of *intelligibilia*. (One could claim that Kant anticipated much of this.)

[2] Hegel, following Aristotle, rejected the Platonic third world: he conflated thought processes and objects of thought. Thus he disastrously attributed consciousness to the objective mind, and deified it. (See especially the end of Hegel's *Encyclopedia* with the very apt quotation from Aristotle's *Metaphysics*, 1072b18–30.)

lated that the first two can interact, and that the last two can interact.[3] Thus the second world, the world of subjective or personal experiences, interacts with each of the other two worlds. The first world and the third world cannot interact, save through the intervention of the second world, the world of subjective or personal experiences.

2. The Causal Relations Between the Three Worlds

It seems to me most important to describe and explain the relationship of the three worlds in this way—that is, with the second world as the mediator between the first and the third. Although rarely stated, this view seems to me clearly involved in the three-world theory. According to this theory, the human mind can see a physical body in the literal sense of 'see' in which the eyes participate in the process. It can also 'see' or 'grasp' an arithmetical or a geometrical object; a number, or a geometrical figure. But although in this sense 'see' or 'grasp' is used in a metaphorical way, it nevertheless denotes a real relationship between the mind and its intelligible object, the arithmetical or geometrical object; and the relationship is closely analogous to 'seeing' in the literal sense. Thus the mind may be linked with objects of both the first world and the third world.

By these links the mind establishes an *indirect* link between the first and the third world. This is of the utmost importance. It cannot seriously be denied that the third world of mathematical and scientific theories exerts an immense influence upon the first world. It does so, for instance, through the intervention of technologists who effect changes in the first world by applying certain consequences of these theories; incidentally, of theories developed originally by other men who may have been unaware of any technological possibilities inherent in their theories. Thus these possibilities were hidden in the theories themselves, in the objective ideas themselves; and they were discovered in them by men who tried to *understand* these ideas.

This argument, if developed with care, seems to me to support the objective reality of all three worlds. Moreover, it seems to me to support not only the thesis that a subjective mental world of personal experiences exists (a thesis denied by the behaviourists), but also the thesis that it is one of the main functions of the second world to grasp the objects of the third world. This is something we all do: it is an essential part of being human to learn a language and this means, essentially, to learn to grasp *objective thought contents* (as Frege called them).[4]

I suggest that one day we will have to revolutionize psychology by looking at

---

[3] I am using here the word 'interact' in a wide sense, so as not to exclude a psychophysical parallelism: it is not my intention to discuss this problem here. (In other places I have argued for interactionism; see, for example, chapters 12 and 13 of my *Conjectures and Refutations,* 1963, 1965, 1969.)

[4] Cp. Gottlob Frege, '*Über Sinn und Bedeutung',* Zeitschrift für Philosophie und philosophische Kritik, 100, 1892, p. 32: 'I understand by thought not the subjective act of thinking but its objective content. . . .'

the human mind as an organ for inter- acting with the objects of the third world; for understanding them, con- tributing to them, participating in them; and for bringing them to bear on the first world.

3. The Objectivity of the Third World

The third world or rather the objects belonging to it, the objective Forms or Ideas which Plato discovered, have been more often than not mistaken for sub- jective ideas or thought processes; that is, for mental states, for objects belong- ing to the second world rather than the third.

This mistake has a long history. It begins with Plato himself. For although Plato clearly recognized the third-world character of his Ideas, it seems that he did not yet realize that the third world contained not only universal concepts or notions, such as the number 7 or the number 77, but also mathematical truths or propositions,[5] such as the proposition '7 times 11 equals 77', and even false propositions, such as '7 times 11 equals 66', and, in addition, all kinds of non- mathematical propositions or theories.

This, it seems, was first seen by the

Stoics who developed a marvellously subtle philosophy of language. Human language, as they realized, belongs to all three worlds.[6] In so far as it consists of physical actions or physical symbols, it belongs to the first world. In so far as it expresses a subjective or psychological state or in so far as grasping or under- standing language involves a change in our subjective state,[7] it belongs to the second world. And in so far as language contains information, in so far as it says or states or describes anything or conveys any meaning or any significant message which may entail another, or agree or clash with another, it belongs to the third world. *Theories, or proposi- tions, or statements are the most im- portant third-world linguistic entities.*

If we say 'I saw something written on papyrus', or 'I saw something en- graved in bronze', we speak of linguistic entities as belonging to the first world: we do not imply that we can read the message. If we say 'I was greatly im- pressed by the earnestness and convic- tion with which the address was de-

---

[5] That for Plato truth and propositions are (usually) not third-world ideas but mental acts (like the mental acts of grasping the notions of likeness, etc., described in *Theaet- etus*, 186 A) seems suggested in *Theaetetus*, 189 EF., where Plato says that 'thought is the talk which the soul has with itself about any ob- ject whatever'. Cp. *Sophist*, 263 E–264 B where the emphasis is on silent speech (true and false), affirmation, negation, and opinion. But in *Phaedrus*, 247 D to 249 B truth is one of the inmates of the third world grasped by the soul.

[6] The Stoics were materialists: they regarded the soul as part of the body, identifying it with 'the breath of life' (Diogenes Laertius, vi. 156 f.). The reasoning power they de- scribed as 'the leading part' of the body (Sextus, *Adv. Math.* vii, 39 ff.). This theory may, however, be interpreted as a special form of body-mind dualism, since it presents a special solution of the body-mind problem. If we add to these two worlds (or two parts of the first world) the *content of 'what has been said' (lecton)* we arrive at the Stoic version of the *third world*.

[7] The idea of a *state* of the mind (such as goodness, or truthfulness) seems to be Stoic; it is of course interpreted as a state of the breath, and thus of the body. Cp. Sextus, loc. cit.

livered', or 'This was not so much a statement as an angry outburst', we speak of linguistic entities as belonging to the second world. If we say 'But James said today precisely the opposite of what John said yesterday' or 'From what James says it follows clearly that John is mistaken', or if we speak of Platonism, or of quantum theory, then we speak of some objective import, of some *objective logical content*; that is, we speak of the third-world significance of the information or the message conveyed in what has been said, or written.

It was the Stoics who first made the important distinction between the (third-world) objective logical *content* of what we are saying, and the *objects* about which we are speaking. These objects, in their turn, can belong to any of the three worlds: we can speak first about the physical world (either about physical things or physical states) or secondly about our subjective mental states (including our grasp of a theory) or thirdly about the contents of some theories, such as some arithmetical propositions and, say, their truth or falsity.

It seems highly advisable to me that we should try to avoid such terms as 'expression' and 'communication' whenever we speak of speech in the third-world sense. For 'expression' and 'communication' are, essentially, psychological terms, and their subjectivist or personal connotations are dangerous in a field where there is so strong a temptation to interpret the third-world contents of thought as second-world thought processes.

It is interesting that the Stoics extended the theory of the third world not merely from Platonic Ideas to theories or propositions. They also included, in addition to such third-world linguistic entities as declarative statements or assertions, such things as problems, arguments, and argumentative inquiries, and besides even commands, admonitions, prayers, treaties, and, of course, poetry and narration. They also distinguished between a personal state of truthfulness, and the truth of a theory or proposition; that is to say, a theory or proposition to which the third-world predicate 'objectively true' applies.

4. The Third World as a Man-Made Product

We can, in the main, distinguish between two groups of philosophers. The first consists of those who, like Plato, accept an autonomous third world and look upon it as superhuman and as divine and eternal. The second consists of those who, like Locke or Mill or Dilthey or Collingwood, point out that *language*, and what it 'expresses' and 'communicates' is *manmade*, and who, for this reason, see everything linguistic as a part of the first and second worlds, rejecting any suggestion that there exists a third world. It is interesting that most students of the humanities belong to this second group which rejects the third world.

The first group, the Platonists, are supported by the fact that we can speak of eternal verities: a proposition is, timelessly, either true or false. This seems to be decisive: eternal verities must have been true before man existed. Thus they cannot be of our making.

The members of the second group agree that eternal verities cannot be of our own making; yet they conclude from this that eternal verities *cannot be 'real'*: 'real' is merely *our usage* of the predicate 'true' and the fact that, at least in certain contexts, we use 'true' as a time-independent predicate. This kind of usage is, they may argue, not so very surprising: while Peter's father Paul may at one time be heavier than Peter, and a year later less heavy, nothing like this can happen to two pieces of metal as long as the one remains a proper one-pound weight and the other a proper two-pound weight. Here the predicate 'proper' plays the same role as the predicate 'true' in connection with statements; in fact, we can replace 'proper' by 'true'. Yet nobody will deny that weights can be man-made, these philosophers may point out.

I think that it is possible to uphold a position which differs from that of both these groups of philosophers: I suggest *that it is possible to accept the reality or (as it may be called) the autonomy of the third world, and at the same time to admit that the third world originates as a product of human activity*. One can even admit that the third world is man-made and, in a very clear sense, superhuman at the same time.[8] It transcends its makers.

[8] Although man-made, the third world (as I understand this term) is super-human in that its contents are virtual rather than actual objects of thought, and in the sense that only a finite number of the infinity of virtual objects can ever become actual objects of thought. We must beware, however, of interpreting these objects as the thoughts of a superhuman consciousness as did, for example, Aristotle, Plotinus, and Hegel. (See my first note above.) For the super-human character of truth, see pp. 29 f. of my *Conjectures and Refutations*, 1963.

That the third world is not a fiction but exists 'in reality' will become clear when we consider its tremendous effect on the first world, mediated through the second world. One need only think of the impact of electrical power transmission or atomic theory on our inorganic and organic environment, or of the impact of economic theories on the decision whether to build a boat or an aeroplane.

According to the position which I am adopting here, the third world (part of which is human language) is the product of men, just as honey is the product of bees, or spiders' webs of spiders. *Like language* (and like honey) human language, and thus larger parts of the third world are *the unplanned product of human actions*,[9] though they may be solutions to biological or other problems.

Let us look at the theory of numbers. I believe (unlike Kronecker) that even the natural numbers are the work of men, the product of human language and of human thought. Yet there is an infinity of such numbers, more than will

[9] See Karl Bühler's theory of the lower and higher functions of human language, and my development of the theory reported in my *Conjectures and Refutations*, 1963, pp. 134 f., and 295, and also in my *Of Clouds and Clocks*, 1966, see pp. 235–8 below. See also F. A. Hayek, *Studies in Philosophy, Politics and Economics*, 1967, especially chapters 3, 4, and 6. Briefly, Bühler points out that animal and human languages are alike in so far as they are always *expressions* (symptoms of a state of the organism) and *communications* (signals). Yet human language is also different since it has, in *addition*, a higher function: it can be *descriptive*. I have pointed out that there are other higher functions, and especially one which is of decisive importance: the *argumentative or critical* function.

ever be pronounced by men, or used by computers. And there is an infinite number of true equations between such numbers, and of false equations; more than we can ever pronounce as true, or false.

But what is even more interesting, unexpected new problems arise as an unintended by-product of the sequence of natural numbers; for instance the unsolved problems of the theory of prime numbers (Goldbach's conjecture, say). These problems are clearly *autonomous*. They are in no sense made by us; rather, they are *discovered* by us; and in this sense they exist, undiscovered, before their discovery. Moreover, at least some of these unsolved problems may be insoluble.

In our attempts to solve these or other problems we may invent new theories. These theories, again, are produced by us: they are the product of our critical and creative thinking, in which we are greatly helped by other existing third-world theories. Yet the moment we have produced these theories, they create new, unintended and unexpected problems, autonomous problems, problems to be discovered.

This explains why the third world which, in its origin, is our product, is *autonomous* in what may be called its ontological status. It explains why we can act upon it, and add to it or help its growth, even though there is no man who can master even a small corner of this world. All of us contribute to its growth, but almost all our individual contributions are vanishingly small. All of us try to grasp it, and none of us could live without being in contact with it, for all of us make use of speech, without which we would hardly be human.[10] Yet the third world has grown far beyond the grasp not only of any man, but even of all men (as shown by the existence of insoluble problems). Its action upon us has become more important for our growth, and even for its own growth, than our creative action upon it. For almost all its growth is due to a feed-back effect: to the challenge of the discovery of autonomous problems, many of which may never be mastered.[11] And there will always be the challenging task of discovering new problems, for an infinity of problems will always remain undiscovered. In spite and also because of the autonomy of the third world, there will always be scope for original and creative work.

---

[10] The humanizing power of her dramatic discovery of speech has been most movingly and convincingly described by Helen Keller. Of the specifically humanizing functions of language the argumentative (or critical) function seems to me the most important one: it is the basis of what is called human rationality.

[11] For it can be shown (A. Tarski, A. Mostowski, R. M. Robinson, *Undecidable Theories*, Amsterdam, 1953; see especially note 13 on pp. 60 f.), that the complete) system of all true propositions in the arithmetic of integers is not axiomatizable and essentially undecidable. It follows that there will always be infinitely many unsolved problems in arithmetic. It is interesting that we are able to make such unexpected discoveries about the third world, which are largely independent of our state of mind. (This result goes largely back to the pioneer work of Kurt Gödel.)

COMMENT

Descartes' Method

The question of method became a matter of keen and widespread interest with the great flowering of science in the seventeenth and eighteenth centuries. The discoveries of such great scientists as Kepler, Galileo, Newton, Gilbert, and Harvey and the rapid development of mathematics and natural science forced men to reflect upon the nature of scientific knowledge and the means to its attainment.

The principal cleavage among the philosophers was between the *rationalists* and the *empiricists*. The rationalists, among them Descartes, Spinoza, and Leibniz, relied chiefly upon reason as the source of genuine knowledge, taking the methods of mathematics, especially geometry, as their model. The empiricists, among them Locke, Berkeley, and Hume, depended mainly upon experience, regarding the methods of hypothesis, observation, and experiment as the principal foundations of knowledge. Actually, the differences between the two groups were not so sharp as they are often represented. Both groups recognized the necessity of a combination of experience and reason, but they veered toward opposite sides in their emphasis.

Of primary significance in considering Descartes' philosophy as an example of rationalism is his intense desire for certainty: "I always had an excessive desire to learn to distinguish the true from the false, in order to see clearly in my actions and to walk with confidence in this life."[1] He believed that the key to certainty, the way in which to dispel his innumerable doubts, lay in a sound and logical method of reasoning. The proper employment of reason, he believed, would make vast provinces accessible to human knowledge.

Descartes asserted that all certain knowledge is based upon two mental operations: *intuition*—which he also called "the natural light of reason"—and *deduction*. His definitions of these terms are contained in his *Rules for the Direction of the Mind*:

> By *intuition* I understand, not the fluctuating testimony of the senses, nor the misleading judgment that proceeds from the blundering constructions of imagination, but the conception which an unclouded and attentive mind gives us so readily and distinctly that we are wholly freed from doubt about that which we understand. Or, what comes to the same thing, *intuition* is the undoubting conception of an unclouded and attentive mind, and springs from the light of reason alone. . . .
>
> By *deduction* . . . we understand all necessary inference from other facts that are known with certainty. . . . Many things are known with certainty, though not by themselves evident, but only deduced from true and known principles by the continuous and uninterrupted action of a mind that has a clear vision of each step in the process. It is in a similar way that we know that the last link in a long chain is connected with the first, even though we do not take in by means

---

[1] *Discourse on Method*, in *The Philosophical Works of Descartes*, translated by Elizabeth S. Haldane and G. R. T. Ross (Cambridge University Press, 1931), I, p. 87.

of one and the same act of vision all the intermediate links on which that connection depends, but only remember that we have taken them successively under review and that each single one is united to its neighbor, from the first even to the last.[2]

In formulating these definitions, Descartes was thinking specifically of the method of mathematics, particularly geometry. The certainty of rigorous mathematical reasoning, he believed, consists in starting with meanings and insights so clear and distinct that they cannot be doubted, and then accepting nothing as true unless it follows no less evidently from these foundations. An intuited truth is such that reason has only to understand its meaning fully to see that it *must* be true. Examples of intuitions are the insights that five is more than four, that a triangle is bounded by only three lines, and that things equal to the same thing are equal to each other. Given such manifest and self-evident premises, our conclusion will be certain provided that it is *necessarily* implied by what precedes and that nothing is admitted in the steps of reasoning that does not thus necessarily follow. Thus, in a chain of reasoning symbolized by letters, if p implies q, and q implies r, and r implies s, then s is certain provided that p is certain and that each subsequent step leading to s is also certain. Descartes believed that thinkers have succeeded in the past and will succeed in the future to the extent that they have rigorously employed, or will employ, intuition and deduction.

With this conception of reasoning in mind, he summed up his method in four rules, which are stated in Part II of the *Discourse*:

1. *The rule of certainty*. This rule is (*a*) to accept nothing as true that we do not unquestionably recognize to be such, and (*b*) carefully to avoid all precipitation and prejudice so as to reach judgments so clear and distinct that they cannot be doubted. Only what we *know* to be true is to be admitted into the sphere of belief: thus Descartes aimed not at mere probability, but at absolute certainty. This rule compelled him to reject all beliefs that are at all dubious.

He recognized two causes as chiefly responsible for error: precipitate judgment, due to insufficient care, and prejudiced judgment, due to habit or emotional bias. Many beliefs are tenaciously held not because they are seen with clearness and distinctness to be true but because, in our haste or bias, we feel a very strong inclination to believe them. "I term that clear," he declared, "which is present and apparent to an attentive mind. . . . But the distinct is that which is so precise and different from all other objects that it contains within itself nothing but what is clear."[3] A judgment is worthy of belief only if all the ideas in it and the judgment as a whole are thus clear and distinct.

2. *The rule of division*. We should analyze each of the difficulties involved in our problem into its smallest and simplest parts. If we then attack each of the subordinate parts separately, we shall find it easier to understand and deal with the simple than the complex. When we have thus discovered elements so simple, so clear, and so distinct that the mind cannot break them down into still more

[2] *Rules for the Direction of the Mind*, in *ibid.*, pp. 7–8.

[3] *The Principles of Philosophy*, in *ibid.*, I, p. 237.

simple parts, we can know these elements by a direct awareness exempt from illusion and error; and after this analysis, reason can more surely reconstruct the complex objects of thought.

3. *The rule of order.* We should carry on our reflections in due order, starting with the simplest ideas and proceeding, step by step, to the more and more complex. Descartes had in mind a deductive chain of reasoning in which each stage follows necessarily from the preceding stage, reason always being careful to follow the one and only order. Every step in this process must command certainty, since it is guaranteed by *intuition*, that "undoubting conception of an unclouded and attentive mind."

4. *The rule of enumeration and review.* In a long chain of reasoning, we are apt to make a slip—to think that we grasp something clearly and distinctly when in fact we do not, or to remember incorrectly some earlier stage in the reasoning. Whenever the smallest link is thus impaired, the chain of reasoning is broken, and all certainty is lost. Hence, it is necessary to recount and review the steps again and again so as to be absolutely sure that there has been no trick of memory or mistake in reasoning. Certainty is attained only when every link is so firmly grasped, and every connection has been so often reviewed, that the mind finally gathers together the links into an indissoluble, self-evident whole, which it views, as it were, all at the same time. Intuition then can grasp this whole as certain, just as it has grasped the initial premises and each successive step as certain.

Systematic Doubt

The success of the Cartesian method depends upon having a sure foundation upon which to build and thereafter upon successfully applying the first rule—to admit nothing that is uncertain. Therefore Descartes resolved to doubt everything that he could possibly doubt, provisionally retaining only those ordinary maxims of conduct that are necessary in order to live decently. To doubt in this methodical way is not to consider something false or improbable but to recognize that it is not *absolutely* certain. The function of systematic doubt is to find a solid foundation for science and philosophy and thus to dispel scepticism.

The kind of indubitable foundation for which Descartes was searching is not any formal principle of logic or mathematics, such as the principle that one and the same proposition cannot be both true and false. Such a principle, although a necessary foundation of reasoning, tells us nothing about *what exists* and hence cannot provide the necessary basis for a philosophy or science of *reality*. The kind of premise that he sought, therefore, must be such that its truth cannot be doubted; it must be self-evident and not deduced from something else; and it must refer to something actually existing.

In resolutely admitting nothing except what is certain, Descartes was forced to doubt almost everything that he had ever believed: sensory experience, memory, expectation, the existence of other people, his body, the external physical world, and even simple mathematical truths such as two plus two equal four. His argument is so lucid that the reader should have no difficulty in understanding it.

It would seem that nothing at all is left to believe; but something remains even when doubt has done its worst. "I suppose myself to be deceived," Descartes exclaimed; "doubtless, then, I exist, since I am deceived." My very act of doubting proves something that I cannot doubt. "I think, therefore I am."

Here is the first principle—the absolute and indubitable certainty—for which Descartes was searching, and here also is the main point of departure of modern epistemology. The certainty of self-consciousness had been proclaimed earlier by St. Augustine (354–430) and St. Thomas Aquinas (1225?–1274). But Descartes gave the idea wide currency, backing it up with systematic doubt, and without admitting the element of faith essential to Augustine and Aquinas. No one before him had so deliberately adopted doubt as a method of procedure or employed it so boldly and sweepingly.

Dualism Attacked

The distinction between mind and body is closely related to the method of doubt. Descartes notes that he can be certain that he exists as a thinking being even when he is still in doubt whether he has a body—hence he concludes that the mind and body must be distinct and that his real essence is to think.

Descartes recognized two distinct realms of being. One is the world described by physics, a world which does not depend upon our thoughts. It would continue to exist and operate if there were no human beings at all. Its essence is to be extended. The other is the world whose essence is thought—perception, willing, feeling, reasoning, imagining, and the corresponding ideas or mental representations.

A human being, as a compound of mind and body, belongs to both realms. How a person can thus be both two and one poses a difficult problem. Despite the apparent paradox, Descartes believed that mind and body, although radically different, are harmoniously combined in the human organism, and that the unextended mind somehow interacts with the extended body.

This dualism is attacked in Gilbert Ryle's famous polemic against "the ghost in the machine." He characterizes the "official theory" of mind and body which stems from Descartes as based upon a "category mistake." A mistake of this sort occurs when something is taken to belong to a different type or class than its true one. For example, it would be a category mistake if a spectator at a baseball game wanted to know which player did the pitching, which the catching, and which the exercising of "team spirit." The mistake, in this instance, would be to suppose that exercising team spirit is the same sort of thing as catching and pitching.

The category mistake involved in dualism is to regard both minds and bodies as things of the same logical type, or to use Descartes' term, as "substances." This leads, declares Ryle, to the false supposition that the mind is an invisible thing somehow having dealings with another thing, the visible body. Each thing is described as having unique and independent properties, bodies being in space and subject to mechanical laws, minds being spaceless and characterized by spiritual capacities. The mental ghost thinks and the bodily machine moves: somehow each influences the other, although it is strange and mysterious how this interaction takes place.

Ryle objects to the tendency to partition off the mental from the physical. For example, he says:

> When we read novels, biographies, and reminiscences, we do not find the chapters partitioned into section "A," covering the hero's "bodily" doings, and section "B," covering his "mental" doings. We find unpartitioned accounts of what he did and thought and felt, of what he said to others and to himself, of the mountains he tried to climb and the problems he tried to solve.[4]

Reacting against introspectionism, Ryle tries to explain mental life in terms of witnessable activities. "Overt intelligent performances," he declares, "are not clues to the workings of minds; they *are* those workings. Boswell described Johnson's mind when he described how he wrote, talked, ate, fidgeted and fumed."[5]

Whether Ryle succeeds in refuting dualism is debatable. Some critics contend that he is too behavioristic and skips over the more private aspects of mental life. A dream, for example, is directly knowable only by the dreamer. It is different from a table which you and I and others can inspect. But Ryle does not deny states of consciousness even though he distrusts introspection. He is quite aware that human beings are more than complicated mechanisms. "Man need not be degraded to a machine by being denied to be a ghost in a machine. . . .," he writes. "There has yet to be ventured the hazardous leap to the hypothesis that perhaps he is a man."[6]

The Three Worlds

Descartes' theory that there are two distinct realms, the objective "world" of physical objects and the subjective "world" of thought, can be denied by insisting that there is only *one* world, whether *mental* as in idealism or *physical* as in materialism. It can also be denied by insisting that there are *more* than two worlds. An example of the latter is Plato's three-world view—visible objects, mental processes, and intelligible objects. (See the passages from the *Republic* on pages 501–508.) Karl Popper espouses a similar tripartite division, but he differs from Plato. He is not disdainful of the first world ("visibilia") and he has a different interpretation of the third world ("intelligibilia"). Unlike Plato's third world of eternal essences—the Good, the Beautiful, the Just, etc.—Popper's third world is

[4] Professor Le Gros Clark (editor), *The Physical Basis of Mind* (Oxford: Basil Blackwell, 1952), p. 77.

[5] *The Concept of Mind*, p. 58.

[6] *Ibid.*, p. 328.

man-made. Its objects are products of the human mind which, once produced, exist independently. They constitute the world of art, science, language, moral ideals, and institutions—the entire cultural heritage—so far as they are intelligible and objective structures. This man-made and yet independent and autonomous third world equals in scope and elaboration the realm of physical artifacts, the products of human craft and industry that belong in the first world. Especially important for human development are languages and linguistic entities—not only concepts but statements, conjectures, hypotheses, and mathematical and scientific theories. These include not only *actual* objects of thought but *virtual* or *potential* objects, such as logical implications as yet unthought and problem-solutions as yet unachieved. Human beings can explore, criticize, revise, and extend this realm but they cannot disregard or arbitrarily change it. Its properties are *hard* facts unalterable by human whim. They transcend their makers, like children, born of parents, but with lives of their own. To think of them as subjective mental processes in world 2 would be a category mistake.

A person's mind interacts not only with the body "beneath" it but with the intelligible objects "above" it. World 2 thus acts as an intermediary between world 1 and world 3. "It cannot seriously be denied," Popper remarks, "that the third world of mathematical and scientific theories exerts an immense influence upon the first world . . . for instance, through the intervention of technologists who effect changes by applying certain consequences of these theories." In turn world 1, acting through the intermediary of mental processes, profoundly influences world 3. The creations of the human mind are encoded and preserved in world 1 objects—for example, books in libraries, instruments in laboratories, and physical media of art. These become the means whereby the mind reacts on world 3 and expands and enriches it. Psycho-physical interaction, in terms of which dualists describe mind-body relations, is only a part, although a central and necessary part, of the interaction of worlds 1, 2, and 3. The reader who compares the theories of Descartes, Plato, and Popper will find a rich subject-matter for reflection.

The Cartesian Method Criticized

Descartes' method as well as his dualistic metaphysics has been subjected to strong attack. An impressive example is the criticism of the American philosopher Charles Peirce. It may be summarized as follows:

1. AGAINST THE METHOD OF DOUBT. Peirce sharply rejected the method of universal doubt. His criticism is partly psychological and partly logical. The crux of the psychological criticism is that *real* doubt arises from the conflict of beliefs and hence involves non-doubt. It is an error to suppose that one can doubt at will. "For belief, while it lasts, is a strong habit, and as such, forces the man to believe until surprise breaks up the habit."[7] The surprise occurs when a belief

---

[7] Unless otherwise indicated, all quotations from Peirce are from *Collected Papers of Charles Sanders Peirce*, edited by Charles Harthshorne and Paul Weiss (Harvard University Press, 1931). I omit page references.

comes into conflict with either some other belief or some novel experience, and a mind empty of belief cannot be surprised. If you try to doubt without such positive occasion for doubting, you are merely feigning doubt. "Do you call it *doubting* to write it down on a piece of paper that you doubt? If so, doubt has nothing to do with any serious business." Underneath all the "paper doubts" will remain a solid core of beliefs, many of which will be implicit and more or less subconscious. The Cartesian method is naive in assuming, first, that people can be thoroughly aware of their beliefs and presuppositions and, second, that they can shed these beliefs at will.

Logically as well as psychologically, inquiry does not begin with an empty mind but involves beliefs as the presuppositions of inquiry. Just what these presuppositions are must be discovered through inquiry; but an investigator who doubted his memory, the principles of logic, the reliability of reason, and all the evidence of his senses would be completely hamstrung. The moment one advances beyond the first "self-evident" premise ("I think, therefore I am"), one must employ some of the very beliefs that one has pretended to doubt. "Descartes and others have endeavored to bolster up the light of reason by make-believe arguments from the 'veracity of God' and the like. They had better not have pretended to call that in question which they intended to prove, since the proofs, themselves, call for the same light to make them evident."

2. AGAINST AN INDIVIDUALISTIC CRITERION OF TRUTH. Peirce rejected individual intuition, or "clear and distinct perception," as the test of truth, substituting a *social* criterion. The Cartesian view, it will be remembered, emphasizes intuition, defined as the individual's immediate insight into self-evident truth, as the ultimate source of knowledge. The reliability of intuition is guaranteed by not only its immediacy but by its clarity and distinctness.

Peirce proposed a quite different approach to truth and clarity. First, he maintained that the way in which to clarify the meaning of an idea or proposition is to envisage its practical consequences. We establish clear meaning by *testing* an idea in *use*—by tracing out its concrete applications and consequences rather than by intuitive inspection or abstract definition. Secondly, Peirce contended that truth is established by public agreement rather than private insight—and not just the agreement of ignorant minds but the agreement of qualified investigators converging toward an ideal limit of accuracy and objectivity. The ultimate test of truth is that it is verified by facts open to inspection and admitted to be such by all qualified observers. So long as an "intuition" remains the object of a single individual's perspective and is not submitted to the test of *social* verification, there is nothing to guarantee its reliability. "Truth is public."[8] Thirdly, Peirce denied that we ever grasp ideas or statements in isolation and immediately discern their truth or clarity. Thinking is fundamentally contextualistic—we understand things when we relate them to other things; we connect the immediately given with the non-given.

[8] Letter to William James quoted in Ralph Barton Perry, *The Thought and Character of William James* (Harvard University Press, 1935), II, p. 437.

3. AGAINST THE PRIMACY OF SELF-CONSCIOUSNESS. Descartes maintained that the awareness each one of us has of himself and his own mental states is the most immediate and indubitable form of knowledge. In the main, modern epistemology has accepted this point of view. Now, Peirce did not deny that in some way and to some degree people are aware of themselves and their own mental states; but he did strenuously deny that this self-knowledge is wholly immediate and private. He believed that children become self-conscious by comparing and contrasting themselves with others, and that this process of interpreting oneself through relations with others continues throughout adulthood. Consequently, self-knowledge is inseparably connected with knowledge of other people. We cannot know ourselves and our own mental states, moreover, unless our thoughts are expressed in words or other signs. Whereas Descartes had maintained that self-knowledge involves a direct two-term relation between a knowing mind and a known object ("myself"), Peirce maintained that people do not know what they are thinking about themselves, unless they can put their thoughts into words or other symbols. Now language or symbolism is a means of social communication, and all words and other symbols are normally expressed in some overt, physical way, such as speaking, writing, or gesturing. Hence self-knowledge involves outward, physical facts, and is social. It is therefore not prior to other forms of knowledge and has no unique, privileged status.

4. AGAINST THE METHOD OF LINEAR INFERENCE. For Descartes, the attainment of knowledge involves a step-by-step process of reasoning from the simplest and clearest intuitions to the more and more complex deductions, following the one and only right order. He found the model of such reasoning in mathematics, especially Euclidean geometry. Peirce denied that it is necessary or desirable to follow such a single thread of reasoning. Even in mathematics, he pointed out, there are usually several ways of proving a theorem, and in empirical science a conclusion may be reached by many routes. "There may . . . be," he declared, "a hundred ways of thinking in passing from a premise to a conclusion." And, again: "Philosophy ought to imitate the successful sciences in its method, . . . and to trust rather to the multitude and variety of its arguments than to the conclusiveness of any one. Its reasoning should not form a chain which is no stronger than its weakest link, but a cable whose fibres may be ever so slender, provided they are sufficiently numerous and intimately connected."

5. AGAINST THE QUEST FOR CERTAINTY. Peirce believed that it is a mistake to seek, as Descartes did, for indubitable first premises and necessary deductions to certain conclusions. The notion that there are such premises and conclusions smacks of dogmatism and "blocks the road of inquiry." In opposition to Descartes, Peirce urged a doctrine that he called "critical common-sensism." This doctrine may be said to consist of three main contentions:

First, the starting point of philosophy is common sense rather than indubitable intuitions. By common sense Peirce meant those fundamental beliefs that we

rationalist

share with almost all human beings and that our human situation forces upon us. Examples of common-sense beliefs are our conviction that fire burns, that some things are red and others blue, that we can usually trust our memories, and that there is a certain amount of order in the universe. Peirce maintained that the human mind has been conditioned by a long course of evolution to have such fundamental beliefs, and that they must be useful and generally sound to have arisen in this natural way.

Second, all opinions about matters of fact, including our common-sense beliefs, are fallible and hence subject to criticism. Peirce did not deny "that people can usually count with accuracy"; he did not question formal reasoning in which the sole objective is logical consistency; and he did not doubt the common-sense position that we should trust our reasoning faculties. What he said is "that people cannot obtain absolute certainty concerning matters of fact." Both the factual premises and the conclusions of philosophy are never more than probable—though perhaps very highly probable.

Third, the correct method of inquiry, in philosophy as well as in science, is not Descartes' rationalistic method of intuition and deduction but an observational and experimental method. By this method we can uncover and criticize our common-sense beliefs and advance to new probable conclusions.

I have summarized Peirce's criticism in some detail to suggest the kind of response that an empiricist would give to Descartes' rationalism. But it would be well to remember that the method of doubt has had a great cleansing effect on modern philosophy in getting rid of superstitions, and that deduction as well as induction has played a great and necessary role in the development of science.

7

Causation, Free Will, and the Limits of Knowledge

DAVID HUME (1711–1776)

(For biographical note see page 39.)

Knowledge and Causality

1. [Impressions and Ideas]

Everyone will readily allow, that there is a considerable difference be-

tween the perceptions of the mind, when a man feels the pain of excessive heat, or the pleasure of moderate

Section 1 combines excerpts from the *Treatise* and the *Enquiry;* sections 2, 4, 5, 6, and 8 are from the *Enquiry;* sections 3 and 7 are from the *Treatise.* The *Treatise* was published in 1739; the *Enquiry* in 1748.

warmth, and when he afterwards recalls to his memory this sensation, or anticipates it by his imagination. These faculties may mimic or copy the perceptions of the senses; but they never can entirely reach the force and vivacity of the original sentiment. The utmost we say of them, even when they operate with greatest vigor, is, that they represent their object in so lively a manner, that we could *almost* say we feel or see it: But, except the mind be disordered by disease or madness, they never can arrive at such a pitch of vivacity, as to render these perceptions altogether undistinguishable. All the colors of poetry, however splendid, can never paint natural objects in such a manner as to make the description be taken for a real landskip. The most lively thought is still inferior to the dullest sensation.

We may observe a like distinction to run through all the other perceptions of the mind. A man in a fit of anger, is actuated in a very different manner from one who only thinks of that emotion. If you tell me, that any person is in love, I easily understand your meaning, and form a just conception of his situation; but never can mistake that conception for the real disorders and agitations of the passion. When we reflect on our past sentiments and affections, our thought is a faithful mirror, and copies its objects truly; but the colors which it employs are faint and dull, in comparison of those in which our original perceptions were clothed. It requires no nice discernment or metaphysical head to mark the distinction between them.

Here therefore we may divide all the perceptions of the mind into two classes or species, which are distinguished by their different degrees of force and vivacity. The less forcible and lively are commonly denominated *Thoughts* or *Ideas.* The other species want a name in our language, and in most others; I suppose, because it was not requisite for any, but philosophical purposes, to rank them under a general term or appellation. Let us, therefore, use a little freedom, and call them *Impressions;* employing that word in a sense somewhat different from the usual. By the term *impression,* then, I mean all our more lively perceptions, when we hear, or see, or feel, or love, or hate, or desire, or will. And impressions are distinguished from ideas, which are the less lively perceptions, of which we are conscious, when we reflect on any of those sensations or movements above mentioned. . . .

Impressions may be divided into two kinds, those of *sensation,* and those of *reflection.* The first kind arises in the soul originally, from unknown causes. The second is derived, in a great measure, from our ideas, and that in the following order. An impression first strikes upon the senses, and makes us perceive heat or cold, thirst or hunger, pleasure or pain, of some kind or other. Of this impression there is a copy taken by the mind, which remains after the impression ceases; and this we call an idea. This idea of pleasure or pain, when it returns upon the soul, produces the new impressions of desire and aversion, hope and fear, which may properly be called impressions of reflection, because derived from it. These again are copied by the memory and imagination, and become ideas: which, perhaps, in their turn, give rise to other impressions and ideas; so that the impressions of reflection, are not only antecedent to their correspondent ideas, but posterior to those of sensation, and derived from them. . . .

We find, by experience, that when any impression has been present with the mind, it again makes its appearance there as an idea; and this it may do after two different ways: either when, in its new appearance, it retains a considerable degree of its first vivacity, and is somewhat intermediate betwixt an impression and an idea; or when it entirely loses that vivacity, and is a perfect idea. The faculty by which we repeat our impressions in the first manner, is called the *memory,* and the other the *imagination.* It is evident, at first sight, that the ideas of the memory are much more lively and strong than those of the imagination, and that the former faculty paints its objects in more distinct colors than any which are employed by the latter. When we remember any past event, the idea of it flows in upon the mind in a forcible manner; whereas, in the imagination, the perception is faint and languid, and cannot, without difficulty, be preserved by the mind steady and uniform for any considerable time. Here, then, is a sensible difference betwixt one species of ideas and another.

There is another difference betwixt these two kinds of ideas, which is no less evident, namely, that though neither the ideas of the memory nor imagination, neither the lively nor faint ideas, can make their appearance in the mind, unless their correspondent impressions have gone before to prepare the way for them, yet the imagination is not restrained to the same order and form with the original impressions; while the memory is in a manner tied down in that respect, without any power of variation.

Nothing, at first view, may seem more unbounded than the thought of man, which not only escapes all human power and authority, but is not even restrained within the limits of nature and reality. To form monsters, and join incongruous shapes and appearances, costs the imagination no more trouble than to conceive the most natural and familiar objects. And while the body is confined to one planet, along which it creeps with pain and difficulty; the thought can in an instant transport us into the most distant regions of the universe; or even beyond the universe, into the unbounded chaos, where nature is supposed to lie in total confusion. What never was seen, or heard of, may yet be conceived; nor is anything beyond the power of thought, except what implies an absolute contradiction.

But though our thought seems to possess this unbounded liberty, we shall find, upon a nearer examination, that it is really confined within very narrow limits, and that all this creative power of the mind amounts to no more than the faculty of compounding, transposing, augmenting, or diminishing the materials afforded us by the senses and experience. When we think of a golden mountain, we only join two consistent ideas, *gold,* and *mountain,* with which we were formerly acquainted. A virtuous horse we can conceive; because, from our own feeling, we can conceive virtue; and this we may unite to the figure and shape of a horse, which is an animal familiar to us. In short, all the materials of thinking are derived either from our outward or inward sentiment: the mixture and composition of these belongs alone to the mind and will. Or, to express myself in philosophical language, all our ideas or more feeble perceptions are copies of our impressions or more lively ones. . . .

Here, therefore, is a proposition, which not only seems, in itself, simple and intelligible; but, if a proper use were made of it, might render every dispute equally intelligible, and banish all that jargon, which has so long taken possession of metaphysical reasonings, and drawn disgrace upon them. All ideas, especially abstract ones, are naturally faint and obscure: the mind has but a slender hold of them: they are apt to be confounded with other resembling ideas; and when we have often employed any term, though without a distinct meaning, we are apt to imagine it has a determinate idea annexed to it. On the contrary, all impressions, that is, all sensations, either outward or inward, are strong and vivid: the limits between them are more exactly determined: nor is it easy to fall into any error or mistake with regard to them. When we entertain, therefore, any suspicion that a philosophical term is employed without any meaning or idea (as is but too frequent), we need but enquire, *from what impression is that supposed idea derived?* And if it be impossible to assign any, this will serve to confirm our suspicion. By bringing ideas into so clear a light we may reasonably hope to remove all dispute, which may arise, concerning their nature and reality.

2. [The Forms of Reasoning]

All the objects of human reason or enquiry may naturally be divided into two kinds, to wit, *Relations of Ideas,* and *Matters of Fact*. Of the first kind are the sciences of Geometry, Algebra, and Arithmetic; and in short, every affirmation which is either intuitively or demonstratively certain. *That the square of the hypothenuse is equal to the square of the two sides,* is a proposition which expresses a relation between these figures. *That three times five is equal to the half of thirty,* expresses a relation between these numbers. Propositions of this kind are discoverable by the mere operation of thought, without dependence on what is anywhere existent in the universe. Though there never were a circle or triangle in nature, the truths demonstrated by Euclid would for ever retain their certainty and evidence.

Matters of fact, which are the second objects of human reason, are not ascertained in the same manner; nor is our evidence of their truth, however great, of a like nature with the foregoing. The contrary of every matter of fact is still possible; because it can never imply a contradiction, and is conceived by the mind with the same facility and distinctness, as if ever so comfortable to reality. *That the sun will not rise tomorrow* is no less intelligible a proposition, and implies no more contradiction than the affirmation, *that it will rise.* We should in vain, therefore, attempt to demonstrate its falsehood. Were it demonstratively false, it would imply a contradiction, and could never be distinctly conceived by the mind.

It may, therefore, be a subject worthy of curiosity, to enquire what is the nature of that evidence which assures us of any real existence and matter of fact, beyond the present testimony of our senses, or the records of our memory. This part of philosophy, it is observable, has been little cultivated, either by the ancients or moderns; and therefore our doubts and errors, in the prosecution of so important an enquiry, may be the more excusable; while we march through such difficult paths without any guide or direction. They may even prove useful, by exciting curiosity, and destroying that implicit faith and security, which is the bane of all reasoning and free enquiry. The discovery of defects in the common philosophy, if any such there be, will not, I presume, be a discouragement, but rather an incitement, as is usual, to attempt something more full and satisfactory than has yet been proposed to the public.

All reasonings concerning matter of fact seem to be founded on the relation of *Cause and Effect.* By means of that relation alone we can go beyond the evidence of our memory and senses. If you were to ask a man, why he believes any matter of fact, which is absent; for instance, that his friend is in the country, or in France; he would give you a reason; and this reason would be some other fact; as a letter received from him, or the knowledge

of his former resolutions and promises. A man finding a watch or any other machine in a desert island, would conclude that there had once been men in that island. All our reasonings concerning fact are of the same nature. And here it is constantly supposed that there is a connection between the present fact and that which is inferred from it. Were there nothing to bind them together, the inference would be entirely precarious. The hearing of an articulate voice and rational discourse in the dark assures us of the presence of some person: Why? because these are the effects of the human make and fabric, and closely connected with it. If we anatomize all the other reasonings of this nature, we shall find that they are founded on the relation of cause and effect, and that this relation is either near or remote, direct or collateral. Heat and light are collateral effects of fire, and the one effect may justly be inferred from the other.

If we would satisfy ourselves, therefore, concerning the nature of that evidence, which assures us of matters of fact, we must enquire how we arrive at the knowledge of cause and effect.

I shall venture to affirm, as a general proposition, which admits of no exception, that the knowledge of this relation is not, in any instance, attained by reasonings *a priori;* but arises entirely from experience, when we find that any particular objects are constantly conjoined with each other. Let an object be presented to a man of ever so strong natural reason and abilities; if that object be entirely new to him, he will not be able, by the most accurate examination of its sensible qualities, to discover any of its causes or effects. Adam, though his rational faculties be supposed, at the very first, entirely perfect, could not have inferred from the fluidity and transparency of water that it would suffocate him, or from the light and warmth of fire that it would consume him. No object ever discovers, by the qualities which appear to the senses, either the causes which produced it, or the effects which will arise from it; nor can our reason, unassisted by experience, ever draw any inference concerning real existence and matter of fact.

This proposition, *that causes and effects are discoverable, not by reason but by experience,* will readily be admitted with regard to such objects, as we remember to have once been altogether unknown to us; since we must be conscious of the utter inability, which we then lay under, of foretelling what would arise from them. Present two smooth pieces of marble to a man who has no tincture of natural philosophy; he will never discover that they will adhere together in such a manner as to require great force to separate them in a direct line, while they make so small a resistance to a lateral pressure. Such events, as bear little analogy to the common course of nature, are also readily confessed to be known only by experience; nor does any man imagine that the explosion of gunpowder, or the attraction of a loadstone, could ever be discovered by arguments *a priori.* In like manner, when an effect is supposed to depend upon an intricate machinery or secret structure of parts, we make no difficulty in attributing all our knowledge of it to experience. Who will assert that he can give the ultimate reason, why milk or bread is proper nourishment for a man, not for a lion or a tiger? . . .

3. [The Idea of Causation]

We must consider the idea of *causation,* and see from what origin it is derived. It is impossible to reason justly, without understanding perfectly the idea concerning which we reason; and it is impossible perfectly to understand any idea, without tracing it up to its origin, and examining that primary impression, from which it arises. The examination of the impression bestows a clearness on the idea; and the examination of the idea bestows a like clearness on all our reasoning.

Let us therefore cast our eye on any two objects, which we call cause and effect, and turn them on all sides, in order to find that impression, which produces an idea of such prodigious consequence. At first sight I perceive, that I must not search for it in any of the particular *qualities* of the objects; since, whichever of these qualities I pitch on, I find some object that is not possessed of it, and yet falls under the denomination of cause or effect. And indeed there is nothing existent, either externally or internally, which is not to be considered either as a cause or an effect; though it is plain there is no one quality which universally belongs to all beings, and gives them a title to that denomination.

The idea then of causation must be derived from some *relation* among objects; and that relation we must now endeavor to discover. I find in the first place, that whatever objects are considered as causes or effects, are *contiguous;* and that nothing can operate in a time or place, which is ever so little removed from those of its existence. Though distant objects may sometimes seem productive of each other, they are commonly found upon examination to be linked by a chain of causes, which are contiguous among themselves, and to the distant objects; and when in any particular instance we cannot discover this connection, we still presume it to exist. We may therefore consider the relation of *contiguity* as essential to that of causation. . . .

The second relation I shall observe as essential to causes and effects, is . . . that of *priority* of time in the cause before the effect. . . .

[A third] relation betwixt cause and effect . . . is their *constant conjunction.* Contiguity and succession are not sufficient to make us pronounce any two objects to be cause and effect, unless we perceive that these two relations are preserved in several instances. . . . Thus we remember to have seen that species of object we call *flame,* and to have felt that species of sensation we call *heat.* We likewise call to mind their constant conjunction in all past instances. Without any farther ceremony, we call the one *cause* and the other *effect,* and infer the existence of the one from that of the other. . . .

There is [also] a *necessary connection* to be taken into consideration; and that relation is of much greater importance. . . .

What is our idea of necessity, when we say that two objects are necessarily connected together? Upon this head I repeat, what I have often had occasion to observe, that as we have no idea that is not derived from an impression, we must find some impression that gives rise to this idea of necessity, if we assert we have really such an idea. In order to this, I consider in what objects necessity is commonly supposed to lie; and, finding that it is always ascribed to causes and effects, I turn my eye to two objects supposed to be placed in that relation, and examine them in all the situations of which they are susceptible. I immediately perceive that they are *contiguous* in time and place, and that the object we call cause *precedes* the other we call effect. In no one instance can I go any further, nor is it possible for me to discover any third relation betwixt these objects. I therefore enlarge my view to comprehend several instances, where I find like objects always existing in like relations of contiguity and succession. At first sight this seems to serve but little to my purpose. The reflection on several instances only repeats the same objects; and therefore can never give rise to a new idea. But upon further enquiry I find, that the repetition is not in every particular the same, but produces a new impression, and by that means the idea which I at present examine. For after a frequent repetition I find, that upon the appearance of one of the objects, the mind is *determined* by custom to consider its usual attendant, and to consider it in a stronger light upon account of its relation to the first object. It is this impression, then, or *determination,* which affords me the idea of necessity. . . .

Suppose two objects to be presented to us, of which the one is the cause and the other the effect; it is plain that, from the simple consideration of one, or both these objects, we never shall perceive the tie by which they are united, or be able certainly to pronounce, that there is a connection betwixt them. It is not, therefore, from any one instance, that we arrive at the idea of cause and effect, of a necessary connection of power, of force, of energy, and of efficacy. Did we never see any but particular conjunctions of objects, entirely different from each other, we should never be able to form any such ideas [as cause and effect].

But, again, suppose we observe several instances in which the same objects are always conjoined together, we immediately conceive a connection betwixt them, and begin to draw an inference from one to another. This multiplicity of resembling instances, therefore, constitutes the very essence of power or connection, and is the source from which the idea of it arises. . . .

Though the several resembling instances, which give rise to the idea of power, have no influence on each other, and can never produce any new quality *in the object,* which can be the model of that idea, yet the *observation* of this resemblance produces a new impression *in the mind,* which is its real model. For after we have observed the resemblance in a sufficient number of instances, we immediately feel a determination of the mind to pass from one object to its usual attendant, and to conceive it in a stronger light upon account of that relation. This determination is the only effect of the resemblance; and,

therefore, must be the same with power or efficacy, whose idea is derived from the resemblance. The several instances of resembling conjunctions lead us into the notion of power and necessity. These instances are in themselves totally distinct from each other, and have no union but in the mind, which observes them, and collects their ideas. Necessity, then, is the effect of this observation, and is nothing but an internal impression of the mind, or a determination to carry our thoughts from one object to another. Without considering it in this view, we can never arrive at the most distant notion of it, or be able to attribute it either to external or internal objects, to spirit or body, to causes or effects. . . .

The idea of necessity arises from some impression. There is no impression conveyed by our senses, which can give rise to that idea. It must, therefore, be derived from some internal impression, or impression of reflection. There is no internal impression which has any relation to the present business, but that propensity, which custom produces, to pass from an object to the idea of its usual attendant. This, therefore, is the essence of necessity. Upon the whole, necessity is something that exists in the mind, not in objects; nor is it possible for us ever to form the most distant idea of it, considered as a quality in bodies. Either we have no idea of necessity, or necessity is nothing but that determination of the thought to pass from causes to effects, and from effects to causes, according to their experienced union.

Thus, as the necessity, which makes two times two equal to four, or three angles of a triangle equal to two right ones, lies only in the act of the understanding, by which we consider and compare these ideas; in like manner, the necessity of power, which unites causes and effects, lies in the determination of the mind to pass from the one to the other. The efficacy or energy of causes is neither placed in the causes themselves, nor in the Deity, nor in the concurrence of these two principles; but belongs entirely to the soul, which considers the union of two or more objects in all past instances. It is here that the real power of causes is placed, along with their connection and necessity. . . .

4. [Of Liberty and Necessity]

I hope . . . to make it appear that all men have ever agreed in the doctrine both of necessity and of liberty, according to any reasonable sense, which can be put on these terms; and that the whole controversy has hitherto turned merely upon words. We shall begin with examining the doctrine of necessity.

It is universally allowed that matter, in all its operations, is actuated by a necessary force, and that every natural effect is so precisely determined by the energy of its cause that no other effect, in such particular circumstances, could possibly have resulted from it. The degree and direction of every motion is, by the laws of nature, prescribed with such exactness that a living creature may as soon arise from the shock of two bodies as motion in any other degree or direction than what is actually produced by it. Would we, therefore, form a just and precise idea of *necessity*, we must con-

sider whence that idea arises when we apply it to the operation of bodies.

It seems evident that, if all the scenes of nature were continually shifted in such a manner that no two events bore any resemblance to each other, but every object was entirely new, without any similitude to whatever had been seen before, we should never, in that case, have attained the least idea of necessity, or of a connexion among these objects. We might say, upon such a supposition, that one object or event has followed another; not that one was produced by the other. The relation of cause and effect must be utterly unknown to mankind. Inference and reasoning concerning the operations of nature would, from that moment, be at an end; and the memory and senses remain the only canals, by which the knowledge of any real existence could possibly have access to the mind. Our idea, therefore, of necessity and causation arises entirely from the uniformity observable in the operations of nature, where similar objects are constantly conjoined together, and the mind is determined by custom to infer the one from the appearance of the other. These two circumstances form the whole of that necessity, which we ascribe to matter. Beyond the constant *conjunction* of similar objects, and the consequent *inference* from one to the other, we have no notion of any necessity or connexion.

If it appear, therefore, that all mankind have ever allowed, without any doubt or hesitation, that these two circumstances take place in the voluntary actions of men, and in the operations of mind; it must follow, that all mankind have ever agreed in the doctrine of necessity, and that they have hitherto disputed, merely for not understanding each other.

As to the first circumstance, the constant and regular conjunction of similar events, we may possibly satisfy ourselves by the following considerations. It is universally acknowledged that there is a great uniformity among the actions of men, in all nations and ages, and that human nature remains still the same, in its principles and operations. The same motives always produce the same actions: The same events follow from the same causes. Ambition, avarice, self-love, vanity, friendship, generosity, public spirit: these passions, mixed in various degrees, and distributed through society, have been, from the beginning of the world, and still are, the source of all the actions and enterprises, which have ever been observed among mankind. . . .

We must not, however, expect that this uniformity of human actions should be carried to such a length as that all men, in the same circumstances, will always act precisely in the same manner, without making any allowance for the diversity of characters, prejudices, and opinions. Such a uniformity in every particular, is found in no part of nature. On the contrary, from observing the variety of conduct in different men, we are enabled to form a greater variety of maxims, which still suppose a degree of uniformity and regularity.

Are the manners of men different in differen ages and countries? We learn thence the great force of custom and education, which mould the human mind from its infancy and form it into a fixed and established character. Is the behaviour and conduct of the one sex very unlike that of the other? Is it thence we become acquainted with the different characters which nature has impressed upon the sexes, and which she preserves with constancy and regularity? Are the actions of the same person much diversified in the different periods of his life, from infancy to old age? This affords room for many general observations concerning the gradual change of our sentiments and inclinations, and the different maxims which prevail in the different ages of human creatures. Even the characters, which are peculiar to each individual, have a uniformity in their influence; otherwise our acquaintance with the persons and our observation of their conduct could never teach us their dispositions, or serve to direct our behaviour with regard to them.

I grant it possible to find some actions, which seem to have no regular connexion with any known motives, and are exceptions to all the measures of conduct which have ever been established for the government of men. But if we would willingly know what judgment should be formed of such irregular and extraordinary actions, we may consider the sentiments commonly entertained with regard to those irregular events which appear in the course of nature, and the operations of external objects. All causes are not conjoined to their usual effects with like uniformity. An artificer, who handles only dead matter, may be disappointed of his aim, as well as the politician, who directs the conduct of sensible and intelligent agents.

The vulgar, who take things according

to their first appearance, attribute the uncertainty of events to such an uncertainty in the causes as makes the latter often fail of their usual influence; though they meet with no impediment in their operation. But philosophers, observing that, almost in every part of nature, there is contained a vast variety of springs and principles, which are hid, by reason of their minuteness or remoteness, find, that it is at least possible the contrariety of events may not proceed from any contingency in the cause, but from the secret operation of contrary causes. This possibility is converted into certainty by farther observation, when they remark that, upon an exact scrutiny, a contrariety of effects always betrays a contrariety of causes, and proceeds from their mutual opposition. A peasant can give no better reason for the stopping of any clock or watch than to say that it does not commonly go right: But an artist easily perceives that the same force in the spring or pendulum has always the same influence on the wheels; but fails of its usual effect, perhaps by reason of a grain of dust, which puts a stop to the whole movement. From the observation of several parallel instances, philosophers form a maxim that the connexion between all causes and effects is equally necessary, and that its seeming uncertainty in some instances proceeds from the secret opposition of contrary causes.

Thus, for instance, in the human body, when the usual symptoms of health or sickness disappoint our expectation; when medicines operate not with their wonted powers; when irregular events follow from any particular cause; the philosopher and physician are not surprised at the matter, nor are ever tempted to deny, in general, the necessity and uniformity of those principles by which the animal economy is conducted. They know that a human body is a mighty complicated machine: That many secret powers lurk in it, which are altogether beyond our comprehension: That to us it must often appear very uncertain in its operations: And that therefore the irregular events, which outwardly discover themselves, can be no proof that the laws of nature are not observed with the greatest regularity in its internal operations and government.

The philosopher, if he be consistent, must apply the same reasoning to the actions and volitions of intelligent agents. The most irregular and unexpected resolutions of men may frequently be accounted for by those who know every particular circumstance of their character and situation. A person of an obliging disposition gives a peevish answer: But he has the toothache, or has not dined. A stupid fellow discovers an uncommon alacrity in his carriage: But he has met with a sudden piece of good fortune. Or even when an action, as sometimes happens, cannot be particularly accounted for, either by the person himself or by others; we know, in general, that the characters of men are, to a certain degree, inconstant and irregular. This is, in a manner, the constant character of human nature; though it be applicable, in a more particular manner, to some persons who have no fixed rule for their conduct, but proceed in a continued course of caprice and inconstancy. The internal principles and motives may operate in a uniform manner, notwithstanding these seeming irregularities; in the same manner as the winds, rain, clouds, and other variations of the weather are supposed to be governed by steady principles; though not easily discoverable by human sagacity and enquiry.

Thus it appears, not only that the conjunction between motives and voluntary actions is as regular and uniform as that between the cause and effect in any part of nature; but also that this regular conjunction has been universally acknowledged among mankind, and has never been the subject of dispute, either in philosophy or common life. Now, as it is from past experience that we draw all inferences concerning the future, and as we conclude that objects will always be conjoined together which we find to have always been conjoined; it may seem superfluous to prove that this experienced uniformity in human actions is a source whence we draw *inferences* concerning them. But in order to throw the argument into a greater variety of lights we shall also insist, though briefly, on this latter topic.

The mutual dependence of men is so great in all societies that scarce any human action is entirely complete in itself, or is performed without some reference to the actions of others, which are requisite to make it answer fully the intention of the agent. The poorest artificer, who labours alone, expects at least the protection of the magistrate, to ensure him the enjoyment of the fruits of his labour. He also expects that, when he carries his goods to market, and offers them at a reasonable price, he shall find purchasers, and shall be able, by the money he acquires, to engage others to supply him with those commodities which are requisite for his subsistence. In proportion as men extend their dealings, and render their intercourse with others more complicated, they always comprehend, in their schemes of life, a greater variety of voluntary actions, which they expect, from the proper motives, to co-operate with their own. In all these conclusions they take their measures from past experience, in the same manner as in their reasonings concerning external objects; and firmly believe that men, as well as all the elements, are to continue, in their operations, the same that they have ever found them. A manufacturer reckons upon the labour of his servants for the execution of any work as much as upon the tools which he employs, and would be equally surprised were his expectations disappointed. In short, this experimental inference and reasoning concerning the actions of others enters so much into human life that no man, while awake, is ever a moment without employing it. Have we not reason, therefore, to affirm that all mankind have always agreed in the doctrine of necessity according to the foregoing definition and explication of it? . . .

I have frequently considered, what could possibly be the reason why all mankind, though they have ever, without hesitation, acknowledged the doctrine of necessity in their whole practice and reasoning, have yet discovered such a reluctance to acknowledge it in words, and have rather shown a propensity, in all ages, to profess the contrary opinion. The matter, I think, may be accounted for after the following manner. If we examine the operations of body, and the production of effects from their causes, we shall find that all our faculties can never carry us farther in our knowledge of this relation than barely to observe that particular objects are *constantly conjoined* together, and that the mind is carried, by a *customary transition,* from the appearance of one to the belief of the other. But though this conclusion concerning human ignorance be the result of the strictest scrutiny of this subject, men still entertain a strong propensity to believe that they penetrate farther into the powers of nature, and perceive something like a necessary connexion between the cause and the effect. When again they turn their reflections towards the operations of their own minds, and *feel* no such connexion of the motive and the action; they are thence apt to suppose, that there is a difference between the effects which result from material force, and those which arise from thought and intelligence. But being once convinced that we know nothing farther of causation of any kind than merely the *constant conjunction* of objects, and the consequent *inference* of the mind from one to another, and finding that these two circumstances are universally allowed to have place in voluntary actions; we may be more easily led to own the same necessity common to all causes. . . .

It would seem, indeed, that men begin at the wrong end of this question concerning liberty and necessity, when they enter upon it by examining the faculties of the soul, the influence of the understanding, and the operations of the will. Let them first discuss a more simple question, namely, the operations

of body and of brute unintelligent matter; and try whether they can there form any idea of causation and necessity, except that of a constant conjunction of objects, and subsequent inference of the mind from one to another. If these circumstances form, in reality, the whole of that necessity, which we conceive in matter, and if these circumstances be also universally acknowledged to take place in the operations of the mind, the dispute is at an end; at least, must be owned to be thenceforth merely verbal. But as long as we will rashly suppose, that we have some farther idea of necessity and causation in the operations of external objects; at the same time, that we can find nothing farther in the voluntary actions of the mind; there is no possibility of bringing the question to any determinate issue, while we proceed upon so erroneous a supposition. The only method of undeceiving us is to mount up higher; to examine the narrow extent of science when applied to material causes; and to convince ourselves that all we know of them is the constant conjunction and inference above mentioned. We may, perhaps, find that it is with difficulty we are induced to fix such narrow limits to human understanding: But we can afterwards find no difficulty when we come to apply this doctrine to the actions of the will. For as it is evident that these have a regular conjunction with motives and circumstances and characters, and as we always draw inferences from one to the other, we must be obliged to acknowledge in words that necessity, which we have already avowed, in every deliberation of our lives, and in every step of our conduct and behaviour. . . .

But to proceed in this reconciling project with regard to the question of liberty and necessity; the most contentious question of metaphysics, the most contentious science; it will not require many words to prove, that all mankind have ever agreed in the doctrine of liberty as well as in that of necessity, and that the whole dispute, in this respect also, has been hitherto merely verbal. For what is meant by liberty, when applied to voluntary actions? We cannot surely mean that actions have so little connexion with motives, inclinations, and circumstances, that one does not follow with a certain degree of uniformity from the other, and that one affords no inference by which we can conclude the existence of the other. For these are plain and acknowledged matters of fact. By liberty, then, we can only mean *a power of acting or not acting, according to the determinations of the will;* that is, if we choose to remain at rest, we may; if we choose to move, we also may. Now this hypothetical liberty is universally allowed to belong to every one who is not a prisoner and in chains. Here, then, is no subject of dispute.

Whatever definition we may give of liberty, we should be careful to observe two requisite circumstances; *first,* that it be consistent with plain matter of fact; *secondly,* that it be consistent with itself. If we observe these circumstances, and render our definition intelligible, I am persuaded that all mankind will be found of one opinion with regard to it.

It is universally allowed that nothing exists without a cause of its existence, and that chance, when strictly examined, is a mere negative word, and means not any real power which has anywhere a being in nature. But it is pretended that some causes are necessary, some not necessary. Here then is the advantage of definitions. Let any one *define* a cause, without comprehending, as a part of the definition, a *necessary connexion* with its effect; and let him show distinctly the origin of the idea, expressed by the definition; and I shall readily give up the whole controversy. But if the foregoing explication of the matter be received, this must be absolutely impracticable. Had not objects a regular conjunction with each other, we should never have entertained any notion of cause and effect; and this regular conjunction produces that inference of the understanding, which is the only connexion, that we can have any comprehension of. Whoever attempts a definition of cause, exclusive of these circumstances, will be obliged either to employ unintelligible terms or such as are synonymous to the term which he endeavours to define. And if the definition above mentioned be admitted; liberty, when opposed to necessity, not to constraint, is the same thing with chance; which is universally allowed to have no existence.

5. [Will the Future Resemble the Past?]

It must certainly be allowed, that nature has kept us at a great distance from all her secrets, and has afforded us only the knowledge of a few superficial qualities of objects; while she conceals from us those powers and principles on which the influence of those objects entirely depends. Our senses inform us of the color, weight, and consistence of bread; but neither sense nor reason can ever inform us of those qualities which fit it for the nourishment and support of a human body. Sight or feeling conveys an idea of the actual motion of bodies; but as to that wonderful force or power, which would carry on a moving body for ever in a continued change of place, and which bodies never lose but by communicating it to others; of this we cannot form the most distant conception. But notwithstanding this ignorance of natural powers and principles, we always presume, when we see like sensible qualities, that they have like secret powers, and expect that effects, similar to those which we have experienced, will follow from them. If a body of like color and consistence with that bread, which we have formerly eat, be presented to us, we make no scruple of repeating the experiment, and foresee, with certainty, like nourishment and support. Now this is a process of the mind or thought, of which I would willingly know the foundation. It is allowed on all hands that there is no known connexion between the sensible qualities and the secret powers; and consequently, that the mind is not led to form such a conclusion concerning their constant and regular conjunction, by anything which it knows of their nature. As to past *Experience,* it can be allowed to give *direct* and *certain* information of those precise objects only, and that precise period of time, which fell under its cognizance: but why this experience should be extended to future times, and to other objects, which for

aught we know, may be only in appearance similar; this is the main question on which I would insist. The bread, which I formerly eat, nourished me; that is, a body of such sensible qualities was, at that time, endued with such secret powers: but does it follow, that other bread must also nourish me at another time, and that like sensible qualities must always be attended with like secret powers? The consequence seems nowise necessary. At least, it must be acknowledged that there is here a consequence drawn by the mind; that there is a certain step taken; a process of thought, and an inference, which wants to be explained. These two propositions are far from being the same, *I have found that such an object has always been attended with such an effect,* and *I foresee, that other objects, which are, in appearance, similar, will be attended with similar effects.* I shall allow, if you please, that the one proposition may justly be inferred from the other: I know, in fact, that it always is inferred. But if you insist that the inference is made by a chain of reasoning, I desire you to produce that reasoning. . . .

All reasonings may be divided into two kinds, namely, demonstrative reasoning, or that concerning relations of ideas, and moral reasoning, or that concerning matter of fact and existence. That there are no demonstrative arguments in the case seems evident; since it implies no contradiction that the cause of nature may change, and that an object, seemingly like those which we have experienced, may be attended with different or contrary effects. May I not clearly and distinctly conceive that a body, falling from the clouds, and which, in all other respects, resembles snow, has yet the taste of salt or feeling of fire? Is there any more intelligible proposition than to affirm, that all the trees will flourish in December and January, and decay in May and June? Now whatever is intelligible, and can be distinctly conceived, implies no contradiction, and can never be proved false by any demonstrative argument or abstract reasoning *a priori.*

If we be, therefore, engaged by arguments to put trust in past experience, and make it the standard of our future judgment, these arguments must be probable only, or such as regard matter of fact and real existence, according to the division above mentioned. But that there is no argument of this kind, must appear, if our explication of that species of reasoning be admitted as solid and satisfactory. We have said that all arguments concerning existence are founded on the relation of cause and effect; that our knowledge of that relation is derived entirely from experience; and that all our experimental conclusions proceed upon the supposition that the future will be conformable to the past. To endeavor, therefore, the proof of this last supposition by probable arguments, or arguments regarding existence, must be evidently going in a circle, and taking that for granted, which is the very point in question. . . .

Should it be said that, from a number of uniform experiments, we *infer* a connexion between the sensible qualities and the secret powers; this, I must confess, seems the same difficulty, couched in different terms. The question still recurs, on what process of argument this *inference* is founded?

Where is the medium, the interposing ideas, which join propositions so very wide of each other? It is confessed that the color, consistence, and other sensible qualities of bread appear not, of themselves, to have any connection with the secret powers of nourishment and support. For otherwise we could infer these secret powers from the first appearance of these sensible qualities, without the aid of experience; contrary to the sentiment of all philosophers, and contrary to plain matter of fact. Here, then, is our natural state of ignorance with regard to the powers and influence of all objects. How is this remedied by experience? It only shows us a number of uniform effects, resulting from certain objects, and teaches us that those particular objects, at that particular time, were endowed with such powers and forces. When a new object, endowed with similar sensible qualities, is produced, we expect similar powers and forces, and look for a like effect. From a body of like color and consistence with bread we expect like nourishment and support. But this surely is a step or progress of the mind, which wants to be explained. When a man says, *I have found in all past instances, such sensible qualities conjoined with such secret powers:* And when he says, *Similar sensible qualities will always be conjoined with similar secret powers,* he is not guilty of a tautology, nor are these propositions in any respect the same. You say that the one proposition is an inference from the other. But you must confess that the inference is not intuitive; neither is it demonstrative: Of what nature is it, then? To say it is experimental, is begging the question. For all inferences from experience suppose, as their foundation, that the future will resemble the past, and that similar powers will be conjoined with similar sensible qualities. If there be any suspicion that the course of nature may change, and that the past may be no rule for the future, all experience becomes useless, and can give rise to no inference or conclusion. It is impossible, therefore, that any arguments from experience can prove this resemblance of the past to the future; since all these arguments are founded on the supposition of that resemblance. Let the course of things be allowed hitherto ever so regular; that alone, without some new argument or inference, proves not that, for the future, it will continue so. In vain do you pretend to have learned the nature of bodies from your past experience. Their secret nature, and consequently all their effects and influence, may change, without any change in their sensible qualities. This happens sometimes, and with regards to some objects: Why may it not happen always, and with regard to all objects? What logic, what process of argument secures you against this supposition? My practice, you say, refutes my doubts. But you mistake the purport of my question. As an agent, I am quite satisfied in the point; but as a philosopher, who has some share of curiosity, I will not say scepticism, I want to learn the foundation of this inference. No reading, no enquiry has yet been able to remove my difficulty, or give me satisfaction in a matter of such importance. Can I do better than propose the difficulty to the public, even though, perhaps, I have small hopes of obtaining a solution? We shall at least,

by this means, be sensible of our ignorance, if we do not augment our knowledge.

6. [Can We Know External Objects?]

It seems evident, that men are carried, by a natural instinct or prepossession, to repose faith in their senses; and that, without any reasoning, or even almost before the use of reason, we always suppose an external universe, which depends not on our perception, but would exist, though we and every sensible creature were absent or annihilated. Even the animal creation are governed by a like opinion, and preserve this belief of external objects, in all their thoughts, designs, and actions.

It seems also evident, that, when men follow this blind and powerful instinct of nature, they always suppose the very images, presented by the senses, to be the external objects, and never entertain any suspicion, that the one are nothing but representations of the other. This very table, which we see white, and which we feel hard, is believed to exist, independent of our perception, and to be something external to our mind, which perceives it. Our presence bestows not being on it: our absence does not annihilate it. It preserves its existence uniform and entire, independent of the situation of intelligent beings, who perceive or contemplate it.

But this universal and primary opinion of all men is soon destroyed by the slightest philosophy, which teaches us, that nothing can ever be present to the mind but an image or perception, and that the senses are only the inlets, through which these images are conveyed, without being able to produce any immediate intercourse between the mind and the object. The table, which we see, seems to diminish, as we remove farther from it: but the real table, which exists independent of us, suffers no alteration: it was, therefore, nothing but its image, which was present to the mind. These are the obvious dictates of reason; and no man, who reflects, ever doubted, that the existences, which we consider, when we say, *this house* and *that tree,* are nothing but perceptions in the mind, and fleeting copies or representations of other existences, which remain uniform and independent.

So far, then, we are necessitated by reasoning to contradict or depart from the primary instincts of nature, and to embrace a new system with regard to the evidence of our senses. But here philosophy finds herself extremely embarrassed, when she would justify this new system, and obviate the cavils and objections of the sceptics. She can no longer plead the infallible and irresistible instinct of nature: for that led us to a quite different system, which is acknowledged fallible and even erroneous. And to justify this pretended philosophical system, by a chain of clear and convincing argument, or even any appearance of argument, exceeds the power of all human capacity.

By what argument can it be proved, that the perceptions of the mind must be caused by external objects, entirely different from them, though resembling them (if that be possible) and could not arise either from the energy of the mind itself, or from the suggestion of some invisible and unknown spirit, or from some other cause still more unknown to us? It is acknowledged, that, in fact, many of these perceptions arise not from anything external, as in dreams, madness, and other diseases. And nothing can be more inexplicable than the manner, in which body should so operate upon mind as ever to convey an image of itself to a substance, supposed of so different, and even contrary a nature.

It is a question of fact, whether the perceptions of the senses be produced by external objects, resembling them: how shall this question be determined? By experience surely; as all other questions of a like nature. But here experience is, and must be entirely silent. The mind has never anything present to it but the perceptions, and cannot possibly reach any experience of their connection with objects. The supposition of such a connexion is, therefore, without any foundation in reasoning.

To have recourse to the veracity of the Supreme Being, in order to prove the veracity of our senses, is surely making a very unexpected circuit. If his veracity were at all concerned in this matter, our senses would be entirely infallible; because it is not possible that he can ever deceive. Not to mention, that, if the external world be once called in question, we shall be at a loss to find arguments, by which we may prove the existence of that Being or any of his attributes.

This is a topic, therefore, in which the profounder and more philosophical sceptics will always triumph, when they endeavor to introduce an universal doubt into all subjects of human knowledge and enquiry. Do you follow the instincts and propensities of nature, may they say, in assenting to the veracity of sense? But these lead you to believe that the very perception or sensible image is the external object. Do you disclaim this principle, in order to embrace a more rational opinion, that the perceptions are only representations of something external? You here depart from your natural propensities and more obvious sentiments; and yet are not able to satisfy your reason, which can never find any convincing argument from experience to prove, that the perceptions are connected with any external objects. . . .

It is universally allowed by modern enquirers, that all the sensible qualities of objects, such as hard, soft, hot, cold, white, black, &c. are merely secondary, and exist not in the objects themselves, but are perceptions of the mind, without any external archetype or model, which they represent. If this be allowed, with regard to secondary qualities, it must also follow, with regard to the supposed primary qualities of extension and solidity; nor can the latter be any more entitled to that denomination than the former. The idea of extension is entirely acquired from the senses of sight and feeling; and if all the qualities, perceived by the senses, be in the mind, not in the object, the same conclusion must reach the idea of extension, which is wholly dependent on the sensible ideas or the ideas of secondary qualities. . . .

Thus the first philosophical objection to the evidence of sense or to the opinion of external existence consists in this, that such an opinion, if rested on natural instinct, is contrary to reason, and if referred to reason, is contrary to natural instinct, and at the same time carries no rational evidence with it, to convince an impartial enquirer. The second objection goes farther, and represents this opinion as contrary to reason: at least, if it be a principle of reason, that all sensible qualities are in the mind, not in the object. Bereave matter of all its intelligible qualities, both primary and secondary, you in a manner annihilate it, and leave only a certain unknown, inexplicable *something,* as the cause of our perceptions; a notion so imperfect, that no sceptic will think it worth while to contend against it.

7. [The Idea of Self]

There are some philosophers, who imagine we are every moment intimately conscious of what we call our *self;* that we feel its existence and its continuance in existence; and are certain, beyond the evidence of a demonstration, both of its perfect identity and simplicity. The strongest sensation, the most violent passion, say they, instead of distracting us from this view, only fix it the more intensely, and make us consider their influence on *self* either by their pain or pleasure. To attempt a further proof of this were to weaken its evidence; since no proof can be derived from any fact of which we are so intimately conscious; nor is there any thing, of which we can be certain, if we doubt of this.

Unluckily all these positive assertions are contrary to that very experience which is pleaded for them; nor have we any idea of *self,* after the manner it is here explained. For, from what impression could this idea be derived? This question it is impossible to answer without a manifest contradiction and absurdity; and yet it is a question which must necessarily be answered, if we would have the idea of self pass for clear and intelligible. It must be some one impression that gives rise to every real idea. But self or person is not any one impression, but that to which our several impressions and ideas are supposed to have a reference. If any impression gives rise to the idea of self, that impression must continue invariably the same, through the whole course of our lives; since self is supposed to exist after that manner. But there is no impression constant and invariable. Pain and pleasure, grief and joy, passions and sensations succeed each other, and never all exist at the same time. It cannot therefore be from any of these impressions, or from any other, that the idea of self is derived; and consequently there is no such idea.

But further, what must become of all our particular perceptions upon this hypothesis? All these are different, and distinguishable, and separable from each other, and may be separately considered, and may exist separately, and have no need of any thing to support their existence. After what manner therefore do they belong to self, and how are they connected with it? For my part, when I enter most intimately into what I call *myself,* I always stumble on some particular perception or other, of heat or cold, light or shade, love or hatred, pain or pleasure. I never can catch *myself* at any time without a perception, and never can observe any thing but the per-

ception. When my perceptions are removed for any time, as by sound sleep, so long am I insensible of *myself,* and may truly be said not to exist. And were all my perceptions removed by death, and could I neither think, nor feel, nor see, nor love, nor hate, after the dissolution of my body, I should be entirely annihilated, nor do I conceive what is further requisite to make me a perfect nonentity. If any one, upon serious and unprejudiced reflection, thinks he has a different notion of *himself,* I must confess I can reason no longer with him. All I can allow him is, that he may be in the right as well as I, and that we are essentially different in this particular. He may, perhaps, perceive something simple and continued, which he calls *himself;* though I am certain there is no such principle in me.

But setting aside some metaphysicians of this kind, I may venture to affirm of the rest of mankind, that they are nothing but a bundle or collection of different perceptions, which succeed each other with an inconceivable rapidity, and are in a perpetual flux and movement. Our eyes cannot turn in their sockets without varying our perceptions. Our thought is still more variable than our sight; and all our other senses and faculties contribute to this change; nor is there any single power of the soul, which remains unalterably the same, perhaps for one moment. The mind is a kind of theater, where several perceptions successively make their appearance; pass, repass, glide away, and mingle in an infinite variety of postures and situations. There is properly no *simplicity* in it at one time, nor identity in different, whatever natural propension we may have to imagine that simplicity and identity. The comparison of the theater must not mislead us. They are the successive perceptions only, that constitute the mind; nor have we the most distant notion of the place where these scenes are represented, or of the materials of which it is composed.

8. [On the Proper Limits of Enquiry]

The *imagination* of man is naturally sublime, delighted with whatever is remote and extraordinary, and running, without control, into the most distant parts of space and time in order to avoid the objects, which custom has rendered too familiar to it. A correct *Judgment* observes a contrary method, and avoiding all distant and high enquiries, confines itself to common life and to such subjects as fall under daily practice and experience; leaving the more sublime topics to the embellishment of poets and orators, or to the arts of priests and politicians. . . . Those who have a propensity to philosophy, will still continue their researches; because they reflect, that, besides the immediate pleasure, attending such an occupation, philosophical decisions are nothing but the reflections of common life, methodized and corrected. But they will never be tempted to go beyond common life, so long as they consider the imperfection of those faculties which they employ, their narrow reach, and their inaccurate operations. While we cannot give a satisfactory reason, why we believe, after a thousand experiments, that a stone will fall, or fire burn; can we ever satisfy ourselves concerning any determination, which we may form, with regard to the origin of worlds, and the situation of nature, from, and to eternity?

This narrow limitation, indeed, of our enquiries, is, in every respect, so reasonable that it suffices to make the slightest examination into the natural powers of the human mind and to compare them with their objects, in order to recommend it to us. We shall then find what are the proper subjects of science and enquiry.

It seems to me, that the only objects of the abstract science or of demonstration are quantity and number, and that all attempts to extend this more perfect species of knowledge beyond these bounds are mere sophistry and illusion. As the component parts of quantity and number are entirely similar, their relations become intricate and involved; and nothing can be more curious, as well as useful, than to trace, by a variety of mediums, their equality or inequality, through their different appearances. But as all other ideas are clearly distinct and different from each other, we can never advance farther, by our utmost scrutiny, than to observe this diversity, and, by an obvious reflection, pronounce one thing not to be another. Or if there be any difficulty in these decisions, it proceeds entirely from the undeterminate meaning of words, which is corrected by juster definitions. That *the square of the hypothenuse is equal to the squares of the other two sides,* cannot be known, let the terms be ever so exactly defined, without a train of reasoning and enquiry. But to convince us of this proposition, *that where there is no property, there can be no injustice,* it is only necessary to define the terms, and explain injustice, to be a violation of property. This proposition is, indeed, nothing but a more imperfect definition. It is the same case with all those pretended syllogistical reasonings, which may be found in every other branch of learning, except the sciences of quantity and number; and these may safely, I think, be pronounced the only proper objects of knowledge and demonstration.

All other enquiries of men regard only matter of fact and existence; and these are evidently incapable of demonstration. Whatever *is* may *not be.* No negation of a fact can involve a contradiction. The nonexistence of any being, without exception, is as clear and distinct an idea as its existence. The proposition, which affirms it not to be, however false, is no less conceivable and intelligible, than that which affirms it to be. The case is different with the sciences, properly so called. Every proposition, which is not true, is there confused and unintelligible. That the cube root of 64 is equal to the half of 10, is a false proposition, and can never be distinctly conceived. But that Cæsar, or the angel Gabriel, or any being never existed, may be a false proposition, but still is perfectly conceivable, and implies no contradiction.

The existence, therefore, of any being can only be proved by arguments from its cause or its effect; and these arguments are founded entirely on experience. If we reason *a priori,* anything may appear able to produce anything. The falling of a pebble may, for aught we know, extinguish the sun; or the wish of a man control the planets in their orbits. It is only experience, which teaches us the nature and bounds of cause and effect, and enables us to infer the existence of one object from that of another. . . .

When we run over libraries, persuaded of these principles, what havoc must we make? If we take in our hand any volume; of divinity or school metaphysics, for instance; let us ask, *Does it contain any abstract reasoning concerning quantity or number?* No. *Does it contain any experimental reasoning concerning matter of fact and existence?* No. Commit it then to the flames: for it can contain nothing but sophistry and illusion.

IMMANUEL KANT (1724–1804)

The fourth child of an humble saddle-maker, Kant was born in Königsberg, East Prussia. His parents belonged to the Pietists, a revivalist sect within the Lutheran Church, and the family life was characterized by simple religious devotion. Kant detested the mechanical discipline and narrow range of ideas of the Pietist school to which he was sent. At sixteen, he enrolled in the University of Königsberg, supporting himself mainly by tutoring well-to-do students. There his intellectual interests turned to physics and astronomy. After six years at the University, Kant became a private tutor in several homes in East Prussia, a profession which he followed for some nine years. Returning to the University in 1755, he obtained a higher degree and a subordinate post on the faculty. For the next fifteen years he lived in academic poverty, until, in 1770, he was finally appointed a full Professor. In his lectures, he enthralled his student audiences with his knowledge, eloquence, and wit. The popular form of his teaching was in marked contrast to the difficult and technical style of his writing.

He never married, and the clocklike regularity of his bachelor ways became proverbial. His servant awakened him at four forty-five every morning; he spent the next hour drinking tea, smoking his pipe, and planning the day's work; from six to seven he prepared his lectures; from seven to nine or ten he taught; then he wrote until half-past eleven; at twelve he ate a hearty dinner; in the afternoon, rain or shine, he took a regular walk; after that, he read or wrote until, at ten, he went to bed. The rigidity of his routine did not prevent him from enjoying the society of ladies and enlivening many social gatherings with his dry wit. He had many friends in the town and, until he was old, he always dined with friends. His gallantry never deserted him; even when he was so old and feeble that he lost his footing and fell in the street, he courteously presented one of the two unknown ladies who helped him to his feet with the rose that he happened to be carrying.

Although he never traveled far from Königsberg, he was fond of travel books and sympathetic with intellectual and political emancipation the world over. "Have the courage to use your own intelligence!" he advised. He applauded the American and French revolutions, but not the Reign of Terror. "It was a time in Königsberg," wrote one of his colleagues, "when anyone who judged the Revolution even mildly, let alone favorably, was put on a black list as a Jacobin. Kant did not allow himself by that fact to be deterred from speaking up for the Revolution even at the table of noblemen."

Except for a remarkable astronomical treatise (1755), in which he anticipated Laplace's nebular hypothesis, all of his more important works were published late in his life, after he was awakened by Hume from his "dogmatic slumber." In an amazing decade, from 1780 to 1790, there appeared a series of epoch-making books, *The Critique of Pure Reason* (1781), *The Prolegomena to All Future Metaphysics* (1783), *The Foundations of the Metaphysic of Morals* (1785), *The Critique of Practical Reason* (1788), and *The Critique of Judgment* (1790). He subsequently published works on politics and religion, but his main task was done. After 1796, his health gradually declined, and he died in 1804, aged nearly eighty.

The Limits
of Knowledge

1. [Kant's Indebtedness to Hume]

Since the essays of Locke and Leibniz were written, or better, since the beginning of metaphysics, as history records it, no event has been more decisive for this science than the attack of David Hume. He shed no light but he did strike a spark from which a light might be kindled in receptive tinder, if its glow were carefully tended.

Hume began with one important metaphysical idea. It was the supposed connection of cause and effect. He challenged the claim that this connection was conceived in the mind itself. He wanted to know how anyone could think anything so constituted that its mere existence necessarily called for the existence of something else; for this is what the notion of cause means. He proved conclusively that it is quite impossible to conceive the connection of cause and effect abstractly, solely by means of thought, because it involves

The following excerpts are from *An Immanuel Kant Reader*, edited and translated by Raymond B. Blakney (New York: Harper & Row, 1960). Reprinted by permission of the publishers. The first section is from *The Prolegomena to All Future Metaphysics* and the final section is from *The Critique of Judgment*. All else is from *The Critique of Pure Reason*.

the idea of necessity. We do not see that if one thing exists, another has to exist in consequence, and we do not know how an abstract idea of this relation could occur to anyone.

Hume concluded that the idea of cause constitutes a delusion which seems to be a human brain child but is just the bastard of imagination sired by experience. Thus, certain perceptions are joined together as the law of association provides. Then habit, which is a psychological necessity, is passed off as objective and as being discovered through insight. He then inferred that we cannot conceive a causal connection between events, even in general; for if we did, our ideas would be fictional, and knowledge, which is supposed to be abstract and necessary, would be nothing but common experience under a false label. This, plainly, means that there is not and cannot be such a thing as metaphysics.

However hasty and mistaken Hume's conclusion may be, it was at least based on investigation. This made it worthwhile for the bright people of the day to co-operate in finding a happier solution to the problem as he explained it. The outcome might well have been a complete reform of the science, but the unhappy genius of metaphysicians caused him not to be understood.

I frankly confess that many years ago it was the memory of David Hume that first interrupted my dogmatic slumber and gave new direction to my studies in the field of speculative philosophy.

I tried first to see if Hume's objection could be put in a general form. I soon found that the idea of a connection between cause and effect was by no means the only idea we conceive abstractly of relations between things. Metaphysics consists first and last of such ideas. I tried to count them and when I had succeeded as I wished, taking first one and then another, I went on to explain them. I was now certain that they are not derived from experience, as Hume has asserted, but that they spring from the mind alone. These explanations had seemed impossible to my smart predecessor and had not even occurred to anyone else, although everyone used such ideas without asking what the security behind them might be. This, I say, was the most difficult work ever undertaken on behalf of metaphysics. The worst of it was that no help at all could be had from metaphysics itself because the very possibility of metaphysics depends on this kind of explanation.

Having now succeeded in the solution of Hume's problem, not only in special cases but with a view to the whole reasoning function of mind, I could proceed safely, if slowly, to survey the field of pure reasoning, its boundaries as well as its contents, and I could do this working from general principles. This is exactly what metaphysics needs to build a system which is securely planned.

2. [A New Way of Thinking]

In metaphysics, thought is continually coming to a dead end, even when laws which common experience supports are under examination, purely as laws. Times without number it is necessary to go back to the fork because the road does not take us where we want to go. As for unanimity among the practitioners of metaphysics, there is so little of it that the discipline seems more like an arena, a ring constructed for those who like to exercise their skills in mock combat. At any rate, no contestant has yet succeeded in getting and holding a spot of his own. It appears, then, that to date, the procedure in metaphysics has just been to grope and worse than that, to grope among ideas.

How can it be explained that in this field, scientific certainty has not yet been found? Can it be impossible? If it is, why has nature visited our minds with a restless drive for certainty, as if this were the most important business of all? Not only that but there would be little reason ever to trust the powers of thought, if they fail in one of the most important projects of human curiosity, proffering illusions and giving at last betrayal. Perhaps it is only that up to now we have failed to read the road signs correctly. If we renew the search, may we hope to have better luck than has been the lot of those who preceded us?

It seems to me that the examples of mathematics and physics, having become what they are by sudden revolution, are remarkable enough to warrant attention to the essential element of their change, the change that proved so beneficial. It may be worth our while also to make the experiment of imitating them, to the degree the analogy between these two rational disciplines and metaphysics permits.

Hitherto it has been assumed that knowledge must conform to the things known; but on this basis all attempts to find out about the world of things by abstract thought, and thus to permit an extension of human knowledge, have come to nothing. Let us then experiment to see whether or not we do better with the problems of metaphysics if we assume that things to be known must conform in advance to our knowing process. This would appear to lead to what we want, namely, knowledge that tells us something about an object of thought before it becomes a part of our experience.

If my perception of an object has to conform to the object, I do not see how there could be any abstract knowledge of it; but if the objects of my perceptions conform to the laws by which I know them, it is easy to conceive of abstract knowledge, for all experience is a kind of knowledge involving the mind, the laws of which I must suppose were a part of me before I ever saw anything. Those laws get expressed in abstract terms but all my experience must agree with them.

This experiment succeeds as well as could be desired. It promises scientific certainty for the part of metaphysics that deals in abstract ideas, the corresponding objects of which may be checked off in experience. It involves a new way of thinking which enables us to explain perfectly how abstract knowledge, knowledge prior to experience, is possible. It also furnishes satisfactory proofs of the laws which form the mental framework of the natural world. Both of these achievements had been impossible heretofore.

3. [Empirical and A Priori Knowledge]

There is no doubt that knowledge begins with experience. How else could mental powers be awakened to action, if not by the objects that excite our senses, in part arousing images and in part stimulating the mental activity by which the images are compared? Images must then be combined or separated and the raw material of sense impressions worked over into the knowledge of things called experience. In the order of time, life begins with experience; there is no knowledge before that.

But if knowledge begins with experience, it does not follow that all of it is derived from experience. It may well be that whatever knowledge we do get from experience is already a combination of impressions and mental activity, the sense impressions being merely the occasion. It may be that the mental additive cannot be distinguished from the basic stuff until long practice makes one alert to it and skilled to pick it out.

This then is a question that needs close study and for which no offhand answer will do: Is there knowledge apart from both experience and sense impressions? This kind of knowledge is called abstract and prior (*a priori*) in contrast to knowledge derived from experience, which is empirical (*a posteriori*).

The word "*a priori*" is not yet definite enough to indicate the full meaning of the question at hand. It is often said of knowledge derived from experience that it is abstract because it does not come immediately from experience, but from some general rule borrowed from experience. Of a man who undermines the foundations of his house, we might say that he might have known *a priori,* that is, abstractly and beforehand, that the house would fall. He need not have waited for the actual experience of seeing it go down. He could not, however, have known about the house falling, from abstract principles only. He needs first to learn that bodies are heavy and that they fall when supports are removed; this would have to be learned from experience.

In what follows, by *abstract* knowledge we do not mean knowledge independent of this or that experience but knowledge *utterly independent of all experience.* In contrast, there is empirical, or *a posteriori* knowledge which we get only through experience. Abstract knowledge is called *pure* when it contains no trace of experience. So, for example, the proposition, "Every change has its cause," is abstract but not pure because *change* is an idea drawn only from experience.

We need now a criterion by which to distinguish pure from empirical knowledge. Experience teaches one that an object is what it is, but not

that it could not be otherwise. So, first, if a proposition cannot be conceived without thinking it *necessary,* it is *abstract.* Secondly, a judgment based on experience is never truly or strictly universal but only relatively so. But if a judgment is strictly *universal* and there is no possible exception to this, then it is not derived from experience and is valid, absolutely *abstract, pure.*

We need also to distinguish between two kinds of judgments, or statements: *analytic,* in which the predicate merely analyzes the subject; and *synthetic,* or *amplifying* in which the predicate adds something to the subject. If A is the subject of a statement and B is the predicate, there are two choices. If B is contained in A, the statement is analytic; if B is not contained in A but is related to it otherwise, the statement is synthetic, or amplifying.

For example, if I say, "All bodies are extended," this is an analytic statement of judgment. I need not go beyond the very idea of "body" to find the idea of "extension." On the other hand when I say, "All bodies are heavy," the predicate is quite different from what I think in the idea of "body" as such, and the addition of this kind of predicate to the subject makes the statement synthetic. Statements of experience always amplify the subject.

In abstract, amplifying judgments, no help can be had from experience. If I go beyond idea A and find idea B related to it, on what could such an amplification be based? Take, for example, the proposition: Everything that happens has a cause. In the idea of "something that happens," I can think of a time before the event and from it derive analytic judgments. But the idea of "cause" is something else; it does not fall within the idea of "something that happens." How then can I say something about this subject that is entirely unrelated to it? How do I know that cause belongs necessarily to that "something that happens," even when that something does not contain any notion of it? What is the unknown X on which one depends when he discovers a predicate B, foreign to A, which is, nevertheless, connected with it?

The unknown X cannot be experience because the principle just discussed adds a second conception (cause) to the first (existence), not only with wider generalization than experience can proffer but with an assertion of necessity. It is therefore wholly abstract and unrelated to experience. The whole aim of our speculative, abstract knowledge depends on synthetic, or amplifying propositions of this kind. Analytic judgments are of the highest importance and necessary, but only to clarify conception. This, in turn, is required for the secure and broader amplification by which something really new may be added to the matter of knowledge.

Examples from science. Mathematical judgments always amplify. One might think at first that $7 + 5 = 12$ is a straight analytic proposition. On closer inspection, it appears that the sum $7 + 5$ contains nothing more than the combination of these two numbers. There is nothing to indicate what number embraces both. Arithmetical propositions always amplify.

Nor are geometric propositions analytic. That a straight line is the shortest distance between two points is an amplifying conception. Straightness has nothing to do with quantity, but only with quality. The idea of shortness is thus additive, and intuition is necessary at this point. Without it, amplification would be impossible.

The science of physics also contains principles which are abstract and amplifying. For example, there is the proposition that in all the changes of the physical world, the total quantity of matter remains unchanged. But in the idea of matter, I do not imagine its permanency. I think only of its presence in the space it fills. So I really have to go beyond the idea of matter itself and attribute something to it abstractly, something I never thought it involved. The proposition is thus not analytic but synthetic, or amplifying and yet it is abstractly conceived.

There must be amplifying and abstract knowledge in metaphysics too, even if metaphysics is regarded only as a pseudo science, necessary to human nature. It is not the duty of metaphysicians merely to dissect subjects and so, analytically, to illustrate abstract ideas. It is their duty to extend abstract knowledge and for this purpose they use principles which add to their ideas matter not originally contained in them. By means of abstract, amplifying judgments they may even go where experience cannot follow, as, for example, in the statement that "the world must have a beginning," and the like. So, metaphysics, at least by aim, consists of pure, amplifying propositions.

The characteristic problem then of pure reason is: How are abstract, amplifying judgments possible? That metaphysics has so far remained in the state of vacillating uncertainty and contradiction, is due to the fact that this problem was not recognized sooner, nor, perhaps, was the difference between analytic and amplifying judgment made clear.

4. [The Matter and Form of Intuition]

Of the varied processes by which things become known, there is one from which all thought stems. It is awareness (intuition), and it alone is direct or immediate. Ultimately all food for thought comes from the outside world through our awareness of it, but among humans this occurs only when mind is involved.

The property of mind by which external things are recognized may be called sensitivity. Objects appear to mind because of its sensitivity, and this is the only way awareness can occur. In functioning mind, then, awareness gives rise to thoughts and finally to concepts. Directly or indirectly, all thought goes back to awareness and so to sensitivity, because there is no other way to know external things. Sensation is the effect an object has on the sensitive mind. If awareness comes through sensation, it is said to be empirical; and the object so revealed, whatever it may be, is called "phenomenon," or simply "thing."

By matter, I mean the substance of a thing, to which sensations are traceable; by form, I refer to my awareness that the substance of something is arranged in a given order.

It is clear that sensations are not put in form by other sensations. The matter of which things are composed may be known through sensation but their form is provided by the mind, and form is therefore separate from sensation.

I call awareness (intuition) which does not participate in sensation, *pure* (that is, belonging only to mind). The pure form which sense impressions take on, the form or order in which the many elements of things are arranged by the mind, must be in mind beforehand. The pure form of sensitivity may be called pure awareness.

If, from your awareness of a body, you subtract the contribution of thought processes such as substance, forces, divisibility, etc., and then take away all that pertains to sensation, such as impenetrability, color, etc., there will still remain extension and form. These belong to pure awareness and exist only in mind, as forms for sense impressions, even if there were present no external objects or sensations from them.

5. [The Pure Forms of Intuition —Space and Time]

There is a sense or sensitivity of mind, by which we reach out to things and see them located in external space. Within this space their form, size, and relative positions are or can be fixed.

There is an internal sense by which the mind is aware of itself or its internal states. This sense does not present the soul as an object to be observed. It is, however, a fixed function without which an awareness of internal states of mind would be impossible. Its operations pertain to the relationships of time. Time cannot appear as an external matter any more than space can appear to be something within.

What then are space and time? Are they real entities? Or if not, are they the delimitations of things or relations between things which exist whether anyone observes them or not? Or are they delimitations and relations which are inherent in one's awareness of the world and thus in the subjective character of the mind? If so, then without these properties of mind, predicates like space and time would never appear anywhere.

To understand this matter more clearly, let us first consider space.

1. Space is not an idea derived from experience of the external world. If my sensations are to be referred to things outside me, i.e., to things located at some point of space other than where I am, or if I am to be able to refer my sensations to differing objects located at several points, the idea of space must be present in advance. My conception of space therefore cannot be the product of experience or borrowed from the relations of things to each other. On the contrary, it is only by means of the idea of space that external experience becomes possible at all.

2. Space is the visualization which is necessary to the mind, and the basis of all external perceptions. One might imagine space with no objects to fill it, but it is impossible to imagine that there should be no space. Space is therefore a condition of the possibility of phenomena and not a form required by them. It is subjective, a vizualization which precedes all external experience.

3. The demonstrable certainty of geometric propositions depends on the necessity of this mental visualization of space. If space were a conception gained empirically or borrowed from general external experience, the first principles of mathematical definition would be merely perceptions. They would be subject to all the accidents of perception and there would be no necessity that there should be only one straight line between two points. A theorem would be something to be learned in each case by experience. Whatever is derived from experience possesses only relative generality, based on reasoning from observations. We should accordingly be able to say only that so far as anyone can see, there is no space having more than three dimensions.

4. Space is not a discursive or general idea of the relations between things. It is pure awareness or mental visualization. First of all, only one space is imaginable, and if many spaces are mentioned, they are all parts of the one space. They are not to be considered as leading up to the one all-embracing space, or the component parts from which an aggregate of space is formed.

Space is essentially one. The general idea of a mutiplicity of spaces is the result of imposing limitations on space. Hence, it follows that the foundation of all ideas of space is a mental awareness, and it is thus not derived from experience. So geometrical principles, such as "The sum of two sides of a triangle is greater than the third," may never be derived from the general conception of sides and triangles but from an awareness or visualization which is purely mental and which is derived thence with demonstrable certainty.

5. Space is visualized as an infinite quantity. The general idea of space, which is to be found in a foot as well as a yard, would furnish no information about the quantity of the space involved if there were not infinity in the reach of awareness. Without this, no conception of relations in space could ever contain the principle of infinity.

Space is not in any sense a property of things or the relation between them. It is nothing but the form the appearances of things take to man's outer senses. It is the mental basis of sensitivity and makes possible one's awareness of the external world.

One may speak of space, extension, etc., only from the human point of view. Apart from one's awareness of the outer world, the idea of space means nothing at all. The space predicate is attributed to things only as they are sensed.

The rule that "things are juxtaposed in space" is valid within the limitation that "things" are taken only as objects of awareness. Add one condition and say that "things as they appear externally are juxtaposed in space," and the rule is universally valid.

This exposition therefore teaches the *reality* (objective validity) of space. Space is as real as anything else in the world. At the same time, it teaches the *ideality* of space, when things are viewed as only the mind can view them, as they are by themselves, apart from the activity of human sense. We also assert the reality of space as veri-fiable fact in human experience of the external world.

The *formal* idea of phenomena in space is a critical reminder that there is nothing of which one is aware that is a thing-itself (that is, something apart from man's perception of it). Space is not the form of things-themselves. The phenomena of which we are aware tell us nothing about things as they are apart from us, and in experience nobody ever asks about them as such.

[*Kant's treatment of time parallels that of space, and need not be quoted. Time, like space, is a form of perception, not a thing perceived. Just as phenomena are spread out in space, above or below, near or far, to the right or the left, so likewise are they ordered in time, before, after, or simultaneous with other events. Anything experienced as spatial is thought of as belonging to the outer world, but temporal order applies to one's psychological acts of apprehension. Hence time is "the form of inner sense, that is, of our awareness of ourselves and our own inner states." But both space and time are necessary forms of human perception, and cannot be ascribed to objects in themselves apart from experience.*]

6. [How the Categories of the Understanding Unify and Organize Our Experience]

Among the many strands from which the complicated web of human knowledge is woven there are some which are destined from the start to be used abstractly and to continue independent of experience. The claims made for these ideas generally require special demonstration (deduction). Their legitimacy is not established by a deduction based on experience, even though we do want to knôw how these ideas can refer to objects within one's experience, and yet be derived apart from it. The explanation of the way abstract and prior ideas refer to objects is to be called *formal deduction.* This is distinguished from *empirical deduction,* which shows how an idea is derived by reflection from experience. *Empirical deduction* applies not to the legitimacy of the use of the ideas but to the facts from which they arise.

Without doubt an investigation of the functioning of man's power to know, beginning with single perceptions and climbing to general ideas, is useful. We have to thank the celebrated John Locke for opening up this avenue. The deduction of pure ideas is not, however, to be achieved along these lines; it is to be worked out in another direction. Their future use, independent of experience, requires for them a very particular birth certificate, in which descent from experience is denied. Locke's attempted psychological derivation is not deduction at all, because it depends on matters of fact. It is rather an explanation of the possession of pure knowledge. It is clear, therefore, that only a formal deduction of pure ideas is usable and that empirical deductions will not do.

Our entire investigation of the formal deduction of pure ideas should be based on this principle: Pure ideas are the abstract and prior conditions of experience. They supply the objective ground of experience and are, accordingly, necessary. To know how they occur, the abstract and prior conditions necessary to experience must be discovered and kept separate from knowledge derived from experience. The categories are pure ideas which express the formal and objective conditions of experience with sufficient generality and which contain the pure thought involved in every experience. It is really a sufficient deduction of the categories and a justification of their objective validity to prove that no object is conceivable without them.

The famous John Locke, lacking these considerations and having come across pure ideas in the course of experience, proceeded to derive them from experience itself. Then, inconsistently, he went far beyond the bounds of experience in studies of knowledge. David Hume saw that to do this, ideas from pure origins are needed. He could not explain, however, how it was that ideas, disconnected in one's mind, came together in some object of thought. It never occurred to him that mind itself might be the author of the experience of its object.

So he, too, was led to derive pure ideas from experience, or habit, i.e., from a subjective necessity begotten of frequent associations of experiences. This finally came to be accepted as objective, but falsely so. Subsequently Hume explained, and quite consistently this time, that with ideas so derived and with their attendant principles, it is not possible to get beyond personal experience. The deduction of pure ideas from experience, as practiced by Locke and Hume, cannot be reconciled with the abstract and prior knowledge encountered in pure mathematics and natural science. It is therefore refuted by the facts.

The first of these men left the door wide open to fantasy. It is hard to keep reasoning within due bounds once it has had unlimited prestige. The second gave in entirely to skepticism because he believed he had found in the knowing process an illusion which generally passed as reasonable. We now turn to study whether or not reasoning can be steered between these two cliffs, its limits indicated, and still keep its proper field of function open.

If every perception or idea were isolated from every other, there could be no knowledge as we know it, because knowledge consists of perceptions and ideas conjoined and compared to each other. Since the senses cover a whole field of awareness, they need a synopsis corresponding to the organization that makes knowledge possible when mind spontaneously comprehends sense data. Spontaneity is the beginning of a threefold organization which is necessary to every kind of knowledge. It consists of (1) *comprehension,* in which awareness is made into perceptions by ideas; (2) imagination in the *recollection* of the various elements necessary to knowledge; (3) *recognition* of the resultant ideas. Thus we have three inner sources of knowledge which make understanding and its empirical product, experience, possible.

However ideas or images arise, whether from the influence of external things or inner causes, or abstractly, or empirically as phenomena, they belong to man's inner sense because they are simply modifications of mind. All knowledge is, accordingly, subject to the formal condition of inner sense, namely, time. Everything is arranged, connected, and related by time. This general remark is fundamental to all subsequent discussion.

Generally speaking, awareness means being aware of many things at once, and this could not be imagined if time were not marked in the mind by a succession of impressions. In any given instant each impression is an absolute unity by itself; so, in order to get unity in awareness (as the idea of space requires), it is first necessary to let the various elements of awareness run in succession through the mind and then pull them together. This is the act which I call the organization of apprehension, or understanding. It is applied directly to awareness, which actually is multiple and so requires organization if it is to be unified or comprehended by means of a single idea.

The synthesis, or organization of understanding must be carried out abstractly and in advance, since ideas which are not empirical are involved. The ideas of space and time would be impossible without it; the many elements of sense data must be organized before they appear. This is how the pure organization of understanding is accomplished.

Again, it is apparent that if I draw an imaginary line, or consider the time lapse from one noon to the next, or even think of a certain number, I must begin by getting a general idea of the aggregates or sets of perceptions involved. If I were to lose from thought the antecedent part of either of them, say the first part of the line, the first hours of the day, or the digits preceding my number, and if I were unable to reproduce the lost parts as I went on, then no general ,idea of either of these sets would be possible to me. Neither could I, in that case, have the foregoing thoughts of even the first and purest ideas of space and time.

The organization of understanding is inseparably connected with recollection. Since the former is the formal basis of all knowledge, both empirical and pure, the organization of recollection by imagination belongs to the formal activity of mind and is here to be called *formal imagination*.

Again, if I were not aware that what I now think is the same as what I was thinking a moment ago, recollection of a lost step in a series of perceptions would be useless. Each perception in its place would be new, and not part of the action that made the series. A series of experiences could never be complete because it would lack the unity which only consciousness can give it. When I count, if I forget how the series of numbers now in my thought has been added up, one by one, I can never understand how the final sum is produced. The sum is a concept which depends on my consciousness of the organized unity of the number series.

The very word "idea" could have been the occasion of these remarks; consciousness gathers up the items in a series or a field, one by one, then recollection pulls them all together in a single idea. The consciousness involved may be so weak that it is felt, not in the act or process of production but only in the final idea. Nevertheless, even though it is not very clear, consciousness must always be there. Without it, ideas and all knowledge of objects would be impossible. . . .

If it is desired to follow up the inward connections among perceptions to their point of convergence, where they are unified as experience requires, we must begin with pure self-consciousness. Awareness amounts to nothing until it merges into consciousness, directly or indirectly. If this did not happen there would be no knowledge. Among all the perceptions of a given moment, we are conscious, abstractly and in advance, of our own identity. This is how any perception becomes possible, and it is a firm principle which may be called the formal principle of unity in one's perception of a field of sense data.

This unity, however, presupposes or involves an organization which is as necessary to knowledge and as prior and abstract as the unity itself. Unification depends on pure imagination to organize a field of perceptions into knowledge. Such an organization is said to be formal if, ignoring differences of awareness, it effects only the necessary unification of the field. The unity involved is also formal when it refers only to the original unity of self and thus becomes prior and necessary. Formal and organizing imagination is thus the pure form of knowledge by means of which, abstractly and in advance, objects of experience become known.

Understanding is the self at work in imagination, unifying and organizing experience; pure understanding is the self at work when imagination effects a formal organization. Understanding, therefore, involves pure, abstract forms for knowledge, which carry the unity the imagination uses to organize the data or experience into phenomena. These forms are the categories; that is, they are the mind's pure conceptions, or ideas. This then is how man learns from experience: Mind focuses on objects of sense by its own necessity, via awareness and by means of an organizing imagination; then phenomena, the data of experience, conform to mind; by means of the categories, pure mind constitutes a formal and organizing principle of experience, and this shows how, necessarily, phenomena are related to mind. . . .

Imagination, therefore, is man's prior and necessary capacity to organize things, and this makes us call it *productive imagination*. If imagination effects only necessary unity in the organization of phenomena, it can be called formal. The foregoing may appear strange, but it must be clear by now that the affinity, the association of phenomena and their recollection according to law, which is to say the whole of human experience, is made possible by formal imagination. Without this, ideas of objects could never foregather in a single experience.

It is the permanent and unchanging "I" (pure apperception) that correlates perceptions when we become conscious of them. All consciousness belongs to one all-embracing pure apperception, "I," as sense awareness belongs to one pure inner awareness, namely, time. So that this "I" may function mentally, imagination is added and the organiza-

tion effected by imagination, though of itself prior and necessary, is carried out in the senses. Phenomena are connected in a field of impressions only as they appear in awareness: for example, a triangle. When the field is once related to the "I," ideas of it fit into the mind, and imagination relates them to sense awareness.

Pure imagination is therefore a fundamental operation of the soul, and abstractly, in advance, all knowledge depends on it. It connects all that one is aware of with the unitary "I." It brings the two extremes of sense and mind together. Without it, the senses might report phenomena but not empirical knowledge, and so experience would be impossible. Real experience comes of apprehension, association, and recognition of phenomena and contains the ultimate and highest ideas, the ideas that formally unify experience and validate empirical knowledge objectively. These ideas constitute the basis on which a field of sense data is recognized. If they concern only the form of experience, they are, accordingly, categories. The whole formal unity of recognition by means of imagination depends on the categories, and in turn the whole empirical use of the categories (in recognition, recollection, association, and apprehension), even down to phenomena, depends on imagination. These four elements of knowing make it possible for a phenomenon to belong to our consciousness and so to ourselves.

It is we who bring order and regularity to phenomena and call the result "nature." These properties would not be discovered in nature if our own minds had not first put them there; for unity in nature means a prior, necessary, and certain connection of phenomena. How indeed could organized unity in nature be conceived in advance, if the original source of knowledge, the inner core of our minds, did not first contain it? What would there be to see if this mental condition of ours were not objectively valid, valid because it is the condition by which objects become part of experience?

7. [Phenomena and Noumena]

We have now explored the land of pure reasoning and carefully surveyed every part of it. We have measured its extent and put everything in its right place. It is an island, by nature enclosed within unchangeable limits. It is the land of truth (enchanting name!), surrounded by a wide and stormy ocean, the native home of illusion, where cloud banks and icebergs falsely prophesy new lands and incessantly deceive adventurous seafarers with empty hopes, engaging them in romantic pursuits which they can neither abandon nor fulfill. Before we venture on this sea, we ought to glance at the map of the island and consider whether or not to be satisfied with it, lest there be no other territory on which to settle. We should know what title we have to it, by which we may be secure against opposing claims.

We have seen that the produce of mind is not borrowed from experience but is for use only in experience. The mind's principles may be either abstract and constitutive, like mathematical principles, or merely regulative, like dynamic principles. In either case they contain nothing but the pure schema of possible experience. Unity comes into experience from the organizing unity of mind, which the mind confers on self-consciousness via imagination; and phenomena, as the data of possible experience, must fit into that unity abstractly and in advance. These rules of mind not only are true but also are the source of all truth, the reason for the agreement of our knowledge with objects. They contain the basis on which experience is possible, that is, experience viewed as the sum of one's knowledge of objects. We are not, however, satisfied with an exposition merely of what is true; we want also to know what mankind otherwise wants to know. This long, critical inquiry would hardly seem worthwhile if at the end of it, we have learned only what would have gone on anyway in everyday mental operations.

Even if our minds do work satisfactorily without such an inquiry as this, the inquiry has one advantage. The mind that is in us is unable to determine for itself the limits of its own uses. That is why the deep inquiry we have set up is required. If we cannot decide whether certain questions lie within our mental horizon, we must be prepared for getting lost among the delusions that result from overstepping our limitations.

If we can know certainly whether the mind can use its principles only within experience and never purely formally, this knowledge will have important consequences. The formal use of an idea is its application to things in general and to entities for which we have no sense data; the empirical use of an idea is its application to phenomena, or to objects of possible experience. It is evident that only the latter application is practicable. For example, consider the ideas of mathematics, first as pure awareness: space has three dimensions; there can be but one straight line between two points; etc. Although these principles are generated abstractly in the mind, they would mean nothing if their meaning could not be demonstrated in phenomena. It is therefore required that a pure idea be made sensible, that is, that one should or can be aware of an object corresponding to it. Otherwise, the idea, we say, would make no sense, i.e., it would be meaningless.

The mathematician meets this need by the construction of a figure which is, to the senses, a phenomenon, even though abstractly produced. In the same science, the idea of size finds its meaning and support in number, whether by fingers, or abacus beads, or in strokes and points on the printed page. The idea is always abstractly conceived, as are the amplifying principles and formulas derived from them; but finally, their use and their relation to their indicated objects appear only in experience, even though they contain the formal conditions of the possibility of that experience.

That this is the case with all the categories and the principles spun out of them, appears as follows. We cannot really define the categories, or make the possibility of their objects intelligible, without descending at once to the conditions of sense and the forms of phenomena, to which, as their only objects, the categories must be limited. If this condition is removed, all meaning, all relation to an object disappears, and no example will make the meaning of such an idea comprehensible....

If *noumenon* means something which is not an object of sense and so is abstracted from awareness, this is the negative sense of the term. If, however, it means an object of nonsensible awareness, we presuppose a special kind of awareness, which is purely mental, not part of our equipment, and of which we cannot imagine even the possibility. That would be *noumenon* in the positive sense of the word. . . .

The division of objects into phenomena and noumena, and the world into a world of the senses and a world of mind, is not admissible in the positive sense, even though the division of ideas as sensible and mental is legitimate. For we cannot conceive a mind which knows objects, not discursively or through categories, but by a nonsensible awareness. What mind acquires through the idea of noumenon is a negative extension. It is not then limited by sense but rather, it limits sense by applying the term "noumena" to things-themselves, which are not phenomena. It also limits itself, since noumena are not to be known by means of categories. They can be thought of only as unknown somethings.

8. [God, Freedom, and Immortality]

God, freedom, and the immortality of the soul are the problems to the solution of which all the labors of metaphysics are directed. It used to be believed that the doctrine of freedom was necessary only as a negative condition of practical philosophy, and that the ideas of God and the soul belonged to theoretical philosophy; they had to be demonstrated separately. Religion was achieved subsequently by adding morality to these ideas.

It soon appears, however, that such an attempt must miscarry. It is absolutely impossible to conceive an original Being whose characteristics make him experienceable, and therefore knowable, if one starts with only simple, abstract, ontological ideas. Neither would an idea based on the experience of physical appropriateness in nature adequately demonstrate morality or acquaintance with God. Just as little would knowledge of the soul, acquired from experience in this life, provide an idea of the soul's spiritual, immortal nature, adequate to morality. Neither theology nor spiritualism can be established by empirical data. They deal with matters that transcend human knowledge. Ideas of God and the immortal soul can be defined only by predicates drawn from supersensible sources, predicates whose reality is demonstrated by experience. This is the only way a supersensible Being can be known.

The freedom of man under moral law conjoined with the final end which freedom prescribes by means of the moral law compose the only predicate of this kind. This combination of ideas contains the conditions necessary to the possibility of both God and man.

An inference can then be made to the actuality and the nature of God and the soul, both of which would otherwise be entirely hidden from us.

Theoretical proofs of God and immortality fail because natural ideas tell us nothing about supersensible matters. Proofs via morality and freedom do succeed because there is causality in these ideas and their roots are supersensible. The causal law of freedom here establishes its own actuality by the way men behave. It also provides means of knowing other supersensible objects, such as the final moral end and its practicability. The conception of freedom's causality is, of course, based on practical considerations, but that happens to be all religion needs.

It is remarkable that of the three pure, rational ideas—God, freedom, and immortality—whose objects are supersensible, freedom alone proves its objective reality in the world of nature by what it can effect there. Freedom, therefore, makes possible the connection of the other two ideas with nature and of all three with religion. We may thus conceive the supersensible realm within man and around him, so that it becomes practical knowledge. Speculative philosophy, which offers only a negative idea even of freedom itself, can never accomplish anything like this. The idea of freedom, fundamental to unconditioned practical law, reaches beyond the limits within which natural, theoretical ideas remain hopelessly restricted.

GERALD DWORKIN (1937–   )

Professor Dworkin received his doctor of philosophy degree at the University of California (Berkeley), and has taught at Harvard and the Massachusetts Institute of Technology. Since 1976 he has been Professor of Philosophy at the University of Illinois in the Chicago Circle. His principal areas of research and publication are ethics, social and political philosophy, and philosophy of law.

Determinism, Free Will, and Moral Responsibility

The famous attorney Clarence Darrow once addressed the prisoners in the Cook County Jail as follows:

There is no such thing as a crime as the word is generally understood. I do not believe there is any sort of distinction between the real moral conditions of the people in and out of jail. One is just as good as the other. The people here can no more help being here than the people outside can avoid being outside. I do not believe that people are in jail because they deserve to be. They are in jail simply because they cannot avoid it on account of circumstances which are entirely beyond their control and for which they are in no way responsible. . . . There are people who think that everything in this world is an accident. But really there is no such thing as an accident. . . . There are a great many people here who have done some of these things [murder, theft, *etc.*] who really do not know themselves why they did them. It looked to you at the time as if you had a chance to do them or not, as you saw fit; but still, after all you had no choice. . . . If you look at the question deeply enough and carefully enough you will see that there were circumstances that drove you to do exactly the thing which you did. You could not help it any more than we outside can help taking the positions that we take.

This is an excellent, if somewhat extreme, statement of a view held by many people regarding the implications of a thesis about the nature of the world which may be called *determinism*. This view has its roots in the earliest attempts to grasp in a rational manner some understanding of the universe, and it remains today a point of controversy among theoretical physicists. It is a philosophical issue which, as the quotation from Darrow illustrates, professes to have important implications for the ways in which we think, talk, and act. This collection of articles is an attempt to introduce to a beginning student of philosophy the problem of determinism and free will.

I

There are basically three questions that can be asked of any philosophical thesis: What does its mean? Is it true? What difference does it make? The organization of this book reflects these questions, as will this introduction.

II

It is by no means easy to define the thesis of determinism in any very precise manner. And the definition of the thesis will determine its implications. If, for example, one defines determinism as "the denial of free will," whatever the latter might be, then it will be a logical truth that if determinism is true, there is no free will. But this way of proceeding, although it has what Bertrand Russell calls "the advantages of theft over honest toil," will not prove intellectually satisfying. If possible one would like a definition of the thesis which meets the following requirements: (1) It does not beg any questions concerning the important implications of the thesis; (2) It does not involve any terms which are at least as problematic as the one being defined; and (3) The thesis seems to have some chance of being true.

The usual model on which a definition is constructed is the kind of knowl-

edge gained by the physical sciences. The classical view as ʼstated by the eighteenth-century mathematician Laplace is that "an intelligence knowing all the forces acting in nature at a given instant, as well as the momentary positions of all things in the universe, would be able to comprehend in one single formula the motions of the largest bodies as well as the lightest atoms. . . . To it nothing would be uncertain, the future as well as the past would be present to its eyes."[1] This statement contains the two fundamental ingredients of any determinism: a belief in universal causal laws and a notion of predictability. Although it is the feature of predictability that has usually been stressed, perhaps because psychologically that is the feature of determinism that bothers people, it is really the presence of causal laws and explanations which characterizes the determinist position. As soon as it is pointed out to the determinist that as a matter of fact he cannot predict, for example, the next three words I am going to write, he falls back on a notion of *predictable-in-principle*. But the only basis for believing that such predictions are in principle possible is the premise that there are causal factors at work determining the future in a unique fashion, such factors being in principle capable of being known. It is, however, possible that the world may be a deterministic system, although its complexity might be such that we could not grasp the causal laws involved and hence could not use them in making predictions.

[3] Laplace, *Théorie Analytique des Probabilités* (2nd ed.), (Paris, 1814), p. ii.

How then shall we formulate the deterministic thesis? Let us consider some given system. It might be a human being or an amoeba or a television set or the solar system. Certain things happen to the system, and it, in turn, does certain things. In scientific jargon, there are inputs and outputs. In addition the system has a certain internal structure of its own. The determinist asserts that the output of the system is a unique function of the input and the internal structure. Given any output, O, there are universally true causal laws which determine O uniquely on the basis of the internal structure of the system and some of the inputs. For every output O there were earlier events which were sufficient for the production of O. That is, if we could now move backwards in time to some earlier point and we kept all the variables of the system at the same values they had at the earlier time, then the system would again produce O as its output. Now determinism asserts that the universe is just such a deterministic system, and it then of course follows that the particular systems we call human beings are deterministic systems.

Determinism should not be confused with what might be called predeterminism, or *fatalism*. Fatalism states that our output is not affected by any efforts or decisions that we make. This is a stronger claim than determinism, in effect not only claiming that our outputs are caused, but also specifying certain factors as being causally irrelevant to the outcome. This thesis suffers from the defect that there is no reason to suppose it true and every reason to regard it as false.

From the intuitive and rough characterization given above we may try and produce more precise formulations. For example: For any event E

1. The occurrence of E was causally necessitated
2. The occurrence of E has a sufficient explanation in causal terms
3. E had sufficient antecedent conditions
4. The occurrence of E was in principle predictable
5. There exist a set of events, C, and a true law of nature, L, which asserts that if C were to occur then E would occur.

We may then define *indeterminism* as the negation of determinism, that is, as the view that there is at least one event E of which the defining conditions for determinism do not hold.

We now see emerging that circle of concepts which encloses the problem: cause, necessity, sufficient conditions, causal explanation, predictability, law of nature. Explaining and clarifying these concepts is one of the main tasks of the philosopher.

III

Given some understanding of the thesis, we can then address ourselves to the existence of evidence for its truth. Why should anyone ever have supposed that the universe is a deterministic system? And are there good reasons for such a belief? The answer to these questions depends on how the thesis is to be construed. Is it supposed to be, for example, just a broad generalization from experience? A child might find that if he drops a ball it falls toward the floor. He then might discover that this is true for all of his toys—balloons excepted. Perhaps then he would observe that this property holds true no matter which room of his house he is in and indeed everywhere he goes. Next he could conjecture that (almost) all objects anywhere on earth fall if left unsupported. His generalization could then be extended to the entire universe. One difficulty with treating determinism in an analogous fashion as an inductive generalization is that if a proposition is a generalization from experience it should be possible to find it false on the basis of further experience. But it is not clear how to do this with the deterministic thesis, for the failure to find causal laws governing the occurrence of any given event does not mean there are none; the determinist can always ask us to look further. Of course, sometimes the best reason for supposing something does not exist is that we have looked very carefully and extensively and have not found it to exist. But sometimes the reasoning for supposing something not to exist will be of a more theoretical nature. The reason I do not believe in the existence of a man who can fly by flapping his arms is not that I have made a thorough search for such a creature and failed to find one, but that on the basis of a well-confirmed anatomical and physical theory there cannot be such a creature. Although there have been few attempts by indeterminists to use such reasoning to show that there are (must be) uncaused events, one such line of reasoning is to be found in the selection by Peirce.

Nagel, on the other hand, does not construe the thesis to be an empirical one but rather interprets it as a regulative principle or postulate, to be judged on its fruitful consequences for scientific investigation of the world. The reader must judge for himself how successful this approach is and whether it avoids Peirce's ironic onslaught.

Finally there are attempts such as Hume's to show that belief in determinism is warranted as the only way in which we can account for the judgments and predictions we make about the behavior of our fellow men. What has to be shown by this line of argument is that we do use a principle as strong as the determinist principle to make judgments, and further that we cannot arrive at the same results by using any weaker theory, that is, one that only assumes that *most* events are determined uniquely or one that makes use of only statistical determinations.

IV

Let us turn now to the issue of *free will.* How is it to be defined? And what are the logical connections between free will and determinism? The intuitive idea underlying the notion of free will is that of an openness of possibilities for the agent. It is commonly believed that although, as a matter of fact, a man did one thing rather than another—for example, went to the movies rather than watch television—it was open to him to have done something else instead. There were alternatives to his action which were genuine possibilities. Similarly, it is commonly believed that at present there are various possibilities which I can bring about. I can either continue writing or stop, decide to pay my income tax or refuse to pay, lift my arm or keep it at my side. The claim that we have free will is, then, the claim that for some actions at least the following condition is true: There is an alternative action (which may be simply refraining from the action to be performed) open to the agent. Put in the past tense after the agent has performed some action A: There was some alternative action which the agent could have performed other than the one which he in fact did.

Both Campbell and Reid attempt to show the truth of this thesis on the basis of appeals to introspective evidence. Reid takes the more cautious line, trying to show that a careful examination of our inner experience produces enough evidence at least to throw the burden of proof on anyone denying free will. The DeValla and Herbst articles are interesting attempts to understand the connection between the possibility of others (including God) making correct and justified predictions about our future actions and the concept of free will.

There are three possible positions that can be taken with respect to the relation between determinism and free will: (1) determinism is inconsistent with free will—that is, the truth of determinism entails the falsity of free will; (2) the truth of determinism entails the truth of free will; or (3) the two positions are logically independent—that is, nothing follows about the truth or falsity of free will from the truth of determinism. For the sake of symmetry, and because there is little reason to suppose (2) is true, (2) and (3) are usually lumped together as the claim that determinism and free will are compatible or consistent, while (1) is the belief that the two theses are inconsistent.

Most of the fuss over this subject has arisen because it has seemed obvious to many philosophers that determinism is inconsistent with free will. Here is a typical argument: Suppose I were faced with a choice between vanilla and chocolate ice cream, and I chose vanilla. Could I have chosen chocolate? If determinism is true, then we can find some causal law linking the choice I made with antecedent conditions such as my upbringing, my tastes, my moods, and so forth. But if the law is true, and if the initial conditions are present, then the law plus initial conditions will entail that this choice and no other takes place. It would be contradictory to admit whenever A, then B, and then to admit A and reject B. If there were indeed sufficient conditions for my choice of vanilla ice cream, then I could not have chosen chocolate ice cream, for then the conditions must not have been sufficient, but at most perhaps necessary. It is no more possible for me to choose chocolate than for a piece of paper to turn to ice when a blow-torch is applied to it.

Those philosophers who have wished to resist this conclusion, to show that determinism and free will are consistent, have proceeded by arguing that words such as "can," "would have," and "possible" are not self-evident terms, and that a proper analysis would show that, correctly understood, I could have chosen differently even if determinism is true. Determinism and free will seem to be inconsistent only because we think that "I could have done otherwise" means "I could have done otherwise in exactly those circumstances in which I did not do otherwise." But, it is suggested, what should be understood by this phrase is, roughly, "I could have done otherwise if such-and-such had been the case (I had chosen differently, I had tried harder, I had had a different upbringing, *etc.*)." The Hume and Moore selections illustrate this approach to the problem.

The reply to this line of argument, as the Broad and Lehrer articles illustrate, is that although this may be one meaning that the phrase "could have done otherwise" may carry, it is not the sense that this phrase must bear if we are to justify our ordinary ways of judging people blameworthy and punishing them. For this we must have a categorical sense of possibility rather than a hypothetical sense. Not "could have done otherwise" *if,* but "could have done otherwise," period.

At this point in the debate it becomes clear that the question of the proper analysis of the notions of "possibility," "could have done otherwise," and so forth, must be tied in with a conception of the puzzles and problems being raised. Determinism is widely supposed to undermine many commonly held beliefs about human responsibility, and the thesis of free will is supposed to rescue us from this quandary.

The following argument attempts to develop the above implications:

1. A necessary condition for holding a person responsible, blaming, or punishing him for an act, A, is that the person did A freely.

2. If determinism is true nobody ever acts freely.
3. Therefore, if determinism is true, no one is ever responsible, blameworthy, or punishable.
4. At least sometimes agents are responsible, blameworthy, or punishable for what they do.
5. Therefore, determinism is false.

To return to the question of the compatibility of free will and determinism, that is, whether premise (2) in the above argument is true, we can now define the problem more accurately. What sense of "acting freely" or "could have done otherwise" is required by premise (1), and is determinism consistent with *that* sense of the term?

Determinists who wish to hold onto our common belief that sometimes we are responsible for what we do analyze the notion of responsibility in such a way that it is consistent with a hypothetical analysis of "could have done otherwise,"—"would have done otherwise, if. . . ." This analysis of responsibility is usually some form of what might be called a "modifiability" theory. According to this theory, a person is morally responsible for an action if and only if he is modifiable by blame and punishment. A wrongdoer is morally responsible if and only if punishment would have affected his choice to do something wrong in the past or will now influence him to avoid such actions in the future. Hence we need a sense of "could have done otherwise" which is relevant to the modifiability of the agent. Now a hypothetical analysis in terms of choice looks plausible. For in those cases where the agent could have done otherwise if he had so chosen, and if his choices in the future will be influenced by blame or punishment, we are justified in holding him responsible, blaming him, and so forth.

Those who insist that the "can" needed is a categorical one, and hence that premise (2) is true, argue that the equation of moral responsibility with modifiability is mistaken and has absurd consequences, that the notions of blame and punishment have other than utilitarian justifications, and that the reason we insist on a "could have done otherwise" condition is not that we are interested in changing behavior but that we are interested in being fair. And it is not simply inefficacious to punish a man who could not have done otherwise (sometimes, indeed it may be efficacious); it is unjust. We are inflicting sanctions (formal or informal) on a man who could not have avoided his wrong conduct. By parody of reasoning, so it is argued, the hypothetical analysis of "could have done otherwise" should apply to a man in a coma; for surely he could have or even would have saved a drowning child if he had so chosen.

There is an interesting parallel between the way in which philosophers in the British empiricist tradition (Locke, Hume, Mill) treat the problem of free will and the way in which they analyze the issue of social freedom or liberty. In both cases freedom is defined, roughly, as being able to do what one wishes or chooses to do. And in both cases the feeling is that pushing the inquiry further into the conditions under which people have acquired the desires they have is unnecessary and illegitimate. Thus for the social freedom

theorist, the question of whether or not members of a society have been indoctrinated, manipulated, or brainwashed into certain needs or desires is irrelevant to issues of liberty. As long as they have those desires and are able to act to satisfy them, they are free men. The parallel argument for free will is that it does not matter whether or not a man's choices have causal antecedents. All that is important is that if he should choose or desire otherwise he would be able to translate those desires and choices into action. In both cases opponents have argued that, although this initial definition is part of the story of freedom, it is merely a part, and that it would be a mockery to insist that a man is free with all the implications of that assessment unless that portion of the story which involves the determinants of a man's choices is brought in as well.

The articles by Smart, Broad, Moore, Thomas, and Lehrer discuss the proper analysis of "could have done otherwise" and its implications for questions of *moral responsibility*.

There has been more sympathy in recent years for the view that determinism is inconsistent with free will and has radical implications for our moral outlook upon the world. If we are to make progress on this problem we must take determinism seriously and not assume that it leaves everything as it is. But even if this position is accepted, it is not enough to argue that because we all believe people are often responsible for their conduct determinism is false. Our intuitions on this matter might have to give way before the theory rather than *vice versa*. Still, if anything will work, it is this type of strategy.

Determinism, like most philosophical theses, will not fall to any single attack or knock-down argument. Rather it must be undermined in as many different ways as we have imagination and ingenuity to conceive. It is only by revealing as many counterintuitive results as possible, covering as broad a range of thought about human beings as possible, that we can successfully dislodge a mistaken view.

Determinists—historically often persons most interested and concerned with human freedom (Spinoza, Marx, Freud) —have assumed that the only things that would disappear as a result of accepting their views are vengeance, vindictiveness, smug views of moral superiority, and so forth. What has to be shown is that the consequences are far more drastic, that the entire notion of a human agent disappears as well.

COMMENT

Impressions and Ideas

The supreme advocate of the sceptical spirit is David Hume. He is a member of the sequence of classic British empiricists, which includes such great figures as Bacon, Hobbes, Locke, Berkeley, and Mill. More consistent in his empiricism than his predecessors, Hume pushed the sceptical implications of this approach to its logical extreme. Many philosophers have tried to refute his arguments, but his influence continues to be immense.

A thorough empiricist, Hume traced all knowledge back to some original basis in experience. The stream of experience, he pointed out, is made up of *perceptions*, a term he employed to designate any mental content whatever. He divided perceptions into *impressions*, the original sensations or feelings, and *ideas*, the images, copies, or representations of these originals. It is important to note that Hume, unlike Locke and Berkeley, reserved the word "idea" for mental copies or representations of original data.

Hume's practice of tracing ideas back to their original impressions becomes a *logical test* of the soundness of concepts. If a concept, such as that of substance, cannot be traced back to some reliable basis in impressions, it immediately becomes suspect. A fertile source of confusion in our thinking is the tendency to impute to outer things the qualities that belong to internal impressions. Thus an internal feeling of necessity may be falsely imputed to some outer chain of events. The human mind, if it does not carefully analyze the sources of its ideas, is prone to fall into such errors. Hume's philosophy consists largely in exposing these pitfalls in our thinking.

Criticism of the Idea of Causation

The most famous example of this critical method is Hume's analysis of the idea of causation. He began by pointing out that this idea is extremely crucial in our thinking. "The only connection or relation of objects," he declared, "which can lead us beyond the immediate impressions of our memory and senses, is that of cause and effect; and that because it is the only one on which we can found a just inference from one object to another."[1] We infer external objects only be-

[1] *An Enquiry Concerning Human Understanding,* edited by L. A. Selby-Bigge (Oxford: Clarendon Press, 1902), p. 89.

cause we suppose them to be the causes of the immediate data of experience. The idea of causation is thus the basis of empirical science and the ultimate ground for belief in an external world. For Hume, scientific knowledge as a whole stands or falls according to whether causation can be validated as a principle of reasoning.

Upon analysis, the idea of causation breaks up into four notions: (1) *succession*, (2) *contiguity*, (3) *constant conjunction*, and (4) *necessary connection*. Hume maintained that the first three notions can be defended—we can verify them by recalling the original sensory impressions from which they are derived. But *necessity* cannot thus be verified—try as we may, we cannot trace it back to any sensory impressions. It turns out, therefore, to be a confused and illegitimate notion. I shall not analyze the details of his argument, since this exercise in analysis is excellent practice for students.

Sceptical Implications

Hume was quick to draw the consequences from his theory of causation. One implication is that our common-sense idea that the future will resemble the past is merely an assumption, an expectation begotten by habit, not a rational conviction. Since we never discover an objective necessity binding effect to cause, we have no reason to assume that this cause-and-effect relation must continue to hold. The sun has risen many times, but this does not mean that it will rise tomorrow. There is no "law" that the sun must rise: there is only inexplicable repetition.

One of the most significant applications of Hume's analysis of causation is his attack upon the arguments for an external world. Both Locke and Berkeley, whose arguments Hume had primarily in mind, inferred the existence of an external world on the basis of a theory of causation. They reasoned that the regular character of experience, which is largely determined for us independently of our wills, must have some external cause. Locke found the cause in material substances and primary qualities; Berkeley in God and the ideas which God imprints upon our minds. Now Hume, in attack, went to the nerve of the argument and maintained that we are not justified in employing the idea of cause in this way.

> The only conclusion we can draw from the existence of one thing to that of another is by means of the relation of cause and effort, which shows that there is a connection betwixt them, and that the existence of one is dependent on that of the other. . . . But as no beings are ever present to the mind but perceptions, it follows that we may observe a conjunction or a relation of cause and effort between different perceptions, but can never observe it between perceptions and objects. 'Tis impossible, therefore, that from the existence of any of the qualities of the former, we can ever form any conclusion concerning the existence of the latter. . . .[2]

[2] *A Treatise of Human Nature*, edited by L. A. Selby-Bigge (Oxford: Clarendon Press 1896), p. 212.

What emerges from this devastating criticism? If we are resolved thus to stay within the closed circle of experience, we can either accept our perceptions as the ultimate character of existence or say that there may be something more—*some kind of external world*—but that we cannot know what that something more is. There is little basis here for positive belief.

A final twist to Hume's scepticism is his denial of a substantial self. Just as Berkeley rejected Locke's doctrine of material substance, so Hume for similar reasons rejected Berkeley's doctrine of a mental substance. He denied that we ever have an *impression* of a self, and in the absence of any such impression, he saw no way of proving that a self exists. All the content of experience is fleeting, evanescent, whereas the self is supposed to be identical through succeeding states. Impressions, being variable and evanescent, are incapable of revealing a permanent self; and to *infer* an unexperienced self as the necessary cause of our mental states is to project illegitimately the relation of cause and effect, which is through and through experiential, beyond the circle of experience.

Hume thus reduced reality, so far as it can be verified, to a stream of "perceptions" neither caused nor sustained by any mental or material substance. Existence is made up of mental facts, perceptions, with no selves to which the perceptions belong and no material world in which they reside.

How Kant Differed from Hume

Kant was struck, as Hume himself had been struck, by the largely negative results of Hume's inquiry. "I am . . . affrighted and confounded with the forlorn solitude in which I am placed by my philosophy," Hume confessed, "and fancy myself some strange uncouth monster, utterly abandoned and disconsolate." The effect of Hume's scepticism upon Kant was different—not to fill his mind with fright and confusion, but to awaken him from his "dogmatic slumbers." Hume convinced Kant that traditional metaphysics was bankrupt and that a new start was necessary. But Kant was also convinced that there must be something fundamentally wrong with an empiricism that led to such devastating conclusions. He was not content to fall back upon "natural instinct" but sought some kind of rationale for his trust in science and his moral and religious convictions. The task that he set himself, in the words of one of his contemporaries, was "to limit Hume's scepticism on the one hand, and the old dogmatism on the other, and to refute and destroy materialism, fatalism, atheism, as well as sentimentalism and superstition."

In the *Critique of Pure Reason*, Kant undertook to prove that all genuine scientific knowledge, whether in mathematics or in the natural sciences, is universally valid, but that speculative metaphysics, which seeks to go beyond experience to determine the ultimate and absolute nature of things, cannot be established upon any sound and dependable basis. Science is reliable because it deals with *phenomena*—things as they *appear* in human experiences; but metaphysics is unreliable because it tries to interpret *noumena*—things as they are in themselves apart from experience. The world of ultimate reality, in contrast to the world of appearance, can never be known to reason. The noumenal realities must be interpreted, if at all, by moral conviction and religious faith—not by science or pure theoretical philosophy.

The phenomena, Kant insisted, exhibit spatial and temporal forms of rational connections, such as cause and effect. In grasping these forms and connections, consciousness is an awareness of meanings—not passive contemplation but active judgment, not mere perception but synthetic interpretation. We can never know things as they are apart from these synthetic modes of apprehension and judgment, which are the necessary conditions of all human experience. To interpret *ultimate* reality as either finite or infinite, one or many, mechanistic or teleological, mental or material, is to attempt to probe the supersensible nature of existence— and this human reason can never do. But if the positive claims of transcendent metaphysics are thus overthrown, so are its negative claims. The metaphysician is as powerless to *disprove* the existence of God as to prove His existence, or to *disprove* an idealistic account of reality as to prove it. When the overweening claims of "pure reason" are thus refuted, our "practical reason" is no longer inhibited by atheism, materialism, or mechanistic determinism.

Let me sum up his answer to Hume's scepticism. He tries to make secure the foundations of natural science by demonstrating that the order and regularity necessary to science—the sensory forms of space and time and the intelligible order of substance, causation, and the other "categories"—inhere necessarily in phenomena because they are contributed by the mind in the very act of knowing (knowledge being a joint-product of mind and things-in-themselves). To Hume's reduction of the mind to a succession of awarenesses, Kant opposes the mind's awareness of succession, which he says is unaccountable without more synthesis and continuity than Hume recognized. While he agrees with Hume that the doctrines of speculative metaphysics cannot be demonstrated, he tries to justify the ideas of God, freedom, and immortality on moral grounds.

I shall not trace the arguments by which Kant reached these conclusions. Since Blakney's translation is remarkably lucid, the reader who studies the text carefully should find no insuperable difficulty in understanding its meaning.

The Question of Free Will

Since the question of free will is fascinating, I shall consider it at greater length. The question has been touched upon in previous chapters. Lucretius, as we have seen, correlated free will in the human being with the indeterministic swerving of the atoms. Far different was Spinoza's monistic cosmic determinism. Even Spinoza, however, contended that God is free because God is the totality, and God's nature is not limited by anything external to it. So far as people share in God's nature, they also are free—not in the sense of being undetermined, but in the sense of participating in God's free and infinite being. Freedom is here opposed to constraint.

Hume rejected Spinoza's metaphysical system but retained the idea that freedom is the absence of constraint. It is a mere confusion of thought to identify freedom and indeterminism, since nothing is more fatal than an accident, and nothing is more accidental than an undetermined event. Necessity, he argued, applies to human life as much as to nature, but in no way destroys our liberty. So long as the necessity springs from the people's nature and does not involve constraint, they are free. Free people are unhindered in the realization of their desires; unfree people are chained, locked up, or otherwise constrained.

Kant rejected this analysis. He believed in a freedom exempt from necessity, and attributed this kind of free action to the transcendental self—the "I" existing outside of the phenomenal order in the realm of things-in-themselves. He thought, paradoxically, that a self could be at once under necessity *qua* phenomenon and free *qua* noumenon. Just how freedom and necessity can thus be joined remains a mystery, since we lack all knowledge of the noumenal world.

Although most philosophers would reject this attempt to reconcile phenomenal necessity with noumenal freedom, many would accept Kants argument that "I ought" implies "I can." One of the better known defenders of free will, C. A. Campbell of Glasgow University, has written:

> Let us put the argument implicit in the common view a little more sharply. The moral 'ought' implies 'can'. If we say that A morally ought to have done X, we imply that in our opinion, he could have done X. But we assign moral blame to a man only for failing to do what we think he morally ought to have done. Hence if we morally blame A for not having done X, we imply that he could have done even though in fact he did not. In other words, we imply that A could have acted otherwise than he did. And that means that we imply, as a necessary condition of a man's being morally blameworthy, that he enjoyed a freedom of a kind not compatible with unbroken causal continuity.[5]

Campbell also agrees with Kant in ascribing to human beings a contra-causal type of freedom that is distinguished sharply from ordinary deterministic causality. At the moment of choice, everyone feels that there are genuinely open possibilities, and Campbell is not prone to dismiss this feeling as illusion. He believes that it is possible, by an effort of will, to "rise to duty" even though we may be strongly inclined to yield to temptation. Similarly William James, in his famous essay "The Dilemma of Determinism," contends that the *modus operandi* of free choice is the resolute effort of attention and will that we direct to one alternative rather than another. There is no way, he thinks, to show that this effort does not occur or that it is inefficacious.

Included in the present chapter is Gerald Dworkin's introduction to a book of

[5] C. A. Campbell, "Is 'Freewill' a Pseudo-Problem?" *Mind*, Vol. 60 (October 1951).

readings on free will, determinism, and moral responsibility. Among the readings are essays by C. A. Campbell, Charles Peirce, Thomas Reid, G. E. Moore, C. D. Broad, Ernest Nagel, and other philosophers. The reader who wishes to pursue the question of free will and determinism can scarcely do better than study this book. I have reproduced Dworkin's introduction because it defines the issues and states the arguments pro and con succinctly. An account so lucid needs no interpretative comment.

Questions for Analysis and Review

The reader may wish to consider the following questions: In what way does Hume carry on the tradition of British empiricism? How does he differ from his predecessors Locke and Berkeley? What is the basis of his sceptical arguments concerning causality and substance? Why does he think that we cannot know by direct experience or by inference the nature of the external world? How does Kant's analysis of knowledge hark back to Hume? How does it differ? How does Kant distinguish between "analytic" and "synthetic" judgments, and what use does he make of this distinction? Why does he think that we can have knowledge of phenomena but not of noumena? How does he justify belief in God, freedom, and immortality? What is his answer to the problem of free will, and how does it differ from that of Hume? Are you more inclined to accept the ideas of Hume or Kant or some other philosopher? Among the alternative doctrines outlined by Dworkin, which seems to you the more plausible and why?

8

Method in Science and Philosophy

CHARLES SANDERS PEIRCE (1839–1914)

Peirce was born in Cambridge, Massachusetts, the second son of Benjamin Peirce, a professor at Harvard and one of America's foremost mathematicians. At the time of Peirce's birth, Cambridge was one of the main centers of American culture, and the Peirce home was a principal gathering place of celebrities. Such famous scientists as Louis Agassiz and Asa Gray and such great literary figures as Longfellow, Emerson, and Oliver Wendell Holmes were frequent guests. Peirce's father, himself remarkable, gave his son Charles an impressive education in logic, mathematics, philosophy, and experimental science. At the age of twelve, Charles set up a chemical laboratory in which he undertook some rather advanced experiments. At Harvard, which he attended from the age of sixteen until he was twenty, he did not buckle down to a strict routine of study but roamed over a vast philosophical and scientific literature. After being graduated, he continued his studies at Harvard, receiving a Master's degree in mathematics and an additional degree in chemistry.

This wide reading and scientific training was supplemented by a great deal of practical experience in scientific research. He was an assistant for three years in the Harvard astronomical observatory, where he carried out the investigations published in *Photometric Researches* (1878), the only one of his books to appear during his lifetime. He also conducted extensive scientific research for the United States Coast and Geodetic Survey, with which he was associated from 1861 to 1891. His researches led to important original contributions in chemistry, astronomy, optics, the theory of gravity and pendulum movement, and the determination of weights and measures.

During the 1860's he found time to give a number of lecture courses at Harvard on logic and the history of science, and from 1879 to 1884, he was a lecturer in logic at the Johns Hopkins University. But he never received a permanent university appointment, largely because his ideas were too bold and original and his personality was too eccentric. Publishers showed themselves indifferent to an author who had no official university backing; and consequently a great deal of his writing was never presented to the public during his own lifetime. His reputation at

Harvard also suffered as a result of his divorce from his first wife, who belonged to a very respectable family and was popular in Cambridge. Although he contracted a happy second marriage to a French woman, he never quite regained his status in the eyes of the community.

Throughout final years of illness and poverty, he heroically preserved in his philosophical labors, often writing the whole night through. Nothing daunted him—not physical pain, the lack of a publisher, the isolation from friends, the failure to achieve public recognition. He continued to write even when he trembled so much that he was compelled to steady one hand against the other. Only death, at the age of seventy-five, could quell his spirit.

How to Make
Our Ideas Clear

I

Whoever has looked into a modern treatise on logic of the common sort, will doubtless remember the two distinctions between *clear* and *obscure* conceptions, and between *distinct* and *confused* conceptions. They have lain in the books now for nigh two centuries, unimproved and unmodified, and are generally reckoned by logicians as among the gems of their doctrine.

A clear idea is defined as one which is so apprehended that it will be recognized wherever it is met with, and so that no other will be mistaken for it. If it fails of this clearness, it is said to be obscure.

This is rather a neat bit of philosophical terminology; yet, since it is clearness that they were defining, I wish the logicians had made their definition a little more plain. Never to fail to recognize an idea, and under no circumstances to mistake another for it, let it come in how recondite a form it may, would indeed imply such prodigious force and clearness of intellect as is seldom met with in this world. On the other hand, merely to have such an acquaintance with the idea as to have become familiar with it, and to have lost all hesitancy in recognizing it in ordinary cases, hardly

seems to deserve the name of clearness of apprehension, since after all it only amounts to a subjective feeling of mastery which may be entirely mistaken. I take it, however, that when the logicians speak of "clearness," they mean nothing more than such a familiarity with an idea, since they regard the quality as but a small merit, which needs to be supplemented by another, which they call *distinctness*.

A distinct idea is defined as one which contains nothing which is not clear. This is technical language; by the *contents* of an idea logicians understand whatever is contained in its definition. So that an idea is *distinctly* apprehended, according to them, when we can give a precise definition of it, in abstract terms. Here the professional logicians leave the subject; and I would not have troubled the reader with what they have to say, if it were not such a striking example of how they have been slumbering through ages of intellectual activity, listlessly disregarding the enginery of modern thought, and never dreaming of applying its lessons to the improvement of logic. It is easy to show that the doctrine that familiar use and abstract distinctness make the perfection of apprehension has its only true place in philosophies which have long been extinct; and it is now time to formulate the method of attaining to a more perfect clearness of

This essay is a sequel to "The Fixation of Belief." Reprinted from *Popular Science Monthly*, 1878, with some omissions.

thought, such as we see and admire in the thinkers of our own time.

When Descartes set about the reconstruction of philosophy, his first step was to (theoretically) permit scepticism and to discard the practice of the schoolmen of looking to authority as the ultimate source of truth. That done, he sought a more natural fountain of true principles, and professed to find it in the human mind; thus passing, in the directest way, from the method of authority to that of a priority, as described in my first paper. Self-consciousness was to furnish us with our fundamental truths, and to decide what was agreeable to reason. But since, evidently, not all ideas are true, he was led to note, as the first condition of infallibility, that they must be clear. The distinction between an idea *seeming* clear and really being so, never occurred to him. Trusting to introspection, as he did, even for a knowledge of external things, why should he question its testimony in respect to the contents of our own minds? But then, I suppose, seeing men, who seemed to be quite clear and positive, holding opposite opinions upon fundamental principles, he was further led to say that clearness of ideas is not sufficient, but that they need also to be distinct, *i.e.,* to have nothing unclear about them. What he probably meant by this (for he did not explain himself with precision) was, that they must sustain the test of dialectical examination; that they must not only seem clear at the outset, but that discussion must never be able to bring to light points of obscurity connected with them.

Such was the distinction of Descartes, and one sees that it was precisely on the level of his philosophy. It was somewhat developed by Leibnitz. This great and singular genius was as remarkable for what he failed to see as for what he saw. That a piece of mechanism could not do work perpetually without being fed with power in some form, was a thing perfectly apparent to him; yet he did not understand that the machinery of the mind can only transform knowledge, but never originate it, unless it be fed with facts of observation. He thus missed the most essential point of the Cartesian philosophy, which is, that to accept propositions which seem perfectly evident to us is a thing which, whether it be logical or illogical, we cannot help doing. Instead of regarding the matter in this way, he sought to reduce the first principles of science to formulas which cannot be denied without self-contradiction, and was apparently unaware of the great difference between his position and that of Descartes. So he reverted to the old formalities of logic, and, above all, abstract definitions played a great part in his philosophy. It was quite natural, therefore, that on observing that the method of Descartes labored under the difficulty that we may seem to ourselves to have clear apprehensions of ideas which in truth are very hazy, no better remedy occurred to him than to require an abstract definition of every important term. Accordingly, in adopting the distinction of *clear* and *distinct* notions, he described the latter quality as the clear apprehension of everything contained in the definition; and the books have ever since copied his words. There is no danger that his chimerical scheme will ever again be overvalued. Nothing new can ever be learned by analyzing definitions. Nevertheless, our existing beliefs can be set in order by this process, and order is an essential element of intellectual economy, as of every other. It may be acknowledged, therefore, that the books are right in making familiarity with a notion the first step toward clearness of apprehension, and the defining of it the second. But in omitting all mention of any higher perspicuity of thought, they simply mirror a philosophy which was exploded a hundred years ago. That much-admired "ornament of logic"— the doctrine of clearness and distinctness—may be pretty enough, but it is high time to relegate to our cabinet of curiosities the antique *bijou,* and to wear about us something better adapted to modern uses.

The very first lesson that we have a right to demand that logic shall teach us is, how to make our ideas clear; and a most important one it is, depreciated only by minds who stand in need of it. To know what we think, to be masters of our own meaning, will make a solid foundation for great and weighty thought. It is most easily learned by those whose ideas are meager and restricted; and far happier they than such as wallow helplessly in a rich mud of conceptions. A nation, it is true, may, in the course of generations, overcome the disadvantage of an excessive wealth of language and its natural concomitant, a vast, unfathomable deep of ideas. We may see it in history, slowly perfecting its literary forms, sloughing at length its metaphysics, and, by virtue of the untirable patience which is often a compensation, attaining great excellence in every branch of mental acquirement.

The page of history is not yet unrolled which is to tell us whether such a people will or will not in the long run prevail over one whose ideas (like the words of their language) are few, but which possesses a wonderful mastery over those which it has. For an individual, however, there can be no question that a few clear ideas are worth more than many confused ones. A young man would hardly be persuaded to sacrifice the greater part of his thoughts to save the rest; and the muddled head is the least apt to see the necessity of such a sacrifice. Him we can usually only commiserate, as a person with a congenital defect. Time will help him, but intellectual maturity with regard to clearness comes rather late, an unfortunate arrangement of Nature, inasmuch as clearness is of less use to a man settled in life, whose errors have in great measure had their effect, than it would be to one whose path lies before him. It is terrible to see how a single unclear idea, a single formula without meaning, lurking in a young man's head, will sometimes act like an obstruction of inert matter in an artery, hindering the nutrition of the brain, and condemning its victim to pine away in the fullness of his intellectual vigor and in the midst of intellectual plenty. Many a man has cherished for years as his hobby some vague shadow of an idea, too meaningless to be positively false; he has, nevertheless, passionately loved it, has made it his companion by day and by night, and has given to it his strength and his life, leaving all other occupations for its sake, and in short has lived with it and for it, until it has become, as it were, flesh of his flesh and bone of his bone; and then he has waked up some bright morning to find it gone, clean vanished away like the beautiful Melusina of the fable, and the essence of his life gone with it. I have myself known such a man; and who can tell how many histories of circle-squarers, metaphysicians, astrologers, and what not, may not be told in the old German story?

II

The principles set forth in the first of these papers lead, at once, to a method of reaching a clearness of thought of a far higher grade than the "distinctness" of the logicians. We have there found that the action of thought is excited by the irritation of doubt, and ceases when belief is attained; so that the production of belief is the sole function of thought. All these words, however, are too strong for my purpose. It is as if I had described the phenomena as they appear under a mental microscope. Doubt and Belief, as the words are commonly employed, relate to religious or other grave discussions. But here I use them to designate the starting of any question, no matter how small or how great, and the resolution of it. If, for instance, in a horse-car, I pull out my purse and find a five-cent nickel and five coppers, I decide, while my hand is going to the purse, in which way I will pay my fare. To call such a question Doubt, and my decision Belief, is certainly to use words very disproportionate to the occasion. To speak of such a doubt as causing an irritation which needs to be appeased, suggests a temper which is uncomfortable to the verge of insanity. Yet, looking at the matter minutely, it must be admitted that, if there is the least hesitation as to whether I shall pay the five coppers or the nickel (as there will be sure to be, unless I act from some previously contracted habit in the matter), though irritation is too strong a word, yet I am excited to such small mental activity as may be necessary to deciding how I shall act. Most frequently doubts arise from some indecision, however momentary, in our action. Sometimes it is not so. I have, for example, to wait in a railway-station, and to pass the time I read the advertisements on the walls, I compare the advantages of different trains and different routes which I never expect to take, merely fancying myself to be in a state of hesitancy, because I am bored with having nothing to trouble me. Feigned hesitancy, whether feigned for mere amusement or with a lofty purpose, plays a great part in the production of scientific inquiry. However the doubt may originate, it stimulates the mind to an activity which may be slight or energetic, calm or turbulent. Images pass rapidly through consciousness, one incessantly melting into another, until at last, when all is over—it may be in a fraction of a second, in an hour, or after long years—we find ourselves decided as to how we should act under such circumstances as those which occasioned our hesitation. In other words, we have attained belief.

In this process we observe two sorts of elements of consciousness, the distinction between which may best be made clear by means of an illustration. In a piece of music there are the separate notes, and there is the air. A single tone may be prolonged for an hour or a day, and it exists as perfectly in each second of that time as in the whole taken together; so that, as long as it is sounding, it might be present to a sense from which everything in the past was as completely absent as the future itself. But it is different with the air, the performance of which occupies a certain time, during the portions of which only portions of it are played. It consists in an orderliness in the succession of sounds which strike the ear at different times; and to perceive it there must be some continuity of consciousness which makes the events of a lapse of time present to us. We certainly only perceive the air by hearing the separate notes; yet we cannot be said to directly hear it, for we hear only what is present at the instant, and an orderliness of succession cannot exist in an instant. These two sorts of objects, what we are *immediately* conscious of and what we are *mediately* conscious of, are found in all consciousness. Some elements (the sensations) are completely present at every instant so long as they last, while others (like thought) are actions having the beginning, middle, and end, and consist in a congruence in the succession of sensations which flow through the mind. They cannot be immediately present to us, but must cover some portion of the past or future. Thought is a thread of melody running through the succession of our sensations.

We may add that just as a piece of music may be written in parts, each part having its own air, so various systems of relationship of succession subsist together between the same sensations. These different systems are distinguished by having different motives, ideas, or functions. Thought is only one such system, for its sole motive, idea, and function, is to produce belief, and whatever does not concern that purpose belongs to some other system of relations. The action of thinking may incidentally have other results; it may serve to amuse us, for example, and among *dillettanti* it is not rare to find those who have so perverted thought to the purposes of pleasure that it seems to vex them to think that the questions upon which they delight to exercise it may ever get finally settled; and a positive discovery which takes a favorite subject out of the arena of literary debate is met with ill-concealed dislike. This disposition is the very debauchery of thought. But the soul and meaning of thought, abstracted from the other elements which accompany it, though it may be voluntarily thwarted, can never be made to direct itself toward anything but the production of belief. Thought in action has for its only possible motive the attainment of thought at rest; and whatever does not refer to belief is no part of the thought itself.

And what, then, is belief? It is the demicadence which closes a musical phrase in the symphony of our intellectual life. We have seen that it has just three properties: First, it is something that we are aware of; second, it appeases the irritation of doubt; and, third, it involves the establishment in our nature of a rule of action, or, say, for short, a *habit*. As it appeases the irritation of doubt, which is the motives for thinking, thought relaxes, and comes to rest for a moment when belief is reached. But, since belief is a rule for action, the application of which involves further doubt and further thought, at the same time that it is a stopping-place, it is also a new starting-place for thought. That is why I have permitted myself to call it thought at rest, although thought is essentially an action. The *final* upshot of thinking is the exercise of volition, and of this thought no longer forms a part; but belief is only a stadium of mental action, an effect upon our nature due to thought, which will influence future thinking.

The essence of belief is the establishment of a habit, and different beliefs are distinguished by the different modes of action to which they give rise. If be-

and the same belief; yet it is conceivable that a man should assert one proposition and deny the other. Such false distinctions do as much harm as the confusion of beliefs really different, and are among the pitfalls of which we ought constantly to beware, especially when we are upon metaphysical ground. One singular deception of this sort, which often occurs, is to mistake the sensation produced by our own unclearness of thought for a character of the object we are thinking. Instead of perceiving that the obscurity is purely subjective, we fancy that we contem-

FIG. 1

FIG. 2

liefs do not differ in this respect, if they appease the same doubt by producing the same rule of action, then no mere differences in the manner of consciousness of them can make them different beliefs, any more than playing a tune in different keys is playing different tunes. Imaginary distinctions are often drawn between beliefs which differ only in their mode of expression;—the wrangling which ensues is real enough, however. To believe that any objects are arranged as in Fig. 1, and to believe that they are arranged [as] in Fig. 2, are one

plate a quality of the object which is essentially mysterious; and if our conception be afterward presented to us in a clear form we do not recognize it as the same, owing to the absence of the feeling of unintelligibility. So long as this deception lasts, it obviously puts an impassable barrier in the way of perspicuous thinking; so that it equally interests the opponent of rational thought to perpetuate it, and its adherents to guard against it.

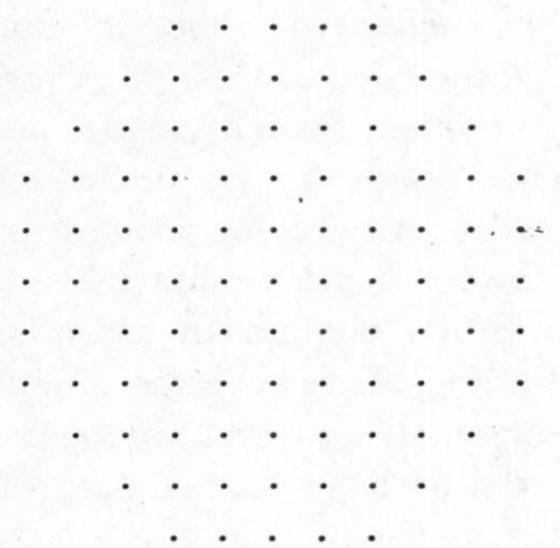

Another such deception is to mistake a mere difference in the grammatical construction of two words for a distinction between the ideas they express. In this pedantic age, when the general mob of writers attend so much more to words than to things, this error is common enough. When I just said that thought is an *action,* and that it consists in a relation, although a person performs an action but not a relation, which can only be the result of an action, yet there was no inconsistency in what I said, but only a grammatical vagueness.

From all these sophisms we shall be perfectly safe so long as we reflect that the whole function of thought is to produce habits of action; and that whatever there is connected with a thought, but irrelevant to its purpose, is an accretion to it, but no part of it. If there be a unity among our sensations which has no reference to how we shall act on a given occasion, as when we listen to a piece of music, why, we do not call that thinking. To develop its meaning, we have, therefore, simply to determine what habits it produces, for what a thing means is simply what habits it involves. Now, the identity of a habit depends on how it might lead us to act, not merely under such circumstances as are likely to arise, but under such as might possibly occur, no matter how improbable they may be. What the habit is depends on *when* and *how* it causes us to act. As for the *when,* every stimulus to action is derived from perception; as for the how, every purpose of action is to produce some sensible result. Thus, we come down to what is tangible and conceivably practical, as the root of every real distinction of thought, no

matter how subtile it may be; and there is no distinction of meaning so fine as to consist in anything but a possible difference of practice.

To see what this principle leads to, consider in the light of it such a doctrine as that of transubstantiation. The Protestant churches generally hold that the elements of the sacrament are flesh and blood only in a tropical sense; they nourish our souls as meat and the juice of it would our bodies. But the Catholics maintain that they are literally just that; although they possess all the sensible qualities of wafer-cakes and diluted wine. But we can have no conception of wine except what may enter into a belief, either—

1. That this, that, or the other, is wine; or,

2. That wine possesses certain properties.

Such beliefs are nothing but self-notification that we should, upon occasion, act in regard to such things as we believe to be wine according to the qualities which we believe wine to possess. The occasion of such an action would be some sensible perception, the motive of it to produce some sensible result. Thus our action has exclusive reference to what affects the senses, our habit has the same bearing as our action, our belief the same as our habit, our conception the same as our belief; and we can consequently mean nothing by wine but what has certain effects, direct or indirect, upon our senses; and to talk of something as having all the sensible characters of wine, yet being in reality blood, is senseless jargon. Now, it is not my object to pursue the theological question; and having used it as a logical example I drop it, without caring to anticipate the theologian's reply. I only desire to point out how impossible it is that we should have an idea in our minds which relates to anything but conceived sensible effects of things. Our idea of anything *is* our idea of its sensible effects; and if we fancy that we have any other we deceive ourselves, and mistake a mere sensation accompanying the thought for a part of the thought itself. It is absurd to say that thought has any meaning unrelated to its only function. It is foolish for Catholics and Protestants to fancy themselves in disagreement about the elements of the sacrament, if they agree in regard to all their sensible effects, here or hereafter.

It appears, then, that the rule for attaining the third grade of clearness of apprehension is as follows: Consider what effects, which might conceivably have practical bearings, we conceive the object of our conception to have. Then, our conception of these effects is the whole of our conception of the object.

III

Let us illustrate this rule by some examples; and, to begin with the simplest one possible, let us ask what we mean by calling a thing *hard*. Evidently that it will not be scratched by many other substances. The whole conception of this quality, as of every other, lies in its conceived effects. There is absolutely no difference between a hard thing and a soft thing so long as they are not brought to the test. Suppose, then, that a diamond could be crystallized in the midst of a cushion of soft cotton, and should remain there until it was finally burned up. Would it be false to say that that diamond was soft? This seems a foolish question, and would be so, in fact, except in the realm of logic. There such questions are often of the greatest utility as serving to bring logical principles into sharper relief than real discussions ever could. In studying logic we must not put them aside with hasty answers, but must consider them with attentive care, in order to make out the principles involved. We may, in the present case, modify our question, and ask what prevents us from saying that all hard bodies remain perfectly soft until they are touched, when their hardness increases with the pressure until they are scratched. Reflection will show that the reply is this: there would be no *falsity* in such modes of speech. They would involve a modification of our present usage of speech with regard to the words hard and soft, but not of their meanings. For they represent no fact to be different from what it is; only they involve arrangements of facts which would be exceedingly maladroit. This leads us to remark that the question of what would occur under circumstances which do not actually arise is not a question of fact, but only of the most perspicuous arrangement of them. For example, the question of free-will and fate in its simplest form, stripped of verbiage, is something like this: I have done something of which I am ashamed; could I, by an effort of the will, have resisted the temptation, and done otherwise? The philosophical reply is, that this is not a question of fact, but only of the arrangement of facts.

Arranging them so as to exhibit what is particularly pertinent to my question —namely, that I ought to blame myself for having done wrong—it is perfectly true to say that, if I had willed to do otherwise than I did, I should have done otherwise. On the other hand, arranging the facts so as to exhibit another important consideration, it is equally true that, when a temptation has once been allowed to work, it will, if it has a certain force, produce its effect, let me struggle how I may. There is no objection to a contradiction in what would result from a false supposition. The *reductio ad absurdum* consists in showing that contradictory results would follow from a hypothesis which is consequently judged to be false. Many questions are involved in the free-will discussion, and I am far from desiring to say that both sides are equally right. On the contrary, I am of opinion that one side denies important facts, and that the other does not. But what I do say is, that the above single question was the origin of the whole doubt; that, had it not been for this question, the controversy would never have arisen; and that this question is perfectly solved in the manner which I have indicated.

Let us next seek a clear idea of weight. This is another very easy case. To say that a body is heavy means simply that, in the absence of opposing force, it will fall. This (neglecting certain specifications of how it will fall, etc., which exist in the mind of the physicist who uses the word) is evidently the whole conception of weight. It is a fair question whether some particular facts may not *account* for grav-

ity; but what we mean by the force itself is completely involved in its effects. . . .

IV

Let us now approach the subject of logic, and consider a conception which particularly concerns it, that of *reality*. Taking clearness in the sense of familiarity, no idea could be clearer than this. Every child uses it with perfect confidence, never dreaming that he does not understand it. As for clearness in its second grade, however, it would probably puzzle most men, even among those of a reflective turn of mind, to give an abstract definition of the real. Yet such a definition may perhaps be reached by considering the points of difference between reality and its opposite, fiction. A figment is a product of somebody's imagination; it has such characters as his thought impresses upon it. That whose characters are independent of how you or I think is an external reality. There are, however, phenomena within our own minds, dependent upon our thought, which are at the same time real in the sense that we really think them. But though their characters depend on how we think, they do not depend on what we think those characters to be. Thus, a dream has a real existence as a mental phenomenon, if somebody has really dreamt it; that he dreamt so and so, does not depend on what anybody thinks was dreamt, but is completely independent of all opinion on the subject. On the other hand, considering, not the fact of dreaming but the thing dreamt, it retains its peculiarities by virtue of no other fact than that it was dreamt to possess them. Thus we may define the real as that whose characters are independent of what anybody may think them to be.

But, however satisfactory such a definition may be found, it would be a great mistake to suppose that it makes the idea of reality perfectly clear. Here, then, let us apply our rules. According to them, reality, like every other quality, consists in the peculiar sensible effects which things partaking of it produce. The only effect which real things have is to cause belief, for all the sensations which they excite emerge into consciousness in the form of beliefs. The question therefore is, how is true belief (or belief in the real) distinguished from false belief (or belief in fiction). Now, as we have seen in the former paper, the ideas of truth and falsehood, in their full development, appertain exclusively to the scientific method of settling opinion. A person who arbitrarily chooses the propositions which he will adopt can use the word truth only to emphasize the expression of his determination to hold on to his choice. Of course, the method of tenacity never prevailed exclusively; reason is too natural to men for that. But in the literature of the dark ages we find some fine examples of it. When Scotus Erigena is commenting upon a poetical passage in which hellebore is spoken of as having caused the death of Socrates, he does not hesitate to inform the inquiring reader that Helleborus and Socrates were two eminent Greek philosophers, and that the latter having been overcome in argument by the former took the matter to heart and died of it! What sort of an idea of truth could a man have who could adopt and teach, without the qualification of a perhaps, an opinion taken so entirely at random? The real spirit of Socrates, who I hope would have been delighted to have been "overcome in argument," because he would have learned something by it, is in curious contrast with the naïve idea of the glossist, for whom discussion would seem to have been simply a struggle. When philosophy began to awake from its long slumber, and before theology completely dominated it, the practice seems to have been for each professor to seize upon any philosophical position he found unoccupied and which seemed a strong one, to intrench himself in it, and to sally forth from time to time to give battle to the others. Thus, even the scanty records we possess of those disputes enable us to make out a dozen or more opinions held by different teachers at one time concerning the question of nominalism and realism. Read the opening part of the "Historia Calamitatum" of Abelard, who was certainly as philosophical as any of his contemporaries, and see the spirit of combat which it breathes. For him, the truth is simply his particular stronghold. When the method of authority prevailed, the truth meant little more than the Catholic faith. All the efforts of the scholastic doctors are directed toward harmonizing their faith in Aristotle and their faith in the Church, and one may search their ponderous folios through without finding an argument which goes any further. It is noticeable that where different faiths flourish side by side, renegades are looked upon with contempt even by the party whose belief they adopt; so completely has the idea of loyalty replaced that of truth-seeking. Since the time of Descartes, the defect in the conception of truth has been less apparent. Still, it will sometimes strike a scientific man that the philosophers have been less intent on finding out what the facts are, than on inquiring what belief is most in harmony with their system. It is hard to convince a follower of the *a priori* method by adducing facts; but show him that an opinion he is defending is inconsistent with what he has laid down elsewhere, and he will be very apt to retract it. These minds do not seem to believe that disputation is ever to cease; they seem to think that the opinion which is natural for one man is not so for another, and that belief will, consequently, never be settled. In contenting themselves with fixing their own opinions by a method which would lead another man to a different result, they betray their feeble hold of the conception of what truth is.

On the other hand, all the followers of science are fully persuaded that the processes of investigation, if only pushed far enough, will give one certain solution to every question to which they can be applied. One man may investigate the velocity of light by studying the transits of Venus and the aberration of the stars; another by the oppositions of Mars and the eclipses of Jupiter's satellites; a third by the method of Fizeau; a fourth by that of Foucault; a fifth by the motions of the curves of Lissajous; a sixth, a seventh, an eighth, and a ninth, may follow the different methods of comparing the measures of statical and dynamical elec-tricity. They may at first obtain different results, but, as each perfects his method and his processes, the results will move steadily together toward a destined center. So with all scientific research. Different minds may set out with the most antagonistic views, but the progress of investigation carries them by a force outside of themselves to one and the same conclusion. This activity of thought by which we are carried, not where we wish, but to a foreordained goal, is like the operation of destiny. No modification of the point of view taken, no selection of other facts for study, no natural bent of mind even, can enable a man to escape the predestinate opinion. This great law is embodied in the conception of truth and reality. The opinion which is fated[1] to be ultimately agreed to by all who investigate, is what we mean by the truth, and the object represented in this opinion is the real. That is the way I would explain reality.

But it may be said that this view is directly opposed to the abstract definition which we have given of reality, inasmuch as it makes the characters of the real to depend on what is ultimately thought about them. But the answer to this is that, on the one hand, reality is independent, not necessarily of thought in general, but only of what you or I or any finite number of men may think about it; and that, on the other hand,

---

[1] Fate means merely that which is sure to come true, and can nohow be avoided. It is a superstition to suppose that a certain sort of events are ever fated, and it is another to suppose that the word fate can never be freed from its superstitious taint. We are all fated to die. [Footnote added in later reprinting.]

though the object of the final opinion depends on what that opinion is, yet what that opinion is does not depend on what you or I or any man thinks. Our perversity and that of others may indefinitely postpone the settlement of opinion; it might even conceivably cause an arbitrary proposition to be universally accepted as long as the human race should last. Yet even that would not change the nature of the belief, which alone could be the result of investigation carried sufficiently far; and if, after the extinction of our race, another should arise with faculties and disposition for investigation, that true opinion must be the one which they would ultimately come to. "Truth crushed to earth shall rise again," and the opinion which would finally result from investigation does not depend on how anybody may actually think. But the reality of that which is real does depend on the real fact that investigation is destined to lead, at last, if continued long enough, to a belief in it.

But I may be asked what I have to say to all the minute facts of history, forgotten never to be recovered, to the lost books of the ancients, to the buried secrets.

Full many a gem of purest ray serene
  The dark, unfathomed caves of ocean bear;
Full many a flower is born to blush unseen,
  And waste its sweetness on the desert air.

Do these things not really exist because they are hopelessly beyond the reach of our knowledge? And then, after the universe is dead (according to the prediction of some scientists), and all life has ceased forever, will not the shock

of atoms continue though there will be no mind to know it? To this I reply that, though in no possible state of knowledge can any number be great enough to express the relation between the amount of what rests unknown and the amount of the known, yet it is unphilosophical to suppose that, with regard to any given question (which has any clear meaning), investigation would not bring forth a solution of it, if it were carried far enough. Who would have said, a few years ago, that we could ever know of what substances stars are made whose light may have been longer in reaching us than the human race has existed? Who can be sure of what we shall not know in a few hundred years? Who can guess what would be the result of continuing the pursuit of science for ten thousand years, with the activity of the last hundred? And if it were to go on for a million, or a billion, or any number of years you please, how is it possible to say that there is any question which might not ultimately be solved?

But it may be objected, "Why make so much of these remote considerations, especially when it is your principle that only practical distinctions have a meaning?" Well, I must confess that it makes very little difference whether we say that a stone on the bottom of the ocean, in complete darkness, is brilliant or not—that is to say, that it *probably* makes no difference, remembering always that that stone *may* be fished up tomorrow. But that there are gems at the bottom of the sea, flowers in the untraveled desert, etc., are propositions which, like that about a diamond being hard when it is not pressed, concern much more the arrangement of our language than they do the meaning of our ideas.

We have, hitherto, not crossed the threshold of scientific logic. It is certainly important to know how to make our ideas clear, but they may be ever so clear without being true. . . . How

to give birth to those vital and procreative ideas which multiply into a thousand forms and diffuse themselves everywhere, advancing civilization and making the dignity of man, is an art not yet reduced to rules, but of the secret of which the history of science affords some hints.

JOHN DEWEY (1859–1952)

John Dewey was born in the beautiful New England town of Burlington, Vermont. "All my forefathers," he has said, "earned an honest living as farmers, wheelwrights, coopers. I was absolutely the first one in seven generations to fall from grace."[1] But his father, a grocer, loved to recite from Shakespeare and Milton, and his parents gave their four sons the advantages of a college education and of a liberal moral and religious outlook. John took his undergraduate degree at the University of Vermont and his Doctor's degree in Philosophy at Johns Hopkins in 1884.

He taught at the University of Michigan from 1884 until 1894 (except for one year at the University of Minnesota), and then, for an additional ten-year period, at the University of Chicago. During these years, he gradually shifted from Hegelian idealism to his own version of pragmatism, or, as he preferred to call it, "instrumentalism." His ideas had begun to cause some controversy even before he went to Chicago, but this was mild compared with the storm that broke out when he began to apply his pragmatic ideals as director of the "Laboratory School" for children at the University of Chicago. Aided by his wife, for seven and a half years Dewey conducted a bold educational experiment based on the concepts of "learning by doing" and "education for democracy." Whereas traditional education had sought to instill obedience and receptivity, he sought to cultivate activity, initiative, diversity, and voluntary cooperation; and in so doing, he wrought a veritable revolution in educational theory and practice. The volume in which he explained what he was trying to do, *School and Society*, was first published in 1899 and has since been translated into a dozen European and Oriental languages and reprinted many times.

---

[1] Edwin E. Slosson, *Six Major Prophets* (Boston: Little, Brown, 1917), p. 268. (From a letter of Dewey to Slosson.)

Having achieved fame both as an educator and as a philosopher, Dewey in 1904 was called to Columbia University, where he remained until his retirement in 1929. With prodigious energy, he poured forth an immense volume of publications and engaged in many educational, political, and civic activities.

During the later years of his life, Dewey's interests continued to broaden, as indicated by the wide range of his writings—on education, religion, art, politics, ethics, logic, epistemology, and metaphysics. His many social and intellectual activities, however, did not prevent him from rearing a large family and forming many warm personal friendships. When he died at the age of ninety-two, he had had a more comprehensive and profound impact on the modern world than any other American philosopher.

Modest, unobstrusive, somewhat halting in speech, and ultra-democratic in manner, Dewey the human being has sometimes seemed to be quite different from Dewey the bold and independent thinker. This contrast has led many people to misinterpret and vulgarize his ideas and to underestimate his native radicalism. But if, as has been claimed, Dewey is more representative of democratic America than any other thinker, it is an intellectually adventurous and daring America that he represents.

The Scientific Factor in Reconstruction of Philosophy

Philosophy starts from some deep and wide way of responding to the difficulties life presents, but it grows only when material is at hand for making this practical response conscious, articulate and communicable. Accompanying the economic, political and ecclesiastical changes which were alluded to in an earlier lecture, was a scientific revolution enormous in scope and leaving unchanged almost no detail of belief about nature, physical and human. In part this scientific transformation was produced by just the change in practical attitude and temper. But as it progressed, it furnished that change an appropriate vocabulary, congenial to its needs, and made it articulate. The advance of science in its larger generalizations and in its specific detail of fact supplied precisely that intellectual equipment of ideas and concrete fact that was needed in order to formulate, precipitate, communicate and propagate the new disposition. Today, accordingly, we shall deal with those contrasting conceptions of the structure and constitution of Nature, which when they are

From *Reconstruction in Philosophy* (originally given as lectures in Japan), New York: Henry Holt and Company, 1920; enlarged edition, Boston: Beacon Press, 1948. Reprinted by permission of the Beacon Press.

accepted on the authority of science (alleged or real), form the intellectual framework of philosophy.

Contrasting conceptions of ancient and modern science have been selected. For I see no way in which the truly philosophic import of the picture of the world painted by modern science can be appreciated except to exhibit it in contrast with that earlier picture which gave classic metaphysics its intellectual foundation and confirmation. The world in which philosophers once put their trust was a closed world, a world consisting internally of a limited number of fixed forms, and having definite boundaries externally. The world of modern science is an open world, a world varying indefinitely without the possibility of assignable limit in its internal make-up, a world stretching beyond any assignable bounds externally. Again, the world in which even the most intelligent men of olden times thought they lived was a fixed world, a realm where changes went on only without immutable limits of rest and permanence, and a world where the fixed and unmoving was, as we have already noted, higher in quality and authority than the moving and altering. And in the third place, the world which men once saw with their eyes, portrayed in their imaginations and repeated in their plans of conduct, was a world of a limited number of classes, kinds, forms, distinct in quality (as kinds and species must be distinct) and arranged in a graded order of superiority and inferiority.

It is not easy to recall the image of the universe which was taken for granted in the world tradition. In spite of its dramatic rendering (as in Dante), of the dialectical elaborations of Aristotle and St. Thomas, in spite of the fact that it held men's minds captive until the last three hundred years, and that its overthrow involved a religious upheaval, it is already dim, faded and remote. Even as a separate and abstract thing of theory it is not easy to recover.

As something pervasive, interwoven with all the details of reflection and observation, with the plans and rules of behavior, it is impossible to call it back again. Yet, as best we can, we need to put before our minds a definitely enclosed universe, something which can be called a universe in a literal and visible sense, having the earth at its fixed and unchanging centre and at a fixed circumference the heavenly arch of fixed stars moving in an eternal round of divine ether, hemming in all things and keeping them forever at one and in order. The earth, though at the centre, is the coarest, grossest, most material, least significant and good (or perfect) of the parts of this closed world. It is the scene of maximum fluctuation and vicissitude. It is the least rational, and therefore the least notable, or knowable; it offers the least to reward contemplation, provoke admiration and govern conduct. Between this grossly material centre and the immaterial, spiritual and eternal heavens lie a definite series of regions of moon, planets, sun, etc., each of which gains in rank, value, rationality and true being as it is farther from earth and nearer the heavens. Each of these regions is composed of its own appropriate stuff of earth, water, air, fire in its own dominant degree, until we reach the heavenly firmament which transcends all these principles, being constituted, as was just said, of that immaterial, inalterable energy called ether.

Within this tight and pent in universe, changes take place of course. But they are only of a small number of fixed kinds; and they operate only within fixed limits. Each kind of stuff has its own appropriate motion. It is the nature of earthly things to be heavy, since they are gross, and hence to move downward. Fire and superior things are light and hence move upward to their proper place; air rises only to the plane of the planets, where it then takes its back and forth motion which naturally belongs to it, as is evident in the winds and in respiration. Ether being the highest of all physical things has a purely circular movement. The daily return of the fixed stars is the closest possible approximation to eternity, and to the self-involved revolution of mind upon its own ideal axis of reason. Upon the earth in virtue of its earthly nature —or rather its lack of virtue—is a scene of mere change. Mere flux, aimless and meaningless, starts at no definite point and arrives at nothing, amounts to nothing. Mere changes of quantity, all purely mechanical changes, are of this kind. They are like the shiftings of the sands by the sea. They may be sensed, but they cannot be "noted" or understood; they lack fixed limits which govern them. They are contemptible. They are casual, the sport of accident.

Only changes which lead to some defined or fixed outcome of form are of any account and can have any account —any *logos* or reason—made of them. The growth of plants and animals illustrates the highest kind of change which is possible in the sublunary or mundane sphere. They go from one definite fixed form to another. Oaks generate only oaks, oysters only oysters, man only man. The material factor of mechanical production enters in, but enters in as accident to prevent the full consummation of the type of the species, and to bring about the meaningless variations which diversify various oaks or oysters from one another; or in extreme cases to produce freaks, sports, monsters, three-handed or four-toed men. Aside from accidental and undesirable variations, each individual has a fixed career to pursue, a fixed path in which to travel. Terms which sound modern, words like potentiality and development abound in Aristotelian thought, and have misled some into reading into his thought modern meanings. But the significance of these words in classic and medieval thought is rigidly determined by their context. Development holds merely of the course of changes which takes place within a particular member of the species. It is only a name for the predetermined movement from the acorn to the oak tree. It takes place not in things generally but only in some one of the numerically insignificant members of the oak species. Development, evolution, never means, as in modern science, origin of new forms, a mutation from an old species, but only

the monotonous traversing of a previously plotted cycle of change. So potentiality never means, as in modern life, the possibility of novelty, of invention, of radical deviation, but only that principle in virtue of which the acorn becomes the oak. Technically, it is the capacity for movement between opposites. Only the cold can become hot; only the dry can become wet; only the babe can become a man; the seed the full-grown wheat and so on. Potentiality instead of implying the emergence of anything novel means merely the facility with which a particular thing repeats the recurrent processes of its kind, and thus becomes a specific case of the eternal forms in and through which all things are constituted.

In spite of the almost infinite numerical diversity of individuals, there are only a limited number of species, kinds or sorts. And the world is essentially a world which falls into sorts; it is prearranged into distinct classes. Moreover, just as we naturally arrange plants and animals into series, ranks and grades, from the lower to the highest, so with all things in the universe. The distinct classes to which things belong by their very nature form a hierarchical order. There are castes in nature. The universe is constituted on an aristocratic, one can truly say a feudal, plan. Species, classes, do not mix or overlap—except in cases of accident, and to the result of chaos. Otherwise, everything belongs in advance to a certain class, and the class has its own fixed place in the hierarchy of Being. The universe is indeed a tidy spot whose purity is interfered with only by those irregular changes in individuals which are due to the presence of an obdurate matter that refuses to yield itself wholly to rule and form. Otherwise it is a universe with a fixed place for everything and where everything knows its place, its station and class, and keeps it. Hence what are known technically as final and formal causes are supreme, and efficient causes are relegated to an inferior place. The so-called final cause is just a name for the fact that there is some fixed form characteristic of a class or sort of things which governs the changes going on, so that they tend toward it as their end and goal, the fulfillment of their true nature. The supralunar region is the end or final cause of the proper movements of air and fire; the earth of the motions of crass, heavy things; the oak of the acorn; the mature form in general of the germinal.

The "efficient cause," that which produces and instigates a movement is only some external change as it accidentally gives a kind of push to an immature, imperfect being and starts it moving toward its perfected or fulfilled form. The final cause is the perfected form regarded as the *explanation* or *reason* of prior changes. When it is not taken in reference to the changes completed and brought to rest in it, but in itself it is the "formal cause": The inherent *nature* or character which "makes" or constitutes a thing *what it is* so far as it truly *is,* namely, what it is so far as it does not change. Logically and practically all of the traits which have been enumerated cohere. Attack one and you attack all. When any one is undermined, all go. This is the reason why the intellectual modification of the last few centuries may truly be called a revolu-

tion. It has substituted a conception of the world differing at every point. It makes little matter at what point you commence to trace the difference, you find yourself carried into all other points.

Instead of a closed universe, science now presents us with one infinite in space and time, having no limits here or there, at this end, so to speak, or at that, and as infinitely complex in internal structure as it is infinite in extent. Hence it is also an open world, an infinitely variegated one, a world which in the old sense can hardly be called a universe at all; so multiplex and far-reaching that it cannot be summed up and grasped in any one formula. And change rather than fixity is now a measure of "reality" or energy of being; change is omnipresent. The laws in which the modern man of science is interested are laws of motion, of generation and consequence. He speaks of law where the ancients spoke of kind and essence, because what he wants is a correlation of changes, an ability to detect one change occurring in correspondence with another. He does not try to define and delimit something remaining constant *in* change. He tries to describe a constant order *of* change. And while the word "constant" appears in both statements, the meaning of the word is not the same. In one case, we are dealing with something constant in *existence,* physical or metaphysical; in the other case, with something constant in *function* and operation. One is a form of independent being; the other is a formula of description and calculation of interdependent changes.

In short, classic thought accepted a feudally arranged order of classes or kinds, each "holding" from a superior and in turn giving the rule of conduct and service to an inferior. This trait reflects and parallels most closely the social situation we were considering at the last hour. We have a fairly definite notion of society as organized upon the feudal basis. The family principle, the principle of kinship is strong, and especially is this true as we ascend in the social scale. At the lower end, individuals may be lost more or less in the mass. Since all are parts of the common herd, there is nothing especial to distinguish their birth. But among the privileged and ruling class the case is quite different. The tie of kinship at once marks a group off externally and gives it distinction, and internally holds all its members together. Kinship, kind, class, genus are synonymous terms, starting from social and concrete facts and going to the technical and abstract. For kinship is a sign of a common nature, of something universal and permanent running through all particular individuals, and giving them a real and objecitve unity. Because such and such persons are kin they are *really,* and not merely conventionally, marked off into a class having something unique about it. All contemporary members are bound into an objective unity which includes ancestors and descendants and excludes all who belong to another kin or kind. Assuredly this parcelling out of the world into separate kinds, each having its qualitatively distinct nature in contrast with other species, binding numerically distinct individuals together, and preventing their diversities from exceeding fixed bounds, may without exaggeration be called a projection of the family principle into the world at large.

In a feudally organized society, moreover, each kinship group or species occupies a definite place. It is marked by the possession of a specific *rank* higher or lower with respect to other grades. This position confers upon it certain privileges, enabling it to enforce certain claims upon those lower in the scale and entailing upon it certain services and homage to be rendered to superiors. The relationship of causation, so to speak, is up and down. Influence, power, proceeds from above to below; the activities of the inferior are performed with respect, quite literally, to what is above. Action and reaction are far from being equal and in opposite directions. All action is of one sort, of the nature of lordship, and proceeds from the higher to the lower. Reaction is of the nature of subjection and deference and proceeds from lower to higher. The classic theory of the constitution of the world corresponds point by point to this ordering of classes in a scale of dignity and power.

A third trait assigned by historians to feudalism is that the ordering of ranks centres about armed service and the relationship of armed defense and protection. I am afraid that what has already been said about the parallelism of ancient cosmology with social organization may seem a fanciful analogy; and if a comparison is also drawn in this last regard, there will be no doubt in your minds that a metaphor is being forced. Such is truly the case if we take the comparison too literally. But not so, if we confine our attention to the notion of rule and command implied in both.

Attention has already been called to the meaning that is now given the term law—a constant relationship among changes. Nevertheless, we often hear about laws which "govern" events, and it often seems to be thought that phenomena would be utterly disorderly were there not laws to keep them in order. This way of thinking is a survival of reading social relationships into nature—not necessarily a feudal relationship, but the relation of ruler and ruled, sovereign and subject. Law is assimilated to a command or order. If the factor of personal will is eliminated (as it was in the best Greek thought) still the idea of law or universal is impregnated with the sense of a guiding and ruling influence exerted from above on what is naturally inferior to it. The universal governs as the end and model which the artisan has in mind "governs" his movements. The Middle Ages added to this Greek idea of control the idea of a command proceeding from a superior will; and hence thought of the operations of nature as if they were a fulfillment of a task set by one who had authority to direct action.

The traits of the picture of nature drawn by modern science fairly spring by contrast into high relief. Modern science took its first step when daring astronomers abolished the distinction of high, sublime and ideal forces operating in the heavens from lower and material forces actuating terrestrial events. The supposed heterogeneity of substances and forces between heaven and earth was denied. It was asserted that the same laws hold everywhere, that there is homogeneity of material and process everywhere throughout nature. The re-mote and esthetically sublime is to be scientifically described and explained in terms of homely familiar events and forces. The material of direct handling and observation is that of which we are surest; it is the better known. Until we can convert the grosser and more superficial observations of far-away things in the heavens into elements identical with those of things directly at hand, they remain blind and not understood. Instead of presenting superior worth, they present only problems. They are not means of enlightenment but challenges. The earth is not superior in rank to sun, moon and stars, but it is equal in dignity, and its occurrences give the key to the understanding of celestial existences. Being *at* hand, they are also capable of being brought *under* our hand; they can be manipulated, broken up, resolved into elements which can be managed, combined at will in old and new forms. The net result may be termed, I think, without any great forcing, the substitution of a democracy of individual facts equal in rank for the feudal system of an ordered gradation of general classes of unequal rank.

One important incident of the new science was the destruction of the idea that the earth is the centre of the universe. When the idea of a fixed centre went, there went with it the idea of a closed universe and a circumscribing heavenly boundary. To the Greek sense, just because its theory of knowing was dominated by esthetic considerations, the finite was the perfect. Literally, the finite was the finished, the ended, the completed, that with no ragged edges and unaccountable operations. The infinite or limitless was lacking in character just because it was in-finite. Being everything, it was nothing. It was unformed and chaotic, uncontrolled and unruly, the source of incalculable deviations and accidents. Our present feeling that associates infinity with boundless power, with capacity for expansion that knows no end, with the delight in a progress that has no external limit, would be incomprehensible were it not that interest has shifted from the esthetic to the practical; from interest in beholding a harmonious and complete scene to interest in transforming an inharmonious one. One has only to read the authors of the transition period, say Giordano Bruno, to realize what a pent-in, suffocating sensation they associated with a closed, finite world, and what a feeling of exhilaration, expansion and boundless possibility was aroused in them by the thought of a world infinite in stretch of space and time, and composed internally of infinitesimal infinitely numerous elements. That which the Greeks withdrew from with repulsion they welcomed with an intoxicated sense of adventure. The infinite meant, it was true, something forever untraversed even by thought, and hence something forever unknown—no matter how great attainment in learning. But this "forever unknown" instead of being chilling and repelling was now an inspiring challenge to ever-renewed inquiry, and an assurance of inexhaustible possibilities of progress.

The student of history knows well that the Greeks made great progress in the science of mechanics as well as of geometry. At first sight, it appears strange that with this advance in mechanics so little advance was made in the direction of modern science. The seeming paradox impels us to ask why it was that mechanics remained a separate science, why it was not used in description and explanation of natural phenomena after the manner of Galileo and Newton. The answer is found in the social parallelism already mentioned. Socially speaking, machines, tools, were devices employed by artisans. The science of mechanics had to do with the kind of things employed by human mechanics, and mechanics were base fellows. They were at the lower end of the social scale, and how could light on the heavens, the highest, be derived from them? The application of considerations of mechanics to natural phenomena would moreover have implied an interest in the practical control and utilization of phenomena which was totally incompatible with the importance attached to final causes as fixed determiners of nature. All the scientific reformers of the sixteenth and seventeenth centuries strikingly agree in regarding the doctrine of final causes as *the* cause of the failure of science. Why? Because this doctrine taught that the processes of nature are held in bondage to certain fixed ends which they must tend to realize. Nature was kept in leading strings; it was cramped down to production of a limited number of stereotyped results. Only a comparatively small number of things could be brought into being, and these few must be similar to the ends which similar cycles of change had effected in the past. The scope of inquiry and understanding was limited to the narrow round of processes eventuating in the fixed ends which the observed world offered to view. At best, invention and production of new results by use of machines and tools must be restricted to articles of transient dignity and bodily, not intellectual, use.

When the rigid clamp of fixed ends was taken off from nature, observation and imagination were emancipated, and experimental control for scientific and practical purposes enormously stimulated. Because natural processes were no longer restricted to a fixed number of immovable ends or results, anything might conceivably happen. It was only a question of what elements could be brought into juxtaposition so that they would work upon one another. Immediately, mechanics ceased to be a separate science and became an organ for attacking nature. The mechanics of the lever, wheel, pulley and inclined plane told accurately what happens when things in space are used to move one another during definite periods of time. The whole of nature became a scene of pushes and pulls, of cogs and levers, of motions of parts or elements to which the formulae of movements produced by well-known machines were directly applicable.

The banishing of ends and forms from the universe has seemed to many an ideal and spiritual impoverishment. When nature was regarded as a set of mechanical interactions, it apparently lost all meaning and purpose. Its glory departed. Elimination of differences of quality deprived it of beauty. Denial to nature of all inherent longings and aspiring tendencies toward ideal ends removed nature and natural science from contact with poetry, religion and divine things. There seemed to be left only a harsh, brutal despiritualized exhibition of mechanical forces. As a consequence, it has seemed to many philosophers that one of their chief problems was to reconcile the existence of this purely mechanical world with belief in objective rationality and purpose—to save life from a degrading materialism. Hence many sought to re-attain by way of an analysis of the process of knowing, or epistemology, that belief in the superiority of Ideal Being which had anciently been maintained on the basis of cosmology. But when it is recognized that the mechanical view is determined by the requirements of an experimental control of natural energies, this problem of reconciliation no longer vexes us. Fixed forms and ends, let us recall, mark fixed limits to change. Hence they make futile all human efforts to produce and regulate change except within narrow and unimportant limits. They paralyze constructive human inventions by a theory which condemns them in advance to failure. Human activity can conform only to ends already set by nature. It was not till ends were banished from nature that purposes became important as factors in human minds capable of reshaping existence. A natural world that does not subsist for the sake of realizing a fixed set of ends is relatively malleable and plastic; it may be used for this end *or* that. That nature can be known through the application of mechanical formulae is the prime condition of turning it to human account. Tools, machines are means to be utilized. Only when nature is regarded as mechanical, is systematic invention and construction of machines relevant to nature's activities. Nature is subdued to human purpose because it is no longer the slave of metaphysical and theological purpose.

Bergson has pointed out that man might well be called *Homo Faber*. He is distinguished as the tool-making animal. This has held good since man was man; but till nature was construed in mechanical terms, the making of tools with which to attack and transform nature was sporadic and accidental. Under such circumstances it would not have occurred even to a Bergson that man's tool-making capacity was so important and fundamental that it could be used to define him. The very things that make the nature of the mechanical-physical scientist esthetically blank and dull are the things which render nature amenable to human control. When qualities were subordinated to quantitative and mathematical relationships, color, music and form disappeared from the object of the scientist's inquiry as such. But the remaining properties of weight, extension, numerable velocity of movement and so on were just the qualities which lent themselves to the substitution of one thing for another, to the conversion of one form of energy into another; to the effecting of transformations. When chemical fertilizers can be used in place of animal manures, when improved grain and cattle can be purposefully bred from inferior animals and grasses, when mechanical energy can be converted into heat and electricity into mechanical energy, man gains power to manipulate nature. Most of all he gains power to frame *new* ends and aims and to proceed in regular system to their actualization. Only indefinite substitution and convertibility regardless of quality render nature man-

ageable. The mechanization of nature is the condition of a practical and progressive idealism in action.

It thus turns out that the old, old dread and dislike of matter as something opposed to mind and threatening it, to be kept within the narrowest bounds of recognition; something to be denied so far as possible lest it encroach upon ideal purposes and finally exclude them from the real world, is as absurd practically as it was impotent intellectually. Judged from the only scientific standpoint, what it does and how it functions, matter means conditions. To respect matter means to respect the conditions of achievement; conditions which hinder and obstruct and which have to be changed, conditions which help and further and which can be used to modify obstructions and attain ends. Only as men have learned to pay sincere and persistent regard to matter, to the conditions upon which depends negatively and positively the success of all endeavor, have they shown sincere and fruitful respect for ends and purposes. To profess to have an aim and then neglect the means of its execution is self-delusion of the most dangerous sort. Education and morals will begin to find themselves on the same road of advance that say chemical industry and medicine have found for themselves when they too learn fully the lesson of wholehearted and unremitting attention to means and conditions—that is, to what mankind so long despised as material and mechanical. When we take means for ends we indeed fall into moral materialism. But when we take ends without regard to means we degenerate into sentimentalism. In the name of the ideal we fall back upon mere luck and chance and magic or exhortation and preaching; or else upon a fanaticism that will force the realization of preconceived ends at any cost.

I have touched in this lecture upon many things in a cursory way. Yet there has been but one point in mind. The revolution in our conceptions of nature and in our methods of knowing it has bred a new temper of imagination and aspiration. It has confirmed the new attitude generated by economic and political changes. It has supplied this attitude with definite intellectual material with which to formulate and justify itself.

In the first lecture it was noted that in Greek life prosaic matter of fact or empirical knowledge was at a great disadvantage as compared with the imaginative beliefs that were bound up with special institutions and moral habitudes. Now this empirical knowledge has grown till it has broken its low and limited sphere of application and esteem. It has itself become an organ of inspiring imagination through introducing ideas of boundless possibility, indefinite progress, free movement, equal opportunity irrespective of fixed limits. It has reshaped social institutions, and in so far developed a new morale. It has achieved ideal values. It is convertible into creative and constructive philosophy.

Convertible, however, rather than already converted. When we consider how deeply embedded in customs of thought and action the classic philosophy came to be and how congenial it is to man's more spontaneous beliefs, the throes that attended the birth of modern science are not to be wondered at. We should rather wonder that a view so upsetting, so undermining, made its way without more persecutions, martyrdoms and disturbances. It certainly is not surprising that its complete and consistent formulation in philosophy has been long delayed. The main efforts of thinkers were inevitably directed to minimizing the shock of change, easing the strains of transition, mediating and reconciling. When we look back upon almost all of the thinkers of the seventeenth and eighteenth centuries, upon all excepting those who were avowedly sceptical and revolutionary, what strikes us is the amount of traditional subject-matter and method that it to be found even among those who were regarded as most advanced. Men cannot easily throw off their old habits of thinking, and never can throw off all of them at once. In developing, teaching and receiving new ideas we are compelled to use some of the old ones as tools of understanding and communication. Only piecemeal, step-by-step, could the full import of the new science be grasped. Roughly speaking, the seventeenth century witnessed its application in astronomy and general cosmology; the eighteenth century in physics and chemistry; the nineteenth century undertook an application in geology and the biological sciences.

It was said that it has now become extremely difficult to recover the view of the world which universally obtained in Europe till the seventeenth century. Yet after all we need only recur to the science of plants and animals as it was before Darwin and to the ideas which even now are dominant in moral and political matters to find the older order of conceptions in full possession of the popular mind. Until the dogma of fixed unchangeable types and species, of arrangement in classes of higher and lower, of subordination of the transitory individual to the universal or kind had been shaken in its hold upon the science of life, it was impossible that the new ideas and method should be made at home in social and moral life. Does it not seem to be the intellectual task of the twentieth century to take this last step? When this step is taken the circle of scientific development will be rounded out and the reconstruction of philosophy be made an accomplished fact.

MORRIS R. COHEN (1880–1947) and ERNEST NAGEL (1901–   )

Morris Raphael Cohen was born in Minsk, Russia. When he was twelve years old, his Jewish parents migrated to New York City in search of freedom and opportunity. Growing up in the metropolis, Cohen attended the College of the City of New York (City College), from which he was graduated in 1900. He then studied philosophy at Harvard as a student of Josiah Royce and William James, receiving his doctor's degree in 1906. Famous as a great teacher, he served on the faculty at City College from 1912 to 1938 and at the University of Chicago from 1938 through 1941. He was also a lecturer or visiting professor at Columbia, Yale, Harvard, Cornell, the New School for Social Research, and other institutions. His works include *Reason and Nature: An Essay on the Meaning of the Scientific Method* (1931), *Law and the Social Order* (1933), *The Meaning of Human History* (1947), and his autobiography, *A Dreamer's Journey* (1949).

Ernest Nagel was born at Nove Mesto, Czechoslovakia. His family migrated to the United States when he was ten years old and he was naturalized in 1919. He studied under Morris Cohen at City College, and received an M.A. degree in mathematics and a Ph.D. degree in philosophy at Columbia University, where he was deeply influenced by John Dewey. As professor of philosophy at Columbia and author of important books and articles, he is noted for his defence of naturalism and his contributions to the philosophy of science. Among his publications are *Sovereign Reason* (1954) and *The Structure of Science* (1961). He and Morris Cohen collaborated in writing *An Introduction to Logic and Scientific Method* (1934).

Scientific Method

Facts and Scientific Method

The method of science does not seek to impose the desires and hopes of men upon the flux of things in a capricious manner. It may indeed be employed to satisfy the desires of men. But its successful use depends upon seeking, in a deliberate manner, and irrespective of what men's desires are, to recognize, as well as to take advantage of, the structure which the flux possesses.

1. Consequently, scientific method aims to discover what the facts truly are, and the use of the method must be guided by the discovered facts. But, as we have repeatedly pointed out, what the facts are cannot be discovered without reflection. Knowledge of the facts cannot be equated to the brute immediacy of our sensations. When our skin comes into contact with objects having high temperatures or with liquid air, the immediate experiences may be similar. We cannot, however, conclude without error that the temperatures of the substances touched are the same.

From *An Introduction to Logic and Scientific Method* by Morris R. Cohen and Ernest Nagel, copyright, 1934, by Harcourt Brace Jovanovich, Inc.; renewed, 1962, by Ernest Nagel and Leonora Cohen Rosenfeld. Reprinted by permission of the publishers.

Sensory experience sets the *problem* for knowledge, and just because such experience is immediate and final it must become informed by reflective analysis before knowledge can be said to take place.

2. Every inquiry arises from some felt problem, so that no inquiry can even get under way unless some selection or sifting of the subject matter has taken place. Such selection requires, we have been urging all along, some hypothesis, preconception, prejudice, which guides the research as well as delimits the subject matter of inquiry. Every inquiry is specific in the sense that it has a definite problem to solve, and such solution terminates the inquiry. It is idle to collect "facts" unless there is a problem upon which they are supposed to bear.

3. The ability to formulate problems whose solution may also help solve other problems is a rare gift, requiring extraordinary genius. The problems which meet us in daily life can be solved, if they can be solved at all, by the application of scientific method. But such problems do not, as a rule, raise far-reaching issues. The most striking applications of scientific method are to be found in the various natural and social sciences.

4. The "facts" for which every in-

quiry reaches out are propositions for whose truth there is considerable evidence. Consequently what the "facts" are must be determined by inquiry, and cannot be determined antecedently to inquiry. Moreover, what we believe to be the facts clearly depends upon the stage of our inquiry. There is therefore no sharp line dividing facts from guesses or hypotheses. During any inquiry the status of a proposition may change from that of hypothesis to that of fact, or from that of fact to that of hypothesis. Every so-called fact, therefore, *may* be challenged for the evidence upon which it is asserted to be a fact, even though no such challenge is actually made.

Hypotheses and Scientific Method

The method of science would be impossible if the hypotheses which are suggested as solutions could not be elaborated to reveal what they imply. The full meaning of a hypothesis is to be discovered in its implications.

1. Hypotheses are suggested to an inquirer by something in the subject matter under investigation, and by his previous knowledge of other subject matters. No rules can be offered for obtaining fruitful hypotheses, any more than rules can be given for discovering significant problems.

2. Hypotheses are required at every stage of an inquiry. It must not be forgotten that what are called general principles or laws (which may have been confirmed in a previous inquiry) can be applied to a present, still unterminated inquiry only with some risk. For they may not in fact be applicable. The general laws of any science func-

tion as hypotheses, which guide the inquiry in all its phases.

3. Hypotheses can be regarded as suggestions of possible connections between actual facts or imagined ones. The question of the truth of hypotheses need not, therefore, always be raised. The necessary feature of a hypothesis, from this point of view, is that it should be statable in a determinate form, so that its implications can be discovered by logical means.

4. The number of hypotheses which may occur to an inquirer is without limit, and is a function of the character of his imagination. There is a need, therefore, for a technique to choose between the alternative suggestions, and to make sure that the alternatives are in fact, and not only in appearance, *different* theories. Perhaps the most important and best explored part of such a technique is the technique of formal inference. For this reason, the structure of formal logic has been examined at some length. The object of that examination has been to give the reader an adequate sense of what formal validity means, as well as to provide him with a synoptic view of the power and range of formal logic.

5. It is convenient to have on hand—in storage, so to speak—different hypotheses whose consequences have been carefully explored. It is the task of mathematics to provide and explore alternative hypotheses. Mathematics receives hints concerning what hypotheses to study from the natural sciences; and the natural sciences are indebted to mathematics for suggestions concerning the type of order which their subject matter embodies.

6. The deductive elaboration of hypotheses is not the sole task of scientific method. Since there is a plurality of possible hypotheses, it is the risk of inquiry to determine which of the possible explanations or solutions of the problem is in best agreement with the facts. Formal considerations are therefore never sufficient to establish the material truth of any theory.

7. No hypothesis which states a general proposition can be demonstrated as absolutely true. We have seen that all inquiry which deals with matters of fact employs probable inference. The task of such investigations is to select that hypothesis which is the most probable on the factual evidence; and it is the task of further inquiry to find other factual evidence which will increase or decrease the probability of such a theory.

Evidence and Scientific Method

Scientific method pursues the road of systematic doubt. It does not doubt *all* things, for this is clearly impossible. But it does question whatever lacks adequate evidence in its support.

1. Science is not satisfied with psychological certitude, for the mere intensity with which a belief is held is no guarantee of its truth. Science demands and looks for logically adequate grounds for the propositions it advances.

2. No single proposition dealing with matters of fact is beyond every significant doubt. No proposition is so well supported by evidence that other evidence may not increase or decrease its probability. However, while no single

proposition is indubitable, the body of knowledge which supports it, and of which it is itself a part, is better grounded than any alternative body of knowledge.

3. Science is thus always ready to abandon a theory when the facts so demand. But the facts must really demand it. It is not unusual for a theory to be modified so that it may be retained in substance even though "facts" contradicted an earlier formulation of it. Scientific procedure is therefore a mixture of a willingness to change, and an obstinacy in holding on to, theories apparently incompatible with facts.

4. The verification of theories is only approximate. Verification simply shows that, within the margin of experimental error, the experiment is *compatible* with the verified hypothesis.

System in the Ideal of Science

The ideal of science is to achieve a systematic interconnection of facts. Isolated propositions do not constitute a science. Such propositions serve merely as an opportunity to find the logical connection between them and other propositions.

1. "Common sense" is content with a miscellaneous collection of information. As a consequence, the propositions it asserts are frequently vague, the range of their application is unknown, and their mutual compatibility is generally very questionable. The advantages of discovering a system among facts is therefore obvious. A condition for achieving a system is the introduction of accuracy in the assertions made. The

limit within which propositions are true is then clearly defined. Moreover, inconsistencies between propositions asserted become eliminated gradually because propositions which are part of a system must support and correct one another. The extent and accuracy of our information is thus increased. In fact, scientific method differs from other methods in the accuracy and number of facts it studies.

2. When, as frequently happens, a science abandons one theory for another, it is a mistake to suppose that science has become "bankrupt" and that it is incapable of discovering the structure of the subject matter it studies. Such changes indicate rather that the science is progressively realizing its ideal. For such changes arise from correcting previous observations or reasoning, and such correction means that we are in possession of more reliable facts.

3. The ideal of system requires that the propositions asserted to be true should be connected without the introduction of further propositions for which the evidence is small or nonexistent. In a system the number of unconnected propositions and the number of propositions for which there is no evidence are at a minimum. Consequently, in a system the requirements of simplicity, as expressed in the principle of Occam's razor, are satisfied in a high degree. For that principle declares that entities should not be multiplied beyond necessity. This may be interpreted as a demand that whatever is capable of proof should be proved. But the ideal of system requires just that.

4. The evidence for propositions which are elements in a system accumulates more rapidly than that for isolated propositions. The evidence for a proposition may come from its own verifying instances, or from the verifying instances of *other* propositions which are connected with the first in a system. It is this systematic character of scientific theories which gives such high probabilities to the various individual propositions of a science.

The Self-Corrective Nature of Scientific Method

Science does not desire to obtain conviction for its propositions in *any* manner and at *any* price. Propostions must be supported by logically acceptable evidence, which must be weighed carefully and tested by the well-known canons of necessary and probable inference. It follows that the *method* of science is more stable, and more important to men of science, than any particular result achieved by its means.

1. In virtue of its method, the enterprise of science is a self-corrective process. It appeals to no special revelation or authority whose deliverances are indubitable and final. It claims no infallibility, but relies upon the methods of developing and testing hypotheses for assured conclusions. The canons of inquiry are themselves discovered in the process of reflection, and may themselves become modified in the course of study. The method makes possible the noting and correction of errors by continued application of itself.

2. General propositions can be established only by the method of repeated

sampling. Consequently, the propositions which a science puts forward for study are either confirmed in all possible experiments or modified in accordance with the evidence. It is this self-corrective nature of the method which allows us to challenge any proposition, but which also assures us that the theories which science accepts are more probable than any alternative theories. By not claiming more certainty than the evidence warrants, scientific method succeeds in obtaining more logical certainty than any other method yet devised.

3. In the process of gathering and weighing evidence, there is a continuous appeal from facts to theories or principles, and from principles to facts. For there is nothing intrinsically indubitable, there are no absolutely first principles, in the sense of principles which are self-evident or which must be known prior to everything else.

4. The method of science is thus essentially circular. We obtain evidence for principles by appealing to empirical material, to what is alleged to be "fact"; and we select, analyze, and interpret empirical material on the basis of principles. In virtue of such give and take between facts and principles, everything that is dubitable falls under careful scrutiny at one time or another.

The Abstract Nature of Scientific Theories

No theory asserts *everything* that can possibly be asserted about a subject matter. Every theory selects certain aspects of it and excludes others. Unless it were

possible to do this—either because such other aspects are irrelevant or because their influence on those selected is very minute—science as we know it would be impossible.

1. All theories involve abstraction from concrete subject matter. No rule can be given as to which aspects of a subject matter should be abstracted and so studied independently of other aspects. But in virtue of the goal of science—the achievement of a systematic interconnection of phenomena—in general those aspects will be abstracted which make a realization of this goal possible. Certain common elements in the phenomenon studied must be found, so that the endless variety of phenomena may be viewed as a system in which their structure is exhibited.

2. Because of the abstractness of theories, science often seems in patent contradiction with "common sense." In "common sense" the unique character and the pervasive character of things are not distinguished, so that the attempt by science to disclose the invariant features often gives the appearance of artificiality. Theories are then frequently regarded as "convenient fictions" or as "unreal." However, such criticisms overlook the fact that it is just certain *selected invariant relations* of things in which science is interested, so that many familiar properties of things are necessarily neglected by the sciences. Moreover, they forget that "common sense" itself operates in terms of abstractions, which are familiar and often confused, and which are inadequate to express the complex structure of the flux of things.

Types of Scientific Theories

Scientific explanation consists in subsuming under some rule or law which expresses an invariant character of a group of events, the particular events it is said to explain. Laws themselves may be explained, and in the same manner, by showing that they are consequences of more comprehensive theories. The effect of such progressive explanation of events by laws, laws by wider laws or theories, is to reveal the interconnection of many apparently isolated propositions.

1. It is clear, however, that the process of explanation must come to a halt at some point. Theories which cannot be shown to be special consequences from a wider connection of facts must be left unexplained, and accepted as a part of the brute fact of existence. Material considerations, in the form of contingent matters of fact, must be recognized in at least two places. There is contingency at the level of sense: just *this* and not *that* is given in sense experience. And there is contingency at the level of explanation: a definite system, although not the only possible one from the point of view of formal logic, is found to be exemplified in the flux of things.

2. In a previous chapter we have enumerated several kinds of "laws" which frequently serve as explanations of phenomena. There is, however, another interesting distinction between theories. Some theories appeal to an easily imagined *hidden mechanism* which will explain the observable phenomena; other theories eschew all reference to such hidden mechanisms, and make use of *relations* abstracted from the phenomena actually observable. The former are called *physical* theories; the latter are called *mathematical* or *abstractive* theories.

It is important to be aware of the difference between these two kinds of theories, and to understand that some minds are especially attracted to one kind, while others are comfortable only with the other kind. But it is also essential not to suppose that either kind of theory is more fundamental or more valid than the other. In the history of science there is a constant oscillation between theories of these two types; sometimes both types of theories are used successfully on the same subject matter. Let us, however, make clear the difference between them.

The English physicist Rankine explained the distinction as follows: There are two methods of framing a theory. In a mathematical or abstractive theory, "a class of objects or phenomena is defined . . . by describing . . . that assemblage of properties which is common to all the objects or phenomena composing the class, as perceived by the senses, without introducing anything hypothetical." In a physical theory "a class of objects is defined . . . as being constituted, in a manner not apparent to the senses, by a modification of some other class of objects or phenomena whose laws are already known."[1]

In the second kind of theory, some visualizable model is made the pattern for a mechanism hidden from the sense. Some physicists, like Kelvin, cannot be satisfied with anything less than a me-

[1] W. J. M. Rankine, *Miscellaneous Scientific Papers,* 1881, p. 210.

chanical explanation of observable phenomena, no matter how complex such a mechanism may be. Examples of this kind of theory are the atomic theory of chemistry, the kinetic theory of matter as developed in thermodynamics and the behavior of gases, the theory of the gene in studies on heredity, the theory of lines of force in electrostatics, and the recent Bohr model of the atom in spectroscopy.

In the mathematical type of theory, the appeal to hidden mechanisms is eliminated, or at any rate is at a minimum. How this may be done is graphically described by Henri Poincaré: "Suppose we have before us any machine; the initial wheel work and the final wheel work alone are visible, but the transmission, the intermediary machinery by which the movement is communicated from one to the other, is hidden in the interior and escapes our view; we do not know whether the communication is made by gearing or by belts, by connecting-rods or by other contrivances. Do we say that it is impossible for us to understand anything about this machine so long as we are not permitted to take it to pieces? You know well we do not, and that the principle of the conservation of energy suffices to determine for us the most interesting point. We easily ascertain that the final wheel turns ten times less quickly than the initial wheel, since these two wheels are visible; we are able thence to conclude that a couple applied to the one will be balanced by a couple ten times greater applied to the other. For that there is no need to penetrate the mechanism of this equilibrium and to know how the forces compensate

each other in the interior of the machine."[2] Examples of such theories are the theory of gravitation, Galileo's laws of falling bodies, the theory of the flow of heat, the theory of organic evolution, and the theory of relativity.

As we suggested, it is useless to quarrel as to which type of theory is the more fundamental and which type should be universally adopted. Both kinds of theories have been successful in coördinating vast domains of phenomena, and fertile in making discoveries of the most important kind. At some periods in the history of a science, there is a tendency to mechanical models and atomicity; at others, to general principles connecting characteristics abstracted from directly observable phenomena; at still others, to a fusion or synthesis of these two points of view. Some scientists, like Kelvin, Faraday, Lodge, Maxwell, show an exclusive preference for "model" theories; other scientists, like Rankine, Ostwald, Duhem, can work best with the abstractive theories; and still others, like Einstein, have the unusual gift of being equally at home with both kinds.

§ 2. The Limits and the Value of Scientific Method

The desire for knowledge for its own sake is more widespread than is generally recognized by anti-intellectualists. It has its roots in the animal curiosity which shows itself in the cosmological questions of children and in the gossip of adults. No ulterior utilitarian motive makes people want to know about the

[2] *Op. cit.,* p. 290–291.

private lives of their neighbors, the great, or the notorious. There is also a certain zest which makes people engage in various intellectual games or exercises in which one is required to find out something. But while the desire to know is wide, it is seldom strong enough to overcome the more powerful organic desires, and few indeed have both the inclination and the ability to face the arduous difficulties of scientific method in more than one special field. The desire to know is not often strong enough to sustain critical inquiry. Men generally are interested in the results, in the story or romance of science, not in the technical methods whereby these results are obtained and their truth continually is tested and qualified. Our first impulse is to accept the plausible as true and to reject the uncongenial as false. We have not the time, inclination, or energy to investigate everything. Indeed, the call to do so is often felt as irksome and joy-killing. And when we are asked to treat our cherished beliefs as mere hypotheses, we rebel as violently as when those dear to us are insulted. This provides the ground for various movements that are hostile to rational scientific procedure (though their promoters do not often admit that it is science to which they are hostile).

Mystics, intuitionists, authoritarians, voluntarists, and fictionalists are all trying to undermine respect for the rational methods of science. These attacks have always met with wide acclaim and are bound to continue to do so, for they strike a responsive note in human nature. Unfortunately they do not offer any reliable alternative method for obtaining verifiable knowledge. The great

French writer Pascal opposed to logic the spirit of subtlety or finesse (*esprit géometrique* and *esprit de finesse*) and urged that the heart has its reasons as well as the mind, reasons that cannot be accurately formulated but which subtle spirits apprehend none the less. Men as diverse as James Russell Lowell and George Santayana are agreed that:

"The soul is oracular still,"

and

"It is wisdom to trust the heart . . . To trust the soul's invincible surmise."

Now it is true that in the absence of omniscience we must trust our soul's surmise; and great men are those whose surmises or intuitions are deep or penetrating. It is only by acting on our surmise that we can procure the evidence in its favor. But only havoc can result from confusing a surmise with a proposition for which there is already evidence. Are all the reasons of the heart sound? Do all oracles tell the truth? The sad history of human experience is distinctly discouraging to any such claim. Mystic intuition may give men absolute subjective certainty, but can give no proof that contrary intuitions are erroneous. It is obvious that when authorities conflict we must weigh the evidence in their favor logically if we are to make a rational choice. Certainly, when a truth is questioned it is no answer to say, "I am convinced," or, "I prefer to rely on this rather than on another authority." The view that physical science is no guide to proof, but is a mere fiction, fails to explain why it has enabled us to anticipate phenomena of nature and to control them. These attacks on scientific method receive a certain color of plausibility because of some indefensible claims made by uncritical enthusiasts. But it is of the essence of scientific method to limit its own pretension. Recognizing that we do not know everything, it does not claim the ability to solve all of our practical problems. It is an error to suppose, as is often done, that science denies the truth of all unverified propositions. For that which is unverified today may be verified tomorrow. We may get at truth by guessing or in other ways. Scientific method, however, is concerned with verification. Admittedly the wisdom of those engaged in this process has not been popularly ranked as high as that of the sage, the prophet, or the poet. Admittedly, also, we know of no way of supplying creative intelligence to those who lack it. Scientists, like all other human beings, may get into ruts and apply their techniques regardless of varying circumstances. There will always be formal procedures which are fruitless. Definitions and formal distinctions may be a sharpening of tools without the wit to use them properly, and statistical information may conform to the highest technical standards and yet be irrelevant and inconclusive. Nevertheless, scientific method is the only way to increase the general body of tested and verified truth and to eliminate arbitrary opinion. It is well to clarify our ideas by asking for the precise meaning of our words, and to try to check our favorite ideas by applying them to accurately formulated propositions.

In raising the question as to the so-cial need for scientific method, it is well to recognize that the suspension of judgment which is essential to that method is difficult or impossible when we are pressed by the demands of immediate action When my house is on fire, I must act quickly and promptly— I cannot stop to consider the possible causes, nor even to estimate the exact probabilities involved in the various alternative ways of reacting. For this reason, those who are bent upon some specific course of action often despise those devoted to reflection; and certain ultramodernists seem to argue as if the need for action guaranteed the truth of our decision. But the fact that I must either vote for candidate X or refrain from doing so does not of itself give me adequate knowledge. The frequency of our regrets makes this obvious. Wisely ordered society is therefore provided with means for deliberation and reflection *before* the pressure of action becomes irresistible. In order to assure the most thorough investigation, all possible views must be canvassed, and this means toleration of views that are *prima facie* most repugnant to us.

In general the chief social condition of scientific method is a widespread desire for truth that is strong enough to withstand the powerful forces which make us cling tenaciously to old views or else embrace every novelty because it is a change. Those who are engaged in scientific work need not only leisure for reflection and material for their experiment, but also a community that respects the pursuit of truth and allows freedom for the expression of intellectual doubt as to its most sacred or established institutions. Fear of offending established dogmas has been an obstacle to the growth of astronomy and geology and other physical sciences; and the fear of offending patriotic or respected sentiment is perhaps one of the strongest hindrances to scholarly history and social science. On the other hand, when a community indiscriminately acclaims every new doctrine the love of truth becomes subordinated to the desire for novel formulations.

On the whole it may be said that the safety of science depends on there being men who care more for the justice of their methods than for any results obtained by their use. For this reason it is unfortunate when scientific research in the social field is largely in the hands of those not in a favorable position to oppose established or popular opinion. We may put it the other way by saying that the physical sciences can be more liberal because we are sure that foolish opinions will be readily eliminated by the shock of facts. In the social field, however, no one can tell what harm may come of foolish ideas before the foolishness is finally, if ever, demonstrated. None of the precautions of scientific method can prevent human life from being an adventure, and no

scientific investigator knows whether he will reach his goal. But scientific method does enable large numbers to walk with surer steps. By analyzing the possibilities of any step or plan, it becomes possible to anticipate the future and adjust ourselves to it in advance. Scientific method thus minimizes the shock of novelty and the uncertainty of life. It enables us to frame policies of actions and of moral judgment fit for a wider outlook than those of immediate physical stimulus or organic response.

Scientific method is the only effective way of strengthening the love of truth. It develops the intellectual courage to face difficulties and to overcome illusions that are pleasant temporarily but destructive ultimately. It settles differences without any external force by appealing to our common rational nature. The way of science, even if it is up a steep mountain, is open to all. Hence, while sectarian and partisan faiths are based on personal choice or temperament and divide men, scientific procedure unites men in something nobly devoid of all pettiness. Because it requires detachment, disinterestedness, it is the finest flower and test of a liberal civilization.

COMMENT

The Empiricist Tradition

Even before Descartes outlined his rationalistic theory of knowledge, Francis Bacon (1561–1626), a prominent figure in the Court of Queen Elizabeth and James I of England, had set forth the basic tenets of empiricism in his two great books *The Advancement of Learning* and *Novum Organum*. With the intensity and earnestness of a prophet, Bacon proclaimed that induction is the true road to knowledge and that none before him had tried this method. The statement is itself, however, a faulty induction, since even a superficial survey of his history of science reveals that a number of Bacon's predecessors—Roger Bacon, Leonardo da Vinci, Telesio, and Campanella, to name but a few—were also heralds of empirical science. Even Aristotle, whom Bacon denounced, knew very well how to handle the inductive method. After the time of Bacon, there was a great succession of English philosophers—Locke, Berkeley, Hume and Mill—whose emphasis was empirical. On the Continent, the method of empiricism has been notably represented by the "positivists" Mach, Comte, and Poincaré.

The American philosophers, Peirce, Dewey, Cohen, and Nagel, may fairly be called empiricists. In temper they are sharply opposed to Plato's emphasis on transcendent essences, Aristotle's emphasis on fixed ends, St. Thomas' emphasis on God and an afterlife, and Descartes' and Spinoza's emphasis on deductive method. As much as Hume and more than Kant, they represent a breaking away from these older modes of thought. In Chapter 5 I have already summarized Peirce's criticism of the Cartesian method. Dewey, in the lecture here reprinted, attacks the "closed" and "hierarchical" world depicted by Aristotle and St. Thomas, and advocates "the scientific reconstruction of philosophy." Cohen and Nagel, in the same tradition, are uncompromising advocates of scientific method.

Peirce and Dewey are frequently characterized as pragmatists, but their pragmatism is an offshoot of scientific empiricism. Just what this means will be clearer if we glance at the pragmatist movement.

The Origin and Development of Pragmatism

The word "pragmatism" was introduced into modern philosophy by Charles Peirce to designate the "method of ascertaining the meaning of hard words and abstract conceptions" which he had advocated in "How to Make Our Ideas Clear" (1878). Even before he wrote this essay, Peirce had expressed the basic principle of his pragmatism in a review (1871) of Fraser's edition of Berkeley's *Works*, in which he offered the following "rule for avoiding the deceits of language": "Do things fulfill the same function practically? Then let them be signified by the same word. Do they not? Then let them be distinguished." In neither of these early statements did Peirce use the word "pragmatism." But in 1898, at the University of California, William James delivered a lecture entitled "Philosophical Conceptions and Practical Results," in which he hailed Peirce not only as the founder of pragmatism but as the originator of the term. It appears that Peirce used the word orally for some time before he first committed it to print in 1902, when he contributed an article on the subject to Baldwin's *Philosophical Dictionary*.

The terms "pragmatic" and "pragmatism" were suggested to Peirce by his study of Kant. In *The Metaphysic of Morals*, Kant distinguished between "pragmatic" and "practical." The former term, deriving from the Greek *pragma* (things done), applies to the rules of art or technique based upon experience; the latter term applies to moral rules which Kant regarded as *a priori*. Hence Peirce, wishing to emphasize an experimental and non-*a priori* type of reasoning, chose the word "pragmatic" to designate his way of clarifying meanings.

The pragmatic movement first sprang to life in the early eighteen-seventies in the "Metaphysical Club," a philosophical discussion group founded by Peirce, which included among its members William James and Oliver Wendell Holmes, Jr. Two of the brilliant young members of the club, Chauncey Wright and Nicholas St. John Green, emphasized the practical bearing and function of ideas. They thus suggested to Peirce the criterion of clarity which he expressed in "How to Make Our Ideas Clear." But this essay lay unnoticed for twenty years until James, in his address of 1898, pointed to Peirce as the founder of an important new philosophical movement.

As Peirce initially used the term, pragmatism referred to a maxim for the clarification of ideas and hypotheses, not for their verification; it was a theory of meaning, not of truth. Later he also used the term to designate the rule that only hypotheses that are *clear* should be admitted in scientific or philosophical inquiry. As interpreted and amplified by James, "pragmatism" became a theory of truth and so changed into something alien to Peirce's way of thinking. "The modern movement known as pragmatism," Ralph Barton Perry has remarked, "is largely the result of James' misunderstanding of Peirce."[1]

While James was developing his own version of pragmatism, John Dewey was working along similar lines at the University of Michigan and later at the University of Chicago. As early as 1886, he and James began to exchange letters, and in 1903, in the Preface to *Studies in Logical Theory*, Dewey acknowledged "a preëminent obligation" to James. In certain ways, however, Dewey shows a closer affinity to Peirce—for example, in his close study of the experimental methods of natural science, in his rejection of James' criterion of emotional satisfaction as a test of truth, in his emphasis on the *social* bearing of ideas, and in his opposition to all "intuitionist" theories of knowledge.

However much he differed in some respects from James, Dewey fully agreed with the forward-looking and empirical temper of James' pragmatism—"the attitude of looking away from first things, principles, 'categories,' supposed necessities; and of looking toward last things, fruits, consequences, facts." He also agreed that thinking is essentially instrumental to the attainment of human purposes, although the purposes of the scientist are to be distinguished from the purposes of the practical man of affairs. Like James, moreover, he vehemently rejected a dualism of experience and nature: the stuff of the world is natural events such as we directly experience. His interpretation of inquiry, however, was more akin to Peirce's experimentalism than to James' ethical pragmatism.[2]

Conceiving philosophical and scientific method in this way, Dewey regarded fruitful inquiry as essentially active and prospective rather than passive and retrospective:

[1] *The Thought and Character of William James*, Briefer Version (Harvard University Press, 1935), p. 281.

[2] For readings from James that illustrate his pragmatic mode of reasoning, see "The One and the Many" in Chapter 8 and "The Will to Believe" in Chapter 12.

> Intelligence develops within the sphere of action for the sake of possibilities not yet given. . . . Intelligence *as* intelligence is inherently forward-looking. . . . A pragmatic intelligence is a creative intelligence, not a routine mechanic. . . . Intelligence is . . . instrumental *through* action to the determination of the qualities of future experience.[3]

Accordingly, Dewey proposes to determine meanings and test beliefs by examining the *consequences* that flow from them. What can the idea or belief promise for the future? How can it help us in resolving our perplexities? What predictions are implied by the hypothesis and how can they be verified?

Such questions apply even to propositions about the past, and even these propositions must be verified in terms of future consequences: "The past event has left effects, consequences, that are present and that will continue in the future. Our belief about it, if genuine, must also modify action in *some* way and so have objective effects. If these two sets of effects interlock harmoniously, then the judgment is true."[4] For example, the assassination of Lincoln *had* consequences, such as records of the event. My belief about it *has* consequences, such as expectations that the records will be so-and-so. If the two sets of consequences harmoniously coincide so that my expectations are fulfilled, the statement is true.

Dewey regarded this emphasis on consequences as the essential characteristic of pragmatism. "The term 'pragmatic,'" he declared, "means only the rule of referring all thinking, all reflective considerations, to *consequences* for final meaning and test."[5] This insistence upon consequent rather than antecedent phenomena is, as we have noted, like the pragmatism of James except that it does not define truth in terms of emotional satisfactions and the play of desires, as James did in his more extreme statements.

There were other important contributors to pragmatism, such as George Herbert Mead (1863–1931) and C. I. Lewis (1883–1964); but Peirce, James, and Dewey are the towering figures. James' pragmatic mode of reasoning is illustrated in his essay on "The One and the Many" in Chapter 5, and Peirce and Dewey are well represented by the readings in the present chapter.

Cohen and Nagel on Scientific Method

Morris R. Cohen was a student of James and Ernest Nagel was a student of Dewey, but it is the more scientific side of the pragmatism of Dewey and James that has influenced their writing. Cohen described his view as realistic rationalism, a view that emphasizes the importance of scientific reasoning as applied to the actual world. Nagel similarly described his philosophy as naturalism, which he carefully distinguished from the kind of materialism that seeks to reduce ideas and values to physical terms such as 'molecules.' Both Cohen and Nagel shared with Dewey certain fundamental convictions: the need for an empirical and naturalistic approach to human problems, the necessity of extending the scientific method into the sphere of social affairs, and the insistence of the factual basis

[3] *Creative Intelligence* (Henry Holt, 1917), p. 65.
[4] *The Influence of Darwin on Philosophy and Other Essays* (Henry Holt, 1910), p. 160.
[5] *Essays in Experimental Logic* (University of Chicago Press, 1916), p. 330.

of sound normative judgments. Although they differed from Dewey in certain respects, their attainment to the scientific method marks them as well as Dewey as empiricists.

Despite the difference between the work of the physicist and the biologist, the astronomer and the sociologist, certain methodological patterns are common to all. This common method of science Cohen and Nagel describe and defend. Since their discussion is a model of clarity, it needs no explication. The reader who seeks an understanding of scientific method would be well advised to study their book.

Conclusion

A number of the leaders of youth's "counterculture" have advocated a mystical and romantic approach to life. Theodore Roszack, who may be cited as typical, thinks that there should be a movement toward "a new culture in which the non-intellective capacities of the personality—those capacities that take fire from visionary splendor and the experience of human communion—become the arbiters of the good, the true, and the beautiful." Scientific and technological priorities must be swept aside in favor of "a new simplicity, a decelerating social pace, a vital leisure" and "the communal opening-up of man to man." "For, after all, science is not everything, and in fact is not very much at all when it comes to creating a creditable way of life for ourselves," and it is better to side with "the non-intellective spontaneity of children and primitives, artists and lovers, those who can lose themselves gracefully in the splendor of the moment."[6] How much truth is there in this view? Is it possible to cultivate "non-intellective" values without the sacrifice of science and technology? Whether the writers in this chapter undervalue nonscientific modes of thought and overvalue science I shall leave my readers to debate.

[6] *The Making of a Counter Culture* (Garden City, N.Y., Doubleday & Company, 1969), pp. 50–51, 54, 68.

9

Existentialism

SÖREN KIERKEGAARD (1813–1855)

The youngest son of rather elderly parents, Kierkegaard was born in Copenhagen and reared in a pious Lutheran family. His father was a wealthy and retired merchant with a strong sense of sin which he impressed upon his children. As a young University student, Sören lived a Bohemian life in revolt against his father and religious pietism. After a moral conversion, he returned to his studies and passed his theological examinations at the University of Copenhagen in 1840. The next year he went to Berlin to attend Schelling's lectures, which confirmed his dislike of Hegel's philosophy. The abstractions of Hegelianism did not supply what he demanded—"a truth which is true *for me,* to find the *idea for which I can live and die (Journal,* Aug. 1, 1935)."

Thenceforth the driving force of his life was to "become a Christian," a task that, in his opinion, would not be easy. Although he was in love with 17-year-old Regine Olsen, he broke the engagement because it seemed incompatible with his religious commitment. This break not only hurt his fiancee's pride but had a profoundly traumatic effect upon him. He thereafter searched his tormented soul for self-knowledge in book after book.

During his later years he was involved in intense controversy with the Danish State Church, which he accused of being pseudo-Christian. On the point of death he refused the sacrament. "Pastors are royal officials," he explained. "Royal officials have nothing to do with Christianity." The epitaph that he composed for himself was simply, "That individual."

Individuality
and Subjective Truth

The Single Individual
and the Crowd[1]

This that follows is in part the expression of a way of thinking and feeling characteristic of my nature, which possibly is in need of revision (which I myself would welcome), and as it does not claim to be more than that, it is at the farthest remove from claiming the reader's adherence and is rather inclined to concessions. In part, however, it is a well-thought-out view of 'the Life', of 'the Truth', of 'the Way'.[2]

There is a view of life which conceives that where the crowd is, there also is the truth, and that in truth itself there is need of having the crowd on its side. There is another view of life which conceives that wherever there is a crowd there is untruth, so that (to consider for a moment the extreme case), even if every individual, each for himself in private, were to be in possession of the truth, yet in case they were all to get together in a crowd—a crowd to which any sort of *decisive* significance is attributed, a voting, noisy, audible crowd—untruth would at once be in evidence.[3]

For a 'crowd' is the untruth. In a godly sense it is true, eternally, Christianly, as St. Paul says, that 'only one attains the goal'—which is not meant in a comparative sense, for comparison takes others into account. It means that every man can be that one, God helping him therein—but only one attains the goal. And again this means that every man should be chary about having to do with 'the others', and essentially should talk only with God and with himself—for only one attains the goal. And again this means that man, or to

[1] From *The Point of View* by Sören Kierkegaard, translated and edited by Dr. Walter Lowrie. London, New York, and Toronto: Oxford University Press, 1939. Reprinted by permission. Footnotes followed by (K) are by Kierkegaard.

[2] Perhaps it may be well to note here once and for all a thing that goes without saying and which I never have denied, that in relation to all temporal, earthly, worldly matters the crowd may have competency, and even decisive competency as a court of last resort. But it is not of such matters I am speaking, nor have I ever concerned myself with such things. I am speaking about the ethical, about the ethico-religious, about 'the truth', and I am affirming the untruth of the crowd, ethico-religiously regarded, when it is treated as a criterion for what 'truth' is. (K)

[3] Perhaps it may be well to note here, although it seems to me almost superfluous, that it naturally could not occur to me to object to the fact, for example, that preaching is done or that the truth is proclaimed, even though it were to an assemblage of hundreds of thousands. Not at all; but if there were an assemblage even of only ten—and if they should put the truth to the ballot, that is to say, if the assemblage should be regarded as the authority, if it is the crowd which turns the scale—then there *is* untruth. (K)

be a man, is akin to deity.—In a worldly and temporal sense, it will be said by the man of bustle, sociability, and amicableness, 'How unreasonable that only one attains the goal; for it is far more likely that many, by the strength of united effort, should attain the goal; and when we are many success is more certain and it is easier for each man severally.' True enough, it is far more *likely*; and it is true also with respect to all earthly and material goods. If it is allowed to have its way, this becomes the only true point of view, for it does away with God and eternity and with man's kinship with deity. It does away with it or transforms it into a fable, and puts in its place the modern (or, we might rather say, the old pagan) notion that to be a man is to belong to a race endowed with reason, to belong to it as a specimen, so that the race or species is higher than the individual, which is to say that there are no more individuals but only specimens. But eternity which arches over and high above the temporal, tranquil as the starry vault at night, and God in heaven who in the bliss of that sublime tranquillity holds in survey, without the least sense of dizziness at such a height, these countless multitudes of men and knows each single individual by name—He, the great Examiner, says that only one attains the goal. That means, every one can and every one should be this *one*—but only one attains the goal. Hence where there is a multitude, a crowd, or where decisive significance is attached to the fact that there is a multitude, *there* it is sure that no one is working, living, striving for the highest aim, but only for one or another earthly aim;

since to work for the eternal decisive aim is possible only where there is one, and to be this one which all can be is to let God be the helper—the 'crowd' is the untruth.

A crowd—not this crowd or that, the crowd now living or the crowd long deceased, a crowd of humble people or of superior people, of rich or of poor, &c.—a crowd in its very concept[4] is the untruth, by reason of the fact that it renders the individual completely impenitent and irresponsible, or at least weakens his sense of responsibility by reducing it to a fraction. Observe that there was not one single soldier that dared lay hands upon Caius Marius—this was an instance of truth. But given merely three or four women with the consciousness or the impression that they were a crowd, and with hope of a sort in the possibility that no one could say definitely who was doing it or who began it—then they had courage for it. What a falsehood! The falsehood first of all is the notion that the crowd does what in fact only the *individual* in the crowd does, though it be every *individual*. For 'crowd' is an abstraction and has no hands: but each individual has ordinarily two hands, and so when

[4] The reader will also remember that here the word 'crowd' is understood in a purely formal sense, not in the sense one commonly attaches to 'the crowd' when it is meant as an invidious qualification, the distinction which human selfishness irreligiously erects between 'the crowd' and superior persons, &c. Good God! How could a religious man hit upon such an inhuman equality! No, 'crowd' stands for number, the numerical, a number of noblemen, millionaires, high dignitaries, &c.—as soon as the numerical is involved it is 'crowd', 'the crowd'. (K)

an individual lays his two hands upon Caius Marius they are the two hands of the individual, certainly not those of his neighbour, and still less those of the . . . crowd which has no hands. In the next place, the falsehood is that the crowd had the 'courage' for it, for no one of the individuals was ever so cowardly as the crowd always is. For every individual who flees for refuge into the crowd, and so flees in cowardice from being an individual (who had not the courage to lay his hands upon Caius Marius, nor even to admit that he had it not), such a man contributes his share of cowardliness to the cowardliness which we know as the 'crowd'.— Take the highest example, think of Christ—and the whole human race, all the men that ever were born or are to be born. But let the situation be one that challenges the individual, requiring each one for himself to be alone with Him in a solitary place and as an individual to step up to Him and spit upon Him—the man never was born and never will be born with courage or insolence enough to do such a thing. This is untruth.

The crowd is untruth. Hence none has more contempt for what it is to be a man than they who make it their profession to lead the crowd. Let some one approach a person of this sort, some individual—that is an affair far too small for his attention, and he proudly repels him. There must be hundreds at the least. And when there are thousands, he defers to the crowd, bowing and scraping to them. What untruth! No, when it is a question of a single individual man, then is the time to give expression to the truth by showing one's respect for what it is to be a man; and if perhaps it was, as it is cruelly said, a poor wretch of a man, then the thing to do is to invite him into the best room, and one who possesses several voices should use the kindest and most friendly. That is truth. If on the other hand there were an assemblage of thousands or more and the truth was to be decided by ballot, then this is what one should do (unless one were to prefer to utter silently the petition of the Lord's Prayer, 'Deliver us from evil'): one should in godly fear give expression to the fact that the crowd, regarded as a judge over ethical and religious matters, is untruth, whereas it is eternally true that every man can be the *one*. This is truth.

The crowd is untruth. Therefore was Christ crucified, because, although He addressed himself to all, He would have no dealings with the crowd, because He would not permit the crowd to aid him in any way, because in this regard He repelled people absolutely, would not found a party, did not permit balloting, but would be what He is, the Truth, which relates itself to the individual.— And hence every one who truly would serve the truth is *eo ipso,* in one way or another, a martyr. If it were possible for a person in his mother's womb to make the decision to will to serve the truth truly, then, whatever his martyrdom turns out to be, he is *eo ipso* from his mother's womb a martyr. For it is not so great a trick to win the crowd. All that is needed is some talent, a certain dose of falsehood, and a little acquaintance with human passions. But no witness for the truth (ah! and that is what every man should be, including you and me)—no witness for the truth dare become engaged with the crowd. The witness for the truth—who naturally has nothing to do with politics and must above everything else be most vigilantly on the watch not to be confounded with the politician—the God-fearing work of the witness to the truth is to engage himself if possible with all, but always individually, talking to every one severally on the streets and lanes . . . in order to disintegrate the crowd, or to talk even to the crowd, though not with the intent of educating the crowd as such, but rather with the hope that one or another individual might return from this assemblage and become a single individual. On the other hand the 'crowd', when it is treated as an authority and its judgement regarded as the final judgement, is detested by the witness for the truth more heartily than a maiden of good morals detests the public dance-floor; and he who addresses the crowd as the supreme authority is regarded by him as the tool of the untruth. For (to repeat what I have said) that which in politics or in similar fields may be justifiable, wholly or in part, becomes untruth when it is transferred to the intellectual, the spiritual, the religious fields. And one thing more I would say, perhaps with a cautiousness which is exaggerated. By 'truth' I mean always 'eternal truth'. But politics, &c., have nothing to do with 'eternal truth'. A policy which in the proper sense of 'eternal truth' were to make serious work of introducing 'eternal truth' into real life would show itself in that very same second to be in the most eminent degree the most 'impolitic' thing that can be imagined.

A crowd is untruth. And I could weep, or at least I could learn to long for eternity, at thinking of the misery of our age, in comparison even with the greatest misery of bygone ages, owing to the fact that the daily press with its anonymity makes the situation madder still with the help of the public, this abstraction which claims to be the judge in matters of 'truth'. For in reality assemblies which make this claim do not now take place. The fact that an anonymous author by the help of the press can day by day find occasion to say (even about intellectual, moral, and religious matters) whatever he pleases to say, and what perhaps he would be very far from having the courage to say as an individual; that every time he opens his mouth (or shall we say his abysmal gullet?) he at once is addressing thousands of thousands; that he can get ten thousand times ten thousand to repeat after him what he has said—and with all this nobody has any responsibility, so that it is not as in ancient times the relatively unrepentant crowd which possesses omnipotence, but the absolutely unrepentant thing, a nobody, an anonymity, who is the producer (*auctor*), and another anonymity, the public, sometimes even anonymous subscribers, and with all this, nobody, nobody! Good God! And yet our states call themselves Christian states! Let no one say that in this case it is possible for 'truth' in its turn by the help of the press to get the better of lies and errors. O thou who speakest thus, dost thou venture to maintain that men regarded as a crowd are just as quick to seize upon truth which is not always palatable as upon falsehood which always is prepared delicately to give delight?— not to mention the fact that acceptance of the truth is made the more difficult by the necessity of admitting that one has been deceived! Or dost thou venture even to maintain that 'truth' can just as quickly be understood as falsehood, which requires no preliminary knowledge, no schooling, no discipline, no abstinence, no self-denial, no honest concern about oneself, no patient labour?

Nay, truth—which abhors also this untruth of aspiring after broad dissemination as the one aim—is not nimble on its feet. In the first place it cannot work by means of the fantastical means of the press, which is the untruth; the communicator of the truth can only be a single individual. And again the communication of it can only be addressed to the individual; for the truth consists precisely in that conception of life which is expressed by the individual. The truth can neither be communicated nor be received except as it were under God's eyes, not without God's help, not without God's being involved as the middle term, He himself being the Truth. It can therefore only be communicated by and received by 'the individual', which as a matter of fact can be every living man. The mark which distinguishes such a man is merely that of the truth, in contrast to the abstract, the fantastical, the impersonal, the crowd—the public which excludes God as the middle term (for the *personal* God cannot be a middle term in an *impersonal* relationship), and thereby excludes also the truth, for God is at once the Truth and the middle term which renders it intelligible.

And to honour every man, absolutely every man, is the truth, and this is what it is to fear God and love one's 'neighbour'. But from an ethico-religious point of view, to recognize the 'crowd' as the court of last resort is to deny God, and it cannot exactly mean to love the 'neighbour'. And the 'neighbour' is the absolutely true expression for human equality. In case every one were in truth to love his neighbour as himself, complete human equality would be attained. Every one who loves his neighbour in truth, expresses unconditionally human equality. Every one who, like me, admits that his effort is weak and imperfect, yet is aware that the task is to love one's neighbour, is also aware of what human equality is. But never have I read in Holy Scripture the commandment, Thou shalt love the crowd—and still less, Thou shalt recognize, ethico-religiously, in the crowd the supreme authority in matters of 'truth'. But the thing is simple enough: this thing of loving one's neighbour is self-denial; that of loving the crowd, or of pretending to love it, of making it the authority in matters of truth, is the way to material power, the way to temporal and earthly advantages of all sorts—at the same time it is the untruth, for a crowd is the untruth.

But he who acknowledges the truth of this view, which is seldom presented (for it often happens that a man thinks that the crowd is the untruth, but when it—the crowd—accepts his opinion *en masse,* everything is all right again), admits for himself that he is weak and impotent; for how could it be possible for an individual to make a stand against the crowd which possesses the power! And he could not wish to get the crowd on his side for the sake of ensuring that his view would prevail, the crowd, ethico-religiously regarded, being the untruth—that would be mocking himself. But although from the first this view involves an admission of weakness and impotence, and seems therefore far from inviting, and for this reason perhaps is so seldom heard, yet it has the good feature that it is even-handed, that it offends no one, not a single person, that it makes no invidious distinctions, not the least in the world. The crowd, in fact, is composed of individuals; it must therefore be in every man's power to become what he is, an individual. From becoming an individual no one, no one at all, is excluded, except he who excludes himself by becoming a crowd. To become a crowd, to collect a crowd about one, is on the contrary to affirm the distinctions of human life. The most well-meaning person who talks about these distinctions can easily offend an individual. But then it is not the crowd which possesses power, influence, repute, and mastery over men, but it is the invidious distinctions of human life which despotically ignore the single individual as the weak and impotent, which in a temporal and worldly interest ignore the eternal truth—the single individual.

How Johannes Climacus Became an Author[5]

It is now about four years since I got the notion of wanting to try my hand

as an author. I remember it quite clearly; it was on a Sunday, yes, that's it, a Sunday afternoon. As usual I was sitting out-of-doors at the café in the Frederiksberg Garden, that wonderful garden which for the child was fairy-land, where the King dwelt with his Queen, that delightful garden which afforded the youth happy diversion in the merriment of the populace, that friendly garden where now for the man of riper years there is such a homely feeling of sad exaltation above the world and all that is of the world, where even the invidious glory of royal dignity is what it is now out there—a queen's remembrance of her deceased lord.[6] There I sat as usual and smoked my cigar. . . .

I had been a student for ten years. Although never lazy, all my activity nevertheless was like a glittering inactivity, a kind of occupation for which I still have a strong predilection, and perhaps even a little talent. I read much, spent the rest of the day idling and thinking, or thinking and idling, but that was all it came to; the earliest sproutings of my productivity barely sufficed for my daily use and were consumed in their first greening. An inexplicable and overwhelming might constantly held me back, by strength as well as by artifice. This might was my indolence. It is not like the vehement

5 This and the following excerpt on "The Subjective Truth: Inwardness" are from *Concluding Unscientific Postscript* translated by David F. Swenson, Lillian Marvin Swenson, and Walter Lowrie, in *A Kierkegaard Anthology,* edited by Robert Bretall. Copyright 1946 by Princeton University Press. Reprinted by permission.

6 Referring to the widow of Frederick VI, who continued to reside there a great part of the year. (Note by Lowrie. The remaining notes are by Kierkegaard.)

aspiration of love, nor like the strong incentive of enthusiasm, it is rather like a housekeeper who holds one back, and with whom one is very well off, so well off that it never occurs to one to get married. This much is sure: though with the comforts of life I am not on the whole unacquainted, of all, indolence is the most comfortable.

So there I sat and smoked my cigar until I lapsed into reverie. Among other thoughts I remember this: "You are now," I said to myself, "on the way to becoming an old man, without being anything, and without really undertaking to do anything. On the other hand, wherever you look about you, in literature and in life, you see the celebrated names and figures, the precious and much heralded men who are coming into prominence and are much talked about, the many benefactors of the age who know how to benefit mankind by making life easier and easier, some by railways, others by omnibuses and steamboats, others by telegraph, others by easily apprehended compendiums and short recitals of everything worth knowing, and finally the true benefactors of the age who by virtue of thought make spiritual existence systematically easier and easier, and yet more and more significant. And what are you doing?"

Here my self-communion was interrupted, for my cigar was burned out and a new one had to be lit. So I smoked again, and then suddenly there flashed through my mind this thought: "You must do something, but inasmuch as with your limited capacities it will be impossible to make anything easier than it has become, you must, with the same humanitarian enthusiasm as the others, undertake to make something harder." This notion pleased me immensely, and at the same time it flattered me to think that I, like the rest of them, would be loved and esteemed by the whole community. For when all combine in every way to make everything easier and easier, there remains only one possible danger, namely, that the easiness might become so great that it would be too great; then only one want is left, though not yet a felt want —that people will want difficulty. Out of love for mankind, and out of despair at my embarrassing situation, seeing that I had accomplished nothing and was unable to make anything easier than it had already been made, and moved by a genuine interest in those who make everything easy, I conceived it my task to create difficulties everywhere. I was struck also by the strange reflection that, after all, I might have to thank my indolence for the fact that this task became mine. For far from having found it, as Aladdin did the lamp, I must rather suppose that my indolence, by hindering me from intervening at an opportune time to make things easy, had forced upon me the only task that was left. . . .

The Subjective Truth: Inwardness Truth is Subjectivity

WHEN *the question of truth is raised in an objective manner, reflection is directed objectively to the truth, as an object to which the knower is related. Reflection is not focused upon the relationship, however, but upon the question of whether it is the truth to which the knower is related. If only the object to which he is related is the truth, the subject is accounted to be in the truth. When the question of the truth is raised subjectively, reflection is directed subjectively to the nature of the individual's relationship: if only the mode of this relationship is in the truth, the individual is in the truth, even if he should happen to be thus related to what is not true.*[7] Let us take as an example the knowledge of God. Objectively, reflection is directed to the problem of whether this object is the true God; subjectively, reflection is directed to the question whether the individual is related to a something *in such a manner* that his relationship is in truth a God-relationship. On which side is the truth now to be found? Ah, may we not here resort to a mediation, and say: It is on neither side, but in the mediation of both? Excellently well said, provided we might have it explained how an existing individual manages to be in a state of mediation. For to be in a state of mediation is to be finished, while to exist is to become. Nor can an existing individual be in two places at the same time—he cannot be an identity of subject and object. When he is nearest to being in two places at the same time he is in passion; but passion is merely momentary, and passion is also the highest expression of subjectivity.

The existing individual who chooses

[7] The reader will observe that the question here is about essential truth, or about the truth which is essentially related to existence, and that it is precisely for the sake of clarifying it as inwardness or as subjectivity that this contrast is drawn. (K)

to pursue the objective way enters upon the entire approximation-process by which it is proposed to bring God to light objectively. But this is in all eternity impossible, because God is a subject, and therefore exists only for subjectivity in inwardness. The existing individual who chooses the subjective way apprehends instantly the entire dialectical difficulty involved in having to use some time, perhaps a long time, in finding God objectively; and he feels this dialectical difficulty in all its painfulness, because he must use God at that very moment, since every moment is wasted in which he does not have God.[8] That very instant he has God, not by virtue of any objective deliberation but by virtue of the infinite passion of inwardness. The objective inquirer, on the other hand, is not embarrassed by such dialectical difficulties as are involved in devoting an entire period of investigation to finding God—since it is possible that the inquirer may die tomorrow; and if he lives he can scarcely regard God as something to be taken along if convenient, since God is precisely that which one takes *a tout prix*, which in the understanding of

[8] In this manner God certainly becomes a postulate, but not in the otiose manner in which this word is commonly understood. It becomes clear rather that the only way in which an existing individual comes into relation with God is when the dialectical contradiction brings his passion to the point of despair, and helps him to embrace God with the "category of despair" (faith). Then the postulate is so far from being arbitrary that it is precisely a life-necessity. It is then not so much that God is a postulate as that the existing individual's postulation of God is a necessity. (K)

passion constitutes the true inward relationship to God.

It is at this point, so difficult dialectically, that the way swings off for everyone who knows what it means to think, and to think existentially; which is something very different from sitting at a desk like a fantastical being and writing about what one has never done, something very different from writing *de omnibus dubitandum,* and at the same time being as existentially credulous as the most sensuous of men. Here is where the way swings off, and the change is marked by the fact that, while objective knowledge rambles comfortably on by way of the long road of approximation without being impelled by the urge of passion, subjective knowledge counts every delay a deadly peril, and the decision so infinitely important and so instantly pressing that it is as if the opportunity had already passed unutilized.

Now when the problem is to reckon up on which side there is most truth, whether on the side of one who seeks the true God objectively, and pursues the approximate truth of the God-idea; or on the side of one who, driven by the infinite passion of his need of God, feels an infinite concern for his own relationship to God in truth (and to be at one and the same time on both sides equally is, as we have noted, not possible for an existing individual, but is merely the happy delusion of an imaginary I-am-I): the answer cannot be in doubt for anyone who has not been demoralized with the aid of science. If one who lives in the midst of Christianity goes up to the house of God, the house of the true God, with the true

conception of God in his knowledge, and prays, but prays in a false spirit; and one who lives in an idolatrous community prays with the entire passion of the infinite, although his eyes rest upon the image of an idol: where is there most truth? The one prays in truth to God though he worships an idol; the other prays falsely to the true God, and hence worships in fact an idol.

When one man investigates objectively the problem of immortality, and another embraces an uncertainty with the passion of the infinite: where is there most truth, and who has the greater certainty? The one has entered upon a never-ending approximation, for the certainty of immortality lies precisely in the subjectivity of the individual; the other is immortal, and fights for his immortality by struggling with the uncertainty. Let us consider Socrates. Nowadays everyone dabbles in a few proofs; some have several such proofs, others fewer. But Socrates! He puts the question objectively in a problematic manner: *if* there is an immortality. Must he therefore be accounted a doubter in comparison with one of our modern thinkers with the three proofs? By no means. On this "if" he risks his entire life, he has the courage to meet death, and he has with the passion of the infinite so determined the pattern of his life that it must be found acceptable—*if* there is an immortality. Can any better proof be given for the immortality of the soul? But those who have the three proofs do not at all determine their lives in conformity therewith; if there is an immortality, it must feel disgust over their manner of life:

can any better refutation be given of the three proofs? The "bit" of uncertainty that Socrates had helped him, because he himself contributed the passion of the infinite; the three proofs that the others have do not profit them at all, because they are and remain dead to spirit and enthusiasm, and their three proofs, in lieu of proving anything else, prove just this. A young girl may enjoy all the sweetness of love on the basis of what is merely a weak hope; but she is beloved, because she rests everything on this weak hope; but many a wedded matron more than once subjected to the strongest expressions of love has in so far indeed had proofs, but strangely enough has not enjoyed *quod erat demonstrandum*. The Socratic ignorance, which Socrates held fast with the entire passion of his inwardness, was thus an expression for the principle that the eternal truth is related to an existing individual, and that this truth must therefore be a paradox for him as long as he exists; and yet it is possible that there was more truth in the Socratic ignorance as it was in him, than in the entire objective truth of the System, which flirts with what the times demand and accommodates itself to *Privatdocents*.

The objective accent falls on WHAT is said, the subjective accent on HOW it is said. This distinction holds even in the aesthetic realm, and receives definite expression in the principle that what is in itself true may in the mouth of such and such a person become untrue. In these times this distinction is particularly worthy of notice for, if we wish to express in a single sentence the difference between ancient times and our own, we should doubtless have to say: "In ancient times only an individual here and there knew the truth; now all know it, but the inwardness of its appropriation stands in an inverse relationship to the extent of its dissemination. Aesthetically the contradiction that truth becomes untruth in this or that person's mouth is best construed comically. In the ethico-religious sphere, the accent is again on the "how." But this is not to be understood as referring to demeanor, expression, delivery, or the like; rather it refers to the relationship sustained by the existing individual, in his own existence, to the content of his utterance. Objectively the interest is focused merely on the thought-content, subjectively on the inwardness. At its maximum this inward "how" is the passion of the infinite, and the passion of the infinite is the truth. But the passion of the infinite is precisely subjectivity, and thus subjectivity becomes the truth. Objectively there is no infinite decision, and hence it is objectively in order to annul the difference between good and evil, together with the principle of contradiction, and therewith also the infinite difference between the true and the false. Only in subjectivity is there decision, to seek objectivity is to be in error. It is the passion of the infinite that is the decisive factor and not its content, for its content is precisely itself. In this manner subjectivity and the subjective "how" constitute the truth.

But the "how" which is thus subjectively accentuated, precisely because the subject is an existing individual, is also subject to a dialectic with respect to time. In the passionate moment of decision, where the road swings away from objective knowledge, it seems as if the infinite decision were thereby realized. But in the same moment the existing individual finds himself in the temporal order, and the subjective "how" is transformed into a striving, a striving which receives indeed its impulse and a repeated renewal from the decisive passion of the infinite, but is nevertheless a striving.

When subjectivity is the truth, the conceptual determination of the truth must include an expression for the antithesis to objectivity, a memento of the fork in the road where the way swings off; this expression will also indicate the tension of the subjective inwardness. Here is such a definition of truth: *An objective uncertainty held fast in an appropriation-process of the most passionate inwardness is the truth, the highest truth attainable for an existing individual.* At the point where the way swings off (and where this is cannot be specified objectively, since it is a matter of subjectivity), there objective knowledge is placed in abeyance. Thus the subject merely has, objectively, the uncertainty; but it is this which precisely increases the tension of that infinite passion which constitutes his

inwardness. The truth is precisely the venture which chooses an objective uncertainty with the passion of the infinite. I contemplate nature in the hope of finding God, and I see omnipotence and wisdom; but I also see much else that disturbs my mind and excites anxiety. The sum of all this is an objective uncertainty. But it is for this very reason that the inwardness becomes as intense as it is, for it embraces this objective uncertainty with the entire passion of the infinite. In the case of a mathematical proposition the objectivity is given, but for this reason the truth of such a proposition is also an indifferent truth.

But the above definition of truth is an equivalent expression for faith. Without risk there is no faith. Faith is precisely the contradiction between the infinite passion of the individual's inwardness and the objective uncertainty. If I am capable of grasping God objectively, I do not believe, but precisely because I cannot do this I must believe. If I wish to preserve myself in faith I must constantly be intent upon holding fast the objective uncertainty, so that in the objective uncertainty I am out "upon the seventy thousand fathoms of water," and yet believe. . . .

MARTIN BUBER (1878–1965)

Born in Vienna of Jewish parentage, Martin Buber studied philosophy and the history of art at the Universities of Vienna and Berlin. From his youth he was active in the Zionist movement, especially in its cultural and religious aspects, and in 1901 he became editor of the Zionist journal *Die Welt*. He also edited for eight years (1916-1924) the influential German periodical *Der Jude*, devoted to the renascence of Jewish life and culture. For a decade (1923-1933) he taught philosophy and religion at the University of Frankfurt. He escaped from Hitler's Germany in 1938 and became, at the age of sixty, professor of philosophy in the Hebrew University in Jerusalem, continuing in this post for fifteen years. In Israel he worked to bring about understanding between the Jews and Arabs and advocated a bi-national state. He also supported, as an alternative to both individualism and collectivism, experiments in communal living within small, autonomous groups. His book, *I and Thou*, more than any other of his numerous publications, established his worldwide fame as a moral and religious existentialist.

Elements
of the Interhuman

The Social
and the Interhuman

It is usual to ascribe what takes place between men to the social realm, thereby blurring a basically important line of division between two essentially different areas of human life. I myself, when I began nearly fifty years ago to find my own bearings in the knowledge of society, making use of the then unknown concept of the interhuman, made the same error. From that time it became increasingly clear to me that we have to do here with a separate category of our existence, even a separate dimension, to use a mathematical term, and one with which we are so familiar that its peculiarity has hitherto almost escaped us. Yet insight into its peculiarity is extremely important not only for our thinking, but also for our living.

We may speak of social phenomena wherever the life of a number of men, lived with one another, bound up together, brings in its train shared experiences and reactions. But to be thus bound up together means only that each individual existence is enclosed

From *The Knowledge of Man* ed. M. Friedman. Trans. Robert Gregor Smith. ©1965 by Martin Buber and Maurice Friedman. Reprinted by permission of Harper & Row and George Allen & Unwin Ltd.

and contained in a group existence. It does not mean that between one member and another of the group there exists any kind of personal relation. They do feel that they belong together in a way that is, so to speak, fundamentally different from every possible belonging together with someone outside the group. And there do arise, especially in the life of smaller groups, contacts which frequently favour the birth of individual relations, but, on the other hand, frequently make it more difficult. In no case, however, does membership in a group necessarily involve an existential relation between one member and another. It is true that there have been groups in history which included highly intensive and intimate relations between two of their members —as, for instance, in the homosexual relations among the Japanese Samurai or among Doric warriors—and these were countenanced for the sake of the stricter cohesion of the group. But in general it must be said that the leading elements in groups, especially in the later course of human history, have rather been inclined to suppress the personal relation in favour of the purely collective element. Where this latter element reigns alone or is predominant, men feel themselves to be carried by the collectivity, which lifts them out of loneliness and fear of the world and lostness. When this happens—and for modern man it is an essential happening—the life between person and person seems to retreat more and more before the advance of the collective. The collective aims at holding in check the inclination to personal life. It is as though those who are bound together in groups should in the main be concerned only with the work of the group and should turn to the personal partners, who are tolerated by the group, only in secondary meetings.

The difference between the two realms became very palpable to me on one occasion when I had joined the procession through a large town of a movement to which I did not belong. I did it out of sympathy for the tragic development which I sensed was at hand in the destiny of a friend who was one of the leaders of the movement. While the procession was forming, I conversed with him and with another, a goodhearted 'wild man', who also had the mark of death upon him. At that moment I still felt that the two men really were there, over against me, each of them a man near to me, near even in what was most remote from me; so different from me that my soul continually suffered from this difference, yet by virtue of this very difference confronting me with authentic being. Then the formations started off, and after a short time I was lifted out of all confrontation, drawn into the procession, falling in with its aimless step; and it was obviously the very same for the two with whom I had just exchanged human words. After a while we passed a café where I had been sitting the previous day with a musician

whom I knew only slightly. The very moment we passed it the door opened, the musician stood on the threshold, saw me, apparently saw me alone, and waved to me. Straightway it seemed to me as though I were taken out of the procession and of the presence of my marching friends, and set there, confronting the musician. I forgot that I was walking along with the same step; I felt that I was standing over there by the man who had called out to me, and without a word, with a smile of understanding, was answering him. When consciousness of the facts returned to me, the procession, with my companions and myself at its head, had left the café behind.

The realm of the interhuman goes far beyond that of sympathy. Such simple happenings can be part of it as, for instance, when two strangers exchange glances in a crowded streetcar, at once to sink back again into the convenient state of wishing to know nothing about each other. But also every casual encounter between opponents belongs to this realm, when it affects the opponent's attitude—that is, when something, however imperceptible, happens between the two, no matter whether it is marked at the time by any feeling or not. The only thing that matters is that for each of the two men the other happens as the particular other, that each becomes aware of the other and is thus related to him in such a way that he does not regard and use him as his object, but as his partner in a living event, even if it is no more than a boxing match. It is well known that some existentialists assert that the basic factor between men is that one is an object for the other. But so far as this is actually the case, the special reality of the interhuman, the fact of the contact, has been largely eliminated. It cannot indeed be entirely eliminated. As a crude example, take two men who are observing one another. The essential thing is not that the one makes the other his object, but the fact that he is not fully able to do so and the reason for his failure. We have in common with all existing beings that we can be made objects of observation. But it is my privilege as man that by the hidden activity of my being I can establish an impassable barrier to objectification. Only in partnership can my being be perceived as an existing whole.

The sociologist may object to any separation of the social and the interhuman on the ground that society is actually built upon human relations, and the theory of these relations is therefore to be regarded as the very foundation of sociology. But here an ambiguity in the concept 'relation' becomes evident. We speak, for instance, of a comradely relation between two men in their work, and do not merely mean what happens between them as comrades, but also a lasting disposition which is actualized in those happenings and which even includes purely psychological events such as the recollection of the absent comrade. But by the sphere of the interhuman I mean solely actual happenings between men, whether wholly mutual or tending to grow into mutual relations. For the participation of both partners is in principle indispensable. The sphere of the interhuman is one in which a person is confronted by the other. We call its unfolding the dialogical.

In accordance with this, it is basically erroneous to try to understand the interhuman phenomena as psychological. When two men converse together, the psychological is certainly an important part of the situation, as each listens and each prepares to speak. Yet this is only the hidden accompaniment to the conversation itself, the phonetic event fraught with meaning, whose meaning is to be found neither in one of the two partners nor in both together, but only in their dialogue itself, in this 'between' which they live together.

Being and Seeming

The essential problem of the sphere of the interhuman is the duality of being and seeming.

Although it is a familiar fact that men are often troubled about the impression they make on others, this has been much more discussed in moral philosophy than in anthropology. Yet this is one of the most important subjects for anthropological study.

We may distinguish between two different types of human existence. The one proceeds from what one really is, the other from what one wishes to seem. In general, the two are found mixed together. There have probably been few men who were entirely independent of the impression they made on others, while there has scarcely existed one who was exclusively determined by the impression made by him. We must be content to distinguish between men in whose essential attitude the one or the other predominates.

This distinction is most powerfully at work, as its nature indicates, in the interhuman realm—that is, in men's personal dealings with one another.

Take as the simplest and yet quite clear example the situation in which two persons look at one another—the first belonging to the first type, the second to the second. The one who lives from his being looks at the other just as one looks at someone with whom he has personal dealings. His look is 'spontaneous', 'without reserve'; of course he is not uninfluenced by the desire to make himself understood by the other, but he is uninfluenced by any thought of the idea of himself which he can or should awaken in the person whom he is looking at. His opposite is different. Since he is concerned with the image which his appearance, and especially his look or glance, produces in the other, he 'makes' this look. With the help of the capacity, in greater or lesser degree peculiar to man, to make a definite element of his being appear in his look, he produces a look which is meant to have, and often enough does have, the effect of a spontaneous utterance—not only the utterance of a psychical event supposed to be taking place at that very moment, but also, as it were, the reflection of a personal life of such-and-such a kind.

This must, however, be carefully distinguished from another area of seeming whose ontological legitimacy cannot be doubted. I mean the realm of 'genuine seeming', where a lad, for instance, imitates his heroic model and while he is doing so is seized by the actuality of heroism, or a man plays the part of a destiny and conjures up authentic destiny. In this situation there is nothing false; the imitation is genuine imitation and the part played is genuine; the mask, too, is a mask and no deceit. But where the semblance originates from the lie and is permeated by it, the interhuman is threatened in its very existence. It is not that someone utters a lie, falsifies some account. The lie I mean does not take place in relation to particular facts, but in relation to existence itself, and it attacks interhuman existence as such. There are times when a man, to satisfy some stale conceit, forfeits the great chance of a true happening between I and Thou.

Let us now imagine two men, whose life is dominated by appearance, sitting and talking together. Call them Peter and Paul. Let us list the different configurations which are involved. First, there is Peter as he wishes to appear to Paul, and Paul as he wishes to appear to Peter. Then there is Peter as he really appears to Paul, that is, Paul's image of Peter, which in general does not in the least coincide with what Peter wishes Paul to see; and similarly there is the reverse situation. Further, there is Peter as he appears to himself, and Paul as he appears to himself. Lastly, there are the bodily Peter and the bodily Paul. Two living beings and six ghostly appearances, which mingle in many ways in the conversation between the two. Where is there room for any genuine interhuman life?

Whatever the meaning of the word 'truth' may be in other realms, in the interhuman realm it means that men communicate themselves to one another as what they are. It does not depend on one saying to the other everything that occurs to him, but only on his letting no seeming creep in between himself and the other. It does not depend on one letting himself go before another, but on his granting to the man to whom he comunicates himself a share in his being. This is a question of the authenticity of the interhuman, and where this is not to be found, neither is the human element itself authentic.

Therefore, as we begin to recognize the crisis of man as the crisis of what is between man and man, we must free the concept of uprightness from the thin moralistic tones which cling to it, and let it take its tone from the concept of bodily uprightness. If a presupposition of human life in primeval times is given in man's walking upright, the fulfilment of human life can only come through the soul's walking upright, through the great uprightness which is not tempted by any seeming because it has conquered all semblance.

But, one may ask, what if a man by his nature makes his life subservient to the images which he produces in others? Can he, in such a case, still become a man living from his being, can he escape from his nature?

The widespread tendency to live from the recurrent impression one makes instead of from the steadiness of one's being is not a 'nature'. It originates, in fact, on the other side of interhuman life itself, in men's dependence upon one another. It is no light thing to be confirmed in one's being by others, and seeming deceptively offers itself as a help in this. To yield to seeming is man's essential cowardice, to resist it is his essential courage. But this is not an inexorable state of affairs which is as it is and must so remain. One can struggle to come to oneself—that is, to come to confidence in being. One struggles, now more successfully, now less, but never in vain, even when one thinks he is defeated. One must at times pay dearly for life lived from the being; but it is never too dear. Yet is there not bad being, do weeds not grow everywhere? I have never known a young person who seemed to me irretrievably bad. Later indeed it becomes more and more difficult to penetrate the increasingly tough layer which has settled down on a man's being. Thus there arises the false perspective of the seemingly fixed 'nature' which cannot be overcome. It is false; the foreground is deceitful; man as man can be redeemed.

Again we see Peter and Paul before us surrounded by the ghost of the semblances. A ghost can be exorcized. Let us imagine that these two find it more and more repellent to be represented by ghosts. In each of them the will is stirred and strengthened to be confirmed in their being as what they really are and nothing else. We see the forces of real life at work as they drive out the ghost, till the semblance vanishes and the depths of personal life call to one another.

Personal Making Present

By far the greater part of what is today called conversation among men would be more properly and precisely described as speechifying. In general, people do not really speak to one another, but each, although turned to the other, really speaks to a fictitious court of appeal whose life consists of nothing but listening to him. Chekhov has given poetic expression to this state of affairs in *The Cherry Orchard,* where the only use the members of a family make of their being together is to talk past one another. But it is Sartre who has raised to a principle of existence what in Chekhov still appears as the deficiency of a person who is shut up in himself. Sartre regards the walls between the partners in a conversation as simply impassable. For him it is inevitable human destiny that a man has directly to do only with himself and his own affairs. The inner existence of the other is his own concern, not mine; there is no direct relation with the other, nor can there be. This is perhaps the clearest expression of the wretched fatalism of modern man, which regards degeneration as the unchangeable nature of *Homo sapiens* and the misfortune of having run into a blind alley as his primal fate, and which brands every thought of a breakthrough as reactionary romanticism. He who really knows how far our generation has lost the way of true freedom, of free giving between I and Thou, must himself, by virtue of the demand implicit in every great knowledge of this kind, practise directness—even if he were the only man on earth who did it—and not depart from it until scoffers are struck with fear, and hear in his voice the voice of their own suppressed longing.

The chief presupposition for the rise of genuine dialogue is that each should regard his partner as the very one he is. I become aware of him, aware that he is different, essentially different from myself, in the definite, unique way which is peculiar to him, and I accept whom I thus see, so that in full earnestness I can direct what I say to him as the person he is. Perhaps from time to time I must offer strict opposition to his view about the subject of our conversation. But I accept this person, the personal bearer of a conviction, in his definite being out of which his conviction has grown—even though I must try to show, bit by bit, the wrongness of this very conviction. I affirm the person I struggle with: I struggle with him as his partner, I confirm him as creature and as creation, I confirm him who is opposed to me as him who is over against me. It is true that it now depends on the other whether genuine dialogue, mutuality in speech arises between us. But if I thus give to the other who confronts me his legitimate standing as a man with whom I am ready to enter into dialogue, then I may trust him and suppose him to be also ready to deal with me as his partner.

But what does it mean to be 'aware' of a man in the exact sense in which I use the word? To be aware of a thing or a being means, in quite general terms, to experience it as a whole and yet at the same time without reduction or abstraction, in all its concreteness. But a man, although he exists as a living being among living beings and even as a thing among things, is nevertheless something categorically different from all things and all beings. A man cannot really be grasped except on the basis of the gift of the spirit which belongs to man alone among all things, the spirit as sharing decisively in the personal life of the living man, that is, the spirit which determines the person. To be aware of a man, therefore, means in particular to perceive his wholeness as a person determined by the spirit; it means to perceive the dynamic centre which stamps his every utterance, action, and attitude with the recognizable sign of uniqueness. Such an awareness is impossible, however, if and so long as the other is the separated object of my contemplation or even observation, for this wholeness and its centre do not let themselves be known to contemplation or observation. It is only possible when I step into an elemental relation with the other, that is, when he becomes present to me. Hence I designate awareness in this special sense as 'personal making present'.

The perception of one's fellow man as a whole, as a unity, and as unique—even if his wholeness, unity, and uniqueness are only partly developed, as is usually the case—is opposed in our time by almost everything that is commonly understood as specifically modern. In our time there predominates an analytical, reductive, and deriving look between man and man. This look is analytical, or rather pseudo analytical, since it treats the whole being as put together and therefore able to be taken apart—not only the so-called unconscious which is accessible to relative objectification, but also the psychic stream itself, which can never, in fact, be grasped as an object. This look is a reductive one because it tries to contract the manifold person, who is nourished by the microcosmic richness of the possible, to some schematically surveyable and recurrent structures. And this look is a deriving one because it supposes it can grasp what a man has become, or even is becoming, in genetic formulae, and it thinks that even the dynamic central principle of the individual in this becoming can be represented by a general concept. An effort is being made today radically to destroy the mystery between man and man. The personal life, the ever near mystery, once the source of the stillest enthusiasms, is levelled down.

What I have just said is not an attack on the analytical method of the human sciences, a method which is indispensable wherever it furthers knowledge of a phenomenon without impairing the essentially different knowledge of its uniqueness that transcends the valid circle of the method. The science of man that makes use of the analytical method must accordingly always keep in view the boundary of such a contemplation, which stretches like a horizon around it. This duty makes the transposition of the method into life dubious; for it is excessively difficult to see where the boundary is in life.

If we want to do today's work and prepare tomorrow's with clear sight, then we must develop in ourselves and in the next generation a gift which lives in man's inwardness as a Cinderella, one day to be a princess. Some call it intuition, but that is not a wholly unambiguous concept. I prefer the name 'imagining the real', for in its essential being this gift is not a looking at the other, but a bold swinging—demanding the most intensive stirring of one's being—into the life of the other. This is the nature of all genuine imagining, only that here the real of my action is not the all-possible, but the particular real person who confronts me, whom I can attempt to make present to myself just in this way, and not otherwise, in his wholeness, unity, and uniqueness, and with his dynamic center which realizes all these things ever anew.

Let it be said again that all this can only take place in a living partnership, that is, when I stand in a common situation with the other and expose myself vitally to his share in the situation as really his share. It is true that my basic attitude can remain unanswered, and the dialogue can die in seed. But if mutuality stirs, then the interhuman blossoms into genuine dialogue.

Imposition and Unfolding

I have referred to two things which impede the growth of life between men: the invasion of seeming, and the inadequacy of perception. We are now faced with a third, plainer than the others, and in this critical hour more powerful and more dangerous than ever.

There are two basic ways of affecting men in their views and their attitude to life. In the first a man tries to impose himself, his opinion and his attitude, on the other in such a way that the latter feels the psychical result of the action to be his own insight, which has only been freed by the influence. In the second basic way of affecting others, a man wishes to find and to further in the soul of the other the disposition toward what he has recognized in himself as the right. Because it is the right, it must also be alive in the microcosm of the other, as one possibility. The other need only be opened out in this potentiality of his; moreover, this opening out takes place not essentially by teaching, but by meeting, by existential communication between someone that is in actual being and someone that is in a process of becoming. The first way has been most powerfully developed in the realm of propaganda, the second in that of education.

The propagandist I have in mind, who imposes himself, is not in the least concerned with the person whom he desires to influence, as a person; various individual qualities are of importance only is so far as he can exploit them to win the other and must get to know them for this purpose. In his indifference to everything personal the propagandist goes a substantial distance beyond the party for which he works. For the party, persons in their difference are of significance because each can be used according to his special qualities in a particular function. It is true that the personal is considered only in respect of the specific use to which it can be put, but within these limits it is recognized in practice. To propaganda as such, on the other hand, individual qualities are rather looked on as a burden, for propaganda is concerned simply with *more*—more members, more adherents, an increasing extent of support. Political methods, where they rule in an extreme form, as here, simply mean winning power over the other by depersonalizing him. This kind of propaganda enters upon different relations with force; it supplements it or replaces it, according to the need or the prospects, but it is in the last analysis nothing but sublimated violence, which has become imperceptible as such. It places men's souls under a pressure which allows the illusion of autonomy. Political methods at their height mean the effective abolition of the human factor.

The educator whom I have in mind lives in a world of individuals, a certain number of whom are always at any one time committed to his care. He sees each of these individuals as in a position to become a unique, single person, and thus the bearer of a special task of existence which can be fulfilled through him and through him alone. He sees every personal life as engaged in such a process of actualization, and he knows from his own experience that the forces making for actualization are all the time involved in a microcosmic struggle with counterforces. He has come to see himself as a helper of the actualizing forces. He knows these forces; they have shaped and they still shape him. Now he puts this person shaped by them at their disposal for a new struggle and a new work. He cannot wish to impose himself, for he believes in the effect of the actualizing forces, that is, he believes that in every man what is right is established in a single and uniquely personal way. No other way may be imposed on a man, but another way, that of the educator, may and must unfold what is right, as in this case it struggles for achievement, and help it to develop.

The propagandist, who imposes himself, does not really believe even in his own cause, for he does not trust it to attain its effect of its own power without his special methods, whose symbols are the loudspeaker and the television advertisement. The educator who unfolds what is there believes in the primal power which has scattered itself, and still scatters itself, in all human beings in order that it may grow up in each man in the special form of that man. He is confident that this growth needs at each moment only that help which is given in meeting, and that he is called to supply that help.

I have illustrated the character of the two basic attitudes and their relation to one another by means of two extremely antithetical examples. But wherever men have dealings with one another, one or the other attitude is to be found in more or less degree.

These two principles of imposing oneself on someone and helping someone to unfold should not be confused with concepts such as arrogance and humility. A man can be arrogant without wishing to impose himself on others, and it is not enough to be humble in order to help another unfold. Arrogance and humility are dispositions of the soul, psychological facts with a moral accent, while imposition and helping to unfold are events between men, anthropological facts which point to an ontology, the ontology of the inherhuman.

In the moral realm Kant expressed the essential principle that one's fellow man must never be thought of and treated merely as a means, but always at the same time as an independent end. The principle is expressed as an 'ought' which is sustained by the idea of human dignity. My point of view, which is near to Kant's in its essential features, has another source and goal. It is concerned with the presuppositions of the interhuman. Man exists anthropologically not in his isolation, but in the completeness of the relation between man and man; what humanity is can be properly grasped only in vital reciprocity. For the proper existence of the interhuman it is necessary, as I have shown, that the semblance not intervene to spoil the relation of personal being to personal being. It is further necessary, as I have also shown, that each one means and makes present the other in his personal being. That neither should wish to impose himself on the other is the third basic presupposition of the interhuman. These presuppositions do not include the demand that one should influence the other in his unfolding; this is, however, an element that is suited to lead to a higher stage of the interhuman.

That there resides in every man the possibility of attaining authentic human existence in the special way peculiar to him can be grasped in the Aristotelian image of entelechy, innate self-realization; but one must note that it is an entelechy of the work of creation. It would be mistaken to speak here of individuation alone. Individuation is only the indispensable personal stamp of all realization of human existence. The self as such is not ultimately the essential, but the meaning of human existence given in creation again and again fulfils itself as self. The help that men give each other in becoming a self leads the life between men to its height.

The dynamic glory of the being of man is first bodily present in the relation between two men each of whom in meaning the other also means the highest to which this person is called, and serves the self-realization of this human life as one true to creation without wishing to impose on the other anything of his own realization.

Genuine Dialogue

We must now summarize and clarify the marks of genuine dialogue.

In genuine dialogue the turning to the partner takes place in all truth, that is, it is a turning of the being. Every speaker 'means' the partner or partners to whom he turns as this personal existence. To 'mean' someone in this connection is at the same time to exercise that degree of making present which is possible to the speaker at that moment. The experiencing senses and the imagining of the real which completes the findings of the senses work together to make the other present as a whole and as a unique being, as the person that he is. But the speaker does not merely perceive the one who is present to him in this way; he receives him as his partner, and that means that he confirms this other being, so far as it is for him to confirm. The true turning of his person to the other includes this confirmation, this acceptance. Of course, such a confirmation does not mean approval; but no matter in what I am against the other, by accepting him as my partner in genuine dialogue I have affirmed him as a person.

Further, if genuine dialogue is to arise, everyone who takes part in it must be willing on each occasion to say what is really in his mind about the subject of the conversation. And that means further that on each occasion he makes the contribution of his spirit without reduction and without shifting his ground. Even men of great integrity are under the illusion that they are not bound to say everything 'they have to say'. But in the great faithfulness which is the climate of genuine dialogue, what I have to say at any one time already has in me the character of something that wishes to be uttered, and I must not keep it back, keep it in myself. It bears for me the unmistakable sign which indicates that it belongs to the common life of the word. Where the dialogical word genuinely exists, it must be given its right by keeping nothing back. To keep nothing back is the exact opposite of unreserved speech. Everything depends on the legitimacy of 'what I have to say'. And of course I must also be intent to raise into an inner word and then into a spoken word what I have to say at this moment but do not yet possess as speech. To speak is both nature and work, something that grows and something that is made, and where it appears dialogically, in the climate of great faithfulness, it has to fulfill ever anew the unity of the two.

Associated with this is that overcoming of semblance to which I have referred. In the atmosphere of genuine dialogue, he who is ruled by the thought of his own effect as the speaker of what he has to speak, has a destructive effect. If instead of what has to be said, I try to bring attention to my *I*, I have irrevocably miscarried what I had to say; it enters the dialogue as a failure, and the dialogue is a failure. Because genuine dialogue is an ontological sphere which is constituted by the authenticity of being, every invasion of semblance must damage it.

But where the dialogue is fulfilled in its being, between partners who have turned to one another in truth, who express themselves without reserve and are free of the desire for semblance, there is brought into being a memorable common fruitfulness which is to be found nowhere else. At such times, at each such time, the word arises in a substantial way between men who have been seized in their depths and opened out by the dynamic of an elemental togetherness. The interhuman opens out what otherwise remains unopened.

This phenomenon is indeed well known in dialogue between two persons; but I have also sometimes experienced it in a dialogue in which several have taken part.

About Easter of 1914 there met a group consisting of representatives of several European nations for a three-day discussion that was intended to be preliminary to further talks.[1] We wanted to discuss together how the catastrophe, which we all believed was imminent, could be avoided. Without our having agreed beforehand on any sort of modalities for our talk, all the presuppositions of genuine dialogue were fulfilled. From the first hour immediacy reigned between all of us, some of whom had just got to know one another; everyone spoke with an unheard-of unreserve, and clearly not

[1] I have set down elsewhere an episode from this meeting. See my essay 'Dialogue' in *Between Man and Man*, especially pp. 4–6.

a single one of the participants was in bondage to semblance. In respect of its purpose the meeting must be described as a failure (though even now in my heart it is still not a certainty that it had to be a failure); the irony of the situation was that we arranged the final discussion for the middle of August, and in the course of events the group was soon broken up. Nevertheless, in the time that followed, not one of the participants doubted that he shared in a triumph of the interhuman.

One more point must be noted. Of course it is not necessary for all who are joined in a genuine dialogue actually to speak; those who keep silent can on occasion be especially important. But each must be determined not to withdraw when the course of the conversation makes it proper for him to say what he has to say. No one, of course, can know in advance what it is that he has to say; genuine dialogue cannot be arranged beforehand. It has indeed its basic order in itself from the beginning, but nothing can be determined, the course is of the spirit, and some discover what they have to say only when they catch the call of the spirit.

But it is also a matter of course that all the participants, without exception, must be of such nature that they are capable of satisfying the presuppositions of genuine dialogue and are ready to do so. The genuineness of the dialogue is called in question as soon as even a small number of those present are felt by themselves and by the others as not being expected to take any active part. Such a state of affairs can lead to very serious problems.

I had a friend whom I account one of the most considerable men of our age. He was a master of conversation, and he loved it: his genuineness as a speaker was evident. But once it happened that he was sitting with two friends and with the three wives, and a conversation arose in which by its nature the women were clearly not joining, although their presence in fact had a great influence. The conversation among the men soon developed into a duel between two of them (I was the third). The other 'duelist', also a friend of mine, was of a noble nature; he too was a man of true conversation, but given more to objective fairness than to the play of the intellect, and a stranger to any controversy. The friend whom I have called a master of conversation did not speak with his usual composure and strength, but he scintillated, he fought, he triumphed. The dialogue was destroyed.

COMMENT

Kierkegaard and Existentialism

The present century has witnessed crises of unparalleled scope and intensity: two world wars, a very severe economic depression, revolutionary movements of tremendous magnitude and fury, the threat of nuclear holocaust. Philosophers have reacted with different degrees of intensity to these world-shaking events. Apart from the Marxists, the existentialists have been the philosophers most responsive. Existentialism, in fact, is a philosophy of crisis—its popularity can be explained largely in these terms. Although Sartre and Camus in France, Heidegger and Jaspers in Germany, and the other existentialist philosophers have been able to agree upon almost nothing else, they are alike in reflecting a time out of joint, when people have been hungry for meaning, for identity, for some roots in existence, for some structure of purpose in human experience, for some protection against anxieties and frustrations.

Certainly the "existentialists" are a strange assortment of figures. Jaspers, for example, is a Protestant, Marcel a Catholic, Buber a religious Jew, Heidegger an agnostic, Sartre an atheist. Their political convictions are no less diverse. As a result, "existentialism" has come to mean so many things that, by itself, it would seem to mean nothing. Nevertheless the existentialists exhibit, as Wittgenstein would say, a "family resemblance." We can best understand this resemblance if we trace the family tree back to its roots in such forerunners as Kierkegaard and Nietzsche. It is Sören Kierkegaard, above all, who is the fountainhead of our contemporary existentialism. His influence, which rapidly increased in the period between the two world wars, has spread beyond the boundaries of the Scandinavian countries, and has largely molded the philosophy of existentialism in Germany, France, Spain, Latin America, and to a lesser degree, the United States.

In the foregoing readings from Kierkegaard there are several themes that are typical of the existentialist movement:

1. EMPHASIS UPON CONCRETE INDIVIDUAL EXISTENCE. Kierkegaard was convinced that his religious and philosophical mission could be fulfilled only through his own personal experience and not through abstract mental processes. He is an existentialist in the sense that his stress is upon the sheer factual existence of the individual. As Master Eckhart, the German mystic, has said:

> That I am a man, this I share with other men. That I see and hear and that I eat and drink is what all animals do likewise. But that I am I is only mine and belongs to me and to nobody else; to no other man nor to an angel nor to God— except inasmuch as I am one with Him.[1]

Every man is an individual. He is "man" in the singular; he is not the abstraction "mankind." He shares many characteristics with other animals and with other men; but there is always a peculiar temperament, a unique blend of talents, a separate and distinctive consciousness. There is always something about me that is never common to you and me. Respect for a person is respect for this core of individuality. It is appreciation of the real person of flesh and blood—the unique *me*.

---

[1] Master Eckhart, *Fragments*, as quoted by Erich Fromm, *Man for Himself* (New York: Holt, Rinehart and Winston, 1947), p. 38.

Individuality for Kierkegaard is opposed to both the stereotypes of mass society and the abstractness of philosophical systems. He detested the anonymity of "the crowd" and every kind of dehumanizing collectivism. "The crowd is untruth," he said again and again. The kind of "truth" that Kierkegaard valued most is realized inwardly in the life of the individual. Hence he had a profound distaste for all *systems* of thought, such as Hegelianism. To exist as an individual is to suffer and to struggle, to develop, to be open to new possibilities, to be incomplete and inconsistent—while a system by its very nature is closed, static, dead, complete. "A logical system is possible," he said, but "an existential system is impossible."[2]

The very titles of Kierkegaard's major works—*Philosophical Fragments* and *Concluding Unscientific Postscript*—suggest the deliberately untidy and fragmentary character of his reflections. He issued a number of his books under pseudonyms, different from book to book, so that he was free to attack his own work under a different pseudonym. He thus avoided even the appearance of trying to construct a single, consistent, systematic body of thought.

2. THE NEED TO MAKE THINGS DIFFICULT. "With everyone engaged everywhere in making things easier," the pseudonymous author Johannes Climacus remarks, "someone was needed to make them difficult again." The passage from which this sentence is taken is a witty piece of fiction, but there is an underlying seriousness about it. The modern world, with its labor-saving devices and pain-killers, its mass stereotypes and oversimplified explanations, has made things too easy. One should face up to the tragic conflicts, paradoxes, and complexities of human existence. Where a rigid scientific rationalism has postulated only one kind of truth—objective scientific truth—and but one kind of good—the value of scientific and technological mastery—someone is needed to stress the truths and values of other modes of experience. Few men have explored more deeply than Kierkegaard the meaning of dread, anguish, alienation, and self-estrangement, "sickness unto death," and the kind of wisdom that can be gleaned from such experiences.

In the "pregnant moment" of crisis, existence and thought are fused into unity, and a person attains, if ever, authentic existence. The individual in a crisis situation may make dramatic and irrevocable choices for which he must assume sole responsibility. One of the persistent themes of existentialism, from Pascal to Sartre, is the need and reality of choice. Sartre speaks as if every action expresses an individual choice, whereas Kierkegaard speaks more often of the choice of a way of life, aesthetic or moral or religious. This transition from one way of life to another is conceived as a kind of conversion, dramatic and sometimes catastrophic. But both Kierkegaard and Sartre agree that people do not have fixed natures or predetermined roles.

---

[2] *Concluding Unscientific Postscript*, in Robert Bretall, *A Kierkegaard Anthology* (Princeton University Press, 1946), p. 196.

3. THE CLAIM THAT TRUTH IS SUBJECTIVITY. Kierkegaard's view of truth is based upon the distinction between what we believe and how we believe. Objectively the interest is focused upon the object of belief, subjectively upon the attitude of the believer. When it comes to matters of scientific truth, it is the object as verifiable that is of primary concern. But Kierkegaard is not much interested in objective truth in this sense. He is primarily concerned with an existential relationship of the individual with God. When it comes to this, what is most important is an intense spirituality. Through faith the individual appropriates in passionate inwardness the eternal truth of God's existence. What is sought is not scientific verification or rational understanding, which in this instance is impossible, but something that passes understanding, namely, a faith so intense that it amounts to salvation. With this kind of "truth" in mind, Kierkegaard proclaims his thesis: truth is subjectivity.

The reader may feel that such a conception of truth is highly paradoxical if not downright contradictory. To call "true" the existential status of the individual in believing may seem to be an abuse of language. In a revealing passage Kierkegaard declares: "It is impossible to express with more intensive inwardness the principle that subjectivity is truth, than when subjectivity is in the first instance untruth, and yet subjectivity is the truth,"[3] In other words, a superstition believed in a certain manner is subjectively "true," regardless of its objective falsity.

Almost everything that Kierkegaard has written is highly controversial. Before committing himself *pro* or *con* the reader might ponder such questions as these: Is Kierkegaard's emphasis upon will and feeling, rather than reason or the scientific method, exaggerated? In his preference for passionate participation and commitment, does he undervalue a disinterested analytical attitude? Does he argue inconsistently both that ultimate choice is criterionless and that the choice of a religious way of life is more correct than any other? Is he a one-sided romanticist, and in that sense a reductionist, despite his proposal to "make things difficult"? In his preference for "existence" over "essence," is he begging the question as to what is "really real"? Does he undervalue the ability to sense the essential and to formulate it in something like a definition? These questions can best be answered if the point of view of Kierkegaard is critically compared with the views of the philosophers studied in the preceding chapters.

We have said that Kierkegaard has little use for the "crowd" or the "public," and that his emphasis is almost invariably on the "single one." In this respect he has struck a note that has reverberated throughout the present century. Human beings have been threatened or abused to a shocking degree by dehumanizing bureaucracies and all-powerful totalitarian states. All of the existentialists join in protest against this mass degradation. But here too there is ground for question or criticism of Kierkegaard's extreme individualism. "If ever a person was self-centered, it was Kierkegaard," H. J. Paton has declared: "He hardly ever thinks

---

[3] *Concluding Unscientific Postscript* (Princeton University Press, 1946), p. 191.

of anyone but himself."[4] Of himself in relation to God, we might add. This pre-occupation with individual religious salvation can be challenged by an attack on either theism or individualism. Existentialists such as Nietzsche and Sartre have attacked the theism, existentialists such as Marcel and Buber have attacked the individualism.

Perhaps Buber, more than any other existentialist, exemplifies the breakaway from a narrow individualism to interpersonal fellowship. To this we shall now turn.

I and Thou

Buber's theory, as set forth in *I and Thou*, is poetic and cryptic. Since the book is difficult in style, I have reproduced instead his essay "Elements of the Inter-human." But it will be helpful in understanding the latter to review some of the central concepts of *I and Thou*.

Basic to his thought is the distinction between two types of relation. He states this distinction in enigmatic language:

> To man the world is twofold, in accordance with his twofold attitude. The attitude of man is twofold, in accordance with the twofold nature of the primary words which he speaks. The primary words are not isolated words, but combined words. The one primary word is the combination *I-Thou*. The other primary word is the combination *I-It*; wherein, without a change in the primary word, one of the words *He* and *She* can replace *it*. Hence the *I* of man is also twofold. For the *I* of the primary word *I-Thou* is a different *I* from that of the primary word *I-It*.[5]

Buber's meaning is this: people adopt a twofold interpretation of their world, according to the "primary word" that they speak. To speak the word is not to use one's vocal cords but to stand before existence and to comport oneself in a certain way. In the I-It relation, I regard the object, even if it be a He or a She, as if it were a mere thing. I stand apart from it in order coldly to scrutinize and exploit it: to observe, measure, categorize, and manipulate it—to bend it to my advantage. In this relation there is no reciprocity: the relation is that of master to instrument. If I treat someone as an *It*, I do not acknowledge *his* right to treat me as an *It* in return. In the I-Thou relation, on the other hand, one's essential being is in direct and sympathetic contact with another essential being. The Thou is cherished for what you are in your "singleness"—not as an *object* but as a *presence,* not as a *type* but as an *individual,* not as a *means* but as an *end*. The I-Thou relation is reciprocal: I-Thou implies Thou-I. I not only give but receive; I not only speak but listen; I not only respond but invite

[4] *The Modern Predicament* (London: George Allen & Unwin, 1955), p. 120.

[5] *I and Thou* (New York: Charles Scribner's Sons, 1937), p. 3.

response. "My *Thou* affects me, as I affect it."[6] The *I* is constituted and remade in this act of meeting: "Through the *Thou* a man becomes I."[7]

Not only does the "Thou" differ from the "It," but the "I" in the first relation differs fundamentally from the "I" in the second. The first "I" is a real person in a world of persons; the second is a depersonalized individual in a world of things. A person is fully a person only in relation to other persons. You are not a real person so far as you regard others as things, as mere objects or implements. The real meeting between person and person comes about only when each regards the other as an end. This is not always possible. To live, we need to use things, and what is more to the point, to use human beings. But in a real community, the means-relation between individuals, the "I-it" relation, is subordinated to the ends-relation between persons, the "I-Thou" relation. "Only men who are capable of truly saying *Thou* to one another can truly say *We* with one another."[8]

The world of the I-Thou and the world of the I-It are not sharply separated. "Every *Thou* in our world must become an *It*."[9] There is nothing wrong with such impersonal relations so long as they remain subordinate to the personal. But "in our age the I-It relation, gigantically swollen, has usurped, practically uncontested, the mastery and the rule. The I of this relation, an I that . . . is unable to say Thou, unable to meet a being essentially, is the lord of the hour."[10]

The essay, "Elements of the Interhuman," develops some of the implications of *I and Thou*. In particular Buber delineates "the sphere of the between." He means by this phrase "the relation between man and man"—a person-to-person relation of genuine mutuality. It stands in sharp contrast to the depersonalization of relations in massive, bureaucratic organizations. The "interhuman" is the I-Thou relation as embodied in the "dialogue" between person and person. To achieve this kind of authentic relationship a person must *be* and not *seem*. The significance of this duality between being and seeming is discussed in the essay.

"Interhuman": Its Implications

The question can be asked whether Buber's ideal of the "interhuman" represents a viable alternative to the social rootlessness of individualism and the mass anonymity of collectivism. He contends that the dilemma, "individualism or collectivism," no longer appears inescapable, and that the choice it presents no longer appears attractive. Neither horn of the dilemma can provide the genuine freedom and realization that each promises, and there is a *third* alternative that avoids the extremes and distortions of the other two. "The essential human

---

[6] *I and Thou*, p. 15.

[7] *I and Thou*, p. 28.

[8] *I and Thou*, p. 176.

[9] *I and Thou*, p. 16.

[10] *Eclipse of God*, translated by Maurice S. Friedman (New York: Harper and Brothers, 1952), p. 166.

reality is neither one of individual nor of collective existence," he declares, "but lies in the relation between man and man, and is a matter between me and you."[11] Here, then, is the ideal of a fraternity whose roots are personal rather than abstract and impersonal. It is based upon free mutuality rather than like-mindedness. It excludes any relation of dominance or exploitation, and it heals the homelessness of the alienated individual. Clearly, modern civilization is desperately in need of reorientation. The student might well consider whether this reorientation should be around Buber's concept of the "interhuman."

A second question is whether the basis of reorientation should be theistic or purely humanistic. Perhaps this question can best be posed if we contrast Buber with Ludwig Feuerbach (1804–1872), a German philosopher who defected from Hegelian idealism to a naturalistic view of man and history. Both he and Buber espoused an existentialist interpretation of love and fellowship, but Feuerbach was an atheist and Buber a theist. In a typical passage Feuerbach declared:

> The other is my thou—the relation being reciprocal—my *alter ego*, man objective to me, the revelation of my own nature, the eye seeing itself. In another I first have the consciousness of humanity; through him I first learn, I first feel, that I am a man: in my love for him it is first clear to me that he belongs to me and I to him, that we two cannot be without each other, that only community constitutes humanity.[12]

Buber has hailed this doctrine as "the Copernican revolution of modern thought," declaring: "I myself in my youth was given a decisive impetus by Feuerbach."[13] Buber, however, clings to theism, as opposed to atheistic humanism. The love of a person for a person and the love of a person for God, he insists, are interdependent. "I-Thou finds its highest intensity and transfiguration in religious reality, in which unlimited Being becomes, as absolute person, my partner."[14] Human beings relate themselves most deeply to each other by thus relating themselves to an eternal Thou. But "real relationship with God cannot be achieved on earth if real relationship to the world and mankind are lacking."[15] The meeting with God is direct and mutual; it is a totality act of personality; it requires that we meet human beings and the world in the same total way. "Meet the

---

[11] Buber's Foreword to E. A. Gutkind, *Community and Environment* (London: C. A. Watts & Co., 1953), p. viii.

[12] Feuerbach, *The Essence of Christianity* (New York: C. Blanchard, 1855), p. 208.

[13] *Between Man and Man* (Boston: Beacon Press, 1955), p. 148.

[14] *Eclipse of God*, p. 61.

[15] *At the Turning* (Farrar, Strauss, and Cudahy, 1952), p. 39.

world with the fullness of your being, and you shall meet God. . . . If you wish to believe, love!"[16] Feuerbach, in contrast, maintained that we have been unfaithful to natural love because we have been distracted by religious supernaturalism. Love as a *human* bond must now come into its own. The transition from theism to humanism, he declared, is destined to be the turning point of human history. Which philosopher, Feuerbach or Buber, is more nearly right?

[16] *At the Turning,* p. 44.

Part Two

THE BASIS
OF MORALITY

In Part Two we shall deal with ethics. The fundamental concepts of ethics are *good* and *bad*, and *right* and *wrong*. Although such words as *good* and *right* can be used in a nonmoral sense, we shall be concerned with their moral usage. Both are closely related to *ought—good* is what ought to exist, and *right* is what ought to be done.

The readers of this book have already been introduced to ethics in Chapter 1. Socrates, in the *Apology*, was criticizing the ethics of custom and expediency and defending the ideal of wisdom. In Part Three, we shall again meet Socrates, this time as a character in Plato's *Republic*. In this dialogue, Socrates maintains that good is the harmonious development of all parts of the soul under the control of reason, and that the good of the state is the harmonious development of all classes under the control of wise men. Some readers of this book will prefer to consider the selections from the *Republic* in connection with the ethical problems of Part Two rather than the social problems of Part Three.

10

Reason and Virtue

ARISTOTLE (384 B.C.–322 B.C.)

Aristotle was born in Stagira, a town in Macedonia colonized by Greeks. At the time of his birth, Socrates had·been dead for fifteen years and Plato was thirty-three. Aristotle's father Nichomachus, having achieved some renown, became court physician to King Amyntas II of Macedonia. Refusing to follow his father's profession, Aristotle at the age of eighteen migrated to Athens, where he lived for twenty years as a member of Plato's school, the Academy. When the master died, Aristotle left Athens to spend four years on the coast of Asia Minor, engaged mainly in biological research. During this period he married, and his wife eventually bore him a daughter. Subsequently he married a second time and had two sons, although one of them was adopted.

Meanwhile Philip, the son of Amyntas, having become King of Macedonia, invited Aristotle to take charge of the education of his son Alexander, then thirteen years old. In consequence of accepting this invitation, Aristotle must have acquired intimate knowledge of court affairs, but he makes no mention of the great Macedonian empire built up by Philip and Alexander the Great. Perhaps he was too close to kings to be greatly impressed by courtly glitter.

He stayed with Philip for seven years, until the monarch's death, and lingered at the court for about a year after Alexander's accession to the throne. Then he returned to Athens to resume his philosophical career. At this time the Academy was being reorganized, and Xenocrates, a second-rate philosopher, was made head. Evidently disappointed at the choice, Aristotle withdrew and founded a school of his own, the Lyceum, which he directed for twelve years. It was during this period that he was his most productive.

Aristotle's reputation and the prosperity of his school suffered from the anti-Macedonian reaction which took place after Alexander's death in 323 B.C. Accused of impiety, Aristotle, unlike Socrates, fled to the island of Euboea, vowing that he would not "give the Athenians a second chance of sinning against philosophy." A year later, in 322 B.C., he died of a stomach disease, at the age of sixty-three.

His writings, as they have come down to us, lack the beauty of Plato's dialogues and are without wit, personal charm, or poetry. He also wrote popular works, including dialogues, which were praised by Cicero for "the incredible flow and sweetness of their diction"; but like many other ancient compositions, these dialogues have been lost. The works that remain touch upon almost every phase of human knowledge, and they establish Aristotle's reputation not only as an extremely versatile philosopher but as an accomplished biologist.

Ethics

1. [The Nature of Happiness]

[*Aristotle begins, in a way characteristic of his method, with a generalization which, if accepted, will lead to a more exact account of his subject. It is a generalization which is fundamental to his philosophy and in his own mind there is no doubt about the truth of it.*

The Ethics of Aristotle, *translated by J. A. K. Thomson, George Allen and Unwin, London, and Barnes and Noble, New York, 1953. Reprinted by permission. The sentences in italics are explanatory comments by the translator except where initialed "M.R."*

Yet he is not at this point asserting its truth. He is content to state a position which he has found reason to hold. It may be defined in some such words as these: The good is that at which all things aim. *If we are to understand this, we must form to ourselves a clear notion of what is meant by an aim or, in more technical language, an "end." The first chapter of the* Ethics *is concerned with making the notion clear.*]

It is thought that every activity, artistic or scientific, in fact every deliberate action or pursuit, has for its object the attainment of some good. We may therefore assent to the view which has been expressed that "the good" is "that at which all things aim." . . . Since modes of action involving the practiced hand and the instructed brain are numerous, the number of their ends is proportionately large. For instance, the end of medical science is health; of military science, victory; of economic science, wealth. All skills of that kind which come under a single "faculty"— a skill in making bridles or any other part of a horse's gear comes under the faculty or art of horsemanship, while horsemanship itself and every branch of military practice comes under the art of war, and in like manner other arts and techniques are subordinate to yet others—in all these the ends of the master arts are to be preferred to those of the subordinate skills, for it is the former that provide the motive for pursuing the latter. . . .

Now if there is an end which as moral agents we seek for its own sake, and which is the cause of our seeking all the other ends—if we are not to go on choosing one act for the sake of another, thus landing ourselves in an infinite progression with the result that desire will be frustrated and ineffectual —it is clear that this must be the good, that is the absolutely good. May we not then argue from this that a knowledge of the good is a great advantage to us in the conduct of our lives? Are we not more likely to hit the mark if we have a target? If this be true, we must do our best to get at least a rough idea of what the good really is, and which of the sciences, pure or applied, is concerned with the business of achieving it.

[*Ethics is a branch of politics. That is to say, it is the duty of the statesman to create for the citizen the best possible opportunity of living the good life. It will be seen that the effect of this injunction is not to degrade morality but to moralize politics. The modern view that "you cannot make men better by act of parliament" would have been repudiated by Aristotle as certainly as by Plato and indeed by ancient philosophers in general.*]

Now most people would regard the good as the end pursued by that study which has most authority and control over the rest. Need I say that this is the science of politics? It is political science that prescribes what subjects are to be taught in states, which of these the different sections of the population are to learn, and up to what point. We see also that the faculties which obtain most regard come under this science: for example, the art of war, the management of property, the ability to state a case. Since, therefore, politics makes use of the other practical sciences, and lays it down besides what we must do and what we must not do, its end must include theirs. And that end, in politics as well as in ethics, can only be the good for man. For even if the good of the community coincides with that of the individual, the good of the community is clearly a greater and more perfect good both to get and to keep. This is not to deny that the good of the individual is worth while. But what is good for a nation or a city has a higher, a diviner, quality.

Such being the matters we seek to investigate, the investigation may fairly be represented as the study of politics. . . .

life, liberty, and the pursuit of Happiness

[. . . *Let us consider what is the end of political science. For want of a better word we call it "Happiness." People are agreed on the word but not on its meaning.*]

. . . Since every activity involving some acquired skill or some moral decision aims at some good, what do we take to be the end of politics—what is the supreme good attainable in our actions? Well, so far as the name goes there is pretty general agreement. "It is happiness," say both intellectuals and the unsophisticated, meaning by "happiness" living well or faring well. But when it comes to saying in what happiness consists, opinions differ and the account given by the generality of mankind is not at all like that given by the philosophers. The masses take it to be something plain and tangible, like pleasure or money or social standing. Some maintain that it is one of these, some that it is another, and the same man will change his opinion about it more than once. When he has caught an illness he will say that it is health, and when he is hard up he will say that it is money. Conscious that they are out of their depths in such discussions, most people are impressed by anyone who pontificates and says something that is over their heads. Now it would no doubt be a waste of time to examine all these opinions; enough if we consider those which are most in evidence or have something to be said for them. Among these we shall have to discuss the view held by some that, over and above particular goods like those I have just mentioned, there is another which is good in itself and the cause of what-

ever goodness there is in all these others. . . .

[*A man's way of life may afford a clue to his genuine views upon the nature of happiness. It is therefore worth our while to glance at the different types of life.*]

. . . There is a general assumption that the manner of a man's life is a clue to what he on reflection regards as the good—in other words happiness. Persons of low tastes (always in the majority) hold that it is pleasure. Accordingly they ask for nothing better than the sort of life which consists in having a good time. (I have in mind the three well-known types of life—that just mentioned, that of the man of affairs, that of the philosophic student.) The utter vulgarity of the herd of men comes out in their preference for the sort of existence a cow leads. Their view would hardly get a respectful hearing, were it not that those who occupy great positions sympathize with a monster of sensuality like Sardanapalus. The gentleman, however, and the man of affairs identify the good with honor, which may fairly be described as the end which men pursue in political or public life. Yet honor is surely too superficial a thing to be the good we are seeking. Honor depends more on those who confer than on him who receives it, and we cannot but feel that the good is something personal and almost inseparable from its possessor. Again, why do men seek honor? Surely in order to confirm the favorable opinion they have formed of themselves. It is at all events by intelligent men who know them personally that they seek to be honored. And for what? For their moral qualities.

The inference is clear; public men prefer virtue to honor. It might therefore seem reasonable to suppose that virtue rather than honor is the end pursued in the life of the public servant. But clearly even virtue cannot be quite the end. It is possible, most people think, to possess virtue while you are asleep, to possess it without acting under its influence during any portion of one's life. Besides, the virtuous man may meet with the most atrocious luck or ill-treatment; and nobody, who was not arguing for argument's sake, would maintain that a man with an existence of that sort was "happy." . . . The third type of life is the "contemplative," and this we shall discuss later.

As for the life of the business man, it does not give him much freedom of action. Besides, wealth obviously is not the good we seek, for the sole purpose it serves is to provide the means of getting something else. So far as that goes, the ends we have already mentioned would have a better title to be considered the good, for they are desired on their own account. But in fact even their claim must be disallowed. We may say that they have furnished the ground for many arguments, and leave the matter at that. . . .

[*What then is the good? If it is what all men in the last resort aim at, it must be happiness. And that for two reasons:* (1) *happiness is everything it needs to be,* (2) *it has everything it needs to have.*]

. . . [The good] is one thing in medicine and another in strategy, and so in the other branches of human skill. We must inquire, then, what is the good which is the end common to all of them. Shall we say it is that for the sake of which everything else is done? In medicine this is health, in military science victory, in architecture a building, and so on—different ends in different arts; every consciously directed activity has an end for the sake of which everything that it does is done. This end may be described as its good. Consequently, if there be some one thing which is the end of all things consciously done, this will be the double good; or, if there be more than one end, then it will be all of these. . . .

In our actions we aim at more ends than one—that seems to be certain—but, since we choose some (wealth, for example, or flutes and tools or instruments generally) as means to something else, it is clear that not all of them are ends in the full sense of the word, whereas the good, that is the supreme good, is surely such an end. Assuming then that there is some one thing which alone is an end beyond which there are no further ends, we may call *that* the good of which we are in search. If there be more than one such final end, the good will be that end which has the highest degree of finality. An object pursued for its own sake possesses a higher degree of finality than one pursued with an eye to something else. A corollary to that is that a thing which is never chosen as a means to some remoter object has a higher degree of finality than things which are chosen both as ends in themselves and as means to such ends. We may conclude, then, that something which is always chosen for its own sake and never for the sake of something else is without qualification a final end.

What defines happiness?

Now happiness more than anything else appears to be just such an end, for we always choose it for its own sake and never for the sake of some other thing. It is different with honor, pleasure, intelligence and good qualities generally. We choose them indeed for their own sake in the sense that we should be glad to have them irrespective of any advantage which might accrue from them. But we also choose them for the sake of our happiness in the belief that they will be instrumental in promoting that. On the other hand nobody chooses happiness as a means of achieving them or anything else whatsoever than just happiness.

The same conclusion would seem to follow from another consideration. It is a generally accepted view that the final good is self-sufficient. By "self-sufficient" is meant not what is sufficient for oneself living the life of a solitary but includes parents, wife and children, friends and fellow-citizens in general. For man is a social animal. . . . A self-sufficient thing, then, we take to be one which on its own footing tends to make life desirable and lacking in nothing. And we regard happiness as such a thing. . . .

[*But we desire a clearer definition of happiness. The way to this may be prepared by a discussion of what is meant by the "function" of a man.*]

But no doubt people will say, "To call happiness the highest good is a truism. We want a more distinct account of what it is." We might arrive at this if we could grasp what is meant by the "function" of a human being. If we take a flutist or a sculptor or any craftsman—in fact any class of men at all

who have some special job or profession —we find that his special talent and excellence comes out in that job, and this is his function. The same thing will be true of man simply as man—that is of course if "man" does have a function. But is it likely that joiners and shoemakers have certain functions or specialized activities, while man as such has none but has been left by Nature a functionless being? Seeing that eye and hand and foot and every one of our members has some obvious function, must we not believe that in like manner a human being has a function over and above these particular functions? Then what exactly is it? The mere act of living is not peculiar to man—we find it even in the vegetable kingdom—and what we are looking for is something peculiar to him. We must therefore exclude from our definition the life that manifests itself in mere nurture and growth. A step higher should come the life that is confined to experiencing sensations. But that we see is shared by horses, cows and the brute creation as a whole. We are left, then, with a life concerning which we can make two statements. First, it belongs to the rational part of man. Secondly, it finds expression in actions. The rational part may be either active or passive: passive in so far as it follows the dictates of reasoning. A similar distinction can be drawn within the rational life; that is to say, the reasonable element in it may be active or passive. Let us take it that what we are concerned with here is the reasoning power in action, for it will be generally allowed that when we speak of "reasoning" we really mean *exercising* our reasoning faculties. (This seems the more correct use of the word.)

Now let us assume for the moment the truth of the following propositions. (*a*) The function of a man is the exercise of his non-corporeal faculties or "soul" in accordance with, or at least not divorced from, a rational principle. (*b*) The function of an individual and of a *good* individual in the same class—a harp player, for example, and a good harp player, and so through the classes—is generically the same, except that we must add superiority in accomplishment to the function, the function of the harp player being merely to play on the harp, while the function of the good harp player is to play on it well. (*c*) The function of man is a certain form of life, namely an activity of the soul exercised in combination with a rational principle or reasonable ground of action. (*d*) The function of a good man is to exert such activity well. (*e*) A function is performed well when performed in accordance with the excellence proper to it.—If these assumptions are granted, we conclude that the good for man is "an activity of soul in accordance with goodness" or (on the supposition that there may be more than one form of goodness) "in accordance with the best and most complete form of goodness."

[*Happiness is more than momentary bliss.*]

There is another condition of happiness; it cannot be achieved in less than a complete lifetime. One swallow does not make a summer; neither does one fine day. And one day, or indeed any brief period of felicity, does not make a man entirely and perfectly happy. . . .

[. . . *Our first principle—our defini-tion of happiness—should be tested not only by the rules of logic but also by the application to it of current opinions on the subject.*]

So we must examine our first principle not only logically, that is as a conclusion from premises, but also in the light of what is currently said about it. For if a thing be true, the evidence will be found in harmony with it; and, if it be false, the evidence is quickly shown to be discordant with it.

But first a note about "goods." They have been classified as (*a*) external, (*b*) of the soul, (*c*) of the body. Of these we may express our belief that goods of the soul are the best and are most properly designated as "good." Now according to our definition happiness is an expression of the soul in considered actions, and that definition seems to be confirmed by this belief, which is not only an old popular notion but is accepted by philosophers. We are justified, too, in saying that the end consists in certain acts or activities, for this enables us to count it among goods of the soul and not among external goods. We may also claim that our description of the happy man as the man who lives or fares well chimes in with our definition. For happiness has pretty much been stated to be a form of such living or faring well. Again, our definition seems to include the elements detected in the various analyses of happiness—virtue, practical wisdom, speculative wisdom, or a combination of these, or one of them in more or less intimate association with pleasure. All these definitions have their supporters, while still others are for adding material prosperity to the conditions of a happy life.

Some of these views are popular convictions of long standing; others are set forth by a distinguished minority. It is reasonable to think that neither the mass of men nor the sages are mistaken altogether, but that on this point or that, or indeed on most points, there is justice in what they say.

Now our definition of happiness as an activity in accordance with virtue is so far in agreement with that of those who say that it *is* virtue, that such an activity *involves* virtue. But of course it makes a great difference whether we think of the highest good as consisting in the *possession* or in the *exercise* of virtue. It is possible for a disposition to goodness to exist in a man without anything coming of it; he might be asleep or in some other way have ceased to exercise his function of a man. But that is not possible with the activity in our definition. For in "doing well" the happy man will of necessity *do*. Just as at the Olympic Games it is not the best-looking or the strongest men present who are crowned with victory but competitors—the successful competitors, so in the arena of human life the honors and rewards fall to those who show their good qualities in action.

Observe, moreover, that the life of the actively good is inherently pleasant. Pleasure is a psychological experience, and every man finds that pleasant for which he has a liking—"fond of" so and so is the expression people use. For example, a horse is a source of pleasure to a man who is fond of horses, a show to a man who is fond of sight-seeing. In the same way just actions are a source of pleasure to a man who likes to see justice done, and good actions in general to one who likes goodness. Now the mass of men do not follow any consistent plan in the pursuit of their pleasures, because their pleasures are not inherently pleasurable. But men of more elevated tastes and sentiments find pleasure in things which are in their own nature pleasant, for instance virtuous actions, which are pleasant in themselves and not merely to such men. So their life does not need to have pleasure fastened about it like a necklace, but possesses it as a part of itself. We may go further and assert that he is no good man who does not find pleasure in noble deeds. Nobody would admit that a man is just, unless he takes pleasure in just actions; or liberal, unless he takes pleasure in acts of liberality; and so with the other virtues. Grant this, and you must grant that virtuous actions are a source of pleasure in themselves. And surely they are also both good and noble, and that always in the highest degree, if we are to accept, as accept we must, the judgment of the good man about them, he judging in the way I have described. Thus, happiness is the best, the noblest, the most delightful thing in the world, and in it meet all those qualities which are separately enumerated in the inscription upon the temple at Delos:

Justice is loveliest, and health is best,
And sweetest to obtain is heart's desire.

All these good qualities inhere in the activities of the virtuous soul, and it is these, or the best of them, which we say constitute happiness.

For all that those are clearly right who, as I remarked, maintain the necessity to a happy life of an addition in the form of material goods. It is difficult, if not impossible, to engage in noble enterprises without money to spend on them; many can only be performed through friends, or wealth, or political influence. There are also certain advantages, such as the possession of honored ancestors or children, or personal beauty, the absence of which takes the bloom from our felicity. For you cannot quite regard a man as happy if he be very ugly to look at, or of humble origin, or alone in the world and childless, or—what is probably worse—with children or friends who have not a single good quality. . . .

[*Our definition of happiness compels us to consider the nature of virtue. But before we can do this we must have some conception of how the human soul is constituted. It will serve our purpose to take over (for what it is worth) the current psychology which divides the soul into "parts."*]

Happiness, then, being an activity of the soul in conformity with perfect goodness, it follows that we must examine the nature of goodness. . . . The goodness we have to consider is human goodness. This—I mean human goodness or (if you prefer to put it that way) human happiness—was what we set out to find. By human goodness is meant not fineness of physique but a right condition of the soul, and by happiness a condition of the soul. That being so, it is evident that the statesman ought to have some inkling of psychology, just as the doctor who is to specialize in diseases of the eye must have a general knowledge of physiology. Indeed, such a general background is even more necessary for the statesman in view of the fact that his science is of a higher order than the doctor's. Now the best kind of doctor takes a good deal of trouble to acquire a knowledge of the human body as a whole. Therefore the statesman should also be a psychologist and study the soul with an eye to his profession. Yet he will do so only as far as his own problems make it necessary; to go into greater detail on the subject would hardly be worth the labor spent on it.

Psychology has been studied elsewhere and some of the doctrines stated there may be accepted as adequate for our present purpose and used by us here. The soul is represented as consisting of two parts, a rational and an irrational. . . . As regards the irrational part there is one subdivision of it which appears to be common to all living things, and this we may designate as having a "vegetative" nature, by which I mean that it is the cause of nutrition and growth, since one must assume the existence of some such vital force in all things that assimilate food. . . . Now the excellence peculiar to this power is evidently common to the whole of animated nature and not confined to man. This view is supported by the admitted fact that the vegetative part of us is particularly active in sleep, when the good and the bad are hardest to distinguish. . . . Such a phenomenon would be only natural, for sleep is a cessation of that function on the operation of which depends the goodness or badness of the soul. . . . But enough of this, let us say no more about the nutritive part of the soul, since it forms no portion of goodness in the specifically *human* character.

But there would seem to be another constituent of the soul which, while irrational, contains an element of rationality. It may be observed in the types of men we call "continent" and "incontinent." They have a principle—a rational element in their souls—which we commend, because it encourages them to perform the best actions in the right way. But such natures appear at the same time to contain an irrational element in active opposition to the rational. In paralytic cases it often happens that when the patient wills to move his limbs to the right they swing instead to the left. Exactly the same thing may happen to the soul; the impulses of the incontinent man carry him in the opposite direction from that towards which he was aiming. The only difference is that, where the body is concerned, we see the uncontrolled limb, while the erratic impulse we do not see. Yet this should not prevent us from believing that besides the rational an irrational principle exists running opposite and counter to the other. . . . Yet, as I said, it is not altogether irrational; at all events it submits to direction in the continent man, and may be assumed to be still more amenable to reason in the "temperate" and in the brave man, in whose moral make-up there is nothing which is at variance with reason.

We have, then, this clear result. The irrational part of the soul, like the soul itself, consists of two parts. The first of these is the vegetative, which has nothing rational about it at all. The second is that from which spring the appetites and desire in general; and this does in a way participate in reason, seeing that it is submissive and obedient to it. . . .

That the irrational element in us need not be heedless of the rational is proved by the fact that we find admonition, indeed every form of censure and exhortation, not ineffective. It may be, however, that we ought to speak of the appetitive part of the soul as rational, too. In that event it will rather be the rational part that is divided in two, one division rational in the proper sense of the word and in its nature, the other in the derivative sense in which we speak of a child as "listening to reason" in the person of its father.

These distinctions within the soul supply us with a classification of the virtues. Some are called "intellectual," as wisdom, intelligence, prudence. Others are "moral," as liberality and temperance. When we are speaking of a man's *character* we do not describe him as wise or intelligent but as gentle or temperate. Yet we praise a wise man, too, on the ground of his "disposition" or settled habit of acting wisely. The dispositions so praised are what we mean by "virtues."

2. [Moral Goodness]

[. . . *We have to ask what moral virtue or goodness is. It is a confirmed disposition to act rightly, the disposition being itself formed by a continuous series of right actions.*]

Virtue, then, is of two kinds, intellectual and moral. Of these the intellectual is in the main indebted to teaching for its production and growth, and this calls for time and experience. Moral goodness, on the other hand, is the child of habit, from which it has got its very name, ethics being derived from *ethos,* "habit." . . . This is an indication that none of the moral virtues is implanted in us by nature, since nothing that nature creates can be taught by habit to change the direction of its development. For instance a stone, the natural tendency of which is to fall down, could never, however often you threw it up in the air, be trained to go in that direction. No more can you train fire to burn downwards. Nothing in fact, if the law of its being is to behave in one way, can be habituated to behave in another. The moral virtues, then, are produced in us neither *by* Nature nor *against* Nature. Nature, indeed, prepares in us the ground for their reception, but their complete formation is the product of habit.

Consider again these powers or faculties with which Nature endows us. We acquire the ability to use them before we do use them. The senses provide us with a good illustration of this truth. We have not acquired the sense of sight from repeated acts of seeing, or the sense of hearing from repeated acts of hearing. It is the other way round. We had these senses before we used them, we did not acquire them as a result of using them. But the moral virtues we do acquire by first exercising them. The same is true of the arts and crafts in general. The craftsman has to learn how to make things, but he learns in the process of making them. So men become builders by building, harp players by playing the harp. By a similar process we become just by performing just actions, temperate by performing temperate actions, brave by performing brave actions. Look at what happens in political societies—it confirms our view.

We find legislators seeking to make good men of their fellows by making good behavior habitual with them. . . .

We may sum it all up in the generalization, "Like activities produce like dispositions." This makes it our duty to see that our activities have the right character, since the differences of quality in them are repeated in the dispositions that follow in their train. So it is a matter of real importance whether our early education confirms us in one set of habits or another. It would be nearer the truth to say that it makes a very great difference indeed, in fact all the difference in the world. . . .

[*There is one way of discovering whether we are in full possession of a virtue or not. We possess it if we feel pleasure in its exercise; indeed, it is just with pleasures and pains that virtue is concerned.*]

We may use the pleasure (or pain) that accompanies the exercise of our dispositions as an index of how far they have established themselves. A man is temperate who abstaining from bodily pleasures finds this abstinence pleasant; if he finds it irksome, he is intemperate. Again, it is the man who encounters danger gladly, or at least without painful sensations, who is brave; the man who has these sensations is a coward. In a word, moral virtue has to do with pains and pleasures. There are a number of reasons for believing this. (1) Pleasure has a way of making us do what is disgraceful; pain deters us from doing what is right and fine. Hence the importance—I quote Plato—of having been brought up to find pleasure and pain in the right things. True education is just such a training. (2) The virtues operate with actions and emotions, each of which is accompanied by pleasure or pain. This is only another way of saying that virtue has to do with pleasures and pains. (3) Pain is used as an instrument of punishment. For in her remedies Nature works by opposites, and pain can be remedial. (4) When any disposition finds its complete expression it is, as we noted, in dealing with just those things by which it is its nature to be made better or worse, and which constitute the sphere of its operations. Now when men become bad it is under the influence of pleasures and pains when they seek the wrong ones among them, or seek them at the wrong time, or in the wrong manner, or in any of the wrong forms which such offenses may take; and in seeking the wrong pleasures and pains they shun the right. . . .

So far, then, we have got this result. Moral goodness is a quality disposing us to act in the best way when we are dealing with pleasures and pains, while vice is one which leads us to act in the worst way when we deal with them. . . .

[*We have now to state the "differentia" of virtue. Virtue is a disposition; but how are we to distinguish it from other dispositions? We may say that it is such a disposition as enables the good man to perform his function well. And he performs it well when he avoids the extremes and chooses the mean in actions and feelings.*]

. . . Excellence of whatever kind affects that of which it is the excellence in two ways. (1) It produces a good state in it. (2) It enables it to perform its function well. Take eyesight. The goodness of your eye is not only that which makes your eye good, it is also that which makes it function well. Or take the case of a horse. The goodness of a horse makes him a good horse, but it also makes him good at running, carrying a rider and facing the enemy. Our proposition, then, seems to be true, and it enables us to say that virtue in a man will be the disposition which (*a*) makes him a good man, (*b*) enables him to perform his function well. . . .

Every form . . . of applied knowledge, when it performs its function well, looks to the mean and works to the standard set by that. It is because people feel this that they apply the *cliché*, "You couldn't add anything to it or take anything from it" to an artistic masterpiece, the implication being that too much and too little alike destroy perfection, while the mean preserves it. Now if this be so, and if it be true, as we say, that good craftsmen work to the standard of the mean, then, since goodness like nature is more exact and of a higher character than any art, it follows that goodness is the quality that hits the mean. By "goodness" I mean goodness of moral character, since it is moral goodness that deals with feelings and actions, and it is in them that we find excess, deficiency and a mean. It is possible, for example, to experience fear, boldness, desire, anger, pity, and pleasures and pains generally, too much or too little or to the right amount. If we feel them too much or too little, we are wrong. But to have these feelings at the right times on the right occasions towards the right people for the right motive and in the right way is to have them in the right measure, that is somewhere between the extremes; and this is what characterizes goodness. The same may be said of the mean and extremes in actions. Now it is in the field of actions and feelings that goodness operates; in them we find excess, deficiency and, between them, the mean, the first two being wrong, the mean right and praised as such. . . . Goodness, then, is a mean condition in the sense that it aims at and hits the mean. Consider, too, that it is possible to go wrong in more ways than one. (In Pythagorean terminology evil is a form of the Unlimited, good of the Limited.) But there is only one way of being right. That is why going wrong is easy, and going right difficult; it is easy to miss the bull's eye and difficult to hit it. Here, then, is another explanation of why the too much and the too little are connected with evil and the mean with good. As the poet says,

Goodness is one, evil is multiform.

[*We are now in a position to state our definition of virtue with more precision. Observe that the kind of virtue meant here is moral, not intellectual, and that Aristotle must not be taken as saying that the kind of virtue which he regards as the highest and truest is any sort of mean.*]

We may now define virtue as a disposition of the soul in which, when it has to choose among actions and feelings, it observes the mean relative to us, this being determined by such a rule or principle as would take shape in the mind of a man of sense or practical wisdom. We call it a mean condition as lying between two forms of badness, one being excess and the other deficiency; and also for this reason, that, whereas badness either falls short of or exceeds the right measure in feelings and actions, virtue discovers the mean and deliberately chooses it. Thus, looked at from the point of view of its essence as embodied in its definition, virtue no doubt is a mean; judged by the standard of what is right and best, it is an extreme.

[*Aristotle enters a caution. Though we have said that virtue observes the mean in actions and passions, we do not say this of all acts and all feelings. Some are essentially evil and, when these are involved, our rule of applying the mean cannot be brought into operation.*]

But choice of a mean is not possible in every action or every feeling. The very names of some have an immediate connotation of evil. Such are malice, shamelessness, envy among feelings, and among actions adultery, theft, murder. All these and more like them have a bad name as being evil in themselves; it is not merely the excess or deficiency of them that we censure. In their case, then, it is impossible to act rightly; whatever we do is wrong. . . .

[*Aristotle now suggests some rules for our guidance.*]

. . . We shall find it useful when aiming at the mean to observe these rules. (1) *Keep away from that extreme which is the more opposed to the mean.* It is Calypso's advice:

Swing round the ship
clear of this surf and surge.

For one of the extremes is always a more dangerous error than the other; and—since it is hard to hit the bull's-eye—we must take the next best course and choose the least of the evils. And it will be easiest for us to do this if we follow the rule I have suggested. (2) *Note the errors into which we personally are most liable to fall.* (Each of us has his natural bias in one direction or another.) We shall find out what ours are by noting what gives us pleasure and pain. After that we must drag ourselves in the opposite direction. For our best way of reaching the middle is by giving a wide berth to our darling sin. It is the method used by a carpenter when he is straightening a warped board. (3) *Always be particularly on your guard against pleasure and pleasant things.* When Pleasure is at the bar the jury is not impartial. So it will be best for us if we feel towards her as the Trojan elders felt towards Helen, and regularly apply their words to her. If we are for packing her off, as they were with Helen, we shall be the less likely to go wrong.

3. [Particular Virtues]

[*Aristotle now embarks upon a long analysis of the virtues and vices. These do not include the characteristically Christian virtues of piety, chastity and humility, which are not regarded by him as independent virtues at all. Yet however he may classify and name the moral feelings and habits which form the material for his analysis, that material is substantially the same for him as for us. The picture of the good man which emerges is perfectly recognizable and even familiar to us.*]

Let us begin with courage.

We have seen that it is a disposition which aims at the mean in situations inspiring fear and confidence. What we fear are of course things of a nature to inspire fear. Now these are, speaking generally, evil things, so that we get the definition of fear as 'an anticipation of evil.' Well, we do fear all evil things—ill-repute, poverty, sickness, friendlessness, death and so on—but in the opinion of most people courage is to be distinguished from the simple fear of all these. There are some evils which it is proper and honourable to fear and discreditable not to fear—disgrace, for example. The man who fears disgrace has a sense of what is due to himself as a man of character and to other people; the man who does not fear it has a forehead of brass. Such a man indeed is occasionally styled a brave fellow, but only by a transference of epithet made possible by the fact that there is one point of similarity between him and the truly brave man, namely their freedom from timidity. Then one ought not, of course, to fear poverty or illness or, indeed, anything at all that is not a consequence of vice or of one's own misconduct; still we do not call a man who is fearless in facing these things 'brave' except once more by analogy. For we find individuals who are cowardly on the field of battle and yet spend money lavishly and meet the loss of it with equanimity. And surely a man is not to be dubbed a coward because he dreads brutality to his wife and children, or the effects of envy towards himself, or anything of that nature. Nor is a man described as brave if he does not turn a hair at the prospect of a whipping.

What, then, are the objects of fear confronting which the brave man comes out in his true colours? Surely one would say the greatest, for it is just in facing fearful issues that the brave man excels. Now the most fearful thing is death; for death is an end, and to the dead man nothing seems good or evil any more for ever. Yet even death may be attended by circumstances which make it seem inappropriate to describe the man confronted by it as 'brave.' For instance, he might be drowned at sea or pass away in his bed. In what dangers, then, is courage most clearly displayed? Shall we not say, in the noblest? Well, the noblest death is the soldier's, for he meets it in the midst of the greatest and most glorious dangers. This is recognized in the honours conferred on the fallen by republics and monarchs alike. So in the strict meaning of the word the brave man will be one who fearlessly meets an honourable death or some instant threat to life; and it is war which presents most opportunities of that sort. Not but what the brave man will be fearless in plague, or in peril by sea, although it will be a different kind of fearlessness from that of the old salt. For in a shipwreck the brave man does not expect to be rescued, and he hates the thought of the inglorious end which threatens him, whereas the seaman who has weathered many a storm never gives up hope. Courage, too, may be shown on occasions when a man can put up a fight or meet a glorious death. But there is no opportunity for either when you are going down in a ship.

All men have not the same views about what is to be feared, although there are some terrors which are admitted to be more than human nature can face. Terrors of that order are experienced of course by every sane person. But there are great diversities in the extent and degree of the dangers that are humanly tolerable; and there is the same variety in the objects which instil courage. What characterizes the brave man is his unshaken courage wherever courage is humanly possible. No doubt even then he will not always be exempt from fear; but when he fears it will be in the right way, and he will meet the danger according to the rule or principle he has taken to guide his conduct, his object being to achieve moral dignity or beauty in what he does, for that is the end of virtue. Yet it is possible to feel such dangers too much, and possible to fear them too little, and possible also to fear things that are not fearful as much as if they were. One may fear what one ought not to fear, and that is one kind of error; one may fear it in the wrong way, and that is another. A third error is committed when one fears at the wrong time. And so on. We have the same possibilities of error when we deal with things that give us confidence. The brave man is the man who faces or fears the right thing for the right purpose in the right manner at the right moment, or who shows courage in the corresponding ways. . . .

The man who goes to the extreme in fear is a coward—one who fears the wrong things in the wrong way and all the rest of it. He also exhibits a deficiency in boldness. But what one particularly notices is the extremity of his fear in the face of pain. We may therefore describe the coward as a poor-spirited person scared of everything. This is the very opposite of the brave man, for a bold heart indicates a confident temper.

We may say, then, that the coward, the rash man, and the brave man work as it were with the same materials, but their attitudes to them are different. The coward has too much fear and too little courage, the rash man too much courage and too little fear. It is the brave man who has the right attitude, for he has the right disposition, enabling him to observe the mean. We may add that the rash man is foolhardy, ready for anything before the danger arrives; but, when it does, sheering off. On the other hand the brave man is gallant in action but undemonstrative beforehand.

Summing up, let us say that courage is the disposition which aims at the mean in conditions which inspire confidence or fear in the circumstances I have described; it feels confidence and faces danger because it is the fine thing to do so and because it is base to shrink from doing it. Yet to kill oneself as a means of escape from poverty or disappointed love or bodily or mental anguish is the deed of a coward rather than a brave man. To run away from trouble is a form of cowardice and, while it is true that the suicide braves death, he does it not for some noble object but to escape some ill.

[*The virtue of which Aristotle now gives an account is* Sophrosyne, *a word which cannot be rendered by any modern English equivalent. It is, however, what our moralists until quite recently called 'temperance,' and this, with its opposite 'intemperance,' will be used*

here. What Aristotle means by Sophrosyne *will gradually appear.*]

Let us next say something about temperance, which like courage is considered to be one of the virtues developed in the irrational parts of the soul.

We have already described it as aiming at the mean in pleasurable experiences. Intemperance is shown in the same field. So we must now say something definite about the quality of the pleasures which are the material on which temperance and its opposite work. Let us begin by drawing a distinction between (*a*) pleasures of the soul and (*b*) pleasures of the body.

(*a*) As an instance of pleasures of the soul consider the love of distinction in public life or in some branch of learning. The devotee in either case takes pleasure in what he loves without any physical sensations. What he feels is a spiritual or intellectual pleasure, and we do not speak of men who seek that kind of pleasure as 'temperate' or 'intemperate.' Nor do we apply these terms to any class of persons whose pleasures are not those of the flesh. For example, the kind of person who likes to swap stories and ancedotes, and wastes his time discussing trivialities, we call a 'gossip' or a 'chatterbox,' but not 'intemperate.' Neither should we so describe a man who makes a tragedy out of some loss he has met with of money or of friends.

(*b*) It is then the pleasures of sense that are the concern of temperance, though not all of these. The people who find pleasure in looking at things like colours and forms and pictures are not called temperate or intemperate. At the same time we must suppose that pleasure in these things can be felt too much or too little or in due measure. It is so with the pleasures of listening. A man may take inordinate delight in music or acting. But nobody is prepared to call him intemperate on that account; nor, if he takes neither too much nor too little, do we think of describing him as temperate. It is the same with the pleasures of smell, except when some association comes in. A man is not called intemperate if he happens to like the smell of apples or roses or incense. Yet he may be, if he inhales essences or the emanations of the cuisine, for these are odours which appeal to the voluptuary, because they remind him of the things that arouse his desires. And not only the voluptuary; everybody likes the smell of things to eat when he is hungry. Still the delight in such things is specially characteristic of the voluptuary or intemperate man, because it is on these that his heart is set. And if we extend our observation to the lower animals, we note that they, too, find nothing intrinsically pleasant in these sensations. A hunting-dog gets no pleasure from the scent of a hare. The pleasure is in eating it; all the scent did was to tell him the hare was there. It is not the lowing of an ox that gratifies a lion but the eating it, though the lowing tells him the ox is somewhere about, and that evidently gives him pleasure. Nor does he, as Homer thinks, rejoice when he has caught sight of 'stag or goat of the wild,' but because he is promising himself a meal.

Such are the pleasures with which temperance and intemperance deal, and they are pleasures in which the lower animals also share. On that account

they have the name of being illiberal and brutish, confined as they are to touch and taste. And even taste seems to count for little or nothing in the practice of temperance. It is the function of taste to discriminate between flavours, as connoisseurs do when they sample wines, and chefs when they prepare entrées; although it is not exactly the flavours that please (except, perhaps, with the intemperate), it is the enjoyment of the flavorous article, and that is wholly a tactile experience, whether in eating, drinking or what are called the pleasures of sex. This explains the anecdote of the epicure who prayed that his throat might be made longer than a crane's—the longer the contact, he thought, the more protracted the pleasure. So the sense in respect of which we give an intemperate man that name is the sense that comes nearest to being universal. This may seem to justify its ill-repute, for it belongs to us not as men but as animals. Therefore to delight in such sensations, and to prefer them to any other pleasure, is brutish.

[*Aristotle discusses other virtues, such as liberality, the golden mean between stinginess and prodigality; dignified self-respect, between humility and vanity; and friendliness, between quarrelsomeness and obsequiousness. He points out that acts like theft, adultery, and murder, and emotions like shamelessness, envy, and spite, are already excesses or defects, and therefore cannot exist in proper moderation. The virtue of justice, as a kind of fairness or impartiality, consists in treating equals equally and unequals unequally in proportion to their deserts. It is a mean, not as the other virtues are, but only in the sense that it produces a state of affairs intermediate between giving too much or too little to one person compared with another.—M.R.*]

4. [Self-love and Friendship]

[*How far, and with what justification, may a man love himself?*]

Another problem is whether one ought to love oneself or another most. The world blames those whose first thoughts are always for themselves and stigmatizes them as self-centred. It is also generally believed that a bad man does everything from a selfish motive, and does this the more, the worse he is.[1] On the other hand the good man is supposed never to act except on some lofty principle—the loftier the principle, the better the man—and to neglect his own interest in order to promote that of his friend. It is a view which is not borne out by the facts. Nor need this surprise us. It is common ground that a man should love his best friend most. But my best friend is the man who in wishing me well wishes it for my sake, whether this shall come to be known or not. Well, there is no one who fulfills this condition so well as I do in my behaviour towards myself; indeed it may be said of every quality which enters into the definition of a friend—I have it in a higher degree than any of my friends. For, as I have already observed, all the affectionate feelings of a man for others are an extension of his feelings for himself. You will find, too,

[1] A bad man is often accused of 'doing nothing until he has to.'

that all the popular bywords agree on this point. ('Two bodies and one soul,' 'Amity is parity,' 'The knee is nearer than the shin.') All the proverbs show how close are the ties of friendship, and they all apply best to oneself. For a man is his own best friend. From this it follows that he ought to love himself best. —Which then of these two opinions ought we to accept in practice? It is a reasonable question, since there is a degree of plausibility in both.

No doubt the proper method of dealing with divergent opinions of this sort is to distinguish between them, and so reach a definite conclusion on the point of how far and in what way each of them is true. So the present difficulty may be cleared up if we can discover what meaning each side attaches to the word 'self-love.' Those who make it a term of reproach give the epithet of 'self-loving' to those who assign to themselves more than they are entitled to in money, public distinctions and bodily pleasures, these being what most men crave for and earnestly pursue as the greatest blessings, so that they contend fiercely for the possession of them. Well, the man who grasps at more than his fair share of these things is given to the gratification of his desires and his passions generally and the irrational part of his soul. Now most men are like that, and we see from this that the censorious use of the epithet 'self-loving' results from the fact that the self-love of most men is a bad thing. Applied to them, the censorious epithet is therefore justified. And unquestionably it is people who arrogate too much of such things to themselves who are called 'self-loving' by the ordinary man. For if anybody were to make it his constant business to take the lead himself over everyone else in the performance of just or temperate or any other kind whatever of virtuous actions, generally claiming the honourable rôle for himself, nobody would stigmatize *him* as a 'self-lover.' Yet the view might be taken that such a man was exceptionally self-loving. At any rate he arrogates to himself the things of greatest moral beauty and excellence, and what he gratifies and obeys throughout is the magistral part of himself, his higher intelligence. Now just as in a state or any other composite body it is the magistral or dominant part of it that is considered more particularly to *be* the state or body, so with a man; his intelligence, the governing part of him, *is* the man. Therefore he who loves and indulges this part is to the fullest extent a lover of himself. Further, we may note that the terms 'continent' and 'incontinent' imply that the intellect is or is not in control, which involves the assumption that the intellect is the man. Again, it is our reasoned acts that are held to be more especially those which we have performed ourselves and by our own volition. All which goes to show that a man is, or is chiefly the ruling part of himself, and that a good man loves it beyond any other part of his nature. It follows that such a man will be self-loving in a different sense from that attached to the word when it is used as a term of reproach. From the vulgar self-lover he differs as far as the life of reason from the life of passion, and as far as a noble purpose differs from mere grasping at whatever presents itself as an expedient. Hence those who are exceptionally devoted to the performance of fine and noble actions receive the approval and commendation of all. And if everyone sought to outdo his neighbour in elevation of character, and laboured strenuously to perform the noblest actions, the common weal would find its complete actualization and the private citizen would realize for himself the greatest of goods, which is virtue.

Therefore it is right for the *good* man to be self-loving, because he will thereby himself be benefited by performing fine actions; and by the same process he will be helpful to others. The bad man on the other hand should not be a self-lover, because he will only be injuring himself and his neighbours by his subservience to base passions. As a result of this subservience what he does is in conflict with what he ought to do, whereas the good man does what he ought to do. For intelligence never fails to choose the course that is best for itself, and the good man obeys his intelligence.

But there is something else which we can truly say about the good man. Many of his actions are performed to serve his friends or his country, even if this should involve dying for them. For he is ready to sacrifice wealth, honours, all the prizes of life in his eagerness to play a noble part. He would prefer one crowded hour of glorious life to a protracted period of quiet existence and mild enjoyment spent as an ordinary man would spend it—one great and dazzling achievement to many small successes. And surely this may be said of those who lay down their lives for others; they choose for themselves a crown of glory. It is also a characteristic

trait of the good man that he is prepared to lose money on condition that
his friends get more. The friend gets
the cash, and he gets the credit, so that
he is assigning the greater good to himself. His conduct is not different when
it comes to public honours and offices.
All these he will freely give up to his
friend, because that is the fine and
praiseworthy thing for him to do. It is
natural then that people should think
him virtuous, when he prefers honour
to everything else. He may even create
opportunities for his friend to do a fine
action which he might have done himself, and this may be the nobler course
for him to take. Thus in the whole field
of admirable conduct we see the good
man taking the larger share of moral
dignity. In this sense then it is, as I
said before, right that he should be self-
loving. But in the vulgar sense no one
should be so.

[*It has been questioned whether the
possession of friends is necessary to happiness. Aristotle has no doubt that it is
so, and gives his reasons.*]

Another debatable point concerning
the happy man is this. Will friends be
necessary to his happiness or not? It is
commonly said that the happy, being
sufficient to themselves, have no need of
friends. All the blessings of life are
theirs already; so, having all resources
within themselves, they are not in need
of anything else, whereas a friend, being an *alter ego*, is only there to supply
what one cannot supply for oneself.
Hence that line in the *Orestes* of Eurip-
ides:

When Fortune smiles on us, what
need of friends?

Yet it seems a strange thing that in the
the process of attributing every blessing
to the happy man we should not assign
him friends, who are thought to be the
greatest of all external advantages. Besides, if it is more like a friend to
confer than to receive benefits, and doing good to others is an activity which
especially belongs to virtue and the virtuous man, and if it is better to do a
kindness to a friend than to a stranger,
the good man will have need of friends
as objects of his active benevolence.
Hence a second question. Does one need
friends more in prosperity than in adversity? There is a case for either of
these alternatives. The unfortunate need
people who will be kind to them; the
prosperous need people to be kind to.

Surely also there is something strange
in representing the man of perfect
blessedness as a solitary or a recluse.
Nobody would deliberately choose to
have all the good things in the world, if
there was a condition that he was to
have them all by himself. Man is a social
animal, and the need for company is
in his blood. Therefore the happy man
must have company, for he has everything that is naturally good, and it
will not be denied that it is better to
associate with friends than with strangers, with men of virtue than with the
ordinary run of persons. We conclude then that the happy man needs
friends. . . .

[*A little chapter on the value and
influence of Friendship.*]

Well then, are we to say that, just as
lovers find their chief delight in gazing
upon the beloved and prefer sight to all
the other senses—for this is the seat and
source of love—so friends find the so-

ciety of one another that which they prefer to all things else? For in the first place friendship is a communion or partnership. Secondly, a man stands in the same relation to his friend as to himself. Now the consciousness which he has of his own existence is something that would be chosen as a good. So the consciousness of his friend's existence must be a good. This consciousness becomes active in the intercourse of the friends, which accordingly they instinctively desire. Thirdly, every man wishes to share with his friends that occupation, whatever it may be, which forms for him the essence and aim of his existence. So we find friends who drink together, and others who dice together, while yet others go in together for physical training, hunting or philosophy. Each set spend their time in one another's company following the pursuit which makes the great pleasure of their lives. As their wish is to be always with their friends, they do what these do and take part with them in these pursuits to the best of their ability. But this means that the friendship of the unworthy is evil, for they associate in unworthy pursuits; and so becoming more and more like each other they turn out badly. But the friendship of the good is good and increases in goodness in consequence of their association. They seem to become positively better men by putting their friendship into operation and correcting each other's faults. For each seeks to transfer to himself the traits he admires in the other. Hence the famous saying:

From noble men you may learn noble deeds . . .

5. [Intellectual Goodness]

[*. . . Aristotle gives reasons for thinking that happiness in its highest and best manifestation is found in cultivating the "contemplative" life.*]

. . . If happiness is an activity in accordance with virtue, it is reasonable to assume that it will be in accordance with the highest virtue; and this can only be the virtue of the best part of us. Whether this be the intellect or something else—whatever it is that is held to have a natural right to govern and guide us, and to have an insight into what is noble and divine, either as being itself also divine or more divine than any other part of us—it is the activity of this part in accordance with the virtue proper to it that will be perfect happiness. Now we have seen already that this activity has a speculative or contemplative character. This is a conclusion which may be accepted as in harmony with our earlier arguments and with the truth. For "contemplation" is the highest form of activity, since the intellect is the highest thing in us and the objects which come within its range are the highest that can be known. But it is also the most continuous activity, for we can think about intellectual problems more continuously than we can keep up any sort of physical action. Again, we feel sure that a modicum of pleasure must be one of the ingredients of happiness. Now it is admitted that activity along the lines of "wisdom" is the pleasantest of all the good activities. At all events it is thought that philosophy ("the pursuit of wisdom") has pleasures marvelous in purity and duration, and it stands to reason that those who have knowledge pass their time more pleasantly than those who are engaged in its pursuit. Again, self-sufficiency will be found to belong in an exceptional degree to the exercise of the speculative intellect. The wise man, as much as the just man and everyone else, must have the necessaries of life. But, given an adequate supply of these, the just man also needs people with and towards whom he can put his justice into operation; and we can use similar language about the temperate man, the brave man, and so on. But the wise man can do more. He can speculate all by himself, and the wiser he is the better he can do it. Doubtless it helps to have fellow workers, but for all that he is the most self-sufficing of men. Finally it may well be thought that the activity of contemplation is the only one that is praised on its own account, because nothing comes of it beyond the act of contemplation, whereas from practical activities we count on gaining something more or less over and above the mere action. Again, it is commonly believed that, to have happiness, one must have leisure; we occupy ourselves in order that we may have leisure, just as we make war for the sake of peace. Now the practical virtues find opportunity for their exercise in politics and in war, but there are occupations which are supposed to leave no room for leisure. Certainly it is true of the trade of war, for no one deliberately chooses to make war for the sake of making it or tries to bring about a war. A man would be regarded as a bloodthirsty monster if he were to make war on a friendly state just to produce battles and slaughter. The business of the poli-

tician also makes leisure impossible. Besides the activity itself, politics aims at securing positions of power and honor or the happiness of the politician himself or his fellow citizens—a happiness obviously distinct from that which we are seeking.

We are now in a position to suggest the truth of the following statements. (*a*) Political and military activities, while preeminent among good activities in beauty and grandeur, are incompatible with leisure, and are not chosen for their own sake but with a view to some remoter end, whereas the activity of the intellect is felt to excel in the serious use of leisure, taking as it does the form of contemplation, and not to aim at any end beyond itself, and to own a pleasure peculiar to itself, thereby enhancing its activity. (*b*) In this activity we easily recognize self-sufficiency, the possibility of leisure and such freedom from fatigue as is humanly possible, together with all the other blessings of pure happiness. Now if these statements are received as true, it will follow that it is this intellectual activity which forms perfect happiness for a man—provided of course that it ensures a complete span of life, for nothing incomplete can be an element in happiness.

Yes, but such a life will be too high for *human* attainment. It will not be lived by us in our merely human capacity but in virtue of something divine within us, and so far as this divine particle is superior to man's composite nature, to that extent will its activity be superior to that of the other forms of excellence. If the intellect is divine compared with man, the life of the intellect must be divine compared with the life of a human creature. And we ought not to listen to those who counsel us *O man, think as man should* and *O mortal, remember your mortality.* Rather ought we, so far as in us lies, to put on immortality and to leave nothing unattempted in the effort to live in conformity with the highest thing within us. Small in bulk it may be, yet in power and preciousness it transcends all the rest. We may in fact believe that this is the true self of the individual, being the sovereign and better part of him. It would be strange, then, if a man should choose to live not his own life but another's. Moreover the rule, as I stated it a little before, will apply here —the rule that what is best and pleasantest for each creature is that which intimately belongs to it. Applying it, we shall conclude that the life of the intellect is the best and pleasantest for man, because the intellect more than anything else *is* the man. Thus it will be the happiest life as well.

COMMENT

In considering the merits of Aristotle's theory, we should keep certain key questions in mind:

1. *Can we deduce good from the nature of things?* The presupposition of Aristotle's ethics is that each kind of thing has certain characteristic tendencies and that the good is the fulfillment of these tendencies. Man's good, accordingly, can be deduced from human nature. It may be objected that this implies an optimistic and undemonstrated premise (that developed reality is fully good) and allows the tendencies of the actual world to dictate our standards of value. Some philosophers, such as Kant, deny that the *ought* (good and right) can be derived from the *is* (mattters of fact), and thus take fundamental issue with the basis of Aristotle's ethics. This issue is especially relevant to Cicero's theory of natural law, which we shall discuss in the next chapter, and hence we shall postpone its consideration.

2. *Is the wider definition of good correct?* We can distinguish, in Aristotle's theory, between a "wide" and a "narrow" definition of ultimate good. In its wide meaning, good is the actualization of potentialities. In its narrow meaning, it is the actualization of *human* potentialities, which are taken to be essentially rational.

Let us first consider the wider definition. It is very wide indeed, for it applies to animals, plants, and even inanimate things. Whether Aristotle would interpret it so broadly is not altogether clear. In his teleological metaphysics, he speaks of "end" or "final cause" in this very inclusive way, but he does not state explicitly that every end is good. If, however, the actualization of potentialities is taken to be the essence of good, there is no logical reason to stop short with conscious or even unconscious organisms.

This very wide definition, a critic might say, confuses an "end" in a temporal sense (the *finis* of a process) with an "end" in an ethical sense (good as an end rather than as a means). Another type of confusion may also be involved. We often say that something is a *good* example of its kind, and good in this sense, a biologist might claim, applies only to a fully developed animal, which clearly exhibits the powers and abilities of its species. But "good" in this sense does not imply positive value; a cancer specialist might speak of a perfectly good case of cancer, meaning a case so far developed that it clearly exhibits the generic characteristics of the malignancy. Has Aristotle confused good in this sense with good in its value import?

The attempt to extend the meaning of intrinsic goodness to include nonconscious things has often been challenged. If there were no feelings, no desires, no thoughts whatsoever—if all things in the universe were as unconscious as sticks and stones—would there be any value? Some philosophers maintain that a world without consciousness would be without value; if this were so, we should have to reject Aristotle's wider interpretation of good.

3. *Is the narrower definition of good correct?* Aristotle's interpretation of human goodness rests upon two premises: (*a*) the good is to be found in the life and work peculiar to people, and (*b*) rationality is the distinctive mark of the human creature. Both premises can be challenged.

(*a*) Why should we suppose that the human good is to be found in what is distinctive to people? That a certain factor is peculiar to a species does not necessarily imply any ethical superiority in that factor. If all human beings were just like other animals except that they alone had bowlegs, this would not prove that human good is bowleggedness. Perhaps Aristotle is taking it for granted that people *are* superior to other animals and that this superiority must lie in that which people alone possess. But some philosophers would question this view. Hedonists, for example, would say that good is pleasure, and the fact that a dog can feel pleasure does not detract from human good. We may or may not believe that this view is mistaken and Aristotle's theory correct—but is there any way of supporting our conviction?

(*b*) Is reason the differentia of humankind? Certain psychologists, such as Wolfgang Köhler, have demonstrated that chimpanzees also have the capacity to reason. These clever animals can figure out ways of piling up and mounting boxes, for example, so as to reach a bunch of bananas hanging high from the top of their cage. Aristotle would no doubt reply that this is only *practical*, not *theoretical*, reason, but it may be that chimpanzees also have curiosity and enjoy satisfying it. At least it is not at all obvious that reason is *the* distinctive mark of human beings, or that any faculty is exclusively human. What fundamentally distinguishes people, it can be argued, is the whole development of their culture, including art and religion and social institutions in addition to philosophy and science. Does Aristotle's rather exclusive emphasis upon reason betray the natural bias of a philosopher?

4. *Does Aristotle, in stressing the generic nature of man, neglect the importance of individuality?* His emphasis is upon the reason that all men share, and

only in rare passages does he speak of self-realization in individualistic terms. He would probably have admitted, for example, that a person with very great musical talent should develop that special gift. But an existentialist such as Kierkegaard would charge that Aristotle shows too little respect for the matchless individuality that is the core of every human life. Who is right?

5. *Is moral virtue to be found in adherence to a mean between the extremes of excess and deficiency?* How adequate is Aristotle's theory of the golden mean? "Be cautious; avoid extremes; follow the mean," it can be argued, is a counsel of prudence and not necessarily of morality—even the wicked and crafty can find it useful. From the standpoint of attaining happiness, does it need to be counterbalanced by a relish for adventure and the careless rapture of intense moments of experience?

Still other questions can be posed. Is pleasure merely contributory to the happy life, as Aristotle supposed, or is it the very essence of happiness, as the hedonists contend? Is the ideal of intellectual contemplation unrealizable by all but the aristocratic few, and, if so, should we favor the development of an intellectual élite rather than the cultivation of the masses? Are ethics and politics inseparable in the way in which Aristotle supposed? Do you agree with his characterization of the nature and value of self-love? Of friendship? Other questions will probably occur to the reader.

11

Nature

MARCUS TULLIUS CICERO (106–43 B.C.)

Statesman, philosopher, and man of letters, Cicero was one of the greatest intellectual figures during the last days of the Roman Republic. He won fame as a young lawyer for his successful defense of Sextus Roscius, the victim of a trumped-up murder charge and enemy of the powerful dictator, Sulla. In 75 B.C., Cicero was sent to Sicily as an administrator, and five years later acted as prosecutor of Verres, an unscrupulous governor whose cruel and corrupt rule had excited the hostility of the Sicilians. So powerful was the indictment that Verres, abandoning all hope of a defense, fled into exile.

In the year 66, Cicero, now a famous man, was elected a magistrate of Rome. Two years later he became Roman consul, at a time when the Republic was in a critical condition because of corruption and sedition. The courage and eloquence with which Cicero defeated the conspiracy of Catiline, whom he denounced before the Roman Senate in four famous orations, won him still greater celebrity. One of his enemies, Publius Clodius, a tribune, thereupon charged him with putting Catiline's fellow conspirators to death without public trial, and he was forced into exile. But he soon returned to public office and brilliantly defended the old forms of the Roman constitution against the encroachments of autocracy. After Caesar's murder, he denounced Mark Antony in a series of impassioned orations before the Senate. His death was then demanded by Antony, and he was assassinated.

Despite his tumultuous public career, Cicero found time to write various philo-

395

sophical and literary works. He developed the Stoic doctrine that the only just government is that based upon law and that the moral foundation of law is the natural kinship and equality of all men.

Natural Law

PERSONS OF THE DIALOGUE: *Marcus Tullius Cicero* himself; *Quintus Tullius Cicero,* his brother; and *Titus Pomponius Atticus,* his friend.

Marcus. . . . Out of all the material of the philosophers' discussions, surely there comes nothing more valuable than the full realization that we are born for Justice, and that right is based, not upon men's opinions, but upon Nature. This fact will immediately be plain if you once get a clear conception of man's fellowship and union with his fellow-men. For no single thing is so like another, so exactly its counterpart, as all of us are to one another. Nay, if bad habits and false beliefs did not twist the weaker minds and turn them in whatever direction they are inclined, no one would be so like his own self as all men would be like all others. And so, however we may define man, a single definition will apply to all. This is a sufficient proof that there is no difference in kind between man and man; for if there were, one defi-

The following excerpts from Books I and II of *The Laws* and Book III of *The Republic* are taken from *De Re Publica, De Legibus,* with an English translation by Clinton Walker Keyes (Loeb Classical Library), Harvard University Press, Cambridge, Mass., 1943. Reprinted by permission.

nition could not be applicable to all men; and indeed reason, which alone raises us above the level of the beasts and enables us to draw inferences, to prove and disprove, to discuss and solve problems, and to come to conclusions, is certainly common to us all, and, though varying in what it learns, at least in the capacity to learn it is invariable. For the same things are invariably perceived by the senses, and those things which stimulate the senses, stimulate them in the same way in all men; and those rudimentary beginnings of intelligence to which I have referred, which are imprinted on our minds, are imprinted on all minds alike; and speech, the mind's interpreter, though differing in the choice of words, agrees in the sentiments expressed. In fact, there is no human being of any race who, if he finds a guide, cannot attain to virtue.

The similarity of the human race is clearly marked in its evil tendencies as well as in its goodness, for pleasure also attracts all men; and even though it is an enticement to vice, yet it has some likeness to what is naturally good. For it delights us by its lightness and agreeableness; and for this reason, by an error of thought, it is embraced as something wholesome. It is through a similar misconception that we shun death as though it were a dissolution of nature, and cling to life because it keeps us in the sphere in which we were born; and that we look upon pain as one of the greatest of evils, not only because of its cruelty, but also because it seems to lead to the destruction of nature. In the same way, on account of the similarity between moral worth and renown, those who are publicly honored are considered happy, while those who do not attain fame are thought miserable. Troubles, joys, desires, and fears haunt the minds of all men without distinction, and even if different men have different beliefs, that does not prove, for example, that it is not the same quality of superstition that besets those races which worship dogs and cats as gods, as that which torments other races. But what nation does not love courtesy, kindliness, gratitude, and remembrance of favors bestowed? What people does not hate and despise the haughty, the wicked, the cruel, and the ungrateful? Inasmuch as these considerations prove to us that the whole human race is bound together in unity, it follows, finally, that knowledge of the principles of right living is what makes men better.

If you approve of what has been said, I will go on to what follows. But if there is anything that you care to have explained, we will take that up first.

Atticus. We have no questions, if I may speak for both of us.

Marcus. The next point, then, is that we are so constituted by Nature as to share the sense of Justice with one another and to pass it on to all men. And in this whole discussion I want it understood that what I shall call Nature is [that which is implanted in us by Nature]; that, however, the corruption caused by bad habits is so great that the sparks of fire, so to speak, which Nature has kindled in us are extinguished by this corruption, and the vices which are their opposites spring up and are established. But, if the judgments of men were in agreement with Nature, so that, as the poet says, they considered "nothing alien to them which concerns mankind," then Justice would be equally observed by all. For those creatures who have received the gift of reason from Nature have also received right reason, and therefore they have also received the gift of Law, which is right reason applied to command and prohibition. And if they have received Law, they have received Justice also. Now, all men have received reason; therefore, all men have received Justice. Consequently, Socrates was right when he cursed, as he often did, the man who first separated utility from Justice; for this separation, he complained, is the source of all mischief. For what gave rise to Pythagoras' famous words about friendship? . . . From this it is clear that, when a wise man shows toward another endowed with equal virtue the kind of benevolence which is so widely diffused among men, that will then have come to pass which, unbelievable as it seems to some, is after all the inevitable result—namely, that he loves himself no whit more than he loves another. For what difference can there be among things which are all equal? But, if the least distinction should be made in friendship, then the very name of friendship would perish forthwith; for its essence is such that, as soon as either friend prefers anything for himself, friendship ceases to exist.

Now, all this is really a preface to what remains to be said in our discussion, and its purpose is to make it more easily understood that Justice is inherent in Nature. After I have said a few words more on this topic, I shall go on to the civil law, the subject which gives rise to all this discourse.

Quintus. You certainly need to say very little more on that head, for from what you have already said, Atticus is convinced, and certainly I am, that Nature is the source of Justice.

Atticus. How can I help being convinced, when it has just been proved to us, first, that we have been provided and equipped with what we may call the gifts of the gods; next, that there is only one principle by which men may live with one another, and that this is the same for all, and possessed equally by all; and, finally, that all men are bound together by a certain natural feeling of kindliness and good-will, and also by a partnership in Justice? Now that we have admitted the truth of these conclusions, and rightly, I think, how can we separate Law and Justice from Nature? . . .

Marcus. Once more, then, before we come to the individual laws, let us look at the character and nature of Law, for fear that, though it must be the standard to which we refer everything, we may now and then be led astray by an incorrect use of terms, and forget the rational principles on which our laws must be based.

Quintus. Quite so, that is the correct method of exposition.

Marcus. Well, then, I find that it has

been the opinion of the wisest men that Law is not a product of human thought, nor is it any enactment of peoples, but something eternal which rules the whole universe by its wisdom in command and prohibition. Thus they have been accustomed to say that Law is the primal and ultimate mind of God, whose reason directs all things either by compulsion or restraint. Wherefore that Law which the gods have given to the human race has been justly praised; for it is the reason and mind of a wise lawgiver applied to command and prohibition.

Quintus. You have touched upon this subject several times before. But before you come to the laws of peoples, please make the character of this heavenly Law clear to us, so that the waves of habit may not carry us away and sweep us into the common mode of speech of such subjects.

Marcus. Ever since we were children, Quintus, we have learned to call, "If one summon another to court,"[1] and other rules of the same kind, laws. But we must come to the true understanding of the matter, which is as follows: this and other commands and prohibitions of nations have the power to summon to righteousness and away from wrongdoing; but this power is not merely older than the existence of nations and States, it is coeval with that God who guards and rules heaven and earth. For the divine mind cannot exist without reason, and divine reason cannot but have this power to establish

[1] A familiar quotation from the Laws of the Twelve Tables, the earliest written code of Roman law.

right and wrong. No written law commanded that a man should take his stand on a bridge alone, against the full force of the enemy, and order the bridge broken down behind him; yet we shall not for that reason suppose that the heroic Cocles[2] was not obeying the law of bravery and following its decrees in doing so noble a deed. Even if there was no written law against rape at Rome in the reign of Lucius Tarquinius, we cannot say on that account that Sextus Tarquinius did not break that eternal Law by violating Lucretia, the daughter of Tricipitinus. For reason did exist, derived from the Nature of the universe, urging men to right conduct and diverting them from wrongdoing, and this reason did not first become Law when it was written down, but when it first came into existence; and it came into existence simultaneously with the divine mind. Wherefore the true and primal Law, applied to command and prohibition, is the right reason of supreme Jupiter.

Quintus. I agree with you, brother, that what is right and true is also eternal, and does not begin or end with written statutes.

Marcus. Therefore, just as that divine mind is the supreme Law, so, when [reason] is perfected in man, [that also is Law; and this perfected reason exists] in the mind of the wise man; but those rules which, in varying forms and for the need of the moment, have been formulated for the guidance of nations, bear the title of laws rather by favor than because they are really such.

---

[2] Horatius Cocles, who, with two companions, held the bridge over the Tiber against the Etruscan army.

For every law which really deserves that name is truly praiseworthy, as they prove by approximately the following arguments. It is agreed, of course, that laws were invented for the safety of citizens, the preservation of States, and the tranquility and happiness of human life, and that those who first put statutes of this kind in force convinced their people that it was their intention to write down and put into effect such rules as, once accepted and adopted, would make possible for them an honorable and happy life; and when such rules were drawn up and put in force, it is clear that men called them "laws." From this point of view it can be readily understood that those who formulated wicked and unjust statutes for nations, thereby breaking their promises and agreements, put into effect anything but "laws." It may thus be clear that in the very definition of the term "law" there inheres the idea and principle of choosing what is just and true. I ask you then, Quintus, according to the custom of the philosophers: if there is a certain thing, the lack of which in a State compels us to consider it no State at all, must we consider this thing a good?

Quintus. One of the greatest goods, certainly.

Marcus. And if a State lacks Law, must it for that reason be considered no State at all?

Quintus. It cannot be denied.

Marcus. Then Law must necessarily be considered one of the greatest goods.

Quintus. I agree with you entirely.

Marcus. What of the many deadly, the many pestilential statutes which nations put in force? These no more deserve to be called laws than the rules a band of robbers might pass in their assembly. For if ignorant and unskilful men have prescribed deadly poisons instead of healing drugs, these cannot possibly be called physicians' prescriptions; neither in a nation can a statute of any sort be called a law, even though the nation, in spite of its being a ruinous regulation, has accepted it. Therefore Law is the distinction between things just and unjust, made in agreement with that primal and most ancient of all things, Nature; and in conformity to Nature's standard are framed those human laws which inflict punishment upon the wicked but defend and protect the good.

Quintus. I understand you completely, and believe that from now on we must not consider or even call anything else a law.

Marcus. Then you do not think the Titian or Apuleian Laws were really laws at all?

Quintus. No; nor the Livian Laws either.[3]

Marcus. And you are right, especially as the Senate repealed them in one sentence and in a single moment. But the Law whose nature I have explained can neither be repealed nor abrogated.

[3] Examples of laws passed in Rome. It is implied that these enacted laws are not laws in the profounder sense that applies to natural laws.

The Republic

. . True law is right reason in agreement with nature; it is of universal application, unchanging and everlasting; it summons to duty by its commands, and averts from wrongdoing by its prohibitions. And it does not lay its commands or prohibitions upon good men in vain, though neither have any effect on the wicked. It is a sin to try to alter this law, nor is it allowable to attempt to repeal any part of it, and it is impossible to abolish it entirely. We cannot be freed from its obligations by senate or people, and we need not look outside ourselves for an expounder or interpreter of it. And there will not be different laws at Rome and at Athens, or different laws now and in the future, but one eternal and unchangeable law will be valid for all nations and all times, and there will be one master and ruler, that is, God, over us all, for he is the author of this law, its promulgator, and its enforcing judge. Whoever is disobedient is fleeing from himself and denying his human nature, and by reason of this very fact he will suffer the worst penalties, even if he escapes what is commonly considered punishment. . . .

MARCUS AURELIUS (121–180 A.D.)

Marcus Aurelius was the adopted son of his uncle, the Emperor Antoninus Pius. In early boyhood he was introduced to the doctrines of Stoicism, and he assumed the simple dress and practiced the austere way of life of the Stoics. After his marriage to the emperor's daughter Faustina, who bore him thirteen children, he was occupied with family affairs and learning the arts of government. At the death of Antoninus in 161 he became the ruler of the vast Roman Empire.

The remaining nineteen years of his life called for all the Stoic fortitude he could muster; for his reign was beset with calamities—floods, fires, earthquakes, pestilences, insurrections, wars, and barbarian invasions. He instituted many reforms and founded charitable institutions, but he violently persecuted the Christians whom he regarded as subversive. His *Meditations*, which apparently were private soliloquies intended for no eyes but his own, were written during military campaigns, the hardships of which eventually caused his death at his headquarters near present-day Vienna.

Harmony with Nature

Book II

Begin the morning by saying to thyself, I shall meet with the busybody, the ungrateful, arrogant, deceitful, envious, unsocial. All these things happen to them by reason of their ignorance of what is good and evil. But I who have seen the nature of the good that it is beautiful, and of the bad that it is ugly, and the nature of him who does wrong, that it is akin to me, not only of the same blood or seed, but that it participates in the same intelligence and the same portion of the divinity, I can neither be injured by any of them, for no one can fix on me what is ugly, nor

From *The Meditations of Marcus Aurelius Antoninus* translated by George Long (1862).

can I be angry with my kinsman, nor hate him. For we are made for co-operation, like feet, like hands, like eyelids, like the rows of the upper and lower teeth. To act against one another then is contrary to nature; and it is acting against one another to be vexed and to turn away.

9. This thou must always bear in mind, what is the nature of the whole, and what is my nature, and how this is related to that, and what kind of a part it is of what kind of a whole; and that there is no one who hinders thee from always doing and saying the things which are according to the nature of which thou are a part.

16. The soul of man does violence to itself, first of all, when it becomes an abscess and, as it were, a tumour on the

universe, so far as it can. For to be vexed at anything which happens is a separation of ourselves from nature, in some part of which the natures of all other things are contained. In the next place, the soul does violence to itself when it turns away from any man, or even moves towards him with the intention of injuring, such as are the souls of those who are angry. In the third place, the soul does violence to itself when it is overpowered by pleasure or by pain. Fourthly, when it plays a part, and does or says anything insincerely and untruly. Fifthly, when it allows any act of its own and any movement to be without an aim, and does anything thoughtlessly and without considering what it is, it being right that even the smallest things be done with reference to an end; and the end of rational animals is to follow the reason and the law of the most ancient city and polity.

17. Of human life the time is a point, and the substance is in a flux, and the perception dull, and the composition of the whole body subject to putrefaction, and the soul a whirl, and fortune hard to divine, and fame a thing devoid of judgement. And, to say all in a word, everything which belongs to the body is a stream, and what belongs to the soul is a dream and vapour, and life is a warfare and a stranger's sojourn, and after-fame is oblivion. What then is that which is able to conduct a man? One thing and only one, philosophy. But this consists in keeping the daemon within a man free from violence and unharmed, superior to pains and pleasures, doing nothing without a purpose, nor yet falsely and with hypocrisy, not

feeling the need of another man's doing or not doing anything; and besides, accepting all that happens, and all that it allotted, as coming from thence, wherever it is, from whence he himself came; and, finally, waiting for death with a cheerful mind, as being nothing else than a dissolution of the elements of which every living being is compounded. But if there is no harm to the elements themselves in each continually changing into another, why should a man have any apprehension about the change and dissolution of all the elements? For it is according to nature, and nothing is evil which is according to nature.

Book III

2. We ought to observe also that even the things which follow after the things which are produced according to nature contain something pleasing and attractive. For instance, when bread is baked some parts are split at the surface, and these parts which thus open, and have a certain fashion contrary to the purpose of the baker's art, are beautiful in a manner, and in a peculiar way excite a desire for eating. And again, figs, when they are quite ripe, gape open; and in the ripe olives the very circumstance of their being near to rottenness adds a peculiar beauty to the fruit. And the ears of corn bending down, and the lion's eyebrows, and the foam which flows from the mouth of wild boars, and many other things—though they are far from being beautiful, if a man should examine them severally—still, because they are consequent upon the things which are formed by nature, help

to adorn them, and they please the mind; so that if a man should have a feeling and deeper insight with respect to the things which are produced in the universe, there is hardly one of those which follow by way of consequence which will not seem to him to be in a manner disposed so as to give pleasure. And so he will see even the real gaping jaws of wild beasts with no less pleasure than those which painters and sculptors show by imitation; and in an old woman and an old man he will be able to see a certain maturity and comeliness; and the attractive loveliness of young persons he will be able to look on with chaste eyes; and many such things will present themselves, not pleasing to every man, but to him only who has become truly familiar with nature and her works.

11. To the aids which have been mentioned let this one still be added:— Make for thyself a definition or description of the thing which is presented to thee, so as to see distinctly what kind of a thing it is in its substance, in its nudity, in its complete entirety, and tell thyself its proper name, and the names of the things of which it has been compounded, and into which it will be resolved. For nothing is so productive of elevation of mind as to be able to examine methodically and truly every object which is presented to thee in life, and always to look at things so as to see at the same time what kind of universe this is, and what kind of use everything performs in it, and what value everything has with reference to the whole, and what with reference to man, who is a citizen of the highest city, of which all other cities are like families; what

each thing is, and of what it is composed, and how long it is the nature of this thing to endure which now makes an impression on me, and what virtue I have need of with respect to it, such as gentleness, manliness, truth, fidelity, simplicity, contentment, and the rest. Wherefore, on every occasion a man should say: this comes from God; and this is according to the apportionment and spinning of the thread of destiny, and such-like coincidence and chance; and this is from one of the same stock, and a kinsman and partner, one who knows not however what is according to his nature. But I know; for this reason I behave towards him according to the natural law of fellowship with benevolence and justice. At the same time however in things indifferent I attempt to ascertain the value of each.

Book IV

4. If our intellectual part is common, the reason also, in respect of which we are rational beings, is common: if this is so, common also is the reason which commands us what to do, and what not to do; if this is so, there is a common law also; if this is so, we are fellow-citizens; if this is so, we are members of some political community; if this is so, the world is in a manner a state. For of what other common political community will any one say that the whole human race are members? And from thence, from this common political community comes also our very intellectual faculty and reasoning faculty and our capacity for law; or whence do they come? For as my earthly part is a portion given to me from certain earth, and

that which is watery from another element, and that which is hot and fiery from some peculiar source (for nothing comes out of that which is nothing, as nothing also returns to non-existence), so also the intellectual part comes from some source.

23. Everything harmonizes with me, which is harmonious to thee, O Universe. Nothing for me is too early nor too late, which is in due time for thee. Everything is fruit to me which thy seasons bring, O Nature: from thee are all things, in thee are all things, to thee all things return. The poet says, Dear city of Cecrops; and wilt not thou say, Dear city of Zeus?

48. Think continually how many physicians are dead after often contracting their eyebrows over the sick; and how many astrologers after predicting with great pretensions the deaths of others; and how many philosophers after endless discourses on death or immortality; how many heroes after killing thousands; and how many tyrants who have used their power over men's lives with terrible insolence as if they were immortal; and how many cities are entirely dead, so to speak, Helice and Pompeii and Herculaneum, and others innumerable. Add to the reckoning all whom thou hast known, one after another. One man after burying another has been laid out dead, and another buries him: and all this in a short time. To conclude, always observe how ephemeral and worthless human things are, and what was yesterday a little mucus tomorrow will be a mummy or ashes. Pass then through this little space of time conformably to nature, and end thy journey in content, just as an olive

falls off when it is ripe, blessing nature who produced it, and thanking the tree on which it grew.

49. Be like the promontory against which the waves continually break, but it stands firm and tames the fury of the water around it.

Unhappy am I, because this has happened to me.—Not so, but happy am I, though this has happened to me, because I continue free from pain, neither crushed by the present nor fearing the future. For such a thing as this might have happened to every man; but every man would not have continued free from pain on such an occasion. Why then is that rather a misfortune than this a good fortune? And dost thou in all cases call that a man's misfortune, which is not a deviation from man's nature? And does a thing seem to thee to be a deviation from man's nature, when it is not contrary to the will of man's nature? Well, thou knowest the will of nature. Will then this which has happened prevent thee from being just, magnanimous, temperate, prudent, secure against inconsiderate opinions and falsehood; will it prevent thee from having modesty, freedom, and everything else, by the presence of which man's nature obtains all that is its own? Remember too on every occasion which leads thee to vexation to apply this principle: not that this is a misfortune, but that to bear it nobly is good fortune.

Book V

In the morning when thou risest unwillingly, let this thought be present— I am rising to the work of a human being. Why then am I dissatisfied if I am going to do the things for which I exist and for which I was brought into the world? Or have I been made for this, to lie in the bed-clothes and keep myself warm?—But this is more pleasant.—Dost thou exist then to take thy pleasure, and not at all for action or exertion? Dost thou not see the little plants, the little birds, the ants, the spiders, the bees working together to put in order their several parts of the universe? And art thou willing to do the work of a human being, and dost thou not make haste to do that which is according to thy nature?—But it is necessary to take rest also.—It is necessary: however nature has fixed bounds to this too: she has fixed bounds both to eating and drinking, and yet thou goest beyond these bounds, beyond what is sufficient; yet in thy acts it is not so, but thou stoppest short of what thou canst do. So thou lovest not thyself, for if thou didst, thou wouldst love thy nature and her will. But those who love their several arts exhaust themselves in working at them unwashed and without food; but thou valuest thy own nature less than the turner values the turning art, or the dancer the dancing art, or the lover of money values his money, or the vainglorious man his little glory. And such men, when they have a violent affection to a thing, choose neither to eat nor to sleep rather than to perfect the things which they care for. But are the acts which concern society more vile in thy eyes and less worthy of thy labour?

2. How easy it is to repel and to wipe away every impression which is troublesome or unsuitable, and immediately to be in all tranquillity.

3. Judge every word and deed which are according to nature to be fit for thee; and be not diverted by the blame which follows from any people nor by their words, but if a thing is good to be done or said, do not consider it unworthy of thee. For those persons have their peculiar leading principle and follow their peculiar movement; which things do not thou regard, but go straight on, following thy own nature and the common nature; and the way of both is one.

16. Such as are thy habitual thoughts, such also will be the character of thy mind; for the soul is dyed by the thoughts. Dye it then with a continuous series of such thoughts as these: for instance, that where a man can live, there he can also live well. But he must live in a place;—well then, he can also live well in a palace. And again, consider that for whatever purpose each thing has been constituted, for this it has been constituted, and towards this it is carried; and its end is in that towards which it is carried; and where the end is, there also is the advantage and the good of each thing. Now the good for the reasonable animal is society; for that we are made for society has been shown above. Is it not plain that the inferior exist for the sake of the superior? But the things which have life are superior to those which have not life, and of those which have life the superior are those which have reason.

Book VI

15. Some things are hurrying into existence, and others are hurrying out of it; and of that which is coming into

existence part is already extinguished. Motions and changes are continually renewing the world, just as the uninterrupted course of time is always renewing the infinite duration of ages. In this flowing stream then, on which there is no abiding, what is there of the things which hurry by on which a man would set a high price? It would be just as if a man should fall in love with one of the sparrows which fly by, but it has already passed out of sight. Something of this kind is the very life of every man, like the exhalation of the blood and the respiration of the air. For such as it is to have once drawn in the air and to have given it back, which we do every moment, just the same is it with the whole respiratory power, which thou didst receive at thy birth yesterday and the day before, to give it back to the element from which thou didst first draw it.

16. Neither is transpiration, as in plants, a thing to be valued, nor respiration, as in domesticated animals and wild beasts, nor the receiving of impressions by the appearances of things, nor being moved by desires as puppets by strings, nor assembling in herds, nor being nourished by food; for this is just like the act of separating and parting with the useless part of our food. What then is worth being valued? To be received with clapping of hands? No. Neither must we value the clapping of tongues, for the praise which comes from the many is a clapping of tongues. Suppose then that thou hast given up this worthless thing called fame, what remains that is worth valuing? This is my opinion, to move thyself and to restrain thyself in conformity to thy proper constitution, to which end both

all employments and arts lead. For every art aims at this, that the thing which has been made should be adapted to the work for which it has been made; and both the vine-planter who looks after the vine, and the horse-breaker, and he who trains the dog, seek this end. But the education and the teaching of youth aim at something. In this then is the value of the education and the teaching. And if this is well, thou wilt not seek anything else. Wilt thou not cease to value many other things too? Then thou wilt be neither free, nor sufficient for thy own happiness, nor without passion. For of necessity thou must be envious, jealous, and suspicious of those who can take away those things, and plot against those who have that which is valued by thee. Of necessity a man must be altogether in a state of perturbation who wants any of these things; and besides, he must often find fault with the gods. But to reverence and honour thy own mind will make thee content with thyself, and in harmony with society, and in agreement with the gods, that is, praising all that they give and have ordered.

Book VII

9. All things are implicated with one another, and the bond is holy; and there is hardly anything unconnected with any other thing. For things have been co-ordinated, and they combine to form the same universe (order). For there is one universe made up of all things, and one God who pervades all things, and one substance, and one law, one common reason in all intelligent animals, and one truth; if indeed there

is also one perfection for all animals which are of the same stock and participate in the same reason.

55. Do not look around thee to discover other men's ruling principles, but look straight to this, to what nature leads thee, both the universal nature through the things which happen to thee, and thy own nature through the acts which must be done by thee. But every being ought to do that which is according to its constitution; and all other things have been constituted for the sake of rational beings, just as among irrational things the inferior for the sake of the superior, but the rational for the sake of one another.

The prime principle then in man's constitution is the social. And the second is not to yield to the persuasions of the body, for it is the peculiar office of the rational and intelligent motion to circumscribe itself, and never to be overpowered either by the motion of the senses or of the appetites, for both are animal; but the intelligent motion claims superiority and does not permit itself to be overpowered by the others. And with good reason, for it is formed by nature to use all of them. The third thing in the rational constitution is freedom from error and from deception. Let then the ruling principle holding fast to these things go straight on, and it has what is its own.

Book VIII

7. Every nature is contented with itself when it goes on its way well; and a rational nature goes on its way well, when in its thoughts it assents to nothing false or uncertain, and when it directs its movements to social acts only, and when it confines its desires and aversions to the things which are in its power, and when it is satisfied with everything that is assigned to it by the common nature. For of this common nature every particular nature is a part, as the nature of the leaf is a part of the nature of the plant; except that in the plant the nature of the leaf is part of a nature which has not perception or reason, and is subject to be impeded; but the nature of man is part of a nature which is not subject to impediments, and is intelligent and just, since it gives to everything in equal portions and according to its worth, times, substance, cause (form), activity, and incident. But examine, not to discover that any one thing compared with any other single thing is equal in all respects, but by taking all the parts together of one thing comparing them with all the parts together of another.

34. If thou didst ever see a hand cut off, or a foot, or a head, lying anywhere apart from the rest of the body, such does a man make himself, as far as he can, who is not content with what happens, and separates himself from others, or does anything unsocial. Suppose that thou hast detached thyself from the natural unity—for thou wast made by nature a part, but now thou hast cut thyself off—yet here there is this beautiful provision, that it is in thy power again to unite thyself. God has allowed this to no other part, after it has been separated and cut asunder, to come together again. But consider the kindness by which he has distinguished man, for he has put it in his power not to be separated at all from the universal; and

when he has been separated, he has allowed him to return and to be united and to resume his place as a part.

47. If thou art pained by any external thing, it is not this thing that disturbs thee, but thy own judgement about it. And it is in thy power to wipe out this judgement now. But if anything in thy own disposition gives thee pain, who hinders thee from correcting thy opinion? And even if thou are pained because thou art not doing some particular thing which seems to thee to be right, why dost thou not rather act than complain?—But some insuperable obstacle is in the way?—Do not be grieved then, for the cause of its not being done depends not on thee.—But it is not worth while to live, if this cannot be done.—Take thy departure then from life contentedly, just as he dies who is in full activity, and well pleased too with things which are obstacles.

Book IX

3. Do not despise death, but be well content with it, since this too is one of those things which nature wills. For such as it is to be young and to grow old, and to increase and to reach maturity, and to have teeth and beard and grey hairs, and to beget, and to be pregnant and to bring forth, and all the other natural operations which the seasons of thy life bring, such also is dissolution. This, then, is consistent with the character of a reflecting man, to be neither careless nor impatient nor contemptuous with respect to death, but to wait for it as one of the operations of nature. As thou now waitest for the time when the child shall come out of

thy wife's womb, so be ready for the time when thy soul shall fall out of this envelope. But if thou requirest also a vulgar kind of comfort which shall reach thy heart, thou wilt be made best reconciled to death by observing the objects from which thou art going to be removed, and the morals of those with whom thy soul will no longer be mingled. For it is no way right to be offended with men, but it is thy duty to care for them and to bear with them gently; and yet to remember that thy departure will be not from men who have the same principles as thyself. For this is the only thing, if there be any, which could draw us the contrary way and attach us to life, to be permitted to live with those who have the same principles as ourselves. But now thou seest how great is the trouble arising from the discordance of those who live together, so that thou mayest say, Come quick, O death, lest perchance I, too, should forget myself.

9. All things which participate in anything which is common to them all move towards that which is of the same kind with themselves. Everything which is earthy turns towards the earth, everything which is liquid flows together, and everything which is of an aërial kind does the same, so that they require something to keep them asunder, and the application of force. Fire indeed moves upwards on account of the elemental fire, but it is so ready to be kindled together with all the fire which is here, that even every substance which is somewhat dry, is easily ignited, because there is less mingled with it of that which is a hindrance to ignition. Accordingly then everything

also which participates in the common intelligent nature moves in like manner towards that which is of the same kind with itself, or moves even more. For so much as it is superior in comparison with all other things, in the same degree also is it more ready to mingle with and to be fused with that which is akin to it. Accordingly among animals devoid of reason we find swarms of bees, and herds of cattle, and the nurture of young birds, and in a manner, loves; for even in animals there are souls, and that power which brings them together is seen to exert itself in the superior degree, and in such a way as never has been observed in plants nor in stones nor in trees. But in rational animals there are political communities and friendships, and families and meetings of people; and in wars, treaties and armistices. But in the things which are still superior, even though they are separated from one another, unity in a manner exists, as in the stars. Thus the ascent to the higher degree is able to produce a sympathy even in things which are separated. See, then, what now takes place. For only intelligent animals have now forgotten this mutual desire and inclination, and in them alone the property of flowing together is not seen. But still though men strive to avoid this union, they are caught and held by it, for their nature is too strong for them; and thou wilt see what I say, if thou only observest. Sooner, then, will one find anything earthy which comes in contact with no earthy thing than a man altogether separated from other men.

42. When thou art offended with any man's shameless conduct, immediately ask thyself, Is it possible, then, that shameless men should not be in the world? It is not possible. Do not, then, require what is impossible. For this man also is one of those shameless men who must of necessity be in the world. Let the same considerations be present to thy mind in the case of the knave, and the faithless man, and of every man who does wrong in any way. For at the same time that thou dost remind thyself that it is impossible that such kind of men should not exist, thou wilt become more kindly disposed towards every one individually. It is useful to perceive this, too, immediately when the occasion arises, what virtue nature has given to man to oppose to every wrongful act. For she has given to man, as an antidote against the stupid man, mildness, and against another kind of man some other power. And in all cases it is possible for thee to correct by teaching the man who is gone astray; for every man who errs misses his object and is gone astray. Besides wherein hast thou been injured? For thou wilt find that no one among those against whom thou art irritated has done anything by which thy mind could be made worse; but that which is evil to thee and harmful has its foundation only in the mind. And what harm is done or what is there strange, if the man who has not been instructed does the acts of an uninstructed man? Consider whether thou shouldst not rather blame thyself, because thou didst not expect such a man to err in such a way. For thou hadst means given thee by the reason to suppose that it was likely that he would commit this error, and yet thou hast forgotten and art amazed that he has

erred. But most of all when thou blamest a man as faithless or ungrateful, turn to thyself. For the fault is manifestly thy own, whether thou didst trust that a man who had such a disposition would keep his promise, or when conferring thy kindness thou didst not confer it absolutely, nor yet in such way as to have received from thy very act all the profit. For what more dost thou want when thou hast done a man a service? Are thou not content that thou hast done something conformable to thy nature, and dost thou seek to be paid for it? Just as if the eye demanded a recompense for seeing, or the feet for walking. For as these members are formed for a particular purpose, and by working according to their several constitutions obtain what is their own; so also as man is formed by nature to acts of benevolence, when he has done anything benevolent or in any other way conducive to the common interest, he has acted conformably to his constitution, and he gets what is his own.

Book X

2. Observe what thy nature requires, so far as thou art governed by nature only: then do it and accept it, if thy nature, so far as thou art a living being, shall not be made worse by it. And next thou must observe what thy nature requires so far as thou art a living being. And all this thou mayest allow thyself, if thy nature, so far as thou art a rational animal, shall not be made worse by it. But the rational animal is consequently also a political (social) animal. Use these rules, then, and trouble thyself about nothing else.

6. Whether the universe is a concourse of atoms, or nature is a system, let this first be established, that I am a part of the whole which is governed by nature; next, I am in a manner intimately related to the parts which are of the same kind with myself. For remembering this, inasmuch as I am a part, I shall be discontented with none of the things which are assigned to me out of the whole; for nothing is injurious to the part, if it is for the advantage of the whole. For the whole contains nothing which is not for its advantage; and all natures indeed have this common principle, but the nature of the universe has this principle besides, that it cannot be compelled even by any external cause to generate anything harmful to itself. By remembering, then, that I am a part of such a whole, I shall be content with everything that happens. And inasmuch as I am in a manner intimately related to the parts which are of the same kind with myself, I shall do nothing unsocial, but I shall rather direct myself to the things which are of the same kind with myself, and I shall turn all my efforts to the common interest, and divert them from the contrary. Now, if these things are done so, life must flow on happily, just as thou mayest observe that the life of a citizen is happy, who continues a course of action which is advantageous to his fellow-citizens, and is content with whatever the state may assign to him.

Book XI

19. There are four principal aberrations of the superior faculty against which thou shouldst be constantly on

thy guard, and when thou hast detected them, thou shouldst wipe them out and say on each occasion thus: this thought is not necessary: this tends to destroy social union: this which thou art going to say comes not from the real thoughts; for thou shouldst consider it among the most absurd of things for a man not to speak from his real thoughts. But the fourth is when thou shalt reproach thyself for anything, for this is an evidence of the diviner part within thee being overpowered and yielding to the less honourable and to the perishable part, the body, and to its gross pleasures.

20. Thy aërial part and all the fiery parts which are mingled in thee, though by nature they have an upward tendency, still in obedience to the disposition of the universe they are overpowered here in the compound mass (the body). And also the whole of the earthy part in thee and the watery, though their tendency is downward, still are raised up and occupy a position which is not their natural one. In this manner then the elemental parts obey the universal, for when they have been fixed in any place perforce they remain there until again the universal shall sound the signal for dissolution. Is it not then strange that thy intelligent part only should be disobedient and discontented with its own place? And yet no force is imposed on it, but only those things which are conformable to its nature: still it does not submit, but is carried in the opposite direction. For the movement towards injustice and intemperance and to anger and grief and fear is nothing else than the act of one who deviates from nature. And also when the ruling faculty is discontented with

anything that happens, then too it deserts its post: for it is constituted for piety and reverence towards the gods no less than for justice. For these qualities also are comprehended under the generic term of contentment with the constitution of things, and indeed they are prior to acts of justice.

Book XII

26. When thou art troubled about anything, thou hast forgotten this, that all things happen according to the universal nature; and forgotten this, that a man's wrongful act is nothing to thee; and further thou hast forgotten this, that everything which happens, always happened so and will happen so, and now happens so everywhere; forgotten this too, how close is the kinship between a man and the whole human race, for it is a community, not of a little blood or seed, but of intelligence. And thou hast forgotten this too, that every man's intelligence is a god, and is an efflux of the deity; and forgotten this, that nothing is a man's own, but that his child and his body and his very soul came from the deity; forgotten this, that everything is opinion; and lastly thou hast forgotten that every man lives the present time only, and loses only this.

36. Man, thou hast been a citizen in this great state (the world): what difference does it make to thee whether for five years (or three)? For that which is conformable to the laws is just for all. Where is the hardship then, if no tyrant nor yet an unjust judge sends thee away from the state, but nature who brought thee into it? The same as if a

praetor who has employed an actor dismisses him from the stage.—'But I have not finished the five acts, but only three of them.'—Thou sayest well, but in life the three acts are the whole drama; for what shall be a complete drama is determined by him who was once the cause of its composition, and now of its dissolution: but thou art the cause of neither. Depart then satisfied, for he also who releases thee is satisfied.

COMMENT

The Ethics of Cicero

At the present time, Cicero is not generally considered to be one of the major figures in the history of philosophy. He is, however, very important in the history of thought, for he wielded an immense influence upon medieval and Renaissance culture. Because of the typicality of his ideas and the clarity and eloquence of his style, we have selected the philosophy of Cicero as representative of the "natural law" tradition. His ethical philosophy may be summarized under three inter-related headings: (1) the concept of a cosmic order as the ground of objective moral laws, (2) the idea of natural law, and (3) the doctrine of the natural kinship of all human beings. Let us glance at each of these tenets.

1. COSMIC ORDER AS THE BASIS OF OBJECTIVE MORAL LAW. The metaphysical background of Cicero's theory is the Stoic conception of nature as rational and divine. "Nature" is the divine reason infused through the cosmos—the inner essence and animating force of all things—and human reason is the divine element in human beings. By means of reason, people can discover the fundamental laws of the universe and can direct their conduct in conformity with these laws. To live according to nature is to develop one's essential faculties and, at the same time, to be in harmony with the divine order of the cosmos.

2. THE LAW OF NATURE. Cicero's theory of natural law is based on the conception of natural harmony. Grounded in the nature of human beings, society, and the universe, natural law is independent of convention, legislation, and all other institutional devices. Far from being an arbitrary construction based on human wish or decree, it is both a law of nature and a moral law, universal, irrevocable, and inalienable. It provides the ultimate standard of right conduct, whether of individuals or of states.

"Natural law" in this sense should be clearly distinguished from what modern science means by *a* natural law. Physicists speak of the law of gravity, but this is a law in a purely descriptive and non-moral sense. Everyone is subject to such a natural law and no one can disobey it, because it is imposed upon our bodies by physical necessity without the cooperation of our will or reason. It is just as binding upon a worm or a rock as it is upon a human being. But "natural law" in Cicero's sense is quite different. We are obliged to obey it only by our reason and conscience: it is not automatically compulsory. The "natural law" that we should live in peace and friendship together, for example, is frequently violated. It orders our conduct only to the extent that it is apprehended by our reason and imposed by our will.

Why, then, should such a thing be called a "law of nature"? Because the good for people depends upon the *nature* of people and their universe. Moral laws are not purely arbitrary. The *"ought"* is based upon what *"is."* Norms are founded on facts. Even when it is broken, the moral law remains a non-arbitrary standard, irrevocable in the sense that it is eternally valid. Those who violate it suffer evil and harm; those who live in harmony with it enjoy the highest blessedness. In this sense, it is enforced by natural sanctions.

This doctrine does not mean that there is a perfect identity between *what is* and *what ought to be*. Cicero does not deny that there are bad people and bad societies. But nature determines certain tendencies that require completion if good is to be achieved. Each individual entity possesses a nature which it shares with other members of the species. This essential nature determines its most fundamental tendencies. Good inheres in the fulfillment of these tendencies; evil, in their frustration.

3. THE NATURAL KINSHIP OF ALL HUMAN BEINGS. In Cicero's philosophy, the doctrine of natural law is combined with the doctrine of natural brotherhood and equality. All people by nature are kin. "No single thing is so like another . . . as all of us are to one another. . . . And so, however we may define man, a single definition will apply to all." This does not mean that all people are equal in learning or that they should be made equal in worldly goods, but, rather, that they all possess a similar psychological constitution and should be treated with the dignity and respect that befits a human being. In opposition to all forms of relativism and parochialism—the bias of race, nation, class, or creed—Cicero asserts the great doctrine of human brotherhood.

One of the momentous implications of this doctrine is that the highest allegiance is not to the local state but to the universal fellowship. All people, as children of nature, are bound in conscience by the same laws and belong, in this sense, to the same "commonwealth." "Those who share Law must also share Justice; and those who share these are to be regarded as members of the same commonwealth. . . . Hence we must now conceive of this whole universe as one commonwealth of which both gods and men are members." Cicero does not deny that we should be citizens of the particular state in which we find ourselves; he even emphasizes the importance of civic duties. Local allegiance, however, is ethically subordinate to the wider allegiance to nature and humanity. If the laws of the state do not conform to the laws of nature, they no more deserve to be called laws than do the dictates of a robber band. Here is the ultimate source of the revolutionary doctrine that people owe a higher allegiance to nature and to nature's God than to any temporal ruler and hence have the inalienable right to revolt against an unjust and tyrannical state. These doctrines are fundamental in the American Declaration of Independence and in the legal tradition of "natural law."

Human Harmony with the Natural Environment

In the writings of both Cicero and Marcus Aurelius, there is a strong overtone of pantheism in their doctrine that people should live in harmony with nature. Just as a soul or life force animates the human body, they maintained, so a spiritual force rolls through all things. This soul or life force can be called God, Nature, Reason—synonyms for the inner essence and animating principle of the universe. It is the productive, formative power, the force that makes for movement and growth. It is divine reason, all pervasive and all-powerful. Hence Marcus Aurelius maintained that there is no sheer evil in the world, and nothing is left to chance. From this standpoint it is also fate—not a blind mechanical necessity but a purposive, providential force, the living activity of the whole expressing itself through every natural event.

The divine essence is in every person: reason is our governing principle, the core and center of our being. What corresponds to this reason and expresses our nature also corresponds to the world soul and expresses the universal nature. To "live according to nature" is to express our rational nature, and to be in harmony with the rational order of the world. The essence of morality is to make the "things in our power"—our inner attitudes—harmonize with the "things not in our power" —the rational outward course of events.

The need to live in harmony with nature is not just an ancient doctrine. It has been echoed and reechoed during our modern ecological crisis. We may choose to express this need more in scientific than in religious terms, but we too must recognize the necessity to live in symbiotic harmony with nature. Willy-nilly, we have to dwell on this earth if we are to live at all. If the future is to be tolerable, we must bring human breeding under sensible control, we must conserve our dwindling natural resources, and we must bring to a halt the air and water pollution and the bulldozed devastation of the landscape.

Some Major Questions

The great question that is posed by the readings in this chapter is the relation between "facts" and "ideals," between "what is" and "what ought to be." This is a question to which the philosophers represented in Part Three will return again and again, and it is one of the most important and difficult questions in ethics. The serious student of philosophy will need to ponder its meaning and implications and to decide as best as possible what is a reasonable answer.

It seems clear that *good*, in the sense of *what ought to be*, and *right*, in the sense of *what ought to be done*, are not natural characteristics, as are rectangularity or absent-mindedness. Many philosophers have concluded that these concepts have a distinctly *ethical* meaning—a meaning which must be grasped by intuition or *a priori* reason or a peculiar moral sense rather than by empirical science or a descriptive metaphysics. If so, does this invalidate the doctrine discussed in this chapter that morality is based on nature? Here is a question which the reader might ponder.

Another very fundamental question is whether the anti-relativistic implications of the theory of natural law are valid. Can we define our legitimate aim as the unfolding of our basic powers according to the laws of our nature and in harmony with our natural environment? Or should we conclude that people are so variously moulded by patterns of culture that "human nature" is largely an empty word? Or that the natural environment counts less and less in comparison with the artificialities of urban civilization? If so, is this a disaster?

Other questions concern the relation between natural rights and democratic theory. The concept of natural rights has often been linked with the "social contract." This is the idea of an original convenant by which individuals, who possessed natural rights in an original nonpolitical "state of nature," joined together and through mutual consent formed a state and placed a fiduciary trust in the supreme power of government. The purpose of the covenant is to make these rights more secure, and if the government fails to do this, it forfeits the right to rule. Thus phrased the theory of the state of nature, natural rights, and the social contract formed the basis of democratic, sometimes, revolutionary, tendencies. In Rousseau's formulation and even more clearly in Kant's the state of nature and the social contract were treated as useful fictions, meant to serve as a criterion for judging the legitimacy of acts of the state. Recently this constellation of ideas has been elaborated by John Rawl's much discussed book, *The Theory of Justice* (Harvard University Press, 1971). The reader may wish to consider whether the tradition of natural law and natural rights is a satisfactory basis for a theory of democratic sovereignty and social justice. Is it an effective way to delineate the meaning of human rights? Or is it too abstract and nonhistorical? Must we seek some other basis for democratic theory, for example, the instrumentalist approach of John Dewey, or the socialist approach of Karl Marx? Or should we reject democracy altogether, as Plato and Nietzsche would have us do?

There is also the question whether Marcus Aurelius' interpretation of nature is coherent. Is he being inconsistent in clinging to the doctrines of both fate and free will, cosmopolitanism and self-sufficiency, tacit admission that certain things are preferable and yet explicit teaching that all happens for the best. If he *is* inconsistent, can we somehow reconcile these clashing doctrines, or must we choose some and abandon others? If so how much can we salvage? Can we still admire the main tenets of his Stoicism: the courage, the tranquility, the cosmopolitanism, the sense of universal fellowship, the attempt to see the rational connections and necessity of things, the poise and magnanimity of outlook that result from identifying oneself with the whole frame of nature?

Finally there is the question of ecological adjustment. As I have already intimated, this is a crucial issue for the whole of humanity. Our present technology is suicidal—so much of it is devoted to the instruments of death rather than to the means of life, and so much is based on the extraction of exhaustible ores and fossil fuels. These diminishing resources are combined with mounting overpopulation. Control is an unsolved problem even in the developed countries, and starvation is the only sure-fire method of controlling population in the undeveloped countries. The present rate of population growth cannot continue indefinitely, for it would rapidly exhaust the physical resources and limit of our world. Can we cope with these threats without a fairly radical interference with cherished freedoms and traditional institutions? Can we limit growth without precipitating a new depression? What far-reaching changes in human values will be required?

12

Duty

IMMANUEL KANT

(For biographical note see pages 264–265.)

The Categorical Imperative

Section I

Transition from Ordinary Moral Conceptions to the Philosophical Conception of Morality

Nothing in the whole world, or even

outside of the world, can possibly be regarded as good without limitation except a *good will*. No doubt it is a good and desirable thing to have intelligence, sagacity, judgment, and other intellectual gifts, by whatever name they may be called; it is also good and

The Philosophy of Kant as Contained in Extracts from His Own Writings, selected and translated by John Watson. Jackson, Wylie and Company, Glasgow, 1888, second edition, 1891. (In this version, the original in *The Foundations of the Metaphysic of Morals* is somewhat condensed.)

417

desirable in many respects to possess by nature such qualities as courage, resolution, and perseverance; but all these gifts of nature may be in the highest degree pernicious and hurtful, if the will which directs them, or what is called the *character,* is not itself good. The same thing applies to *gifts of fortune.* Power, wealth, honor, even good health, and that general well-being and contentment with one's lot which we call *happiness,* give rise to pride and not infrequently to insolence, if a man's will is not good; nor can a reflective and impartial spectator ever look with satisfaction upon the unbroken prosperity of a man who is destitute of the ornament of a pure and good will. A good will would therefore seem to be the indispensable condition without which no one is even worthy to be happy.

A man's will is good, not because the consequences which flow from it are good, nor because it is capable of attaining the end which it seeks, but it is good in itself, or because it wills the good. By a good will is not meant mere well-wishing; it consists in a resolute employment of all the means within one's reach, and its intrinsic value is in no way increased by success or lessened by failure.

This idea of the absolute value of mere will seems so extraordinary that, although it is endorsed even by the popular judgment, we must subject it to careful scrutiny.

If nature had meant to provide simply for the maintenance, the well-being, in a word the happiness, of beings which have reason and will, it must be confessed that, in making use of their reason, it has hit upon a very poor way of attaining its end. As a matter of fact the very worst way a man of refinement and culture can take to secure enjoyment and happiness is to make use of his reason for that purpose. Hence there is apt to arise in his mind a certain degree of *misology,* or hatred of reason. Finding that the arts which minister to luxury, and even the sciences, instead of bringing him happiness, only lay a heavier yoke on his neck, he at length comes to envy, rather than to despise, men of less refinement, who follow more closely the promptings of their natural impulses, and pay little heed to what reason tells them to do or to leave undone. It must at least be admitted, that one may deny reason to have much or indeed any value in the production of happiness and contentment, without taking a morose or ungrateful view of the goodness with which the world is governed. Such a judgment really means that life has another and a much nobler end than happiness, and that the true vocation of reason is to secure that end.

The true object of reason then, in so far as it is practical, or capable of influencing the will, must be to produce a will which is *good in itself,* and not merely good *as a means* to something else. This will is not the only or the whole good, but it is the highest good, and the condition of all other good, even of the desire for happiness itself. It is therefore not inconsistent with the wisdom of nature that the cultivation of reason which is essential to the furtherance of its first and unconditioned object, the production of a good will, should, in this life at least, in many ways limit, or even make impossible, the attainment of happiness, which is its second and conditioned object.

To bring to clear consciousness the conception of a will which is good in itself, a conception already familiar to the popular mind, let us examine the conception of *duty,* which involves the idea of a good will as manifested under certain subjective limitations and hindrances.

I pass over actions which are admittedly violations of duty, for these, however useful they may be in the attainment of this or that end, manifestly do not proceed *from* duty. I set aside also those actions which are not actually inconsistent with duty, but which yet are done under the impulse of some natural inclination, although *not a direct inclination* to do these particular actions; for in these it is easy to determine whether the action that is consistent with duty, is done *from duty* or with some selfish object in view. It is more difficult to make a clear distinction of motives when there is a *direct* inclination to do a certain action, which is itself in conformity with duty. The preservation of one's own life, for instance, is a duty; but, as everyone has a natural inclination to preserve his life, the anxious care which most men usually devote to this object, has no intrinsic value, nor the maxim from which they act any moral import. They preserve their life *in accordance with* duty, but not *because of* duty. But, suppose adversity and hopeless sorrow to have taken away all desire for life; suppose that the wretched man would welcome death as a release, and yet takes means to prolong his life simply from a sense of duty: then his maxim has a genuine moral import.

But, secondly, an action that is done from duty gets its moral value, *not from the object* which it is intended to secure, but from the maxim by which it is determined. Accordingly, the action has the same moral value whether the object is attained or not, if only the *principle* by which the will is determined to act is independent of every object of sensuous desire. What was said above makes it clear, that it is not the object aimed at, or, in other words, the consequences which flow from an action when these are made the end and motive of the will, that can give to the action an unconditioned and moral value. In what, then, can the moral value of an action consist, if it does not lie in the will itself, as directed to the attainment of a certain object? It can lie only in the principle of the will, no matter whether the object sought can be attained by the action or not. For the will stands as it were at the parting of the ways, between its *a priori* principle, which is formal, and its *a posteriori* material motive. As so standing it must be determined by something, and, as no action which is done from duty can be determined by a material principle, it can be determined only by the formal principle of all volition.

From the two propositions just set forth a third directly follows, which may be thus stated. *Duty is the obligation to act from reverence for law.* Now, I may have a natural *inclination* for the object that I expect to follow from my action, but I can never have *reverence* for that which is not a spontaneous activity of my will, but merely an effect of it; neither can I have reverence for any natural inclination, whether it is my own or another's. If it is my own, I can at most only approve of it; if it is manifested by another, I may regard it as conducive to my own interest, and hence I may in certain cases even be said to have a love for it. But the only thing which I can reverence or which can lay me under an obligation to act, is the law which is connected with my will, not as a consequence, but as a principle; a principle which is not dependent upon natural inclination, but overmasters it, or at least allows it to have no influence whatever in determining my course of action. Now if an action which is done out of regard for duty sets entirely aside the influence of natural inclination and along with it every object of the will, nothing else is left by which the will can be determined but objectively the *law* itself, and subjectively *pure reverence* for the law as a principle of action. Thus there arises the maxim, to obey the moral law even at the sacrifice of all my natural inclinations.

The supreme good which we call moral can therefore be nothing but the *idea of the law* in itself, in so far as it is this idea which determines the will, and not any consequences that are expected to follow. Only a *rational* being can have such an idea, and hence a man who acts from the idea of the law is already morally good, no matter whether the consequences which he expects from his action follow or not.

Now what must be the nature of a law, the idea of which is to determine the will, even apart from the effects expected to follow, and which is therefore itself entitled to be called good absolutely and without qualification? As the will must not be moved to act from any desire for the results expected to follow from obedience to a certain law, the only principle of the will which remains is that of the conformity of actions to universal law. In all cases I must act in such a way *that I can at the same time will that my maxim should become a universal law*. This is what is meant by conformity to law pure and simple; and this is the principle which serves, and must serve, to determine the will, if the idea of duty is not to be regarded as empty and chimerical. As a matter of fact the judgments which we are wont to pass upon conduct perfectly agree with this principle, and in making them we always have it before our eyes.

May I, for instance, under the pressure of circumstances, make a promise which I have no intention of keeping? The question is not, whether it is prudent to make a false promise, but whether it is morally right. To enable me to answer this question shortly and conclusively, the best way is for me to ask myself whether it would satisfy me that the maxim to extricate myself from embarrassment by giving a false promise should have the force of a universal law, applying to others as well as to myself. And I see at once, that, while I can certainly will the lie, I cannot will that lying should be a universal law. If lying were universal, there would, properly speaking, be no promises whatever. I might say that I intended to do a certain thing at some future time, but nobody would believe me, or if he did at the moment trust to my promise, he would afterwards pay me back in my own coin. My maxim thus proves itself to be self-destructive, so soon as it is taken as a universal law.

Duty, then, consists in the obligation to act from *pure* reverence for the moral law. To this motive all others must give way, for it is the condition of a will which is good *in itself,* and which has a value with which nothing else is comparable.

There is, however, in man a strong feeling of antagonism to the commands of duty, although his reason tells him that those commands are worthy of the highest reverence. For man not only possesses reason, but he has certain natural wants and inclinations, the complete satisfaction of which he calls happiness. These natural inclinations clamorously demand to have their seemingly reasonable claims respected; but reason issues its commands inflexibly, refusing to promise anything to the natural desires, and treating their claims with a sort of neglect and contempt. From this there arises a *natural dialectic,* that is, a disposition to explain away the strict laws of duty, to cast doubt upon their validity, or at least, upon their purity and stringency, and in this way to make them yield to the demands of the natural inclinations.

Thus men are forced to go beyond the narrow circle of ideas within which their reason ordinarily moves, and to take a step into the field of *moral philosophy,* not indeed from any perception of speculative difficulties, but simply on practical grounds. The practical reason of men cannot be long exercised any more than the theoretical,

without falling insensibly into a dialectic, which compels it to call in the aid of philosophy; and in the one case as in the other, rest can be found only in a thorough criticism of human reason.

Section II

Transition from Popular Moral Philosophy to the Metaphysic of Morality

So far, we have drawn our conception of duty from the manner in which men employ it in the ordinary exercise of their practical reason. The conception of duty, however, we must not suppose to be therefore derived from experience. On the contrary, we hear frequent complaints, the justice of which we cannot but admit, that no one can point to a single instance in which an action has undoubtedly been done purely from a regard for duty; that there are certainly many actions which are not *opposed* to duty, but none which are indisputably done *from* duty and therefore have a moral value. Nothing indeed can secure us against the complete loss of our ideas of duty, and maintain in the soul a well-grounded respect for the moral law, but the clear conviction, that reason issues its commands on its own authority, without caring in the least whether the actions of men have, as a matter of fact, been done purely from ideas of duty. For reason commands inflexibly that certain actions should be done, which perhaps never have been done; actions, the very possibility of which may seem doubtful to one who bases everything upon experience. Perfect disinterestedness in friendship, for instance, is demanded of every man, although there may never have been a sincere friend; for pure friendship is bound up with the idea of duty as duty, and belongs to the very idea of a reason which determines the will on *a priori* grounds, prior to all experience.

It is, moreover, beyond dispute, that unless we are to deny to morality all truth and all reference to a possible object, the moral law has so wide an application that it is binding, not merely upon man, but upon all *rational beings,* and not merely under certain contingent conditions, and with certain limitations, but absolutely and necessarily. . . .

Only a rational being has the faculty of acting in conformity with the *idea* of law, or from principles; only a rational being, in other words, has a will. And as without reason actions cannot proceed from laws, will is simply practical reason. If the will is infallibly determined by reason, the actions of a rational being are subjectively as well as objectively necessary; that is, will must be regarded as a faculty of choosing *that only* which reason, independently of natural inclination, declares to be practically necessary or good. On the other hand, if the will is not invariably determined by reason alone, but is subject to certain subjective conditions or motives, which are not always in harmony with the objective conditions; if the will, as actually is the case with man, is not in perfect conformity with reason; actions which are recognized to be objectively necessary, are subjectively contingent. The determination of such a will according to objective laws is therefore called *obligation.* That is to say, if the will of a rational being is not

absolutely good, we conceive of it as capable of being determined by objective laws of reason, but not as by its very nature necessarily obeying them.

The idea that a certain principle is objective, and binding upon the will, is a command of reason, and the statement of the command in a formula is an *imperative.*

All imperatives are expressed by the word *ought,* to indicate that the will upon which they are binding is not by its subjective constitution necessarily determined in conformity with the objective law of reason. An imperative says, that the doing, or leaving undone of a certain thing would be good, but it addresses a will which does not always do a thing simply because it is good. Now, that is practically *good* which determines the will by ideas of reason, in other words, that which determines it, not by subjective influences, but by principles which are objective, or apply to all rational beings as such. *Good* and *pleasure* are quite distinct. Pleasure results from the influence of purely subjective causes upon the will of the subject, and these vary with the susceptibility of this or that individual, while a principle of reason is valid for all.

A perfectly good will would, like the will of man, stand under objective laws, laws of the good, but it could not be said to be under an *obligation* to act in conformity with those laws. Such a will by its subjective constitution could be determined only by the idea of the good. In reference to the Divine will, or any other holy will, imperatives have no meaning; for here the will is by its very nature necessarily in harmony with the law, and therefore *ought* has no application to it. Imperatives are formulae, which express merely the relation of objective laws of volition in general to the imperfect will of this or that rational being, as for instance, the will of man.

Now, all imperatives command either *hypothetically* or *categorically*. A hypothetical imperative states that a certain thing must be done, if something else which is willed, or at least might be willed, is to be attained. The categorical imperative declares that an act is in itself or objectively necessary, without any reference to another end.

Every practical law represents a possible action as good, and therefore as obligatory for a subject that is capable of being determined to act by reason. Hence all imperatives are formulae for the determination of an action which is obligatory according to the principle of a will that is in some sense good. If the action is good only because it is a means to *something else,* the imperative is *hypothetical;* if the action is conceived to be good *in itself,* the imperative, as the necessary principle of a will that in itself conforms to reason, is *categorical.*

An imperative, then, states what possible action of mine would be good. It supplies the practical rule for a will which does not at once do an act simply because it is good, either because the subject does not know it to be good, or because, knowing it to be good, he is influenced by maxims which are opposed to the objective principles of a practical reason.

The hypothetical imperative says only that an action is good relatively to a certain *possible* end or to a certain *actual* end. In the former case it is *problematic,* in the latter case *assertoric.* The categorical imperative, which affirms that an action is in itself or objectively necessary without regard to an end, that is, without regard to any other end than itself, is an *apodictic* practical principle.

Whatever is within the power of a rational being may be conceived to be capable of being willed by some rational being, and hence the principles which determine what actions are necessary in the attainment of certain possible ends, are infinite in number.

Yet there is one thing which we may assume that all finite rational beings actually make their end, and there is therefore one object which may safely be regarded, not simply as something that they *may* seek, but as something that by a necessity of their nature they actually *do* seek. This object is *happiness.* The hypothetical imperative, which affirms the practical necessity of an action as the means of attaining happiness, is *assertoric.* We must not think of happiness as simply a possible and problematic end, but as an end that we may with confidence presuppose *a priori* to be sought by everyone, belonging as it does to the very nature of man. Now skill in the choice of means to his own greatest well-being may be called *prudence,* taking the word in its more restricted sense. An imperative, therefore, which relates merely to the choice of means to one's own happiness, that is, a maxim of prudence, must be hypothetical; it commands an action, not absolutely, but only as a means to another end.

Lastly, there is an imperative which directly commands an action, without presupposing as its condition that some other end is to be attained by means of that action. This imperative is *categorical*. It has to do, not with the matter of an action and the result expected to follow from it, but simply with the form and principle from which the action itself proceeds. The action is essentially good if the motive of the agent is good, let the consequences be what they may. This imperative may be called the imperative of *morality*.

How are all these imperatives possible? The question is not, How is an action which an imperative commands actually realized? but, How can we think of the will as placed under obligation by each of those imperatives? Very little need be said to show how an imperative of skill is possible. He who wills the end, wills also the means in his power which are indispensable to the attainment of the end. Looking simply at the act of will, we must say that this proposition is analytic. If a certain object is to follow as an effect from my volition, my causality must be conceived as active in the production of the effect, or as employing the means by which the effect will take place. The imperative, therefore, simply states that in the conception of the willing of this end there is directly implied the conception of actions necessary to this end. No doubt certain synthetic propositions are required to determine the particular means by which a given end may be attained, but these have nothing to do with the principle or act of the will, but merely state how the object may actually be realized.

Were it as easy to give a definite conception of happiness as of a particular end, the imperatives of prudence would be of exactly the same nature as the imperatives of skill, and would therefore be analytic. For, we should be able to say, that he who wills the end wills also the only means in his power for the attainment of the end. But, unfortunately, the conception of happiness is so indefinite, that, although every man desires to obtain it, he is unable to give a definite and self-consistent statement of what he actually desires and wills. The truth is, that, strictly speaking, the imperatives of prudence are not commands at all. They do not say that actions are objective or *necessary*, and hence they must be regarded as counsels, not as commands of reason. Still, the imperative of prudence would be an analytic proposition, if the means to happiness could only be known with certainty. For the only difference in the two cases is that in the imperative of skill the end is merely possible, in the imperative of prudence it is actually given; and as in both all that is commanded is the means to an end which is assumed to be willed, the imperative which commands that he who wills the end should also will the means, is in both cases analytic. There is therefore no real difficulty in seeing how an imperative of prudence is possible.

The only question which is difficult of solution, is, how the imperative of morality is possible. Here the imperative is not hypothetical, and hence we cannot derive its objective necessity from any presupposition. Nor must it for a moment be forgotten, that an imperative of this sort cannot be established by instances taken from experience. We must therefore find out by careful investigation, whether imperatives which seem to be categorical may not be simply hypothetical imperatives in disguise.

One thing is plain at the very outset, namely, that only a categorical imperative can have the dignity of a practical *law,* and that the other imperatives, while they may no doubt be called *principles* of the will, cannot be called laws. An action which is necessary merely as a means to an arbitrary end, may be regarded as itself contingent, and if the end is abandoned, the maxim which prescribes the action has no longer any force. An unconditioned command, on the other hand, does not permit the will to choose the opposite, and therefore it carries with it the necessity which is essential to a law.

It is, however, very hard to see how there can be a categorical imperative or law of morality at all. Such a law is an *a priori* synthetic proposition, and we cannot expect that there will be less difficulty in showing how a proposition of that sort is possible in the sphere of morality than we have found it to be in the sphere of knowledge.

In attempting to solve this problem, we shall first of all inquire, whether the mere conception of a categorical imperative may not perhaps supply us with a formula, which contains the only proposition that can possibly be a categorical imperative. . . .

If I take the mere conception of a hypothetical imperative, I cannot tell what it may contain until the condition under which it applies is presented to me. But I can tell at once from the very conception of a categorical imperative what it must contain. Viewed apart from the law, the imperative simply affirms that the maxim, or subjective principle of action, must conform to the objective principle or law. Now the law contains no condition to which it is restricted, and hence nothing remains but the statement, that the maxim ought to conform to the universality of the law as such. It is only this conformity to law that the imperative can be said to represent as necessary.

There is therefore but one categorical imperative, which may be thus stated: *Act in conformity with that maxim, and that maxim only, which you can at the same time will to be a universal law.* . . .

The universality of the law which governs the succession of events, is what we mean by *nature,* in the most general sense, that is, the existence of things, in so far as their existence is determined in conformity with universal laws. The universal imperative of duty might therefore be put in this way: *Act as if the maxim from which you act were to become through your will a universal law of nature.*

If we attend to what goes on in ourselves in every transgression of a duty, we find, that we do not will that our maxim should become a universal law. We find it in fact impossible to do so, and we really will that the opposite of our maxim should remain a universal law, at the same time that we assume the liberty of making an exception in favor of natural inclination in our own case, or perhaps only for this particular occasion. Hence, if we looked at all cases from the same point of view, that is, from the point of view of reason, we should see that there was here a contradiction in our will. The contradiction is, that a certain principle is admitted to be necessary objectively or as a universal law, and yet is held not to be universal subjectively, but to admit of exceptions. What we do is, to consider our action at one time from the point of view of a will that is in perfect conformity with reason, and at another time from the point of view of a will that is under the influence of natural inclination. There is, therefore, here no real contradiction, but merely an antagonism of inclination to the command of reason. The universality of the principle is changed into a mere generality, in order that the practical principle of reason may meet the maxim half way. Not only is this limitation condemned by our own impartial judgment, but it proves that we actually recognize the validity of the categorical imperative, and merely allow ourselves to make a few exceptions in our own favor which we try to consider as of no importance, or as a necessary concession to circumstances.

This much at least we have learned, that if the idea of duty is to have any meaning and to lay down the laws of our actions, it must be expressed in categorical and not in hypothetical imperatives. We have also obtained a clear and distinct conception (a very important thing), of what is implied in a categorical imperative which contains the principle of duty for all cases, granting such an imperative to be possible at all. But we have not yet been able to prove *a priori*, that there actually is such an imperative; that there is a practical law which commands absolutely on its own authority, and is independent of all sensuous impulses; and that duty consists in obedience to this law.

In seeking to reach this point, it is of the greatest importance to observe, that the reality of this principle cannot possibly be derived from the *peculiar constitution of human nature*. For by duty is meant the practically unconditioned necessity of an act, and hence we can show that duty is a law for the will of all human beings, only by showing that it is applicable to all rational beings, or rather to all rational beings to whom an imperative applies at all. . . .

Practical principles that abstract from all subjective ends are *formal;* those that presuppose subjective ends, and therefore natural inclinations, are *material*. The ends which a rational being arbitrarily sets before himself as material ends to be produced by his actions, are all merely relative; for that which gives to them their value is simply their relation to the peculiar susceptibility of the subject. They can therefore yield no universal and necessary principles, or practical laws, applicable to all rational beings, and binding upon every will. Upon such relative ends, therefore, only hypothetical imperatives can be based.

Suppose, however, that there is something the existence of which has in itself an absolute value, something which, *as an end in itself*, can be a ground of definite laws; then, there would lie in that, and only in that, the ground of a possible categorical imperative or practical law.

Now, I say, that man, and indeed every rational being as such, *exists* as an end in himself, *not merely as a means* to be made use of by this or that will, and therefore man in all his actions, whether these are directed towards himself or towards other rational beings, must always be regarded as an end. No object of natural desire has more than a conditioned value; for if the natural desires, and the wants to which they give rise, did not exist, the object to which they are directed would have no value at all. So far are the natural desires and wants from having an absolute value, so far are they from being sought simply for themselves, that every rational being must wish to be entirely free from their influence. The value of every object which human action is the means of obtaining, is, therefore, always conditioned. And even beings whose existence depends upon nature, not upon our will, if they are without reason, have only the relative value of means, and are therefore called *things*. Rational beings, on the other hand, are called *persons*, because their very nature shows them to be ends in themselves, that is, something which cannot be made use of simply as a means. A person being thus an object of respect, a certain limit is placed upon arbitrary will. Persons are not purely subjective ends, whose existence has a value *for us* as the effect of our actions, but they are *objective ends*, or beings whose existence is an end in itself, for which no other end can be substituted. If all value were conditioned, and therefore contingent, it would be impossible to show that there is any supreme practical principle whatever.

If, then, there is a supreme practical principle, a principle which in relation to the human will is a categorical imperative, it must be an *objective* principle of the will, and must be able to serve as a universal practical law. For, such a principle must be derived from the idea of that which is necessarily an end for every one because it is an *end in itself*. Its foundation is this, that *rational nature exists as an end in itself*. Man necessarily conceives of his own existence in this way, and so far this is a *subjective* principle of human action. But in this way also every other rational being conceives of his own existence, and for the very same reason; hence the principle is also *objective,* and from it, as the highest practical ground, all laws of the will must be capable of being derived. The practical imperative will therefore be this: *Act so as to use humanity, whether in your own person or in the person of another, always as an end, never as merely a means.*

The principle, that humanity and every rational nature is an end in itself, is not borrowed from experience. For, in the first place, because of its universality it applies to all rational beings, and no experience can apply so widely. In the second place, it does not regard humanity subjectively, as an end of man, that is, as an object which the subject of himself actually makes his end, but as an objective end, which ought to be regarded as a law that constitutes the supreme limiting condition of all subjective ends, and which must therefore have its source in pure reason. The objective ground of all practical laws consists in the *rule* and the form of universality, which makes them capable of serving as laws, but their *subjective* ground consists in the *end* to which they are directed. Now, by the second principle, every rational being, as an end in himself, is the subject of all ends. From this follows the third practical principle of the will, which is the supreme condition of its harmony with universal practical reason, namely, the idea of *the will of every rational being as a will which lays down universal laws of action*. . . .

At the point we have now reached, it does not seem surprising that all previous attempts to find out the principle of morality should have ended in failure. It was seen that man is bound under law by duty, but it did not strike anyone, that the *universal* system of laws to which he is subject are laws which he *imposes upon himself,* and that he is only under obligation to act in conformity with his own will, a will which by the purpose of nature prescribes universal laws. Now so long as man is thought to be merely subject to law, no matter what the law may be, he must be regarded as stimulated or constrained to obey the law from interest of some kind; for as the law does not proceed from *his own* will, there must be *something external* to his will which compels him to act in conformity with it. This perfectly necessary conclusion frustrated every attempt to find a supreme principle of duty. Duty was never established, but merely the necessity of acting from some form of interest, private or public. The imperative was therefore necessarily always conditioned, and could not possibly have the force of a moral command. The supreme principle of morality I shall therefore call the principle of the *autonomy* of the will, to distinguish it

from all other principles, which I call principles of *heteronomy*.

The conception that every rational being in all the maxims of his will must regard himself as prescribing universal laws, by reference to which himself and all his actions are to be judged, leads to a cognate and very fruitful conception, that of a *kingdom of ends*.

By *kingdom,* I mean the systematic combination of different rational beings through the medium of common laws. Now, laws determine certain ends as universal, and hence, if abstraction is made from the individual differences of rational beings, and from all that is peculiar to their private ends, we get the idea of a complete totality of ends combined in a system; in other words, we are able to conceive of a kingdom of ends, which conforms to the principles formulated above.

All rational beings stand under the law, that each should treat himself and others, *never simply as means,* but always as *at the same time ends in themselves.* Thus there arises a systematic combination of rational beings through the medium of common objective laws. This may well be called a kingdom of ends, because the object of those laws is just to relate all rational beings to one another as ends and means. Of course this kingdom of ends is merely an ideal.

Morality, then, consists in the relation of all action to the system of laws which alone makes possible a kingdom of ends. These laws must belong to the nature of every rational being, and must proceed from his own will. The principle of the will, therefore, is, that no action should be done from any other maxim than one which is consistent with a universal law. This may be expressed in the formula: *Act so that the will may regard itself as in its maxims laying down universal laws.* Now, if the maxims of rational beings are not by their very nature in harmony with this objective principle, the principle of a universal system of laws, the necessity of acting in conformity with that principle is called practical obligation or *duty.* . . . *Autonomy* is thus the foundation of the moral value of man and of every other rational being.

The three ways in which the principle of morality has been formulated are at bottom simply different statements of the same law, and each implies the other two.

COMMENT

Some Main Issues Presented by Kant's Ethics

The ethics of Kant is the most famous example of a "deontological" type of ethics. The adjective "deontological" is derived from the Greek words *deon* (duty) and *logos* (science, or theory). A deontological ethics is one based on the theory of duty. As the term is commonly used, it means an ethics of duty for duty's sake, expressed in its most uncompromising form in the motto, "Let me do right though the heavens fall." The opposite, or utilitarian, point of view, is that an act would be wrong, because disastrous, *if* the heavens fell. As indicated by the next chapter, utilitarians such as Bentham and Mill judge the morality of actions in terms of their consequences for weal or woe. Quite different is the point of view of Kant that the moral quality of acts depends upon conformtiy to laws, rules, or principles of action rather than upon goals or results.

Whatever our opinion of Kant's ethics—and there is much to admire as well as to criticize—we cannot deny that he presents issues of great importance. Some of these are as follows:

1. ARE ETHICAL PRINCIPLES EMPIRICAL OR A PRIORI? The motive of Kant's philosophy is the discovery and justification of *a priori* forms, concepts, and principles. In ethics, he draws a sharp distinction between "is" and "ought" and contends that the moral *ought* must be formulated in *a priori* principles. Is he correct?

If empirical science is a knowledge of *existence*, and if an "ideal" or "norm" is what ought to be but *is not*, the conception of a "normative empirical science" is contradictory. And if so, ethics is either merely subjective—as the advocates of the emotive theory contend—or it is *a priori*. Modern philosophers have been deeply disturbed by the problem thus posed.

The proponents of natural law, such as Cicero, try to solve the problem by denying the sharp antithesis between *what is* and *what ought to be*—and on this point they receive support from utilitarians such as Mill and pragmatists such as Dewey. What ought to be, it can be argued, is what satisfies genuine needs. A need arises when there is an uncompleted tendency in human nature—a frustrated, or at least unconsummated, impulse or desire. These needs can be determined scientifically, and plans to satisfy them can be elaborated with due regard to facts. The objective of securing the greatest possible fulfillment should determine which needs are to receive preferential treatment, and here, too, there are facts to guide us.

Kant would reply that such an empirical procedure is a mere begging of the question. It *assumes* that morality consists in the fulfillment of our needs—but this assumption he would sharply challenge. If *need* is interpreted in a nonmoral sense, it is not a moral concept and hence is irrelevant; but if it is interpreted in a moral sense, it must be connected with obligation—and obligation is not the sort of thing that empirical science can discover and justify. *Moral* objectivity is quite different from *scientific* objectivity, and an objective moral *ought* can never be determined scientifically. Rejecting the emotive view that morality is subjective, Kant concludes that moral objectivity must rest upon *a priori* foundations.

2. Is Good Will, and Good Will Alone, Unconditionally Good? Let us consider Kant's contention that pleasure is good if combined with a good will but evil if combined with a bad will. A hedonist would agree that pleasure gained from wanton torture is bad, but would say that it is bad not *in* and *of itself* but in its evil consequences. Its bad effects greatly outweigh its intrinsic goodness— but *as pleasure*, it is intrinsically good. The hedonist would add that what makes good will "intrinsically good" is simply the pleasure that it involves, rather than the accompanying sense of duty. A nonhedonist might admit that good will is intrinsically good, but maintain that there are other intrinsic goods, such as truth and beauty, that are no less ultimate and unconditional.

We can ask the question whether there is *any* unconditional good—pleasure or love or respect for duty or anything else. Pleasure can be sadistic, respect for duty can be chill and puritanical, and anything else can be degraded by its context.

3. Is Kant's Distinction between a Hypothetical and a Categorical Imperative Sound? If the criterion of right volition is neither inclination nor consequences, what is it? Kant answers that the rightness of the volition depends upon two factors: *right incentive* and *right maxim*.

The right incentive is respect and reverence for moral law. A moral act must be done for duty's sake (although other motivations may be involved). This requirement has already been discussed under the name, "good will."

The right maxim is the principle of "the categorical imperative." An imperative is an injunction or command; it says that a person ought to do so and so. A hypothetical imperative always takes a conditional form: "*If* you want to achieve *x,* then you ought to do *y.*" Rules of skill and counsels of prudence are hypothetical imperatives: they tell us what we ought to do—"ought" in the sense of what we would be well advised to do—*if* we desire certain ends. They may be legitimate but they are not moral. A categorical imperative, on the other hand, asserts unconditionally, "You ought to act so and so." There is no "if" in front of the "ought." Obligation is not determined by inclination or expediency but by objective moral necessity, which can be stated in a universal rule.

The question is whether this distinction between a categorical and a hypothetical imperative is sound? Has Kant drawn the distinction too sharply? Is he, in pressing this distinction, too much the absolutist, not enough the relativist? Or is Kant right? Don't we believe that moral imperatives are, somehow or other, distinctive? And has he not correctly formulated the distinction? These are questions for the reader to ponder.

4. DOES KANT'S ETHICS PROVIDE A SOUND TEST OF RIGHT? An opponent might concede that there are categorical imperatives, and still find Kant's formulae for determining them unsatisfactory.

His first formula is: "Act only on that maxim which you can will as a universal law." One may object that this does not take account of individual differences which may be ethically decisive. Consider Kant's dispute with the French philosopher Benjamin Constant. The moral duty to tell the truth, Constant argued, is not unconditional. It would be ethically right to lie to a would-be murderer in order to save the intended victim, for a person bent on murder has forfeited all right to a truth which would abet a plot. To this contention Kant replied, "The duty of truthfulness makes no distinction between persons to whom one has this duty and to whom one can exempt himself from this duty; rather, it is an unconditional duty which holds in all circumstances."[1] Hence, we are duty-bound to tell even a truth that would result in murder. This is an extreme position that very few thinkers, whether philosophers or laymen, would endorse. In the case cited by Constant, there is a conflict between two duties: the duty to tell the truth and the duty to save a life. In such instances, how can we decide which duty is paramount without a consideration of consequences?

Kant would reply that there are "perfect duties," and that the duty to tell the truth is such a duty. We recognize a perfect obligation when we see that it is possible to universalize it and impossible to universalize its violation. For example, it is impossible to universalize lying (the violation of truth-telling) because if everybody lied, no one would believe you—lying is parasitic upon truth-telling. Hence telling the truth, which can be universalized with perfect consistency, is an absolute duty, and lying is an absolute violation of this duty. The duty to protect a life that is threatened is only an "imperfect duty"—derived from the fact that no one could consistently will that his own life be unprotected under such circumstances. The duties of perfect obligation, forbidding us to lie, break promises, steal, murder, and so forth, admit of no exceptions whatever in favor of duties of imperfect obligation.

Some writers have argued, in Kant's defense, that his universalization formula can be interpreted flexibly enough to meet common-sense objections. For example,

---

[1] "On a Supposed Right to Lie from Altruistic Motives," *Critique of Practical Reason and Other Writings in Moral Philosophy*, translated by L. W. Beck (University of Chicago Press, 1949), p. 349.

we could universalize the principle that people should steal rather than starve to death. Or (to revert to the question that Constant raised) we could universalize the principle that one should lie in order to save an innocent person from the threat of murder. But can we reason in this way without a more empirical approach to ethics than Kant was prepared to admit? Can we do so without setting aside his concept of "perfect duties"?

A utilitarian could agree with Kant up to a certain point: granted that an act is right for one person, it must be right *under the same conditions* for everybody. But when the conditions (physical or psychological or cultural) vary, philanthropic exception to the general rule may be warranted. If this is so, can morality be *a priori* and universal, as Kant supposed?

His second formula of the categorical imperative is: "Act so as to treat humanity, whether in your own person or in that of another, always as an end and never as a means only." This formula expresses our sense of the intrinsic value of the human spirit, and it has a profound moral appeal. But is it possible to carry out the formula without a view to the effects of our actions? Must we not have some positive idea of the ends of humanity and how to achieve them? If so, is the second formula consistent with the first formula? The first formula, it could be argued, is a right for right's sake principle, and the second is a right for good's sake principle.

The third formula is: "Act as a member of a kingdom of ends." Spelled out, this means that every person, as a rational agent, is ideally a member of a moral community, in which one is both sovereign (free) and subject (responsible), willing the universal laws of morality for oneself and others. The moral law, according to this formula, must be the person's own free voice and is not a whit less a universal law for being freely chosen. But is genuine freedom consistent with Kant's interpretation of universality? Freedom, it might be objected, does not consist merely in willing the dictates of universal abstract reason; it is warmer, more personal, and creative. In maintaining that morality is obedience to universal law, without regard to the individual and his peculiar circumstances, Kant dissolves the individual personality in an ocean of ethical abstraction, like an individual grain of sand dissolved in a vast sea. In so doing, he undermines his very demand for a moral community of free and responsible human beings. So at least might an existentialist, with his strong emphasis upon human individuality, argue.

In Kant's defense, it can be pointed out that *The Foundations of the Metaphysic of Morals,* from which our selection is taken, is the most abstract and formalistic of his ethical works. In the *Critique of Practical Reason,* Kant corrects the one-sidedness of the *Foundations* by discoursing at length on the concept of "good" as well as "duty," and in his *Lectures on Ethics* and *Metaphysics of Morals* (not to be confused with the *Foundations*) Kant discusses particular duties in a concrete way. The more teleological and less absolutistic elements in his theory emerge in these works.

13

Happiness and Utility

JEREMY BENTHAM (1748–1832)

The son of a well-to-do London barrister, Bentham studied law but never practiced it. He set himself to work out a new system of jurisprudence and to reform both the penal and the civil law. In pursuit of this aim he wrote thousands of pages, but was curiously indifferent about publishing them. Although his works were collected in eleven large volumes, the only major theoretical work that he published himself was the *Introduction to the Principles of Morals and Legislation* (1789), which contains an exposition of his hedonistic and utilitarian ethics.

Painfully shy, he could hardly endure the company of strangers, and yet he became a powerful political force. As a leader of the "Philosophical Radicals," he attracted such distinguished followers as James Mill and John Stuart Mill. He established the *Westminster Review,* at his own expense, as an organ of his movement, and he and his associates succeeded in founding University College, London. There his embalmed body, dressed in his customary clothes and topped with a wax model of his head, is still to be seen.

Pleasure, Pain, and
the Hedonistic Calculus

Chapter I

Of the Principle of Utility

I. Nature has placed mankind under the governance of two sovereign masters, *pain* and *pleasure*. It is for them alone to point out what we ought to do, as well as to determine what we shall do. On the one hand the standard of right and wrong, on the other the chain of causes and effects, are fastened to their throne. They govern us in all we do, in all we say, in all we think: every effort we can make to throw off our subjection, will serve but to demonstrate and confirm it. In words a man may pretend to abjure their empire: but in reality he will remain subject to it all the while. The *principle of utility*[1] recognizes this subjection, and

From *An Introduction to the Principles of Morals and Legislation*, new edition, Oxford, 1823. Some of Bentham's footnotes have been omitted. First published in 1789.

[1] Note by the Author, July 1822: To this denomination has of late been added, or substituted, the *greatest happiness or greatest felicity* principle: this for shortness, instead of saying at length *that principle* which states the greatest happiness of all those whose interest is in question, as being the right and

assumes it for the foundation of that system, the object of which is to rear the fabric of felicity by the hands of reason and of law. Systems which attempt to question it, deal in sounds instead of sense, in caprice instead of reason, in darkness instead of light.

But enough of metaphor and declamation: it is not by such means that moral science is to be improved.

---

proper, and only right and proper and universally desirable, end of human action: of human action in every situation, and in particular in that of a functionary or set of functionaries exercising the powers of Government. The word *utility* does not so clearly point to the ideas of *pleasure* and *pain* as the words *happiness* and *felicity* do: nor does it lead us to the consideration of the *number,* of the interests affected; to the *number,* as being the circumstance, which contributes, in the largest proportion, to the formation of the standard here in question; the *standard of right and wrong,* by which alone the propriety of human conduct, in every situation can with propriety be tried. This want of a sufficiently manifest connexion between the ideas of *happiness* and *pleasure* on the one hand, and the idea of *utility* on the other, I have every now and then found operating, and with but too much efficiency, as a bar to the acceptance, that might otherwise have been given, to this principle.

II. The principle of utility is the foundation of the present work: it will be proper therefore at the outset to give an explicit and determinate account of what is meant by it. By the principle of utility is meant that principle which approves or disapproves of every action whatsoever, according to the tendency which it appears to have to augment or diminish the happiness of the party whose interest is in question: or, what is the same thing in other words, to promote or to oppose that happiness. I say of every action whatsoever; and therefore not only of every action of a private individual, but of every measure of government.

III. By utility is meant that property in any object, whereby it tends to produce benefit, advantage, pleasure, good, or happiness, (all this in the present case comes to the same thing) or (what comes again to the same thing) to prevent the happening of mischief, pain, evil, or unhappiness to the party whose interest is considered: if that party be the community in general, then the happiness of the community: if a particular individual, then the happiness of that individual.

IV. The interest of the community is one of the most general expressions that can occur in the phraseology of morals: no wonder that the meaning of it is often lost. When it has a meaning, it is this. The community is a fictitious *body,* composed of the individual persons who are considered as constituting as it were its *members.* The interest of the community then is, what? —the sum of the interests of the several members who compose it.

V. It is in vain to talk of the interest of the community, without understanding what is the interest of the individual. A thing is said to promote the interest, or to be *for* the interest, of an individual, when it tends to add to the sum total of his pleasures: or, what comes to the same thing, to diminish the sum total of his pains.

VI. An action then may be said to be conformable to the principle of utility, or, for shortness sake, to utility, (meaning with respect to the community at large) when the tendency it has to augment the happiness of the community is greater than any it has to diminish it.

VII. A measure of government (which is but a particular kind of action, performed by a particular person or persons) may be said to be conformable to or dictated by the principle of utility, when in like manner the tendency which it has to augment the happiness of the community is greater than any which it has to diminish it.

VIII. When an action, or in particular a measure of government, is supposed by a man to be conformable to the principle of utility, it may be convenient, for the purposes of discourse, to imagine a kind of law or dictate, called a law or dictate of utility: and to speak of the action in question, as being conformable to such law or dictate.

IX. A man may be said to be a partizan of the principle of utility, when the approbation or disapprobation he annexes to any action, or to any measure, is determined by and proportioned to the tendency which he conceives it to have to augment or to diminish the happiness of the community: or in other words, to its conformity or unconformity to the laws or dictates of utility.

X. Of an action that is conformable to the principle of utility one may always say either that it is one that ought to be done, or at least that it is not one that ought not to be done. One may say also, that it is right it should be done; at least that it is not wrong it should be done: that it is a right action; at least that it is not a wrong action. When thus interpreted, the words *ought,* and *right* and *wrong,* and others of that stamp, have a meaning: when otherwise, they have none.

XI. Has the rectitude of this principle been ever formally contested? It should seem that it had, by those who have not known what they have been meaning. Is it susceptible of any direct proof? it should seem not: for that which is used to prove every thing else, cannot itself be proved: a chain of proofs must have their commencement somewhere. To give such proof is as impossible as it is needless.

XII. Not that there is or ever has been that human creature breathing, however stupid or perverse, who has not on many, perhaps on most occasions of his life, deferred to it. By the natural constitution of the human frame, on most occasions of their lives men in general embrace this principle, without thinking of it: if not for the ordering of their own actions, yet for the trying of their own actions, as well as those of other men. There have been, at the same time, not many, perhaps,

even of the most intelligent, who have been disposed to embrace it purely and without reserve. There are even few who have not taken some occasion or other to quarrel with it, either on account of their not understanding always how to apply it, or on account of some prejudice or other which they were afraid to examine into, or could not bear to part with. For such is the stuff that man is made of: in principle and in practice, in a right track and in a wrong one, the rarest of all human qualities is consistency.

XIII. When a man attempts to combat the principle of utility, it is with reasons drawn, without his being aware of it, from that very principle itself. His arguments, if they prove any thing, prove not that the principle is *wrong,* but that, according to the applications he supposes to be made of it, it is *misapplied.* Is it possible for a man to move the earth? Yes; but he must first find out another earth to stand upon.

XIV. To disprove the propriety of it by arguments is impossible; but, from the causes that have been mentioned, or from some confused or partial view of it, a man may happen to be disposed not to relish it. Where this is the case, if he thinks the settling of his opinions on such a subject worth the trouble, let him take the following steps, and at length, perhaps, he may come to reconcile himself to it.

1. Let him settle with himself, whether he would wish to discard this principle altogether; if so, let him consider what it is that all his reasonings (in matters of politics especially) can amount to?

2. If he would, let him settle with himself, whether he would judge and act without any principle, or whether there is any other he would judge and act by?

3. If there be, let him examine and satisfy himself whether the principle he thinks he has found is really any separate intelligible principle; or whether it be not a mere principle in words, a kind of phrase, which at bottom expresses neither more nor less than the mere averment of his own unfounded sentiments; that is, what in another person he might be apt to call caprice?

4. If he is inclined to think that his own approbation or disapprobation, annexed to the idea of an act, without any regard to its consequences, is a sufficient foundation for him to judge and act upon, let him ask himself whether his sentiment is to be a standard of right and wrong, with respect to every other man, or whether every man's sentiment has the same privilege of being a standard to itself?

5. In the first case, let him ask himself whether his principle is not despotical, and hostile to all the rest of the human race?

6. In the second case, whether it is not anarchical, and whether at this rate there are not as many different standards of right and wrong as there are men? and whether even to the same man, the same thing, which is right to-day, may not (without the least change in its nature) be wrong tomorrow? and whether the same thing is not right and wrong in the same place at the same time? and in either case, whether all argument is not at an end? and whether, when two men have said, 'I like this,' and 'I don't like it,' they can (upon such a principle) have any thing more to say?

7. If he should have said to himself, No: for that sentiment which he proposes as a standard must be grounded on reflection, let him say on what particulars the reflection is to turn? if on particulars having relation to the utility of the act, then let him say whether this is not deserting his own principle, and borrowing assistance from that very one in opposition to which he sets it up: or if not on those particulars, on what other particulars?

8. If he should be for compounding the matter, and adopting his own principle in part, and the principle of utility in part, let him say how far he will adopt it?

9. When he has settled with himself where he will stop, then let him ask himself how he justifies to himself the adopting it so far? and why he will not adopt it any farther?

10. Admitting any other principle than the principle of utility to be a right principle, a principle that it is right for a man to pursue; admitting (what is not true) that the word *right* can have a meaning without reference to utility, let him say whether there is any such thing as a *motive* that a man can have to pursue the dictates of it: if there is, let him say what that motive is, and how it is to be distinguished from those which enforce the dictates of utility: if not, then lastly let him say what it is this other principle can be good for? . . .

Value of a Lot of Pleasure or Pain, How To Be Measured

I. PLEASURES then, and the avoidance of pains, are the *ends* which the legislator has in view: it behoves him therefore to understand their *value*. Pleasures and pains are the *instruments* he has to work with: it behoves him therefore to understand their force, which is again, in other words, their value.

II. To a person considered *by himself,* the value of a pleasure or pain considered *by itself,* will be greater or less, according to the four following circumstances:[2]

1. Its *intensity.*
2. Its *duration.*
3. Its *certainty* or *uncertainty.*
4. Its *propinquity* or *remoteness.*

III. These are the circumstances which are to be considered in estimating a pleasure or a pain considered each of them by itself. But when the value of any pleasure or pain is considered for the purpose of estimating

the tendency of any *act* by which it is produced, there are two other circumstances to be taken into the account; these are,

5. Its *fecundity,* or the chance it has of being followed by sensations of the *same* kind: that is, pleasures, if it be a pleasure: pains, if it be a pain.

6. Its *purity,* or the chance it has of *not* being followed by sensations of the *opposite* kind: that is, pains, if it be a pleasure: pleasures, if it be a pain.

These two last, however, are in strictness scarcely to be deemed properties of the pleasure or the pain itself; they are not, therefore, in strictness to be taken into the account of the value of that pleasure or that pain. They are in strictness to be deemed properties only of the act, or other event, by which such pleasure or pain has been produced; and accordingly are only to be taken into the account of the tendency of such act or such event.

IV. To a *number* of persons, with reference to each of whom the value of a pleasure or a pain is considered, it will be greater or less, according to seven circumstances: to wit, the six preceding ones; viz.

1. Its *intensity.*
2. Its *duration.*
3. Its *certainty* or *uncertainty.*
4. Its *propinquity* or *remoteness.*
5. Its *fecundity.*
6. Its *purity.*

And one other; to wit:

7. Its *extent;* that is, the number of persons to whom it *extends;* or (in other words) who are affected by it.

V. To take an exact account then of the general tendency of any act, by

[2] These circumstances have since been denominated *elements* or *dimensions* of *value* in a pleasure or a pain.

Not long after the publication of the first edition, the following memoriter verses were framed, in the view of lodging more effectually, in the memory, these points, on which the whole fabric of morals and legislation may be seen to rest.

Intense, long, certain, speedy, fruitful, pure—
Such marks in *pleasures* and in *pains* endure.
Such pleasures seek, if *private* be thy end:
If it be *public,* wide let them *extend.*
Such *pains* avoid, whichever be thy view:
If pains *must* come, let them *extend* to few.

which the interests of a community are affected, proceed as follows. Begin with any one person of those whose interests seem most immediately to be affected by it: and take an account,

1. Of the value of each distinguishable *pleasure* which appears to be produced by it in the *first* instance.

2. Of the value of each *pain* which appears to be produced by it in the *first* instance.

3. Of the value of each pleasure which appears to be produced by it *after* the first. This constitutes the *fecundity* of the first *pleasure* and the *impurity* of the first *pain*.

4. Of the value of each *pain* which appears to be produced by it after the first. This constitutes the *fecundity* of the first *pain*, and the *impurity* of the first *pleasure*.

5. Sum up all the values of all the *pleasures* on the one side, and those of all the *pains* on the other. The balance, if it be on the side of pleasure, will give the *good* tendency of the act upon the whole, with respect to the interests of that *individual* person; if on the side of pain, the *bad* tendency of it upon the whole.

6. Take an account of the *number* of persons whose interests appear to be concerned; and repeat the above process with respect to each. *Sum up* the numbers expressive of the degrees of *good* tendency which the act has, with respect to each individual, in regard to whom the tendency of it is *good* upon the whole: . . . do this again with respect to each individual, in regard to whom the tendency of it is *bad* upon the whole. Take the *balance;* which, if on the side of *pleasure,* will give the general *good tendency* of the act, with respect to the total number or community of individuals concerned; if on the side of pain, the general *evil tendency,* with respect to the same community.

VI. It is not to be expected that this process should be strictly pursued previously to every moral judgment, or to every legislative or judicial operation. It may, however, be always kept in view: and as near as the process actually pursued on these occasions approaches to it, so near will such process approach to the character of an exact one.

VII. The same process is alike applicable to pleasure and pain, in whatever shape they appear: and by whatever denomination they are distinguished: to pleasure, whether it be called *good* (which is properly the cause or instrument of pleasure) or *profit* (which is distant pleasure, or the cause or instrument of distant pleasure,) or *convenience,* or *advantage, benefit, emolument, happiness,* and so forth: to pain, whether it be called *evil,* (which corresponds to *good*) or *mischief,* or *inconvenience,* or *disadvantage,* or *loss,* or *unhappiness,* and so forth.

VIII. Nor is this a novel and unwarranted, any more than it is a useless theory. In all this there is nothing but what the practice of mankind, wheresoever they have a clear view of their own interest, is perfectly conformable to. An article of property, an estate in land, for instance, is valuable, on what account? On account of the pleasures of all kinds which it enables a man to produce, and what comes to the same thing the pains of all kinds which it enables him to avert. But the value of such an article of property is universally understood to rise or fall according to the length or shortness of the time which a man has in it: the certainty or uncertainty of its coming into possession: and the nearness or remoteness of the time at which, if at all, it is to come into possession. As to the *intensity* of the pleasures which a man may derive from it, this is never thought of, because it depends upon the use which each particular person may come to make of it; which cannot be estimated till the particular pleasures he may come to derive from it, or the particular pains he may come to exclude by means of it, are brought to view. For the same reason, neither does he think of the *fecundity* or *purity* of those pleasures.

JOHN STUART MILL (1806–1873)

Mill was reared in London and was educated privately by his father, James Mill, a famous political philosopher. No child ever received a more prodigious education. Mill was reading Plato and Thucydides in the original Greek at an age when most children are reading nursery stories in their native language. His father set him to learn Greek at the age of three; Latin, algebra, and geometry at the age of eight; logic at twelve; and political economy at thirteen. Jeremy Bentham was an intimate friend of the family, and young John was thoroughly indoctrinated in his philosophy.

When Mill reached the age of seventeen, he was appointed a clerk in the East India Company, in whose service he remained for thirty-five years, rising steadily to the highest post in his department, that of examiner of correspondence and dispatches to India. This position afforded him considerable leisure for his intense intellectual pursuits.

In his twenty-first year, he fell into a deep mental depression, evidently the result of his unnatural childhood and years of intellectual cramming. He gradually emerged from this illness, but with a new sense of the insufficiency of his father's doctrinaire philosophy and a keener appreciation of the value of poetry, especially Wordsworth's. Thereafter he sought to broaden his outlook and succeeded in becoming a much better rounded (though less consistent) philosopher than either Bentham or his father. An important influence upon Mill was Harriet Taylor, the beautiful and talented wife of a London merchant, who finally married him (in 1851) after her husband died. They lived happily together for seven years, until they were separated by her untimely death. It was through her, Mill said, that he came to be more of a democrat and socialist, and *On Liberty* was their joint work.

After his long service in the India Office, he retired on a pension at the age of fifty-two. The remaining fifteen years of his life, although marred by ill health, were packed with intellectual and political activity. In 1865, he consented to run for Parliament as a representative of the working man for the constituency of Westminster; and during his single term of office (1866–1868), he made a considerable impression by his vigorous championing of reform. In 1869, he retired with his stepdaughter, Helen Taylor, to a small white stone cottage near Avignon, in France, where he continued to write. In May 1873 he died, the victim of a local fever.

Among his important books were *Logic* (1843), *The Principles of Political Economy* (1848), *On Liberty* (1859), *Utilitarianism* (1863), *Examination of Sir William Hamilton's Philosophy* (1865), and *Autobiography* (published after his death, in 1873).

Utilitarianism

What Utilitarianism Is

A passing remark is all that needs be given to the ignorant blunder of supposing that those who stand up for utility as the test of right and wrong use the term in that restricted and merely colloquial sense in which utility is opposed to pleasure. An apology is due to the philosophical opponents of utilitarianism, for even the momentary appearance of confounding them with anyone capable of so absurd a misconception; which is the more extraordinary, inasmuch as the contrary accusation, of referring everything to pleasure, and that, too, in its grossest form, is another of the common charges against utilitarianism: and, as has been pointedly remarked by an able writer,

From *Utilitarianism* published serially in *Fraser's Magazine* in 1861 and in book form, London, 1863.

the same sort of persons, and often the very same persons, denounce the theory "as impracticably dry when the word 'utility' precedes the word 'pleasure,' and as too practically voluptuous when the word 'pleasure' precedes the word 'utility'." Those who know anything about the matter are aware that every writer, from Epicurus to Bentham, who maintained the theory of utility, meant by it, not something to be contradistinguished from pleasure, but pleasure itself, together with exemption from pain; and instead of opposing the useful to the agreeable or the ornamental, have always declared that the useful means these, among other things. Yet the common herd, including the herd of writers, not only in newspapers and periodicals, but in books of weight and pretension, are perpetually falling into this shallow mistake. Having caught up the word "utilitarian," while knowing nothing whatever about it but its sound, they habitually express by it the rejection or the neglect of pleasure in some of its forms: of beauty, of ornament, or of amusement. Nor is the term thus ignorantly misapplied solely in disparagement, but occasionally in compliment, as though it implied superiority to frivolity and the mere pleasures of the moment. And this perverted use is the only one in which the word is popularly known, and the one from which the new generation are acquiring their sole notion of its meaning. Those who introduced the word, but who had for many years discontinued it as a distinctive appellation, may well feel themselves called upon to resume it if by doing so they can hope to contribute anything towards rescuing it from this utter degradation.

The creed which accepts as the foundation of morals "utility" or the "greatest happiness principle" holds that actions are right in proportion as they tend to promote happiness, wrong as they tend to produce the reverse of happiness. By happiness is intended pleasure, and the absence of pain; by unhappiness, pain, and the privation of pleasure. To give a clear view of the moral standard set up by the theory, much more requires to be said; in particular, what things it includes in the ideas of pain and pleasure; and to what extent this is left an open question. But these supplementary explanations do not affect the theory of life on which this theory of morality is grounded—namely, that pleasure and freedom from pain are the only things desirable as ends; and that all desirable things (which are as numerous in the utilitarian as in any other scheme) are desirable either for the pleasure inherent in themselves, or as means to the promotion of pleasure and the prevention of pain.

Now such a theory of life excites in many minds, and among them in some of the most estimable in feeling and purpose, inveterate dislike. To suppose that life has (as they express it) no higher end than pleasure—no better and nobler object of desire and pursuit—they designate as utterly mean and groveling; as a doctrine worthy only of swine, to whom the followers of Epicurus were, at a very early period, contemptuously likened; and modern holders of the doctrine are occasionally made the subject of equally polite comparisons by its German, French, and English assailants.

When thus attacked, the Epicureans have always answered that it is not they, but their accusers, who represent human nature in a degrading light, since the accusation supposes human beings to be capable of no pleasures except those of which swine are capable. If this supposition were true, the charge could not be gainsaid, but would then be no longer an imputation; for if the sources of pleasure were precisely the same to human beings and to swine, the rule of life which is good enough for the one would be good enough for the other. The comparison of the Epicurean life to that of beasts is felt as degrading, precisely because a beast's pleasures do not satisfy a human being's conceptions of happiness. Human beings have faculties more elevated than the animal appetites and, when once made conscious of them, do not regard anything as happiness which does not include their gratification. I do not, indeed, consider the Epicureans to have been by any means faultless in drawing out their scheme of consequences from the utilitarian principle. To do this in any sufficient manner, many Stoic, as well as Christian, elements require to be included. But there is no known Epicurean theory of life which does not assign to the pleasures of the intellect, of the feelings and imagination, and of the moral sentiments, a much higher value as pleasures than to those of mere sensation. It must be admitted, however, that utilitarian writers in general have placed the superiority of mental over bodily pleasures chiefly in the greater permanency, safety, uncostliness, etc., of the former—that is, in their circumstantial advantages rather than in their intrinsic nature. And on all these points utilitarians have fully proved their case; but they might have taken the other and, as it may be called, higher ground with entire consistency. It is quite compatible with the principle of utility to recognize the fact that some kinds of pleasure are more desirable and more valuable than others. It would be absurd that, while, in estimating all other things, quality is considered as well as quantity, the estimation of pleasures should be supposed to depend on quantity alone.

If I am asked what I mean by difference of quality in pleasures, or what makes one pleasure more valuable than another, merely as a pleasure, except its being greater in amount, there is but one possible answer. Of two pleasures, if there be one to which all or almost all who have experience of both give a decided preference, irrespective

of any feeling of moral obligation to prefer it, that is the more desirable pleasure. If one of the two is, by those who are competently acquainted with both, placed so far above the other that they prefer it, even though knowing it to be attended with a greater amount of discontent, and would not resign it for any quantity of the other pleasure which their nature is capable of, we are justified in ascribing to the preferred enjoyment a superiority in quality so far outweighing quantity as to render it, in comparison, of small account.

Now it is an unquestionable fact that those who are equally acquainted with and equally capable of appreciating and enjoying both, do give a most marked preference to the manner of existence which employs their higher faculties. Few human creatures would consent to be changed into any of the lower animals for a promise of the fullest allowance of a beast's pleasures; no intelligent human being would consent to be a fool, no instructed person would be an ignoramus, no person of feeling and conscience would be selfish and base, even though they should be persuaded that the fool, the dunce, or the rascal is better satisfied with his lot than they are with theirs. They would not resign what they possess more than he for the most complete satisfaction of all the desires which they have in common with him. If they ever fancy they would, it is only in cases of unhappiness so extreme that to escape from it they would exchange their lot for almost any other, however undesirable in their own eyes. A being of higher faculties requires more to make him happy, is capable probably of more acute suffering, and certainly accessible to it at more points, than one of an inferior type; but in spite of these liabilities, he can never really wish to sink into what he feels to be a lower grade of existence. We may give what explanation we please of this unwillingness; we may attribute it to pride, a name which is given indiscriminately to some of the most and to some of the least estimable feelings of which mankind are capable: we may refer it to the love of liberty and personal independence, an appeal to which was with the Stoics one of the most effective means for the inculcation of it; to the love of power or to the love of excitement, both of which do really enter into and contribute to it; but its most appropriate appellation is a sense of dignity, which all human beings possess in one form or other, and in some, though by no means in exact, proportion to their higher faculties, and which is so essential a part of the happiness of those in whom it is strong that- nothing which conflicts with it could be otherwise than momentarily an object of desire to them. Whoever supposes that this preference takes place at a sacrifice of happiness—that the superior being, in anything like equal circumstances, is not happier than the inferior—confounds the two very different ideas of happiness and content. It is undisputable that the being whose capacities of enjoyment are low has the greatest chance of having them fully satisfied; and a highly endowed being will always feel that any happiness which he can look for, as the world is constituted, is imperfect. But he can learn to bear its imperfections, if they are at all bearable; and they will not make him envy the being who is indeed unconscious of the imperfections, but only because he feels not at all the good which those imperfections qualify. It is better to be a human being dissatisfied than a pig satisfied; better to be Socrates dissatisfied than a fool satisfied. And if the fool, or the pig, are of a different opinion, it is because they only know their own side of the question. The other party to the comparison knows both sides.

It may be objected that many who are capable of the higher pleasures occasionally, under the influence of temptation, postpone them to the lower. But this is quite compatible with a full appreciation of the intrinsic superiority of the higher. Men often, from infirmity of character, make their election for the nearer good, though they know it to be the less valuable; and this no less when the choice is between two bodily pleasures than when it is between bodily and mental. They pursue sensual indulgences to the injury of health, though perfectly aware that health is the greater good. It may be further objected that many who begin with youthful enthusiasm for everything noble, as they advance in years, sink into indolence and selfishness. But I do not believe that those who undergo this very common change voluntarily choose the lower description of pleasures in preference to the higher. I believe that, before they devote themselves exclusively to the one, they have already become incapable of the other. Capacity for the nobler feelings is in most natures a very tender plant, easily killed, not only by hostile influences, but by mere want of sustenance; and in the majority of young persons it speedily dies away if the occupations to which their position in life has devoted them, and the society into which it has thrown them, are not favorable to keeping that higher capacity in exercise. Men lose their high aspirations as they lose their intellectual tastes, because they have not time or opportunity for indulging them; and they addict themselves to inferior pleasures, not because they deliberately prefer them, but because they are either the only ones to which they have access, or the only ones which they are any longer capable of enjoying. It may be questioned whether any one who has remained equally susceptible to both classes of pleasures, ever knowingly and calmly preferred the lower, though many, in all ages, have broken down in an ineffectual attempt to combine both.

From this verdict of the only competent judges, I apprehend there can be no appeal. On a question which is the best worth having of two pleasures, or which of two modes of existence is the most grateful to the feelings, apart from its moral attributes and from its consequences, the judgment of those who are qualified by knowledge of both, or, if they differ, that of the majority of them, must be admitted as final. And there needs be the less hesitation to accept this judgment respecting the quality of pleasures, since there is no other tribunal to be referred to even on the question of quantity. What means are there of determining which is the acutest of two pains, or the intensest of two pleasurable sensations, except the general suffrage of those who are familiar with both? Neither pains nor pleasures are homogeneous, and pain is always heterogeneous with pleasure. What is there to decide whether a particular pleasure is worth purchasing at the cost of a particular pain, except the feelings and judgment of the experienced? When, therefore, those feelings and judgment declare the pleasures derived from the higher faculties to be preferable *in kind,* apart from the question of intensity, to those of which the animal nature, disjointed from the higher faculties, is susceptible, they are entitled on this subject to the same regard.

I have dwelt on this point, as being a necessary part of a perfectly just conception of utility or happiness considered as the directive rule of human conduct. But it is by no means an indispensable condition to the acceptance of the utilitarian standard; for that standard is not the agent's own greatest happiness, but the greatest amount of happiness altogether; and if it may possibly be doubted whether a noble character is always the happier for its nobleness, there can be no doubt that it makes other people happier, and that the world in general is immensely a gainer by it. Utilitarianism, therefore, could only attain its end by the general cultivation of nobleness of character, even if each individual were only benefited by the nobleness of others, and his own, so far as happiness is concerned, were a sheer deduction from the benefit. But the bare enunciation of such an absurdity as this last renders refutation superfluous.

According to the greatest happiness principle, as above explained, the ultimate end, with reference to and for the sake of which all other things are desirable—whether we are considering our own good or that of other people—is an existence exempt as far as possible from pain, and as rich as possible in enjoyments, both in point of quantity and quality; the test of quality and the rule for measuring it against quantity being the preference felt by those who, in their opportunities of experience, to which must be added their habits of self-consciousness and self-observation, are best furnished with the means of comparison. This, being, according to the utilitarian opinion, the end of human action, is necessarily also the standard of morality, which may accordingly be defined "the rules and precepts for human conduct," by the observance of which an existence such as has been described might be, to the greatest extent possible, secured to all mankind; and not to them only, but, so far as the nature of things admits, to the whole sentient creation. . . .

[*The remainder of the chapter is devoted to Mill's answer to objections. Some of these objections, for example, that happiness is unobtainable, that utilitarianism is a "godless doctrine," that the doctrine is "worthy only of swine," would no longer be advanced by reputable philosophers, and can here be omitted. But a few of the objections and Mill's answers to them are worthy of attention. We shall begin with his reply to the objection that we should learn to do without happiness, since self-sacrifice is a duty.*]

. . . The utilitarian morality does recognize in human beings the power of sacrificing their own greatest good for the good of others. It only refuses to admit that the sacrifice is itself a good. A sacrifice which does not increase or tend to increase the sum total of happiness, it considers as wasted. The only self-renunciation which it applauds is devotion to the happiness, or to some of the means of happiness, of others, either of mankind collectively or of individuals within the limits imposed by the collective interests of mankind.

I must again repeat what the assailants of utilitarianism seldom have the justice to acknowledge, that the happiness which forms the utilitarian standard of what is right in conduct is not the agent's own happiness but that of all concerned. As between his own happiness and that of others, utilitarianism requires him to be as strictly impartial as a disinterested and benevolent spectator. In the golden rule of Jesus of Nazareth, we read the complete spirit of the ethics of utility. "To do as you would be done by," and "to love your neighbor as yourself," constitute the ideal perfection of utilitarian morality. As the means of making the nearest approach to this ideal, utility would enjoin, first, that laws and social arrangements should place the happiness or (as, speaking practically, it may be called) the interest of every individual as nearly as possible in harmony with the interest of the whole; and, secondly, that education and opinion, which have so vast a power over human character, should so use that power as to establish in the mind of every individual an indissoluble association between his own happiness and the good of the whole, especially between his own happiness and the practice of such modes of conduct, negative and positive, as regard for the universal happiness prescribes; so that not only he may be unable to conceive the possibility of happiness to himself, consistently with conduct opposed to the general good, but also that a direct impulse to promote the general good may be in every individual one of the habitual motives of action, and the sentiments connected therewith may fill a large and prominent place in every human being's sentient existence. If the impugners of the utilitarian morality represented it to their own minds in this its true character, I know not what recommendation possessed by any other morality they could possibly affirm to be wanting to it; what more beautiful or more exalted developments of human nature any other ethical system can be supposed to foster, or what springs of action, not accessible to the utilitarian, such systems rely on for giving effect to their mandates.

The objectors to utilitarianism cannot always be charged with representing it in a discreditable light. On the contrary, those among them who entertain anything like a just idea of its disinterested character sometimes find fault with its standard as being too high for humanity. They say it is exacting too much to require that people shall always act from the inducement of promoting the general interests of society. But this is to mistake the very meaning of a standard of morals, and confound the rule of action with the motive of it. It is the business of ethics to tell us what are our duties, or by what test we may know them; but no system of ethics requires that the sole motive of all we do shall be a feeling of duty; on the contrary, ninety-nine hundredths of all our actions are done from other motives, and rightly so done if the rule of duty does not condemn them. It is the more unjust to utilitarianism that this particular misapprehension should be made a ground of objection to it, inasmuch as utilitarian moralists have gone beyond almost all others in affirming that the motive has nothing to do with the morality of the action, though much with the worth of the agent. He who saves a fellow creature from drowning does what is morally right, whether his motive be duty or the hope of being paid for his trouble; he who betrays the friend that trusts him is guilty of a crime, even if his object be to serve another friend to whom he is under greater obligations. But to speak only of actions done from the motive of duty, and in direct obedience to principle: it is a misapprehension to the utilitarian mode of thought to conceive it as implying that people should fix their minds upon so wide a generality as the world, or society at large. The great majority of good actions are intended not for the benefit of the world, but for that of individuals, of which the good of the world is made up; and the thoughts of the most virtuous man need not on these occasions travel beyond the particular persons concerned, except so far as is necessary to assure himself that in benefiting them he is not violating the rights, that is, the legitimate and authorized expectations, of any one else. The multiplication of happiness is, according to the utilitarian ethics, politician

the object of virtue: the occasions on which any person (except one in a thousand) has it in his power to do this on an extended scale, in other words, to be a public benefactor, are but exceptional; and on these occasions alone is he called on to consider public utility; in every other case, private utility, the interest or happiness of some few persons, is all he has to attend to. Those alone the influence of whose actions extends to society in general need concern themselves habitually about so large an object. In the case of abstinences indeed—of things which people forbear to do from moral considerations, though the consequences in the particular case might be beneficial—it would be unworthy of an intelligent agent not to be consciously aware that the action is of a class which, if practiced generally, would be generally injurious, and that this is the ground of the obligation to abstain from it. The amount of regard for the public interest implied in this recognition is no greater than is demanded by every system of morals, for they all enjoin to abstain from whatever is manifestly pernicious to society.

The same considerations dispose of another reproach against the doctrine of utility, founded on a still grosser misconception of the purpose of a standard of morality, and of the very meaning of the words "right" and "wrong." It is often affirmed that utilitarianism renders men cold and unsympathizing; that it chills their moral feelings towards individuals; that it makes them regard only the dry and hard consideration of the consequences of actions, not taking into their moral estimate the qualities from which those actions emanate. If the assertion means that they do not allow their judgment respecting the rightness or wrongness of an action to be influenced by their opinion of the qualities of the person who does it, this is a complaint not against utilitarianism, but against any standard of morality at all; for certainly no known ethical standard decides an action to be good or bad because it is done by a good or a bad man, still less because done by an amiable, a brave, or a benevolent man, or the contrary. These considerations are relevant, not to the estimation of actions, but of persons; and there is nothing in the utilitarian theory inconsistent with the fact that there are other things which interest us in persons besides the rightness and wrongness of their actions. The Stoics, indeed, with the paradoxical misuse of language which was part of their system, and by which they strove to raise themselves above all concern about anything but virtue, were fond of saying that he who has that has everything; that he, and only he, is rich, is beautiful, is a king. But no claim of this description is made for the virtuous man by the utilitarian doctrine. Utilitarians are quite aware that there are other desirable possessions and qualities besides virtue, and are perfectly willing to allow to all of them their full worth. They are also aware that a right action does not necessarily indicate a virtuous character, and that actions which are blamable often proceed from qualities entitled to praise. When this is apparent in any particular case, it modifies their estimation, not certainly of the act, but of the agent. . . .

Again, utility is often summarily stigmatized as an immoral doctrine by giving it the name of "expediency," and taking advantage of the popular use of that term to contrast it with principle. But the expedient, in the sense in which it is opposed to the right, generally means that which is expedient for the particular interest of the agent himself; as when a minister sacrifices the interests of his country to keep himself in place. When it means anything better than this, it means that which is expedient for some immediate object, some temporary purpose, but which violates a rule whose observance is expedient in a much higher degree. The expedient, in this sense, instead of being the same thing with the useful, is a branch of the hurtful. Thus it would often be expedient, for the purpose of getting over some momentary embarrassment, or attaining some object immediately useful to ourselves or others, to tell a lie. But inasmuch as the cultivation in ourselves of a sensitive feeling on the subject of veracity is one of the most useful, and the enfeeblement of that feeling one of the most hurtful, things to which our conduct can be instrumental; and inasmuch as any, even unintentional, deviation from truth does that much towards weakening the trustworthiness of human assertion, which is not only the principal support of all present social well-being, but the insufficiency of which does more than any one thing that can be named to keep back civilization, virtue, everything on which human happiness on the largest scale depends—we feel that the violation, for a present advantage, of a rule

of such transcendent expediency is not expedient, and that he who, for the sake of convenience to himself or to some other individual, does what depends on him to deprive mankind of the good, and inflict upon them the evil, involved in the greater or less reliance which they can place in each other's word, acts the part of one of their worst enemies. Yet that even this rule, sacred as it is, admits of possible exceptions is acknowledged by all moralists; the chief of which is when the withholding of some fact (as of information from a malefactor, or of bad news from a person dangerously ill) would save an individual (especially an individual other than oneself) from great and unmerited evil, and when the withholding can only be effected by denial. But in order that the exception may not extend itself beyond the need, and may have the least possible effect in weakening reliance on veracity, it ought to be recognized and, if possible, its limits defined; and, if the principle of utility is good for anything, it must be good for weighing these conflicting utilities against one another, and marking out the region within which one or the other preponderates.

Again, defenders of utility often find themselves called upon to reply to such objections as this—that there is not time, previous to action, for calculating and weighing the effects of any line of conduct on the general happiness. This is exactly as if any one were to say that it is impossible to guide our conduct by Christianity because there is not time, on every occasion on which anything has to be done, to read through the Old and New Testaments. The answer to the objection is that there has been ample time, namely, the whole past duration of the human species. During all that time, mankind have been learning by experience the tendencies of actions; on which experience all the prudence, as well as all the morality, of life are dependent. People talk as if the commencement of this course of experience had hitherto been put off, and as if, at the moment when some man feels tempted to meddle with the property or life of another, he had to begin considering for the first time whether murder and theft are injurious to human happiness. Even then I do not think that he would find the question very puzzling; but, at all events, the matter is now done to his hand. It is truly a whimsical supposition that, if mankind were agreed in considering utility to be the test of morality, they would remain without any agreement as to what *is* useful, and would take no measures for having their notions on the subject taught to the young, and enforced by law and opinion. There is no difficulty in proving any ethical standard whatever to work ill if we suppose universal idiocy to be conjoined with it; but on any hypothesis short of that, mankind must by this time have acquired positive beliefs as to the effects of some actions on their happiness; and the beliefs which have thus come down are the rules of morality for the multitude, and for the philosopher until he has succeeded in finding better. That philosophers might easily do this, even now, on many subjects; that the received code of ethics is by no means of divine right;

and that mankind have still much to learn as to the effects of actions on the general happiness, I admit or rather earnestly maintain. The corollaries from the principle of utility, like the precepts of every practical art, admit of indefinite improvement, and, in a progressive state of the human mind, their improvement is perpetually going on. But to consider the rules of morality as improvable is one thing; to pass over the intermediate generalization entirely and endeavor to test each individual action directly by the first principle is another. It is a strange notion that the acknowledgment of a first principle is inconsistent with the admission of secondary ones. To inform a traveler respecting the place of his ultimate destination is not to forbid the use of landmarks and direction-posts on the way. The proposition that happiness is the end and aim of morality does not mean that no road ought to be laid down to that goal, or that persons going thither should not be advised to take one direction rather than another. Men really ought to leave off talking a kind of nonsense on this subject, which they would neither talk nor listen to on other matters of practical concernment. Nobody argues that the art of navigation is not founded on astronomy because sailors cannot wait to calculate the nautical almanac. Being rational creatures, they go to sea with it ready calculated; and all rational creatures go out upon the sea of life with their minds made up on the common questions of right and wrong, as well as on many of the far more difficult questions of wise and foolish. And this, as long as foresight is a human quality, it is to be presumed they will continue to do. Whatever we adopt as the fundamental principle of morality, we require subordinate principles to apply it by; the impossibility of doing without them, being common to all systems, can afford no argument against any one in particular; but gravely to argue as if no such secondary principles could be had, and as if mankind had remained till now, and always must remain, without drawing any general conclusions from the experience of human life, is as high a pitch, I think, as absurdity has ever reached in philosophical controversy. . . .

We are told that a utilitarian will be apt to make his own particular case an exception to moral rules, and, when under temptation, will see a utility in the breach of a rule, greater than he will see in its observance. But is utility the only creed which is able to furnish us with excuses for evil doing, and means of cheating our own conscience? They are afforded in abundance by all doctrines which recognize as a fact in morals the existence of conflicting considerations, which all doctrines do that have been believed by sane persons. It is not the fault of any creed, but of the complicated nature of human affairs, that rules of conduct cannot be so framed as to require no exceptions, and that hardly any kind of action can safely be laid down as either always obligatory or always condemnable. There is no ethical creed which does not temper the rigidity of its laws by giving a certain latitude, under the moral responsibility of the agent, for accommodation to peculiarities of circumstances; and under

every creed, at the opening thus made, self-deception and dishonest casuistry get in. There exists no moral system under which there do not arise unequivocal cases of conflicting obligation. These are the real difficulties, the knotty points both in the theory of ethics and in the conscientious guidance of personal conduct. They are overcome practically, with greater or with less success, according to the intellect and virtue of the individual; but it can hardly be pretended that anyone will be the less qualified for dealing with them, from possessing an ultimate standard to which conflicting rights and duties can be referred. If utility is the ultimate source of moral obligations, utility may be invoked to decide between them when their demands are incompatible. Though the application of the standard may be difficult, it is better than none at all; while in other systems the moral laws all claiming independent authority, there is no common umpire entitled to interfere between them; their claims to precedence one over another rest on little better than sophistry, and, unless determined, as they generally are, by the unacknowledged influence of considerations of utility, afford a free scope for the action of personal desires and partialities. We must remember that only in these cases of conflict between secondary principles is it requisite that first principles should be appealed to. There is no case of moral obligation in which some secondary principle is not involved; and if only one, there can seldom be any real doubt which one it is, in the mind of any person by whom the principle itself is recognized.

Of What Sort of Proof the Principle of Utility Is Susceptible

It has already been remarked that questions of ultimate ends do not admit of proof, in the ordinary acceptation of the term. To be incapable of proof by reasoning is common to all first principles, to the first premises of our knowledge, as well as to those of our conduct. But the former, being matters of fact, may be the subject of a direct appeal to the faculties which judge of fact—namely, our senses and our internal consciousness. Can an appeal be made to the same faculties on questions of practical ends? Or by what other faculty is cognizance taken of them?

Questions about ends are, in other words, questions what things are desirable. The utilitarian doctrine is that happiness is desirable, and the only thing desirable, as an end; all other things being only desirable as means to that end. What ought to be required of this doctrine, what conditions is it requisite that the doctrine should fulfill—to make good its claim to be believed?

The only proof capable of being given that an object is visible is that people actually see it. The only proof that a sound is audible is that people hear it; and so of the other sources of our experience. In like manner, I apprehend, the sole evidence it is possible to produce that anything is desirable is that people do actually desire it. If the end which the utilitarian doctrine proposes to itself were not, in theory and in practice, acknowledged to be an end, nothing could ever convince any person that

it was so. No reason can be given why the general happiness is desirable, except that each person, so far as he believes it to be attainable, desires his own happiness. This, however, being a fact, we have not only all the proof which the case admits of, but all which it is possible to require, that happiness is a good; that each person's happiness is a good to that person, and the general happiness, therefore, a good to the aggregate of all persons. Happiness has made out its title as *one* of the ends of conduct, and consequently one of the criteria of morality.

But it has not, by this alone, proved itself to be the sole criterion. To do that, it would seem, by the same rule, necessary to show, not only that people desire happiness, but that they never desire anything else. Now it is palpable that they do desire things which, in common language, are decidedly distinguished from happiness. They desire, for example, virtue and the absence of vice, no less really than pleasure and the absence of pain. The desire of virtue is not as universal, but it is as authentic a fact as the desire of happiness. And hence the opponents of the utilitarian standard deem that they have a right to infer that there are other ends of human action besides happiness, and that happiness is not the standard of approbation and disapprobation.

But does the utilitarian doctrine deny that people desire virtue, or maintain that virtue is not a thing to be desired? The very reverse. It maintains not only that virtue is to be desired, but that it is to be desired disinterestedly, for itself.

Whatever may be the opinion of utilitarian moralists as to the original conditions by which virtue is made virtue, however they may believe (as they do) that actions and dispositions are only virtuous because they promote another end than virtue, yet this being granted, and it having been decided, from considerations of this description, what *is* virtuous, they not only place virtue at the very head of the things which are good as means to the ultimate end, but they also recognize as a psychological fact the possibility of its being, to the individual, a good in itself, without looking to any end beyond it; and hold that the mind is not in a right state, not in a state conformable to utility, not in the state most conducive to the general happiness, unless it does love virtue in this manner—as a thing desirable in itself, even although, in the individual instance, it should not produce those other desirable consequences which it tends to produce, and on account of which it is held to be virtue. This opinion is not, in the smallest degree, a departure from the happiness principle. The ingredients of happiness are very various, and each of them is desirable in itself, and not merely when considered as swelling an aggregate. The principle of utility does not mean that any given pleasure, as music, for instance, or any given exemption from pain, as for example health, is to be looked upon as means to a collective something termed happiness, and to be desired on that account. They are desired and desirable in and for themselves; besides being means, they are a part of the end. Virtue, according to the utilitarian doctrine, is not naturally

and originally part of the end, but it is capable of becoming so; and in those who love it disinterestedly it has become so, and is desired and cherished, not as a means to happiness, but as a part of their happiness.

To illustrate this further, we may remember that virtue is not the only thing originally a means, and which if it were not a means to anything else would be and remain indifferent, but which by association with what it is a means to comes to be desired for itself, and that too with the utmost intensity. What, for example, shall we say of the love of money? There is nothing originally more desirable about money than about any heap of glittering pebbles. Its worth is solely that of the things which it will buy; the desires for other things than itself, which it is a means of gratifying. Yet the love of money is not only one of the strongest moving forces of human life, but money is, in many cases, desired in and for itself; the desire to possess it is often stronger than the desire to use it, and goes on increasing when all the desires which point to ends beyond it, to be compassed by it, are falling off. It may, then, be said truly that money is desired not for the sake of an end, but as part of the end. From being a means to happiness, it has come to be itself a principal ingredient of the individual's conception of happiness. The same may be said of the majority of the great objects of human life: power, for example, or fame, except that to each of these there is a certain amount of immediate pleasure annexed, which has at least the semblance of being naturally inherent in them—a thing which cannot be said of money. Still, however, the strongest natural attraction, both of power and of fame, is the immense aid they give to the attainment of our other wishes; and it is the strong association thus generated between them and all our objects of desire which gives to the direct desire of them the intensity it often assumes, so as in some characters to surpass in strength all other desires. In these cases the means have become a part of the end, and a more important part of it than any of the things which they are means to. What was once desired as an instrument for the attainment of happiness has come to be desired for its own sake. In being desired for its own sake it is, however, desired as *part* of happiness. The person is made, or thinks he would be made, happy by its mere possession; and is made unhappy by failure to obtain it. The desire of it is not a different thing from the desire of happiness any more than the love of music or the desire of health. They are included in happiness. They are some of the elements of which the desire of happiness is made up. Happiness is not an abstract idea but a concrete whole; and these are some of its parts. And the utilitarian standard sanctions and approves their being so. Life would be a poor thing, very ill provided with sources of happiness, if there were not this provision of nature by which things originally indifferent, but conducive to, or otherwise associated with, the satisfaction of our primitive desires, become in themselves sources of pleasure more valuable than the primitive pleasures, both in permanency, in the space of human existence that they are capable of covering, and even in intensity.

Virtue, according to the utilitarian conception, is a good of this description. There was no original desire of it, or motive to it, save its conduciveness to pleasure, and especially to protection from pain. But through the association thus formed it may be felt a good in itself, and desired as such with as great intensity as any other good; and with this difference between it and the love of money, of power, or of fame, that all of these may, and often do, render the individual noxious to the other members of the society to which he belongs, whereas there is nothing which makes him so much a blessing to them as the cultivation of the disinterested love of virtue. And consequently, the utilitarian standard, while it tolerates and approves those other acquired desires, up to the point beyond which they would be more injurious to the general happiness than promotive of it, enjoins and requires the cultivation of the love of virtue up to the greatest strength possible, as being above all things important to the general happiness.

It results from the preceding considerations that there is in reality nothing desired except happiness. Whatever is desired otherwise than as a means to some end beyond itself, and ultimately to happiness, is desired as itself a part of happiness, and is not desired for itself until it has become so. Those who desire virtue for its own sake desire it either because the consciousness of it is a pleasure, or because the consciousness of being without it is a pain, or for both reasons united; as in truth the pleasure and pain seldom exist separately, but almost always together—the same person feeling pleasure in the degree of virtue attained, and pain in not having attained more. If one of these gave him no pleasure, and the other no pain, he would not love or desire virtue, or would desire it only for the other benefits which it might produce to himself or to persons whom he cared for.

We have now, then, an answer to the question, of what sort of proof the principle of utility is susceptible. If the opinion which I have now stated is psychologically true—if human nature is so constituted as to desire nothing which is not either a part of happiness or a means of happiness, we can have no other proof, and we require no other, that these are the only things desirable. If so, happiness is the sole end of human action, and the promotion of it the test by which to judge of all human conduct; from whence it necessarily follows that it must be the criterion of morality, since a part is included in the whole.

And now to decide whether this is really so, whether mankind do desire nothing for itself but that which is a pleasure to them, or of which the absence is a pain, we have evidently arrived at a question of fact and experience, dependent, like all similar questions, upon evidence. It can only be determined by practised self-consciousness and self-observation, assisted by observation of others. I believe that these sources of evidence, impartially consulted, will declare that desiring a thing and finding it pleasant, aversion to it and thinking of it as painful, are phenomena entirely inseparable or rather two parts of the same phenomenon; in strictness of language, two different modes of naming the same psycholog-

ical fact; that to think of an object as desirable (unless for the sake of its consequences) and to think of it as pleasant are one and the same thing; and that to desire anything except in proportion as the idea of it is pleasant, is a physical and metaphysical impossibility.

So obvious does this appear to me that I expect it will hardly be disputed; and the objection made will be, not that desire can possibly be directed to anything ultimately except pleasure and exemption from pain, but that the will is a different thing from desire; that a person of confirmed virtue or any other person whose purposes are fixed carries out his purposes without any thought of the pleasure he has in contemplating them or expects to derive from their fulfilment, and persists in acting on them, even though these pleasures are much diminished by changes in his character or decay of his passive sensibilities, or are outweighed by the pains which the pursuit of the purposes may bring upon him. All this I fully admit and have stated it elsewhere as positively and emphatically as anyone. Will, the active phenomenon, is a different thing from desire, the state of passive sensibility, and, though originally an offshoot from it, may in time take root and detach itself from the parent stock, so much so that in the case of an habitual purpose, instead of willing the thing because we desire it, we often desire it only because we will it. This, however, is but an instance of that familiar fact, the power of habit, and is nowise confined to the case of virtuous actions. Many indifferent things which men originally did from a motive of some sort, they continue to do from habit. Sometimes this is done unconsciously; the consciousness coming only after the action; at other times with conscious volition, but volition which has become habitual and is put in operation by the force of habit, in opposition perhaps to the deliberate preference, as often happens with those who have contracted habits of vicious or hurtful indulgence. Third and last comes the case in which the habitual act of will in the individual instance is not in contradiction to the general intention prevailing at other times, but in fulfilment of it; as in the case of the person of confirmed virtue and of all who pursue deliberately and consistently any determinate end. The distinction between will and desire thus understood is an authentic and highly important psychological fact; but the fact consists solely in this—that will, like all other parts of our constitution, is amenable to habit, and that we may will from habit what we no longer desire for itself, or desire only because we will it. It is not the less true that will, in the beginning, is entirely produced by desire; including in that term the repelling influence of pain as well as the attractive one of pleasure. Let us take into consideration no longer the person who has a confirmed will to do right, but him in whom that virtuous will is still feeble, conquerable by temptation, and not to be fully relied on; by what means can it be strengthened? How can the will to be virtuous, where it does not exist in sufficient force, be implanted or awakened? Only by making the person *desire* virtue—by making him think of it in a pleasurable light, or of its absence

in a painful one. It is by associating the doing right with pleasure, or the doing wrong with pain, or by eliciting and impressing and bringing home to the person's experience the pleasure naturally involved in the one or the pain in the other, that it is possible to call forth that will to be virtuous which, when confirmed, acts without any thought of either pleasure or pain. Will is the child of desire, and passes out of the dominion of its parent only to come under that of habit. That which is the result of habit affords no presumption of being intrinsically good; and there would be no reason for wishing that the purpose of virtue should become independent of pleasure and pain were it not that the influence of the pleasurable and painful associations which prompt to virtue is not sufficiently to be depended on for unerring constancy of action until it has acquired the support of habit. Both in feeling and in conduct, habit is the only thing which imparts certainty; and it is because of the importance to others of being able to rely absolutely on one's feelings and conduct, and to oneself of being able to rely on one's own, that the will to do right ought to be cultivated into this habitual independence. In other words, this state of the will is a means to good, not intrinsically a good; and does not contradict the doctrine that nothing is a good to human beings but in so far as it is either itself pleasurable or a means of attaining pleasure or averting pain.

But if this doctrine be true, the principle of utility is proved. Whether it is so or not, must now be left to the consideration of the thoughtful reader.

ALFRED CYRIL EWING (1899–1973)

Ewing received his education at Oxford and taught at Cambridge University. He has been a Visiting Professor of Philosophy at Princeton and Northwestern University and has lectured in India. His many contributions to philosophy include books and articles in the history of philosophy, metaphysics, ethics, and social philosophy. He is distinguished by the clarity and cogency of his thought.

Selfishness and Unselfishness

One of the first questions that presents itself in Ethics is—Why ought I to sacrifice myself for the sake of somebody else? If it is shown to me that some action will have bad consequences for myself, this gives an obvious reason why I should not do it, but it is often felt that it is not so obvious why I should not do what is to my own interest because it has bad consequences for others. Yet every system of ethics has prescribed duties to others as well as to oneself, and no good man is uninfluenced by the prospect of his proposed actions producing bad effects on other men. Confronted with this situation one is tempted to reply by trying to show that the fulfilment of his duties to others is really to the agent's own interests in the long run, either in this life or in another. And some philosophers who ought to have known better, thinking that this can be done, have actually taken the view that ultimately we cannot be under an obligation to pursue anything but our own greatest happiness and that our duties towards others are to be commended solely as

efficient, though indirect, means of attaining this happiness. That view is known as egoistic hedonism. "Hedonism" is derived from a Greek word meaning pleasure, and stands for the ethical doctrine that pleasure is the only good, no distinction being ordinarily made by hedonists between "pleasure" and "happiness"; "egoistic" brings out the point that the ultimate aim is *one's own* pleasure. To be fair to the theory we must realize that "pleasure" is intended to cover all satisfactions, not only the mundane pleasures of good dinners and amusements, but the joy of the most selfless and spiritualized love, the unselfish satisfaction of the righteous in furthering the general good, and the delight of the religious mystic in communion with God. Nor does the theory maintain that we should always aim directly at our own pleasure: on the contrary it maintains that we can get pleasure for ourselves best by aiming directly at other things than our own pleasure, particularly the happiness of other men, only it maintains that the sole reason why we ought to aim at the other things is because they are the best means to our own pleasure, not because we are under any obligation to pursue them for their own sake.

The first inclination of most unsophisticated people is to reject egoistic hedonism as blatantly immoral, but even if this turns out to be our final conclusion we must first examine the theory more carefully. And we may feel surprised when we find that such a theory has been held by a number of people of excellent character distinguished for what would normally be described as unselfish devotion to others. This does not indeed prove that the theory is not really in conflict with the most fundamental principles of any tolerable ethics, for a man's practice is often inconsistent with his theory, but it prevents us from dismissing it as mere wickedness or sophistry. And in fact the behaviour that such a theory, consistently carried out, would require of us is not usually by any means so different as one would at first sight expect from the behaviour normally approved ethically. It can easily be shown that under most circumstances the more obvious forms of wrong-doing simply do not pay in happiness even from a completely selfish point of view. Most wicked acts are also highly imprudent, though it is very difficult to get the people who do them to realize this till it is too late. Our happiness is dependent very largely on our relations with other men, and they will be alienated if we are thoroughly unscrupulous and selfish. Happiness also depends very largely on our mind being at peace with itself, and vicious conduct has a very strong tend-ency to destroy that internal peace. It is a mistake to think of the good as if it were a limited store not capable of increase so that I must inevitably have less if others have more. This is not true even of material wealth, since the common stock may be greatly increased by effort and ingenuity so that there is more to distribute, and since in a commercial exchange both parties commonly benefit. Still less is it true of happiness, which does not depend chiefly on material goods (though a minimum of the latter is necessary). If I acquire more money, it may (though it need not) mean that somebody else will be poorer; but if I gain in happiness through forming more satisfactory relations with others, increasing my ability to appreciate, or becoming more contented with my lot, it will not have the slightest tendency to make anybody else less happy, but rather the reverse. And one of the chief sources of happiness is the consciousness that one is performing a useful function in life and contributing to the welfare of others. The egoist need not deny that we have what are normally called unselfish desires, i.e. desires for the good of others, but he will insist that we gain in happiness ourselves through indulging these desires even more than through indulging the desires which are purely selfish. Bentham, the best known British advocate of the theory I am discussing, was also a great philanthropist, and he was asked whether he was not inconsistent in being so. He replied to the effect that he was not inconsistent, because people took their pleasure in different ways, and he happened to be so constituted that he took his pleasure in philanthropy, whereas another man might, say, take it in drink.

I think, however, that this argument is often pushed too far. It is by no means possible to show that a man always gains in happiness in proportion to what would generally be regarded as his goodness. Society may punish men for doing wrong, but it can only take cognizance of a small proportion of wrong acts, and suppose society itself is corrupt and punishes people for doing right? It is by no means clear that a good man was at all likely to be happier in Nazi Germany than a bad. Again, in all civilizations of which we know it has been held that it was sometimes a man's duty to risk gravely and even sacrifice his health and life. That is a strange way of acquiring the greatest pleasure possible for the agent! It is not legitimate for the hedonistic egoist to reply that the man will be rewarded in a future life, for even if we grant this we must admit that the only reason for thinking that the action will be rewarded is that we already think it right and admirable, and we cannot, therefore, without committing a vicious circle also hold that the reward makes it right. If our only duty is to pursue our own greatest pleasure, why should we be rewarded for sacrificing our pleasure on this earth to others? *Prima facie* we should be punished. It has often been said that we shall be rendered unhappy by pangs of conscience if we do not sacrifice ourselves for the greater good of others, but we may make a similar reply to this point. Why should we suffer from pangs of conscience if we do not first recognize

the action as wrong? And, whilst it may be true of some few people that, if they thought they had saved their own lives by neglecting their duty, they would feel so unhappy about it as to outweigh any pleasure in life, we cannot possibly maintain that this is true of everybody. Surely a man is not excused from the duty to help others because he is so constituted that he can escape the uneasiness about not having helped them by thinking of other things. People's sensitiveness in this matter varies enormously; and when an egoist dwells on the joy of serving others it is difficult to see what he could say if somebody met him with the retort—It is all very well for you, but tastes differ and I am so constituted that I enjoy the selfish pleasures much better than the unselfish.

It seems to me indeed that some of the worst acts ever done could be justified if egoistic hedonism were true. In Ibsen's play, *The Pretenders*, there is a well-known scene in which the villain lying on his deathbed has an opportunity of avenging himself on an enemy by giving rise to a misapprehension about the succession to the throne, knowing that if he does so he will gratuitously cause a civil war in which thousands will be slain. The situation in the play is complicated by the fear of punishment hereafter, but we have seen this to be irrelevant unless the proposed action can be seen to be wrong independently of the punishment, and in any case we may suppose the man thus tempted to be an atheist. Now if the sole criterion of the rightness or wrongness of an action is its conduciveness to one's own pleasure, I think one would have to say that the act of revenge was right because it would make the last few moments of his life happier than they would otherwise have been. It is true that he would have been likely to be a happier man on the whole if he had not indulged his vindictive desires to such an appalling extent in the past as he must have done to make such an act even a serious temptation, but it is too late for him to alter this now. We could not say to him—Control your vindictive desires now and your character will be improved so that you will be capable of greater pleasure in the future, for he would reply—I have no future. For the egoistic hedonist to make oneself miserable for the good of another man should be positively wicked in the only sense in which anything could be wicked at all.

But, even if the egoistic hedonist could show that his view was compatible with the ordinary canons of morality as regards the external nature of actions, he would still not have justified his position. For it is not only the external act, but the motive which counts in ethics, and the motive he suggests is one which we must regard as essentially unethical. Suppose a man admitted that he only refrains from stealing for fear of being sent to prison, or from ill-treating his children because he has been promised a sum of money if he does not ill-treat them, and we believed him, should we regard him as morally worthy? Not at all, we should condemn him as much or almost as much as if he had been guilty of theft and cruelty, for we should not recognize his motive as a proper one at all. And if so, why should we regard his conduct as any more moral if he refrains from

wrong acts in general merely because he is bribed by the prospect of happiness or deterred by the fear of unhappiness whether in this life or in another, even if the happiness or unhappiness is not viewed as coming in such crude ways and as further removed in time? The best we could say is that he shows prudence and far-sightedness, not that he is good. The occasions when we feel markedly under a moral obligation are just *not* the occasions when we are exercised about our own happiness, but the occasions on which we feel an obligation to somebody else that strikes us as such quite independently of whether obedience to it is or is not conducive to our happiness. If a man sacrifices his own happiness needlessly without apparently harming others, the natural word that springs to the lips of the observer in speaking of him is "foolish"; if he sacrifices the happiness of another to further his own apparent happiness, the natural word is not "foolish" but "bad" (in the moral sense of that word). I do not deny that some egoistic hedonists were good men, but I do say that they had a wrong theory of the motives which determined and ought to determine their conduct.

In making these criticisms I have argued from what I called "common-sense ethics", namely, I have appealed to what we cannot help believing in particular ethical situations when we try to look reasonably at the question what one ought to do or approve of doing. If anybody says that all our ethical beliefs are illusions, I must admit that I cannot refute him, only prevent him from refuting me by meeting his arguments, but this completely sceptical position about ethics is one which we may indeed defend in a philosophical argument but not seriously hold in daily life. I note that the people who are most sceptical about the truth of ethical judgements commonly show a righteous moral indignation about at least ethical intolerance, and insist very strongly that we "ought" to seek and accept the truth. And I find it extremely difficult to believe that even the most pronounced ethical sceptic would not be convinced that my actions were bad if he saw me, e.g. wantonly torturing a little child. I shall say something more about the sceptic in a later chapter, but in the meantime we must go on the assumption, which I made in the first chapter, that the ordinary moral judgments which we on reflection cannot help making are the main clue to what is right in Ethics, subject to the test of coherence, and we shall have to ask about each rival theory whether it gives a coherent account of these. I have no hesitation in making the above assumption, and if we do not make it we shall have no Ethics at all, because we shall have no ethical data to organize. Of course this rejection of sheer ethical scepticism is compatible with very much disagreement as to what we do exactly when we make ethical judgements and as to many of the ethical judgements we are called on to make.

However, even complete ethical scepticism should certainly not lead to egoistic hedonism. For even the egoistic hedonist makes some ethical assumptions of a positive kind: he assumes at least that his own pleasure is good in itself, and his pain bad. That this is so he does not and cannot prove. It must

therefore be something he sees to be true without proof. And it does seem an obvious enough truth. But in admitting it he has already accepted some ethical convictions without proof just because he sees them to be true, which is what philosophers usually mean by "intuition". Now, if he accepts any at all because he sees them intuitively, ought he not, at least in the absence of positive arguments against them, to accept all those which after careful reflection seem to him intuitively obvious in a like degree? And is it not plain that it is intuitively at least as obvious that it is wrong to do things which hurt others needlessly as that it is wrong unnecessarily to hurt oneself? There are other ethical intuitions incompatible with egoistic hedonism which might be cited, but this one is sufficient. If it is wrong to do things which hurt others for our own amusement, and we see it to be wrong just because it does hurt them, egoistic hedonism is false. For according to egoistic hedonism the only reason why anything is wrong is because it is not conducive to the agent's greatest pleasure. Even if in fact it is the case that it is never conducive to my own greatest pleasure to hurt others, it should be plain that this is not the main reason why it is wrong. If we can see clearly that our own pleasure is good, we can see just as clearly that the fact that an action needlessly and intentionally hurts another is quite sufficient to make it wrong, whether it also hurts me or not. So if we are to be consistent, we must accept both intuitions or neither, unless there are positive arguments which show one to be false, and I do not see what these could possibly be. As a matter of fact it may be doubted whether any important philosophers accept the doctrine of egoistic hedonism to-day, but very many have done so in the past, and it is a view which naturally suggests itself to very many people when they start to think about Ethics, so it is important to settle accounts with it before we move on.

It remains to answer the question how it was that such an obviously mistaken view ever acquired an important influence on ethical thinkers. It seems to me that there were two main reasons for this. In the first place it is plain that the fact that a course of action is conducive to one's own happiness is, as far as it goes, a reason for adopting it. It is a subject for dispute whether this makes it morally obligatory or merely prudent to act in the way proposed, but at least it is a good reason of some sort for doing so. Wantonly to sacrifice one's happiness or incur unhappiness is at least irrational, and that something is rational is a reason for doing it if anything is. Now the project of bringing all Ethics under a single principle so that there is just one kind of circumstance which decides whether an act is right or wrong is very attractive to thinkers, and so when we have found a principle which obviously does give valid reasons for action, there is a temptation to bring all ethical judgements under it. Thinkers have again and again succumbed to such temptations to a premature unification, but knowledge and life are not so simple as that.

Secondly, there is a plausible psychological doctrine which seemed to support egoistic hedonism. The doctrine, commonly known as *hedonistic psychology*, developed in this way. It is plain that a man can only desire what pleases him. Even if we take the case of the martyr who sacrifices all mundane advantages in order to do what he conceives to be his duty, it may be pointed out that he certainly would not have done this if he had not cared a farthing whether he did his duty or did not. Obviously the thought of doing his duty pleased him or at least the thought of not doing it displeased him. Therefore it was concluded that what he really desired was the pleasure of doing his duty and a similar conclusion was reached as regards every human desire. According to this view what an affectionate mother desires is not her children's happiness but the happiness she will herself get from believing them happy; what the martyr is seeking is not to do his duty or defend his faith, but to avoid the discomfort he would feel at having done that for which his conscience reproached him. In that case the aim of the good and the bad man is the same, their own happiness, only the latter is short-sighted in his views as to what will give him happiness. And since we cannot possibly seek anything else but our own happiness, we cannot be under any obligation to do so. It is only a question whether we seek it wisely or blunder into sacrificing a greater happiness for a lesser.

The people who defined this view in popular argument would have had much excuse if they had been living a hundred years ago, but they do not realize that it is completely rejected by modern psychology, not to say philosophy. To modern psychologists and philosophers it is plain that desire comes on the whole first and pleasure second and that the desire for pleasure as such plays only a small part in life. It is true that I could not desire something that was not in some way pleasant to me (though it might in other respects be very painful), but this does not prove that I only desire anything for the sake of the pleasure it will give. On the contrary in most cases the pleasure is rather the result of the desire than the desire of the anticipation of pleasure. Hedonists say that we avoid doing wrong because we shun the pain of a bad conscience, but should we feel this pain if we had not an aversion to wrongdoing for its own sake? And, though it is perfectly true that a mother almost always feels unhappy herself if her children are unhappy, is this not because she wants her children to be happy for their own sake? It is a mistake to equate even all *selfish* action with action motived by desire for one's own pleasure. Far more evil has been done and on the whole worse traits of character displayed under the influence of the desire for power than under that of the desire for pleasure. We need only think of certain military dictators, to say nothing of the many tyrannical employers, husbands and parents in private life. To seek power for oneself regardless of whether it benefits or harms others is just as selfish as thus to seek pleasure. No doubt the dictators, etc., took pleasure in their power, but that was only because they desired power for its own sake. A thoroughly bad act may be disinterested in the sense of not being aimed at one's own pleasure, as is illustrated by the phrase

"disinterested cruelty". If A hates B and gives way to the temptation of hate, what he wants is not his own pleasure but the pain of B, yet of all human actions the worst perhaps are those which show this kind of disinterestedness.

There is a place for the attitude of the egoistic hedonist, since there are many actions, at least when on holiday, where the only or chief relevant point is the amount of pleasure likely to be gained for oneself, but there is nothing specifically moral about it, and unless kept within strict bounds it carries with it a punishment which illustrates the falsity of hedonistic psychology as a general account of human action and desire. It is a well-known truth attested by much experience that, if we seek pleasure too much, it flies, because we are then concentrating our attention on pleasure and not on the objective sources from which alone pleasure can be derived. In order to get pleasure we must be interested in other things besides pleasure for their own sake. Even to enjoy a game we must develop an artificial desire for victory and concentrate our thoughts on this end and not on our pleasure in seeking it. And, while it is legitimate and rational to choose the more pleasant course rather than the less pleasant for oneself where other things are equal, the egoistic hedonist has certainly produced no valid argument against the ordinary view that it is wrong to sacrifice another's greater to one's own lesser pleasure.

But the egoist may resume the contest more plausibly at a higher level. So far I have dealt only with the kind of egoist who will admit only one good, pleasure. But suppose the egoist abandons hedonism and admits that good character or virtue is also an end in itself. He may then argue like this:—I ought always to pursue my own greatest good, for my greatest good is to act virtuously, and I obviously ought always to act virtuously. Even supposing I sacrifice every other personal advantage in order to do my duty, I shall only have sacrificed my lesser good for my greater: If it is argued that this kind of egoism is inconsistent with my duty to help others not only for the sake of my own good but for their own sake, it may be replied that part of virtue just consists in seeking the good of others disinterestedly. It is not only that seeking the good of others is a means to my own but that my own good actually consists partly in seeking theirs. This higher egoism, though rarely found among contemporary philosophers, seems in some form to have been the generally accepted doctrine of classical Greek philosophy, except for those hedonistic philosophers who defended the lower type of egoism which I have already criticized. Thus both Plato and Aristotle base morality on the conception that it is to our own true good to act rightly, though they do not identify good with pleasure but regard the latter as a resultant of the good rather than as constituting it.

A weak point in the egoist's case shows itself when he is asked whether it can ever be a man's duty to sacrifice his life for another. It may be granted that it is very virtuous and therefore a very great good to do so, but can we possibly say that it is such a great good as to outweigh all the goods that the

person who sacrificed his life would, if he had continued to live, have attained and enjoyed? Five minutes' or an hour's virtuous action in which he laid down his life could not outweigh the good of years of virtue which he might still have had if he had not made the sacrifice in question. A similar reply may be made if the emphasis is laid not on the goodness displayed in the sacrifice, but on the moral evil of refusing to make it. There is a story of an Irishman who, when he was called a coward for running away in battle, said—I would rather be a coward for five minutes than a corpse all the rest of my life. I should certainly advise you, if you wish to take up philosophy, to aim at higher standards in respect of logical and accurate expression than did the Irishman, but I think the substance of his objection is such that it is beyond the power of the egoist to answer it. Yet such sacrifice, the conditions for which are by no means limited to battles, is enjoined on occasion and praised in a very high degree by almost every system of ethics.

Further, is it not priggish, and indeed selfish in a bad sense, to make other men a mere means to our own good, even if that good be conceived in its highest and widest sense as the development of our character? Would not a man be a prig rather than a saint if he decided all actions by reference only to their effects on his own character? Nor is it clear that it would always be to the good of others to be treated in this fashion. To take an example, it is a commonplace that power and a rise in the social scale tend to be detrimental to character, yet it by no means follows that a man who realized that he was subject to the temptations which these things bring would be justified in there-fore rejecting an important post with a high remuneration, though he had good cause to anticipate it as highly likely that acceptance of it would lead to some deterioration in his own morality. What should we have thought if Churchill or some member of his cabinet had brought forward these objections against hold-ing office in 1940, thus subordinating the nation's welfare to the good of his own character?

An important modern philosopher, Professor G. E. Moore, has tried to show egoism to be self-contradictory.* He was thinking mainly of egoistic hedonism, but the same argument, if valid at all, would, as he recognizes, apply to any theory which held it a man's sole duty to pursue his own good, whether this good was conceived more widely or identified with pleasure. Moore argued that the egoistic hedonist is committed to maintaining that his own pleasure is the only good there is. Now, if this is so, the same would apply equally to you and me and every one of the two thousand or so million inhabitants of the earth, so there follows from his view the completely absurd conclusion that every one of over two thousand million things is the one and only thing good-in-itself, than which you could hardly have a conclusion more self-contradic-tory. Obviously the same objection would, if valid at all, apply to whatever we regarded as good, provided we took the egoistic point of view. It would be just as self-contradictory to say of every man's virtue that it was the only good

as it would be to say it of every man's pleasure. But I think the egoist (and even the egoistic hedonist) has a reply which will enable him to escape the charge of actual self-contradiction. The usual view of the egoist is surely not that each man's own good is the only good, but that it is the only good at which he is under any obligation to aim. Other people's good would on his view be equally good, only they would not impose on him any obligation to further them for their own sake. The position appears self-contradictory only if it is assumed that it is our duty to produce the greatest good, to whomever the good belongs, and this assumption, though highly plausible, is not abso-lutely necessary. We may be under an obligation to produce some good things and not others, and the egoist is main-taining that the only good things which we are under an obligation to produce are those which will belong to ourselves.

But, although there is no actual self-contradiction in the egoist position, a similar argument may be used to make it appear at least very unplausible. For, granted the amount of good be the same, why on earth should the mere fact that it belongs not to me but to someone else exempt me from all obli-gation in regard to it? It is not as if the sense of obligation were specially connected with *our* good. On the con-trary it seems to be an essential feature of the developed moral sense that it aims at being impartial between oneself and others, and forbids us to treat a good as more important because it is our own good. This being so, it seems hard indeed to maintain that we are under a paramount obligation to de-

* *Principia Ethica*, p. 98 ff.

velop goodness in ourselves but have no direct obligation whatever to further it in other men. This is not to say that we should always be setting out directly to improve the morals of other people, a policy which, if not very carefully carried out, may easily defeat its own ends, though on the other hand it would be a gross exaggeration to deny that one man can very often help another to be morally better.

In sharp contrast to even the higher egoism and still more to egoistic hedonism the ethical view popularly preached in Christian countries has usually been that the primary virtue is unselfishness viewed as the readiness to sacrifice oneself for other men. But this view cannot, any more than egoistic hedonism, be carried to its absolute extreme. A society in which everybody spent his life sacrificing all his pleasure for others would be even more absurd than a society whose members all lived by taking in each other's washing. In a society of such completely unselfish people who would be prepared to accept and benefit by the sacrifice? And the purposeless surrender of one's happiness is mere folly. This suggests the view that self-sacrifice is only required or indeed justified where it is necessary in order to secure for somebody else a *greater* good than that sacrificed, for otherwise (except in the rare case where the good sacrificed and the good gained are exactly equal) there is a net loss of good on the whole, which is undesirable. But it is not practicable to measure happiness with such mathematical exactitude, and the good man will not grudge it if he loses a little more than the man he benefits gains or count his own sacri-

fices so carefully. That would be niggardliness rather than generosity. Further, since most people are more likely to be too selfish than too unselfish, it is generally better, if in doubt, to risk going too far rather than too short a way in the direction of sacrifice. But the other error is possible, and not very uncommon. If committed out of genuine kindness it is a highly pardonable error and usually results in no harm except a slight loss of pleasure, but the motives are often rather more dubious, e.g. desire for power, desire to feel "what a good person I am", sexual desire more or less perverted. Psychologists have pointed out a "masochistic" tendency in many people which leads them to unnecessary and harmful sacrifices for particular individuals, which is of course quite compatible with general selfishness towards others. Further, whatever the motive of the sacrifice, we must take account not only of the loss of pleasure by the benefactor, which may be easily compensated by satisfaction in the act, direct or indirect, but of the effect on the character of the beneficiary. It can hardly be good for a person to be the constant recipient of unreasonable sacrifices, and is likely to make him selfish and exigent. Yet there is nothing that calls for greater admiration than devoted and cheerful sacrifice of great goods or incurring of great hardships where it is really called for if another person is to be saved from unhappiness. And even if we think that the sacrifice will be rewarded by greater happiness for the agent in this life or another, we cannot make this desire of reward the motive without gravely spoiling the spirit of the action.

We cannot therefore define an unselfish man as one who sacrifices his welfare to others, but only as one who does so within reason. We ought not to treat either other people as a mere means to our own happiness or ourselves as a mere means to the happiness of others. The point is that the interests of others should be treated on just the same level as one's own, so that the antithesis between self and others is made as little prominent in one's ethical thinking as possible. It is impossible even for the best man to feel the misfortunes of others as much as his own (except for a very few individuals of whom he is specially fond), and if he did he would be crushed by the misery in the world to and beyond the point of complete mental collapse, but it is still possible to treat their misfortunes as equally important. The principle "Do unto others as you would be done by", cannot indeed be applied literally, because people wish different things, and because it is not always right to give people what they wish, e.g. I might wish not to be punished when punishment was deserved and right. But it serves epigrammatically to express the impartiality towards ourselves and others at which we ought to aim in ethics, though we shall sometimes have to consider rather what men ought to wish than what they actually do wish. All this suggests another theory of Ethics, which has been widely held, namely the theory that what we ought to do is to seek to promote the greatest happiness, not only of ourselves, but of people in general.

COMMENT

Although Mill begins his discussion of Utilitarianism with remarks that appear to be in perfect agreement with Bentham's theory, he soon exhibits his independence. This divergence gives rise to some of the most fundamental issues in the whole field of ethics. Let us now consider some of these issues.

The Question of Qualities of Pleasure

In estimating the intrinsic value of pleasures, Mill subordinates Bentham's quantitative standards—intensity and duration—to a standard of quality. The pleasures of the cultivated life, he maintains, are superior in *kind* to the pleasures of the uncultivated. Hence the pleasures of a human being are qualitatively superior to the pleasures of a pig, and the pleasures of a Socrates are qualitatively superior to the pleasures of an uncultivated fool. This is a radical break with Bentham's quantitative hedonism, which maintains that the pleasure of a dolt is no better or worse intrinsically than the quantitatively equal pleasure of a highly developed person.

Is Mill correct in supposing that there are different kinds of pleasure? At first glance, the facts seem to bear out his view. The pleasure of reading a good philosophical book, for example, apparently differs qualitatively from the pleasure of playing a brisk game of handball. But is the qualitative difference in the *pleasures*, or is it in the differing *accompaniments* of the pleasures? If we consider pleasant *experiences*, and not bare pleasures, there *are* genuine qualitative differences; but these differences may be not in the pleasures but in the very different *contents* of experience that have the common property of pleasing. In the case of reading, the experience is quiet, meditative, and relaxed; in the case of playing handball, it is exciting, kinesthetic, and strenuous. Some psychologists, such as Edward Titchener, in his *Textbook on Psychology*, have maintained that the pleasures in such diverse experiences differ only in intensity and duration, and that the only qualitative differences are in such accompaniments as we have just pointed out. Mill inadvertently lends support to this interpretation, since he speaks of the "nobility," "dignity," "intellectuality," and so on, of the "pleasures" that he prefers. It would seem that he is talking not about bare pleasures, abstracted from any content, but, rather, about *experiences* which contain not only pleasure but various intellectual, moral, and esthetic qualities.

It is theoretically possible to maintain that there are qualitative differences in pure pleasures and that these differences are ethically important. Just as there are different kinds of colors—red, blue, green, and so on—so there might be different kinds of pleasures. And just as one might hold that warm colors, let us say, are qualitatively superior to cool colors, so one might contend that certain kinds of pleasures are qualitatively superior to others. One difficulty with this view is that we do not find such indisputable qualitative differences in pleasures. Even if we did, we might still be unable to tell whether some kinds of pleasure are really better than others.

This sort of qualitative hedonism, in any event, is not Mill's view. He *appears* to be advocating hedonism, but he is really maintaining, albeit unclearly and inconsistently, that the good is the pleasant *development* of the personality. This is a kind of synthesis of hedonism and self-realizationism rather than hedonism pure and simple.

The Question of Moral Arithmetic

Bentham maintained that the business of the legislator or moralist is to calculate the probable effects of alternative acts with a view to maximizing pleasure and minimizing pain. This entails the quantitative assessment of pleasures and pains. That there are great difficulties in comparing intensities with durations, adding up pleasures and pains, and subtracting pains from pleasures has often been pointed out. Bentham might reply that such calculation, although difficult, should be carried out as best we can, and that at least a rough estimation of the hedonic consequences of acts is indispensable to any rational direction of our lives.

By introducing questions of quality, Mill greatly restricts the applicability of Bentham's moral arithmetic. His qualitative test is *preference*—not the preference of the average person but that of the moral connoisseur. He tells us that wise persons, such as Socrates, are more competent than the unwise to compare pleasures, to judge which are qualitatively superior, and to decide whether, in a particular instance, considerations of quantity should be sacrificed to considerations of quality. "From this verdict of the only competent judges," he declares, "I apprehend there can be no appeal."

The difference between the approaches of Bentham and of Mill gives rise to a number of questions: To what extent does utilitarianism entail the measurement of pleasures and pains? Are intensities commensurable with durations, and pains with pleasures? Is the preference of the wise a better guide than quantitative assessment? Is the concept of a moral connoisseur sound?

The Question of the Social Distribution of Good

Bentham proposes that the morality of acts be determined by their contribution to "the greatest happiness of the greatest number"—and Mill, at times, employs the same phrase. But does this formula mean the greatest amount of happiness among people, or the greatest number of people who are happy? And, supposing that there is a conflict between greatest happiness and greatest number, should we sacrifice the greatest number to the greatest happiness, or the greatest happiness to the greatest number? The ambiguous formula of Bentham and Mill provides us with no answer.

There are indications, however, that Bentham is more democratic and equalitarian in his approach to the problem of distribution than Mill. Each person, he declared, should count for one, and no one for more than one. This tenet could be interpreted as meaning that the pleasure of any person is as intrinsically good as the quantitatively equal pleasure of any other person. But it could also be interpreted to mean that a smaller amount of pleasure *equally* distributed is morally preferable (at least on occasion) to a greater amount *unequally* distributed. If this was Bentham's real conviction, he was not a strict utilitarian and hedonist—for the principle of equality so interpreted is based upon a sense of distributive justice rather than upon the utilitarian principle of maximizing pleasure and minimizing pain.

The second part of the ethical philosophy of Bentham and the two Mills is a theory about the nature of ultimate good and evil. Here again, as we have seen, there is disagreement between John Stuart Mill, who embraced a kind of hedonic self-realizationism, and Bentham, who clung to pure quantitative hedonism. The issue is extremely important, but it is not one that can be decided by any conclusive proof. Mill (not realizing the extent of his divergence from Bentham) undertook to "prove" that pleasure alone is ultimately good, but his so-called proof (he admits that *strict* or *conclusive* proof is impossible) contains some of the most widely advertised fallacies in the history of philosophy. We shall refrain from pointing out these fallacies, leaving to the reader the exercise of discovering them. Whether the fallacies are apparent only, being due to carelessness in the use of language, or whether they are *real* fallacies resulting from mental confusion, is a question of interpretation.

To decide the question what is ultimately good we must summon up whatever insight we can muster. If we imagine a world of people and a world of lower animals, *equal in the amount of pleasure they contain*, it might not follow that the two worlds are equal in ultimate goodness—because the people, in addition to experiencing pleasure, have insight into truth, love, imagination, excellence of character, enjoyment of beauty, and so forth. The reply of the hedonist, that all these things are good as means because they *give* pleasure, would not seem to the antihedonist an adequate answer. The antihedonist would say that it is important not merely to feel pleasure, but to feel pleasure in certain ways, with certain accompaniments rather than others. *Real* happiness embraces the great goods of beauty and truth and nobility of character as having intrinsic and not merely instrumental value. To decide who is right, the hedonist or the antihedonist, is a very important question for the reader to answer.

Utilitarianism and Justice

A frequent criticism of utilitarianism is that it cannot be reconciled with our ideas of a just social order. According to the utilitarian standard, any distribution of goods and evils, however, unjust, ought to be preferred to any other distribution, however just, if it would yield a greater surplus of happiness over unhappiness ("net good"). The sole aim of morals is to produce as much net-good as possible. To maintain such a view, the anti-utilitarian will argue, is shockingly to neglect the right of every person to fair treatment.

Take, for example, the matter of punishment. "If some kind of very cruel crime becomes common, and none of the criminals can be caught," remarks E. F. Carritt, "it might be highly expedient, as an example, to hang an innocent man, if a charge against him could be so framed that he were universally thought guilty."[1] Carritt concludes that a utilitarian would be logically bound in this instance to approve the hanging of an innocent person.

Or take the matter of the distribution of goods. Arguing on grounds that "each person possesses an inviolability founded on justice that even the welfare of society as a whole cannot override," John Rawls concludes that "all social primary goods —liberty and opportunity, income and wealth, and the bases of self-respect—are to be distributed equally unless an unequal distribution of any or all of these goods is to the advantage of the least favored."[2] How these "primary goods," which are instrumental to the chances of attaining all other goods, should be

---

[1] *Ethical and Political Thinking* (New York: Oxford University Press, 1947), p. 65.

[2] *A Theory of Justice* (Cambridge, Mass.: Harvard University Press), pp. 3, 302–303.

distributed raises the question of what distribution justice demands. Rawls believes that his standard of justice as fairness should take precedence over the utilitarian standard of net-good.

Consider Bentham's position. According to Bentham, any respect to be paid to justice is strictly derivative from the single end of attaining the greatest balance of pleasure over pain. Under certain conditions, slavery might yield the greatest balance, yet it would according to Rawls be unjust and immoral.

Bentham might reply as follows. We are never justified in imposing an evil that is not compensated by good results. Every person, being capable of enjoyment and suffering, is a locus of ultimate values, and is to be respected and treated as such. This means that every person is entitled to as much good and as little evil as possible, so long as this does not interfere with the greater net-good of others. Another important consideration is "the law of diminishing utility." This is the principle that, as men and women become more affluent, there is a diminishing return in happiness for every unit of money or resources expended. For example, if you give a half dollar to a poor and hungry person for a bowl of soup, you will contribute more to human satisfaction than if you give an equivalent sum to a wealthy person. This is a powerful reason for coming to the aid of the more destitute. It is also a reason for an equitable distribution of income, limiting the maximum as well as raising the minimum. With these principles in mind, Bentham could agree with his critics that it is wrong to distribute goods arbitrarily or unfairly, but he would say that it is not arbitrary or unfair to be governed by best results.

This sort of defense is available to a quantitative utilitarian. Mill, with his theory of qualitative good, has an additional answer. In estimating best results, we should consider not only the quantity but the quality of the good-making property. States of experience that involve fairness may be qualitatively superior (other things being equal) to states that involve unfairness. The pleasures involving injustice are qualitatively inferior to the pleasures free from this taint. If so, it would be consistent with utilitarianism to prefer the pleasures of justice ("fairness") on the grounds of their qualitative superiority, and the conflict of justice with utility could be avoided.

The concept of "justice as fairness" is difficult to reduce to utilitarian criteria, unless we admit that fairness itself has intrinsic value and include it among the goods to be maximized. If we should nevertheless decide that justice cannot be wholly explained on utilitarian grounds, our principal duty may still be to promote the good, subject only to the constraint that justice should either not be violated or that the good in the particular instance is so great that it outweighs the violation. Rawls would not accept this compromise, because he believes that justice as a principle of right must have absolute priority over ultimate good, whether it be conceived as happiness, fulfillment of interest, or in any other manner. Here is a profound difference of philosophical conviction that the reader may well ponder.

Act-Utilitarianism and Rule-Utilitarianism

We can distinguish between "extreme" and "restricted" utilitarianism. The former is more often called "act-utilitarianism," and the latter "rule-utilitarianism." Extreme- or act-utilitarianism judges rightness in terms of the consequences of *individual* acts. According to this point of view, the right act is that which brings the best results in the particular circumstances. Since it may be inconvenient or difficult or impossible to estimate the consequences of individual acts, we are often forced to fall back upon "rules of thumb," but if breaking the rule *does* produce the best possible consequences, then the rule ought to be broken.

Restricted- or rule-utilitarianism maintains that acts are to be tested by rules and rules by consequences. The only exceptions are when rules conflict or when the particular act falls under no rules. Just as the rules of a game determine what is permissible, so the rules of moral practice determine what is *morally* permissible. When the umpire calls the batter out after three strikes, it would be absurd for him to plead with the umpire for another try. The batter has no choice but to abide by the rules. So likewise the rule-utilitarian insists upon obedience to the relevant moral rule, while justifying the rule by the consequences.

Note that the rule-utilitarian would have an answer to Carritt (see above) that the act-utilitarian would not have. Punishment is a practice, and in a civilized society this practice is highly instituitonalized. For a judge or jury to condemn a person known to be innocent, even though there is some great advantage in doing so, is to violate the whole concept of punishment as a practice. The safeguards against such miscarriage of justice are built-in features of the institution of punishment. If the institution is justified on utilitarian grounds, so are these safeguards.

The choice between act-utilitarianism and rule-utilitarianism need not be exclusive. Both may be valid within limits, act-utilitarianism applying in the absence of institutionalized practice, and rule-utilitarianism applying when there is not only such practice but good utilitarian reasons for keeping the practice inviolate.

A number of philosophers have raised the interesting question whether Mill was an act-utilitarian or a rule-utilitarian. Here is a question of interpretation that the reader may wish to consider. You may also wish to ponder the question whether act-utilitarianism or rule-utilitarianism is the sounder theory, or whether and how it is best to combine them.

Part Three

SOCIAL PHILOSOPHY

SOCIAL PHILOSOPHY IS not a sharply distinct and separate field. The fundamental issues that divide social philosophers are ultimately metaphysical, epistemological, or ethical. Among the questions debated are the following: What is the basis of political obligation? What is the nature of a good social order? What is right social action? Are the actions of government to be justified by reference to the ends of the individual or of society? Does history have a pattern that can be known and predicted? All these questions involve metaphysical, epistemological, or ethical issues.

14

Aristocracy

PLATO

(For biographical note see pages 9-10.)

The Republic

Scene: The home of Cephalus, a retired manufacturer living at Piraeus, the harbor town about five miles from Athens.

Characters (in the following sections of the dialogue): Glaucon, Adeimantus, and Socrates, who narrates the entire conversation to an unspecified audience.

[In the section of the Republic *preceding our selections, Plato set forth some of the essential premises of his thought. He begins by a refutation of the Sophist theory that moral principles are purely relative; on the contrary, he maintains, they have a rational and absolute basis. Thrasymachus, a Sophist, is introduced as a rather cynical advocate of the theory that "just or right*

Translated with introduction and notes by Francis MacDonald Cornford, Oxford University Press, London, 1941; New York, 1945. Reprinted by permission. Some of Cornford's footnotes have been omitted. The italicized glosses are his except for those supplied by the present editor and marked by the initials "M. R".

means nothing but what is to the interest of the stronger party." This doctrine is similar to Karl Marx's declaration, in the Communist Manifesto, *that "the ruling ideas of every age are the ideas of the ruling class." But Marx looked forward to an all-human morality based upon the eventual achievement of a classless society, whereas Thrasymachus champions the doctrine that right means nothing but the interest of the dominant political force. Socrates, in reply, argues that every art, including the art of government, serves the interests of its subjects. A physician, for example, serves his patients, and a shepherd takes good care of his sheep. Similarly any statesman deserving of the name cares for the good of the citizens within his jurisdiction. At this point, Thrasymachus abruptly drops his defense of "justice" and champions injustice, which he compares to fattening sheep for slaughter. M.R.]*

Socrates, have you a nurse?

Why do you ask such a question as

that? I said. Wouldn't it be better to answer mine?

Because she lets you go about sniffling like a child whose nose wants wiping. She hasn't even taught you to know a shepherd when you see one, or his sheep either.

What makes you say that?

Why, you imagine that a herdsman studies the interests of his flocks or cattle, tending and fattening them up with some other end in view than his master's profit or his own; and so you don't see that, in politics, the genuine ruler regards his subjects exactly like sheep, and thinks of nothing else, night and day, but the good he can get out of them for himself. You are so far out in your notions of right and wrong, justice and injustice, as not to know that 'right' actually means what is good for someone else, and to be 'just' means serving the interest of the stronger who rules, at the cost of the subject who obeys; whereas injustice is just the reverse, asserting its authority over those innocents who are called just, so that they minister solely to their master's advantage and happiness, and not in the least degree to their own. Innocent as you are yourself, Socrates, you must see that a just man always has the worst of it. Take a private business: when a partnership is wound up, you will never find that the more honest of two partners comes off with the larger share; and in their relations to the state, when there are taxes to be paid, the honest man will pay more than the other on the same amount of property; or if there is money to be distributed, the dishonest will get it all. When either of them hold some public office, even if the just

man loses in no other way, his private affairs at any rate will suffer from neglect, while his principles will not allow him to help himself from the public funds; not to mention the offence he will give to his friends and relations by refusing to sacrifice those principles to do them a good turn. Injustice has all the opposite advantages. I am speaking of the type I described just now, the man who can get the better of other people on a large scale: you must fix your eye on him, if you want to judge how much it is to one's own interest not to be just. You can see that best in the most consummate form of injustice, which rewards wrongdoing with supreme welfare and happiness and reduces its victims, if they won't retaliate in kind, to misery. That form is despotism, which uses force or fraud to plunder the goods of others, public or private, sacred or profane, and to do it in a wholesale way. If you are caught committing any one of these crimes on a small scale, you are punished and disgraced; they call it sacrilege, kidnapping, burglary, theft and brigandage. But if, besides taking their property, you turn all your countrymen into slaves, you will hear no more of those ugly names; your countrymen themselves will call you the happiest of men and bless your name, and so will everyone who hears of such a complete triumph of injustice; for when people denounce injustice, it is because they are afraid of suffering wrong, not of doing it. So true is it, Socrates, that injustice, on a grand enough scale, is superior to justice in strength and freedom and autocratic power; and 'right,' as I said at first, means simply what serves the interest of the stronger party; 'wrong' means what is for the interest and profit of oneself.

[*Socrates advances a number of objections to this defense of injustice on a grand scale. He argues that the thirst for power results in uncontrolled competition; the wise ruler puts a limit to his personal ambitions. Unbridled power produces strife; true justice produces harmony. The human soul has its characteristic function, which is not the lust for power or sensual gratification, but the subordination of impulse to rational principles of conduct. Socrates thus maintains that there are objective principles of morality and justice—a contention which requires the entire dialogue which follows to substantiate.*

When Thrasymachus, worsted in the argument, sullenly withdraws, Glaucon and Adeimantus—Plato's elder brothers—step into the discussion. They ask Socrates to criticize a theory which they find both plausible and disturbing—that people prefer a just to an unjust life for reasons of mere expediency. A person, they are inclined to think, would be quite ready to commit injustice if he could escape the penalties. Socrates agrees to carry on the dialogue. M.R.]

The Ring of Gyges

Good, said Glaucon. Listen then, and I will begin with my first point: the nature and origin of justice.

What people say is that to do wrong is, in itself, a desirable thing; on the other hand, it is not at all desirable to suffer wrong, and the harm to the sufferer outweighs the advantage to the doer. Consequently, when men have had a taste of both, those who have not the power to seize the advantage and escape the harm decide that they would be better off if they made a compact neither to do wrong nor to suffer it. Hence they began to make laws and covenants with one another; and whatever the law prescribed they called lawful and right. That is what right or justice is and how it came into existence; it stands half-way between the best thing of all—to do wrong with impunity—and the worst, which is to suffer wrong without the power to retaliate. So justice is accepted as a compromise, and valued, not as good in itself, but for lack of power to do wrong; no man worthy of the name, who had that power, would ever enter into such a compact with anyone; he would be mad if he did. That, Socrates, is the nature of justice according to this account, and such the circumstances in which it arose.

The next point is that men practise it against the grain, for lack of power to do wrong. How true that is, we shall best see if we imagine two men, one just, the other unjust, given full licence to do whatever they like, and then follow them to observe where each will be led by his desires. We shall catch the just man taking the same road as the unjust; he will be moved by self-interest, the end which it is natural to every creature to pursue as good, until forcibly turned aside by law and custom to respect the principle of equality.

Now, the easiest way to give them that complete liberty of action would be to imagine them possessed of the talisman found by Gyges, the ancestor of the famous Lydian. The story tells how he was a shepherd in the King's service. One day there was a great storm, and the ground where his flock was feeding was rent by an earthquake. Astonished at the sight, he went down into the chasm and saw, among other wonders of which the story tells, a brazen horse, hollow, with windows in its sides. Peering in, he saw a dead body, which seemed to be of more than human size. It was naked save for a gold ring, which he took from the finger and made his way out. When the sheperds met, as they did every month, to send an account to the King of the state of his flocks, Gyges came wearing the ring. As he was sitting with the others, he happened to turn the bezel of the ring inside his hand. At once he became invisible, and his companions, to his surprise, began to speak of him as if he had left them. Then, as he was fingering the ring, he turned the bezel outwards and became visible again. With that, he set about testing the ring to see if it really had this power, and always with the same result: according as he turned the bezel inside or out he vanished and reappeared. After this discovery he contrived to be one of the messengers sent to the court. There he seduced the Queen, and with her help murdered the King and seized the throne.

Now suppose there were two such magic rings, and one were given to the just man, the other to the unjust. No one, it is commonly believed, would have such iron strength of mind as to stand fast in doing right or keep his hands off other men's goods, when he could go to the market-place and fearlessly help himself to anything he wanted, enter houses and sleep with any woman he chose, set prisoners free and kill men at his pleasure, and in a word go about among men with the powers of a god. He would behave no better than the other; both would take the same course. Surely this would be strong proof that men do right only under compulsion; no individual thinks of it as good for him personally, since he does wrong whenever he finds he has the power. Every man believes that wrongdoing pays him personally much better, and, according to this theory, that is the truth. Granted full licence to do as he liked, people would think him a miserable fool if they found him refusing to wrong his neighbours or to touch their belongings, though in public they would keep up a pretence of praising his conduct, for fear of being wronged themselves. So much for that.

Finally, if we are really to judge between the two lives, the only way is to contrast the extremes of justice and injustice. We can best do that by imagining our two men to be perfect types, and crediting both to the full with the qualities they need for their respective ways of life. To begin with the unjust man: he must be like any consummate master of a craft, a physician or a captain, who, knowing just what his art can do, never tries to do more, and can always retrieve a false step. The unjust man, if he is to reach perfection, must be equally discreet in his criminal attempts, and he must not be found out, or we shall think him a bungler; for the highest pitch of injustice is to seem just when you are not. So we must endow our man with the full complement of injustice; we must allow him to have secured a spotless reputation for virtue while committing the blackest crimes; he must be able to retrieve any mistake, to defend himself with convincing eloquence if his misdeeds are denounced, and, when force is required, to bear down all opposition by his courage and strength and by his command of friends and money.

Now set beside this paragon the just man in his simplicity and nobleness, one who, in Aeschylus' words, "would be, not seem, the best." There must, indeed, be no such seeming; for if his character were apparent, his reputation would bring him honours and rewards, and then we should not know whether it was for their sake that he was just or for justice's sake alone. He must be stripped of everything but justice, and denied every advantage the other enjoyed. Doing no wrong, he must have the worst reputation for wrong-doing, to test whether his virtue is proof against all that comes of having a bad name; and under this lifelong imputation of wickedness, let him hold on his course of justice unwavering to the point of death. And so, when the two men have carried their justice and injustice to the last extreme, we may judge which is the happier.

My dear Glaucon, I exclaimed, how vigorously you scour these two characters clean for inspection, as if you were burnishing a couple of statues![1]

[1] At Elis and Athens officials called *phaidryntai*, 'burnishers,' had the duty of cleaning cult statues (A. B. Cook, *Zeus*, iii. 967). At 612 c, where this passage is recalled, it is admitted to be an extravagant supposition, that the just and unjust should exchange reputations.

I am doing my best, he answered. Well, given two such characters, it is not hard, I fancy, to describe the sort of life that each of them may expect; and if the description sounds rather coarse, take it as coming from those who cry up the merits of injustice rather than from me. They will tell you that our just man will be thrown into prison, scourged and racked, will have his eyes burnt out, and, after every kind of torment, be impaled. That will teach him how much better it is to seem virtuous than to be so. In fact those lines of Aeschylus I quoted are more fitly applied to the unjust man, who, they say, is a realist and does not live for appearances: "he would be, not seem" unjust,

. . . reaping the harvest sown
In those deep furrows of the thoughtful heart
Whence wisdom springs.

With his reputation for virtue, he will hold offices of state, ally himself by marriage to any family he may choose, become a partner in any business, and, having no scruples about being dishonest, turn all these advantages to profit. If he is involved in a lawsuit, public or private, he will get the better of his opponents, grow rich on the proceeds, and be able to help his friends and harm his enemies. Finally, he can make sacrifices to the gods and dedicate offerings with due magnificence, and, being in a much better position than the just man to serve the gods as well as his chosen friends, he may reasonably hope to stand higher in the favour of heaven. So much better, they say, Socrates, is the life prepared for the unjust by gods and men.

[*Socrates sees no way of immediately refuting the theory advanced by Glaucon and suggests that an answer can best be found if the argument is projected from the level of the individual to that of the community. He proposes to study the origin and nature of the state, in the hope of thereby discovering the nature of justice and other virtues. —M.R.*]

The Virtues in the State

[*Plato's original aim in constructing an ideal state was to find in it justice exemplified on a larger scale than in the individual. Assuming that four cardinal qualities make up the whole of virtue, he now asks wherein consist the wisdom, courage, temperance, and justice of the state, or, in other words, of the individuals composing the state in their public capacity as citizens.*

Wisdom in the conduct of state affairs will be the practical prudence or good counsel of the deliberative body. Only the philosophic Rulers will possess the necessary insight into what is good for the community as a whole. They will have "right belief" grounded on immediate knowledge of the meaning of goodness in all its forms. The Auxiliaries will have only a right belief accepted on the authority of the Rulers. Their functions will be executive, not deliberative.

The Courage of the state will obviously be manifested in the fighting force. Socrates had defined courage as knowledge of what really is, or is not, to be feared, and he had regarded it as an inseparable part of all virtue, which consists in knowing what things are

really good or evil. If the only real evil is moral evil, then poverty, suffering, and all the so-called evils that others can inflict on us, including death itself, are not to be feared, since, if they are met in the right spirit, they cannot make us worse people. This knowledge only the philosophic Rulers will possess to the full. The courage of the Auxiliaries will consist in the power of holding fast to the conviction implanted by their education.

Temperance is not, as we might expect, the peculiar virtue of the lowest order in the state. As self-mastery, it means the subordination of the lower elements to the higher; but government must be with the willing consent of the governed, and temperance will include the unanimous agreement of all classes as to who should rule and who obey.[2] *It is consequently like a harmony pervading and uniting all parts of the whole, a principle of solidarity. In the* Laws, *which stresses the harmonious union of different and complementary elements, this virtue overshadows even Justice.*

Justice is the complementary principle of differentiation, keeping the parts distinct. It has been before us all through the construction of the state since it first appeared on the economic level as the division of labor based on natural aptitudes. "Doing one's own work" now has the larger sense of a concentration on one's peculiar duty or function in the community. This conception of "doing and possessing what properly belongs to one" is wide enough

[2] At *Statesman* 276 E the true king is distinguished from the despot by the voluntary submission of his subjects to his rule.

to cover the justice of the law-courts,
assuring to each person his due rights.
Injustice will mean invasion and encroachment upon the rights and duties
of others.

*The virtue described in this chapter
is what Plato calls "civic" or "popular"
virtue. Except in the Rulers, it is not
directly based on that ultimate knowledge of good and evil which is wisdom,
to be attained only at the end of the
higher education of the philosopher.*]

So now at last, son of Ariston, said I,
your commonwealth is established. The
next thing is to bring to bear upon it
all the light you can get from any
quarter, with the help of your brother
and Polemarchus and all the rest, in
the hope that we may see where justice
is to be found in it and where injustice,
how they differ, and which of the two
will bring happiness to its possessor, no
matter whether gods and men see that
he has it or not.

Nonsense, said Glaucon; you promised to conduct the search yourself, because it would be a sin not to uphold
justice by every means in your power.

That is true; I must do as you say,
but you must all help.

We will.

I suspect, then, we may find what we
are looking for in this way. I take it
that our state, having been founded and
built up on the right lines, is good in
the complete sense of the word.

It must be.

Obviously, then, it is wise, brave,
temperate, and just.

Obviously.

Then if we find some of these qualities in it, the remainder will be the one
we have not found. It is as if we were

looking somewhere for one of any four
things: if we detected that one immediately, we should be satisfied; whereas
if we recognized the other three first,
that would be enough to indicate the
thing we wanted; it could only be the
remaining one. So here we have four
qualities. Had we not better follow that
method in looking for the one we
want?

Surely.

To begin then: the first quality to
come into view in our state seems to be
its wisdom; and there appears to be
something odd about this quality.[3]

What is there odd about it?

I think the state we have described
really has wisdom; for it will be prudent in counsel, won't it?

Yes.

And prudence in counsel is clearly a
form of knowledge; good counsel cannot be due to ignorance and stupidity.

Clearly.

But there are many and various
kinds of knowledge in our commonwealth. There is the knowledge possessed by the carpenters or the smiths,
and the knowledge how to raise crops.
Are we to call the state wise and prudent on the strength of these forms of
skill?

No; they would only make it good at
furniture-making or working in cop-
per or agriculture.

Well then, is there any form of
knowledge, possessed by some among
the citizens of our new-founded commonwealth, which will enable it to take
thought, not for some particular inter-

---

[3] Because the wisdom of the whole resides
in the smallest part, as explained below.

est, but for the best possible conduct of the state as a whole in its internal and external relations?

Yes, there is.

What is it, and where does it reside?

It is precisely that art of guardianship which resides in those Rulers whom we just now called Guardians in the full sense.

And what would you call the state on the strength of that knowledge?

Prudent and truly wise.

And do you think there will be more or fewer of these genuine Guardians in our state than there will be smiths?

Far fewer.

Fewer, in fact, than any of those other groups who are called after the kind of skill they possess?

Much fewer.

So, if a state is constituted on natural principles, the wisdom it possesses as a whole will be due to the knowledge residing in the smallest part, the one which takes the lead and governs the rest. Such knowledge is the only kind that deserves the name of wisdom, and it appears to be ordained by nature that the class privileged to possess it should be the smallest of all.

Quite true.

Here then we have more or less made out one of our four qualities and its seat in the structure of the commonwealth.

To my satisfaction, at any rate.

Next there is courage. It is not hard to discern that quality or the part of the community in which it resides so as to entitle the whole to be called brave.

Why do you say so?

Because anyone who speaks of a state as either brave or cowardly can only be thinking of that part of it which takes the field and fights in its defence; the reason being, I imagine, that the character of the state is not determined by the bravery or cowardice of the other parts.

No.

Courage, then, is another quality which a community owes to a certain part of itself. And its being brave will mean that, in this part, it possesses the power of preserving, in all circumstances, a conviction about the sort of things that it is right to be afraid of—the conviction implanted by the education which the law-giver has established. Is not that what you mean by courage?

I do not quite understand. Will you say it again?

I am saying that courage means preserving something.

Yes, but what?

The conviction, inculcated by lawfully established education, about the sort of things which may rightly be feared. When I added "in all circumstances," I meant preserving it always and never abandoning it, whether under the influence of pain or of pleasure, of desire or of fear. If you like, I will give an illustration.

Please do.

You know how dyers who want wool to take a purple dye, first select the white wool from among all the other colors, next treat it very carefully to make it take the dye in its full brilliance, and only then dip it in the vat. Dyed in that way, wool gets a fast color, which no washing, even with soap, will rob of its brilliance; whereas if they choose wool of any color but white, or if they neglect to prepare it, you know what happens.

Yes, it looks washed-out and ridiculous.

That illustrates the result we were doing our best to achieve when we were choosing our fighting men and training their minds and bodies. Our only purpose was to contrive influences whereby they might take the color of our institutions like a dye, so that, in virtue of having both the right temperament and the right education, their convictions about what ought to be feared and on all other subjects might be indelibly fixed, never to be washed out by pleasure and pain, desire and fear, solvents more terribly effective than all the soap and fuller's earth in the world. Such a power of constantly preserving, in accordance with our institutions, the right conviction about the things which ought, or ought not, to be feared, is what I call courage. That is my position, unless you have some objection to make.

None at all, he replied; if the belief were such as might be found in a slave or an animal—correct, but not produced by education—you would hardly describe it as in accordance with our institutions, and you would give it some other name than courage.

Quite true.

Then I accept your account of courage.

You will do well to accept it, at any rate as applying to the courage of the ordinary citizen;[4] if you like we will go

into it more fully some other time. At present we are in search of justice, rather than of courage; and for that purpose we have said enough.

I quite agree.

Two qualities, I went on, still remain to be made out in our state, temperance and the object of our whole inquiry, justice. Can we discover justice without troubling ourselves further about temperance?

I do not know, and I would rather not have justice come to light first, if that means that we should not go on to consider temperance. So if you want to please me, take temperance first.

Of course I have every wish to please you.

Do go on then.

I will. At first sight, temperance seems more like some sort of concord or harmony than the other qualities did.

How so?

Temperance surely means a kind of orderliness, a control of certain pleasures and appetites. People use the expression, "master of oneself," whatever that means, and various other phrases that point the same way.

Quite true.

Is not "master of oneself" an absurd expression? A man who was master of himself would presumably be also subject to himself, and the subject would be master; for all these terms apply to the same person.

No doubt.

I think, however, the phrase means that within the man himself, in his soul, there is a better part and a worse; and that he is his own master when the part which is better by nature has the worse

---

[4] As distinct from the perfect courage of the philosophic Ruler, based on immediate knowledge of values.

under its control. It is certainly a term of praise; whereas it is considered a disgrace, when, through bad breeding or bad company, the better part is overwhelmed by the worse, like a small force outnumbered by a multitude. A man in that condition is called a slave to himself and intemperate.

Probably that is what is meant.

Then now look at our newly founded state and you will find one of these two conditions realized there. You will agree that it deserves to be called master of itself, if temperance and self-mastery exist where the better part rules the worse.

Yes, I can see that is true.

It is also true that the great mass of multifarious appetites and pleasures and pains will be found to occur chiefly in children and women and slaves, and, among free men so called, in the inferior multitude; whereas the simple and moderate desires which, with the aid of reason and right belief, are guided by reflection, you will find only in a few, and those with the best inborn dispositions and the best educated.

Yes, certainly.

Do you see that this state of things will exist in your commonwealth, where the desires of the inferior multitude will be controlled by the desires and wisdom of the superior few? Hence, if any society can be called master of itself and in control of pleasures and desires, it will be ours.

Quite so.

On all these grounds, then, we may describe it as temperate. Furthermore, in our state, if anywhere, the governors and the governed will share the same conviction on the question who ought to rule.[5] Don't you think so?

I am quite sure of it.

Then, if that is their state of mind, in which of the two classes of citizens will temperance reside—in the governors or in the governed?

In both, I suppose.

So we were not wrong in divining a resemblance between temperance and some kind of harmony. Temperance is not like courage and wisdom, which made the state wise and brave by residing each in one particular part. Temperance works in a different way; it extends throughout the whole gamut of the state, producing a consonance of all its elements from the weakest to the strongest as measured by any standard you like to take—wisdom, bodily strength, numbers, or wealth. So we are entirely justified in identifying with temperance this unanimity or harmonious agreement between the naturally superior and inferior elements on the question which of the two should govern, whether in the state or in the individual.

I fully agree.

Good, said I. We have discovered in our commonwealth three out of our four qualities, to the best of our present judgment. What is the remaining one, required to make up its full complement of goodness? For clearly this will be justice.

[5] This principle of freedom—government with consent of the governed—is thus recognized. The "democratic" freedom to "do whatever you like" is condemned in later chapters.

Clearly.

Now is the moment, then, Glaucon, for us to keep the closest watch, like huntsmen standing round a covert, to make sure that justice does not slip through and vanish undetected. It must certainly be somewhere hereabouts; so keep your eyes open for a view of the quarry, and if you see it first, give me the alert.

I wish I could, he answered; but you will do better to give me a lead and not count on me for more than eyes to see what you show me.

Pray for luck, then, and follow me. The thicket looks rather impenetrable, said I; too dark for it to be easy to start up the game. However, we must push on.

Of course we must.

Here I gave the view halloo. Glaucon, I exclaimed, I believe we are on the track and the quarry is not going to escape us altogether.

That is good news.

Really, I said, we have been extremely stupid. All this time the thing has been under our very noses from the start, and we never saw it. We have been as absurd as a person who hunts for something he has all the time got in his hand. Instead of looking at the thing, we have been staring into the distance. No doubt that is why it escaped us.

What do you mean?

I believe we have been talking about the thing all this while without ever understanding that we were giving some sort of account of it.

Do come to the point. I am all ears.

Listen, then, and judge whether I am right. You remember how, when we first began to establish our common-wealth and several times since, we have laid down, as a universal principle, that everyone ought to perform the one function in the community for which his nature best suited him. Well, I believe that that principle, or some form of it, is justice.

We certainly laid that down.

Yes, and surely we have often heard people say that justice means minding one's own business and not meddling with other men's concerns; and we have often said so ourselves.

We have.

Well, my friend, it may be that this minding of one's own business, when it takes a certain form, is actually the same thing as justice, Do you know what makes me think so?

No, tell me.

I think that this quality which makes it possible for the three we have already considered, wisdom, courage, and temperance, to take their place in the commonwealth, and so long as it remains present secures their continuance, must be the remaining one. And we said that, when three of the four were found, the one left over would be justice.

It must be so.

Well now, if we had to decide which of these qualities will contribute most to the excellence of our commonwealth, it would be hard to say whether it was the unanimity of rules and subjects, or the soldier's fidelity to the established conviction about what is, or is not, to be feared, or the watchful intelligence of the Rulers; or whether its excellence were not above all due to the observance by everyone, child or woman, slave or freeman or artisan, ruler or ruled, of this principle that one should do his own proper work without interfering with others.

It would be hard to decide, no doubt.

It seems, then, that this principle can at any rate claim to rival wisdom, temperance, and courage as conducing to the excellence of a state. And would you not say that the only possible competitor of these qualities must be justice?

Yes, undoubtedly.

Here is another thing which points to the same conclusion. The judging of law-suits is a duty that you will lay upon your Rulers, isn't it?

Of course.

And the chief aim of their decisions will be that neither party shall have what belongs to another or be deprived of what is his own.

Yes.

Because that is just?

Yes.

So here again justice admittedly means that a man should possess and concern himself with what properly belongs to him.[6]

True.

Again, do you agree with me that no great harm would be done to the community by a general interchange of most forms of work, the carpenter and the cobbler exchanging their positions and their tools and taking on each other's jobs, or even the same man undertaking both?

Yes, there would not be much harm in that.

But I think you will also agree that another kind of interchange would be disastrous. Suppose, for instance, some-

one whom nature designed to be an artisan or tradesman should be emboldened by some advantage, such as wealth or command of votes or bodily strength, to try to enter the order of fighting men; or some member of that order should aspire, beyond his merits, to a seat in the council-chamber of the Guardians. Such interference and exchange of social positions and tools, or the attempt to combine all these forms of work in the same person, would be fatal to the commonwealth.

Most certainly.

Where there are three orders, then, any plurality of functions or shifting from one order to another is not merely utterly harmful to the community, but one might fairly call it the extreme of wrongdoing. And you will agree that to do the greatest of wrongs to one's own community is injustice.

Surely.

This, then, is injustice. And, conversely, let us repeat that when each order—tradesman, Auxiliary, Guardian—keeps to its own proper business in the commonwealth and does its own work, that is justice and what makes a just society.

I entirely agree.

The Three Parts of the Soul

[*It has been shown that justice in the state means that the three chief social functions—deliberative and governing, executive, and productive—are kept distinct and rightly performed. Since the qualities of a community are those of the component individuals, we may expect to find three corresponding elements in the individual soul. All three*

---

[6] Here the legal conception of justice is connected with its moral significance.

will be present in every soul; but the structure of society is based on the fact that they are developed to different degrees in different types of character.

The existence of three elements or "parts" of the soul is established by an analysis of the conflict of motives. A simple case is the thirsty person's appetite for drink, held in check by the rational reflection that to drink will be bad. That two distinct elements must be at work here follows from the general principle that the same thing cannot act or be affected in two opposite ways at the same time. By "thirst" is meant simply the bare craving for drink; it must not be confused with a desire for some good (e.g., health or pleasure) expected as a consequence of drinking. This simple craving says, "Drink"; Reason says, "Do not drink": the contradiction shows that two elements are at work.

A third factor is the "spirited" element, akin to our "sense of honor," manifested in indignation, which takes the side of reason against appetite, but cannot be identified with reason, since it is found in childen and animals and it may be rebuked by reason.

This analysis is not intended as a complete outline of psychology; that could be reached only by following "a longer road." It is concerned with the factors involved in moral behavior. . . .]

The Virtues in the Individual

[The virtues in the state were the qualities of the citizen, as such, considered as playing the special part in society for which the citizen was qualified by the predominance in the citizen's

nature of the philosophic, the pugnacious, or the commercial spirit. But all three elements exist in every individual, who is thus a replica of society in miniature. In the perfect person reason will rule, with the spirited element as its auxiliary, over the bodily appetites. Self-control or temperance will be a condition of internal harmony, all the parts being content with their legitimate satisfactions. Justice finally appears, no longer only as a matter of external behavior toward others, but as an internal order of the soul, from which right behavior will necessarily follow. Injustice is the opposite state of internal discord and faction. To ask whether justice or injustice pays the better is now seen to be as absurd as to ask whether health is preferable to disease.]

And so, after a stormy passage, we have reached the land. We are fairly agreed that the same three elements exist alike in the state and in the individual soul.

That is so.

Does it not follow at once that state and individual will be wise or brave by virtue of the same element in each and in the same way? Both will possess in the same manner any quality that makes for excellence.

That must be true.

Then it applies to justice: we shall conclude that a man is just in the same way that a state was just. And we have surely not forgotten that justice in the state meant that each of the three orders in it was doing its own proper work. So we may henceforth bear in mind that each one of us likewise will be a just person, fulfilling his proper function, only if the several parts of our nature fulfill theirs.

Certainly.

And it will be the business of reason to rule with wisdom and forethought on behalf of the entire soul; while the spirited element ought to act as its subordinate and ally. The two will be brought into accord, as we said earlier, by that combination of mental and bodily training which will tune up one string of the instrument and relax the other, nourishing the reasoning part on the study of noble literature and allaying the other's wildness by harmony and rhythm. When both have been thus nurtured and trained to know their own true functions, they must be set in command over the appetites, which form the greater part of each man's soul and are by nature insatiably covetous. They must keep watch lest this part, by battening on the pleasures that are called bodily, should grow so great and powerful that it will no longer keep to its own work, but will try to enslave the others and usurp a dominion to which it has no right, thus turning the whole of life upside down. At the same time, those two together will be the best of guardians for the entire soul and for the body against all enemies from without: the one will take counsel, while the other will do battle, following its ruler's commands and by its own bravery giving effect to the ruler's designs.

Yes, that is all true.

And so we call an individual brave in virtue of this spirited part of his nature, when, in spite of pain or pleasure, it holds fast to the injunctions of reason about what he ought or ought not to be afraid of.

True.

And wise in virtue of that small part which rules and issues these injunctions, possessing as it does the knowledge of what is good for each of the three elements and for all of them in common.

Certainly.

And, again, temperate by reason of the unanimity and concord of all three, when there is no internal conflict between the ruling element and its two subjects, but all are agreed that reason should be ruler.

Yes, that is an exact account of temperance, whether in the state or in the individual.

Finally, a man will be just by observing the principle we have so often stated.

Necessarily.

Now is there any indistinctness in our vision of justice, that might make it seem somehow different from what we found it to be in the state?

I don't think so.

Because, if we have any lingering doubt, we might make sure by comparing it with some commonplace notions. Suppose, for instance, that a sum of money were entrusted to our state or to an individual of corresponding character and training, would anyone imagine that such a person would be specially likely to embezzle it?

No.

And would he not be incapable of sacrilege and theft, or of treachery to friend or country; never false to an oath or any other compact; the last to be guilty of adultery or of neglecting parents or the due service of the gods?

Yes.

And the reason for all this is that each part of his nature is exercising its proper function, of ruling or of being ruled.

Yes, exactly.

Are you satisfied, then, that justice is the power which produces states or individuals of whom that is true, or must we look further?

There is no need; I am quite satisfied.

And so our dream has come true—I mean the inkling we had that, by some happy chance, we had lighted upon a rudimentary form of justice from the very moment when we sat about founding our commonwealth. Our principle that the born shoemaker or carpenter had better stick to his trade turns out to have been an adumbration of justice; and that is why it has helped us. But in reality justice, though evidently analogous to this principle, is not a matter of external behavior, but of the inward self and of attending to all that is, in the fullest sense, a man's proper concern. The just man does not allow the several elements in his soul to usurp one another's functions; he is indeed one who sets his house in order, by self-mastery and discipline coming to be at peace with himself, and bringing into tune those three parts, like the terms in the proportion of a musical scale, the highest and lowest notes and the mean between them, with all the intermediate intervals. Only when he has linked these parts together in well-tempered harmony and has made himself one man instead of many, will he be ready to go about whatever he may have to do, whether it be making money and satisfying bodily wants, or business transactions, or the affairs of state. In all these fields when he speaks of just and honorable conduct, he will mean the behavior that helps to produce and to preserve this habit of mind; and by wisdom he will mean the knowledge which presides over such conduct. Any action which tends to break down this habit will be for him unjust; and the notions governing it he will call ignorance and folly.

That is perfectly true, Socrates.

Good, said I. I believe we should not be thought altogether mistaken, if we claimed to have discovered the just man and the just state, and wherein their justice consists.

Indeed we should not.

Shall we make that claim, then?

Yes, we will.

So be it, said I. Next, I suppose, we have to consider injustice.

Evidently.

This must surely be a sort of civil strife among the three elements, whereby they usurp and encroach upon one another's functions and some one part of the soul rises up in rebellion against the whole, claiming a supremacy to which it has no right because its nature fits it only to be the servant of the ruling principle. Such turmoil and aberration we shall, I think, identify with injustice, intemperance, cowardice, ignorance, and in a word with all wickedness.

Exactly.

And now that we know the nature of justice and injustice, we can be equally clear about what is meant by acting justly and again by unjust action and wrong-doing.

How do you mean?

Plainly, they are exactly analogous to those wholesome and unwholesome activities which respectively produce a healthy or unhealthy condition in the body; in the same way just and unjust conduct produce a just or unjust character. Justice is produced in the soul, like health in the body, by establishing the elements concerned in their natural relations of control and subordination, whereas injustice is like disease and means that this natural order is inverted.

Quite so.

It appears, then, that virtue is as it were the health and comeliness and well-being of the soul, as wickedness is disease, deformity, and weakness.

True.

And also that virtue and wickedness are brought about by one's way of life, honorable or disgraceful.

That follows.

So now it only remains to consider which is the more profitable course: to do right and live honorably and be just, whether or not anyone knows what manner of man you are, or to do wrong and be unjust, provided that you can escape the chastisement which might make you a better man.

But really, Socrates, it seems to me ridiculous to ask that question now that the nature of justice and injustice has been brought to light. People think that all the luxury and wealth and power in the world cannot make life worth living when the bodily constitution is going to rack and ruin; and are we to believe that, when the very principle whereby we live is deranged and corrupted, life will be worth living so long as a man can do as he will, and wills to do anything rather than to free himself from vice and wrongdoing and to win justice and virtue?

Yes, I replied, it is a ridiculous question. . . .

The Paradox: Philosophers Must Be Kings

[*Challenged to show that the ideal state can exist, Socrates first claims that an ideal is none the worse for not being realizable on earth. The assertion that theory comes closer than practice to truth or reality is characteristically Platonic. The ideal state or person is the* true *state or person; for if 'men, who are in fact always imperfect, could reach perfection, they would only be realizing all that their nature aims at being and might conceivably be. Further, the realm of ideas is the* real *world, unchanging and eternal, which can be known by thought. The visible and tangible things commonly called real are only a realm of fleeting appearance, where the ideal is imperfectly manifested in various degrees of approximation. . . .*

An ideal has an indispensable value for practice, in that thought thereby gives to action its right aim. So, instead of proving that the ideal state or person can exist here, it is enough to discover the least change, within the bounds of possibility, that would bring the actual state nearest to the ideal. This change would be the union, in the same persons, of political power and the love of wisdom, so as to close the gulf, which had been growing wider since the age of Pericles, between the people of thought and the people of action. The corresponding change in the individual is the supremacy of the reason, the divine element in us, over the rest of our nature.]

But really, Socrates, Glaucon continued, if you are allowed to go on like this, I am afraid you will forget all about the question you thrust aside some time ago: whether a society so constituted can ever come into existence, and if so, how. No doubt, if it did exist, all manner of good things would come about. I can even add some that you have passed over. Men who acknowledged one another as fathers, sons, or brothers and always used those names among themselves would never desert one another; so they would fight with unequalled bravery. And if their womenfolk went out with them to war, either in the ranks or drawn up in the rear to intimidate the enemy and act as a reserve in case of need, I am sure all this would make them invincible. At home, too, I can see many advantages you have not mentioned. But, since I admit that our commonwealth would have all these merits and any number more, if once it came into existence, you need not describe it in further detail. All we have now to do is to convince ourselves that it can be brought into being and how.

This is a very sudden onslaught, said I; you have no mercy on my shilly-shallying. Perhaps you do not realize that, after I have barely escaped the first two waves,[7] the third, which you are now bringing down upon me, is the most formidable of all. When you have seen what it is like and heard my reply, you will be ready to excuse the very

natural fears which made me shrink from putting forward such a paradox for discussion.

The more you talk like that, he said, the less we shall be willing to let you off from telling us how this constitution can come into existence; so you had better waste no more time.

Well, said I, let me begin by reminding you that what brought us to this point was our inquiry into the nature of justice and injustice.

True; but what of that?

Merely this: suppose we do find out what justice is,[8] are we going to demand that a man who is just shall have a character which exactly corresponds in every respect to the ideal of justice? Or shall we be satisfied if he comes as near to the ideal as possible and has in him a larger measure of that quality than the rest of the world?

That will satisfy me.

If so, when we set out to discover the essential nature of justice and injustice and what a perfectly just and a perfectly unjust man would be like, supposing them to exist, our purpose was to use them as ideal patterns: we were to observe the degree of happiness or unhappiness that each exhibited, and to draw the necessary inference that our own destiny would be like that of the one we most resembled. We did not set out to show that these ideals could exist in fact.

That is true.

Then suppose a painter had drawn an ideally beautiful figure complete to

---

[7] The equality of women and the abolition of the family. [These concepts have been spoken of as waves, and the wave metaphor is now continued.]

[8] Justice, as a "civic" virtue, has been defined . . . ; but the wise man's virtue, based on knowledge, has still to be described.

the last touch, would you think any the worse of him, if he could not show that a person as beautiful as that could exist?

No, I should not.

Well, we have been constructing in discourse the pattern of an ideal state. Is our theory any the worse, if we cannot prove it possible that a state so organized should be actually founded?

Surely not.

That, then, is the truth of the matter. But if, for your satisfaction, I am to do my best to show under what conditions our ideal would have the best chance of being realized, I must ask you once more to admit that the same principle applies here. Can theory ever be fully realized in practice? Is it not in the nature of things that action should come less close to truth than thought? People may not think so; but do you agree or not?

I do.

Then you must not insist upon my showing that this construction we have traced in thought could be reproduced in fact down to the last detail. You must admit that we shall have found a way to meet your demand for realization, if we can discover how a state might be constituted in the closest accordance with our description. Will not that content you? It would be enough for me.

And for me too.

Then our next attempt, it seems, must be to point out what defect in the working of existing states prevents them from being so organized, and what is the least change that would effect a transformation into this type of government—a single change if possible, or perhaps two; at any rate let us make the changes as few and insignificant as may be.

By all means.

Well, there is one change which, as I believe we can show, would bring about this revolution—not a small change, certainly, nor an easy one, but possible.

What is it?

I have now to confront what we called the third and greatest wave. But I must state my paradox, even though the wave should break in laughter over my head and drown me in ignominy. Now mark what I am going to say.

Go on.

Unless either philosophers become kings in their countries or those who are now called kings and rulers come to be sufficiently inspired with a genuine desire for wisdom; unless, that is to say, political power and philosophy meet together, while the many natures who now go their several ways in the one or the other direction are forcibly debarred from doing so, there can be no rest from troubles, my dear Glaucon, for states, nor yet, as I believe, for all mankind; nor can this commonwealth which we have imagined ever till then see the light of day and grow to its full stature. This it was that I have so long hung back from saying; I knew what a paradox it would be, because it is hard to see that there is no other way of happiness either for the state or for the individual. . . .

Definition of the Philosopher: The Two Worlds

[*The word "philosophy" originally meant curiosity, the desire for fresh experience, such as led Solon to travel and see the world* (Herod. i. 30), *or the pursuit of intellectual culture, as in Pericles' speech: "We cultivate the mind* (φιλοσοφοῦμεν) *without loss of manliness"* (Thuc. ii. 40). *This sense has to be excluded: the Rulers are not to be dilettanti or mere amateurs of the arts. They are to desire knowledge of the whole of truth and reality, and hence of the world of essential Forms, in contrast with the world of appearances.*

The doctrine of Forms is here more explicitly invoked. Corresponding to the two worlds, the mind has two faculties: Knowledge of the real and Belief in appearances (doxa). *Faculties can be distinguished only by* (1) *the states of mind they produce, and* (2) *their fields of objects. By both tests Knowledge and Belief differ.* (1) *Knowledge is infallible* (*there is no false knowledge*); *Belief may be true or false.* (2) *Knowledge, by definition, is of unique, unchanging objects. Just in this respect the Forms resemble the laws of nature sought by modern natural science: a law is an unseen intelligible principle, a unity underlying an unlimited multiplicity of similar phenomena, and supposed to be unalterable. The Forms, however, are not laws of the sequence or coexistence of phenomena, but ideals or patterns, which have a real existence independent of our minds*[9] *and of which the many individual things called by their names in the world of appearances are*

like images or reflections. If we are disposed, with Aristotle, to deny that Platonic Forms or ideals exist apart from individual things in the visible world, we should remember that the essence of the doctrine is the conviction that the differences between good and evil, right and wrong, true and false, beautiful and ugly, are absolute, not 'relative' to the customs or tastes or desires of individual men or social groups. We can know them or (*as is commonly the case*) *not know them; they cannot change or vary from place to place or from time to time. This conviction has been, and is, held by many who cannot accept, at its face value, Plato's mode of expressing it.*

A Form, such as Beauty itself, excludes its opposite, Ugliness: it can never be or become ugly. But any particular beautiful thing may be also ugly in some aspects or situations: it may cease to be beautiful and become ugly; it may seem beautiful to me, ugly to you; and it must begin and cease to exist in time. Such things cannot be objects of knowledge. Our apprehension of these many changing things is here called doxa *and compared to dream experience, which is neither wholly real nor utterly non-existent.* Doxa *is usually rendered by "Opinion." Here 'Belief' is preferred as having a corresponding verb which, unlike* 'opine,' *is in common use. But both terms are inadequate.* Doxa *and its cognates denote our apprehension of anything that 'seems':* (1) *what seems to exist, sensible appearances, phenomena;* (2) *what seems true, opinions, beliefs, whether really true or false;* (3) *what seems right, legal and delib-*

---

[9] Hence most modern critics avoid the term 'Idea,' though this is Plato's word, because it now suggests a thought existing only 'in our minds.'

erative decisions, and the "many con-
ventional notions" of current morality
(479 D), which vary from place to place
and from time to time. The amateur
of the arts and the politician live in
the twilight realm of these fluctuating
beliefs.]

Now, I continued, if we are to elude
those assailants you have described, we
must, I think, define for them whom
we mean by these lovers of wisdom
who, we have dared to assert, ought
to be our rulers. Once we have a clear
view of their character, we shall be
able to defend our position by pointing
to some who are naturally fitted to
combine philosophic study with political leadership, while the rest of the
world should accept their guidance and
let philosophy alone.

Yes, this is the moment for a definition.

Here, then, is a line of thought which
may lead to a satisfactory explanation.
Need I remind you that a man will
deserve to be called a lover of this or
that, only if it is clear that he loves
that thing as a whole, not merely in
parts?

You must remind me, it seems; for
I do not see what you mean.

That answer would have come better
from someone less susceptible to love
than yourself, Glaucon. You ought not
to have forgotten that any boy in the
bloom of youth will arouse some sting
of passion in a man of your amorous
temperament and seem worthy of his
attentions. Is not this your way with
your favourites? You will praise a snub
nose as piquant and a hooked one as
giving a regal air, while you call a

straight nose perfectly proportioned;
the swarthy, you say, have a manly
look, the fair are children of the gods;
and what do you think is that word
'honey-pale,' if not the euphemism of
some lover who had no fault to find
with sallowness on the cheek of youth?
In a word, you will carry pretence and
extravagance to any length sooner than
reject a single one that is in the flower
of his prime.

If you insist on taking me as an
example of how lovers behave, I will
agree for the sake of argument.

Again, do you not see the same behaviour in people with a passion for
wine? They are glad of any excuse to
drink wine of any sort. And there are
the men who covet honour, who, if
they cannot lead an army, will command a company, and if they cannot
win the respect of important people,
are glad to be looked up to by no-
bodies, because they must have someone
to esteem them.

Quite true.

Do you agree, then, that when we
speak of a man as having a passion
for a certain kind of thing, we mean
that he has an appetite for everything
of that kind without discrimination?

Yes.

So the philosopher, with his passion
for wisdom, will be one who desires
all wisdom, not only some part of it.
If a student is particular about his
studies, especially while he is too young
to know which are useful and which
are not, we shall say he is no lover of
learning or of wisdom; just as, if he
were dainty about his food, we should
say he was not hungry or fond of eating, but had a poor appetite. Only the

man who has a taste for every sort of knowledge and throws himself into acquiring it with an insatiable curiosity will deserve to be called a philosopher. Am I not right?

That description, Glaucon replied, would include a large and ill-assorted company. It is curiosity, I suppose, and a delight in fresh experience that gives some people a passion for all that is to be seen and heard at theatrical and musical performances. But they are a queer set to reckon among philosophers, considering that they would never go near anything like a philosophical discussion, though they run round at all the Dionysiac festivals in town or country as if they were under contract to listen to every company of performers without fail. Will curiosity entitle all these enthusiasts, not to mention amateurs of the minor arts, to be called philosophers?

Certainly not; though they have a certain counterfeit resemblance?

And whom do you mean by the genuine philosophers?

Those whose passion it is to see the truth.

That must be so; but will you explain?

It would not be easy to explain to everyone; but you, I believe, will grant my premiss.

Which is—?

That since beauty and ugliness are opposite, they are two things; and consequently each of them is one. The same holds of justice and injustice, good and bad, and all the essential Forms: each in itself is one; but they manifest themselves in a great variety of combinations, with actions, with material things, and with one another, and so each seems to be many.[10]

That is true.

On the strength of this premiss, then, I can distinguish your amateurs of the arts and men of action from the philosophers we are concerned with, who are alone worthy of the name.

What is your distinction?

Your lovers of sights and sounds delight in beautiful tones and colours and shapes and in all the works of art into which these enter; but they have not the power of thought to behold and to take delight in the nature of Beauty itself. That power to approach Beauty and behold it as it is in itself, is rare indeed.

Quite true.

Now if a man believes in the existence of beautiful things, but not of Beauty itself, and cannot follow a guide who would lead him to a knowledge of it, is he not living in a dream? Consider: does not dreaming, whether one is awake or asleep, consist in mistaking a semblance for the reality it resembles?

I should certainly call that dreaming.

Contrast with him the man who holds that there is such a thing as Beauty itself and can discern that essence as well as the things that partake of its character, without ever confusing the one with the other—is he a dreamer or living in a waking state?

He is very much awake.

---

[10] At 523 A ff., it is explained how confused impressions of opposite qualities in sense-perception provoke reflection to isolate and define the corresponding universals or Forms.

So may we say that he knows, while the other has only a belief in appearances; and might we call their states of mind knowledge and belief?

Certainly.

But this person who, we say, has only belief without knowledge may be aggrieved and challenge our statement. Is there any means of soothing his resentment and converting him gently, without telling him plainly that he is not in his right mind?

We surely ought to try.

Come then, consider what we are to say to him. Or shall we ask him a question, assuring him that, far from grudging him any knowledge he may have, we shall be only too glad to find that there is something he knows? But, we shall say, tell us this: When a man knows, must there not be something that he knows? Will you answer for him, Glaucon?

My answer will be, that there must.

Something real or unreal?

Something real; how could a thing that is unreal ever be known?

Are we satisfied, then, on this point, from however many points of view we might examine it: that the perfectly real is perfectly knowable, and the utterly unreal is entirely unknowable?

Quite satisfied.

Good. Now if there is something so constituted that it both *is* and *is not,* will it not lie between the purely real and the utterly unreal?

It will.

Well then, as knowledge corresponds to the real, and absence of knowledge necessarily to the unreal, so, to correspond to this intermediate thing, we must look for something between ig-

norance and knowledge, if such a thing there be.

Certainly.

Is there not a thing we call belief?

Surely.

A different power from knowledge, or the same?

Different.

Knowledge and belief, then, must have different objects, answering to their respective powers.

Yes.

And knowledge has for its natural object the real—to know the truth about reality. However, before going further, I think we need a definition. Shall we distinguish under the general name of "faculties"[11] those powers which enable us—or anything else—to do what we can do? Sight and hearing, for instance, are what I call faculties, if that will help you to see the class of things I have in mind.

Yes, I understand.

Then let me tell you what view I take of them. In a faculty I cannot find any of those qualities, such as colour or shape, which, in the case of many other things, enable me to distinguish one thing from another. I can only look to its field of objects and the state of mind it produces, and regard these as sufficient to identify it and to distinguish it from faculties which have different fields and produce different states. Is that how you would go to work?

Yes.

[11] The Greek here uses only the common word for "power" (*dynamics*), but Plato is defining the special sense we express by "faculty."

Let us go back, then, to knowledge. Would you class that as a faculty?

Yes; and I should call it the most powerful of all.

And is belief also a faculty?

It can be nothing else, since it is what gives us the power of believing.

But a little while ago you agreed that knowledge and belief are not the same thing.

Yes; there could be no sense in identifying the infallible with the fallible.[12]

Good. So we are quite clear that knowledge and belief are different things?

They are.

If so, each of them, having a different power, must have a different field of objects.

Necessarily.

The field of knowledge being the real; and its power, the power of knowing the real as it is.

Yes.

Whereas belief, we say, is the power of believing. Is its object the same as that which knowledge knows? Can the same things be possible objects of knowledge and of belief?[13]

Not if we hold to the principles we agreed upon. If it is of the nature of a different faculty to have a different field, and if both knowledge and belief are faculties and, as we assert, different ones, it follows that the same things cannot be possible objects of both.

So if the real is the object of knowledge, the object of belief must be something other than the real.

Yes.

Can it be the unreal? Or is that an impossible object even for belief? Consider: if a man has a belief, there must be something before his mind; he cannot be believing nothing, can he?

No.

He is believing something, then; whereas the unreal could only be called nothing at all.

Certainly.

Now we said that ignorance must correspond to the unreal, knowledge to the real. So what he is believing cannot be real nor yet unreal.

True.

Belief, then, cannot be either ignorance or knowledge.

It appears not.

Then does it lie outside and beyond these two? Is it either more clear and certain than knowledge or less clear and certain than ignorance?

No, it is neither.

It rather seems to you to be something more obscure than knowledge, but not so dark as ignorance, and so to lie between the two extremes?

Quite so.

Well, we said earlier that if some object could be found such that it both *is* and at the same time *is not,* that object would lie between the perfectly real and the utterly unreal; and that

[12] This marks one distinction between the two states of mind. Further, even if true, belief, unlike knowledge, is (1) produced by persuasion, not by instruction; (2) cannot "give an account" of itself; and (3) can be shaken by persuasion (*Timaeus* 51 E).

[13] If "belief" bore its common meaning, we might answer, yes. But in this context it is essentially belief in *appearances.* It includes perception by the senses, and these can never perceive objects of thought, such as Beauty itself.

the corresponding faculty would be neither knowledge nor ignorance, but a faculty to be found situated between the two.

Yes.

And now what we have found between the two is the faculty we call belief.

True.

It seems, then, that what remains to be discovered is that object which can be said both to be and not to be and cannot properly be called either purely real or purely unreal. If that can be found, we may justly call it the object of belief, and so give the intermediate faculty the intermediate object, while the two extreme objects will fall to the extreme faculties.

Yes.

On these assumptions, then, I shall call for an answer from our friend who denies the existence of Beauty itself or of anything that can be called an essential Form of Beauty remaining unchangeably in the same state for ever, though he does recognize the existence of beautiful things as a plurality—that lover of things seen who will not listen to anyone who says that Beauty is one, Just is one, and so on. I shall say to him, Be so good as to tell us: of all these many beautiful things is there one which will not appear ugly? Or of these many just or righteous actions, is there one that will not appear unjust or unrighteous?

No, replied Glaucon, they must inevitably appear to be in some way both beautiful and ugly; and so with all the other terms your question refers to.

And again the many things which are doubles are just as much halves as they are doubles. And the things we call large or heavy have just as much right to be called small or light.

Yes; any such thing will always have a claim to both opposite designations.

Then, whatever any one of these many things may be said to be, can you say that it absolutely *is* that, any more than that it *is not* that?

They remind me of those punning riddles people ask at dinner parties, or the child's puzzle about what the eunuch threw at the bat and what the bat was perched on.[14] These things have the same ambiguous character, and one cannot form any stable conception of them either as being or as not being, or as both being and not being, or as neither.

Can you think of any better way of disposing of them than by placing them between reality and unreality? For I suppose they will not appear more obscure and so less real than unreality, or clearer and so more real than reality.

Quite true.

It seems, then, we have discovered that the many conventional notions of the mass of mankind about what is beautiful or honourable or just and so on are adrift in a sort of twilight between pure reality and pure unreality.

We have.

And we agreed earlier that, if any

---

[14] A man who was not a man (eunuch), seeing and not seeing (seeing imperfectly) a bird that was not a bird (bat) perched on a bough that was not a bough (a reed), pelted and did not pelt it (aimed at it and missed) with a stone that was not a stone (pumice-stone).

such object were discovered, it should be called the object of belief and not of knowledge. Fluctuating in that half-way region, it would be seized upon by the intermediate faculty.

Yes.

So when people have an eye for the multitude of beautiful things or of just actions or whatever it may be, but can neither behold Beauty or Justice itself nor follow a guide who would lead them to it, we shall say that all they have is beliefs, without any real knowledge of the objects of their belief.

That follows.

But what of those who contemplate the realities themselves as they are for ever in the same unchangeable state? Shall we not say that they have, not mere belief, but knowledge?

That too follows.

And, further, that their affection goes out to the objects of knowledge, whereas the others set their affections on the objects of belief; for it was they, you remember, who had a passion for the spectacle of beautiful colours and sounds, but would not hear of Beauty itself being a real thing.

I remember.

So we may fairly call them lovers of belief rather than of wisdom—not philosophical, in fact, but philodoxical. Will they be seriously annoyed by that description?

Not if they will listen to my advice. No one ought to take offence at the truth.

The name of philosopher, then, will be reserved for those whose affections are set, in every case, on the reality.

By all means.

The Philosopher's Fitness to Rule

[*The above definition of the philosopher might suggest an unpractical head-in-air, unfit to control life in the state. But the qualities most valuable in a ruler will follow naturally from the master passion for truth in a nature of the type described earlier, when it is perfected by time and education.*]

So at last, Glaucon, after this long and weary way, we have come to see who are the philosophers and who are not.

I doubt if the way could have been shortened.

Apparently not. I think, however, that we might have gained a still clearer view if this had been the only topic to be discussed; but there are so many others awaiting us, if we mean to discover in what ways the just life is better than the unjust.

Which are we to take up now?

Surely the one that follows next in order. Since the philosophers are those who can apprehend the eternal and unchanging, while those who cannot do so, but are lost in the mazes of multiplicity and change, are not philosophers, which of the two ought to be in control of a state?

I wonder what would be a reasonable solution.

To establish as Guardians whichever of the two appear competent to guard the laws and ways of life in society.

True.

Well, there can be no question whether a Guardian who is to keep watch over anything needs to be keen-sighted or blind. And is not blindness precisely the condition of men who are entirely cut off from knowledge of any reality, and have in their soul no clear pattern of perfect truth, which they might study in every detail and constantly refer to, as a painter looks at his model, before they proceed to embody notions of justice, honour, and goodness in earthly institutions or, in their character of Guardians, to preserve such institutions as already exist?

Certainly such a condition is very like blindness.

Shall we, then, make such as these our Guardians in preference to men who, besides their knowledge of realities, are in no way inferior to them in experience and in every excellence of character?

It would be absurd not to choose the philosophers, whose knowledge is perhaps their greatest point of superiority, provided they do not lack those other qualifications.

What we have to explain, then, is how those qualifications can be combined in the same persons with philosophy.

Certainly.

The first thing, as we said at the outset, is to get a clear view of their inborn disposition.[15] When we are satisfied on that head, I think we shall agree that such a combination of qualities is possible and that we need look no further for men fit to be in control of a commonwealth. One trait of the philosophic nature we may take as already granted: a constant passion for any knowledge that will reveal to them something of that reality which endures for ever and is not always passing into and out of existence. And, we may add, their desire is to know the whole of that reality; they will not willingly renounce any part of it as relatively small and insignificant, as we said before when we compared them to the lover and to the man who covets honour.

True.

Is there not another trait which the nature we are seeking cannot fail to possess—truthfulness, a love of truth and a hatred of falsehood that will not tolerate untruth in any form?

Yes, it is natural to expect that.

It is not merely natural, but entirely necessary that an instinctive passion for any object should extend to all that is closely akin to it; and there is nothing more closely akin to wisdom than truth. So the same nature cannot love wisdom and falsehood; the genuine lover of knowledge cannot fail, from his youth up, to strive after the whole of truth.

I perfectly agree.

Now we surely know that when a man's desires set strongly in one direction, in every other channel they flow more feebly, like a stream diverted into another bed. So when the current has set towards knowledge and all that goes with it, desire will abandon those pleasures of which the body is the instrument and be concerned only with the pleasure which the soul enjoys independently—if, that is to say, the love

---

[15] The subject of the present chapter. The next will explain why the other qualifications, of experience and character, are too often lacking.

of wisdom is more than a mere pretence. Accordingly, such a one will be temperate and no lover of money; for he will be the last person to care about the things for the sake of which money is eagerly sought and lavishly spent.

That is true.

Again, in seeking to distinguish the philosophic nature, you must not overlook the least touch of meanness. Nothing could be more contrary than pettiness to a mind constantly bent on grasping the whole of things, both divine and human.

Quite true.

And do you suppose that one who is so high-minded and whose thought can contemplate all time and all existence will count this life of man a matter of much concern?

No, he could not.

So for such a man death will have no terrors.

None.

A mean and cowardly nature, then, can have no part in the genuine pursuit of wisdom.

I think not.

And if a man is temperate and free from the love of money, meanness, pretentiousness, and cowardice, he will not be hard to deal with or dishonest. So, as another indication of the philosophic temper, you will observe whether, from youth up, he is fairminded, gentle, and sociable.

Certainly.

Also you will not fail to notice whether he is quick or slow to learn. No one can be expected to take a reasonable delight in a task in which much painful effort makes little headway. And if he cannot retain what he learns, his forgetfulness will leave no room in his head for knowledge; and so, having all his toil for nothing, he can only end by hating himself as well as his fruitless occupation. We must not, then, count a forgetful mind as competent to pursue wisdom; we must require a good memory.

By all means.

Further, there is in some natures a crudity and awkwardness that can only tend to a lack of measure and proportion; and there is a close affinity between proportion and truth. Hence, besides our other requirements, we shall look for a mind endowed with measure and grace, which will be instinctively drawn to see every reality in its true light.

Yes.

Well then, now that we have enumerated the qualities of a mind destined to take its full part in the apprehension of reality, have you any doubt about their being indispensable and all necessarily going together?

None whatever.

Then have you any fault to find with a pursuit which none can worthily follow who is not by nature quick to learn and to remember, magnanimous and gracious, the friend and kinsman of truth, justice, courage, temperance?

No; Momus[16] himself could find no flaw in it.

Well then, when time and education have brought such characters as these to maturity, would you entrust the care of your commonwealth to anyone else? . . .

---

[16] The spirit of faultfinding, one of the children of Night in Hesiod's *Theogony*.

Four Stages of Cognition: The Line

[*Socrates has contrasted the realm of sensible appearances and shifting beliefs with the realm of eternal and unchanging Forms, dominated (as we now know) by the Good. The philosopher was he whose affections were set on knowledge of that real world. The Guardians' primary education in literature and art was mainly confined to the world of appearance and belief, though it culminated in the perception of "images" of the moral ideals, the beauty of which would excite love for the individual person in whose soul they dwelt (402). The higher intellectual training now to be described is to detach the mind from appearances and individuals and to carry it across the boundary between the two worlds and all the way beyond to the vision of the Good. It thus corresponds to the* "greater mysteries" *of which Diotima speaks in the* Symposium *(210),* where *Eros,* detached from its individual object, advances to the vision of Beauty itself (the Good considered as the object of desire). The next chapter will give an allegorical picture of this progress.*

The allegory is here prefaced by a diagram. A line is divided into two parts, whose inequality symbolizes that the visible world has a lower degree of reality and truth than the intelligible. Each part is then subdivided in the same proportion as the whole line, (thus $A + B : C + D = A : B = C : D$). *The four sections correspond to four states of mind or modes of cognition, each clearer and more certain than the one below.*

The lower part $(A + B)$ *is at first called "the Visible," but elsewhere the field of* doxa *in the wide sense explained above (p. 689); and so it in-*

Objects		States of Mind
The Good		
		Intelligence (*noesis*) or
Forms	D	Knowledge (*episteme*)
Intelligible World		
Mathematical objects	C	Thinking (*dianoia*)
Visible Things	B	Belief (*pistis*)
World of Appearances		
Images	A	Imaging (*eikasia*)

cludes the *"many conventional no-*
tions of the multitude" about morality
(479 D). *It is the physical and moral*
world as apprehended by those "lovers
of appearance" who do not recognize
the absolute ideals which Plato calls
real.

(*A*) *The lowest form of cognition*
is called eikasia. *The word defies trans-*
lation, being one of those current terms
to which Plato gives a peculiar sense,
to be inferred from the context. It is
etymologically connected with eikon =
image, likeness, and with eikos =
likely, and it can mean either likeness
(*representation*) *or likening* (*compari-*
son) *or estimation of likelihood* (*con-*
jecture). *Perhaps "imagining" is the*
least unsatisfactory rendering. It seems
to be the wholly unenlightened state
of mind which takes sensible appear-
ances and current moral notions at
their face value—the condition of the
unreleased prisoners in the Cave alle-
gory below, who see only images of
images.

(*B*) *The higher section stands for*
common-sense belief (pistis) *in the re-*
ality of the visible and tangible things
commonly called substantial. In the
moral sphere it would include "correct
beliefs without knowledge" (506 c),
such as the young Guardians were
taught to hold. True beliefs are sufficient
guides for action, but are insecure un-
til based on knowledge of the reasons
for them (Meno 97).

Higher education is to effect an es-
cape from the prison of appearances
by training the intellect, first in mathe-
matics, and then in moral philosophy.
(*C*) *The lower section of the intel-*
ligible contains the subject-matter of

the mathematical sciences (511 B).[17]
Two characteristics of mathematical
procedure are mentioned: (a) *the use*
of visible diagrams and models as im-
perfect illustrations of the objects and
truths of pure thought. Here is a sort
of bridge carrying the mind across
from the visible thing to the intelli-
gible reality, which it must learn to
distinguish. (b) *Each branch of mathe-*
matics starts from unquestioned assump-
tions (*postulates, axioms, definitions*)
and reasons from them deductively.
The premises may be true and the
conclusions may follow, but the whole
structure hangs in the air until the
assumptions themselves shall have been
shown to depend on an uncondi-
tional principle. (*This may be conjec-*
tured to be Unity itself, an aspect of
the Good.) *Meanwhile the state of*
mind is dianoia, *the ordinary word for*
"thought" or "thinking," here imply-
ing a degree of understanding which
falls short of perfect knowledge (533 D).
Dianoia *suggests discursive thinking or*
reasoning from premise to conclusion,
whereas noesis *is constantly compared*
to the immediate act of vision and sug-
gests rather the direct intuition or ap-
prehension of its object.

(*D*) *The higher method is called*
Dialectic, a word which since Hegel
has acquired misleading associations.
In the Republic *it simply means the*
technique of philosophic conversation
(*dialogue*) *carried on by question and*
answer and seeking to render, or to
receive from a respondent, an "account"
(logos) *of some Form, usually a moral*

[17] The interpretation of the higher part
of the Line is the subject of a long controversy which cannot be pursued here.

Form such as Justice in this dialogue. At this stage visible illustrations are no longer available, and the movement at first is not downward, deducing conclusions from premises, but upward, examining the premises themselves and seeking the ultimate principle on which they all depend. It is suggested that, if the mind could ever rise to grasp the supreme Form, it might then descend by a deduction confirming the whole structure of moral and mathematical knowledge. The state of mind is called intelligence or rational intuition (noesis) *and knowledge* (episteme, 533 E) *in the full sense. . . .]*

CONCEIVE, then, that there are these two powers I speak of, the Good reigning over the domain of all that is intelligible, the Sun over the visible world—or the heaven as I might call it; only you would think I was showing off my skill in etymology.[18] At any rate you have these two orders of things clearly before your mind: the visible and the intelligible?

I have.

Now take a line divided into two unequal parts, one to represent the visible order, the other the intelligible and divide each part again in the same proportion, symbolizing degrees of comparative clearness or obscurity. Then (A) one of the two sections in the visible world will stand for images. By images I mean first shadows, and then reflections in water or in close-grained, polished surfaces, and every-

thing of that kind, if you understand.

Yes, I understand.

Let the second section (B) stand for the actual things of which the first are likenesses, the living creatures about us and all the works of nature or of human hands.

So be it.

Will you also take the proportion in which the visible world has been divided as corresponding to degrees of reality and truth, so that the likeness shall stand to the original in the same ratio as the sphere of appearances and belief to the sphere of knowledge?

Certainly.

Now consider how we are to divide the part which stands for the intelligible world. There are two sections. In the first (C) the mind uses as images those actual things which themselves had images in the visible world; and it is compelled to pursue its inquiry by starting from assumptions and travelling, not up to a principle, but down to a conclusion. In the second (D) the mind moves in the other direction, from an assumption up towards a principle which is not hypothetical; and it makes no use of the images employed in the other section, but only of Forms, and conducts its inquiry solely by their means.

I don't quite understand what you mean.

Then we will try again; what I have just said will help you to understand. (C) You know, of course, how students of subjects like geometry and arithmetic begin by postulating odd and even numbers, or the various figures and the three kinds of angle, and other such data in each subject. These

---

[18] Some connected the word for heaven (οὐρανός) with ὁρᾶν 'to see' (*Cratylus*, 396 B). It is sometimes used for the whole of the visible universe.

data they take as known; and, having adopted them as assumptions, they do not feel called upon to give any account of them to themselves or to anyone else, but treat them as self-evident. Then, starting from these assumptions, they go on until they arrive, by a series of consistent steps, at all the conclusions they set out to investigate.

Yes, I know that.

You also know how they make use of visible figures and discourse about them, though what they really have in mind is the originals of which these figures are images: they are not reasoning, for instance, about this particular square and diagonal which they have drawn, but about *the* Square and *the* Diagonal; and so in all cases. The diagrams they draw and the models they make are actual things, which may have their shadows or images in water; but now they serve in their turn as images, while the student is seeking to behold those realities which only thought can apprehend.[19]

True.

This, then, is the class of things that I spoke of as intelligible, but with two qualifications: first, that the mind, in studying them, is compelled to employ assumptions, and, because it cannot rise above these, does not travel upwards to a first principle; and second, that it uses as images those actual things which have images of their own

in the section below them and which, in comparison with those shadows and reflections, are reputed to be more palpable and valued accordingly.

I understand: you mean the subject-matter of geometry and of the kindred arts.

(D) Then by the second section of the intelligible world you may understand me to mean all that unaided reasoning apprehends by the power of dialectic, when it treats its assumptions, not as first principles, but as *hypotheses* in the literal sense, things 'laid down' like a flight of steps up which it may mount all the way to something that is not hypothetical, the first principle of all; and having grasped this, may turn back and, holding on to the consequences which depend upon it, descend at last to a conclusion, never making use of any sensible object, but only of Forms, moving through Forms from one to another, and ending with Forms.

I understand, he said, though not perfectly; for the procedure you describe sounds like an enormous undertaking. But I see that you mean to distinguish the field of intelligible reality studied by dialectic as having a greater certainty and truth than the subject-matter of the 'arts,' as they are called, which treat their assumptions as first principles. The students of these arts are, it is true, compelled to exercise thought in contemplating objects which the senses cannot perceive; but because they start from assumptions without going back to a first principle, you do not regard them as gaining true understanding about those objects, although the objects themselves, when connected

[19] Conversely, the fact that the mathematician can use visible objects as illustrations indicates that the realities and truths of mathematics are embodied, though imperfectly, in the world of visible and tangible things; whereas the counterparts of the moral Forms can only be beheld by thought.

with a first principle, are intelligible'. And I think you would call the state of mind of the students of geometry and other such arts, not intelligence, but thinking, as being something between intelligence and mere acceptance of appearances.

You have understood me quite well enough, I replied. And now you may take, as corresponding to the four sections, these four states of mind: *intelligence* for the highest, *thinking* for the second, *belief* for the third, and for the last *imagining*.[20] These you may arrange as the terms in a proportion, assigning to each a degree of clearness and certainty corresponding to the measure in which their objects possess truth and reality.

I understand and agree with you. I will arrange them as you say.

The Allegory of the Cave

[*The progress of the mind from the lowest state of unenlightenment to knowledge of the Good is now illustrated by the famous parable comparing the world of appearance to an underground Cave. In Empedocles' religious poem the powers which conduct the soul to its incarnation say, "We have come under this cavern's roof." The image was probably taken from mysteries held in caves or dark chambers representing the underworld, through which the candidates for initiation were led to the revelation of sacred objects in a blaze of light. The idea that the body is a prison-house, to which the*

soul is condemned for past misdeeds, is attributed by Plato to the Orphics.

One moral of the allegory is drawn from the distress caused by a too sudden passage from darkness to light. The earlier warning against plunging untrained minds into the discussion of moral problems (498 A), as the Sophists and Socrates himself had done, is reinforced by the picture of the dazed prisoner dragged out into the sunlight. Plato's ten years' course of pure mathematics is to habituate the intellect to abstract reasoning before moral ideas are called in question (537 E, ff.).]

Next, said I, here is a parable to illustrate the degrees in which our nature may be enlightened or unenlightened. Imagine the condition of men living in a sort of cavernous chamber underground, with an entrance open to the light and a long passage all down the cave.[21] Here they have been from childhood, chained by the leg and also by the neck, so that they cannot move and can see only what is in front of them, because the chains will not let them turn their heads. At some distance higher up is the light of a fire burning behind them; and between the prisoners and the fire is a track[22] with a parapet built along it, like the screen at a puppet-show, which hides the performers while they show their puppets over the top.

---

[20] Plato never uses hard and fast technical terms. The four here proposed are not defined or strictly employed in the sequel.

[21] The *length* of the "way in" (*eisodos*) to the chamber where the prisoners sit is an essential feature, explaining why no daylight reaches them.

[22] The track crosses the passage into the cave at right angles, and is *above* the parapet built along it.

I see, said he.

Now behind this parapet imagine persons carrying along various artificial objects, including figures of men and animals in wood or stone or other materials, which project above the parapet. Naturally, some of these persons will be talking, others silent.[23]

It is a strange picture, he said, and a strange sort of prisoners.

Like ourselves, I replied; for in the first place prisoners so confined would have seen nothing of themselves or of one another, except the shadows thrown by the fire-light on the wall of the Cave facing them, would they?

Not if all their lives they had been prevented from moving their heads.

And they would have seen as little of the objects carried past.

Of course.

Now, if they could talk to one another, would they not suppose that their words referred only to those passing shadows which they saw?[24]

Necessarily.

And suppose their prison had an echo from the wall facing them? When one of the people crossing behind them spoke, they could only suppose that the sound came from the shadow passing before their eyes.

No doubt.

In every way, then, such prisoners would recognize as reality nothing but the shadows of those artificial objects.[25]

Inevitably.

Now consider what would happen if their release from the chains and the healing of their unwisdom should come about in this way. Suppose one of them set free and forced suddenly to stand up, turn his head, and walk with eyes lifted to the light; all these movements would be painful, and he would be too dazzled to make out the objects whose shadows he had been used to see. What do you think he would say, if someone told him that what he had formerly seen was meaningless illusion, but now, being somewhat nearer to reality and turned towards more real objects, he was getting a truer view? Suppose further that he were shown the various objects being carried by and were made to say, in reply to questions, what each of them was. Would he not be perplexed and believe the objects now shown him to be not so real as what he formerly saw?[26]

Yes, not nearly so real.

And if he were forced to look at the fire-light itself, would not his eyes ache, so that he would try to escape and turn

[23] A modern Plato would compare his Cave to an underground cinema, where the audience watch the play of shadows thrown by the film passing before a light at their backs. The film itself is only an image of "real" things and events in the world outside the cinema. For the film Plato has to substitute the clumsier apparatus of a procession of artificial objects carried on their heads by persons who are merely part of the machinery, providing for the movement of the objects and the sounds whose echo the prisoners hear. The parapet prevents these person's shadows from being cast on the wall of the Cave.

[24] Adam's text and interpretation. The prisoners, having seen nothing but shadows, cannot think their words refer to the objects carried past behind their backs. For them shadows (images) are the only realities.

[25] The state of mind called *eikasia* in the previous chapter.

[26] The first effect of Socratic questioning is perplexity.

back to the things which he could see distinctly, convinced that they really were clearer than these other objects now being shown to him?

Yes.

And suppose someone were to drag him away forcibly up the steep and rugged ascent and not let him go until he had hauled him out into the sunlight, would he not suffer pain and vexation at such treatment, and, when he had come out into the light, find his eyes so full of its radiance that he could not see a single one of the things that he was now told were real?

Certainly he would not see them all at once.

He would need, then, to grow accustomed before he could see things in that upper world.[27] At first it would be easiest to make out shadows, and then the images of men and things reflected in water, and later on the things themselves. After that, it would be easier to watch the heavenly bodies and the sky itself by night, looking at the light of the moon and stars rather than the Sun and the Sun's light in the day-time.

Yes, surely.

Last of all, he would be able to look at the Sun and contemplate its nature, not as it appears when reflected in water or any alien medium, but as it is in itself in its own domain.

No doubt.

And now he would begin to draw the conclusion that it is the Sun that produces the seasons and the course of the year and controls everything in the visible world, and moreover is in a way the cause of all that he and his companions used to see.

Clearly he would come at last to that conclusion.

Then if he called to mind his fellow prisoners and what passed for wisdom in his former dwelling-place, he would surely think himself happy in the change and be sorry for them. They may have had a practice of honouring and commending one another, with prizes for the man who had the keenest eye for the passing shadows and the best memory for the order in which they followed or accompanied one another, so that he could make a good guess as to which was going to come next.[28] Would our released prisoner be likely to covet those prizes or to envy the men exalted to honour and power in the Cave? Would he not feel like Homer's Achilles, that he would far sooner "be on earth as a hired servant in the house of a landless man"[29] or endure anything rather than go back to his old beliefs and live in the old way?

Yes, he would prefer any fate to such a life.

Now imagine what would happen if he went down again to take his former seat in the Cave. Coming suddenly out of the sunlight, his eyes would be filled with darkness. He might be required once more to deliver his opinion on

[27] Here is the moral—the need of habituation by mathematical study before discussing moral ideas and ascending through them to the Form of the Good.

[28] The empirical politician, with no philosophic insight, but only a "knack of remembering what usually happens" (*Gorg.* 501 A). He has *eikasia* = conjecture as to what is likely (*eikos*).

[29] This verse (already quoted at 386 c), being spoken by the ghost of Achilles, suggests that the Cave is comparable with Hades.

those shadows, in competition with the prisoners who had never been released, while his eyesight was still dim and unsteady; and it might take some time to become used to the darkness. They would laugh at him and say that he had gone up only to come back with his sight ruined; it was worth no one's while even to attempt the ascent. If they could lay hands on the man who was trying to set them free and lead them up, they would kill him.[30]

Yes, they would.

Every feature in this parable, my dear Glaucon, is meant to fit our earlier analysis. The prison dwelling corresponds to the region revealed to us through the sense of sight, and the firelight within it to the power of the Sun. The ascent to see the things in the upper world you may take as standing for the upward journey of the soul into the region of the intelligible; then you will be in possession of what I surmise, since that is what you wish to be told. Heaven knows whether it is true; but this, at any rate, is how it appears to me. In the world of knowledge, the last thing to be perceived and only with great difficulty is the essential Form of Goodness. Once it is perceived, the conclusion must follow that, for all things, this is the cause of whatever is right and good; in the visible world it gives birth to light and to the lord of light, while it is itself sovereign in the intelligible world and the parent of intelligence and truth. Without having had a vision of this Form no one can act with wisdom, either in his own life or in matters of state.

[30] An allusion to the fate of Socrates.

So far as I can understand, I share your belief.

Then you may also agree that it is no wonder if those who have reached this height are reluctant to manage the affairs of men. Their souls long to spend all their time in that upper world—naturally enough, if here once more our parable holds true. Nor, again, is it at all strange that one who comes from the contemplation of divine things to the miseries of human life should appear awkward and ridiculous when, with eyes still dazed and not yet accustomed to the darkness, he is compelled, in a law-court or elsewhere, to dispute about the shadows of justice or the images that cast those shadows, and to wrangle over the notions of what is right in the minds of men who have never beheld Justice itself.[31]

It is not at all strange.

No; a sensible man will remember that the eyes may be confused in two ways—by a change from light to darkness or from darkness to light; and he will recognize that the same thing happens to the soul. When he sees it troubled and unable to discern anything clearly, instead of laughing thoughtlessly, he will ask whether, coming from a brighter existence, its unaccustomed vision is obscured by the darkness, in which case he will think its condition enviable and its life a happy one; or whether, emerging from the depths of ignorance, it is dazzled by excess of light. If so, he will rather feel

[31] In the *Gorgias* 486 A, Callicles, forecasting the trial of Socrates, taunts him with the philosopher's inability to defend himself in a court.

sorry for it; or, if he were inclined to laugh, that would be less ridiculous than to laugh at the soul which has come down from the light.

That is a fair statement.

If this is true, then, we must conclude that education is not what it is said to be by some, who profess to put knowledge into a soul which does not possess it, as if they could put sight into blind eyes. On the contrary, our own account signifies that the soul of every man does possess the power of learning the truth and the organ to see it with; and that, just as one might have to turn the whole body round in order that the eye should see light instead of darkness, so the entire soul must be turned away from this changing world, until its eye can bear to contemplate reality and that supreme splendour which we have called the Good. Hence there may well be an art whose aim would be to effect this very thing, the conversion of the soul, in the readiest way; not to put the power of sight into the soul's eye, which already has it, but to ensure that, instead of looking in the wrong direction, it is turned the way it ought to be.

Yes, it may well be so.

It looks, then, as though wisdom were different from those ordinary virtues, as they are called, which are not far removed from bodily qualities, in that they can be produced by habituation and exercise in a soul which has not possessed them from the first. Wisdom, it seems, is certainly the virtue of some diviner faculty, which never loses its power, though its use for good or harm depends on the direction towards which it is turned. You must have noticed in dishonest men with a reputation for

sagacity the shrewd glance of a narrow intelligence piercing the objects to which it is directed. There is nothing wrong with their power of vision, but it has been forced into the service of evil, so that the keener its sight, the more harm it works.

Quite true.

And yet if the growth of a nature like this had been pruned from earliest childhood, cleared of those clinging overgrowths which come of gluttony and all luxurious pleasure and, like leaden weights charged with affinity to this mortal world, hang upon the soul, bending its vision downwards; if, freed from these, the soul were turned round towards true reality, then this same power in these very men would see the truth as keenly as the objects it is turned to now.

Yes, very likely.

Is it not also likely, or indeed certain after what has been said, that a state can never be properly governed either by the uneducated who know nothing of truth or by men who are allowed to spend all their days in the pursuit of culture? The ignorant have no single mark before their eyes at which they must aim in all the conduct of their own lives and of affairs of state; and the other will not engage in action if they can help it, dreaming that, while still alive, they have been translated to the Islands of the Blest.

Quite true.

It is for us, then, as founders of a commonwealth, to bring compulsion to bear on the noblest natures. They must be made to climb the ascent to the vision of Goodness, which we called the highest object of knowledge; and, when they have looked upon it long enough, they must not be allowed, as they now are, to remain on the heights, refusing to come down again to the prisoners or to take any part in their labours and rewards, however much or little these may be worth.

Shall we not be doing them an injustice, if we force on them a worse life than they might have?

You have forgotten again, my friend, that the law is not concerned to make any one class specially happy, but to ensure the welfare of the commonwealth as a whole. By persuasion or constraint it will unite the citizens in harmony, making them share whatever benefits each class can contribute to the common good; and its purpose in forming men of that spirit was not that each should be left to go his own way, but that they should be instrumental in binding the community into one.

You will see, then, Glaucon, that there will be no real injustice in compelling our philosophers to watch over and care for the other citizens. We can fairly tell them that their compeers in other states may quite reasonably refuse to collaborate: there they have sprung up, like a self-sown plant, in despite of their country's institutions; no one has fostered their growth, and they cannot be expected to show gratitude for a care they have never received. "But," we shall say, "it is not so with you. We have brought you into existence for your country's sake as well as for your own, to be like leaders and king-bees in a hive; you have been better and more thoroughly educated than those others and hence you are more capable of playing your part both as men of

thought and as men of action. You must go down, then, each in his turn, to live with the rest and let your eyes grown accustomed to the darkness. You will then see a thousand times better than those who live there always; you will recognize every image for what it is and know what it represents, because you have seen justice, beauty, and goodness in their reality; and so you and we shall find life in our commonwealth no mere dream, as it is in most existing states, where men live fighting one another about shadows and quarrelling for power, as if that were a great prize; whereas in truth government can be at its best and free from dissension only where the destined rulers are least desirous of holding office."

Quite true.

Then will our pupils refuse to listen and to take their turns at sharing in the work of the community, though they may live together for most of their time in a purer air?

No; it is a fair demand, and they are fair-minded men. No doubt, unlike any ruler of the present day, they will think of holding power as an unavoidable necessity.

Yes, my friend; for the truth is that you can have a well-governed society only if you can discover for your future rulers a better way of life than being in office; then only will power be in the hands of men who are rich, not in gold, but in the wealth that brings happiness, a good and wise life. All goes wrong when, starved for lack of anything good in their lives, men turn to public affairs hoping to snatch from thence the happiness they hunger for. They set about fighting for power, and this internecine conflict ruins them and their country. The life of true philosophy is the only one that looks down upon offices of state; and access to power must be confined to men who are not in love with it; otherwise rivals will start fighting. So whom else can you compel to undertake the guardianship of the commonwealth, if not those who, besides understanding best the principles of government, enjoy a nobler life than the politician's and look for rewards of a different kind?

There is indeed no other choice.

The Means of Achieving the Ideal

Since the foregoing excerpts from the *Republic* state Plato's ideal as well as his philosophical premises, I need add, to complete the exposition, only a few remarks about the way in which he believed the ideal could be implemented.

If the Guardians are to be wise, they must be very carefully bred, selected, reared, and educated. The biological fiitness of the ruling class should be guaranteed by a comprehensive program of eugenics; the most select parents should be induced to have the greatest number of children. Even more important is education, which Plato regards as the main foundation of the state.

He conceives education as a journey of the mind from the concrete practicalities of sensory experience to the eternal and abstract realities of the intellect. It begins with the arts and gymnastics and mounts upward through mathematics, atsronomy, and harmonics (the mathematical theory of musical form), to philosophy. The preliminary education continues until about the age of eighteen; then follows two years of military training, for males and females alike. The Guardians are then provisionally selected by "ordeals of toil and pain," and only those who manifest the proper character and intelligence will receive the highest training. The program of mathematical and scientific training will occupy the prospective Guardians from the age of twenty to thirty, and they will then have intensive training in philosophy ("dialectics") for five additional years, or until they have "grasped by pure intelligence the very nature of Goodness itself." The students who have distinguished themselves throughout this long and arduous training will serve a political apprenticeship for about fifteen years, discharging the subordinate functions "suitable to the young." Finally, those who have fully proved their mettle, both men and women, will be selected at the age of fifty to fulfill the high function of philosopher-kings. Others, fit to be soldiers but incapable of the highest intellectual flights, remain Auxiliaries; and the great mass of the people, as members of the producing class, receive the lesser education appropriate to their station.

Every precaution should be taken to ward off temptations and keep the Guardians and Auxiliaries faithful to the state. The chief temptations arise from private interests. The competitive struggle for property, Plato believes, is incompatible with full devotion to the social good. Hence he proposes that the Guardians and Auxiliaries should have no private possessions or acquisitive occupations and that they should receive their maintenance from the state. This proposal is not the same as modern communism, since it applies only to the Auxiliaries and Guardians and not to the producers who constitute the bulk of the population.

Plato also believes that normal marriage and family life are incompatible with a wholehearted devotion to the state, since there is always a temptation to prefer family interests to community welfare. Hence he proposes to abolish private homes and monogamous marriage among the Guardians and Auxiliaries. They should live and share their meals together, realizing the principle that "friends have all things in common." Sexual intercourse should be strictly controlled in the interests of the eugenics program.

Such is the pattern of the aristocratic state. But even the "best" of states may decay, and Plato imaginatively sketches, in a section here omitted, the decline of the state through successive stages of timocracy—the rule of the military class; oligarchy—the rule of the wealthy; democracy—the rule of the many; and tyranny—the rule of the irresponsible dictator. Finally, he discusses art and rewards and punishments after death, but these topics do not now concern us.

Some Main Issues

No one will agree with all the details of Plato's argument, but even when we least agree we can find his ideas challenging. Among the principal issues that he presents are the following:

1. FORCE VERSUS MORALITY. In Books I and II of the *Republic,* Plato raises one of the basic issues in political philosophy—the question as to whether force or morality is the foundation of the state. Against Thrasymachus, Socrates (as a character in the dialogue) argues that the authority of the ruler is morally based on right rather than might. In reply to Glaucon and Adeimantus, he maintains that social obligation is based on duty rather than selfish expdiency. The policies of the state, he insists, should conform to the pattern of the Good, which wise men, long disciplined by education, can alone discern. He distinguishes between *opinion* and *knowledge* about goodness, and maintains that genuine knowledge requires an intellectual grasp of *"forms."* The form is the universal essence that is somehow exemplified in particular instances. All beautiful things, for example, exemplify the form of beauty, and all just acts and institutions exemplify the form of justice.

According to Plato, these forms or universals are real, but they exist in their full and essential reality apart from particular things. The perfection, unity, and eternality of the forms separates them from the imperfection, multiplicity, and impermanence of particular things. The sensible nature of the thing declares itself as relative and contingent and points to the imperishable essence which is connected with it and yet independent of it—a form free from limitation, change, defilement. The nature of this super-reality is hard to define—Plato appears to have struggled with the problem throughout his whole philosophical career. In the *Phaedo,* the particulars are said to "participate" in the forms, or the forms are said to be "present" in the particulars. Elsewhere in Plato's dialogues the individual things are said to "imitate" the forms, or to be related as an imperfect "copy" to a pattern or archetype. But all such language is metaphorical, and the essential truth is that the universal somehow transcends the particulars. In the *Republic,* this is taken to mean that the pattern of the ideal state is eternal and hence exempt from the relativities of power politics and shifting expediency.

Whether Plato's theory—or any doctrine of eternal and objective universals—is sound has been one of the principal questions of philosophy from his day until the present. It is possible to agree with him that universals are real, and yet to differ from him in holding that they are immanent in particulars rather than separate and transcendent. "Justice" really exists, but in particular instances—not in "a heaven above the heavens" or as a separate, eternal essence. The "form," in this sense, is simply the characteristic common to all members of the class of things (in this case, the class of just things). The human mind has the power to notice resemblances and to abstract (that is, mentally to extricate) the common characteristics. Thus, universals can be said to consist, on the one hand, of common properties in things, and on the other hand, of concepts which represent these properties. This theory of real but immanent universals is the doctrine of Aristotle, and it serves as well as Plato's theory as an alternative to moral relativism. What is required is that moral concepts must conform to real objective distinctions, and on this point Plato and Aristotle agree.

2. The "Closed" versus the "Open" Society. With his vision fixed upon eternal forms, Plato wishes, after a fundamental revolution in human affairs, to arrest history and preserve the ideal state in its static perfection. As means to this end, he proposes rigorous censorship of the arts and religion, the use of myths and "noble lies" to reconcile the lower classes to their subordinate status, and the regulation of many details of social life, including marriage and the ownership of property, among the Guardians and Auxiliaries. In effect, he insists upon a tight, "closed" unity of the body politic. Whether he is abandoning the Socratic ideal of inquiry portrayed in the *Apology,* and if so whether he is justified in doing so, are questions worth considering.

His emphasis on social unity is related to his organic theory of the state. He maintains that the state is the human soul writ large, just as the soul is the state writ small. There is some question as to how literally we should understand this doctrine, but it seems to imply that the state, like the individual personality, is an organism—that is, a living being with a life and worth of its own. Individuals appear mainly to derive their character and value from their relation to this organic whole. This sort of ethical organicism receives its most express and elaborate expression in the social philosophy of Hegel, but it is foreshadowed in the *Republic*.

The contrasting ideal of an "open" society—in which the freedom and intrinsic value of the individual are primarily emphasized—was eloquently formulated by John Stuart Mill in *On Liberty* (see Chap. 25). Both Mill and Plato, in a sense, maintain an ethics of self-realization, but Plato contends that the private interest of the individual is at one with the interest of the state, whereas Mill is distrustful of the state and believes that self-realization lies in the cultivation of individuality.

We can roughly divide political philosophers into two schools of thought corresponding to their positions on this issue. In one camp are the organic theorists —Plato, Rousseau, Hegel, and Marx—who stress the importance of the general will and the value and significance of collective processes. In the other group are the individualistic theorists—Hume, Bentham, Mill, and Jefferson—who disbelieve in the organic nature of society and regard social institutions as means to the happiness of individuals. The dispute between these two schools of thought is perhaps the most important conflict in the whole of political philosophy.

3. ARISTOCRACY VERSUS DEMOCRACY. The basic tenet of Plato's social philosophy, as we have seen, is that philosopher-kings should rule. This conviction is consistent with his general attitude toward life: he habitually prefers the choice goods to the common goods. Hence he ranks democracy, whose slogan is "equality," as fourth in his classification of five types of government, superior only to tyranny and inferior to aristocracy, timocracy, and oligarchy. The typical democrat seems to him an ill-educated and superficial person who wishes to drag all excellent things down to the mediocre level of the average.

The democrat might reply that philosopher-kings are difficult to find or to produce and that a government *of* the few is almost certain to be a government *for* the few. No one can be trusted with irresponsible power, not even the so-called wise. It is the wearer of the shoe who knows where it pinches, and consequently one cannot allow the few aristocrats to choose one's own shoes. If the state exacts duties of its citizens, moreover, it should grant them rights—for responsibility implies freedom. It is only by living as free people—by participating in government and exercising self-rule—that we cease to be mere imitators and become fully developed human beings. With such arguments, the democrat might answer Plato.

If we democrats and liberals are sensible, however, we will not indiscriminately reject the whole of Plato's social philosophy. We need experts in our government and wisdom in our lives. We should adapt to our own ends Plato's great ideal of a state based upon education, and we should seek to reconcile the aristocratic ideal of excellence with the democratic ideal of sharing. Our goal should be a culture both high in attainment and broad in terms of democratic participation. So it seems to me—but the questions remain whether this synthesis is attainable and whether it is worth attaining.

15

History
and
Freedom

GEORG WILHELM FRIEDRICH HEGEL (1770–1831)

Hegel was born at Stuttgart, where his father held a minor governmental position. Trained in theology at a seminary in Tübingen, he was a rather indifferent student and was often reprimanded for cutting classes. He joined his student-friend Friedrich von Schelling in founding a radical club devoted to discussing the ideas of the French Revolution. His chief interest, however, lay in classical literature, especially in the tragedies of Sophocles. After receiving his doctoral degree, he spent the next six years as a private tutor, first at Berne, and then at Frankfurt. In 1801 he was appointed an instructor at the University of Jena, where he collaborated with Schelling in editing a philosophical journal. The years 1801–1806 were the period of his philosophical awakening, culminating in the publication of his *Phenomenology of Mind*. Threatened by the victorious advance of Napoleon's army, he rushed the manuscript to the printer just before the battle of Jena in 1806.

Forced to flee, he settled down for the next eight years as headmaster of a boy's school in Nuremberg. There he married and his two sons were born. In 1816 he accepted a professorship at Heidelberg, and two years later he moved on to the University of Berlin where he became the acknowledged leader of philosophic thought in Germany. Nevertheless, his intellectual independence aroused the hostility of the conservative elements at the Prussian court, and in the last year of his life he ran into trouble with the Prussian censorship. In the autumn of 1831 he was suddenly taken ill with cholera, and a day later— November 14, 1831—he was dead.

On the Philosophy of History

1. [Dialectic and Change]

It is of the highest importance to ascertain and understand rightly the nature of Dialectic. Wherever there is movement, wherever there is life, wherever anything is carried into effect in the actual world, there Dialectic is at work. It is also the soul of all knowledge which is truly scientific. In the popular way of looking at things, the refusal to be bound by the abstract deliverances of understanding appears as fairness, which, according to the proverb Live and let live, demands that each should have its turn; we admit the one, but we admit the other also. But when we look more closely, we find that the limitations of the finite do not merely come from without; that its own nature is the cause of its abrogation, and

Section 1 is from *The Logic of Hegel*, translated from *The Encyclopedia of the Philosophical Sciences* by William Wallace (Oxford: Clarendon Press, 1892). The other sections are from the Introduction to *The Philosophy of History*, translated by J. Sibree (London, 1857).

that by its own act it passes into its counterpart. We say, for instance, that man is mortal, and seem to think that the ground of his death is in external circumstances only; so that if this way of looking were correct, man would have two special properties, vitality and —also—mortality. But the true view of the matter is that life, as life, involves the germ of death, and that the finite, being radically self-contradictory, involves its own self-suppression.

Nor, again, is Dialectic to be confounded with mere Sophistry. The essence of Sophistry lies in giving authority to a partial and abtract principle, in its isolation, as may suit the interest and particular situation of the individual at the time. For example, a regard to my existence, and my having the means of existence, is a vital motive of conduct, but if I exclusively emphasise this consideration or motive of my welfare, and draw the conclusion that I may steal or betray my country, we have a case of Sophistry. Similarly, it is a vital principle in conduct that I should be subjectively free, that is to say, that I should have an insight into what I am doing, and a conviction that it is right. But if my pleading insists on this principle alone I fall into Sophistry, such as would overthrow all the principles of morality. From this sort of party-pleading Dialectic is wholly different; its purpose is to study things in their own being and movement and thus to demonstrate the finitude of the partial categories of understanding.

Dialectic, it may be added, is no novelty in philosophy. Among the ancients Plato is termed the inventor of Dialectic; and his right to the name rests on the fact, that the Platonic philosophy first gave the free scientific, and thus at the same time the objective, form to Dialectic. Socrates, as we should expect from the general character of his philosophising, has the dialectic element in a predominantly subjective shape, that of Irony. He used to turn his Dialectic, first against ordinary consciousness, and then especially against the Sophists. In his conversations he used to simulate the wish for some clearer knowledge about the subject under discussion, and after putting all sorts of questions with that intent, he drew on those with whom he conversed to the opposite of what their first impressions had pronounced correct. If, for instance, the Sophists claimed to be teachers, Socrates by a series of questions forced the Sophist Protagoras to confess that all learning is only recollection. In his more strictly scientific dialogues Plato employs the dialectical method to show the finitude of all hard and fast terms of understanding. Thus in the Parmenides he deduces the many from the one, and shows nevertheless that the many

cannot but define itself as the one. In this grand style did Plato treat Dialectic. In modern times it was, more than any other, Kant who resuscitated the name of Dialectic, and restored it to its post of honour. He did it . . . by working out the Antinomies of the reason. The problem of these Antinomies is no mere subjective piece of work oscillating between one set of grounds and another; it really serves to show that every abstract proposition of understanding, taken precisely as it is given, naturally veers round into its opposite.

However reluctant Understanding may be to admit the action of Dialectic, we must not suppose that the recognition of its existence is peculiarly confined to the philosopher. It would be truer to say that Dialectic gives expression to a law which is felt in all other grades of consciousness, and in general experience. Everything that surrounds us may be viewed as an instance of Dialectic. We are aware that everything finite, instead of being stable and ultimate, is rather changeable and transient; and this is exactly what we mean by that Dialectic of the finite, by which the finite, as implicitly other than what it is, is forced beyond its own immediate or natural being to turn suddenly into its opposite. We have before this identified Understanding with what is implied in the popular idea of the goodness of God; we may now remark of Dialectic, in the same objective signification, that its principle answers to the idea of his power. All things, we say,— that is, the finite world as such,—are doomed; and in saying so, we have a vision of Dialectic as the universal and irresistible power before which nothing can stay, however secure and stable it may deem itself. The category of power does not, it is true, exhaust the depth of the divine nature or the notion of God; but it certainly forms a vital element in all religious consciousness.

Apart from this general objectivity of Dialectic, we find traces of its presence in each of the particular provinces and phases of the natural and the spiritual world. Take as an illustration the motion of the heavenly bodies. At this moment the planet stands in this spot, but implicitly it is the possibility of being in another spot; and that possibility of being otherwise the planet brings into existence by moving. Similarly the 'physical' elements prove to be Dialectical. The process of meteorological action is the exhibition of their Dialectic. It is the same dynamic that lies at the root of every other natural process, and, as it were, forces nature out of itself. To illustrate the presence of Dialectic in the spiritual world, especially in the provinces of law and morality, we have only to recollect how general experience shows us the extreme of one state or action suddenly shifting into its opposite: a Dialectic which is recognised in many ways in common proverbs. Thus *summum jus summa injuria*: which means, that to drive an abstract right to its extremity is to do a wrong. In political life, as every one knows, extreme anarchy and extreme despotism naturally lead to one another. The perception of Dialectic in the province of individual Ethics is seen in the well-known adages, Pride comes before a fall: Too much wit outwits itself. Even feeling, bodily as well as mental, has its Dialectic. Every one knows how the extremes of pain and pleasure pass into each other: the heart overflowing with joy seeks relief in tears, and the deepest melancholy will at times betray its presence by a smile. . . .

Positive and negative are supposed to express an absolute difference. The two however are at bottom the same: the name of either might be transferred to the other. Thus, for example, debts and assets are not two particular, self-subsisting species of property. What is negative to the debtor, is positive to the creditor. A way to the east is also a way to the west. Positive and negative are therefore intrinsically conditioned by one another, and are only in relation to each other. The north pole of the magnet cannot be without the south pole, and *vice versa*. If we cut a magnet in two, we have not a north pole in one piece, and a south pole in the other. Similarly, in electricity, the positive and the negative are not two diverse and independent fluids. In opposition, the different is not confronted by any other, but by *its* other. Usually we regard different things as unaffected by each other. Thus we say: I am a human being, and around me are air, water, animals, and all sorts of things. Everything is thus put outside of every other. But the aim of philosophy is to banish indifference, and to ascertain the necessity of things. By that means the other is seen to stand over against *its* other. Thus, for example, inorganic nature is not to be considered merely something else than organic nature, but the necessary antithesis of it. Both are in essential relation to one another; and the one of the two is, only in so far as it excludes the other from it, and thus relates itself thereto. Nature in like manner is not without mind, nor mind without na.ture. An important step has been taken, when we cease in thinking to use phrases like: Of course something else is also possible. While we so speak, we are still tainted with contingency: and all true thinking, we have already said, is a thinking of necessity.

In modern physical science the opposition, first observed to exist in magnetism as polarity, has come to be regarded as a universal law pervading the whole of nature. This would be a real scientific advance, if care were at the same time taken not to let mere variety revert without explanation, as a valid category, side by side with opposition. Thus at one time the colours are regarded as in polar opposition to one another, and called complementary colours: at another time they are looked at in their indifferent and merely quantitative difference of red, yellow, green, &c.

Instead of speaking by the maxim of Excluded Middle (which is the maxim of abstract understanding) we should rather say: Everything is opposite. Neither in heaven nor in earth, neither in the world of mind nor of nature, is there anywhere such an abstract 'Either —or' as the understanding maintains. Whatever exists is concrete, with difference and opposition in itself. The finitude of things will then lie in the want of correspondence between their immediate being, and what they essentially are. Thus, in inorganic nature, the acid is implictly at the same time the base: in other words, its only being consists in its relation to its other. Hence also the acid is not something that persists quietly in the contrast: it is always in effort to realise what it potentially is. Contradiction is the very moving principle of the world: and it is ridiculous to say that contradiction is unthinkable. The only thing correct in that statement is that contradiction is not the end of the matter, but cancels itself. But contradiction, when cancelled, does not leave abstract identity; for that is itself only one side of the contrariety. The proximate result of opposition (when realised as contradiction) is the Ground, which contains identity as well as difference superseded and deposed to elements in the completer notion.[1]

2. [History as a Rational Pattern]

The only Thought which Philosophy brings with it to the contemplation of History, is the simple conception of *Reason*; that Reason is the Sovereign of the World; that the history of the world, therefore, presents us with a rational process. This conviction and intuition is a hypothesis in the domain of history as such. In that of Philosophy it is no hypothesis. It is there proved by speculative cognition, that Reason—and this term may here suffice us, without investigating the relation sustained by the Universe to the Divine Being—is *Substance*, as well as *Infinite Power*; its

[1] Hegel's concept of the Ground involves the interdependence of opposites. Because the negative depends on the positive, the positive is the ground of the negative. Similarly the negative is the ground of the positive. In Hegel's example, the north pole of the magnet cannot exist without the south pole, and *vice versa*. Each is equally the ground, and in this sense, the ground is the synthesis, or identity, of difference.—M.R.

own *Infinite Material* underlying all the natural and spiritual life which it originates, as also the *Infinite Form*—that which sets this Material in motion. On the one hand, Reason is the *substance* of the Universe; viz. that by which and in which all reality has its being and subsistence. On the other hand, it is the *Infinite Energy* of the Universe; since Reason is not so powerless as to be incapable of producing anything but a mere ideal, a mere intention—having its place outside reality, nobody knows where; something separate and abstract, in the heads of certain human beings. It is *the infinite complex of things*, their entire Essence and Truth. It is its own material which it commits to its own Active Energy to work up; not needing, as finite action does, the conditions of an external material of given means from which it may obtain its support, and the objects of its activity. It supplies its own nourishment, and is the object of its own operations. While it is exclusively its own basis of existence, and absolute final aim, it is also the energizing power realizing this aim; developing it not only in the phenomena of the Natural, but also of the Spiritual Universe—the History of the World. That this "Idea" or "Reason" is the *True*, the *Eternal*, the absolutely *powerful* essence; that it reveals itself in the World, and that in that World nothing else is revealed but this and its honor and glory—is the thesis which, as we have said, has been proved in Philosophy, and is here regarded as demonstrated.

In those of my hearers who are not acquainted with Philosophy, I may fairly presume, at least, the existence of a *belief* in Reason, a desire, a thirst for acquaintance with it, in entering upon this course of Lectures. It is, in fact, the wish for rational insight, not the ambition to amass a mere heap of requirements, that should be presupposed in every case as possessing the mind of the learner in the study of science. If the clear idea of Reason is not already developed in our minds, in beginning the study of Universal History, we should at least have the firm, unconquerable faith that Reason *does* exist there; and that the World of intelligence and conscious volition is not abandoned to chance, but must show itself in the light of the self-cognizant Idea. Yet I am not obliged to make any such preliminary demand upon your faith. What I have said thus provisionally, and what I shall have further to say, is, even in reference to *our* branch of science, not to be regarded as hypothetical, but as a summary view of the whole; the *result of the investigation* we are about to pursue; a result which happens to be known to *me*, because I have traversed the entire field. It is only an inference from the history of the World, that its development has been a rational process; that the history in question has constituted the rational necessary course of the World-Spirit—that Spirit whose nature is always one and the same, but which unfolds this its one nature in the phenomena of the World's existence. This must, as before stated, present itself as the ultimate *result* of History. But we have to take the latter as it is. We must proceed historically—empirically. . . .

We might then announce it as the first condition to be observed, that we should faithfully adopt all that is historical. But in such general expressions themselves, as "faithfully" and "adopt," lies the ambiguity. Even the ordinary, the "impartial" historiographer, who believes and professes that he maintains a simply receptive attitude; surrendering himself only to the data supplied him—is by no means passive as regards the exercise of his thinking powers. He brings his categories with him, and sees the phenomena presented to his mental vision, exclusively through these media. And, especially in all that pretends to the name of science, it is indispensable that Reason should not sleep—that reflection should be in full play. To him who looks upon the world rationally, the world in its turn presents a rational aspect. The relation is mutual. . . .

The inquiry into the *essential destiny* of Reason—as far as it is considered in reference to the World—is identical with the question, *what is the ultimate design of the world?* And the expression implies that that design is destined to be realized. Two points of consideration suggest themselves: first, the *import* of this design—its abstract definition; and secondly, its *realization*.

It must be observed at the outset, that the phenomenon we investigate—Universal History—belongs to the realm of *Spirit*. The term "*World*," includes both physical and psychical Nature. Physical Nature also plays its part in the World's History, and attention will have to be paid to the fundamental natural relations thus involved. But Spirit, and the course of its development, is our substantial object. Our task does not require us to contemplate Nature as a Rational System in itself—though in its own proper domain it proves itself such—but simply in its relation to *Spirit*. On the stage on which we are observing it —Universal History—Spirit displays itself in its most concrete reality. Notwithstanding this (or rather for the very purpose of comprehending the *general* principles which this, its form of *concrete reality*, embodies) we must premise some abstract characteristics of the *nature of Spirit*. Such an explanation, however, cannot be given here under any other form than that of bare assertion. The present is not the occasion for unfolding the idea of Spirit speculatively; for whatever has a place in an Introduction, must, as already observed, be taken as simply historical; something assumed as having been explained and proved elsewhere; or whose demonstration awaits the sequel of the Science of History itself.

We have therefore to mention here:

1. The abstract characteristics of the nature of Spirit.

2. What means Spirit uses in order to realize its Idea.

3. Lastly, we must consider the shape which the perfect embodiment of Spirit assumes—the State.

3. [Freedom as the Essence of Spirit]

1. The nature of Spirit may be understood by a glance at its direct opposite— *Matter*. As the essence of Matter is Gravity, so, on the other hand, we may affirm that the substance, the essence of Spirit is Freedom. All will readily as-

sent to the doctrine that Spirit, among other properties, is also endowed with Freedom; but philosophy teaches that all the qualities of Spirit exist only through Freedom; that all are but means for attaining freedom; that all seek and produce this and this alone. It is a result of speculative Philosophy, that Freedom is the sole truth of Spirit.

The destiny of the spiritual World, and—since this is the *substantial World*, while the physical remains subordinate to it, or, in the language of speculation, has no truth *as against* the spiritual—the *final cause of the World at large*, we allege to be the consciousness of its own freedom on the part of Spirit, and *ipso facto*, the *reality* of that freedom. But that this term "Freedom," without further qualification, is an indefinite, and incalculable ambiguous term; and that while that which it represents is the *ne plus ultra* of attainment, it is liable to an infinity of misunderstandings, confusions and errors, and to become the occasion for all imaginable excesses—has never been more clearly known and felt than in modern times. Yet, for the present, we must content ourselves with the term itself without further definition. Attention was also directed to the importance of the infinite difference between a principle in the abstract, and its realization in the concrete. In the process before us, the essential nature of freedom—which involves in it absolute necessity—is to be displayed as coming to a consciousness of itself (for it is in its very nature self-consciousness) and thereby realizing its existence. Itself is its own object of attainment, and the sole aim of Spirit. This result it is, at which the process of

the World's History has been continually aiming; and to which the sacrifices that have ever and anon been laid on the vast altar of the earth, through the long lapse of ages, have been offered. This is the only aim that sees itself realized and fulfilled; the only pole of repose amid the ceaseless change of events and conditions, and the sole efficient principle that pervades them. This final aim is God's purpose with the world; but God is the absolutely perfect Being, and can, therefore, will nothing other than himself—his own Will. The Nature of His Will—that is, His Nature itself—is what we here call the Idea of Freedom; translating the language of Religion into that of Thought. The question, then, which we may next put, is: What means does this principle of Freedom use for its realization? This is the second point we have to consider.

4. [The Means by which Freedom Is Realized]

2. The question of the *means* by which Freedom develops itself to a World, conducts us to the phenomenon of History itself. Although Freedom is, primarily, an undeveloped idea, the means it uses are external and phenomenal; presenting themselves in History to our sensuous vision. The first glance at History convinces us that the actions of men proceed from their needs, their passions, their characters and talents; and impresses us with the belief that such needs, passions and interests are the sole springs of action—the efficient agents in this scene of activity. Among these may, perhaps, be found aims of a liberal or universal kind—benevolence

it may be, or noble patriotism; but such virtues and general views are but insignificant as compared with the World and its doings. We may perhaps see the Ideal of Reason actualized in those who adopt such aims, and within the sphere of their influence; but they bear only a trifling proportion to the mass of the human race; and the extent of that influence is limited accordingly. Passions, private aims, and the satisfaction of selfish desires, are, on the other hand, most effective springs of action. Their power lies in the fact that they respect none of the limitations which justice and morality would impose on them; and that these natural impulses have a more direct influence over man than the artificial and tedious discipline that tends to order and self-restraint, law and morality. When we look at this display of passions, and the consequences of their violence; the Unreason which is associated not only with them, but even (rather we might say *especially*) with *good* designs and righteous aims; when we see the evil, the vice, the ruin that has befallen the most flourishing kingdoms which the mind of man ever created; we can scarce avoid being filled with sorrow at this universal taint of corruption; and, since this decay is not the work of mere Nature, but of the Human Will—a moral imbitterment—a revolt of the Good Spirit (if it have a place within us) may well be the result of our reflections. Without rhetorical exaggeration, a simply truthful combination of the miseries that have overwhelmed the noblest of nations and polities, and the finest exemplars of private virtue—forms a picture of most fearful aspect, and excites emotions of the profoundest and most hopeless sadness, counterbalanced by no consolatory result. We endure in beholding it a mental torture, allowing no defence or escape but the consideration that what has happened could not be otherwise; that it is a fatality which no intervention could alter. And at last we draw back from the intolerable disgust with which these sorrowful reflections threaten us into the more agreeable environment of our individual life—the Present formed by our private aims and interests. In short we retreat into the selfishness that stands on the quiet shore, and thence enjoys in safety the distant spectacle of "wrecks confusedly hurled." But even regarding History as the slaughter-bench at which the happiness of peoples, the wisdom of States, and the virtue of individuals have been victimized—the question involuntarily arises—to what principle, to what final aim these enormous sacrifices have been offered. . . .

The *first* remark we have to make, and which—though already presented more than once—cannot be too often repeated when the occasion seems to call for it—is that what we call *principle, aim, destiny,* or the nature and idea of Spirit, is something merely general and abstract. Principle—Plan of Existence—Law—is a hidden, undeveloped essence, which *as such*—however true in itself—is not completely real. Aims, principles, etc., have a place in our thoughts, in our subjective design only; but not yet in the sphere of reality. That which exists for itself only, is a possibility, a potentiality; but has not yet emerged into Existence. A *second* element must be introduced in order to produce actuality

—viz. actuation, realization; and whose motive power is the Will—the activity of man in the widest sense. It is only by this activity that that Idea as well as abstract characteristics generally, are realized, actualized; for of themselves they are powerless. The motive power that puts them in operation, and gives them determinate existence, is the need, instinct, inclination, and passion of man. . . .

We assert then that nothing has been accomplished without interest on the part of the actors; and—if interest be called passion, inasmuch as the whole individuality, to the neglect of all other actual or possible interests and claims, is devoted to an object with every fibre of volition, concentrating all its desires and powers upon it—we may affirm absolutely that *nothing great in the World* has been accomplished without *passion*. Two elements, therefore, enter into the object of our investigation; the first the Idea, the second the complex of human passions; the one the warp, the other the woof of the vast arras-web of Universal History. . . .

From this comment on the second essential element in the historical embodiment of an aim, we infer—glancing at the institution of the State in passing—that a State is then well constituted and internally powerful, when the private interest of its citizens is one with the common interest of the State; when the one finds its gratification and realization in the other—a proposition in itself very important. But in a State many institutions must be adopted, much political machinery invented, accompanied by appropriate political arrangements—necessitating long struggles of the understanding before what is really appropriate can be discovered—involving, moreover, contentions with private interest and passions, and a tedious discipline of these latter, in order to bring about the desired harmony. The epoch, when a State attains this harmonious condition, marks the period of its bloom, its virtue, its vigor, and its prosperity. But the history of mankind does not begin with a *conscious* aim of any kind, as it is the case with the particular circles into which men form themselves of set purpose. The mere social instinct implies a conscious purpose of security for life and property; and when society has been constituted, this purpose becomes more comprehensive. The History of the World begins with its general aim—the realization of the Idea of Spirit—only in an *implicit* form (*an sich*) that is, as Nature; a hidden, most profoundly hidden, unconscious instinct; and the whole process of History (as already observed) is directed to rendering this unconscious impulse a conscious one. Thus appearing in the form of merely natural existence, natural will—that which has been called the subjective side—physical craving, instinct, passion, private interest, as also opinion and subjective conception—spontaneously present themselves at the very commencement. This vast congeries of volitions, interests and activities constitute the instruments and means of the World-Spirit for attaining its object; bringing it to consciousness, and realizing it. And this aim is none other than finding itself—coming to itself—and contemplating itself in concrete actuality. But that those manifestations of vitality on the part of individuals and peoples, in which they seek and satisfy their own purposes, are, at the same time, the means and instruments of a higher and broader purpose of which they know nothing—which they realize unconsciously—might be made a matter of question; rather has been questioned, and in every variety of form negatived, decried and condemned as mere dreaming and "Philosophy." But on this point I announced my view at the very outset, and asserted our hypothesis—which, however, will appear in the sequel, in the form of a legitimate inference—and our belief, that Reason governs the world, and has consequently governed its history. In relation to this independently universal and substantial existence—all else is subordinate, subservient to it, and the means for its development. . . .

5. [Great Men and the Cunning of Reason]

He is happy who finds his condition suited to his special character, will, and fancy, and so enjoys himself in that condition. The History of the World is not the theatre of happiness. Periods of happiness are blank pages in it, for they are period of harmony—periods when the antithesis is in abeyance. Reflection on self—the Freedom above described—is abstractly defined as the formal element of the activity of the absolute Idea. The realizing *activity* of which we have spoken is the middle term of the Syllogism, one of whose extremes is the Universal essence, the *Idea*, which reposes in the penetralia of Spirit; and the other, the complex of external things—objective matter. That

activity is the medium by which the universal latent principle is translated into the domain of objectivity.

I will endeavor to make what has been said more vivid and clear by examples.

The building of a house is, in the first instance, a subjective aim and design. On the other hand we have, as means, the several substances required for the work—Iron, Wood, Stones. The elements are made use of in working up this material: fire to melt the iron, wind to blow the fire, water to set wheels in motion, in order to cut the wood, etc. The result is, that the wind, which has helped to build the house; is shut out by the house; so also are the violence of rains and floods, and the destructive powers of fire, so far as the house is made fireproof. The stones and beams obey the law of gravity—press downward—and so high walls are carried up. Thus the elements are made use of in accordance with their nature, and yet to co-operate for a product, by which their operation is limited. Thus the passions of men are gratified; they develop themselves and their aims in accordance with their natural tendencies, and build up the edifice of human society; thus fortifying a position for Right and Order *against themselves*.

The connection of events above indicated involves also the fact, that in history an additional result is commonly produced by human actions beyond that which they aim at and obtain—that which they immediately recognize and desire. They gratify their own interest; but something further is thereby accomplished, latent in the actions in question, though not present to their consciousness, and not included in their design. An analogous example is offered in the case of a man who, from a feeling of revenge—perhaps not an unjust one, but produced by injury on the other's part—burns that other man's house. A connection is immediately established between the deed itself and a train of circumstances not directly included in it, taken abstractedly. In itself it consisted in merely presenting a small flame to a small portion of a beam. Events not involved in that simple act follow of themselves. The part of the beam which was set fire to is connected with its remote portions; the beam itself is united with the woodwork of the house generally, and this with other houses; so that a wide conflagration ensues, which destroys the goods and chattels of many other persons besides his against whom the act of revenge was first directed; perhaps even costs not a few men their lives. This lay neither in the deed abstractedly, nor in the design of the man who committed it. But the action has a further general bearing. In the design of the doer it was only revenge executed against an individual in the destruction of his property, but it is moreover a crime, and that involves punishment also. This may not have been present to the mind of the perpetrator, still less in his intention; but his deed itself, the general principles it calls into play, its substantial content entails it. By this example I wish only to impress on you the consideration that in a simple act, something further may be implicated than lies in the intention and consciousness of the agent. The example before us involves, however, this additional consideration, that the sub-

stance of the act, consequently we may say the act itself, recoils upon the perpetrator—reacts upon him with destructive tendency. This union of the two extremes—the embodiment of a general idea in the form of direct reality, and the elevation of a speciality into connection with universal truth—is brought to pass, at first sight, under the conditions of an utter diversity of nature between the two, and an indifference of the one extreme toward the other. The aims which the agents set before them are limited and special; but it must be remarked that the agents themselves are intelligent thinking beings. The purport of their desires is interwoven with *general, essential* considerations of justice, good, duty, etc.; for mere desire—volition in its rough and savage forms—falls not within the scene and sphere of Universal History. Those general considerations, which form at the same time a norm for directing aims and actions, have a determinate purport; for such an abstraction as "good for its own sake," has no place in living reality. If men are to act, they must not only intend the Good, but must have decided for themselves whether this or that particular thing is a Good. What special course of action, however, is good or not, is determined, as regards the ordinary contingencies of private life, by the laws and customs of a State; and here no great difficulty is presented. Each individual has his position; he knows on the whole what a just, honorable course of conduct is. As to ordinary, private relations, the assertion that it is difficult to choose the right and good—the regarding it as the mark of an exalted morality to find difficulties and raise scruples on that score—may be set down to an evil or perverse will, which seeks to evade duties not in themselves of a perplexing nature; or, at any rate, to an idly reflective habit of mind—where a feeble will affords no sufficient exercise to the faculties—leaving them therefore to find occupation within themselves, and to expend themselves on moral self-adulation.

It is quite otherwise with the comprehensive relations that History has to do with. In this sphere are presented those momentous collisions between existing, acknowledged duties, laws, and rights, and those contingencies which are adverse to this fixed system; which assail and even destroy its foundations and existence; whose tenor may nevertheless seem good—on the large scale advantageous—yes, even indispensable and necessary. These contingencies realize themselves in History: they involve a general principle of a different order from that on which depends the *permanence* of a people or a State. This principle is an essential phase in the development of the *creating* Idea, of Truth, striving and urging toward [consciousness of] itself. Historical men—*World-Historical Individuals*—are those in whose aim such a general principle lies.

Caesar, in danger of losing a position, not perhaps at that time of superiority, yet at least of equality with the others who were at the head of the State, and of succumbing to those who were just on the point of becoming his enemies—belongs essentially to this category. These enemies—who were at the same time pursuing *their* personal aims —had the form of the constitution, and the power conferred by an appearance of justice, on their side. Caesar was contending for the maintenance of his position, honor, and safety; and, since the power of his opponents included the sovereignty over the provinces of the Roman Empire, his victory secured for him the conquest of that entire Empire; and he thus became (though leaving the form of the constitution) the Autocrat of the State. That which secured for him the execution of a design, which in the first instance was of negative import—the Autocracy of Rome—was, however, at the same time an independently necessary feature in the history of Rome and of the world. It was not then his private gain merely, but an unconscious impulse that occasioned the accomplishment of that for which the time was ripe. Such are all great historical men—whose own particular aims involve those large issues which are the will of the World-Spirit. They may be called Heroes, inasmuch as they have derived their purposes and their vocation, not from the calm, regular course of things, sanctioned by the existing order; but from a concealed fount—one which has not attained to phenomenal, present existence—from that inner Spirit, still hidden beneath the surface, which, impinging on the outer world as on a shell, bursts it in pieces, because it is another kernel than that which belonged to the shell in question. They are men, therefore, who appear to draw the impulse of their life from themselves; and whose deeds have produced a condition of things and a complex of historical relations which appear to be only *their* interest, and *their* work.

Such individuals had no conscious-

ness of the general Idea they were unfolding, while prosecuting those aims
of theirs; on the contrary, they were
practical, political men. But at the same
time they were thinking men, who had
an insight into the requirements of the
time—*what was ripe for development.*
This was the very Truth for their age,
for their world; the species next in
order, so to speak, and which was already formed in the womb of time. It
was theirs to know this nascent principle; the necessary, directly sequent
step in progress, which their world was
to take; to make this their aim, and to
expend their energy in promoting it.
World-historical men—the Heroes of an
epoch—must, therefore, be recognized
as its clear-sighted ones; *their* deeds,
their words are the best of that time.
Great men have formed purposes to
satisfy themselves, not others. Whatever prudent designs and counsels they
might have learned from others, would
be the more limited and inconsistent
features in their career; for it was they
who best understood affairs; from
whom *others* learned, and approved, or
at least acquiesced in—their policy. For
that Spirit which had taken this fresh
step in history is the inmost soul of all
individuals; but in a state of uncon-
sciousness which the great men in question aroused. Their fellows, therefore,
follow these soul-leaders; for they feel
the irresistible power of their own inner
Spirit thus embodied. If we go on to
cast a look at the fate of these World-
Historical persons, whose vocation it
was to be the agents of the World-
Spirit—we shall find it to have been no
happy one. They attained no calm enjoyment; their whole life was labor and
trouble; their whole nature was naught
else but their master-passion. When
their object is attained they fall off like
empty hulls from the kernel. They die
early, like Alexander; they are murdered, like Caesar; transported to St.
Helena, like Napoleon. This fearful
consolation—that historical men have
not enjoyed what is called happiness,
and of which only private life (and this
may be passed under very various external circumstances) is capable—this
consolation those may draw from history, who stand in need of it; and it is
craved by Envy—vexed at what is great
and transcendent—striving, therefore, to
depreciate it, and to find some flaw in it.
Thus in modern times it has been demonstarted *ad nauseam* that princes are
generally unhappy on their thrones; in
consideration of which the possession
of a throne is tolerated, and men ac-
quiesce in the fact that not themselves
but the personages in question are its
occupants. The Free Man, we may observe, is not envious, but gladly recognizes what is great and exalted, and re-
joices that it exists.

It is in the light of those common
elements which constitute the interest
and therefore the passions of individuals, that these historical men are to be
regarded. They are *great* men, because
they willed and accomplished something great; not a mere fancy, a mere
intention, but that which met the case
and fell in with the needs of the age.
This mode of considering them also
excludes the so-called "psychological"
view, which—serving the purpose of
envy most effectually—contrives so to
refer all actions to the heart—to bring
them under such a subjective aspect—

as that their authors appear to' have done everything under the impulse of some passion, mean or grand—some *morbid craving*—and on account of these passions and cravings to have been not moral men. Alexander of Macedon partly subdued Greece, and then Asia; therefore he was possessed by a *morbid craving* for conquest. He is alleged to have acted from a craving for fame, for conquest; and the proof that these were the impelling motives is that he did that which resulted in fame. What pedagogue has not demonstrated of Alexander the Great—of Julius Caesar—that they were instigated by such passions, and were consequently immoral men?— whence the conclusion immediately follows that he, the pedagogue, is a better man than they, because he has not such passions; a proof of which lies in the fact that he does not conquer Asia— vanquish Darius and Porus—but while he enjoys life himself, lets others enjoy it too. These psychologists are particularly fond of contemplating those peculiarities of great historical figures which appertain to them as private persons. Man must eat and drink; he sustains relations to friends and acquaintances; he has passing impulses and ebullitions of temper. "No man is a hero to his valet-de-chambre," is a well-known proverb; I have added—and Goethe repeated it ten years later—"but not because the former is no hero, but because the latter is a valet." He takes off the hero's boots, assists him to bed, knows that he prefers champagne, etc. Historical personnages waited upon in historical literature by such psychological valets, come poorly off; they are brought down by these their attendants to a level with

—or rather a few degrees below the level of—the morality of such exquisite discerners of spirits. The Thersites of Homer who abuses the kings is a standing figure for all times. Blows—that is, beating with a solid cudgel—he does not get in every age, as in the Homeric one; but his envy, his egotism, is the thorn which he has to carry in his flesh; and the undying worm that gnaws him is the tormenting consideration that his excellent views and vituperations remain absolutely without result in the world. But our satisfaction at the fate of Thersitism also, may have its sinister side.

A World-historical individual is not so unwise as to indulge a variety of wishes to divide his regards. He is devoted to the One Aim, regardless of all else. It is even possible that such men may treat other great, even sacred interests, inconsiderately; conduct which is indeed obnoxious to moral reprehension. But so mighty a form must trample down many an innocent flower— crush to pieces many an object in its path.

The special interest of passion is thus inseparable from the active development of a general principle: for it is from the special and determinate and from its negation that the Universal results. Particularity contends with its like, and some loss is involved in the issue. *It* is not the general idea that is implicated in opposition and combat, and that is exposed to danger. It remains in the background, untouched and uninjured. This may be called the *cunning of reason*—that it sets the passions to work for itself, while that which develops its existence through such impulsion pays the penalty, and suffers loss. For it is *phenomenal* being that is so treated, and of this, part is of no value, part is positive and real. The particular is for the most part of too trifling value as compared with the general: individuals are sacrificed and abandoned. The Idea pays the penalty of determinate existence and of corruptibility, not from itself, but from the passions of individuals. . . .

6. [The State as the Embodiment of Freedom]

The third point to be analyzed is, therefore—what is the object to be realized by these means; *i.e.* what is the form it assumes in the realm of reality. We have spoken of *means*; but in the carrying out of a subjective, limited aim, we have also to take into consideration the element of a *material*, either already present or which has to be procured. Thus the question would arise: What is the material in which the Ideal of Reason is wrought out? The primary answer would be—Personality itself—human desires—Subjectivity generally. In human knowledge and volition, as its material element, Reason attains positive existence. We have considered subjective volition where it has an object which is the truth and essence of a reality; viz. where it constitutes a great world-historical passion. As a subjective will, occupied with limited passions, it is dependent, and can gratify its desires only within the limits of this dependence. But the subjective will has also a substantial life—a reality—in which it moves in the region of *essen-*

tial being, and has the essential itself as the object of its existence. This essential being is the union of the *subjective* with the *rational* Will: it is the moral Whole, the *State*, which is that form of reality in which the individual has and enjoys his freedom; but on the condition of his recognizing, believing in and willing that which is common to the Whole. And this must not be understood as if the subjective will of the social unit attained its gratification and enjoyment through that common Will; as if this were a means provided for its benefit; as if the individual, in his relations to other individuals, thus limited his freedom, in order that this universal limitation—the mutual constraint of all— might secure a small space of liberty for each. Rather, we affirm, are Law, Morality, Government, and they alone, the positive reality and completion of Freedom. Freedom of a low and limited order is mere caprice, which finds its exercise in the sphere of particular and limited desires.

Subjective volition—Passion—is that which sets men in activity, that which effects "practical" realization. The Idea is the inner spring of action; the State is the actually existing, realized moral life. For it is the Unity of the universal, essential Will, with that of the individual; and this is "Morality." The Individual living in this unity has a moral life; possesses a value that consists in this substantiality alone. Sophocles in his Antigone, says, "The divine commands are not of yesterday, nor of today; no, they have an infinite existence, and no one could say whence they came." The laws of morality are not accidental, but are the essentially Rational. It is the very object of the State that what is essential in the practical activity of men, and in their dispositions, should be duly recognized; that it should have a manifest existence, and maintain its position. It is the absolute interest of Reason that this moral Whole should exist: and herein lies the justification and merit of heroes who have founded states—however rude these may have been. In the history of the World, only those peoples can come under our notice which form a state. For it must be understood that this latter is the realization of Freedom, *i.e.* of the absolute final aim, and that it exists for its own sake. It must further be understood that all the worth which the human being possesses—all spiritual reality, he possesses only through the State. For his spiritual reality consists in this, that his own essence—Reason— is objectively present to him, that it possesses objective immediate existence for him. Thus only is he fully conscious; thus only is he a partaker of morality— of a just and moral social and political

life. For Truth is the Unity of the universal and subjective Will; and the Universal is to be found in the State, in its laws, its universal and rational arrangements. The State is the Divine Idea as it exists on Earth. We have in it, therefore, the object of History in a more definite shape than before; that in which Freedom obtains objectivity, and lives in the enjoyment of this objectivity. For Law is the objectivity of Spirit; volition in its true form. Only that will which obeys law, is free; for it obeys itself—it is independent and so free. When the State or our country constitutes a community of existence; when the subjective will of man submits to laws—the contradiction between Liberty and Necessity vanishes. The Rational has necessary existence, as being the reality and substance of things, and we are free in recognizing it as law, and following it as the substance of our own being. The objective and the subjective will are then reconciled, and present one identical homogeneous whole.

COMMENT

Both Berkeley and Hegel are "idealists," but the idealism of the one is very different from the idealism of the other. The principal difference is the contrast between Berkeley's pluralistic and Hegel's monistic idealism. According to Berkeley, perception is the result of the direct action of God on finite and independent spirits. The objects we perceive have their cause in God since they are not of our own making. Nature is the "visual language" through which God's power is revealed to us, and through which finite spirits, with the help of God's coordinating influence, communicate with one another. But although God acts upon us, God is nonetheless distinct, and each one of us has our own individual identity.

Thus the Universe is a pluralistic society of minds or spirits, the central position and coordinating role being assigned to God. According to Hegel, Berkeley is correct in maintaining that reality is spiritual but incorrect in maintaining that God is distinct from people and each spirit distinct from every other. For Hegel the Universe is an integrated system and all spirits are members one of another. The fundamental emphasis of absolute idealism, of which Hegel is the supreme exemplar, is upon total integration.

This point of view, then, states that the whole of reality is a system in which each part is relational. Hence the part cannot be understood in isolation—any more than a single line in a well-integrated painting can be understood and appreciated in isolation from the rest of the painting, or a single theorem in geometry understood in isolation from the geometrical system of which it is a part. Thus, to see things together, in their interconnection and unity, is to see them truly; to see things apart, as isolated, fragmentary, and contradictory, is to see them falsely. No proposition taken in isolation is wholly true because no thing taken in isolation is wholly real. Complete or absolute truth is attained only when all fragmentariness disappears and all contradictions vanish within a final, all-inclusive organization of meanings.

Hegel's sense of interrelatedness was reinforced by his theory of a new kind of logic, which would take account of the continuities and gradations of reality. He had noticed that there is a characteristic pattern of thought in the give-and-take of fruitful argument. The first stage tends to be that of unqualified assertion (the thesis), an idea being advanced as unqualifiedly true and intelligible in and of itself. The second stage is a sceptical rejoinder (the antithesis); the original idea, opposed by a counter notion, is shown to be false and incomplete when taken in its initial and unqualified form. As the argument proceeds each person is made to see the strength in the opposing position, and the disputants, if the outcome is fruitful, finally reach an agreement involving a more inclusive organization of thought (the synthesis). Thus a larger truth emerges from the strife of partisan views.

It must not be supposed that all development can be fitted into a neat, triadic pattern. The terms "thesis," "antithesis," and "synthesis" have been used much more frequently by expositors of Hegel than by Hegel himself. In his preface to *The Phenomenology of the Spirit*, he warns against a violent forcing of any and every sort of material into the triadic pattern. His own philosophical thinking, although predominantly "dialectical," is too rich and various to reduce to any simple scheme.

Hegel bases his philosophy of history on his idealism and dialectical logic. Contradiction and its resolution in the realm of pure thought are paralleled by a similar spiritual movement in human history. Here, too, there are antithetical tendencies, each bent on destroying its opposite, and producing a kind of crisis by its inordinate onesidedness. The clash of these tendencies exposes the ridiculousness of each factor taken in isolation, and thus releases corrective forces which restore the balance. In this way the whole process leads on to more coherent and comprehensive states of equilibrium. The "inward guiding soul" of this process is the development of the idea of freedom. People are free by nature in the sense that their destiny is to be free, but we realize this destiny only by historical stages amid incalculable waste and suffering. It is impossible to skip over the stages of development and to realize an idea before its time has come. Thought will fall on barren soil if it is premature; it will take root and become fertile only if it corresponds to the spirit of the age.

Some Critical Questions

1. THE CONCEPT OF UNCONSCIOUS TELEOLOGY. Hegel denies that there is a God outside of history, manipulating it according to plan. For him God is not a transcendent deity but a cosmic spirit both within and beyond our worldly sphere. History is the march through time of the Spirit realizing itself. The lone individual cannot direct history toward personally envisioned goals. Human passion and unreason, not reasoned foresight, are the instruments through which objective reason comes to historical fruition. History is a teleology within a human mind, a purposeful development without a human governing purpose. It is like Adam Smith's "invisible hand" guiding people's selfish economic acts to a favorable social end. Smith's notion has been much criticized. Likewise Aristotle's notion of unconscious teleology has often been attacked as self-contradictory. How sound is Hegel's concept of "the cunning of reason"?

2. THE THEORY OF HISTORICAL PROGRESS. Hegel advances a theory of progress according to which the world is rational. When evil appears it is the negative element (the antithesis) in a dialectical process. Evil though it be, it is necessary for historical development. "Spirit . . . makes war upon itself—consumes its own existence; but in this very destruction it works up that existence into a new form, and each successive phase becomes in turn a material, working on which it exalts itself to a new grade." This entire theory, that history has an overall discoverable pattern and that this pattern is dialectical and progressive, has been subjected to severe criticism. Can Hegel's theory stand the test of critical examination? If some of his ideas of historical development have to be rejected, can others be salvaged?

3. THE CONCEPT OF SOCIAL CONFIGURATION. The term *gestalt* or *configuration* is used to designate a unity in which the parts are essentially related to one another and to the whole. A national culture, according to Hegel, is such a configuration. It is a unique pattern of religion, art, language, morality, ideology, political and economic activity, embodied in customs, traditions, institutions, and such artifacts as books, laws, tools, and works of art. Impressed upon individuals, it pervasively molds their mentality and behaviour; but it endures and develops from stage to stage even though individuals come and go. This is a powerful

concept that has had a profound influence on social ideals and historical interpretations. To what extent is it valid?

4. THE THEORY OF THE STATE. For Hegel the state is the great agency of integration and synthesis, and as such it is the means to and embodiment of freedom. Very different is the interpretation of Marx, who defines the state as the supreme coercive agency within the society. The police and the military are at the very foundation of the state. The state, as the organ of class-domination, is not an agency of integration but an agency of repression. Which interpretation, Hegel's or Marx's, is more nearly correct?

5. LAW AND FREEDOM. Closely related to the state is the rule of law. For liberal individualists such as Thoreau, freedom is a condition in which there is as little law as possible. Law curbs and restricts freedom. The duty of the individual is to follow one's own conscience even at the cost of civil disobedience. This is an anti-Hegelian notion. Freedom, according to Hegel, is achieved when law is internalized and made part of one's conscience. An antisocial "freedom" is mere caprice. The reader might ask to what extent Socrates in the *Apology* agrees with Hegel? Who is right?

6. THE ROLE OF THE GREAT MAN. The greatness of "world-historical individuals," according to Hegel, is that they are the instruments and embodiments of the World-Spirit. They sense and articulate the next stage of historical development, foreshadowing the new and subverting the old. But they do not create their own destiny, they are the agents of a Spirit far greater than themselves. How sound is this interpretation?

7. THE IDEALISTIC INTERPRETATION OF HISTORY. Basic to Hegel's philosophy of history is his idealistic approach. History, he contends, is a rational pattern in which ideas and passions are the dynamic forces of change and development. Opposed to this approach is Marx's "materialistic interpretation of history." We shall postpone the question of the idealistic *versus* the materialistic interpretation until we have examined the Marxian theory.

16

Communism

KARL MARX (1818–1883)

Born in Treves in the German Rhineland, Marx was the son of well-to-do Jewish parents who had been converted to Christianity. He studied law, history, and philosophy at the Universities of Bonn, Berlin, and Jena, imbibing the doctrines of Hegel, then at the height of his fame. His Doctor's thesis was on the materialism of Democritus and Epicurus. In 1842–1843 he edited a newspaper at Cologne, which was suppressed by the Prussian government because of its advanced ideas. After marrying Jennie von Westphalen, a beautiful young woman of aristocratic lineage, he went to Paris, where he studied the socialist movement. There he met Friedrich Engels, a young German who worked in the family business of Ermen and Engels, cotton spinners in Manchester, first as clerk, eventually as manager and part owner. On the basis of the socialist convictions which they shared, the two young men formed a friendship that endured throughout their lives.

In 1845, the Prussian government, incensed by Marx's continued attacks, persuaded the French authorities to deport him. He then went with Engels to live in Brussels, where he continued his political and journalistic activities. During this period he wrote, singly or in collaboration with Engels, a number of socialist works, the most famous of which was the *Communist Manifesto*, published on the eve of the revolutionary disturbances of 1848. Expelled in turn from Belgium, Marx returned to Cologne, where he founded a radical newspaper and participated in the revolutionary uprisings of 1848–1849. The ensuing political reaction compelled him to seek refuge in England.

With his family, he spent the remainder of his life in London. There he worked for years in the British Museum, accumulating the research materials for his indictment of capitalist society. Having only a small income as a correspondent for the *New York Tribune*, he lived with his wife and children in a squalid attic, often without sufficient food, decent clothing, or other basic necessities. His later years were saddened by ill health and the death of three of his children, but nothing could divert him from unremitting service to his ideals. In 1864, he helped to organize the First International, a radical political organization which continued under his direction until 1872. His major work was *Capital*, a detailed historical and economic analysis of capitalist society, which he referred to as "the task to which I have sacrificed my health, my happiness in life, and my family." Volume One was published in 1867 and the two remaining volumes after his death.

Communism
and History

I. The Materialist Conception of History

I was led by my studies to the conclusion that legal relations as well as forms of state could neither be understood by themselves, nor explained by the co-called general progress of the human mind, but that they are rooted in the material conditions of life, which are summed up by Hegel after the fashion of the English and French writers of the eighteenth century under the name *civil society*, and the anatomy of civil society is to be sought in political economy. The study of the latter which I had begun in Paris, I continued in Brussels where I had emigrated on account of an expulsion order issued by M. Guizot. The general conclusion at which I arrived and which, once reached, continued to serve as the guiding thread in my studies, may be formulated briefly as follows: In the social

All passages except the Speech at the Anniversary of the *People's Paper* and the selection from *The Grundrisse: Foundations of the Critique of Political Economy* are taken from *Karl Marx: Selected Writings in Sociology and Social Philosophy*, edited by T. B. Bottomore and M. Rubel (London: C. A. Watts & Co. Ltd., 1956), or *Karl Marx: Early Writings*, edited by T. B. Bottomore (London: C. A. Watts & Co. Ltd., 1963). Translations are by Bottomore. Reprinted by permission of the publisher. The passage from *The Grundrisse*, edited and translated by David McLellan and copyright © 1971 by McLellan, is quoted by permission of Harper & Row, Publishers, Inc. Each passage is followed by a reference to its original source.

production which men carry on they enter into definite relations that are indispensable and independent of their will; these relations of production correspond to a definite stage of development of their material powers of production. The totality of these relations of production constitutes the economic structure of society—the real foundation, on which legal and political superstructures arise and to which definite forms of social consciousness correspond. The mode of production of material life determines the general character of the social, political and spiritual processes of life. It is not the consciousness of men that determines their being, but, on the contrary, their social being determines their consciousness. At a certain stage of their development, the material forces of production in society come in conflict with the existing relations of production, or—what is but a legal expression for the same thing—with the property relations within which they had been at work before. From forms of development of the forces of production these relations turn into their fetters. Then occurs a period of social revolution. With the change of the economic foundation the entire immense superstructure is more or less rapidly transformed. In considering such transformations the distinction should always be made between the material transformation of the economic conditions of production which can be determined with the precision of natural science, and the legal, political, religious, aesthetic or philosophical —in short ideological, forms in which men become conscious of this conflict and fight it out. Just as our opinion of an individual is not based on what he thinks of himself, so can we not judge of such a period of transformation by its own consciousness; on the contrary, this consciousness must rather be explained from the contradictions of material life, from the existing conflict between the social forces of production and the relations of production. No social order ever disappears before all the productive forces for which there is room in it have been developed; and new, higher relations of production never appear before the material conditions of their existence have matured in the womb of the old society. Therefore, mankind always sets itself only such problems as it can solve; since, on closer examination, it will always be found that the problem itself arises only when the material conditions necessary for its solution already exist or are at least in the process of formation. In broad outline we can designate the Asiatic, the ancient, the feudal, and the modern bourgeois modes of production as progressive epochs in the economic formation of society. The bourgeois relations of production are the last antagonistic form of the social process of production; not in the sense of individual antagonisms, but of conflict arising from conditions surrounding the life of individuals in society. At the same time the productive forces developing in the womb of bourgeois society create the material conditions for the solution of that antagonism. With this social formation, therefore, the prehistory of human society comes to an end.

Preface to *A Contribution to the Critique of Political Economy* (1859)

The premises from which we begin are not arbitrary ones, not dogmas, but real premises from which abstraction can be made only in the imagination. They are the real individuals, their activity and their material conditions of life, including those which they find already in existence and those produced by their activity. These premises can thus be established in a purely empirical way.

The first premise of all human history is, of course, the existence of living human individuals. The first fact to be established, therefore, is the physical constitution of these individuals and their consequent relation to the rest of Nature. Of course we cannot here investigate the actual physical nature of man or the natural conditions in which man finds himself—geological, orohydrographical, climatic and so on. All historiography must begin from these natural bases and their modification in the course of history by men's activity.

Men can be distinguished from animals by consciousness, by religion, or by anything one likes. They themselves begin to distinguish themselves from animals as soon as they begin to *produce* their means of subsistence, a step which is determined by their physical constitution. In producing their means of subsistence men indirectly produce their actual material life.

The way in which men produce their means of subsistence depends in the first place on the nature of the existing means which they have to reproduce. This mode of production should not be regarded simply as the reproduction of the physical existence of individuals. It is already a definite form of activity of these individuals, a definite way of expressing their life, a definite *mode of life*. As individuals express their life, so they are. What they are, therefore, coincides with their production, with *what* they produce and with *how* they produce it. What individuals are, therefore, depends on the material conditions of their production. . . .

This conception of history, therefore, rests on the exposition of the real process of production, starting out from the simple material production of life, and on the comprehension of the form or intercourse connected with and created by this mode of production, i.e. of civil society in its various stages as the basis of all history, and also in its action as the State. From this starting point, it explains all the different theoretical productions and forms of consciousness, religion, philosophy, ethics, etc., and traces their origins and growth, by which means the matter can of course be displayed as a whole (and consequently, also the reciprocal action of these various sides on one another). Unlike the idealist view of history, it . . . remains constantly on the real ground of history; it does not explain practice from the idea but explains the formation of ideas from material practice, and accordingly comes to the conclusion that all the forms of and products of consciousness can be dissolved, not by intellectual criticism, . . . but only by the practical overthrow of the actual social relations . . . ; that not criticism but revolution is the driving force of history, as well as of religion, philosophy, and all other types of theory. It shows that history does not end by being resolved into "self-consciousness," as "spirit of the spirit," but that at each stage of history there is found a material result, a sum of productive forces, a historically created relation of individuals to Nature and to one another, which is handed down to each generation from its predecessors, a mass of productive forces, capital, and circumstances, which is indeed modified by the new generation but which also prescribes for it its conditions of life and gives it a definite development, a special character. It shows that circumstances make men just as much as men make circumstances. . . .

The fact is, therefore, that determinate individuals, who are productively active in a definite way, enter into these determinate social and political relations. Empirical observation must, in each particular case, show empirically, and without any mystification or speculation, the connection of the social and political structure with production. The social structure and the State are continually evolving out of the life-process of determinate individuals, of individuals not as they may appear in their own or other people's imagination, but as they really are: i.e. as they act, produce their material life, and are occupied within determinate material limits, presuppositions and conditions, which are independent of their will.

The production of ideas, conceptions and consciousness is at first directly interwoven with the material activity and the material intercourse of men, the language of real life. Representation and thought, the mental intercourse of men, still appear at this stage as the direct emanation of their material behaviour. The same applies to mental production as it is expressed in the political, legal, moral, religious and metaphysical language of a people. Men are the producers of their conceptions, ideas, etc.,—real, active men, as they are conditioned by a determinate development of their productive forces, and of the intercourse which corresponds to these, up to its most extensive forms. Consciousness can never be anything else than conscious existence, and the existence of men is their actual life process. If in all ideology men and their circumstances appear upside down as in a *camera obscura*, this phenomenon arises from their historical life process just as the inversion of objects on the retina does from their physical life-process.

In direct contrast to German philosophy, which descends from heaven to earth, here we ascend from earth to heaven. That is to say, we do not set out from what men say, imagine, or conceive, nor from what has been said, thought, imagined, or conceived of men, in order to arrive at men in the flesh. We begin with real, active men, and from their real life-process show the development of the ideological reflexes and echoes of this life-process. The phantoms of the human brain also are necessary sublimates of men's material life-process, which can be empirically established and which is bound to material preconditions. Morality, religion, metaphysics, and other ideologies, and their corresponding forms of consciousness, no longer retain therefore their appearance of autonomous existence. They have no history, no development; it is men, who, in developing their material production and their material intercourse, change, along with this their real existence, their thinking and the products of their thinking. Life is not determined by consciousness, but consciousness by life. Those who adopt the first method of approach begin with consciousness, regarded as the living individual; those who adopt the second, which corresponds with real life, begin with the real living individuals themselves, and consider consciousness only as *their* consciousness. . . .

The ideas of the ruling class are, in every age, the ruling ideas: i.e. the class which is the dominant *material* force in society is at the same time its dominant *intellectual* force. The class which has the means of material production at its disposal, has control at the same time over the means of mental production, so that in consequence the ideas of those who lack the means of mental production are, in general, subject to it. The dominant ideas are nothing more than the ideal expression of the dominant material realationships, the dominant material relationships grasped as ideas, and thus of the relationships which make one class the ruling one; they are consequently the ideas of its dominance. The individuals composing the ruling class possess among other things consciousness, and therefore think. In so far, therefore, as they rule as a class and determine the whole extent of an epoch, it is self-evident that they do this in their whole range and thus, among other things, rule also as thinkers, as producers of ideas, and regulate the production and distribution of the ideas of their age. Consequently their ideas are the ruling ideas of the age. For instance, in an age and in a country

where royal power, aristocracy and the bourgeoisie are contending for domination and where, therefore, domination is shared, the doctrine of the separation of powers appears as the dominant idea and is enunciated as an "eternal law." The division of labour, which we saw earlier as one of the principal forces of history up to the present time, manifests itself also in the ruling class, as the division of mental and material labour, so that within this class one part appears as the thinkers of the class (its active conceptualizing ideologies, who make it their chief source of livelihood to develop and perfect the illusions of the class about itself), while the others have a more passive and receptive attitude to these ideas and illusions, because they are in reality the active members of this class and have less time to make up ideas and illusions about themselves. This cleavage within the ruling class may even develop into a certain opposition and hostility between the two parts, but in the event of a practical collision in which the class itself is endangered, it disappears of its own accord and with it also the illusion that the ruling ideas were not the ideas of the ruling class and had a power distinct from the power of this class. The existence of revolutionary ideas in a particular age presupposes the existence of a revolutionary class. . . .

If, in considering the course of history, we detach the ideas of the ruling class from the ruling class itself and attribute to them an independent existence, if we confine ourselves to saying that in a particular age these or those ideas were dominant, without paying attention to the conditions of production and the world conditions which are the source of the ideas, it is possible to say, for instance, that during the time that the aristocracy was dominant the concepts honour, loyalty, etc., were dominant; during the dominance of the bourgeoisie the concepts freedom, equality, etc. The ruling class itself in general imagines this to be the case. This conception of history which is common to all historians, particularly since the eighteenth century, will necessarily come up against the phenomenon that increasingly abstract ideas hold sway, i.e. ideas which increasingly take on the form of universality. For each new class which puts itself in the place of the one ruling before it, is compelled, simply in order to achieve its aims, to represent its interest as the common interest of all members of society, i.e. employing an ideal formula, to give its ideas the form of universality and to represent them as the only rational and universally valid ones. The class which makes a revolution appears from the beginning not as a class but as the representative of the whole of society, simply because it is opposed to a *class*. It appears as the whole mass of society confronting the single ruling class. It can do this because at the beginning its interest really is more closely connected with the common interest of all other non-ruling classes and has been unable under the constraint of the previously existing conditions to develop as the particular interest of a particular class. Its victory, therefore, also benefits many individuals of the other classes which are not achieving a dominant position, but only in so far as it now puts these individuals in a position to raise them-

selves into the ruling class. When the French bourgeoisie overthrew the rule of the aristocracy it thereby made it possible for many proletarians to raise themselves above the proletariat, but only in so far as they became bourgeois. Every new class, therefore, achieves its domination only on a broader basis than that of the previous ruling class. On the other hand, the opposition of the non-ruling class to the new ruling class later develops all the more sharply and profoundly. These two characteristics entail that the struggle to be waged against this new ruling class has as its object a more decisive and radical negation of the previous conditions of society than could have been accomplished by all previous classes which aspired to rule.

The German Ideology (with Engels, 1845–1846)

III. Alienation

We shall begin from a *contemporary* economic fact. The worker becomes poorer the more wealth he produces and the more his production increases in power and extent. The worker becomes an ever cheaper commodity the more goods he creates. The *devaluation* of the human world increases in direct relation with the *increase in value* of the world of things. Labor does not only create goods; it also produces itself and the worker as a *commodity*, and indeed in the same proportion as it produces goods.

This fact simply implies that the object produced by labor, its product, now stands opposed to it as an *alien being*, as a *power independent* of the producer. The product of labor is labor which has been embodied in an object and turned into a physical thing; this product is an *objectification* of labor. The performance of work is at the same time its objectification. The performance of work appears in the sphere of political economy as a *vitiation* of the worker, objectification as a *loss* and as *servitude to the object*, and appropriation as *alienation*.

So much does the performance of work appear as vitiation that the worker is vitiated to the point of starvation. So much does objectification appear as loss of the object that the worker is deprived of the most essential things not only of life but also of work. Labor itself becomes an object which he can acquire only by the greatest effort and with unpredictable interruptions. So much does the appropriation of the object appear as alienation that the more objects the worker produces the fewer he can possess and the more he falls under the domination of his product, of capital.

All these consequences follow from the fact that the worker is related to the *product of his labor* as to an *alien object*. For it is clear on this presupposition that the more the worker expends himself in work the more powerful becomes the world of objects which he creates in face of himself, the poorer he becomes in his inner life, and the less he belongs to himself. It is just the same as in religion. The more of himself man attributes to God the less he has left in himself. The worker puts his life into the object, and his life then belongs no longer to himself but to the object. The greater his activity, therefore, the less he possesses. What is embodied in the product of his labor is no longer his own. The greater this product is, therefore, the more he is diminished. The *alienation* of the worker in his product means not only that his labor becomes an object, assumes an external existence, but that it exists independently, *outside himself*, and alien to him, and that it stands opposed to him as an autonomous power. The life which he has given to the object sets itself against him as an alien and hostile force.

Let us now examine more closely the phenomenon of *objectification*, the worker's production and the *alienation* and *loss* of the object it produces, which is involved in it. The worker can create nothing without *nature*, without the *sensuous external world*. The latter is the material in which his labor is realized, in which it is active, out of which and through which it produces things.

But just as nature affords the *means of existence* of labor in the sense that labor cannot *live* without objects upon which it can be exercised, so also it provides the *means of existence* in a narrower sense; namely the means of physical existence for the *worker* himself. Thus, the more the worker *appropriates* the external world of sensuous nature by his labor the more he deprives himself of *means of existence*, in two repects: first, that the sensuous external world becomes progressively less an object belonging to his labor or a means of existence of his labor, and secondly, that it becomes progressively less a means of existence in the direct sense, a means for the physical subsistence of the worker.

In both respects, therefore, the worker becomes a slave of the object; first, in that he receives an *object of work*, i.e., receives *work*, and secondly that he receives *means of subsistence*. Thus the object enables him to exist, first as a *worker* and secondly, as a *physical subject*. The culmination of this enslavement is that he can only maintain himself as a *physical subject* so far as he is worker, and that it is only as a *physical subject* that he is a worker.

(The alienation of the worker in his object is expressed as follows in the laws of political economy: the more the worker produces the less he has to consume; the more value he creates the more worthless he becomes; the more refined his product the more crude and misshapen the worker; the more civilized the product the more barbarous the worker; the more powerful the work the more feeble the worker; the more the work manifests intelligence the more the worker declines in intelligence and becomes a slave of nature.)

Political economy conceals the alienation in the nature of labor insofar as it does not examine the direct relationship between the worker (work) and production. Labor certainly produces marvels for the rich but it produces privation for the worker. It produces palaces, but hovels for the worker. It produces beauty, but deformity for the worker. It replaces labor by machinery, but it casts some of the workers back into a barbarous kind of work and turns the others into machines. It produces intelligence, but also stupidity and cretinism for the workers.

The direct relationship of labor to its products is the relationship of the worker to the objects of his production. The relationship of property owners to the objects of production and to production itself is merely a *consequence* of this first relationship and confirms it. We shall consider this second aspect later.

Thus, when we ask what is the important relationship of labor, we are concerned with the relationship of the *worker* to production.

So far we have considered the alienation of the worker only from one aspect; namely, *his relationship with the products of his labor*. However, alienation appears not only in the result, but also in the *process*, of *production*, within *productive activity* itself. How could the worker stand in an alien relationship to the product of his activity if he did not alienate himself in the act of production itself? The product is indeed only the *résumé* of activity, of production. Consequently, if the product of labor is alienation, production itself must be active alienation—the alienation of activity and the activity of alienation. The alienation of the object of labor merely summarizes the alienation in the work activity itself.

What constitutes the alienation of labor? First, that the work is *external* to the worker, that it is not part of his nature; and that, consequently, he does not fulfill himself in his work but denies himself, has a feeling of misery rather than well being, does not develop freely his mental and physical energies but is physically exhausted and mentally debased. The worker therefore feels himself at home only during his leisure time, whereas at work he feels homeless. His work is not voluntary but imposed, *forced labor*. It is not the satisfaction of a need, but only a *means* for satisfying other needs. Its alien character is clearly shown by the fact that as soon as there is no physical or other compulsion it is avoided like the plague. External labor, labor in which man alienates himself, is a labor of self-sacrifice, of mortification. Finally, the external character of work for the worker is shown by the fact that it is not his own work but work for someone else, that in work he does not belong to himself but to another person.

Just as in religion the spontaneous activity of human fantasy, of the human brain and heart, reacts independently as an alien activity of gods or devils upon the individual, so the activity of the worker is not his own spontaneous activity. It is another's activity and a loss of his own spontaneity.

We arrive at the result that man (the worker) feels himself to be freely active only in his animal functions—eating, drinking and procreating, or at most also in his dwelling and in personal adornment—while in his human functions he is reduced to an animal. The animal becomes human and the human becomes animal.

Eating, drinking and procreating are of course also genuine human functions. But abstractly considered, apart from the environment of other human activities, and turned into final and sole ends, they are animal functions.

We have now considered the act of alienation of practical human activity, labor, from two aspects: (1) the relationship of the worker to the *product of labor* as an alien object which dominates him. This relationship is at the same time the relationship to the sensuous external world, to natural objects, as an alien and hostile world, (2) the relationship of labor to the *act of production* within *labor*. This is the relationship of the worker to his own activity as something alien and not belonging to him, activity as suffering (passivity), strength as powerlessness, creation as emasculation, the *personal* physical and mental energy of the worker, his personal life (for what is life but activity?) as an activity which is directed against himself, independent of him and not belonging to him. This is *self-alienation* as against the above-mentioned alienation of the *thing*.

We have now to infer a third characteristic of *alienated labor* from the two we have considered.

Man is a species-being[5] not only in the sense that he makes the community (his own as well as those of other things) his objects both practically and theoretically, but also (and this is simply another expression for the same thing) in the sense that he treats himself as the present, living species, as a *universal* and consequently free being.

Species-life, for man as for animals, has its physical basis in the fact that man (like animals) lives from inorganic nature, and since man is more universal than an animal so the range of inorganic nature from which he lives is more universal. Plants, animals, minerals, air, light, etc. constitute, from the theoretical aspect, a part of human consciousness as objects of natural science and art; they are man's spiritual inorganic nature, his intellectual means of life, which he must first prepare for enjoyment and perpetuation. So also, from the practical aspect they form a part of human life and activity. In practice man lives only from these natural products, whether in the form of food, heating, clothing, housing, etc. The universality of man appears in practice in the universality which makes the whole of nature into his inorganic body: (1) as a direct means of life; and equally (2) as the material object and instrument of his life activity. Nature is the *inorganic body* of man;

---

[5] The term "species-being" is taken from Feuerbach's *Das Wesen des Christentums* (The Essence of Christianity). Feuerbach used the notion in making a distinction between consciousness in man and in animals. Man is conscious not merely of himself as an individual but of the human species or "human essence."—*Tr. Note*

that is to say, nature excluding the human body itself. To say that man *lives* from nature means that nature is his *body* with which he must remain in a continuous interchange in order not to die. The statement that the physical and mental life of man, and nature, are interdependent means simply that nature is interdependent with itself, for man is a part of nature.

Since alienated labor: (1) alienates nature from man; and (2) alienates man from himself, from his own active function, his life activity; so it alienates him from the species. It makes *species-life* into a means of individual life. In the first place it alienates species-life and individual life, and secondly, it turns the latter, as an abstraction, into the purpose of the former, also in its abstract and alienated form.

For labor, *life activity, productive life*, now appear to man only as *means* for the satisfaction of a need, the need to maintain his physical existence. Productive life is, however, species-life. It is life creating life. In this type of life activity resides the whole character of a species, its species-character; and free, conscious activity is the species-character of human beings. Life itself appears only as a *means of life*.

The animal is one with its life activity. It does not distinguish the activity from itself. It is *its activity*. But man makes his life activity itself an object of his will and consciousness. He has a conscious life activity. It is not a determination with which he is completely identified. Conscious life activity distinguishes man from the life activity of animals. Only for this reason is he a species-being. Or rather, he is only a self-conscious being, i.e. his own life is an object for him, because he is a species-being. Only for this reason is his activity free activity. Alienated labor reverses the relationship, in that man because he is a self-conscious being makes his life activity, his *being*, only a means for his *existence*.

The practical construction of an *objective world*, the *manipulation* of inorganic nature, is the confirmation of man as a conscious species-being, i.e. a being who treats the species as his own being or himself as a species-being. Of course, animals also produce. They construct nests, dwellings, as in the case of bees, beavers, ants, etc. But they only produce what is strictly necessary for themselves or their young. They produce only in a single direction, while man produces universally. They produce only under the compulsion of direct physical need, while man produces when he is free from physical need and only truly produces in freedom from such need. Animals produce only themselves, while man reproduces the whole of nature. The products of animal production belong directly to their physical bodies, while man is free in face of his product. Animals construct only in accordance with the standards and needs of the species to which they belong, while man knows how to produce in accordance with the standards of every species and knows how to apply the appropriate standard to the object. Thus man constructs also in accordance with the laws of beauty.

It is just in his work upon the objective world that man really proves himself as a *species-being*. This production is his active species life. By means of it nature appears as *his* work and his reality. The object of labor is, therefore, the *objectification of man's species life*; for he no longer reproduces himself merely intellectually, as in consciousness, but actively and in a real sense, and he sees his own reflection in a world which he has constructed. While, therefore, alienated labor takes away the object of production from man, it also takes away his *species life*, his real objectivity as a species-being, and changes his advantage over animals into a disadvantage in so far as his inorganic body, nature, is taken from him.

Just as alienated labor transforms free and self-directed activity into a means, so it transforms the species life of man into a means of physical existence.

Consciousness, which man has from his species, is transformed through alienation so that species life becomes only a means for him.

(3) Thus alienated labor turns the *species life of man*, and also nature as his mental species-property, into an *alien* being and into a *means* for his *individual existence*. It alienates from man his own body, external nature, his mental life and his *human* life.

(4) A direct consequence of the alienation of man from the product of his activity and from his species life is that *man is alienated* from other *men*. When man confronts himself he also confronts *other* men. What is true of man's relationship to his work, to the product of his work and to himself, is also true of his relationship to other

men, to their labor and to the objects of their labor.

In general, the statement that man is alienated from his species life means that each man is alienated from others, and that each of the others is likewise alienated from human life.

Human alienation, and above all the relation of man to himself, is first realized and expressed in the relationship between each man and other men. Thus in the relationship of alienated labor every man regards other men according to the standards and relationships in which he finds himself placed as a worker.

We began with an economic fact, the alienation of the worker and his production. We have expressed this fact in conceptual terms as *alienated labor*, and in analyzing the concept we have merely analyzed an economic fact.

Let us now examine further how this concept of alienated labor must express and reveal itself in reality. If the product of labor is alien to me and confronts me as an alien power, to whom does it belong? If my own activity does not belong to me but is an alien, forced activity, to whom does it belong? To a being *other* than myself. And who is this being? The *gods*? It is apparent in the earliest stages of advanced production, e.g., temple building, etc. in Egypt, India, Mexico, and in the service rendered to gods, that the product belonged to the gods. But the gods alone were never the lords of labor. And no more was *nature*. What a contradiction it would be if the more man subjugates nature by his labor, and the more the marvels of the gods are

rendered superfluous by the marvels of industry, he should abstain from his joy in producing and his enjoyment of the product for love of these powers.

The *alien* being to whom labor and the product of labor belong, to whose service labor is devoted, and to whose enjoyment the product of labor goes, can only be *man* himself. If the product of labor does not belong to the worker, but confronts him as an alien power, this can only be because it belongs to *a man other than the worker*. If his activity is a torment to him it must be a source of enjoyment and pleasure to another. Not the gods, nor nature, but only man himself can be this alien power over men.

Economic and Philosophical Manuscripts (1844)

The so-called Revolutions of 1848 were but poor incidents—small fractures and fissures in the dry crust of European society. However, they denounced the abyss. Beneath the apparently solid surface, they betrayed oceans of liquid matter, only needing expansion to rend into fragments continents of hard rock. Noisedly and confusedly they proclaimed the emancipation of the proletarian, *i.e.*, the secret of the nineteenth century, and of the revolution of that century. That social revolution, it is true, was no novelty invented in 1848. Steam, electricity, and the self-acting mule were revolutionists of a rather more dangerous character than even citizens Barbès, Raspail and Blanqui. But, although the atmosphere in which we live weighs upon everyone with a

20,000 pound force, do you feel it? No more than European society before 1848 felt the revolutionary atmosphere enveloping and pressing it from all sides.

There is one great fact, characteristic of this, our nineteenth century, a fact which no party dares deny. On the one hand, there have started into life industrial and scientific forces, which no epoch of the former human history had ever suspected. On the other hand, there exist symptoms of decay, far surpassing the horrors recorded of the latter times of the Roman empire. In our days everything seems pregnant with its contrary; machinery gifted with the wonderful power of shortening and fructifying human labor, we behold starving and overworking it. The new-fangled sources of wealth, by some strange weird spell, are turned into sources of want. The victories of art seem bought by the loss of character. At the same pace that mankind masters nature, man seems to become enslaved to other men or to his own infamy. Even the pure light of science seems unable to shine but on the dark background of ignorance. All our inventions and progress seem to result in endowing material forces with intellectual life, and in stultifying human life into a material force. This antagonism between modern industry and science on the one hand, modern misery and dissolution on the other hand; this antagonism between the productive powers and the social relations of our epoch, is a fact, palpable, overwhelming, and not to be controverted. Some parties may wail over it; others may wish to get rid of modern arts in order to get rid of modern conflicts. Or they may imagine that so signal a progress in industry wants to be completed by as signal a regress in politics.

On our part, we do not mistake the shape of the shrewd spirit that continues to mark all these contradictions. We know that to work well the new-fangled forces of society, they only want to be mastered by new-fangled men—and such are the working men. They are as much the invention of modern times as machinery itself. In the signs that bewilder the middle class, the aristocracy and the poor prophets of regression, we do recognize our brave friend, Robin Goodfellow, the old mole that can work in the earth so fast, that worthy pioneer—the revolution. The English working men are the first born sons of modern industry. They will then, certainly, not be the last in aiding the social revolution produced by that industry, a revolution, which means the emancipation of their own class all over the world, which is as universal as capital-rule and wages-slavery. I know the heroic struggles the English working class have gone through since the middle of the last century—struggles less glorious because they are shrouded in obscurity and buried by the middle class historians. To revenge the misdeeds of the ruling class there existed in the middle ages in Germany a secret tribunal, called the "Vehmgericht." If a red cross was seen marked on a house people knew that its owner was doomed by the "Vehm." All the houses of Europe are now marked with the mysterious red cross.

History is the judge—its executioner, the proletarian.

Speech by Marx at the anniversary celebration of the *People's Paper*, a Chartist publication, in April 1856.

IV. Communist Revolution and Future Society

(1) In the development of the productive forces a stage is reached where productive forces and means of intercourse are called into being which, under the existing relations, can only work mischief, and which are, therefore, no longer productive, but destructive, forces (machinery and money). Associated with this is the emergence of a class which has to bear all the burdens of society without enjoying its advantages, which is excluded from society and is forced into the most resolute opposition to all other classes; a class which comprises the majority of the members of society and in which there develops a consciousness of the need for a fundamental revolution, the communist consciousness. This consciousness can, of course, also arise in other classes from the observation of the situation of this class.

(2) The conditions under which determinate productive forces can be used are also the conditions for the dominance of a determinate social class, whose social power, derived from its property ownership, invariably finds its *practical* and ideal expression in a particular form of the State. Consequently, every revolutionary struggle is directed against the class which has so far been dominant.

(3) In all former revolutions the form of activity was always left unaltered and it was only a question of redistributing this activity among different people, of introducing a new division of labour. The communist revolution, however, is directed against the former *mode* of activity, does away with *labour*, and abolishes all class rule along with the classes themselves, because it is effected by the class which no longer counts as a class in society, which is not recognized as a class, and which is the expression of the dissolution of all classes, nationalities, etc., within contemporary society.

(4) For the creation on a mass scale of this communist consciousness, as well as for the success of the cause itself, it is necessary for men themselves to be changed on a large scale, and this change can only occur in a practical movement, in a *revolution*. Revolution is necessary not only because the *ruling* class cannot be overthrown in any other way, but also because only in a revolution can *the class which overthrows it* rid itself of the accumulated rubbish of the past and become capable of reconstructing society. . . .

The transformation of personal powers (relationships) into material powers through the division of labour cannot be undone again merely by dismissing the idea of it from one's mind, but only by the action of individuals who reestablish their control over these material powers and abolish the division of labour. This is not possible without a community. Only in association with others has each individual the means of cultivating his talents in all directions. Only in a community therefore is personal freedom possible. In the previous substitutes for community, in the State, etc., personal freedom existed only for those individuals who grew up in the ruling class and only in so far as they were members of this class. The illusory community in which, up to the present, individuals have combined, always acquired an independent existence apart from them, and since it was a union of one class against another it represented for the dominated class not only a completely illusory community but also a new shackle. In a genuine community individuals gain their freedom in and through their association.

The German Ideology (1845–1846)

The possessing class and the proletarian class express the same human alienation. But the former is satisfied with its situation, feels itself well established in it, recognizes this self-alienation as *its own* power, and thus has the appearance of a human existence. The latter feels itself crushed by this self-alienation, sees in it its own impotence and the reality of an inhuman situation. It is, to use an expression of Hegel's, "in the midst of degradation the *revolt* against degradation," a revolt to which it is forced by the contradiction between its *humanity* and its situation, which is an open, clear and absolute negation of its humanity. Within the framework of alienation, therefore, the property owners are the *conservative* and the proletarians the *destructive* party.

It is true that, in its economic development, private property advances towards its own dissolution; but it only does this through a development which is independent of itself, unconscious and achieved against its will—solely because it produces the proletariat *as* proletariat, poverty conscious of its moral and physical poverty, degradation conscious of its degradation, and for this reason trying to abolish itself. The proletariat carries out the sentence which private property, by creating the proletariat, passes upon itself, just as it carries out the sentence which wage-labour, by creating wealth for others and poverty for itself, passes upon itself. If the proletariat triumphs this does not mean that it becomes the absolute form of society, for it is only victorious by abolishing itself as well as its opposite. Thus the proletariat disappears along with the opposite which conditions it, private property.

If socialist writers attribute this world-historical role to the proletariat this is not at all . . . because they regard the proletarians as *gods*. On the contrary, in the fully developed proletariat, everything human is taken away, even the *appearance* of humanity. In the conditions of existence of the proletariat are condensed, in their most inhuman form, all the conditions of existence of present-day society. Man has lost himself, but he has not only acquired, at the same time, a theoretical consciousness of his loss, he has been forced, by an ineluctable and imperious *distress*—by practical *necessity*—to revolt against this inhumanity. It is for these reasons that the proletariat can and must emancipate itself. But it can only emancipate itself by destroying its own conditions of existence. It can only destroy its own conditions of existence by destroying *all* the inhuman conditions of existence of present-day society, conditions which are epitomized in its situation. It is not in vain that it passes through the rough but stimulating school of *labour*. It is not a matter of knowing what this or that proletarian, or even the proletariat as a whole, *conceives* as its aims at any particular moment. It is a question of knowing *what* the proletariat *is*, and what it must historically accomplish in accordance with its *nature*. Its aim and its historical activity are ordained for it, in a tangible and irrevocable way, by its own situation as well as by the whole organization of present-day civil society. It is unnecessary to show here that a large part of the English and French proletariat has already become *aware* of its historic mission, and works incessantly to clarify this awareness.

The Holy Family (with Engels, 1845)

. . . [A]s heavy industry develops, the creation of real wealth depends less on labor time and on the quantity of labor utilized than on the power of mechanical agents which are set in motion during labor time. The powerful effectiveness of these agents, in its turn bears no relation to the immediate labor time that their production costs. It depends rather on the general state of science and on technological progress, or the application of this science to production. (The development of science—especially of the natural sciences and with them all of the others—is itself once more related to the development of material production.) Agriculture, for example, is a pure application of the science of material metabolism, and the most advantageous way of employing it for the good of society as a whole.

Real wealth develops much more (as is disclosed by heavy industry) in the enormous disproportion between the labor time utilized and its product, and also in the qualitative disproportion between labor that has been reduced to a mere abstraction, and the power of the production process that it supervises. Labor does not seem any more to be an essential part of the process of production. The human factor is restricted to watching and supervising the production process. (This applies not only to machinery, but also to the combination of human activities and the development of human commerce.)

The worker no longer inserts transformed natural objects as intermediaries between the material and himself; he now inserts the natural process that he has transformed into an industrial one between himself and inorganic nature, over which he has achieved mastery. He is no longer the principal agent of the production process: He exists alongside it. In this transformation, what appears as the mainstay of production and wealth is neither the immediate labor performed by the worker, nor the time that he works, but the appropriation by man of his own general productive force, his understanding of nature and the mastery of it; in a word, the development of the social individual. The theft of others' labor time upon which wealth depends today seems to be a miserable basis compared with this newly developed foundation that has been created by heavy industry itself. As soon as labor, in its direct form, has ceased to be the main source of wealth, then labor time ceases, and must cease, to be its standard of measurement, and thus exchange value must cease to be the measurement of use value. The surplus labor of the masses has ceased to be a condition for the development of wealth in general; in the same way that the nonlabor of the few has ceased to be a condition for the development of the general powers of the human mind. Production based on exchange value therefore falls apart, and the immediate process of material production finds itself stripped of its impoverished, antagonistic form. Individuals are then in a position to develop freely. It is no longer a question of reducing the necessary labor time in order to create surplus labor, but of reducing the necessary labor of society to a minimum. The counterpart of this reduction is that all members of society can develop their education in the arts, sciences, etc., thanks to the free time and means available to all.

—*The Grundrisse: Foundations of the Critique of Political Economy* (1857–1858; translated 1971 by David McLellan)

The realm of freedom only begins, in fact, where that labour which is determined by need and external purposes, ceases; it is therefore, by its very nature, outside the sphere of material production proper. Just as the savage must wrestle with Nature in order to satisfy his wants, to maintain and reproduce his life, so also must civilized man, and he must do it in all forms of society and under any possible mode of production. With his development the realm of natural necessity expands, because his wants increase, but at the same time the forces of production, by which these wants are satisfied, also increase. Freedom in this field cannot consist of anything else but the fact that socialized mankind, the associated producers, regulate their interchange with Nature rationally, bring it under their common control, instead of being ruled by it as by some blind power, and accomplish their task with the least expenditure of energy and under such conditions as are proper and worthy for human beings. Nevertheless, this always remains a realm of necessity. Beyond it begins that development of human potentiality for its own sake, the true realm of freedom, which however can only flourish upon that realm of necessity as its basis. The shortening of the working day is its fundamental prerequisite.

Capital, Vol. III (published posthumously)

What we have to deal with here is a communist society, not as it has *developed* on its own foundation, but, on the contrary, just as it *emerges* from capitalist society; and which is thus in every respect, economically, morally and intellectually, still stamped with the birth-marks of the old society from whose womb it emerges. Accordingly, the individual producer receives back from society—after the deductions have been made—exactly what he contributes to it. What he has contributed to it is his individual quantum of labour. For example, the social working day consists of the sum of the individual hours of work; the individual labour-time of the individual producer is the part of the social working day contributed by him, his share in it. He receives a certificate from society that he has furnished such and such an amount of labour (after deducting his labour for the common funds), and with this certificate he draws from the social stock of means of consumption as much as costs the same amount of labour. The same amount of labour which he has given to society in one form he receives back in another.

Here obviously the same principle prevails as that which regulates the exchange of commodities, as far as this is exchange of equal values. Content and form are changed, because under the altered conditions no one can give anything except his labour, and because on the other hand, nothing can pass into the ownership of individuals except individual means of consumption. But, as far as the distribution of the latter among the individual producers is concerned, the same principle prevails as in the exchange of commodity-equivalents: a given amount of labour in another form.

Hence, *equal right* here is still in principle—*bourgeois right*, although principle and practice are no longer at loggerheads, whereas the exchange of equivalents in commodity exchange only exists *on the average* and not in the individual case.

In spite of this advance, *equal right* is still burdened with bourgeois limitations. The right of the producers is *proportional* to the labour they supply; the equality consists in the fact that measurement is made with an *equal standard, labour.*

But one man is superior to another physically or mentally and so supplies more labour in the same time, or can labour for a longer time; and labour, to serve as a measure, must be defined by its duration or intensity, otherwise it ceases to be a standard of measurement. The *equal* right is an unequal right for unequal labour. It recognizes no class differences, because everyone is only a worker like everyone else; but it tacitly recognizes unequal individual endowment, and thus natural privileges in respect of productive capacity. *It is, therefore, in its content, a right of inequality, like every right.* Right by its very nature can consist only in the application of an equal standard; but unequal individuals (and they would not be different individuals if they were not unequal) can only be assessed by an equal standard in so far as they are regarded from a single aspect, from one particular side only, as for instance, in the present case, they are regarded *only as workers,* and nothing more is seen in them, everything else being ignored. Further, one worker is married, another not; one has more children than another, and so on. Thus, with an equal performance of labour, and hence an equal share in the social consumption fund, one individual will in fact receive more than another, one will be richer than another, and so on. To avoid all these defects, right instead of being equal would have to be unequal.

But these defects are inevitable in the first phase of communist society as it is when it has just emerged after prolonged birth-pangs from capitalist society. Right can never be higher than the economic structure of society and the cultural development conditioned by it.

In a higher phase of communist society, when the enslaving subordination of the individual to the division of labour, and with it the antithesis between mental and physical labour, has vanished; when labour is no longer merely a means of life but has become life's principal need; when the productive forces have also increased with the all-round development of the individual, and all the springs of co-operative wealth flow more abundantly—only then will it be possible completely to transcend the narrow outlook of bourgeois right and only then will society be able to inscribe on its banners: From each according to his ability, to each according to his needs!

Critique of the Gotha Program (1875)

COMMENT

In this chapter we are dealing with an extremely complex thinker whose ideas were not only ambiguous but subject to change and development. Marx once even remarked, "One thing I know and that is that I am not a Marxist."[1] He was aware of the common tendency among "Marxists" to reduce and distort his ideas, being perhaps as misinterpreted by friend as by foe.

Despite some unguarded statements, his theory was not a simple-minded economic determinism. An example of the ambiguity and complexity of his doctrine is the passage that we have quoted from his Preface to *A Contribution to the Critique of Political Economy*. One interpretation is that the economic system is the "base" that "determines" the political and cultural "superstructure." According to this view, the various strata in the social order—the economy, the state with its laws, and the cultural spheres of art, science, philosophy, religion, and morality—are all distinct and externally related factors, in which the "higher," the political and cultural, are determined by the "lower," the economic. This interpretation becomes less convincing when we ask certain questions. When Marx repeatedly uses the word "material," does he mean simply "economic," or does he mean to include the biological constitution of the human being and the interaction between man and external nature? Does Marx believe that thought processes are no more than epiphenomena or echoes of economic factors? Or is he saying that a certain form of thought—ideology—is an echo, but that there are other forms of thought that are relatively independent? Can we characterize the base without introducing something from the superstructure, such as science, law, or art? If not, is the base-superstructure metaphor awkward and misleading?

We should be on our guard against interpreting the Marxian theory as a pure economic determinism. Marx refers in many passages to the influence of political and cultural factors on the economic system. The following statement is an example:

> All circumstances . . . which affect man . . . have a greater or lesser influence upon all his functions and activities, including his functions and activities as the

<hr>

[1] Karl Marx and Friedrich Engels, *Selected Correspondence* (New York: International Publishers, 1936), p. 472.

creator of material wealth, or commodities. In this sense, it can truly be asserted that all human relations and functions, however and wherever they manifest themselves, influence material production and have a more or less determining effect upon it.[2]

Marx thus maintained that all sorts of forces enter into the very complex interaction of causal factors. It is an interaction of unequal forces of which the economic, in the long run, are by far the most powerful.

Contrary to the usual interpretation of his doctrine, he did not suppose that all history can be arranged in a definite series of stages, beginning with primitive communism and going on to slavery, feudalism, capitalism, socialism, and finally advanced communism. In his Preface to *Capital*, we must admit, he seems to be espousing a rigid scheme of historical development." "The natural laws of capitalist production," he said, are "working with iron necessity toward inevitable results. The country that is more developed industrially only shows, to the less developed, the image of its own future." But commenting on this statement in a letter to a Russian sympathizer, Vera Zasulich, he explained that he meant to restrict "the historical inevitability of this line of development to the countries of Western Europe." Elsewhere he pointed out that the historical development in India, China, and Russia deviated greatly from the pattern in Western Europe. In his *Economic and Philosophical Manuscripts* (1844), he distinguished between democratic and autocratic forms of communism, and in his famous speech at the Hague in 1872 he declared that the "emancipation of the workers" may be achieved peacefully in the more democratic countries. Thus he advocated a complex multilinear theory of history rather than the simple unilinear theory that is usually attributed to him.

In a passage in the *Manuscripts* referring to some radical theories then extant, he condemned raw and repressive forms of communism. "This entirely crude and unreflective communism," he declared, "would negate the personality of man in every sphere. . . . It would be a system in which universal envy sets itself up as a power, and . . . in this form of envy, it would reduce everything to a common level." "Crude communism," he went on to say, "is only the culmination of such envy and levelling down to a preconceived minimum." He spoke of it as "the negation of the whole world of culture and civilization.[3]

These remarks were made in 1844, but in his later works, Marx occasionally recognized the dangers of collectivism and bureaucracy. In the 1850s he wrote articles for the New York *Daily Tribune* in which he characterized "Oriental despotism," the state managerialism of the old Asiatic societies, as dooming the masses to a kind of "general [state] slavery."[4] In his comments of 1871 on the

[3] *Economic and Philosophical Manuscripts*, in T. B. Bottomore, *Karl Marx: Early Writings* (London: C. A. Watts & Co., 1963), pp. 153–154.

[2] *Theories of Surplus Value*, in Marx, *Selected Writings in Sociology and Social Philosophy*, edited by T. B. Bottomore and M. Rubel (C. A. Watts & Co. Ltd., 1956), p. 100.

[4] See Karl Wittfogel, *Oriental Despotism* (New Haven, Conn.: Yale University Press, 1959).

Paris Commune, he emphasized the need for popular control of the revolutionary government, warning against bureaucracy and militarism. His ultimate ideal was to abolish the coercive state and to organize society on a decentralized basis. His works contain an impassioned protest against the dehumanizing process of mass industry, with its tendency toward the depersonalization of life. Although expressed most fully in the early *Economic and Philosophical Manuscripts*, his theory of "alienation" remains basic in the later works, but more often implicit than explicit. For example, Marx's speech at the anniversary celebration of the *People's Paper* (1856), mentions two basic sides of the process of alienation: first, material forces taking on "life" and dominating human beings, and second, life being stultified into a material force. Marx seldom used the *word* "alienation" in his later publications, but in his unpublished manuscript *Grundrisse der Kritik der politischen Ökonomie* (1857–1858) the word occurs frequently. In these later works, he still thought of man as estranged from other men, from his work, from his products, from his society, from nature. He also clung to the ideal of dealienation, demanding that human beings be treated as human beings, and things as things. A nonalienated man would be truly a man, free, creative, well-rounded, no longer the victim of impersonal forces.

Hegel and Marx

A comparison of Marx and Hegel on the philosophy of history will throw light on both men. I shall first summarize the ideas that they share. History is visualized in terms of historical stages. The dynamism of historical change is the conflict of opposites: in Hegel, the battle of great ideas or cultural forces; in Marx, the conflict between static class-structure and dynamic technology, and between the bourgeoisie and the proletariat, or between other historical classes. Each stage is at first an advance, but contradictions develop: the old fetters the new, the traditions fetter the innovations. A social crisis results from this state of conflict and disequilibrium: legitimate wants are frustrated, resources are unused or misused, potentialities are fettered by the disproportionate development of societal factors, and dissenters arise to challenge and overthrow the existing order. Mankind thus evolves from stage to stage through conflict and alienation. Human beings become more or less conscious of their alienation, and they move through it and out of it into a new measure of freedom. The conflicts in history, the sufferings and the alienations, are necessary for human progress. The ideal— "the transition from the kingdom of necessity to the kingdom of freedom"— comes only at the end of the process. So much for the similarities.

The differences are sharp and profound. Marx's emphasis upon economic forces and material needs is very different from Hegel's emphasis on human reason and spirituality. The Marxian vision of history as culminating in the abolition of economic classes and "the withering away of the state" has no counterpart in Hegel. The final stages in Hegel's scenario are the strong national state and the hierarchical class-structure in a world of competing states and classes. So far as there is reconciliation it is within and through the state. All this is contrary to Marx.

Criticism

Marx has been subjected to intense criticism. Among the complaints or grounds of attack are the following:

1. CLASHING INTERPRETATIONS AND THE CHARGE OF INCONSISTENCY. The gulf that separates the humanistic and the antihumanistic interpretations of Marx is wide. Some interpreters consider him an economic or technological determinist—others believe that he had a wider, holistic concept of historical forces. Some find an almost exclusive emphasis on "external" factors, such as industrial technology and class-structure—others find a strong emphasis on the "inner" factors of need, alienation, and activist ideals. Some regard him as a forerunner of twentieth-century totalitarianism—others hail him as a sincere advocate of social democracy. Faced with this babble of voices, still others dismiss his theories as muddled and inconsistent.

2. THE UNRELIABILITY OF HISTORICAL PROPHECY. History has not altogether turned out as Marx expected. He apparently thought that capitalism would crumble before the end of the nineteenth century, but in much of the world it is still entrenched. Intermediate forms—such as the "social welfare state" and state-regulated capitalism—have flourished to an extent that he did not foresee. Where socialist revolution initially occurred, it has been in backward countries such as Czarist Russia and nonindustrialized China, not as Marx expected in advanced industrial countries. Evils of the old order, such as massive repression, have lingered on and in some cases have been intensified.

A defender of Marx might reply that he foresaw the future better than most of his contemporaries. Quite so. But the question can be raised whether long-range historical prophecies ever can be very accurate. Karl Popper has said that the error of Marxists has been to mistake historical trends for inexorable laws. Trends depend on underlying conditions that are subject to change; whereas laws, such as Newton's law of gravity, are fixed in the nature of things. Popper also points out that discoveries and inventions cannot be known in advance—otherwise they would not be *real* inventions and discoveries. Hence there is a *built-in* unpredictability in a scientific-technological type of society, where inventions and discoveries abound.

3. THE QUESTION OF HOLISM. In a number of important passages Marx uses such terms as "totality" and "social organism" to characterize the structure and interdependence of social phenomena. In this respect he illustrates a common trend in recent social theory. Although naive comparisons of societies and biological organ-

isms have generally been abandoned, holistic interpretations under such names as "functionalism," "system theory," "structuralism," "totality," "organicism," and "methodological holism" are as prevalent as ever. Opposed to these interpretations are theories of an individualistic or pluralistic type. Corresponding to this division in theory is a division in practice—on the one hand, "holistic social engineering," on the other hand, "piecemeal social engineering"—the one revolutionary, the other limited and experimental. We have touched upon questions of far-reaching implications that transcend the necessary limits of the present book.

4. THE QUESTION OF UTOPIANISM. Marx was severely critical of the "Utopian socialists," such as Robert Owen in England and Charles Fourier in France. Nevertheless, he has been charged with being Utopian himself. Charles Taylor, for example, speaks of his "terribly unreal notion of freedom" and "wildly, unrealistic notion of the transition" to communism.[5] Whether Marx was as unrealistic as Taylor charges is debatable. The passage that I have quoted from the *Grundrisse*, for example, is a shrewd anticipation of the automation so prevalent in the late twentieth century. Marx, it can be argued, was realistically aware that freedom can flourish only on the basis of advanced technology.

I have touched upon a few of the critical questions to which Marx's theory gives rise. The arguments pro and con are worth careful consideration.

[5] *Hegel* (Cambridge University Press, 1975), pp. 554, 557.

17

Liberal Democracy

JOHN STUART MILL

(For biographical note see pages 440.)

On Liberty

Chapter I

Introductory

. . . The object of this Essay is to asssert one very simple principle, as entitled to govern absolutely the dealings of society with the individual in the way of compulsion and control, whether the means used be physical force in the form of legal penalties, or the moral coercion of public opinion. That principle is, that the sole end for which mankind are warranted, in-

On Liberty was first published in London in 1859.

dividually or collectively, in interfering with the liberty of action of any of their number, is self-protection. That the only purpose for which power can be rightfully exercised over any member of a civilized community, against his will, is to prevent harm to others. His own good, either physical or moral, is not a sufficient warrant. He cannot rightfully be compelled to do or forbear because it will be better for him to do so, because it will make him happier, because, in the opinions of others, to do so would be wise, or even right. These are good reasons for remonstrating with him, or reasoning with him, or persuading him, or entreating him, but not for compelling him, or visiting him with any evil in case he do otherwise. To justify that, the conduct from which it is desired to deter him must be calculated to produce evil to some one else. The only part of the conduct of anyone, for which he is amenable to society, is that which concerns others. In the part which merely concerns himself, his independence is, of right, absolute. Over himself, over his own body and mind, the individual is sovereign.

It is perhaps hardly necessary to say that this doctrine is meant to apply only to human beings in the maturity of their faculties. We are not speaking of children, or of young persons below the age which the law may fix as that of manhood or womanhood. Those who are still in a state to require being taken care of by others, must be protected against their own actions as well as against external injury. For the same reason, we may leave out of consideration those backward states of society in which the race itself may be considered as in its nonage. The early difficulties in the way of spontaneous progress are so great, and there is seldom any choice of means for overcoming them; and a ruler full of the spirit of improvement is warranted in the use of any expedients that will attain an end, perhaps otherwise unattainable. Despotism is a legitimate mode of government in dealing with barbarians, provided the end be their improvement, and the means justified by actually effecting that end. Liberty, as a principle, has no application to any state of things anterior to the time when mankind have become capable of being improved by free and equal discussion. Until then, there is nothing for them but implicit obedience to an Akbar or a Charlemagne, if they are so fortunate as to find one. But as soon as mankind have attained the capacity of being guided to their own improvement by conviction or persuasion (a period long since reached in all nations with whom we need here concern ourselves), compulsion, either in the direct form or in that of pains and penalties for noncompliance, is no longer admissible as a means to their own good, and justifiable only for the security of others.

It is proper to state that I forego any advantage which could be derived to my argument from the idea of abstract right, as a thing independent of utility. I regard utility as the ultimate appeal on all ethical questions; but it must be utility in the largest sense, grounded on the permanent interests of a man as a progressive being. Those interests, I contend, authorized the subjection of individual spontaneity to external control, only in respect to those actions of each which concern the interest of other people. If anyone does an act hurtful to others, there is a *prima facie* case for punishing him, by law, or, where legal penalties are not safely applicable, by general disapprobation. There are also many positive acts for the benefit of others, which he may rightfully be compelled to perform: such as to give evidence in a court of justice; to bear his fair share in the common defense, or in any other joint work necessary to the interest of the society of which he enjoys the protection; and to perform certain acts of individual beneficence, such as saving a fellow-creature's life, or interposing to protect the defenseless against ill-usage, things which wherever it is obviously a man's duty to do, he may rightfully be made responsible to society for not doing. A person may cause evil to others not only by his actions but by his inaction, and in either case he is justly accountable to them for the injury. The latter case, it is true, requires a much more cautious exercise of compulsion than the former. To make anyone answerable for doing evil to others is the rule; to make him answerable for not preventing evil is, comparatively speaking, the exception. Yet there are many cases clear enough and grave enough to justify that exception. In all things which regard the external relations of the individual, he is *de jure* amenable to those whose interests are concerned, and, if need be, to society as their protector. There are often good reasons for not holding him to the responsibility; but these reasons must arise from the special expediencies of the case: either because it is a kind of case in which he is on the whole likely to act better, when left to his own discretion, than when controlled in any way in which society have it in their power to control him; or because the attempt to exercise control would produce other evils, greater than those which it would prevent. When such reasons as these preclude the enforcement of responsibility, the conscience of the agent himself should step into the vacant judgment seat, and protect those interests of others which have no external protection; judging himself all the more rigidly, because the case does not admit of his being made accountable to the judgment of his fellow-creatures.

But there is a sphere of action in which society, as distinguished from the individual, has, if any, only an indirect interest; comprehending all that portion of a person's life and conduct which affects only himself, or if it also affects others, only with their free, voluntary, and undeceived consent and participation. When I say only himself, I mean directly, and in the first instance; for whatever affects himself, may affect others through himself; and the objection which may be grounded on this contingency, will receive consideration in the sequel. This, then, is the appropriate region of human liberty. It comprises, *first,* the inward domain of consciousness; demanding liberty of conscience in the most comprehensive sense; liberty of thought and feeling; absolute freedom of opinion and sentiment on all subjects, practical or speculative, scientific, moral or theological. The liberty of expressing and publishing opinions may seem to fall under a different principle, since it belongs to that part of the conduct of an individual which concerns other people; but, being almost of as much importance as the liberty of thought itself, and resting in great part on the same reasons, is practically inseparable from it. *Secondly,* the principle requires liberty of tastes and pursuits; of framing the plan of our life to suit our own character; of doing as we like, subject to such consequences as may follow: without impediment from our fellow-creatures, so long as what we do does not harm them, even though they should think our conduct foolish, perverse, or wrong. *Thirdly,* from this liberty of each individual, follows the liberty, within the same limits, of combination among individuals; freedom to unite, for any purpose not involving harm to others: the persons combining being supposed to be of full age, and not forced or deceived.

No society in which these liberties are not, on the whole, respected, is free, whatever may be its form of government; and none is completely free in which they do not exist absolute and unqualified. The only freedom which deserves the name, is that of pursuing our own good in our own way, so long as we do not attempt to deprive others of theirs, or impede their efforts to obtain it. Each is the proper guardian of his own health, whether bodily, or mental and spiritual. Mankind are greater gainers by suffering each other to live as seems good to themselves, than by compelling each to live as seems good to the rest.

Though this doctrine is anything but new, and, to some persons, may have the air of a truism, there is no doctrine which stands more directly opposed to the general tendency of existing opinion and practice. . . . There is . . . an inclination to stretch unduly the powers of society over the individual, both by the force of opinion and even by that of legislation; and as the tendency of all the changes taking place in the world is to strengthen society, and diminish the power of the individual, this encroachment is not one of the evils which tend spontaneously to disappear, but, on the contrary, to grow more and more formidable. The disposition of mankind, whether as rulers or as fellow-citizens,

to impose their own opinions and inclinations as a rule of conduct on others, is so energetically supported by some of the best and by some of the worst feelings incident to human nature, that it is hardly ever kept under restraint by anything but want of power; and as the power is not declining, but growing, unless a strong barrier of moral conviction can be raised against the mischief, we must expect, in the present circumstances of the world, to see it increase. . . .

Chapter II

Of the Liberty of Thought and Discussion

The time, it is to be hoped, is gone by, when any defence would be necessary of the "liberty of the press" as one of the securities against corrupt or tyrannical government. . . . Speaking generally, it is not, in constitutional countries, to be apprehended that the government, whether completely responsible to the people or not, will often attempt to control the expression of opinion, except when in doing so it makes itself the organ of the general intolerance of the public. Let us suppose, therefore, that the government is entirely at one with the people, and never thinks of exerting any power of coercion unless in agreement with what it conceives to be their voice. But I deny the right of the people to exercise such coercion, either by themselves or by their government. The power itself is illegitimate. The best government has no more title to it than the worst. It is as noxious, or more noxious, when exerted in accordance with public opinion, than when in opposition to it. If all mankind minus one were of one opinion, and only one person were of the contrary opinion, mankind would be no more justified in silencing that one person, than he, if he had the power, would be justified in silencing mankind. Were an opinion a personal possession of no value except to the owner; if to be obstructed in the enjoyment of it were simply a private injury, it would make some difference whether the injury was inflicted only on a few persons or on many. But the peculiar evil of silencing the expression of an opinion is, that it is robbing the human race: posterity as well as the existing generation; those who dissent from the opinion, still more than those who hold it. If the opinion is right, they are deprived of the opportunity of exchanging error for truth; if wrong, they lose, what is almost as great a benefit, the clearer perception and livelier impression of truth, produced by its collision with error.

It is necessary to consider separately these two hypotheses, each of which has a distinct branch of the argument corresponding to it. We can never be sure that the opinion we are endeavoring to stifle is a false opinion; and if we were sure, stifling it would be an evil still.

First: the opinion which it is attempted to suppress by authority may possibly be true. Those who desire to suppress it, of course deny its truth; but they are not infallible. They have no authority to decide the question for all mankind, and exclude every other person from the means of judging. To refuse a hearing to an opinion, because they are sure that it is false, is to assume

that *their* certainty is the same thing as *absolute* certainty. All silencing of discussion is an assumption of infallibility. Its condemnation may be allowed to rest on this common argument, not the worse for being common.

Unfortunately for the good sense of mankind, the fact of their fallibility is far from carrying the weight in their practical judgment which is always allowed to it in theory; for while everyone well knows himself to be fallible, few think it necessary to take any precautions against their own fallibility, or admit the supposition that any opinion of which they feel very certain, may be one of the examples of the error to which they acknowledge themselves to be liable. Absolute princes, or others who are accustomed to unlimited deference, usually feel this complete confidence in their own opinions on nearly all subjects. People more happily situated, who sometimes hear their opinons disputed, and are not wholly unused to be set right when they are wrong, place the same unbounded reliance only on such of their opinions as are shared by all who surround them, or to whom they habitually defer; for in proportion to a man's want of confidence in his own solitary judgment, does he usually repose, with implicit trust, on the infallibility of "the world" in general. And the world, to each individual, means the part of it with which he comes in contact—his party, his sect, his church, his class of society; the man may be called, by comparison, almost liberal and large-minded to whom it means anything so comprehensive as his own country or his own age. Nor is his faith in this collective authority at all shaken by his being aware that other ages, countries, sects, churches, classes, and parties have thought, and even now think, the exact reverse. He devolves upon his own world the responsibility of being in the right against the dissentient worlds of other people; and it never troubles him that mere accident has decided which of these numerous worlds is the object of his reliance, and that the same causes which make him a Churchman in London, would have made him a Buddhist or a Confucian in Peking. Yet it is as evident in itself as any amount of argument can make it, that ages are no more infallible than individuals; every age having held many opinions which subsequent ages have deemed not only false but absurd; and it is as certain that many opinions now general will be rejected by future ages, as it is that many, once general, are rejected by the present.

The objection likely to be made to this argument would probably take some such form as the following. There is no greater assumption of infallibility in forbidding the propagation of error, than in any other thing which is done by public authority on its own judgment and responsibility. Judgment is given to men that they may use it. Because it may be used erroneously, are men to be told that they ought not to use it at all? To prohibit what they think pernicious, is not claiming exemption from error, but fulfilling the duty incumbent on them, although fallible, of acting on their conscientious conviction. If we were never to act on our opinions, because those opinions may be wrong, we should leave all our interests uncared for, and all our duties un-

performed. An objection which applies to all conduct can be no valid objection to any conduct in particular. It is the duty of governments, and of individuals, to form the truest opinions they can; to form them carefully, and never impose them upon others unless they are quite sure of being right. But when they are sure (such reasoners may say), it is not conscientiousness but cowardice to shrink from acting on their opinions, and allow doctrines which they honestly think dangerous to the welfare of mankind, either in this life or in another, to be scattered abroad without restraint, because other people, in less enlightened times, have persecuted opinions now believed to be true. Let us take care, it may be said, not to make the same mistake; but governments and nations have made mistakes in other things, which are not denied to be fit subjects for the exercise of authority: they have laid on bad taxes, made unjust wars. Ought we therefore to lay on no taxes, and, under whatever provocation, make no wars? Men, and governments, must act to the best of their ability. There is no such thing as absolute certainty, but there is assurance sufficient for the purposes of human life. We may, and must, assume our opinion to be true for the guidance of our own conduct: and it is assuming no more when we forbid bad men to pervert society by the propagation of opinions which we regard as false and pernicious.

I answer that it is assuming very much more. There is the greatest difference between presuming an opinion to be true because, with every opportunity for contesting it, it has not been refuted, and assuming its truth for the purpose of not permitting its refutation. Complete liberty of contradicting and disproving our opinion is the very condition which justifies us in assuming its truth for purposes of action; and on no other terms can a being with human faculties have any rational assurance of being right.

When we consider either the history of opinion, or the ordinary conduct of human life, to what is it to be ascribed that the one and the other are no worse than they are? Not certainly to the inherent force of the human understanding; for, on any matter not self-evident, there are ninety-nine persons totally incapable of judging of it for one who is capable; and the capacity of the hundredth person is only comparative: for the majority of the eminent men of every past generation held many opinions now known to be erroneous, and did or approved numerous things which no one will now justify. Why is it, then, that there is on the whole a preponderance among mankind of rational opinions and rational conduct? If there really is this preponderance—which there must be unless human affairs are, and have always been, in an almost desperate state—it is owing to a quality of the human mind, the source of everything respectable in man either as an intellectual or as a moral being, namely, that his errors are corrigible. He is capable of rectifying his mistakes, by discussion and experience. Not by experience alone. There must be discussion, to show how experience is to be interpreted. Wrong opinions and practices gradually yield to fact and argument; but facts and arguments, to produce any effect on the mind, must be brought before it. Very

few facts are able to tell their own story, without comments to bring out their meaning. The whole strength and value, then, of human judgment, depending on the one property, that it can be set right when it is wrong, reliance can be placed on it only when the means of setting it right are kept constantly at hand. In the case of any person whose judgment is really deserving of confidence, how has it become so? Because he has kept his mind open to criticism of his opinions and conduct. Because it has been his practice to listen to all that could be said against him; to profit by as much of it as was just, and expound to himself, and upon occasion to others, the fallacy of what was fallacious. Because he has felt that the only way in which a human being can make some approach to knowing the whole of a subject, is by hearing what can be said about it by persons of every variety of opinion, and studying all modes in which it can be looked at by every character of mind. No wise man ever acquired his wisdom in any mode but this; nor is it in the nature of human intellect to become wise in any other manner. The steady habit of correcting and completing his own opinion by collating it with those of others, so far from causing doubt and hesitation in carrying it into practice, is the only stable foundation for a just reliance on it: for, being cognizant of all that can, at least obviously, be said against him, and having taken up his position against all gainsayers—knowing that he has sought for objections and difficulties, instead of avoiding them, and has shut out no light which can be thrown upon the subject from any quarter—he has a right to think his judgment better than that of any person, or any multitude, who have not gone through a similar process.

It is not too much to require that what the wisest of mankind, those who are best entitled to trust their own judgment, find necessary to warrant their relying on it, should be submitted to by that miscellaneous collection of a few wise and many foolish individuals, called the public. The most intolerant of churches, the Roman Catholic Church, even at the canonization of a saint, admits, and listens patiently to, a "devil's advocate." The holiest of men, it appears, cannot be admitted to posthumous honors, until all that the devil could say against him is known and weighed. If even the Newtonian philosophy were not permitted to be questioned, mankind could not feel as complete assurance of its truth as they now do. The beliefs which we have most warrant for, have no safeguard to rest on but a standing invitation to the whole world to prove them unfounded. If the challenge is not accepted, or is accepted and the attempt fails, we are far enough from certainty still; but we have done the best that the existing state of human reason admits of; we have neglected nothing that could give the truth a chance of reaching us: if the lists are kept open, we may hope that if there be a better truth, it will be found when the human mind is capable of receiving it; and in the meantime we may rely on having attained such approach to truth as is possible in our own day. This is the amount of certainty attainable by a fallible being, and this the sole way of attaining it.

Strange it is that men should admit the validity of the arguments for free discussion, but object to their being "pushed to an extreme"; not seeing that unless the reasons are good for an extreme case, they are not good for any case. Strange that they should imagine that they are not assuming infallibility, when they acknowledge that there should be free discussion on all subjects which can possibly be *doubtful,* but think that some particular principle or doctrine should be forbidden to be questioned because it is so *certain,* that is, because *they are certain* that it is certain. To call any proposition certain while there is anyone who would deny its certainty if permitted, but who is not permitted, is to assume that we ourselves, and those who agree with us, are the judges of certainty, and judges without hearing the other side.

In the present age—which has been described as "destitute of faith, but terrified at scepticism"—in which people feel sure, not so much that their opinions are true, as that they should not know what to do without them—the claims of an opinion to be protected from public attack are rested not so much on its truth, as on its importance to society. There are, it is alleged, certain beliefs so useful, not to say indispensable, to well-being that it is as much the duty of governments to uphold those beliefs, as to protect any other of the interests of society. In a case of such necessity, and so directly in the line of their duty, something less than infallibility may, it is maintained, warrant, and even bind, governments to act on their own opinion, confirmed by the general opinion of mankind. It is also often argued, and still oftener thought, that none but bad men would desire to weaken these salutary beliefs; and there can be nothing wrong, it is thought, in restraining bad men, and prohibiting what only such men would wish to practice. This mode of thinking makes the justification of restraints on discussion not a question of the truth of doctrines, but of their usefulness; and flatters itself by that means to escape the responsibility of claiming to be an infallible judge of opinions. But those who thus satisfy themselves, do not perceive that the assumption of infallibility is merely shifted from one point to another. The usefulness of an opinion is itself matter of opinion: as disputable, as open to discussion, and requiring discussion as much as the opinion itself. There is the same need of an infallible judge of opinions to decide an opinion to be noxious, as to decide it to be false, unless the opinion condemned has full opportunity of defending itself. And it will not do to say that the heretic may be allowed to maintain the utility or harmlessness of his opinion, though forbidden to maintain its truth. The truth of an opinion is part of its utility. If we would know whether or not it is desirable that a proposition should be believed, is it possible to exclude the consideration of whether or not it is true? In the opinion, not of bad men, but of the best men, no belief which is contrary to truth can be really useful; and can you prevent such men from urging that plea, when they are charged with culpability for denying some doctrine which they are told is useful, but which they believe to be false? Those who are on the side of received opinions never fail to take all possible advantages of this plea: you do not find *them* handling the question of utility as if it could be completely abstracted from that of truth; on the contrary, it is, above all, because their doctrine is "the truth," that the knowledge or the belief of it is held to be so indispensable. There can be no fair discussion of the question of usefulness when an argument so vital may be employed on one side, but not on the other. And in point of fact, when law or public feeling do not permit the truth of an opinion to be disputed, they are just as little tolerant of a denial of its usefulness. The utmost they allow is an extenuation of its absolute necessity, or of the positive guilt of rejecting it.

In order more fully to illustrate the mischief of denying a hearing to opinions because we, in our own judgment, have condemned them, it will be desirable to fix down the discussion to a concrete case; and I choose, by preference, the cases which are least favorable to me—in which the argument against freedom of opinion, both on the score of truth and on that of utility, is considered the strongest. Let the opinions impugned be the belief in a God and in a future state, or any of the commonly received doctrines of morality. To fight the battle on such ground gives a great advantage to an unfair antagonist; since he will be sure to say (and many who have no desire to be unfair will say it internally), "Are these the doctrines which you do not deem sufficiently certain to be taken under the protection of laws? Is the belief in a God one of the opinions to feel sure of which you hold to be assuming infallibility?" But I must be permitted to observe that it is not the feeling sure of a doctrine (be it what it may) which I call an assumption of infallibility. It is the undertaking to decide that question *for others,* without allowing them to hear what can be said on the contrary side. And I denounce and reprobate this pretension not the less if put forth on the side of my most solemn convictions. However positive anyone's persuasion may be, not only of the falsity but of the pernicious consequences—not only of the pernicious consequences, but (to adopt expressions which I altogether condemn) the immorality and impiety of an opinion; yet if, in pursuance of that private judgment, though backed by the public judgment of his country or his contemporaries, he prevents the opinion from being heard in its defense, he assumes infallibility. And so far from the assumption being less objectionable or less dangerous because the opinion is called immoral or impious, this is the case of all others in which it is most fatal. These are exactly the occasions on which the men of one generation commit those dreadful mistakes which excite the astonishment and horror of posterity. It is among such that we find the instances memorable in history, when the arm of the law has been employed to root out the best men and the noblest doctrines; with deplorable success as to the men, though some of the doctrines have survived to be (as if in mockery) invoked in defense of similar conduct toward those who dissent from *them,* or from their received interpretation.

Mankind can hardly be too often reminded, that there was once a man named Socrates, between whom and the legal authorities and public opinion of his time there took place a memorable collision. Born in an age and country abounding in individual greatness, this man has been handed down to us by those who best knew both him and the age, as the most virtuous man in it; while *we* know him as the head and prototype of all subsequent teachers of virtue, the source equally of the lofty inspiration of Plato and the judicious utilitarianism of Aristotle, . . . the two head-springs of ethical as of all other philosophy. This acknowledged master of all the eminent thinkers who have since lived—whose fame, still growing after more than two thousand years, all but outweighs the whole remainder of the names which make his native city illustrious—was put to death by his countrymen, after a judicial conviction, for impiety and immorality. Impiety, in denying the gods recognized by the State; indeed his accuser asserted (see the *Apologia*) that he believed in no gods at all. Immorality, in being, by his doctrines and instructions, a "corruptor of youth." Of these charges the tribunal, there is every ground for believing, honestly found him guilty, and condemned the man who probably of all then born had deserved best of mankind to be put to death as a criminal.

To pass from this to the only other instance of judicial iniquity, the mention of which, after the condemnation of Socrates, would not be an anticlimax: the event which took place on Calvary rather more than eighteen hundred years ago. The man who left on the memory of those who witnessed his life and conversation such an impression of his moral grandeur that eighteen subsequent centuries have done homage to him as the Almighty in person, was ignominiously put to death, as what? As a blasphemer. Men did not merely mistake their benefactor; they mistook him for the exact contrary of what he was, and treated him as that prodigy of impiety which they themselves are now held to be for their treatment of him. The feelings with which mankind now regard these lamentable transactions, especially the later of the two, render them extremely unjust in their judgment of the unhappy actors. These were, to all appearance, not bad men—not worse than men commonly are, but rather the contrary; men who possessed in a full, or somewhat more than a full measure, the religious, moral, and patriotic feelings of their time and people: the very kind of men who, in all times, our own included, have every chance of passing through life blameless and respected. The high-priest who rent his garments when the words were pronounced which, according to all the ideas of his country, constituted the blackest guilt, was in all probability quite as sincere in his horror and indignation as the generality of respectable and pious men now are in the religious and moral sentiments they profess; and most of those who now shudder at his conduct, if they had lived in his time, and been born Jews, would have acted precisely as he did. Orthodox Christians who are tempted to think that those who stoned to death the first martyrs must have been worse

men than they themselves are, ought to remember that one of those persecutors was Saint Paul.

Let us add one more example, the most striking of all, if the impressiveness of an error is measured by the wisdom and virtue of him who falls into it. If ever anyone possessed of power had grounds for thinking himself the best and most enlightened among his contemporaries, it was the Emperor Marcus Aurelius. Absolute monarch of the whole civilized world, he preserved through life not only the most unblemished justice, but what was less to be expected from his Stoical breeding, the tenderest heart. The few failings which are attributed to him were all on the side of indulgence; while his writings, the highest ethical product of the ancient mind, differ scarcely perceptibly, if they differ at all, from the most characteristic teachings of Christ. This man, a better Christian in all but the dogmatic sense of the word than almost any of the ostensibly Christian sovereigns who have since reigned, persecuted Christianity. Placed at the summit of all the previous attainments of humanity, with an open, unfettered intellect, and a character which led him of himself to embody in his moral writings the Christian ideal, he yet failed to see that Christianity was to be a good and not an evil to the world, with his duties to which he was so deeply penetrated. Existing society he knew to be in a deplorable state. But such as it was, he saw, or thought he saw, that it was held together, and prevented from being worse, by belief and reverence of the received divinities. As a ruler of mankind, he deemed it his duty not to suffer society to fall in pieces; and saw not how, if its existing ties were removed, any others could be formed which could again knit it together. The new religion openly aimed at dissolving these ties: unless, therefore, it was his duty to adopt that religion, it seemed to be his duty to put it down. Inasmuch then as the theology of Christianity did not appear to him true or of divine origin; inasmuch as this strange history of a crucified God was not credible to him, and a system which purported to rest entirely upon a foundation to him so wholly unbelievable, could not be foreseen by him to be that renovating agency which, after all abatements, it has in fact proved to be; the gentlest and most amiable of philosophers and rulers, under a solemn sense of duty, authorized the persecution of Christianity. To my mind this is one of the most tragical facts in all history. It is a bitter thought, how different a thing the Christianity of the world might have been, if the Christian faith had been adopted as the religion of the empire under the auspices of Marcus Aurelius instead of those of Constantine. But it would be equally unjust to him and false to truth to deny that no one plea which can be urged for punishing anti-Christian teaching was wanting to Marcus Aurelius for punishing as he did the propagation of Christianity. No Christian more firmly believes that atheism is false, and tends to the dissolution of society, than Marcus Aurelius believed the same things of Christianity; he who, of all men then living, might have been thought the most capable of appreciating it. Unless anyone who ap-

proves of punishment for the promulgation of opinions, flatters himself that he is a wiser and better man than Marcus Aurelius—more deeply versed in the wisdom of his time, more elevated in his intellect above it—more earnest in his search for truth, or more single-minded in his devotion to it when found; let him abstain from that assumption of the joint infallibility of himself and the multitude, which the great Antoninus made with so unfortunate a result.

Aware of the impossibility of defending the use of punishment for restraining irreligious opinions by any argument which will not justify Marcus Antoninus, the enemies of religious freedom, when hard pressed, occasionally accept this consequence, and say, with Dr. Johnson, that the persecutors of Christianity were in the right; that persecution is an ordeal through which truth ought to pass, and always passes successfully, legal penalties being, in the end, powerless against truth, though sometimes beneficially effective against mischievous errors. This is a form of the argument for religious intolerance sufficiently remarkable not to be passed without notice.

A theory which maintains that truth may justifiably be persecuted because persecution cannot possibly do it any harm, cannot be charged with being intentionally hostile to the reception of new truths; but we cannot commend the generosity of its dealing with the persons to whom mankind are indebted for them. To discover to the world something which deeply concerns it, and of which it was previously ignorant; to prove to it that it had been mistaken on some vital point of temporal or spiritual interest, is as important a service as a human being can render to his fellow-creatures, and in certain cases, as in those of the early Christians and of the Reformers, those who think with Dr. Johnson believe it to have been the most precious gift which could be bestowed on mankind. That the authors of such splendid benefits should be requited by martyrdom, that their reward should be to be dealt with as the vilest of criminals, is not, upon this theory, a deplorable error and misfortune, for which humanity should mourn in sackcloth and ashes, but the normal and justifiable state of things. The propounder of a new truth, according to this doctrine, should stand, as stood, in the legislation of the Locrians, the proposer of a new law, with a halter round his neck to be instantly tightened if the public assembly did not, on hearing his reasons, then and there adopt his proposition. People who defend this mode of treating benefactors cannot be supposed to set much value on the benefit; and I believe this view of the subject is mostly confined to the sort of persons who think that new truths may have been desirable once, but that we have had enough of them now.

But, indeed, the dictum that truth always triumphs over persecution is one of those pleasant falsehoods which men repeat after one another till they pass into commonplaces, but which all experience refutes. History teems with instances of truth put down by persecution. If not suppressed forever, it may be thrown back for centuries. To speak only of religious opinions: the Reformation broke out at least twenty times before Luther, and was put down. Arnold of Brescia was put down. Fra Dolcino was put down. Savonarola was put down. The Albigeois were put down. The Vaudois were put down. The Lollards were put down. The Hussites were put down. Even after the era of Luther, wherever persecution was persisted in, it was successful. In Spain, Italy, Flanders, the Austrian Empire, Protestantism was rooted out; and, most likely, would have been so in England, had Queen Mary lived, or Queen Elizabeth died. Persecution has always succeeded, save where the heretics were too strong a party to be effectually persecuted. No reasonable person can doubt that Christianity might have been extirpated in the Roman Empire. It spread, and became predominant, because the persecutions were only occasional, lasting but a short time, and separated by long intervals of almost undisturbed propagandism. It is a piece of idle sentimentality that truth, merely as truth, has any inherent power denied to error of prevailing against the dungeon and the stake. Men are not more zealous for truth than they often are for error, and a sufficient application of legal or even of social penalties will generally succeed in stopping the propagation of either. The real advantage which truth has, consists in this, that when an opinion is true, it may be extinguished once, twice, or many times, but in the course of ages there will generally be found persons to rediscover it, until some one of its reappearances falls on a time when from favorable circumstances it escapes persecution until it has made such head as to withstand all subsequent attempts to suppress it.

It will be said that we do not now put to death the introducers of new opinions: we are not like our fathers who slew the prophets, we even build sepulchres to them. It is true we no longer put heretics to death; and the amount of penal infliction which modern feeling would probably tolerate, even against the most obnoxious opinions, is not sufficient to extirpate them. . . . But though we do not now inflict so much evil on those who think differently from us as it was formerly our custom to do, it may be that we do ourselves as much evil as ever by our treatment of them. Socrates was put to death, but the Socratic philosophy rose like the sun in heaven, and spread its illumination over the whole intellectual firmament. Christians were cast to the lions, but the Christian church grew up a stately and spreading tree, overtopping the older and less vigorous growths, and stifling them by its shade. Our merely social intolerance kills no one, roots out no opinions, but induces men to disguise them, or to abstain from any active effort for their diffusion. With us, heretical opinions do not perceptibly gain, or even lose, ground in each decade or generation; they never blaze out far and wide, but continue to smolder in the narrow circles of thinking and studious persons among whom they originate, without ever lighting up the general affairs of mankind with either a true or a deceptive light. And thus is kept up a state of things very satisfactory to some minds, because, without the unpleasant process of fining or imprisoning anybody, it maintains all prevailing opinions outwardly undisturbed, while it does not absolutely interdict the exercise of reason by dissentients afflicted with the malady of thought. A convenient plan for having peace in the intellectual world, and keeping all things going on therein very much as they do already! But the price paid for this sort of intellectual pacification is the sacrifice of the entire moral courage of the human mind. A state of things in which a large portion of the most active and inquiring intellects find it advisable to keep the general principles and grounds of their convictions within their own breasts, and attempt, in what they address to the public, to fit as much as they can of their own conclusions to premises which they have internally renounced, cannot send forth the open, fearless characters, and logical, consistent intellects who once adorned the thinking world. The sort of men who can be looked for under it, are either mere conformers to commonplace, or time-servers for truth, whose arguments on all great subjects are meant for their hearers, and are not those which have convinced themselves. Those who avoid this alternative, do so by narrowing their thoughts and interest to things which can be spoken of without venturing within the region of principles—that is, to small practical matters which would come right of themselves if but the minds of mankind were strengthened and enlarged, and which will never be made effectually right until then; while that which would strengthen and enlarge men's minds, free and daring speculation on the highest subjects, is abandoned.

Those in whose eyes this reticence on the part of heretics is no evil should consider, in the first place, that in consequence of it there is never any fair and thorough discussion of heretical opinions; and that such of them as could not stand such a discussion, though they may be prevented from spreading, do not disappear. But it is not the minds of heretics that are deteriorated most by the ban placed on all inquiry which does not end in the orthodox conclusions. The greatest harm done is to those who are not heretics, and whose whole mental development is cramped, and their reason cowed, by the fear of heresy. Who can compute what the world loses in the multitude of promising intellects combined with timid characters, who dare not follow out any bold, vigorous, independent train of thought, lest it should land them in something which would admit of being considered irreligous or immoral? Among them we may occasionally see some man of deep conscientousness, and subtle and refined understanding, who spends a life in sophisticating with an intellect which he cannot silence, and exhausts the resources of ingenuity in attempting to reconcile the promptings of his conscience and reason with orthodoxy, which he does not, perhaps, to the end succeed in doing. No one can be a great thinker who does not recognize that as a thinker it is his first duty to follow his intellect to whatever conclusions it may lead. Truth gains more even by the errors of one who, with due study and preparation, thinks for

himself, than by the true opinions of those who only hold them because they do not suffer themselves to think. Not that it is solely, or chiefly, to form great thinkers, that freedom of thinking is required. On the contrary, it is as much and even more indispensable to enable average human beings to attain the mental stature which they are capable of. There have been, and may again be, great individual thinkers in a general atmosphere of mental slavery. But there never has been, nor ever will be, in that atmosphere an intellectually active people. Where any people has made a temporary approach to such a character, it has been because the dread of heterodox speculation was for a time suspended. Where there is a tacit convention that principles are not to be disputed; where the discussion of the greatest questions which can occupy humanity is considered to be closed, we cannot hope to find that generally high scale of mental activity which has made some periods of history so remarkable. Never when controversy avoided the subjects which are large and important enough to kindle enthusiasm, was the mind of a people stirred up from its foundations, and the impulse given which raised even persons of the most ordinary intellect to something of the dignity of thinking beings. Of such we have had an example in the condition of Europe during the times immediately following the Reformation; another, though limited to the Continent and to a more cultivated class, in the speculative movement of the latter half of the eighteenth century; and a third, of still briefer duration, in the intellectual fermentation of Germany during the Goethean and Fichtean period. These periods differed widely in the particular opinions which they developed; but were alike in this, that during all three the yoke of authority was broken. In each, an old mental despotism had been thrown off, and no new one had yet taken its place. The impulse given at these three periods has made Europe what it now is. Every single improvement which has taken place either in the human mind or in institutions, may be traced distinctly to one or other of them. Appearances have for some time indicated that all three impulses are well nigh spent; and we can expect no fresh start until we again assert our mental freedom.

Let us now pass to the second division of the argument, and dismissing the supposition that any of the received opinions may be false, let us assume them to be true, and examine into the worth of the manner in which they are likely to be held, when their truth is not freely and openly canvassed. However unwilling a person who has a strong opinion may admit the possibility that his opinion may be false, he ought to be moved by the consideration that, however true it may be, if it is not fully, frequently, and fearlessly discussed, it will be held as a dead dogma, not a living truth.

There is a class of persons (happily not quite so numerous as formerly) who think it enough if a person assents undoubtingly to what they think true, though he has no knowledge whatever of the grounds of the opinion, and could not make a tenable defense of it

against the most superficial objections. Such persons, if they can once get their creed taught from authority, naturally think that no good, and some harm, comes of its being allowed to be questioned. Where their influence prevails, they make it nearly impossible for the received opinion to be rejected wisely and considerately, though it may still be rejected rashly and ignorantly; for to shut out discussion entirely is seldom possible, and when it once gets in, beliefs not grounded on conviction are apt to give way before the slightest semblance of an argument. Waiving, however, this possibility—assuming that the true opinion abides in the mind, but abides as a prejudice, a belief independent of, and proof against, argument—this is not the way in which truth ought to be held by a rational being. This is not knowing the truth. Truth, thus held, is but one superstition the more, accidentally clinging to the words which enunciate a truth.

If the intellect and judgment of mankind ought to be cultivated, a thing which Protestants at least do not deny, on what can these faculties be more appropriately exercised by anyone, than on the things which concern him so much that it is considered necessary for him to hold opinions on them? If the cultivation of the understanding consists in one thing more than in another, it is surely in learning the grounds of one's own opinions. Whatever people believe, on subjects on which it is of the first importance to believe rightly, they ought to be able to defend against at least the common objections. But, some one may say, "Let them be *taught* the grounds of their opinions. It does not follow that opinions must be merely parroted because they are never heard controverted. Persons who learn geometry do not simply commit the theorems to memory, but understand and learn likewise the demonstrations; and it would be absurd to say that they remain ignorant of the grounds of geometrical truths, because they never hear any one deny, and attempt to disprove them." Undoubtedly: and such teaching suffices on a subject like mathematics, where there is nothing at all to be said on the wrong side of the question. The peculiarity of the evidence of mathematical truths is that all the argument is on one side. There are no objections, and no answers to objections. But on every subject on which difference of opinion is possible, the truth depends on a balance to be struck between two sets of conflicting reasons. Even in natural philosophy, there is always some other explanation possible of the same facts—some geocentric theory instead of heliocentric, some phlogiston instead of oxygen—and it has to be shown why that other theory cannot be the true one; and until this is shown, and until we know how it is shown, we do not understand the grounds of our opinion. But when we turn to subjects infinitely more complicated, to morals, religion, politics, social relations, and the business of life, three-fourths of the arguments for every disputed opinion consist in dispelling the appearances which favor some opinion different from it. The greatest orator, save one, of antiquity, has left it on record that he always studied his adversary's case with as great, if not still greater, intensity than even his own. What Cicero practiced as the means of forensic success requires to be imitated by all who study any subject in order to arrive at the truth. He who knows only his own side of the case, knows little of that. His reasons may be good, and no one may have been able to refute them. But if he is equally unable to refute the reasons on the opposite side; if he does not so much as know what they are, he has no ground for preferring either opinion. The rational position for him would be suspension of judgment, and unless he contents himself with that, he is either led by authority, or adopts, like the generality of the world, the side to which he feels most inclination. Nor is it enough that he should hear the arguments of adversaries from his own teachers, presented as they state them, and accompanied by what they offer as refutations. That is not the way to do justice to the arguments, or bring them into real contact with his own mind. He must be able to hear them from persons who actually believe them; who defend them in earnest, and do their very utmost for them. He must know them in their most plausible and persuasive form; he must feel the whole force of the difficulty which the true view of the subject has to encounter and dispose of; else he will never really possess himself of the portion of truth which meets and removes that difficulty. Ninetynine in a hundred of what are called educated men are in this condition; even of those who can argue fluently for their opinions. Their conclusion may be true, but it might be false for anything they know: they have never thrown themselves into the mental position of those who think differently from them, and considered what such persons may have to say; and consequently they do not, in any proper sense of the word, know the doctrine which they themselves profess. They do not know those parts of it which explain and justify the remainder; the considerations which show that a fact which seemingly conflicts with another is reconcilable with it, or that, of two apparently strong reasons, one and not the other ought to be preferred. All that part of the truth which turns the scale, and decides the judgment of a completely informed mind, they are strangers to; nor is it ever really known but to those who have attended equally and impartially to both sides, and endeavored to see the reasons of both in the strongest light. So essential is this discipline to a real understanding of moral and human subjects, that if opponents of all important truths do not exist, it is indispensable to imagine them, and supply them with the strongest arguments which the most skilful devil's advocate can conjure up. . . .

If, however, the mischievous operation of the absence of free discussion, when the received opinions are true, were confined to leaving men ignorant of the grounds of those opinions, it might be thought that this, if an intellectual, is no moral evil, and does not affect the worth of the opinions, regarded in their influence on the character. The fact, however, is that not only the grounds of the opinion are forgotten in the absence of discussion, but too often the meaning of the opinion itself. The words which convey it

cease to suggest ideas, or suggest only a small portion of those they were originally employed to communicate. Instead of a vivid conception and a living belief, there remain only a few phrases retained by rote; or, if any part, the shell and husk only of the meaning is retained, the finer essence being lost. The great chapter in human history which this fact occupies and fills, cannot be too earnestly studied and meditated on.

It is illustrated in the experience of almost all ethical doctrines and religious creeds. They are full of meaning and vitality to those who originate them, and to the direct disciples of the originators. Their meaning continues to be felt in undiminished strength, and is perhaps brought out into even fuller consciousness, so long as the struggle lasts to give the doctrine or creed an ascendancy over other creeds. At last it either prevails, and becomes the general opinion, or its progress stops; it keeps possession of the ground it has gained, but ceases to spread further. When either of these results has become apparent, controversy on the subject flags, and gradually dies away. The doctrine has taken its place, if not as a received opinion, as one of the admitted sects or divisions of opinion: those who hold it have generally inherited, not adopted it; and conversion from one of these doctrines to another, being now an exceptional fact, occupies little place in the thoughts of their professors. Instead of being, as at first, constantly on the alert either to defend themselves against the world, or to bring the world over to them, they have subsided into acquiescence, and neither listen, when they can help it, to arguments against their creed, nor trouble dissentients (if there be such) with arguments in its favor. From this time may usually be dated the decline in the living power of the doctrine. We often hear the teachers of all creeds lamenting the difficulty of keeping up in the minds of believers a lively apprehension of the truth which they nominally recognize, so that it may penetrate the feelings, and acquire a real mastery over the conduct. No such difficulty is complained of while the creed is still fighting for its existence: even the weaker combatants then know and feel what they are fighting for, and the difference between it and other doctrines; and in that period of every creed's existence, not a few persons may be found, who have realized its fundamental principles in all the forms of thought, have weighed and considered them in all their important bearings, and have experienced the full effect on the character which belief in that creed ought to produce in a mind thoroughly imbued with it. But when it has come to be an hereditary creed, and to be received passively, not actively; when the mind is no longer compelled, in the same degree as at first, to exercise its vital powers on the questions which its belief presents to it: there is a progressive tendency to forget all of the belief except the formularies, or to give it a dull and torpid assent, as if accepting it on trust dispensed with the necessity of realizing it in consciousness, or testing it by personal experience, until it almost ceases to connect itself at all with the inner life of the human being. Then are seen the cases, so frequent in this age of the world as almost to form the majority, in which the creed remains as it were outside the mind, incrusting and petrifying it against all other influences addressed to the higher parts of our nature; manifesting its power by not suffering any fresh and living conviction to get in, but itself doing nothing for the mind or heart, except standing sentinel over them to keep them vacant.

To what an extent doctrines intrinsically fitted to make the deepest impression upon the mind may remain in it as dead beliefs, without being ever realized in the imagination, the feelings, or the understanding, is exemplified by the manner in which the majority of believers hold the doctrines of Christianity. By Christianity I here mean what is accounted such by all churches and sects—the maxims and precepts contained in the New Testament. These are considered sacred, and accepted as laws, by all professing Christians. Yet it is scarcely too much to say that not one Christian in a thousand guides or tests his individual conduct by reference to those laws. The standard to which he does refer it, is the custom of his nation, his class, or his religious profession. He has thus, on the one hand, a collection of ethical maxims, which he believes to have been vouchsafed to him by infallible wisdom as rules for his government; and on the other a set of every-day judgments and practices, which go a certain length with some of those maxims, not so great a length with others, stand in direct opposition to some, and are, on the whole, a compromise between the Christian creed and the interests and suggestions of worldly life. To the first of these standards he gives his homage; to the other his real allegiance. . . .

The same thing holds true, generally speaking, of all traditional doctrines—those of prudence and knowledge of life, as well as of morals or religion. All languages and literatures are full of general observations on life, both as to what it is, and how to conduct oneself in it; observations which everybody knows, which everybody repeats, or hears with acquiescence, which are received as truisms, yet of which most people first truly learn the meaning when experience, generally of a painful kind, has made it a reality to them. How often, when smarting under some unforeseen misfortune or disappointment, does a person call to mind some proverb or common saying, familiar to him all his life, the meaning of which, if he had ever before felt it as he does now, would have saved him from the calamity. There are indeed reasons for this, other than the absence of discussion; there are many truths of which the full meaning *cannot* be realized until personal experience has brought it home. But much more of the meaning even of these would have been understood, and what was understood would have been far more deeply impressed on the mind, if the man had been accustomed to hear it argued *pro* and *con* by people who did understand it. The fatal tendency of mankind to leave off thinking about a thing when it is no longer doubtful, is the cause of half their errors. A contemporary author has well spoken of "the deep slumber of a decided opinion."

But what! (it may be asked) Is the absence of unanimity an indispensable condition of true knowledge? Is it necessary that some part of mankind should persist in error to enable any to realize the truth? Does a belief cease to be real and vital as soon as it is generally received; and is a proposition never thoroughly understood and felt unless some doubt of it remains? As soon as mankind have unanimously accepted a truth, does the truth perish within them? The highest aim and best result of improved intelligence, it has hitherto been thought, is to unite mankind more and more in the acknowledgment of all important truths; and does the intelligence only last as long as it has not achieved its object? Do the fruits of conquest perish by the very completeness of the victory?

I affirm no such thing. As mankind improve, the number of doctrines which are no longer disputed or doubted will be constantly on the increase: and the well-being of mankind may almost be measured by the number and gravity of the truths which have reached the point of being uncontested. The cessation, on one question after another, of serious controversy, is one of the necessary incidents of the consolidation of opinion; a consolidation as salutary in the case of true opinions, as it is dangerous and noxious when the opinions are erroneous. But though this gradual narrowing of the bounds of diversity of opinion is necessary in both senses of the term, being at once inevitable and indispensable, we are not therefore obliged to conclude that all its consequences must be beneficial. The loss of so important an aid to the intelligent and living apprehension of a truth, as is afforded by the necessity of explaining it to, or defending it against, opponents, though not sufficient to outweigh, is no trifling drawback from, the benefit of its universal recognition. Where this advantage can no longer be had, I confess I should like to see the teachers of mankind endeavoring to provide a substitute for it; some contrivance for making the difficulties of the question as present to the learner's consciousness, as if they were pressed upon him by a dissentient champion, eager for his conversion. . . .

It is the fashion of the present time to disparage negative logic—that which points out weaknesses in theory or errors in practice, without establishing positive truths. Such negative criticism would indeed be poor enough as an ultimate result; but as a means to attaining any positive knowledge or conviction worthy the name, it cannot be valued too highly; and until people are again systematically trained to it, there will be few great thinkers, and a low general average of intellect, in any but the mathematical and physical departments of speculation. On any other subject no one's opinions deserve the name of knowledge, except so far as he has either had forced upon him by others, or gone through of himself, the same mental process which would have been required of him in carrying on an active controversy with opponents. That, therefore, which when absent, it is so indispensable, but so difficult, to create, how worse than absurd it is to forego, when spontaneously offering itself! If there are any persons who contest a received opinion, or who will do so if law or opinion will let them, let us

thank them for it, open our minds to listen to them, and rejoice that there is some one to do for us what we otherwise ought, if we have any regard for either the certainty or the vitality of our convictions, to do with much greater labor for ourselves.

It still remains to speak of one of the principal causes which make diversity of opinion advantageous, and will continue to do so until mankind shall have entered a stage of intellectual advancement which at present seems at an incalculable distance. We have hitherto considered only two possibilities: that the received opinion may be false, and some other opinion consequently true; or that, the received opinion being true, a conflict with the opposite error is essential to a clear apprehension and deep feeling of its truth. But there is a commoner case than either of these: when the conflicting doctrines, instead of being one true and the other false, share the truth between them; and the nonconforming opinion is needed to supply the remainder of the truth, of which the received doctrine embodies only a part. Popular opinions, on subjects not palpable to sense, are often true, but seldom or never the whole truth. They are a part of the truth; sometimes a greater, sometimes a smaller part, but exaggerated, distorted, and disjointed from the truths by which they ought to be accompanied and limited. Heretical opinions, on the other hand, are generally some of these suppressed and neglected truths, bursting the bonds which kept them down, and neither seeking reconciliation with the truth contained in the common opinion, or fronting it as enemies, and setting themselves up, with similar exclusiveness, as the whole truth. The latter case is hitherto the most frequent, as, in the human mind, one-sidedness has always been the rule, and many-sidedness the exception. Hence, even in revolutions of opinion, one part of the truth usually sets while another rises. Even progress, which ought to superadd, for the most part only substitutes, one partial and incomplete truth for another; improvement consisting chiefly in this, that the new fragment of truth is more wanted, more adapted to the needs of the time, than that which it displaces. Such being the partial character of prevailing opinions, even when resting on a true foundation, every opinion which embodies somewhat of the portion of truth which the common opinion omits, ought to be considered precious, with whatever amount of error and confusion that truth may be blended. No sober judge of human affairs will feel bound to be indignant because those who force on our notice truths which we should otherwise have overlooked, overlook some of those which we see. Rather, he will think that so long as popular truth is one-sided, it is more desirable than otherwise that unpopular truth should have one-sided assertors too; such being usually the most energetic, and the most likely to compel reluctant attention to the fragment of wisdom which they proclaim as if it were the whole.

Thus, in the eighteenth century, when nearly all the instructed, and all those of the uninstructed who were led by them, were lost in admiration of what is called civilization, and of the marvels of modern science, literature, and philosophy, and while greatly overrating the amount of unlikeness between the men of modern and those of ancient times, indulged the belief that the whole of the difference was in their own favor; with what a salutary shock did the paradoxes of Rousseau explode like bombshells in the midst, dislocating the compact mass of one-sided opinion, and forcing its elements to recombine in a better form and with additional ingredients. Not that the current opinions were on the whole farther from the truth than Rousseau's were: on the contrary, they were nearer to it: they contained more of positive truth, and very much less of error. Nevertheless there lay in Rousseau's doctrine, and has floated down the stream of opinion along with it, a considerable amount of exactly those truths which the popular opinion wanted; and these are the deposit which was left behind when the flood subsided. The superior worth of simplicity of life, the enervating and demoralizing effect of the trammels and hypocrisies of artificial society, are ideas which have never been entirely absent from cultivated minds since Rousseau wrote; and they will in time produce their due effect, though at present needing to be asserted as much as ever, and to be asserted by deeds, for words, on this subject, have nearly exhausted their power.

In politics, again, it is almost a commonplace, that a party of order or stability, and a party of progress or reform, are both necessary elements of a healthy state of political life; until the one or the other shall have so enlarged its mental grasp as to be a party equally of order and of progress, knowing and distinguishing what is fit to be preserved from what ought to be swept away. Each of these modes of thinking derives its utility from the deficiencies of the other; but it is in a great measure the opposition of the other that keeps each within the limits of reason and sanity. Unless opinions favorable to democracy and to aristocracy, to property and to equality, to coöperation and to competition, to luxury and to abstinence, to sociality and individuality, to liberty and discipline, and all the other standing antagonisms of practical life, are expressed with equal freedom, and enforced and defended with equal talent and energy, there is no chance of both elements obtaining their due: one scale is sure to go up, and the other down. Truth, in the great practical concerns of life, is so much a question of the reconciling and combining of opposites, that very few have minds sufficiently capacious and impartial to make the adjustment with an approach to correctness, and it has to be made by the rough process of a struggle between combatants fighting under hostile banners. On any of the great open questions just enumerated, if either of the two opinions has a better claim than the other, not merely to be tolerated, but to be encouraged and countenanced, it is the one which happens at the particular time and place to be in a minority. That is the opinion which, for the time being, represents the neglected interests, the side of human well-being which is in danger of obtaining less than its share. I am aware that there is not, in this country, any intolerance of

differences of opinion on most of these topics. They are adduced to show, by admitted and multiplied examples, the universality of the fact that only through diversity of opinion is there, in the existing state of human intellect, a chance of fair play to all sides of the truth. When there are persons to be found who form an exception to the apparent unanimity of the world on any subject, even if the world is in the right, it is always probable that dissentients have something worth hearing to say for themselves, and that truth would lose something by their silence. . . .

We have now recognized the necessity to the mental well-being of mankind (on which all their other well-being depends) of freedom of opinion, and freedom of the expression of opinion, on four distinct grounds; which we will now briefly recapitulate.

First, if any opinion is compelled to silence, that opinion may, for aught we can certainly know, be true. To deny this is to assume our own infallibility.

Secondly, though the silenced opinion be an error, it may, and very commonly does, contain a portion of truth; and since the general or prevailing opinion on any subject is rarely or never the whole truth, it is only by the collision of adverse opinions that the remainder of the truth has any chance of being supplied.

Thirdly, even if the received opinion be not only true, but the whole truth; unless it is suffered to be, and actually is, vigorously and earnestly contested, it will, by most of those who receive it, be held in the manner of a prejudice, with little comprehension or feeling of its rational grounds. And not only this, but, fourthly, the meaning of the doctrine itself will be in danger of being lost, or enfeebled, and deprived of its vital effect on the character and conduct: the dogma becoming a mere formal procession, inefficacious for good, but cumbering the ground, and preventing the growth of any real and heartfelt conviction, from reason or personal experience. . . .

Chapter III

Of Individuality, As One of the Elements of Well-being

Such being the reasons which make it imperative that human beings should be free to form opinions, and to express their opinions without reserve; and such the baneful consequences to the intellectual, and through that to the moral nature of man, unless this liberty is either conceded, or asserted in spite of prohibition; let us next examine whether the same reasons do not require that men should be free to act upon their opinions—to carry these out in their lives, without hindrance, either physical or moral, from their fellow-men, so long as it is at their own risk and peril. This last proviso is of course indispensable. No one pretends that actions should be as free as opinions. On the contrary, even opinions lose their immunity when the circumstances in which they are expressed are such as to constitute their expression a positive instigation to some mischievous act. An opinion that corn-dealers are starvers of the poor, or that private property is robbery, ought to be unmolested when simply circulated

through the press, but may justly incur punishment when delivered orally to an excited mob assembled before the house of a corn-dealer, or when handed about among the same mob in the form of a placard. Acts, of whatever kind, which without justifiable cause do harm to others, may be, and in the more important cases absolutely require to be, controlled by the unfavorable sentiments, and, when needful, by the active interference of mankind. The liberty of the individual must be thus far limited; he must not make himself a nuisance to other people. But if he refrains from molesting others in what concerns them, and merely acts according to his own inclination and judgment in things which concern himself, the same reasons which show that opinion should be free, prove also that he should be allowed, without molestation, to carry his opinions into practice at his own cost. That mankind are not infallible; that their truths, for the most part, are only half-truths; that unity of opinion, unless resulting from the fullest and freest comparison of opposite opinions, is not desirable, and diversity not an evil, but a good, until mankind are much more capable than at present of recognizing all sides of the truth, are principles applicable to men's modes of action, not less than to their opinions. As it is useful that while mankind are imperfect there should be different opinions, so it is that there should be different experiments of living; that free scope should be given to varieties of character, short of injury to others; and that the worth of different modes of life should be proved practically, when any one thinks fit to try them. It is desirable, in short, that in things which do not primarily concern others, individuality should assert itself. Where not the person's own character, but the traditions or customs of other people are the rule of conduct, there is wanting one of the principal ingredients of human happiness, and quite the chief ingredient of individual and social progress.

In maintaining this principle, the greatest difficulty to be encountered does not lie in the appreciation of means toward an acknowledged end, but in the indifference of persons in general to the end in itself. If it were felt that the free development of individuality is one of the leading essentials of well-being; that it is not only a coördinate element with all that is designated by the terms civilization, instruction, education, culture, but is itself a necessary part and condition of all those things; there would be no danger that liberty should be undervalued, and the adjustment of the boundaries between it and social control would present no extraordinary difficulty. But the evil is, that individual spontaneity is hardly recognized by the common modes of thinking as having any intrinsic worth, or deserving any regard on its own account. The majority, being satisfied with the ways of mankind as they now are (for it is they who make them what they are), cannot comprehend why those ways should not be good enough for everybody; and what is more, spontaneity forms no part of the ideal of the majority of moral and social reformers, but is rather looked on with jealousy, as a troublesome and perhaps rebellious obstruction to the general acceptance of what these reformers, in their own judgment, think

would be best for mankind. Few persons, out of Germany, even comprehend the meaning of the doctrine which Wilhelm von Humboldt, so eminent both as a *savant* and as a politician, made the text of a treatise—that "the end of man, or that which is prescribed by the eternal or immutable dictates of reason, and not suggested by vague and transient desires, is the highest and most harmonious development of his powers to a complete and consistent whole"; that, therefore, the object "towards which every human being must ceaselessly direct his efforts, and on which especially those who design to influence their fellow-men must ever keep their eyes, is the individuality of power and development"; that for this there are two requisites, "freedom, and variety of situations"; and that from the union of these arise "individual vigor and manifold diversity," which combine themselves in "originality."[1]

He who lets the world, or his own portion of it, choose his plan of life for him, has no need of any other faculty than the ape-like one of imitation. He who chooses his plan for himself, employs all his faculties. He must use observation to see, reasoning and judgment to foresee, activity to gather materials for decision, discrimination to decide, and when he has decided, firmness and self-control to hold to his deliberate decision. And these qualities he requires and exercises exactly in proportion as the part of his conduct which he determines according to his own judgment and feelings is a large one. It is possible

[1] *The Sphere and Duties of Government,* from the German of Baron Wilhelm von Humboldt, pp. 11–13.

that he might be guided in some good path, and kept out of harm's way, without any of these things. But what will be his comparative worth as a human being? It really is of importance, not only what men do, but also what manner of men they are that do it. Among the works of man which human life is rightly employed in perfecting and beautifying, the first in importance surely is man himself. Supposing it were possible to get houses built, corn grown, battles fought, causes tried, and even churches erected and prayers said, by machinery—by automatons in human form—it would be a considerable loss to exchange for these automatons even the men and women who at present inhabit the more civilized parts of the world, and who assuredly are but starved specimens of what nature can and will produce. Human nature is not a machine to be built after a model, and set to do exactly the work prescribed for it, but a tree, which requires to grow and develop itself on all sides, according to the tendency of the inward forces which make it a living thing. . . .

It is not by wearing down into uniformity all that is individual in themselves, but by cultivating it, and calling it forth, within the limits imposed by the rights and interests of others, that human beings become a noble and beautiful object of contemplation; and as the works partake the character of those who do them, by the same process human life also becomes rich, diversified, and animating, furnishing more abundant aliment to high thoughts and elevating feelings, and strengthening the tie which binds every individual to the race, by making the race infinitely bet-ter worth belonging to. In proportion to the development of his individuality, each person becomes more valuable to himself, and is therefore capable of being more valuable to others. There is a greater fullness of life about his own existence, and when there is more life in the units there is more in the mass which is composed of them. As much compression as is necessary to prevent the stronger specimens of human nature from encroaching on the rights of others cannot be dispensed with; but for this there is ample compensation even in the point of view of human development. The means of development which the individual loses by being prevented from gratifying his inclinations to the injury of others, are chiefly obtained at the expense of the development of other people. And even to himself there is a full equivalent in the better development of the social part of his nature, rendered possible by the restraint put upon the selfish part. To be held to rigid rules of justice for the sake of others, develops the feelings and capacities which have the good of others for their object. But to be restrained in things not affecting their good, by their mere displeasure, develops nothing valuable, except such force of character as may unfold itself in resisting the restraint. If acquiesced in, it dulls and blunts the whole nature. To give any fair play to the nature of each, it is essential that different persons should be allowed to lead different lives. In proportion as this latitude has been exercised in any age, has that age been noteworthy to posterity. Even despotism does not produce its worst effects, so long as individuality exists under it;

and whatever crushes individuality is despotism, by whatever name it may be called, and whether it professes to be enforcing the will of God or the injunctions of men. . . .

I have said that it is important to give the freest scope possible to uncustomary things, in order that it may in time appear which of these are fit to be converted into customs. But independence of action, and disregard of custom, are not solely deserving of encouragement for the chance they afford that better modes of action, and customs more worthy of general adoption, may be struck out; nor is it only persons of decided mental superiority who have a just claim to carry on their lives in their own way. There is no reason that all human existence should be constructed on some one or some small number of patterns. If a person possesses any tolerable amount of common sense and experience, his own mode of laying out his existence is the best, not because it is the best in itself, but because it is his own mode. Human beings are not like sheep; and even sheep are not undistinguishably alike. A man cannot get a coat or a pair of boots to fit him unless beings more like one another in their whole physical and spiritual conforma-tion than in the shape of their feet? If it were only that people have diversities of taste, that is reason enough for not attempting to shape them all after one model. But different persons also require different conditions for their spiritual development; and can no more exist healthily in the same moral, than all the variety of plants can in the same physical, atmosphere and climate. The same things which are helps to one person towards the cultivation of his higher nature are hindrances to another. The same mode of life is a healthy excitement to one, keeping all his faculties of action and enjoyment in their best order, while to another it is a distracting burthen, which suspends or crushes all internal life. Such are the differences among human beings in their sources of pleasure, their susceptibilities of pain, and the operation on them of different physical and moral agencies, that unless there is a corresponding diversity in their modes of life, they neither obtain their fair share of happiness, nor grow up to the mental, moral, and æsthetic stature of which their nature is capable. . . .

[*The remainder of Chapter III and all of Chapters IV and V are omitted.*]

The Basis of Mill's Argument

The older liberals, especially Locke and Jefferson, espoused liberty as an inalienable natural right. Mill, in contrast, avowedly based his argument upon "utility, in the largest sense." Progress, he maintained, is desirable for human welfare, and free thought and action are necessary for that end. The ultimate standard for judging social institutions is their contribution to happiness. Mill thus began by running up the banner of utilitarianism.

The real premise of his argument, however, is not the calculation of pleasure and pain but the inner value of character and unhampered individuality. In

Chapter III of *On Liberty*, he mentions with approval the doctrine of "self-realization" advocated by Wilhelm von Humboldt. "The end of man," according to this German writer, "is the highest and most harmonious development of his powers to a complete and consistent whole," and for this there are two requisites, "freedom and variety of situations." This theory of self-realization is the focus of Mill's teaching. It underlies his decided preference for highly developed individuals rather than "ape-like imitators." Liberty enables a person to be a person—to attain the full use and development of one's powers. To live freely is to unfold one's individual human capacities; to live servilely—by custom, imitation, social pressure, or repressive political rule—is to be less than a human being. Liberty is the acknowledgment of the peculiar dignity of a person as a person—and of *each* person's matchless individuality. There is slight trace in this essay of the earlier teaching of the Utilitarians that it does not matter what people are like provided that they have as much pleasure and as little pain as possible.

Mill had become convinced that the modern enemy of liberty is the tyranny of the majority. No longer is the problem that of overthrowing a tyrannical king or the oligarchy of a few. It is the much more difficult problem of freeing dissident individuals and minorities from the pressure of a mass-society. Mill had been shocked by Alexis de Tocqueville's classic study, *Democracy in America* (1835–1840), which maintained that the ultimate triumph of democracy is inevitable and that its tendency is to reduce all people to a level of equal mediocrity. Sharing de Tocqueville's alarm, Mill believed that a truly liberal society must be created as a safeguard against mass illiberalism. Such a society would be deeply respectful of human freedom. His argument, therefore, is primarily a defense of individuality against the conventionalities of society, the despotism of social custom, and the overweening powers of government.

Individual and Social Standards of Human Fulfillment

The traditional theory of democracy is the doctrine of natural rights which we reviewed in Chapter 11. The language of the American Declaration of Independence and the French Declaration of the Rights of Man, for example, is largely derived from this tradition. Mill believed that his doctrine of the supreme importance of individuality contradicts the natural rights tradition, but his standard of self-realization is not so far removed from that of natural rights as might be supposed at first glance. What distinguishes his doctrine from most theories of natural right is the strong emphasis upon the diversity of human nature. To live freely is to unfold one's *individual* human capacities. His theory in this sense is complementary rather than contradictory to the natural rights theory. It calls attention to the individual, and not merely the generic, elements in human nature.

More than the older natural rights theorists, such as Locke and Rousseau, Mill was aware that society must adapt itself to changing historical circumstances. Similarly Dewey, in his version of democratic liberalism, was keenly aware of the tides of historical change and their relevance to democratic ideals. This is also the characteristic approach of Marxists who insist that "democracy," "socialism," and "communism" are historical concepts with changing meaning and content. Typical is Marx's remark in *The Critique of the Gotha Program* that "right can never be higher than the economic structure of the society and the cultural development conditioned by it." But Mill, more than Marx, insisted on the autonomy and self-fulfillment of the individual.

The contrast between the more individualistic emphasis of Mill and the more social emphasis of Marx should incite lively discussion. While thinking about these differences, however, we should not overlook the similarities. Mill became increasingly convinced as he grew older that real freedom requires the resources and opportunities that enable a person to fulfill his potentialities and effectuate his choices. In his essay on Coleridge, he contended that "a State ought to be considered a great benefit society, or mutual insurance company, for helping (under the necessary regulations for preventing abuse) that large proportion of its members who cannot help themselves." He was inclined to favor cooperative ownership and management of industry by the workers instead of either capitalistic or state-socialistic operation. "There can be little doubt," he said in *Principles of Political Economy*, "that the relation of masters and workpeople will be gradually superseded by partnership in one of two forms: in some cases, association of the labourers with the capitalist; in others, and perhaps finally in all, association of labourers among themselves." In his *Autobiography*, he declared that "the social problem of the future" is "how to unite the greatest individual liberty of action with a common ownership of the raw materials of the globe, and an equal participation of all in the benefits of combined labour." He was nevertheless opposed to state intervention "to chain up the free agency of individuals."

Conclusion

In Part Four we have examined the ideas of three major figures in social philosophy—Plato, Marx, and Mill. They differ in many respects, and not least in their attitudes toward democracy. Plato believed in the cultivation of excellence by the rule of wise men—he rejected democracy because its leaders are neither wise nor devoted to excellence. Marx regarded democracy in a capitalist society as a facade for the rule of wealth and privilege, and he predicted that it would be superseded by a socialist state. Socialism, in turn, will develop into a cooperative anarchism, and the state, as a coercive organization, will "wither away." Mill regarded representative democracy as the best form of government for a modern civilized society, but he warned against the tyranny of the majority and he defended the liberties of the dissident individual. If we add to these characterizations other relevant ideas, such as the concept of natural rights, we have a wide and rich gamut of theories.

18

The Control
of Human Behavior

We conclude with a symposium in which two famous psychologists, B. F. Skinner and Carl Rogers, debate the philosophical issues involved in the educational and political moulding of human beings. In a discussion highly pertinent to our scientific and technological age, some of the most crucial issues that have been raised in preceding chapters are brought to a sharp focus. Faced by "the spectre of predictable man," we are forced to reconsider our most basic concepts and ideals.

BURRHUS FREDERIC SKINNER (1904–   )
and CARL RANSOM ROGERS (1902–   )

B. F. Skinner studied English and Greek classics at Hamilton College in Clinton, New York. Turning from literature to psychology, he received his Master's degree in 1930 and Doctor's degree in 1931 at Harvard, where he has taught since 1947. During World War II he worked for the Office of Scientific Research and Development, training pigeons to pilot bombs and torpedoes through a guidance system activated by the birds' pecking in response to radar. His other remarkable exploits include teaching pigeons how to play ping-pong, and the invention of mechanical baby-tenders and teaching machines. The machines, combined with his theory of "programmed instruction," could revolutionize teaching methods. His novel, *Walden Two* (1948), depicts a Utopian community run on the principles of behavioral psychology. In other widely read books, *Science and Human Behavior* (1953), *Cumulative Record* (revised, 1961), and *Beyond Freedom and Dignity* (1971), he applies his theory to the full range of human phenomena.

Carl Rogers received his M.A. in 1928 and Ph.D. in 1931 from Teachers' College, Columbia University. He has worked as a clinical psychologist in Rochester, New York, and at the Universities of Ohio and Chicago. In 1957 he became Professor of Psychology and Psychiatry at the University of Wisconsin, and since 1964 he has been a resident fellow at the Western Behavioral Sciences Institute at La Jolla, California. He is best known for his "client-centered" theory of psychotherapy, which prescribes a person-to-person relationship between therapist and patient and encourages the patient, within wide limits, to control the course, pace, and length of his treatment. Rogers and his wife Helen love isolated spots in Mexico and the Carribean, where they paint, take colored photographs, swim and lie on the beach. In these spots, he has said, his most important ideas have come to him. Like Skinner, he is deeply interested in the philosophical implications of psychology.

Some Issues Concerning the Control of Human Behavior: A Symposium

I [Skinner]

Science is steadily increasing our power to influence, change, mold—in a word, control—human behavior. It has extended our "understanding" (whatever that may be) so that we deal more successfully with people in nonscientific ways, but it has also identified conditions or variables which can be used to predict and control behavior in a new,

From *Science*, Vol. 124, November 30, 1956. Copyright 1956 by the American Association for the Advancement of Science. Reprinted by permission of *Science* and the authors.

and increasingly rigorous, technology. The broad disciplines of government and economics offer examples of this, but there is special cogency in those contributions of anthropology, sociology, and psychology which deal with individual behavior. Carl Rogers has listed some of the achievements to date in a recent paper.[1] Those of his examples which show or imply the control of the single organism are primarily due, as we should expect, to psychology. It is the experimental study of behavior

[1] Carl Rogers, *Teachers College Record*, Vol. 57 (1956), p. 316.

which carries us beyond awkward or inaccessible "principles," "factors," and so on, to variables which can be directly manipulated.

It is also, and for more or less the same reasons, the conception of human behavior emerging from an experimental analysis which most directly challenges traditional views. Psychologists themselves often do not seem to be aware of how far they have moved in this direction. But the change is not passing unnoticed by others. Until only recently it was customary to deny the possibility of a rigorous science of human behavior by arguing, either that a lawful science was impossible because man was a free agent, or that merely statistical predictions would always leave room for personal freedom. But those who used to take this line have become most vociferous in expressing their alarm at the way these obstacles are being surmounted.

Now, the control of human behavior has always been unpopular. Any undisguised effort to control usually arouses emotional reactions. We hesitate to admit, even to ourselves, that we are engaged in control, and we may refuse to control, even when this would be helpful, for fear of criticism. Those who have explicitly avowed an interest in control have been roughly treated by history. Machiavelli is the great prototype. As Macaulay said of him, "Out of his surname they coined an epithet for a knave and out of his Christian name a synonym for the devil." There were obvious reasons. The control that Machiavelli analyzed and recommended, like most political control, used techniques that were aversive to the con-

trollee. The threats and punishments of the bully, like those of the government operating on the same plan, are not designed—whatever their success—to endear themselves to those who are controlled. Even when the techniques themselves are not aversive, control is usually exercised for the selfish purposes of the controller and, hence, has indirectly punishing effects upon others.

Man's natural inclination to revolt against selfish control has been exploited to good purpose in what we call the philosophy and literature of democracy. The doctrine of the rights of man has been effective in arousing individuals to concerted action against governmental and religious tyranny. The literature which has had this effect has greatly extended the number of terms in our language which express reactions to the control of men. But the ubiquity and ease of expression of this attitude spells trouble for any science which may give birth to a powerful technology of behavior. Intelligent men and women, dominated by the humanistic philosophy of the past two centuries, cannot view with equanimity what Andrew Hacker has called "the specter of predictable man."[2] Even the statistical or actuarial prediction of human events, such as the number of fatalities to be expected on a holiday weekend, strikes many people as uncanny and evil, while the prediction and control of individual behavior is regarded as little less than the work of the devil. I am not so much concerned here with the political or economic consequences for psychology,

[2] Andrew Hacker, *Antioch Review,* Vol. 14 (1954), p. 195.

although research following certain channels may well suffer harmful effects. We ourselves, as intelligent men and women, and as exponents of Western thought, share these attitudes. They have already interfered with the free exercise of a scientific analysis, and their influence threatens to assume more serious proportions. . . .

Education

The techniques of education were once frankly aversive. The teacher was usually older and stronger than his pupils and was able to "make them learn." This meant that they were not actually taught but were surrounded by a threatening world from which they could escape only by learning. Usually they were left to their own resources in discovering how to do so. Claude Coleman has published a grimly amusing reminder of these older practices. He tells of a schoolteacher who published a careful account of his services during 51 years of teaching, during which he administered: ". . . 911,527 blows with a cane; 124,010 with a rod; 20,989 with a ruler; 136,715 with the hand; 10,295 over the mouth; 7,905 boxes on the ear; [and] 1,115,800 slaps on the head. . . ."[3]

Progressive education was a humanitarian effort to substitute positive reinforcement for such aversive measures, but in the search for useful human values in the classroom it has never fully replaced the variables it abandoned. Viewed as a branch of behavioral technology, education remains relatively in-

[3] Claude Coleman, *Bulletin of the American Association of University Professors,* Vol. 39 (1953), p. 457.

efficient. We supplement it, and rationalize it, by admiring the pupil who learns *for himself*; and we often attribute the learning process, or knowledge itself, to something *inside* the individual. We admire behavior which seems to have inner sources. Thus we admire one who *recites* a poem more than one who simply *reads* it. We admire one who *knows* the answer more than one who *knows where to look it up*. We admire the *writer* rather than the reader. We admire the arithmetician who can do a problem in his head rather than with a slide rule or calculating machine, or in "original" ways rather than by a strict application of rules. In general we feel that any aid or "crutch"—except those aids to which we are now thoroughly accustomed—reduces the credit due. In Plato's *Phædrus,* Thamus, the king, attacks the invention of the alphabet on similar grounds! He is afraid "it will produce forgetfulness in the minds of those who learn to use it, because they will not practice their memories. . . ." In other words, he holds it more admirable to remember than to use a memorandum. He also objects that pupils "will read many things without instruction. . . [and] will therefore seem to know many things when they are for the most part ignorant." In the same vein we are today sometimes contemptuous of book learning, but, as educators, we can scarcely afford to adopt this view without reservation.

By admiring the student for knowledge and blaming him for ignorance, we escape some of the responsibility of teaching him. We resist any analysis of the educational process which threatens the notion of inner wisdom or questions the contention that the fault of ignorance lies with the student. More powerful techniques which bring about the sáme changes in behavior by manipulating *external* variables are decried as brainwashing or thought control. We are quite unprepared to judge *effective* educational measures. As long as only a few pupils learn much of what is taught, we do not worry about uniformity or regimentation. We do not fear the feeble technique; but we should view with dismay a system under which every student learned everything listed in a syllabus—although such a condition is far from unthinkable. Similarly, we do not fear a system which is so defective that the student must *work* for an education; but we are loath to give credit for anything learned without effort—although this could well be taken as an ideal result—and we flatly refuse to give credit if the student already knows what a school teaches.

A world in which people are wise and good without trying, without "having to be," without "choosing to be," could conceivably be a far better world for everyone. In such a world we should not have to "give anyone credit"—we should not need to admire anyone—for being wise and good. From our present point of view we cannot believe that such a world would be admirable. We do not even permit ourselves to imagine what it would be like.

Government

Government has always been the special field of aversive control. The state is frequently defined in terms of the power to punish, and jurisprudence leans heavily upon the associated notion of personal responsibility. Yet it is becoming increasingly difficult to reconcile current practice and theory with these earlier views. In criminology, for example, there is a strong tendency to drop the notion of responsibility in favor of some such alternative as capacity or controllability. But no matter how strongly the facts, or even practical expedience, support such a change, it is difficult to make the change in a legal system designed on a different plan. When governments resort to other techniques (for example, positive reinforcement), the concept of responsibility is no longer relevant and the theory of government is no longer applicable.

The conflict is illustrated by two decisions of the Supreme Court in the 1930's which dealt with, and disagreed on, the definition of control or coercion.[4] The Agricultural Adjustment Act proposed that the Secretary of Agriculture make "rental or benefit payments" to those farmers who agreed to reduce production. The government agreed that the Act would be unconstitutional if the farmer had been *compelled* to reduce production but was not, since he was merely *invited* to do so. Justice Roberts expressed the contrary majority view of the court that "The power to confer or withhold unlimited benefits is the power to coerce or destroy." This recognition of positive reinforcement was withdrawn a few years later in another case in which Justice Cardozo wrote "To hold that motive or temptation is equiv-

---

[4] P. A. Freund and others, *Constitutional Law: Cases and Other Problems* (Boston: Little, Brown, 1954), p. 233.

alent to coercion is to plunge the law in endless difficulties."[5] We may agree with him, without implying that the proposition is therefore wrong. Sooner or later the law must be prepared to deal with all possible techniques of governmental control.

The uneasiness with which we view government (in the broadest possible sense) when it does not use punishment is shown by the reception of my utopian novel, *Walden Two*. This was essentially a proposal to apply a behavioral technology to the construction of a workable, effective, and productive pattern of government. It was greeted with wrathful violence. *Life* magazine called it "a travesty on the good life," and "a menace . . . a triumph of mortmain or the dead hand not envisaged since the days of Sparta . . . a slur upon a name, a corruption of an impulse." Joseph Wood Krutch devoted a substantial part of his book, *The Measure of Man,* to attacking my views and those of the protagonist, Frazier, in the same vein, and Morris Viteles has recently criticized the book is a similar manner in *Science*.[6] Perhaps the reaction is best expressed in a quotation from *The Quest for Utopia* by Negley and Patrick: "Halfway through this contemporary utopia, the reader may feel sure, as we did, that this is a beautifully ironic satire on what has been called 'behavioral engineering.' The longer one stays in this better world of the psychologist, however, the plainer it becomes that the inspiration is not satiric, but messianic. This is indeed the behaviorally engi-

neered society, and while it was to be expected that sooner or later the principle of psychological conditioning would be made the basis of a serious construction of utopia—Brown anticipated it in *Limanora*—yet not even the effective satire of Huxley is adequate preparation for the shocking horror of the idea when positively presented. Of all the dictatorships espoused by utopists, this is the most profound, and incipient dictators might well find in this utopia a guidebook of political practice."[7]

One would scarcely guess that the authors are talking about a world in which there is food, clothing, and shelter for all, where everyone chooses his own work and works on the average only 4 hours a day, where music and the arts flourish, where personal relationships develop under the most favorable circumstances, where education prepares every child for the social and intellectual life which lies before him, where—in short—people are truly happy, secure, productive, creative, and forward-looking. What is wrong with it? Only one thing: someone "planned it that way." If these critics had come upon a society in some remote corner of the world which boasted similar advantages, they would undoubtedly have hailed it as providing a pattern we all might well follow—provided that it was clearly the result of a natural process of cultural evolution. Any evidence that intelligence had been used in arriving at this version of the good life would, in their eyes, be a serious flaw. No mat-

[5] Freund: *Constitutional Law,* p. 244.
[6] M. Viteles, *Science,* Vol. 122 (1955), p. 1167.

[7] Glenn Negley and J. M. Patrick, *The Quest for Utopia* (New York: Schuman, 1952).

ter if the planner of *Walden Two* diverts none of the proceeds of the community to his own use, no matter if he has no current control or is, indeed, unknown to most of the other members of the community (he planned that, too), somewhere back of it all he occupies the position of prime mover. And this, to the child of the democratic tradition, spoils it all.

The dangers inherent in the control of human behavior are very real. The possibility of the misuse of scientific knowledge must always be faced. We cannot escape by denying the power of a science of behavior or arresting its development. It is no help to cling to familiar philosophies of human behavior simply because they are more reassuring. As I have pointed out elsewhere,[8] the new techniques emerging from a science of behavior must be subject to the explicit countercontrol which has already been applied to earlier and cruder forms. Brute force and deception, for example, are now fairly generally suppressed by ethical practices and by explicit governmental and religious agencies. A similar countercontrol of scientific knowledge in the interests of the group is a feasible and promising possibility. Although we cannot say how devious the course of its evolution may be, a cultural pattern of control and countercontrol will presumably emerge which will be most widely supported because it is most widely reinforcing.

If we cannot foresee all the details of this (as we obviously cannot), it is important to remember that this is true of

[8] B. F. Skinner, *Transactions of the New York Academy of Sciences,* Vol. 17 (1955), p. 547.

the critics of science as well. The dire consequences of new techniques of control, the hidden menace in original cultural designs—these need some proof. It is only another example of my present point that the need for proof is so often overlooked. Man has got himself into some pretty fixes, and it is easy to believe that he will do so again. But there is a more optimistic possibility. The slow growth of the methods of science, now for the first time being applied to human affairs, *may* mean a new and exciting phase of human life to which historical analogies will not apply and in which earlier political slogans will not be appropriate. If we are to use the knowledge that a science of behavior is now making available with any hope of success, we must look at human nature as it is brought into focus through the methods of science rather than as it has been presented to us in a series of historical accidents.

If the advent of a powerful science of behavior causes trouble, it will not be because science itself is inimical to human welfare but because older conceptions have not yielded easily or gracefully. We expect resistance to new techniques of control from those who have heavy investments in the old, but we have no reason to help them preserve a series of principles that are not ends in themselves but rather outmoded means to an end. What is needed is a new conception of human behavior which is compatible with the implications of a scientific analysis. All men control and are controlled. The question of government in the broadest possible sense is not how freedom is to be preserved but what kinds of control are to be used and to what ends. Control must be analyzed and considered in its proper proportions. No one, I am sure, wishes to develop new master-slave relationships to bend the will of the people to despotic rulers in new ways. These are patterns of control appropriate to a world without science. They may well be the first to go when the experimental analysis of behavior comes into its own in the design of cultural practices.

II [Rogers]

There are, I believe, a number of matters in connection with this important topic on which the authors of this article, and probably a large majority of psychologists, are in agreement. These matters then are not issues as far as we are concerned, and I should like to mention them briefly in order to put them to one side.

Points of agreement

I am sure we agree that men—as individuals and as societies—have always endeavored to understand, predict, influence, and control human behavior—their own behavior and that of others.

I believe we agree that the behavioral sciences are making and will continue to make increasingly rapid progress in the understanding of behavior, and that as a consequence the capacity to predict and to control behavior is developing with equal rapidity.

I believe we agree that to deny these advances, or to claim that man's behavior cannot be a field of science, is unrealistic. Even though this is not an issue for us, we should recognize that many intelligent men still hold strongly to the view that the actions of men are free in some sense such that scientific knowledge of man's behavior is impossible. Thus Reinhold Niebuhr, the noted theologian, heaps scorn on the concept of psychology as a science of man's behavior and even says, "In any event, no scientific investigation of past behavior can become the basis of predictions of future behavior."[9] So, while this is not an issue for psychologists, we should at least notice in passing that it is an issue for many people.

I believe we are in agreement that the tremendous potential power of a science which permits the prediction and control of behavior may be misused, and that the possibility of such misuse constitutes a serious threat.

Consequently Skinner and I are in agreement that the whole question of the scientific control of human behavior is a matter with which psychologists and the general public should concern themselves. As Robert Oppenheimer told the American Psychological Association last year[10] the problems that psychologists will pose for society by their growing ability to control behavior will be much more grave than the problems posed by the ability of physicists to control the reactions of matter. I am not sure whether psychologists generally recognize this. My impression is that by and large they hold a laissez-faire attitude. Obviously Skinner and I do not hold this laissez-faire view, or we would not have written this article.

[9] Reinhold Niebuhr, *The Self and the Dramas of History* (New York: Scribner's, 1955), p. 47.
[10] Robert Oppenheimer, *American Psychologist*, Vol. 11 (1956), p. 127.

Points at issue

With these several points of basic and important agreement, are there then any issues that remain on which there are differences? I believe there are. They can be stated very briefly: Who will be controlled? Who will exercise control? What type of control will be exercised? Most important of all, toward what end or what purpose, or in the pursuit of what value, will control be exercised?

It is on questions of this sort that there exist ambiguities, misunderstandings, and probably deep differences. These differences exist among psychologists, among members of the general public in this country, and among various world cultures. Without any hope of achieving a final resolution of these questions, we can, I believe, put these issues in clearer form.

Some meanings

To avoid ambiguity and faulty communication, I would like to clarify the meanings of some of the terms we are using.

Behavioral science is a term that might be defined from several angles but in the context of this discussion it refers primarily to knowledge that the existence of certain describable conditions in the human being and/or in his environment is followed by certain describable consequences in his actions.

Prediction means the prior identification of behaviors which then occur. Because it is important in some things I wish to say later, I would point out that one may predict a highly specific behavior, such as an eye blink, or one may predict a class of behaviors. One might

correctly predict "avoidant behavior," for example, without being able to specify whether the individual will run away or simply close his eyes.

The word *control* is a very slippery one, which can be used with any one of several meanings. I would like to specify three that seem most important for our present purposes. *Control* may mean: (i) The setting of conditions by *B* for *A*, *A* having no voice in the matter, such that certain predictable behaviors then occur in *A*. I refer to this as external control. (ii) The setting of conditions by *B* for *A*, *A* giving some degree of consent to these conditions, such that certain predictable behaviors then occur in *A*. I refer to this as the influence of *B* on *A*. (iii) The setting of conditions by *A* such that certain predictable behaviors then occur in himself. I refer to this as internal control. It will be noted that Skinner lumps together the first two meanings, external control and influence, under the concept of control. I find this confusing.

Usual concept of control of human behavior

With the underbrush thus cleared away (I hope), let us review very briefly the various elements that are involved in the usual concept of the control of human behavior as mediated by the behavioral sciences. I am drawing here on the previous writings of Skinner, on his present statements, on the writings of others who have considered in either friendly or antagonistic fashion the meanings that would be involved in such control. I have not excluded the science fiction writers, as reported recently by Vandenburg,[11] since they often show an awareness of the issues involved, even though the methods described are as yet fictional. These then are the elements that seem common to these different concepts of the application of science to human behavior.

1) There must first be some sort of decision about goals. Usually desirable goals are assumed, but sometimes, as in George Orwell's book *1984,* the goal that is selected is an aggrandizement of individual power with which most of us would disagree. In a recent paper Skinner suggests that one possible set of goals to be assigned to the behavioral technology is this: "Let men be happy, informed, skillful, well-behaved and productive."[12] In the first draft of his part of this article, which he was kind enough to show me, he did not mention such definite goals as these, but desired "improved" education practices, "wiser" use of knowledge in government, and the like. In the final version of his article he avoids even these value-laden terms, and his implicit goal is the very general one that scientific control of behavior is desirable, because it would perhaps bring "a far better world for everyone."

Thus the first step in thinking about the control of human behavior is the choice of goals, whether specific or general. It is necessary to come to terms in some way with the issue, "For what purpose?"

2) A second element is that, whether the end selected is highly specific or is a very general one such as wanting "a

better world," we proceed by the methods of science to discover the means to these ends. We continue through further experimentation and investigation to discover more effective means. The method of science is self-correcting in thus arriving at increasingly effective ways of achieving the purpose we have in mind.

3) The third aspect of such control is that as the conditions or methods are discovered by which to reach the goals, some person or some group establishes these conditions and uses these methods, having in one way or another obtained the power to do so.

4) The fourth element is the exposure of individuals to the prescribed conditions, and this leads, with a high degree of probability, to behavior which is in line with the goals desired. Individuals are now happy, if that has been the goal, or well-behaved, or submissive, or whatever it has been decided to make them.

5) The fifth element is that if the process I have described is put in motion then there is a continuing social organization which will continue to produce the types of behavior that have been valued.

Some flaws

Are there any flaws in this way of viewing the control of human behavior? I believe there are. In fact the only element in this description with which I find myself in agrement is the second. It seems to me quite incontrovertibly true that the scientific method is an excellent way to discover the means by which to achieve our goals. Beyond that,

---

[11] S. G. Vandenberg, *American Psychologist,* Vol. 11 (1956), p. 339.

[12] B. F. Skinner, *American Scholar,* Vol. 25 (1955–1956), p. 47.

I feel many sharp differences, which I will try to spell out.

I believe that in Skinner's presentation here and in his previous writings, there is a serious underestimation of the problem of power. To hope that the power which is being made available by the behavioral sciences will be exercised by the scientists, or by a benevolent group, seems to me a hope little supported by either recent or distant history. It seems far more likely that behavioral scientists, holding their present attitudes, will be in the position of the German rocket scientists specializing in guided missiles. First they worked devotedly for Hitler to destroy the U.S.S.R. and the United States. Now, depending on who captured them, they work devotedly for the U.S.S.R. in the interest of detroying the United States, or devotedly for the United States in the interest of detroying the U.S.S.R. If behavioral scientists are concerned solely with advancing their science, it seems most probable that they will serve the purposes of whatever individual or group has the power.

But the major flaw I see in this review of what is involved in the scientific control of human behavior is the denial, misunderstanding, or gross underestimation of the place of ends, goals or values in their relationship to science. This error (as it seems to me) has so many implications that I would like to devote some space to it.

Ends and values in relation to science

In sharp contradiction to some views that have been advanced, I would like to propose a two-pronged thesis: (i) In any scientific endeavor—whether "pure" or applied science—there is a prior subjective choice of the purpose or value which that scientific work is perceived as serving. (ii) This subjective value choice which brings the scientific endeavor into being must always lie outside of that endeavor and can never become a part of the science involved in that endeavor.

Let me illustrate the first point from Skinner himself. It is clear that in his earlier writing it is recognized that a prior value choice is necessary, and it is specified as the goal that men are to become happy, well-behaved, productive, and so on. I am pleased that Skinner has retreated from the goals he then chose, because to me they seem to be stultifying values. I can only feel that he was choosing these goals for others, not for himself. I would hate to see Skinner become "well-behaved," as that term would be defined for him by behavioral scientists. His recent article in the *American Psychologist*[13] shows that he certainly does not want to be "productive" as that value is defined by most psychologists. And the most awful fate I can imagine for him would be to have him constantly "happy." It is the fact that he is very unhappy about many things which makes me prize him.

In the first draft of his part of this article, he also included such prior value choices, saying for example, "We must decide how we are to use the knowledge which a science of human behavior is now making available." Now he

[13] B. F. Skinner, *American Psychologist,* Vol. 11 (1956), p. 221.

has dropped all mention of such choices, and if I understand him correctly, he believes that science can proceed without them. He has suggested this view in another recent paper, stating that "We must continue to experiment in cultural design . . . testing the consequences as we go. Eventually the practices which make for the greatest biological and psychological strength of the group will presumably survive."[14]

I would point out, however, that to choose to experiment is a value choice. Even to move in the direction of perfectly random experimentation is a value choice. To test the consequences of an experiment is possible only if we have first made a subjective choice of a criterion value. And implicit in his statement is a valuing of biological and psychological strength. So even when trying to avoid such choice, it seems inescapable that a prior subjective value choice is necessary for any scientific endeavor, or for any application of scientific knowledge. . . .

Is the situation hopeless?

The thoughtful reader may recognize that, although my remarks up to this point have introduced some modifications in the conception of the processes by which human behavior will be controlled, these remarks may have made such control seem, if anything, even more inevitable. We might sum it up this way: Behavioral science is clearly moving forward; the increasing power

[14] B. F. Skinner, *Transactions of the New York Academy of Sciences,* Vol. 17 (1955), p. 549.

for control which it gives will be held by someone or some group; such an individual or group will surely choose the values or goals to be achieved; and most of us will then be increasingly controlled by means so subtle that we will not even be aware of them as controls. Thus, whether a council of wise psychologists (if this is not a contradiction in terms), or a Stalin, or a Big Brother has the power, and whether the goal is happiness, or productivity, or resolution of the Oedipus complex, or submission, or love of Big Brother, we will inevitably find ourselves moving toward the chosen goal and probably thinking that we ourselves desire it. Thus, if this line of reasoning is correct, it appears that some form of *Walden Two* or of *1984* (and at a deep philosophic level they seem indistinguishable) is coming. The fact that it would surely arrive piecemeal, rather than all at once, does not greatly change the fundamental issues. In any event, as Skinner has indicated in his writings, we would then look back upon the concepts of human freedom, the capacity for choice, the responsibility for choice, and the worth of the human individual as historical curiosities which once existed by cultural accident as values in a prescientific civilization.

I believe that any person observant of trends must regard something like the foregoing sequence as a real possibility. It is not simply a fantasy. Something of that sort may even be the most likely future. But is it an inevitable future? I want to devote the remainder of my remarks to an alternative possibility.

Alternative set of values

Suppose we start with a set of ends, values, purposes, quite different from the type of goals we have been considering. Suppose we do this quite openly, setting them forth as a possible value choice to be accepted or rejected. Suppose we select a set of values that focuses on fluid elements of process rather than static attributes. We might then value: man as a process of becoming, as a process of achieving worth and dignity through the development of his potentialities; the individual human being as a self-actualizing process, moving on to more challenging and enriching experiences; the process by which the individual creatively adapts to an ever-new and changing world; the process by which knowledge transcends itself, as, for example, the theory of relativity transcended Newtonian physics, itself to be transcended in some future day by a new perception.

If we select values such as these we turn to our science and technology of behavior with a very different set of questions. We will want to know such things as these: Can science aid in the discovery of new modes of richly rewarding living? more meaningful and satisfying modes of interpersonal relationships? Can science inform us on how the human race can become a more intelligent participant in its own evolution—its physical, psychological and social evolution? Can science inform us on ways of releasing the creative capacity of individuals, which seem so necessary if we are to survive

in this fantastically expanding atomic age? Oppenheimer has pointed out[15] that knowledge, which used to double in millenia or centuries, now doubles in a generation or a decade. It appears that we must discover the utmost in release of creativity if we are to be able to adapt effectively. In short, can science discover the methods by which man can most readily become a continually developing and self-transcending process, in his behavior, his thinking, his knowledge? Can science predict and release an essentially "unpredictable" freedom?

It is one of the virtues of science as a method that it is as able to advance and implement goals and purposes of this sort as it is to serve static values, such as states of being well-informed, happy, obedient. Indeed we have some evidence of this. . . .

Possible concept of the control of human behavior

It is quite clear that the point of view I am expressing is in sharp contrast to the usual conception of the relationship of the behavioral sciences to the control of human behavior. In order to make this contrast even more blunt, I will state this possibility in paragraphs parallel to those used before.

1) It is possible for us to choose to value man as a self-actualizing process of becoming; to value creativity, and the process by which knowledge becomes self-transcending.

[15] Robert Oppenheimer, *Roosevelt University Occasional Papers,* Vol. 2 (1956).

2) We can proceed, by the methods of science, to discover the conditions which necessarily precede these processes and, through continuing experimentation, to discover better means of achieving these purposes.

3) It is possible for individuals or groups to set these conditions, with a minimum of power or control. According to present knowledge, the only authority necessary is the authority to establish certain qualities of interpersonal relationships.

4) Exposed to these conditions, present knowledge suggests that individuals become more self-responsible, make progress in self-actualization, become more flexible, and become more creatively adaptive.

5) Thus such an initial choice would inaugurate the beginnings of a social system or subsystem in which values, knowledge, adaptive skills, and even the concept of science would be continually changing and self-transcending. The emphasis would be upon man as a process of becoming.

I believe it is clear that such a view as I have been describing does not lead to any definable utopia. It would be impossible to predict its final outcome. It involves a step-by-step development, based on a continuing subjective choice of purposes, which are implemented by the behavioral sciences. It is in the direction of the "open society," as that term has been defined by Popper,[16] where individuals carry responsibility for personal decisions. It is at the opposite pole from his concept of the closed

[16] Karl R. Popper, *The Open Society and Its Enemies* (London: Routledge and Kegan Paul, 1945).

society, of which *Walden Two* would be an example.

I trust it is also evident that the whole emphasis is on process, not on end-states of being. I am suggesting that it is by choosing to value certain qualitative elements of the process of becoming that we can find a pathway toward the open society.

The choice

It is my hope that we have helped to clarify the range of choice which will lie before us and our children in regard to the behavioral sciences. We can choose to use our growing knowledge to enslave people in ways never dreamed of before, depersonalizing them, controlling them by means so carefully selected that they will perhaps never be aware of their loss of personhood. We can choose to utilize our scientific knowledge to make men happy, well-behaved, and productive, as Skinner earlier suggested. Or we can insure that each person learns all the syllabus which we select and set before him, as Skinner now suggests. Or at the other end of the spectrum of choice we can choose to use the behavioral sciences in ways which will free, not control; which will bring about constructive variability, not conformity; which will develop creativity, not contentment; which will facilitate each person in his self-directed process of becoming; which will aid individuals, groups, and even the concept of science to become self-transcending in freshly adaptive ways of meeting life and its problems. The choice is up to us, and, the human race being what it is, we are likely to stumble about, making at times some nearly disastrous value choices and at other times highly constructive ones.

I am aware that to some, this setting forth of a choice is unrealistic, because a choice of values is regarded as not possible. Skinner has stated: "Man's vaunted creative powers . . . his capacity to choose and our right to hold him responsible for his choice—none of these is conspicuous in this new self-portrait (provided by science). Man, we once believed, was free to express himself in art, music, and literature, to inquire into nature, to seek salvation in his own way. He could initiate action and make spontaneous and capricious changes of course. . . . But science insists that action is initiated by forces impinging upon the individual, and that caprice is only another name for behavior for which we have not yet found a cause."[17]

I can understand this point of view, but I believe that it avoids looking at the great paradox of behavioral science. Behavior, when it is examined scientifically, is surely best understood as determined by prior causation. This is one great fact of science. But responsible personal choice, which is the most essential element in being a person, which is the core experience in psychotherapy, which exists prior to any scientific endeavor, is an equally prominent fact in our lives. To deny the experience of responsible choice is, to me, as restricted a view as to deny the possibility of a behavioral science. That these two important elements of our experience appear to be in contradiction has perhaps the same significance as the contradiction between the wave theory and the corpuscular theory of light, both of which can be shown to be true, even though incompatible. We cannot profitably deny our subjective life, any more than we can deny the objective description of that life.

In conclusion then, it is my contention that science cannot come into being without a personal choice of the values we wish to achieve. And these values we choose to implement will forever lie outside of the science which implements them; the goals we select, the purposes we wish to follow, must always be outside of the science which achieves them. To me this has the encouraging meaning that the human person, with his capacity of subjective choice, can and will always exist, separate from and prior to any of his scientific undertakings. Unless as individuals and groups we choose to relinquish our capacity of subjective choice, we will always remain persons, not simply pawns of a self-created science.

III [Skinner]

. . . The values I have occasionally recommended (and Rogers has not led me to recant) are transitional. Other things being equal, I am betting on the group whose practices make for healthy, happy, secure, productive, and creative people. And I insist that the values recommended by Rogers are transitional, too, for I can ask him the same kind of question. Man as a process of becoming—*what?* Self-actualization—

---

[17] B. F. Skinner, *American Scholar,* Vol. 25 (1955–1956), p. 47.

for what? Inner control is no more a goal than external.

What Rogers seems to me to be proposing, both here and elsewhere, is this: Let us use our increasing power of control to create individuals who will not need and perhaps will no longer respond to control. Let us solve the problem of our power by renouncing it. At first blush this seems as implausible as a benevolent despot. Yet power has occasionally been foresworn. A nation has burned its Reichstag, rich men have given away their wealth, beautiful women have become ugly hermits in the desert, and psychotherapists have become nondirective. When this happens, I look to other possible reinforcements for a plausible explanation. A people relinquish democratic power when a tyrant promises them the earth. Rich men give away wealth to escape the accusing finger of their fellowmen. A woman destroys her beauty in the hope of salvation. And a psychotherapist relinquishes control because he can thus help his client more effectively.

The solution that Rogers is suggesting is thus understandable. But is he correctly interpreting the result? What evidence is there that a client ever becomes truly *self*-directing? What evidence is there that he ever makes a truly *inner* choice of ideal or goal? Even though the therapist does not do the choosing, even though he encourages "self-actualization"—he is not out of control as long as he holds himself ready to step in when occasion demands —when, for example, the client chooses the goal of becoming a more accomplished liar or murdering his boss. But supposing the therapist does withdraw

completely or is no longer necessary— what about all the other forces acting upon the client? Is the self-chosen goal independent of his early ethical and religious training? of the folk-wisdom of his group? of the opinions and attitudes of others who are important to him? Surely not. The therapeutic situation is only a small part of the world of the client. From the therapist's point of view it may appear to be possible to relinquish control. But the control passes, not to a "self," but to forces in other parts of the client's world. The solution of the therapist's problem of power cannot be *our* solution, for we must consider *all* the forces acting upon the individual.

The child who must be prodded and nagged is something less than a fully developed human being. We want to see him hurrying to his appointment, not because each step is taken in response to verbal reminders from his mother, but because certain temporal contigencies, in which dawdling has been punished and hurrying reinforced, have worked a change in his behavior. Call this a state of better organization, a greater sensitivity to reality, or what you will. The plain fact is that the child passes from a temporary verbal control exercised by his parents to control by certain inexorable features of the environment. I should suppose that something of the same sort happens in successful psychotherapy. Rogers seems to me to be saying this: Let us put an end, as quickly as possible, to any pattern of master-and-slave, to any direct obedience to command, to the submissive following of suggestions. Let the individual be free to adjust himself to more rewarding features of the world about him. In the end, let his teachers and counselors "wither away," like the Marxist state. I not only agree with this as a useful ideal, I have constructed a fanciful world to demonstrate its advantages. It saddens me to hear Rogers say that "at a deep philosophic level" *Walden Two* and George Orwell's *1984* "seem indistinguishable." They could scarcely be more unlike—at any level. The book *1984* is a picture of immediate aversive control for vicious selfish purposes. The founder of *Walden Two*, on the other hand, has built a community in which neither he nor any other person exerts any *current* control. His achievement lay in his original *plan*, and when he boasts of this ("It is enough to satisfy the thirstiest tyrant") we do not fear him but only pity him for his weakness.

Another critic of *Walden Two*, Andrew Hacker,[18] has discussed this point in considering the bearing of mass conditioning upon the liberal notion of autonomous man. In drawing certain parallels between the Grand Inquisition passage in Dostoevsky's *Brothers Karamazov*, Huxley's *Brave New World*, and *Walden Two*, he attempts to set up a distinction to be drawn in any society between conditioners and conditioned. He assumes that "the conditioner can be said to be autonomous in the traditional liberal sense." But

[18] Andrew Hacker, *Journal of Politics*, Vol. 17 (1955), p. 17.

then he notes: "Of course the conditioner has been conditioned. But he has not been conditioned by the conscious manipulation of another *person*." But how does this affect the resulting behavior? Can we not soon forget the origins of the "artificial" diamond which is identical with the real thing? Whether it is an "accidental" cultural pattern, such as is said to have produced the founder of *Walden Two*, or the engineered environment which is about to produce his successors, we are dealing with sets of conditions generating human behavior which will ultimately be measured by their contribution to the strength of the group. We look to the future, not the past, for the test of "goodness" or acceptability.

If we are worthy of our democratic heritage we shall, of course, be ready to resist any tyrannical use of science for immediate or selfish purposes. But if we value the achievements and goals of democracy we must not refuse to apply science to the design and construction of cultural patterns, even though we may then find ourselves in some sense in the position of controllers. Fear of control, generalized beyond any warrant, has led to a misinterpretation of valid practices and the blind rejection of intelligent planning for a better way of life. In terms which I trust Rogers will approve, in conquering this fear we shall become more mature and better organized and shall, thus, more fully actualize ourselves as human beings.

COMMENT

The discussion between Skinner and Rogers is a fitting conclusion to this book. It surveys "the enduring questions" from a fresh and contemporary perspective. Among these questions are the following:

1. WHAT IS THE CORRECT METHOD OF INQUIRY? Skinner, as a brilliant experimentalist, operates in the tradition of empiricists such as Locke, Hume, and Peirce. He rejects the introspective method and traces knowledge back to experience rather than to innate mental factors. Scientific method as he interprets it is based upon sensory and, therefore, public observation. The study of human activities, he insists, should concentrate upon the forms of external behavior, exhibited with various regularities and probabilities. He thinks that there is no great difference in method between animal and human psychology.

Rogers, as a clinical psychologist and psychotherapist, seeks to understand the unfolding development of inner needs and purposes. Although he could not be called a rationalist, he agrees with Descartes in recognizing an innate structure to the mind and in distinguishing rather sharply between the human and animal levels of behavior. For him, we to be studied at our own level and each person is to be understood in their own terms. Like the existentialists, Kierkegaard and Buber, he seeks to penetrate behind all masks and false fronts to "that self which one truly is." Using language identical with Buber's, he has said that the deepest and most satisfying interpersonal contact is "a real I-Thou relationship, not an I-It relationship."[1]

2. WHAT IS THE RELATION BETWEEN MIND AND BODY? Skinner opposes Cartesian dualism. Although he is too sophisticated to deny that there are thoughts and feelings, he declares that a scientific psychology must wholly abandon the conception of psychic causes. He has defined such mental factors as "intentions" in terms of observable relations that refer exclusively to antecedent stimulus conditions and motions of bodies. Everything that a psychologist legitimately wants to say about mental events, he believes, can be said in purely behavioral terms.

Although Rogers does not accept so sharp a dualism as that of Descartes, he insists that the inner life is causally important and nonreducible. Man is a psychophysiological organism, and it is a mistake to slight or disregard the mental side of his nature.

---

[1] For Rogers' sympathy with Kierkegaard, see Clark E. Moustakes (ed.), *The Self* (New York: Harper & Row, 1956), pp. 197–198; and for his relation to Buber, see Maurice S. Friedman, *Martin Buber: The Life of Dialogue* (New York: Harper & Row, 1960), pp. 191–195. Also see the dialogue between Buber and Rogers in Martin Buber, *The Knowledge of Man* (New York: Harper & Row, 1965), pp. 166–184.

3. Do Men Have Free Will? Skinner agrees with Spinoza in rejecting the possibility of undetermined choices and final causes. He has said that a scientific theory of human behavior "must abolish the conception of the individual as a doer, as an originator of action."[2] Explaining behavior in terms of stimuli impinging upon the individual, he is sceptical that a person "ever becomes truly *self*-directing," or "that he ever makes a truly *inner* choice of ideal or goal." Although, like Hume, he speaks of freedom of action, it is within the context of a deterministic theory.

Rogers aligns himself with free-will advocates. He is as insistent upon the importance and reality of "subjective value choice" as Skinner is on "conditioning." His aim as a therapist is to liberate the individual from both inner and outer blocks so as to permit more freedom and self-direction. Granted that there are limits to our environmental opportunities and our given and potential nature, we are free within these limits to guide our growth by reflective goals.

4. What Is the Natural Basis of Ethics? Skinner tends toward an "evolutionary ethics" based upon the principle of "the survival of the fittest." When pressed for justification of his ethical preferences, he falls back upon the criterion of "the strength of the group" and "the survival of mankind." He is much more inclined than Rogers to think that science can supply the norms for the control of human behavior.

Rogers believes that human beings, by nature, are loaded and cocked to develop in certain ways, and that it is good to realize this potential. The ethical goal is fulfillment of what is deepest in a man's nature. He thus approximates the humanism of the natural-law tradition that stems from Aristotle and Cicero, but he differs in putting greater emphasis upon the freedom and uniqueness of the individual person. "Basic human nature," he has said, "is something that is really to be *trusted*. . . . It's been very much my experience in therapy that one does not need to supply motivation toward the positive or toward the constructive. That exists in the individual. . . . If we can release what is most basic in the individual . . . it will be constructive."[3] To pursue this goal calls for a "subjective value choice" that lies outside the scope of science.

5. How Should Human Behavior Be Controlled? In view of the contrasting answers of Skinner and Rogers to the foregoing questions, we should not be surprised that they differ radically in their educational and political ideals.

Skinner approaches education as a technological problem, believing that the art of teaching should be based upon the science of learning. He puts great stress upon "what are called contingencies of reinforcement—the relations which prevail between behavior on the one hand and the consequences of that behavior

---

[2] B. F. Skinner, *Cumulative Record* (New York: Appleton-Century-Crofts, 1959), p. 236.
[3] Martin Buber, *The Knowledge of Man*, pp. 179–180.

on the other."[4] These consequences he proposes to manipulate by rewards ("positive reinforcement") more than punishments ("aversive control" or "negative reinforcement"). He advocates "programmed instruction" with the aid of ingenious teaching machines. The sad thing, he declares, is that we are not making use of a tenth of the knowledge about learning that we have at our disposal.

In sketching his Utopia in *Walden Two,* he applies the same basic principle as in his educational theory—namely, control over positive and negative reinforcements (the carrot and stick approach, with emphasis upon the carrot). His proposal for social reconstruction resembles Plato's in the *Republic,* except that psychological-engineers replace philosopher-kings. Having found that he can do amazing things with rats and pigeons, he believes that equally amazing results can be achieved by the scientific and technological reshaping of human beings within an "engineered environment." For him, the viable choice is not between freedom and control but between scientific control, on the one hand, and caprice and unscientific control, on the other. He is convinced that we gain freedom *through* control and not otherwise. Although he recognizes that authoritarian figures may shape people the wrong way, he thinks that countercontrols can be devised that will minimize this danger.

For Rogers the idea of manipulating human beings, whether in school or in society, is highly distasteful. He draws a sharper distinction than does Skinner between the training of animals and the education of human beings. For the latter he advocates something like the "Socratic method" when liberally interpreted. This method was described by Ralph Cudworth, the seventeenth-century Platonist, as based upon the belief that "knowledge was not to be poured into the soul like liquor, but rather to be invited and gently drawn forth from it; nor the mind so much to be filled therewith from without, like a vessel, as to be kindled and awaked."[5] Rogers, I think, would put more emphasis than Cudworth upon environmental factors in the teaching process, but he too wishes to release inner potentialities and to awaken and kindle the mind.

Because he dislikes the manipulation of human beings even by "positive reinforcement," he sees a deeper affinity between *Walden Two* and Orwell's *1984* than Skinner is willing to admit. He is convinced that the freedom of persons ought categorically to be respected, and that the goal of happiness by contrived reinforcement should not override the demands of freedom. In the tradition of Mill and Dewey he proposes a liberal set of values to guide us politically as well as educationally. "We can choose the behavioral sciences," he says, "in ways which will free, not control." He warns against the danger that science will be used, as in Hitler's Germany or Stalin's Russia, for vicious or totalitarian ends.

---

[4] B. F. Skinner, *The Technology of Teaching* (New York: Appleton-Century-Crofts, 1968), p. 9.

[5] Ralph Cudworth, *Treatise Concerning Eternal and Immutable Morality,* American ed. of *Works,* ed. T. Birch, 1838, p. 427. I am indebted to Noam Chomsky, *Cartesian Linguistics,* for this reference.

There is nothing in science itself, in the absence of "subjective value choice," that can prevent such abuse.

In this clash of opinion between Rogers and Skinner there are exciting grounds for debate and discussion.

Selected Bibliography

CHAPTER 1. THE QUEST FOR WISDOM

Blum, Alan F., *Socrates: The Original and Its Images*. London: Routledge, 1978.

Cornford, F. M., *Before and After Socrates*. London: Cambridge University Press, 1932.

Cross, Robert Nicol, *Socrates: The Man and His Mission*. London: Methuen, 1914.

Ferguson, John (ed.), *Socrates: A Source Book*. London: Macmillan, 1970.

Guardini, Romano, *The Death of Socrates*. New York: Sheed & Ward, 1948.

Gulley, Norman, *The Philosophy of Socrates*. New York: St. Martin's, 1968.

Guthrie, W. K. C., *Socrates*. London: Cambridge University Press, 1971.

Jaeger, Werner, *Paideia: The Idea of Greek Culture*. Oxford: Blackwell, 1947.

O'Brien, Michael John, *The Socratic Paradoxes and the Greek Mind*. Chapel Hill: University of North Carolina Press, 1967.

Sauyage, Micheline, *Socrates and the Human Conscience*. New York: Harper & Row, 1961.

Taylor, A. E., *Socrates*. New York: Appleton, 1933.

Versenyi, Laszlo, *Socratic Humanism*. New Haven: Yale University Press, 1963.

Vlastos, Gregory (ed.), *The Philosophy of Socrates*. New York: Doubleday, 1971.

CHAPTER 2. GOD AND MAN

Alexander, Samuel, *Space, Time and Deity*. New York: Macmillan, 1920, Vol. 2.

Anselm, St., *Proslogion: With a Reply on Behalf of the Fool by Gaunilo and the Author's Reply to Gaunilo* (including an introduction and commentary by M. J. Charlesworth). Oxford: Clarendon Press, 1965.

Barnes, Jonathan, *The Ontological Argument*. New York: St. Martin's, 1972.

Broad, C. D., *Religion, Philosophy and Psychical Research*. New York: Harcourt, 1953.

Copleston, F. C., *Aquinas*. Harmondsworth: Penguin, 1955. Ch. 3.

Flew, Anthony, *God and Philosophy*. London: Hutchinson, 1966.

———, *Hume's Philosophy of Belief*. New York: Humanities Press, 1961.

——— and Alasdair MacIntyre, *New Essays in Philosophical Theology*. New York: Macmillan, 1955.

Freud, Sigmund, *The Future of an Illusion*. New York: Norton, 1976.

Garrigou-Lagrange, R., *God, His Existence and His Nature*, 2 Vols. St. Louis: Herter, 1934, 1936.

Gaskin, J. C. A., *Hume's Philosophy of Religion*. New York: Barnes & Noble, 1978.

Gibson, A. Boyce, *Theism and Empiricism*. New York: Schocken Books, 1970.

Gilson, Etienne, *God and Philosophy*. London: Oxford University Press, 1941.

———, *The Philosophy of St. Thomas Aquinas*. Cambridge: Heffner, 1929.

Hartshorne, Charles, *Anselm's Discovery*. La Salle, Ill.: Open Court, 1965.

———, *The Logic of Perfection*. La Salle, Ill.: Open Court, 1962.

——— (ed.), *Philosopher's Speak of God*. Chicago: University of Chicago Press, 1953.

Hick, John, *Evil and the God of Love*. London: Macmillan, 1966.

——— (ed.), *The Existence of God*. New York: Macmillan, 1964. (Classical and contemporary readings on the arguments for the existence of God.)

———, *God and the Universe of Faiths*. New York: St. Martin's, 1973.

Hicks, G. Dawes, *The Philosophical Bases of Theism*. London: Allen & Unwin, 1937.

Hume, David, *Dialogues Concerning Natural Religion*, ed. by Norman Kemp Smith. New York: Nelson, 1947. (Contains background material and detailed analysis of Hume's arguments.)

Hurlbutt, Robert H., *Hume, Newton, and the Design Argument*. Lincoln: University of Nebraska Press, 1965.

Kaufmann, Walter (ed.), *Religion from Tolstoy to Camus*. New York: Harper & Row, 1961.

Kenny, Anthony, *The Five Ways: St. Thomas Aquinas' Proofs of God's Existence*. New York: Schocken Books, 1969.

McPherson, Thomas, *The Argument from Design*. New York: St. Martin's, 1972.

McTaggart, J. M. E., *Some Dogmas of Religion*. London: Arnold, 1930.

Malcolm, Norman, "Anselm's Ontological Arguments," *Philosophical Review*, Vol. 69 (1960).

Matson, Wallace, *The Existence of God*. Ithaca, N.Y.: Cornell University Press, 1965.

Otto, Rudolf, *The Idea of the Holy*, 2nd ed. New York: Oxford University Press, 1950.

Plantinga, Alvin, *God, Freedom, and Evil*. New York: Harper & Row, 1974.

—— (ed.), *The Ontological Argument: From Anselm to Contemporary Philosophers*. New York: Doubleday, 1967.

Pike, Nelson (ed.), *God and Evil*. Englewood Cliffs, N.J.: Prentice-Hall, 1964.

Rowe, William L., *The Cosmological Argument*. Princeton, N.J.: Princeton University Press, 1975.

Schufreider, Gregory, *An Introduction to Anselm's Argument*. Philadelphia: Temple University Press, 1978.

Taylor, A. E., *Does God Exist?* New York: Macmillan, 1947.

Tennant, F. R., *Philosophical Theology*, 2 Vols. Cambridge University Press, 1928, 1930.

Urban, Linwood, and Douglas N. Walton (eds.), *The Power of God: Readings on Omnipotence and Evil*. New York: Oxford University Press, 1978.

Vahanian, Gabriel, *The Death of God*. New York: Braziller, 1961.

Ward, Keith, *The Concept of God*. New York: St. Martin's, 1974.

Whitehead, Alfred North, *Religion in the Making*. New York: Macmillan, 1926.

Wisdom, John, "Gods" in Anthony Flew (ed.), *Logic and Language*. London: Blackwell, 1960.

CHAPTER 3. ONE OR MANY

Curley, E. M., *Spinoza's Metaphysics*. Cambridge, Mass.: Harvard University Press, 1969.

Freeman, Eugene, and Maurice Mandelbaum (eds.), *Spinoza: Essays in Interpretation*. La Salle, Ill.: Open Court, 1975.

Grene, Marjorie (ed.), *Spinoza: A Collection of Critical Essays*. Garden City, N.Y.: Doubleday, 1973.

Hall, Roland, "Monism and Pluralism" in Paul Edwards (ed.), *The Encyclopedia of Philosophy*. New York: Macmillan and Free Press, 1967. Bibliography.

Hallett, H. F., *Benedict Spinoza*. London: Athlone, 1957.

Hampshire, Stuart, *Spinoza*. Harmondsworth: Penguin, 1951.

James, William, *A Pluralistic Universe*. London: Longmans, 1909.

Jaspers, Karl, *Spinoza*. New York: Harcourt, 1974.

Kashap, S. Paul (ed.), *Studies in Spinoza*. Berkeley: University of California Press, 1972.

Oko, Adolph, *The Spinoza Bibliography*. Boston: Hall, 1964.

Parkinson, G. H. R., *Spinoza's Theory of Knowledge*. Oxford: Clarendon Press, 1964.

Quinton, A. M., "Pluralism and Monism," *Encyclopedia Britannica*, 1971. Vol. 18, pp. 66–68.

Shahan, Robert W., and J. I. Biro (eds.), *Spinoza: New Perspectives*. Norman: University of Oklahoma Press, 1978.

Sullivan, Celestine, *Critical and Historical Reflections on Spinoza's "Ethics"*. Berkeley: University of California Press, 1958.

CHAPTER 4. MATERIALISM

Wettesen, Jon, *The Saga and the Way: Studies in Spinoza's Ethics of Freedom.* Assen: Van Gorcum, 1978.

Armstrong, D. M., *A Materialistic Theory of the Mind.* New York: Humanities Press, 1968.

Cloud, Preston, *Cosmos, Earth and Man: A Short History of the Universe.* New Haven: Yale University Press, 1978. (The universe as depicted by science.)

Feyerabend, Paul, "Materialism and the Mind-Body Problem," *Review of Metaphysics,* 17 (1963).

Lange, F. A., *The History of Materialism.* New York: Harcourt, 1925.

Laslett, P. (ed.), *The Physical Basis of Mind.* Oxford: Blackwell, 1951.

McDougall, William, *Modern Materialism and Emergent Evolution.* New York: Van Nostrand, 1929.

Malcolm, Norman, "Scientific Materialism and the Identity Theory," *Dialogue,* 3 (1964).

Margolis, Joseph, *Persons and Minds: The Prospects of Nonreductive Materialism.* Boston: Reidel, 1978.

Nagel, T., "Physicalism," *Philosophical Review,* 74 (1965).

O'Connor, John M. (ed.), *Modern Materialism.* New York: Harcourt, 1969.

Place, U. T., "Materialism as a Scientific Hypothesis," *Philosophical Review,* 74 (1965).

Rosenthal, David M. (ed.), *Materialism and the Mind-Body Problem.* Englewood Cliffs, N.J.: Prentice-Hall, 1971.

Smart, J. J. C., *Philosophy and Scientific Realism.* London: Routledge, 1963.

Winspear, Alban D., *Lucretius and Scientific Thought.* Montreal: Harvest House, 1963.

Minds and Machines

Anderson, A. R. (ed.), *Minds and Machines.* Englewood Cliffs, N.J.: Prentice-Hall, 1964.

Dreyfus, Herbert L., "A Critique of Artificial Intelligence," *Thought* 43 (1968).

La Mettrie, Julien, *Man a Machine.* Chicago: Open Court, 1912.

Sayre, Kenneth M. *Cybernetics and the Philosophy of Mind.* London: Routledge, 1976.

Sluckin, W., *Minds and Machines.* Baltimore: Penguin, 1960. (Bibliography.)

Thompson, Dennis, "Can a Machine Be Conscious?" *British Journal for the Philosophy of Science,* 16 (1965).

For further references on the mind-body problem see bibliography for Chapter 6.

CHAPTER 5. IDEALISM

Berkeley

Bennett, Jonathan, *Locke, Berkeley, Hume.* Oxford: Clarendon Press, 1971.

Berkeley, George, *Principles, Dialogues, and Philosophical Correspondence,* ed. by Colin Turbayne. Indianapolis: Bobbs-Merrill, 1965. (Full text with excellent introduction.)

Bracken, Harry M., *Berkeley.* New York: St. Martin's, 1974.

Hicks, G. Dawes, *Berkeley.* London: Oxford University Press, 1932.

Jessop, T. E., *George Berkeley.* London: Longman, 1959.

Johnston, G. A., *The Development of Berkeley's Philosophy.* London: Russell & Russell, 1965.

Luce, Arthur A., *Berkeley's Immaterialism.* London: Russell & Russell, 1968.

Martin, C. B., and D. M. Armstrong (eds.), *Locke and Berkeley: A Collection of Critical Essays.* Notre Dame: Notre Dame University Press, 1968.

Pitcher, George, *Berkeley.* London: Routledge, 1977.

Ritchie, A. D., *George Berkeley: A Reappraisal.* Manchester University Press, 1967.

Sillem, Edward A., *George Berkeley and the Proofs of the Existence of God.* London: Longmans, 1957.

Steinkraus, Warren E. (ed.), *New Studies in Berkeley's Philosophy.* New York: Holt, Rinehart and Winston, 1966.

Tipton, I. C., *Berkeley*. London: Methuen, 1974.
Warnock, G. J., *Berkeley*. Harmondsworth: Penguin, 1953.
Wild, John, *George Berkeley: A Study of His Life and Philosophy*. Cambridge, Mass.: Harvard University Press, 1936.
Wisdom, J. O., *The Unconscious Origins of Berkeley's Philosophy*. New York: Hillary House, 1957.

The Idealist Tradition

Acton, H. B., "Idealism" in Paul Edwards (ed.), *The Encyclopedia of Philosophy*, New York: Macmillan and Free Press, 1967.
Adams, George P., *Idealism and the Modern Age*. New Haven: Yale University Press, 1919.
Blanshard, Brand, *The Nature of Thought*, 2 vols. New York: Macmillan, 1940.
Bradley, F. H., *Appearance and Reality*. Oxford: Clarendon Press, 1930.
Ewing, A. C., *Idealism: A Critical Survey*. London: Methuen, 1934.
———— (ed.), *The Idealist Tradition from Berkeley to Blanshard*. New York: Free Press, 1957.
Hoernle, R. F. A., *Idealism as a Philosophy*. New York: Doran, 1927.
Royce, Josiah, *The Spirit of Modern Philosophy*. New York: Tudor, 1955.
Schopenhauer, Arthur, *The World as Will and Idea*. New York: AMS, 1976.
For references on Hegel see bibliography for Chapter 15.

CHAPTER 6. DUALISM

Descartes

Balz, A. G. A., *Descartes and the Modern Mind*. New Haven: Yale University Press, 1952.
Beck, Leslie, *The Metaphysics of Descartes*. Oxford: Clarendon Press, 1965.
Bouwsma, O. K., *Philosophical Essays*. Lincoln: University of Nebraska Press, 1965.
Butler, R. J. (ed.), *Cartesian Studies*. Oxford: Blackwell, 1972.
Curley, Edwin M., *Descartes Against the Sceptics*. Cambridge, Mass.: Harvard University Press, 1978.
Doney, Willis (ed.), *Descartes*. New York: Doubleday, 1968.
Gibson, A. Boyce, *The Philosophy of Descartes*. London: Russell & Russell, 1967.
Grayeff, Felix, *Descartes*. London: Philip Goodall, 1977.
Hooker, Michael (ed.), *Descartes: Critical and Interpretive Essays*. Baltimore: Johns Hopkins Press, 1978.
Keeling, Stanley V., *Descartes,* 2nd ed. New York: Oxford University Press, 1968.
Kenny, Anthony, *Descartes*. New York: Random House, 1968.
Malcolm, Norman, *Problems of Mind: Descartes to Wittgenstein*. New York: Harper & Row, 1971.
Popkin, Richard H., *The History of Skepticism from Erasmus to Descartes*. New York: Harper & Row, 1968.
Sesonske, Alexander, and Noel Fleming (eds.), *Meta-Meditations*. Belmont, Cal.: Wadsworth, 1965.
Smith, Norman Kemp, *New Studies in the Philosophy of Descartes*. New York: Russell & Russell, 1963.
Vrooman, Jack R., *Rene Descartes: A Biography*. New York: Putnam, 1970.
Williams, Bernard, *Descartes*. Atlantic Highlands, N.J.: Humanities Press, 1978.
Wilson, Margaret D., *Descartes*. London: Routledge, 1978.

The Body-Mind Problem

Broad, C. D., *The Mind and Its Place in Nature*. New York: Harcourt, 1925.
Borst, Clive Vernon (ed.), *The Mind-Body Identity Theory*. New York: St. Martin's, 1970.

Campbell, Keith, *Body and Mind*. New York: Doubleday, 1970.

Chappell, Vere Claiborne (ed.), *The Philosophy of Mind*. Englewood Cliffs, N.J.: 1962.

Ducasse, C. J., *Nature, Mind, and Death*. La Salle, Ill.: Open Court, 1951.

Feigel, Herbert, *The "Mental" and the "Physical"*. Minneapolis: University of Minnesota Press, 1967.

Findlay, John M., *Psyche and Cerebrum*. Milwaukee: Marquette University Press, 1972.

Hampshire, Stuart (ed.), *Philosophy of Mind*. New York: Harper & Row, 1966.

Hook, Sidney (ed.), *Dimensions of Mind*. New York: New York University Press, 1960.

Laird, John, *Our Minds and Their Bodies*. London: Oxford University Press, 1925.

Laslett, Peter (ed.), *The Physical Basis of Mind*. Oxford: Blackwell, 1950.

Morick, Harold (ed.), *Introduction to the Philosophy of Mind: Readings from Descartes to Strawson*. Glenview, Ill.: Scott, Foresman, 1970.

Penfield, W., *The Mystery of the Mind*. Princeton University Press, 1975.

Peursen, C. A. van, *Body, Soul, Spirit*. London: Oxford University Press, 1966.

Popper, Karl, and John C. Eccles, *The Self and Its Brain*. New York: Springer, 1977. (Extensive bibliography.)

Schilpp, Paul A. (ed.), *The Philosophy of Karl Popper*, 2 Vols. La Salle, Ill.: Open Court, 1974.

Sherrington, Charles, *Man on His Nature*. London: Cambridge University Press, 1940.

Smythies, J. R. (ed.), *Brain and Mind*. New York: Humanities Press, 1965.

Spicker, Stuart F. (ed.), *The Philosophy of the Body: Rejections of Cartesian Dualism*. Chicago: Quadrangle, 1970.

Strawson, P. F., *Individuals*. London: Methuen, 1959.

Vesey, G. N. A. (ed.), *Body and Mind*. London: Allen & Unwin, 1964.

Taylor, Richard, "How To Bury the Mind-Body Problem," *American Philosophical Quarterly*, 6 (1969).

Teichman, Jenny, *The Mind and the Soul*. London: Routledge, 1974.

Wisdom, John, *Problems of Mind and Matter*. Cambridge University Press, 1934.

Wisdom, J. O., "A New Model for the Mind-Body Relationship," *British Journal for the Philosophy of Science*, 2 (1952).

CHAPTER 7. CAUSATION, FREE WILL, AND THE LIMITS OF KNOWLEDGE

Hume

Basson, Anthony H., *David Hume*. Harmondsworth: Penguin, 1958.

Beck, Lewis White, *Essays on Kant and Hume*. New Haven: Yale University Press, 1978.

Bennett, Jonathan, *Locke, Berkeley, Hume*. Oxford: Clarendon Press, 1971.

Cavendish, A. P., *David Hume*. New York: Dover, 1968.

Chappell, Vere C. (ed.), *Hume: A Collection of Critical Essays*. South Bend, Ind.: University of Notre Dame Press, 1974.

Church, R. W., *Hume's Theory of the Understanding*. Ithaca, N.Y.: Cornell University Press, 1935.

Flew, Anthony, *Hume's Philosophy of Belief*. New York: Humanities Press, 1961.

Greig, J. Y. T., *David Hume*. New York: Oxford University Press, 1931.

Hendel, C. W., *Studies in the Philosophy of Hume*, rev. ed. Indianapolis: Bobbs-Merrill, 1963.

Laing, B. M., *David Hume*. London: Oxford University Press, 1932.

Laird, John, *Hume's Philosophy of Human Nature*. London: Methuen, 1932.

Livingstone, Donald W., and James T. King (eds.), *Hume: A Re-Evaluation*. New York: Fordham University Press, 1976.

Macnabb, D. G. C., *David Hume*, 2nd ed. Oxford: Blackwell, 1966.

Noxon, James H., *Hume's Philosophical Development*. Oxford: Clarendon Press, 1973.

Pears, David (ed.), *David Hume*. New York: St. Martin's, 1963.
Penelhum, Terence, *Hume*. New York: St. Martin's, 1963.
Price, H. H., *Hume's Theory of the External World*. Oxford: Clarendon Press, 1940.
Smith, Norman Kemp, *The Philosophy of David Hume*. London: Macmillan, 1941.
Stove, David C., *Probability and Hume's Inductive Scepticism*. Oxford: Clarendon Press, 1973.
Vesey, Godfrey, *Personal Identity*. Ithaca: Cornell University Press, 1977.
Zabeeh, Farhang, *Hume: Precursor of Modern Empiricism*. The Hague: Nijhoff, 1973.

Kant

Beck, Lewis White (ed.), *Kant Studies Today*. La Salle, Ill.: Open Court, 1969.
Bennett, Jonathan, *Kant's Dialectic*. New York: Cambridge University Press, 1974.
Brittan, Gordon G., *Kant's Theory of Science*. Princeton University Press, 1978.
Broad, C. D., *Kant*. New York: Cambridge University Press, 1978.
Ewing, A. C., *A Short Commentary on Kant's Critique of Pure Reason*. London: Methuen, 1938. (Less difficult than the commentaries of H. J. Paton and Norman Kemp Smith.)
Goldmann, Lucien, *Immanuel Kant*. London: NLB, 1971.
Hartnack, Justus, *Immanuel Kant*. Atlantic Highlands, N.J.: Humanities Press, 1974.
Kemp, John, *The Philosophy of Kant*. London: Oxford University Press, 1968.
Körner, S., *Kant*. Harmondsworth: Penguin, 1955.
Strawson, P. F., *The Bounds of Sense*. London: Methuen, 1966.
Walker, Ralph C. S., *Kant*. London: Routledge, 1978.
Wilkerson, T. E., *Kant's Critique of Pure Reason: A Commentary for Students*. London: Oxford University Press, 1976.
Wolff, Robert Paul (ed.), *Kant*. New York: Doubleday, 1967.
————, *Kant's Theory of Mental Activity*. Cambridge, Mass.: Harvard University Press, 1963.
Wood, Allen W., *Kant's Rational Theology*. Ithaca: Cornell University Press, 1978.
Yovel, Yirmiahu, *History of Kant's System*. Princeton University Press, 1979.

The Limits of Knowledge

Ayer, A. J., *The Problem of Knowledge*. Harmondsworth: Penguin, 1965.
Gellner, Ernest, *Legitimation of Belief*. London: Cambridge University Press, 1974.
Hintikka, Jaakko, *Knowledge and Belief*. Ithaca, N.Y.: Cornell University Press, 1962.
Johnson, Oliver A., *Skepticism and Cognitivism*. Berkeley: University of California Press, 1978.
Lehrer, Keith, *Knowledge*. Oxford: Clarendon Press, 1974.
Levensky, Mark (ed.), *Human Factual Knowledge*. Englewood Cliffs, N.J.: Prentice-Hall, 1971.
Malcolm, Norman, *Thought and Knowledge*. Ithaca, N.Y.: Cornell University Press, 1977.
Margolis, Joseph, *Knowledge and Existence*. New York: Oxford University Press, 1973.
Nagel, Ernest, and Richard Brandt (eds.), *Meaning and Knowledge*. New York: Harcourt, 1965.
Pears, David, *What Is Knowledge?* New York: Harper & Row, 1971.
Russell, Bertrand, *Human Knowledge*. New York: Simon & Schuster, 1948.
Weigel, Gustav E., and Arthur Madden, *Knowledge: Its Values and Limits*. Englewood Cliffs, N.J.: Prentice-Hall, 1961.
Will, F., *Induction and Justification*. Ithaca, N.Y.: Cornell University Press, 1974.

Free Will and Determinism

Ayer, J. L., "Ifs and Cans" in *Philosophical Papers*. London: Macmillan, 1951.
Bergson, Henri, *Time and Free Will*. New York: Macmillan, 1921.
Berofsky, Bernard (ed.), *Free Will and Determinism*. New York: Harper & Row, 1966.
Bradley, F. H., *Ethical Studies*. Oxford: Clarendon Press, 1927. First Essay.
Broad, C. D., *Determinism, Indeterminism, and Libertarianism*. New York: Macmillan, 1934.
Campbell, C. A., *In Defence of Free Will*. New York: Humanities Press, 1968.

————, *On Selfhood and Godhood*. London: Allen & Unwin, 1957.

Enteman, Willard F. (ed.), *The Problem of Free Will*. New York: Scribner's, 1967.

Farrer, Austin, *The Freedom of the Will*. New York: Scribner's, 1960.

Hampshire, Stuart, *Freedom of the Individual*. New York: Harper & Row, 1965.

Hook, Sidney (ed.), *Determinism and Freedom in the Age of Science*. New York: Collier, 1961.

Hospers, John, "Free-Will and Psychoanalysis," in Wilfred Sellars and John Hospers (eds.), *Readings in Ethical Theory*. New York: Appleton, 1952.

Lehrer, Keith (ed.), *Freedom and Determinism*. New York: Random House, 1966.

Lucas, J. R., *The Freedom of the Will*. Oxford: Clarendon Press, 1970.

Morgenbesser, Sidney, and James Walsh (eds.), *Free Will*. Englewood Cliffs, N.J.: Prentice-Hall, 1962. (Bibliography).

Morris, Herbert (ed.), *Freedom and Responsibility*. Stanford University Press, 1961.

O'Connor, D. J., *Free Will*. New York: Doubleday, 1971.

Sartre, Jean Paul, *Being and Nothingness*. New York: Philosophical Library, 1956.

Schlick, Moritz, *Problems of Ethics*. Englewood Cliffs, N.J.: Prentice-Hall, 1939, Ch. 1. (Defence of Hume's view of free will.)

CHAPTER 8. METHOD IN SCIENCE AND PHILOSOPHY

Peirce, Dewey, and Pragmatism

Bernstein, Richard J., *John Dewey*. New York: Washington Square Press, 1966.

————, *Perspectives on Peirce*. New Haven: Yale University Press, 1965.

Boydston, Jo Ann, *Checklist of Writings about John Dewey*. Carbondale, Ill.: Southern Illinois University Press, 1974.

Buchler, Justus, *Charles Peirce's Empiricism*. New York: Harcourt, 1939.

———— (ed.), *The Philosophy of Peirce: Selected Writings*. New York: Harcourt, 1940.

Dewey, John, *Experience and Nature*, rev. ed. La Salle, Ill.: Open Court, 1929.

————, *The Quest for Certainty*. New York: Minton, Balch, 1929.

Gallie, W. B., *Peirce and Pragmatism*. Harmondsworth: Penguin, 1952.

McDermott, John J. (ed.), *The Philosophy of John Dewey*. New York: Putnam, 1973.

Moore, Edward C., *American Pragmatism: Peirce, James, and Dewey*. New York: Columbia University Press, 1961.

Reilly, Francis E., *Charles Peirce's Theory of Scientific Method*. New York: Fordham University Press, 1970.

Rescher, Nicholas, *Peirce's Philosophy of Science*. Notre Dame: Notre Dame University Press, 1978.

Scheffler, Israel, *Four Pragmatists: A Critical Introduction to Peirce, James, Mead, and Dewey*. New York: Humanities Press, 1974.

Schilpp, Paul A. (ed.), *The Philosophy of John Dewey*. La Salle, Ill.: Open Court, 1975.

Turley, Peter T., *Peirce's Cosmology*. New York: Philosophical Library, 1977.

Wiener, Philip P. and Frederick H. Young (eds.), *Studies in the Philosophy of Charles Sanders Peirce*, 2 vols. Cambridge, Mass.: Harvard University Press, 1952, 1964.

Scientific Method

Braithwaite, R. B., *Scientific Explanation*. Cambridge University Press, 1953.

Beveridge, W. I. B., *The Art of Scientific Investigation*. New York: Random House, 1961.

Blake, R. M., Ducasse, C. J., and Madden, E. H., *Theories of Scientific Method*. Seattle: University of Washington Press, 1960.

Broad, C. D., *Scientific Thought*. New York: Harcourt, 1927.

Burks, Arthur W., *Cause, Chance, Reason: An Inquiry into the Nature of Scientific Evidence.* University of Chicago Press, 1975.

Cohen, Morris R., *Reason and Nature: An Essay on the Meaning of Scientific Method.* Glencoe, Ill.: Free Press, 1953.

———, *Studies in Philosophy and Science.* New York: Ungar, 1959.

Columbia Associates, *Introduction to Reflective Thinking.* Boston: Houghton Mifflin, 1923.

Feigel, Herbert, and May Brodbeck (eds.), *Readings in the Philosophy of Science.* New York: Appleton, 1953.

Gingerich, Owen, *Nature of Scientific Discovery.* Washington: Smithsonian Institution, 1945.

Hanson, Norwood Russell, *Perception and Discovery.* San Francisco: Freeman, Cooper, 1970.

Harre, R., *An Introduction to the Logic of the Sciences.* London: Macmillan, 1960.

Hesse, Mary, *The Structure of Scientific Inference.* Berkeley: University of California Press, 1974.

Kuhn, Thomas S., *The Essential Tension: Selected Studies in Scientific Tradition.* University of Chicago Press, 1977.

———, *The Structure of Scientific Revolutions.* University of Chicago Press, 1970.

Nagel, Ernest, *Sovereign Reason.* Glencoe, Ill.: Free Press, 1954.

———, *The Structure of Science.* New York: Harcourt, 1961.

———, Patrick Suppes, and A. Tarski, *Logic, Methodology and Philosophy of Science.* Stanford University Press, 1932.

Popper, Karl R., *Conjectures and Refutations: The Growth of Scientific Knowledge.* New York: Harper & Row, 1965.

———, *The Logic of Scientific Discovery.* London: Hutchinson, 1959.

———, *Objective Knowledge.* Oxford: Clarendon Press, 1975.

Salmon, Wesley C., *The Foundations of Scientific Inference.* Pittsburgh: University of Pittsburgh Press, 1967.

CHAPTER 9. EXISTENTIALISM

Kierkegaard

Bretall, Robert (ed.), *A Kierkegaard Anthology.* New York: Random House, 1946.

Collins, James, *The Mind of Kierkegaard.* Chicago: Regnery, 1953.

Dupre, Louis, *Kierkegaard as Theologian.* New York: Sheed & Ward, 1968.

Johnson, Howard, and Niels Thulstrup (eds.), *A Kierkegaard Critique.* New York: Harper & Row, 1962.

Lowrie, Walter, *Kierkegaard,* 2 Vols. New York: Oxford University Press, 1938.

Malantschuk, Gregor, *Kierkegaard's Thought.* Princeton University Press, 1971.

Murphy, Arthur E., "On Kierkegaard's Claim that Truth Is Subjectivity," *Reason and the Common Good.* Englewood Cliffs, N.J.: Prentice-Hall, 1963.

Price, George, *The Narrow Pass: A Study of Kierkegaard's Concept of Man.* London: Hutchinson, 1963.

Shestov, Lev, *Kierkegaard and the Existentialist Philosophy.* Athens, Ohio: Ohio University Press, 1969.

Shmüeli, Adi, *Kierkegaard and Consciousness.* Princeton University Press, 1971.

Thompson, Josiah (ed.), *Kierkegaard.* New York: Knopf, 1973.

Thulstrup, Niels, *Kierkegaard and Hegel.* Princeton University Press, 1979.

Buber and Community

Berdyaev, Nicolai, *Solitude and Society.* London: Bles, 1938.

Brownell, Baker, *The Human Community.* New York: Harper & Row, 1950.

Buber, Martin, *Between Man and Man.* Boston: Beacon Press, 1958.

————, *I and Thou*, 2nd ed. New York: Scribner's, 1958.

————, *The Knowledge of Man*. New York: Harper & Row, 1965.

Cohen, A. A., *Martin Buber*. London: Bowes and Bowes, 1957.

Diamond, Malcolm, *Martin Buber*. New York: Oxford University Press, 1960.

Drengson, Alan R., "Toward a Philosophy of Community," *Philosophical Forum*, 16 (1979).

Edwards, Paul, *Buber and Buberism*. Lawrence: University of Kansas, 1970.

Friedman, Maurice S., *Martin Buber: The Life of Dialogue*, 3rd ed. University of Chicago Press, 1976.

Herbert, Will (ed.), *The Writings of Martin Buber*. New York: Meridian, 1956.

Hodes, Aubrey, *Martin Buber: An Intimate Portrait*. New York: Viking, 1971.

MacMurray, John, *Persons in Relation*. London: Faber, 1961.

Marcel, Gabriel, *Man against Mass Society*. Chicago: Regnery, 1962.

Mead, George Herbert, *Mind, Self, and Society*. University of Chicago Press, 1934.

Pfuetze, Paul, *The Social Self*. New York: Bookman Associates, 1954. (On Mead and Buber.)

Rader, Melvin, *Ethics and the Human Community*. New York: Holt, Rinehart and Winston, 1964. Chs. 11, 14–16.

Schilpp, Paul A., and Maurice Friedman (eds.), *The Philosophy of Martin Buber*. La Salle, Ill.: Open Court, 1965. (Contains extensive bibliography.)

Tönnies, Ferdinand, *Community and Society*. East Lansing: Michigan State University Press, 1957.

Existentialism

Barnes, Hazel, *An Existentialist Ethics*. New York: Knopf, 1967.

Barrett, William, *Irrational Man*. New York: Doubleday, 1958.

————, *What Is Existentialism?* New York: Grove, 1964.

Berdyaev, Nicolai, *The Divine and the Human*. London: Bles, 1949.

Blackham, H. J., *Six Existentialist Thinkers*. London: Routledge, 1951.

Camus, Albert, *The Myth of Sisyphus*. New York: Random House, 1955.

Collins, James, *The Existentialists*. Chicago: Regnery, 1959.

Gill, Richard, *The Fabric of Existentialism*. Englewood Cliffs, N.J.: Prentice-Hall, 1973.

Grene, Marjorie, *Introduction to Existentialism*. University of Chicago Press, 1959.

Hanna, Thomas, *The Lyrical Existentialists*. New York: Atheneum, 1962.

Harper, Ralph, *The Existential Experience*. Baltimore: Johns Hopkins University Press, 1972.

Heidegger, Martin, *Being and Time*. New York: Harper & Row, 1962.

Heinemann, F. H., *Existentialism and the Modern Predicament*. New York: Harper & Row, 1953.

Jaspers, Karl, *Reason and Existenz*. London: Routledge, 1956.

Kaufmann, Walter (ed.), *Existentialism from Dostoevsky to Sartre*. New York: World, 1956.

Kuhn, Helmut, *Encounter with Nothingness*. London: Methuen, 1951.

Macquarrie, John, *Existentialism*. Baltimore: Penguin, 1973. (Bibliography.)

Molina, Fernando, *Existentialism as Philosophy*. Englewood Cliffs, N.J.: Prentice-Hall, 1962.

Olafson, Frederick, *Principles and Persons: An Ethical Interpretation of Existentialism*. Baltimore: Johns Hopkins University Press, 1967.

Sanborn, Patricia, *Existentialism*. New York: Pegasus, 1968.

Sartre, Jean-Paul, *Being and Nothingness*. New York: Philosophical Library, 1956.

Shinn, Roger L., *Restless Adventure: Essays on Contemporary Expressions of Extentialism*. New York: Scribner's, 1968.

Tillich, Paul, *The Courage To Be*. New Haven: Yale University Press, 1952.

————, "Existential Philosophy," *Journal of the History of Ideas*, 5 (1944).

Wahl, Jean, *Philosophies of Existence*. New York: Schocken Books, 1969.

————, *A Short History of Existentialism*. New York: Philosophical Library, 1972.

Zaner, Richard M., *Phenomenology and Existentialism*. New York: Putnam, 1973.

CHAPTER 10. REASON AND VIRTUE

Clark, Stephen R., *Aristotle's Man: Speculations on Aristotelian Anthropology*. Oxford: Clarendon Press, 1975.

Cooper, John M., *Reason and Human Good in Aristotle*. Cambridge, Mass.: Harvard University Press, 1975.

Kenny, Anthony, *The Aristotelian Ethics*. Oxford: Clarendon Press, 1978.

Monan, J. Donald, *Moral Knowledge and Its Methodology in Aristotle*. Oxford: Clarendon Press, 1968.

Moravcsik, Julius (ed.), *Aristotle*. Garden City, N.Y.: Doubleday, 1967.

Mure, G. R. G., *Aristotle*. New York: Oxford University Press, 1939, Ch. 7.

Oates, Whitney J., *Aristotle and the Problem of Value*. Princeton University Press, 1961.

Randall, John H., *Aristotle*. New York: Columbia University Press, 1960.

Ross, W. D., *Aristotle*, 2nd ed. London: Methuen, 1930, Ch. 7.

Veatch, Henry B., *Aristotle*. Bloomington, Ind.: Indiana University Press, 1974.

———, *Rational Man: A Modern Interpretation of Aristotelian Ethics*. Bloomington, Ind.: Indiana University Press, 1962.

Walsh, James J., *Aristotle's Conception of Moral Weakness*. New York: Columbia University Press, 1963.

——— and H. L. Shapiro (eds.), *Aristotle's Ethics*. Belmont, Cal.: Wadsworth, 1967.

Wild, John, *Introduction to Realistic Philosophy*. New York: Harper & Row, 1948. Part I.

CHAPTER 11. NATURE

Crowe, M. B., *The Changing Profile of Natural Law*. Oxford: Blackwell, 1977.

D'Entreves, A. P., *Natural Law*. London: Hutchinson, 1951.

Gierke, Otto, *Natural Law and the Theory of Society*. London: Cambridge University Press, 1934.

Huxley, Thomas Henry and Julian, *Touchstone for Ethics*. New York: Harper & Row, 1947.

Maritain, Jacques, *The Rights of Man and Natural Law*. New York: Scribner's, 1945.

Midgley, E. B. F., *The Natural Law Tradition and the Theory of International Relations*. New York: Barnes & Noble, 1975.

Mill, John Stuart, "Nature" in *Three Essays on Religion*. London: Longmans, 1885.

Needham, Joseph, *Human Law and the Laws of Nature in China and the West*. New York: Oxford University Press, 1951.

O'Connor, D. J., *Aquinas and Natural Law*. London: Macmillan, 1968.

Rist, John Michael, *Stoic Philosophy*. New York: Cambridge University Press, 1969.

——— (ed.), *The Stoics*. Berkeley: University of California Press, 1978.

Sandbach, F. H., *The Stoics*. New York: Norton, 1975.

Simon, Yves, *The Tradition of Natural Law*. New York: Fordham University Press, 1964.

Veatch, Henry B., "Natural Law: Dead or Alive?" *Literature of Liberty: A Review of Contemporary Liberal Thought*, 1 (1978).

Wild, John, *Plato's Modern Enemies and the Theory of Natural Law*. University of Chicago Press, 1953.

CHAPTER 12. DUTY

Acton, H. B., *Kant's Moral Philosophy*. New York: St. Martin's, 1970.

Beck, Lewis W., *Commentary on Kant's Critique of Practical Reason*. University of Chicago Press, 1960.

Ewing, A. C., "What Would Happen If Everybody Acted Like Me?" *Philosophy*, 28 (1953).

Hare, R. M., "Universalizability," *Proceedings of the Aristotelian Society*, (1954–1955).

Jones, Hardy E., *Kant's Principle of Personality*. Madison: University of Wisconsin Press, 1971.

Murphy, Jeffrie G., *Kant: The Philosophy of Right.* New York: St. Martin's, 1970.
Nell, Onara, *Acting on Principle: An Essay on Kantian Ethics.* New York: Columbia University Press, 1975.
Paton, H. J., *The Categorical Imperative.* London: Hutchinson, 1947.
Prichard, H. A., *Moral Obligation.* New York: Oxford University Press, 1950.
Ross, W. D., *Kant's Ethical Theory.* New York: Oxford University Press, 1954.
Scheler, Max, *Formalism in Ethics.* Evanston: Northwestern University Press, 1973.
Singer, Marcus G., *Generalization in Ethics.* New York: Knopf, 1961.
Teale, Alfred E., *Kantian Ethics.* New York: Oxford University Press, 1951.
Ward, Keith, *The Development of Kant's View of Ethics.* Oxford: Blackwell, 1972.
Williams, T. C., *The Concept of the Categorical Imperative.* Oxford: Clarendon Press, 1968.
Wolff, Robert Paul, *The Autonomy of Morals: A Commentary on Kant's Groundwork of the Metaphysics of Morals.* New York: Harper & Row, 1973.
—— (ed.), *Kant.* New York: Doubleday, 1967. Part Two.

CHAPTER 13. HAPPINESS AND UTILITY

Anschutz, Richard P., *The Philosophy of John Stuart Mill.* Oxford: Clarendon Press, 1953.
Baumgardt, R. B., *Bentham and the Ethics of Today.* Princeton University Press, 1952.
Bayles, Michael D. (ed.), *Contemporary Utilitarianism.* New York: Doubleday, 1968.
Blake, Ralph, "Why Not Hedonism? A Protest," *Ethics,* 37 (1926).
Britton, Karl, *John Stuart Mill.* Harmondsworth: Penguin, 1953.
Gorovitz, Samuel (ed.), *Utilitarianism: John Stuart Mill.* Indianapolis: Bobbs-Merrill, 1971.
Hearn, T. K., *Studies in Utilitarianism.* New York: Appleton, 1971.
Hodgson, D. H., *Consequences of Utilitarianism.* Oxford: Clarendon Press, 1967.
Long, Douglas, *Bentham on Liberty . . . in Relation to His Utilitarianism.* University of Toronto Press, 1977.
Lyons, David, *Forms and Limits of Utilitarianism.* Oxford: Clarendon Press, 1965.
——, *In the Interest of the Governed: A Study in Bentham's Philosophy of Utility and Law.* Oxford: Clarendon Press, 1973.
McCloskey, H. J., *John Stuart Mill.* London: Macmillan, 1971.
Moore, G. E., *Ethica Principia.* New York: Cambridge University Press, 1949.
Nagel, Thomas, *The Possibility of Altruism.* Oxford: Clarendon Press, 1970.
Narveson, Jan, *Morality and Utility.* Baltimore: Johns Hopkins University Press, 1966.
Plamenatz, John, *The English Utilitarians.* Oxford: Blackwell, 1958.
Rawls, John, "Two Concepts of Rules," *Philosophical Review,* 64 (1955).
Rescher, Nicholas, *Distributive Justice: A Constructive Critique of the Utilitarian Theory of Distribution.* Indianapolis: Bobbs-Merrill, 1966.
——, *Unselfishness.* Pittsburgh: University of Pittsburgh Press, 1975.
Ryan, Alan, *John Stuart Mill.* New York: Pantheon, 1970.
Schlick, Moritz, *The Problems of Ethics.* Englewood Cliffs, N.J.: Prentice-Hall, 1938.
Schneewind, Jerome (ed.), *Mill: A Collection of Critical Essays.* New York: Doubleday, 1968.
Smart, J. J. C., *An Outline of a System of Utilitarian Ethics.* Melbourne University Press, 1961.
—— and Bernard Williams, *Utilitarianism: For and Against.* Cambridge University Press, 1973.
Smith, James M. and Ernest Sosa (eds.), *Mill's Utilitarianism.* Belmont, Cal.: Wadsworth, 1969.

CHAPTER 14. ARISTOCRACY

Barker, Ernest, *Greek Political Thought: Plato and His Predecessors.* London: Methuen, 1918.
Barrow, Robin, *Plato, Utilitarianism and Education.* London: Routledge, 1975.
Brumbaugh, R. S., *Plato and the Modern Age.* New York: Crowell-Collier, 1962.

Cross, R. C., and A. D. Woozley, *Plato's Republic*. New York: St. Martin's, 1964.

Crossman, R. H. S., *Plato Today*. New York: Oxford University Press, 1959.

Field, G. C., *The Philosophy of Plato,* 2nd ed. London: Oxford University Press, 1969.

Findlay, J. N., *Plato and Platonism*. New York: Times Books, 1978.

——, *Plato: The Written and Unwritten Doctrines*. New York: Humanities Press, 1974.

Gosling, J. C. B., *Plato*. London: Routledge, 1973.

Gould, John, *The Development of Plato's Ethics*. New York: Columbia University Press, 1955.

Grube, G. M. A., *Plato's Thought*. Boston: Beacon Press, 1935.

Havelock, Eric, *The Greek Concept of Justice: From Its Shadow in Homer to Its Substance in Plato*. London: Brill, 1978.

——, *Preface to Plato*. Cambridge, Mass.: Harvard University Press, 1963.

Jaeger, Werner, *Paidea*. Oxford: Blackwell, 1947, Vol. 2.

Koyre, Alexander, *Discovering Plato*. New York: Columbia University Press, 1945.

Levinson, Ronald, *In Defense of Plato*. Cambridge, Mass.: Harvard University Press, 1953.

Murphy, N. R., *The Interpretation of Plato's Republic*. Oxford: Clarendon Press, 1951.

Popper, Karl R., *The Open Society and Its Enemies*, rev. ed. London: Routledge and K. Paul, 1966, Vol. 1.

Thorson, T. L. (ed.), *Plato: Totalitarian or Democrat?* Englewood Cliffs, N.J.: Prentice-Hall, 1963.

Vlastos, Gregory, *Plato*. New York: Doubleday, 1971.

——, *Plato's Universe*. Seattle: University of Washington Press, 1975.

Wild, John, *Plato's Modern Enemies and the Theory of Natural Law*. University of Chicago Press, 1953.

——, *Plato's Theory of Man*. Cambridge, Mass.: Harvard University Press, 1946.

Winspear, Alban, *The Genesis of Plato's Thought*, 2nd ed. New York: S. A. Russell, 1956.

Woodbridge, F. J. E., *The Son of Apollo*. Boston: Houghton Mifflin, 1929.

CHAPTER 15. HISTORY AND FREEDOM

Avineri, Shlomo, *Hegel's Theory of the Modern State*. Cambridge University Press, 1972.

Findlay, J. N., *Hegel: A Re-Examination*. New York: Macmillan, 1958.

Gadamer, Hans-Georg, *Hegel's Dialectic*. New Haven: Yale University Press, 1976.

Hegel, G. W. F., *Lectures on the Philosophy of World History*, ed. by D. Forbes and H. B. Nisbet. Cambridge University Press, 1975.

Kaufmann, Walter, *Hegel: A Reinterpretation*. New York: Doubleday, 1966.

—— (ed.), *Hegel's Political Philosophy*. New York: Atherton Press, 1970.

Kelly, George A., *Idealism, Politics and History: Sources of Hegelian Thought*. Cambridge University Press, 1969.

Lukács, György, *The Young Hegel*. London: Merlin Press, 1975.

——, *Hegel's False and His Genuine Ontology*. London: Merlin Press, 1978.

MacIntyre, Alasdair (ed.), *Hegel*. New York: Doubleday, 1972.

—— (ed.), *Hegel: A Collection of Critical Essays*. Notre Dame, Ind.: University of Notre Dame Press, 1976.

Marcuse, Herbert, *Reason and Revolution: Hegel and the Rise of Social Theory*. New York: Humanities Press, 1954.

Mueller, Gustav, *Hegel: The Man, His Vision and Work*. New York: Pageant Press, 1968.

Mure, G. R. G., *Idealist Epilogue*. Oxford: Clarendon Press, 1978.

O'Brien, George D., *Hegel on Reason and History*. University of Chicago Press, 1975.

Rosen, Stanley, *G. W. F. Hegel*. New Haven: Yale University Press, 1974.

Steinkraus, Warren E. (ed.), *New Studies in Hegel's Philosophy*. New York: Holt, Rinehart and Winston, 1971.

Taylor, Charles, *Hegel*. Cambridge University Press, 1975.
———, *Hegel and Modern Society*. Cambridge University Press, 1979.
Wilkins, B. F., *Hegel's Philosophy of History*. Ithaca, N.Y.: Cornell University Press, 1974.

CHAPTER 16. COMMUNISM

Avineri, Shlomo, *The Social and Political Thought of Karl Marx*. London: Cambridge University Press, 1969.
Cohen, G. A., *Karl Marx's Theory of History: A Defence*. Princeton University Press, 1978.
Fromm, Erich, *Marx's Concept of Man*. New York: Ungar, 1961.
Garaudy, Roger, *Karl Marx: The Evolution of His Thought*. Westport, Conn.: Greenwood Press, 1976.
Heller, Agnes, *The Theory of Need in Marx*. New York: St. Martin's, 1976.
Hook, Sidney, *From Hegel to Marx*. New York: Reynal, 1963.
Kamenka, Eugene, *The Ethical Foundations of Marxism*. London: Routledge, 1962.
Kolakowski, Leszek, *Main Currents of Marxism*, 3 Vols. Oxford: Clarendon Press, 1978.
Lefebrvre, Henri, *The Sociology of Marx*. New York: Random House, 1969.
Lichtheim, George, *Marxism*. New York: Praeger, 1961.
Maguire, John, *Marx's Paris Writings*. Dublin: Gill and Macmillan, 1972.
McBridge, William, *The Philosophy of Marx*. New York: St. Martin's, 1977.
McLellan, David, *Karl Marx: His Life and Thought*. New York: Harper & Row, 1973.
——— (ed.), *Karl Marx: Selected Writings*. Oxford University Press, 1977. (Comprehensive selections and bibliography.)
McMurtry, John, *The Structure of Marx's World View*. Princeton University Press, 1978.
Meszaros, Istvan, *Marx's Theory of Alienation*. London: Merlin Press, 1970.
Ollman, Bertell, *Alienation: Marx's Conception of Man in Capitalist Society*. Cambridge University Press, 1971.
Plamenatz, John, *German Marxism and Russian Communism*. New York: Harper & Row, 1965.
———, *Karl Marx's Philosophy of Man*. Oxford: Clarendon Press, 1975.
Popper, Karl R., *The Open Society and Its Enemies*, rev. ed. London: Routledge, 1966, Vol. 2.
Rader, Melvin, *Marx's Interpretation of History*. New York: Oxford University Press, 1979.
Seigel, Jerrold, *Marx's Fate: The Shape of a Life*. Princeton University Press, 1978.
Seliger, Martin, *The Marxist Conception of Ideology*. Cambridge University Press, 1977.
Shaw, William H., *Marx's Theory of History*. Stanford University Press, 1978.
Swingewood, Alan, *Marx and Modern Social Theory*. New York: Wiley, 1975.
Torrance, John, *Estrangement, Alienation, and Exploitation: A Sociological Approach to Historical Materialism*. London: Macmillan, 1977.
Tucker, Robert C., *Philosophy and Myth in Karl Marx*. Cambridge University Press, 1972.
Venable, Vernon, *Human Nature: The Marxian View*. New York: Knopf, 1945.
Wittfogel, Karl A., *Oriental Despotism*. New Haven: Yale University Press, 1957.

CHAPTER 17. LIBERALISM

Bay, Christian, *The Structure of Freedom*. Stanford University Press, 1958.
Berlin, Isaiah, *Four Essays on Liberty*. London: Oxford University Press, 1969.
———, *Two Concepts of Liberty*. London: Oxford University Press, 1969.
Britton, Karl, *John Stuart Mill*. Baltimore: Penguin, 1953.
Cowling, Maurice, *Mill and Liberalism*. Cambridge University Press, 1963.
Dewey, John, *Liberalism and Social Action*. New York: Putnam, 1935.
Duncan, Graeme, *Marx and Mill*. Cambridge University Press, 1973.

Halliday, R. J., *John Stuart Mill*. New York: Barnes & Noble, 1976.

Laski, Harold, *The Rise of Liberalism*. New York: Harper & Row, 1936.

MacPherson, C. B., *The Political Theory of Possessive Individualism*. Oxford: Clarendon Press, 1962.

Meiklejohn, Alexander, *Free Speech and Its Relation to Self Government*. New York: Harper & Row, 1948.

Packe, Michael St. John, *The Life of John Stuart Mill*. New York: Macmillan, 1954.

Plamenatz, John, *Consent, Freedom and Political Obligation*. London: Oxford University Press, 1968.

Radcliff, Peter (ed.), *Limits of Liberty: Studies of Mill's On Liberty*. Belmont, Cal.: Wadsworth, 1966.

Rawls, John, *A Theory of Justice*. Cambridge, Mass.: Belknap, 1971.

Robson, John M., *The Improvement of Mankind: The Social and Political Thought of John Stuart Mill*. London: Routledge, 1968.

——— and Michael Lane (eds.), *James and John Stuart Mill*. Toronto: University of Toronto Press, 1976.

Russell, Bertrand, *Authority and the Individual*. New York: Simon & Schuster, 1949.

———, *Freedom and Organization, 1814–1914*. New York: Norton, 1914.

Ryan, Alan, *John Stuart Mill*. New York: Pantheon, 1970.

CHAPTER 18. THE CONTROL OF HUMAN BEHAVIOR

Allport, Gordon, *Personality and Social Encounter*. Boston: Beacon Press, 1960.

Carpenter, Finley, *The Skinner Primer: Behind Freedom and Dignity*. New York: Free Press, 1974.

Chomsky, Noam, *Problems of Knowledge and Freedom*. New York: Pantheon, 1971.

Erwin, Edward, *Behavior Therapy: Scientific, Philosophical and Moral Foundations*. Cambridge University Press, 1978.

Freedman, Daniel G., *Human Socialbiology: A Holistic Approach*. Riverside, N.J.: Free Press, 1979.

Geiser, Robert L., *Behavior Mod and the Managed Society*. Boston: Beacon Press, 1976.

Karen, R. L., *An Introduction to Behavior Theory and Its Applications*. New York: Harper & Row, 1974.

Machan, T. R., *The Pseudo-Science of B. F. Skinner*. New York: Arlington House, 1974.

Marcuse, Herbert, *One Dimensional Man*. Boston: Beacon Press, 1964.

Maslow, Alexander H., *Toward a Psychology of Being*, 2nd ed. New York: Van Nostrand, 1968. ("Holistic-dynamic psychology" opposed to Skinner's behaviorism.)

Milholland, Frank, *From Skinner to Rogers: Contrasting Approaches to Education*. Lincoln, Neb.: Professional Educators Publications, 1972.

Puligandla, R., *Fact and Fiction in Skinner's Science and Utopia*. St. Louis: W. H. Green, 1974.

Rogers, Carl R., *On Becoming a Person*. Boston: Houghton Mifflin, 1961.

Rothblatt, R. (ed.), *Changing Perspectives on Man*. University of Chicago Press, 1968.

Skinner, B. F., *Beyond Freedom and Dignity*. New York: Knopf, 1971.

———, *Particulars of My Life*. New York: Knopf, 1976.

———, *Science and Human Behavior*. New York: Macmillan, 1953.

———, *Walden Two*. New York: Macmillan, 1948.

Wann, T. W. (ed.), *Behaviorism and Phenomenology*. University of Chicago Press, 1964. (See especially the essays by B. F. Skinner and Norman Malcolm.)

Weigel, John A., *B. F. Skinner*. Boston: Twayne, 1977.

Wheeler, John Harvey (ed.), *Beyond the Punitive Society*. San Francisco: Freeman, 1973.

Index

Political Economy —
the political scheme of things
covers the Economic structure

communism is not inevitable because

democracy gives the workers rights politically (4

despite the class distinctions — add to that

nationalism and the systems can survive